Mark Jarrett holds an MA in International History from the London School of Economics, a PhD in History from Stanford, and a Law degree from the University of California, Berkeley. He has taught at Hofstra and Stanford and has worked as an attorney at the world's largest international law firm.

'The system established by the Congress of Vienna is of great interest to both historians and political scientists, and Mark Jarrett's is one of the rare treatments that will appeal to both groups. His narrative gives a clear guidance through the complexities of the era and his analysis engages the central arguments about the period. It is a model treatment.'

—**Robert Jervis, Professor of International and Public Affairs and Adlai E. Stevenson Professor of Political Science, Columbia University**

'This book is more than a comprehensive and richly detailed account of the complex diplomatic and international relations in post-Napoleonic Europe, which will undoubtedly become a standard reference in the curricula of university students. It is, more importantly, a fascinating journey through the Europe of early the nineteenth century, from Sicily to Russia, from England to the Balkans. Whereas other historians mostly focus on the great powers that defeated Napoleon in 1815 (England, Prussia, Austria and Russia), Mark Jarrett avidly researched and brilliantly presents the diverse constellation of diplomatic interests and political movements that contributed to reshaping the European system.

Breaking free from the ideological prejudices still prevalent in the field (whether "international", "national", or "post-colonial"), Jarrett boldly assumes a broader perspective, where characters are seen as actors playing their respective roles within a bigger game of War and Peace: the Congress System. His is therefore not the ordinary Manichean account of "heroes" or "villains", "victories" or "defeats"—except in the minds of the characters themselves, which he depicts in a compassionate manner, regardless of the sides they happened to take.

He does so with an impressive display of scholarship; he is among the first English-speaking authors to take the measure of southeastern Europe and Russia in that crucial period—an accomplishment that has been long awaited. Under his pen, the Eastern Question (the ongoing division of the Ottoman Empire) and the independence of Greece are not presented as a mere chess game between ministries of colonial powers for land and commerce; it is also a story of real people, involved in a game of life and death.

In short, *The Congress of Vienna and its Legacy* successfully combines well-balanced historical research with fresh and vivid history-telling in the best sense of the word, truly enjoyable for all kinds of readers. This is one of the most comprehensively

documented and captivating books on the history of the Congress System published in years.'
—**Stella Ghervas, Institut d'études avancées, Paris, and author of** *Réinventer la tradition. Alexandre Stourdza et l'Europe de la Sainte-Alliance* **(winner of the Guizot Prize of the Académie Française, 2009)**

'Mark Jarrett's beautifully written book deploys a great deal of information without ever getting lost in detail. It weaves together personality and policy, providing a clear analysis of political structures as well as a vivid portrait of personalities.'
—**James J. Sheehan, Dickason Professor in the Humanities and Professor of Modern European History emeritus, Stanford University**

'This will become the definitive work on the Congress of Vienna with all its personalities, intrigues and significance for the nation-state and how we think of diplomacy today. As someone who recently had responsibility for US policy at the UN and other international organizations, the challenges of multilateral diplomacy continue, only with more actors and problems of global scope. I wonder how a Castlereagh or Metternich would deal with the frustrations and intransigence we see in the UN Security Council. Or whether such persons could even emerge. It's interesting that the Congress of Vienna still holds value for a new kind of diplomacy that has taken shape. Traditional multilateral organizations are often unable to address our greatest challenges, and what is emerging is a system of "variable geometry" where organizations, countries or individuals come together informally to develop a common approach. Look at the emergence of the G-20 in the financial crisis, the six-party talks for the DPRK, or 6+1 on Iran. And there are many more examples. These are no longer "conferences" or traditional bilateral diplomacy but are coalitions that form usually among the like-minded for a limited purpose and period. The Congress of Vienna seems to be a forerunner of this modern model, whether to contain France or put in place a "system" for addressing future issues. I can understand the common view that the Congress of Vienna was the model for how nation-states would conduct "modern" diplomacy. I'm sure this book will become a required read at the State Department's Foreign Service Institute, whether in our classes in negotiations or on leadership.'
—**James Warlick, former US Ambassador to Bulgaria**

'Mastering all the relevant primary sources as well as the secondary literature, encompassing all the latest research and analyses of international historians as well as the theories of international relations specialists, Mark Jarrett illuminates a vital two decades in European history that have long been neglected. His is indeed a wonderful book—clearly written, extremely well-researched, open to a whole variety of explanations from historians and political scientists, well balanced, fair in its judgements of historical characters and contemporary academic opinion, and seminal in its allusions to present-day events. I have little doubt that this book will become the standard work on the Congress System.'
—**Alan Sked, Professor of International History, London School of Economics and Political Science, from the Foreword to this book**

THE CONGRESS OF VIENNA AND ITS LEGACY

War and Great Power Diplomacy after Napoleon

MARK JARRETT

BLOOMSBURY ACADEMIC
LONDON • NEW YORK • OXFORD • NEW DELHI • SYDNEY

BLOOMSBURY ACADEMIC
Bloomsbury Publishing Plc
50 Bedford Square, London, WC1B 3DP, UK
1385 Broadway, New York, NY 10018, USA
29 Earlsfort Terrace, Dublin 2, Ireland

BLOOMSBURY, BLOOMSBURY ACADEMIC and the Diana logo are trademarks
of Bloomsbury Publishing Plc

First published in Great Britain by I.B. Tauris 2013
New paperback edition published 2014
This edition published by Bloomsbury Academic 2021, 2024

Copyright © Mark Jarrett, 2013, 2014

Mark Jarrett has asserted his right under the Copyright, Designs and Patents Act,
1988, to be identified as Author of this work.

For legal purposes the Acknowledgements on pp. xv–xvi constitute an extension of
this copyright page.

All rights reserved. No part of this publication may be reproduced or transmitted
in any form or by any means, electronic or mechanical, including photocopying,
recording, or any information storage or retrieval system, without prior permission
in writing from the publishers.

Bloomsbury Publishing Plc does not have any control over, or responsibility for, any
third-party websites referred to or in this book. All internet addresses given in this
book were correct at the time of going to press. The author and publisher regret any
inconvenience caused if addresses have changed or sites have ceased to exist, but
can accept no responsibility for any such changes.

A catalogue record for this book is available from the British Library.

A catalog record for this book is available from the Library of Congress.

ISBN: PB: 978-1-5013-8471-4
ePDF: 978-0-8577-2234-8
eBook: 978-0-8577-3570-6

To find out more about our authors and books visit www.bloomsbury.com
and sign up for our newsletters.

CONTENTS

List of Plates vii
List of Maps ix
Foreword by Alan Sked xi
Preface xiii
Acknowledgements xv

PART ONE: WAR

1 **The European State System and the Napoleonic Wars** 3
   The European state system of the eighteenth century 3
   The challenge of the French Revolution 19
   The rise of Napoleon 25
   The birth of the Napoleonic Empire and the War of the
      Third Coalition 27
   The Napoleonic Empire at its height 31
   The plans of Czartoryski and Pitt for the reconstruction of Europe 35
2 **The Collapse of the Napoleonic Empire, 1812–14** 43
   Napoleon's invasion of Russia and the Fourth Coalition 43
   Castlereagh's mission to the Continent 50
   The negotiations at Châtillon 54
   The Treaty of Chaumont 56
   The Bourbon restoration 58
   The first Peace of Paris 63

PART TWO: PEACE

3 **The Congress of Vienna, 1814–15** 69
   The decision to convene a Congress 69
   Preliminary negotiations in Paris and London 70
   The characters of the statesmen 72
   Diplomatic aims on the eve of the Congress 84
   The procedural question 89
   The social life of the Congress 94
   The Polish Question and Alexander's diplomatic triumph 96

	The Saxon Question and the secret treaty of 3 January 1815	111
	Other questions at the Congress	131
	The question of a general guarantee	146
	Assessments of the settlement	149
4	**The Birth of the Congress System, 1815–18**	**158**
	The Hundred Days	158
	The second Peace of Paris and the Quadruple Alliance	164
	The Holy Alliance	173
	The allied occupation of France	178
	The Congress of Aix-la-Chapelle	180

PART THREE: DIPLOMACY

5	**The Alliance in Operation, 1819–20**	**209**
	Central Europe and the Carlsbad Decrees	209
	Peterloo and the Six Acts	220
	The revolution in Spain and Castlereagh's State Paper of 5 May 1820	223
	The Neapolitan Revolution and Metternich's dilemma	231
6	**Rift and Reunion, 1820–22**	**248**
	The Congress of Troppau and the Principles of Intervention	248
	The Congress of Laibach and the Piedmontese insurrection	270
	The Greek Revolution, the Hanover interview and the threat of a Russo-Turkish war	285
7	**The Twilight of the Congress System, 1822–23**	**309**
	The Congress of Verona	309
	The French expedition to Spain	338
	The end of the Congress System	344
8	**The Legacy of the Congress System: Success or Failure?**	**353**
	Salient characteristics of the Congress System	357
	A post-hegemonic international security regime?	360
	Why the system failed	363
	The legacy of the Congress System	369

Chronology	380
Dramatis Personae	384
Notes	390
Select Bibliography	498
Index	515

LIST OF PLATES

1a Napoleon in 1812 (by Jacques Louis David). National Gallery, Washington DC
1b The Battle of Leipzig, also known as the 'Battle of the Nations', in October 1813. Pushkin Museum (public domain)
2a The Allied Sovereigns entering Paris on 31 March 1814. Author's Collection
2b View of Vienna from the Belvedere Palace, 1820. Wien Museum
3a Equestrian portrait of Tsar Alexander I of Russia in 1812 (by Franz Alkruger). Hermitage Museum (public domain)
3b Prince Metternich in 1815 (by Sir Thomas Lawrence). The Royal Collection/Bridgeman Art Library
4a Viscount Castlereagh in 1810 (by Sir Thomas Lawrence). National Portrait Gallery
4b Prince de Talleyrand in 1809 (by François Gerard). Gianni Dagli Orti/The Art Archive at Art Resource, NY
5a Prince Adam Jerzy Czartoryski, the Polish prince who advised Tsar Alexander I
5b Friedrich von Gentz, the 'Secretary' of the Congresses
5c The leading statesmen of the Congress of Vienna, as depicted by the French painter Jean-Baptiste Isabey. De Agostini Picture Library/A. Dagli Orti/Bridgeman Art Library
6a Map showing the central district of Vienna in 1814. Wien Museum
6b Room in the Austrian State Chancellery where conferences were frequently held during the Congress of Vienna. Erich Lessing/Art Resource, NY
7a Military festival at the Prater on 18 October 1814, commemorating the victory at Leipzig one year earlier (by Balthasar Wigand). Wien Museum
7b A masked ball in the Hofburg Redoutensaal during the Congress of Vienna (by Joseph Schütz). Wien Museum
8a Jousting at the 'Grand Carousel' in the Spanish Riding School on 23 November 1814 (by Carl Beyer). Wien Museum

8b 'La Balance Politique', a political caricature of the Congress of Vienna. Deutsches Historisches Museum, Berlin, Germany/© DHM/The Bridgeman Art Library
9a Louis XVIII and the French royal family. National Portrait Gallery.
9b The Duke of Wellington in 1814 (by Sir Thomas Lawrence). Apsley House/English Heritage Photo Library
10a The Battle of Waterloo on 18 June 1815 (by William Sadler)
10b Prince Karl August von Hardenberg, Chancellor of Prussia (by Johann Tischbein) bpk, Berlin/Art Resource, NY
11a German students march at the Wartburg Festival, 1817
11b The assassination of Kotzebue by Karl Sand in 1819 (by A.P. Eisen)
12a Contemporary view of the Peterloo Massacre on 16 August 1819 (by Richard Carlile). Manchester Library Services (public domain)
12b Portrait of Ferdinand VII of Spain in 1814 (by Goya), Museo del Prado, Madrid. Erich Lessing/Art Resource, NY
13a Count John Capodistrias, Corfiote adviser to Tsar Alexander I and the first President of Greece. National Historical Museum, Athens (public domain)
13b Colonel Rafael del Riego, hero of the Spanish Revolution of 1820
13c Ferdinand IV of Naples (Ferdinand I of the Two Sicilies) reigned for 66 years but enjoyed hunting more than governing. Museo Nazionale di Capodimonte, Naples/Alinari/Art Resource, NY (by Gennaro Maldarelli)
14a General Guglielmo Pepe helped to plan the Neapolitan Revolution of 1820. Archive Dr. Agazio Mellace
14b Sultan Mahmud II (by John Young)
14c The trial of Queen Caroline in 1820 (by Sir George Hayter). National Portrait Gallery
15a Laibach in the early nineteenth century (by Leander Russ). Albertina, Vienna (public domain)
15b The massacre of Greek Christians in Constantinople in 1821, showing the Patriarch hanging from the church door. Athens Gennadios Library (public domain)
16a George Canning in 1825 (by Richard Evans). National Portrait Gallery
16b A political caricature of the Congress of Verona, 1822

LIST OF MAPS

Europe on the Eve of the French Revolution, 1789	xvii
Europe at the Height of the Napoleonic Empire, 1812	xviii–xix
Europe after the Congress of Vienna, 1815	xx–xxi
Europe of the Congresses, 1814–24	xxii
The Partitions of Poland	7
The Frontiers of France, 1814–15	51
The 'Polish-Saxon' Question	97
Spain at the Time of the Revolution of 1820	226
Italy in the 1820s	232
The Danubian Principalities and Greece in the 1820s	286

To my parents, Beverly and Paul, for their love and patience.

To my children, Alexander and Julia, for the joy they have given me.

To the memory of those of my teachers who did not live to see this publication: Gordon A. Craig, Alexander L. George, Kenneth Bourne, Marc Raeff, J.M.W. Bean, Matthew S. Anderson and John Dinwiddy.

And finally, to my wife, Małgorzata, who grew up in Puławy in the shadow of the Czartoryski Palace, where Tsar Alexander met the Polish nobility on his journey to the Congress of Vienna almost exactly two centuries ago.

FOREWORD

NINETEENTH-century European history is no longer fashionable. A century once remembered as an 'age of progress' is now remembered as an age of nationalism and imperialism, dominated by largely undemocratic regimes with cultural values—religious, racist or Social Darwinist—which strike quite the wrong note today. That is not to say that it lacks memorable characters; parliamentary leaders like Palmerston, Gladstone and Disraeli, *Realpolitiker* like Cavour, Napoleon III and Bismarck, heroes like Kossuth and Garibaldi, statesmen like Metternich and Salisbury, military leaders like Radetzky, Moltke and Kitchener. But, it lacks the drama and terror of the twentieth century with its tyrants like Lenin, Stalin, Hitler and Mao along with their mass-murdering regimes. It also lacks world wars.

And yet ... the nineteenth century was born in world war as Europe, East and West, North and South, struggled to free itself from the grip of the tyrant, Napoleon. True, he was more educated, more intelligent, more enlightened and sophisticated—even much more progressive—than twentieth century tyrants (whatever their own warped views of progress), but he was still the military conqueror rather than the legitimate ruler of the Continent and had ambitions to extend his rule beyond its shores. Fortunately, he was eventually defeated in 1813–15 by the military planning of Radetzky and the combined allied armies under military leaders like Schwarzenberg, Blücher and Wellington.

The people who organized his defeat diplomatically—principally Prince Metternich, Lord Castlereagh and Tsar Alexander I of Russia—are the main characters of Mark Jarrett's book. This tells the story of Europe's diplomatic development and organization from 1813 until 1823 with a look towards the present. Mastering all the relevant primary sources as well as the secondary literature, encompassing all the latest research and analyses of international historians as well as the theories of international relations specialists, Mark Jarrett illuminates a vital two decades in European history that have long been neglected.

His is indeed a wonderful book—clearly written, extremely well-researched, open to a whole variety of explanations from historians and political scientists, well-balanced, fair in its judgements of historical characters and contemporary academic opinion, never dogmatic but always imaginative, exemplary in its structure and length and seminal in its allusions to present-day events.

It is a first-rate textbook on a neglected period, now brought vividly back to life by excellent scholarship and a compelling narrative. The detail never overwhelms but always clarifies; the quotes are always apposite and often arresting; the endnotes are fascinating; the chronology is excellent; and the conclusions are fluid, thoughtful and worth re-reading several times over. So, too, is the book. It really is that good.

As a historian of the period, it is not for me to enter into historical debate in this Foreword. Suffice it to say that Mark Jarrett's portraits of the leading figures are excellent; that he understands their fixation with the balance of power; that he is well aware of the tensions in both the policies and personality of Alexander I; that he has the measure of both Castlereagh and Metternich; and that, although he notes their differences of approach diplomatically, he can see how they complement each other. He also manages to slip in enough of the personal and social background to make all these characters come to life.

I have little doubt that his book will become the standard work on 'the Congress System'. I recommend it unreservedly.

Alan Sked
Professor of International History
LSE

PREFACE

In early September 1814, carriages from throughout Europe were rolling across hot and dusty roads on their way to Vienna. In response to a public invitation from the victorious allied powers, monarchs, ministers, and dignitaries of every conceivable status and description were descending upon the Habsburg capital to participate in the reconstruction of Europe. The visitors included the Emperor of Russia, the Kings of Prussia, Bavaria and Denmark, scores of princes and high ranking nobles, German imperial knights, ambassadors, scholars, musicians, artists, writers, cooks, tradesmen and servants in the thousands. Most of them, as it turned out, would play no role at all in the high-stakes diplomacy to be conducted behind closed doors, but their presence provided a splendid backdrop and a fitting end to two decades of revolution and war.

The Congress of Vienna and the so-called 'Congress System' that dominated Europe for the next ten years can best be understood as reactions to the previous epoch. The very fabric of European political and social life had been torn asunder by the French revolutionaries and decades of warfare with Napoleon. The challenge of the postwar period was to come to terms with these new forces while restoring the rudiments of order and stability lost in the years of revolution and strife.

Although the French Bourbons and other toppled dynasties were suddenly restored to their thrones, the statesmen at Vienna recognized there could be no turning back of the clock to the days of the *ancien régime*, whose very imperfections had led to revolutionary upheavals. For the most part, the Congress statesmen looked to a reshaping of the international system to provide an anchor for maintaining the existing social order. They agreed on the general desirability of conducting international politics through consensus rather than by force of arms, and the need to treat one another, if not the lesser powers, with some degree of moderation and restraint.

In the years immediately following the Vienna Congress, the European great powers launched a bold new experiment in the history of international relations. Their ministers met for periodic summit conferences in which they attempted to resolve the major issues confronting Europe—from boundary disputes between Norway and Sweden to Greek Orthodox uprisings in the Sultan's domains. This noble attempt at international cooperation was initially strengthened by a common fear of revolution, but eventually foundered on a deepening division among the powers on the extent to which their alliance could be used to suppress domestic uprisings and prop up unpopular regimes.

Later nineteenth-century historians often judged this generation harshly. Liberals such as Harriet Martineau condemned the Congress System as an alliance of kings against peoples. French historians resented the very existence of a European alliance directed against France, while German scholars like Heinrich von Treitschke believed the Vienna settlement did not go far enough in satisfying the demands of German nationalists. In the twentieth century, the reputation of the peacemakers of 1814–15 suddenly experienced a resurgence, in part because the chaos of that century placed their earlier achievement in greater prominence. Unlike the Paris Peace Conference of 1919, the Vienna Congress had been followed by a century of relative peace. Moreover, the systematic researches of modern scholars, such as Sir Charles Webster, Harold Temperley, August Fournier, Heinrich von Srbik, Guillaume de Bertier de Sauvigny, Francis Ley, Paul Schroeder, Enno Kraehe, W.H. Zawadzki, Stella Ghervas and Alan Sked, have led to a far better understanding of the motives and methods of the Congress statesmen.

The work of these historians has been supplemented by the efforts of political scientists, who have increased our knowledge of leadership styles, decision-making processes, public opinion, military and economic power, national interests and the international system. Students of international politics, such as Kenneth Waltz, have introduced the notion of 'levels of analysis'—the critical insight that international events can best be explained when viewed from three different perspectives: those of the individual actors, the national forces behind those actors, and the structure of the international system itself.

The chief question posed by the Congress of Vienna and the Congress System nevertheless remains much the same today as in the nineteenth century. The Congress statesmen proved to be astonishingly adept at developing mechanisms for a new international order. But was their aim the purely negative one of shoring up the power and privileges of European elites—and if so, did this limitation doom their effort to failure?

ACKNOWLEDGEMENTS

This book could not have been completed without the help of family, teachers and friends. First and foremost, I would like to thank Alan Sked of the London School of Economics and Peter Stansky at Stanford for their encouragement and support. James Sheehan at Stanford, Robert Jervis at Columbia, Stella Ghervas at the University of Geneva, Benjamin Ginsberg at Johns Hopkins, and James Warlick, then US Ambassador to Bulgaria, also each read through the entire manuscript. Peter Paret, Maria Mavroudi, Frances Malino, Heath Pearson, Susan Bell and the late Edwin Dunbaugh kindly read and commented on various sections. The late Roger Lockyer of the University of London originally suggested a book that dealt with both the Congress of Vienna and the Congress System. Elena Speed, a former colleague at the San Francisco office of the international law firm of Baker & McKenzie, helped with Russian translations; my wife, Małgorzata Jarrett, helped with Polish sources; and three students at Stanford, Simone Federico Bianchi, Greta Barilla, and Margherita Loro Piana, helped by translating passages from Italian. My good friend from Vienna, Helene Schuster, was helpful on my trips to that city, and especially obliging in arranging to obtain images from the Wien Museum and in helping me find the location of Metternich's original suburban villa on the Rennweg. Dr. Walter Öhlinger spent an afternoon showing me prints and maps at the Wien Museum, Dr. Helmut Selzer was kind enough to arrange reproductions from the same source, and Dr. Janusz Pezda showed my wife and myself some of Prince Adam Czartoryski's original letters to the Tsar and to his father, when we were at the Czartoryski Foundation Archives in Kraków. Dr. Agazio Mellace of Squillace was kind enough to furnish an image of General Pepe, and Dr. Christian Gottlieb of the Queen's Reference Library in Copenhagen corresponded with me regarding the possible use of images. For the splendid maps in this book, I wish to thank Helen Stirling of www.helenstirlingmaps.com; for the base relief image, Mountain High Maps® Copyright © 1993 Digital Wisdom®, Inc. I also wish to thank Barbara Loeb for typing and Pat FitzGerald for her thorough copyediting. I extend my special gratitude to Dr. Lester Crook, Joanna Godfrey and Alexandra Higson, the editors at I.B.Tauris, for their expertise, patience and above all generosity with respect to deadlines, manuscript length and every other rule that a reprobate author could break. I also wish to acknowledge the assistance of the staffs of the National Archives in Kew, the Reading Room of the British Library, the Public Record Office of Northern Ireland, the Haus-, Hof- und Staatsarchiv in Vienna, the Archives des Affaires Étrangères at La Courneuve (in the northeast of Paris), the Centre for Kentish Studies in Maidstone, the Durham County Record Office in Durham, the National Library of Scotland in Edinburgh, the London Library, and the libraries of Stanford and the University of California at Berkeley. And finally I wish to thank my wife, Małgorzata, for her patience, forbearance and tender affection; our two wonderful and talented children—Alexander, named in part after the mercurial Tsar, and Julia—simply for bringing joy to our lives each day, and for sharing a love of history and of Europe; and my parents, Beverly and Paul Jarrett, for their unflagging support.

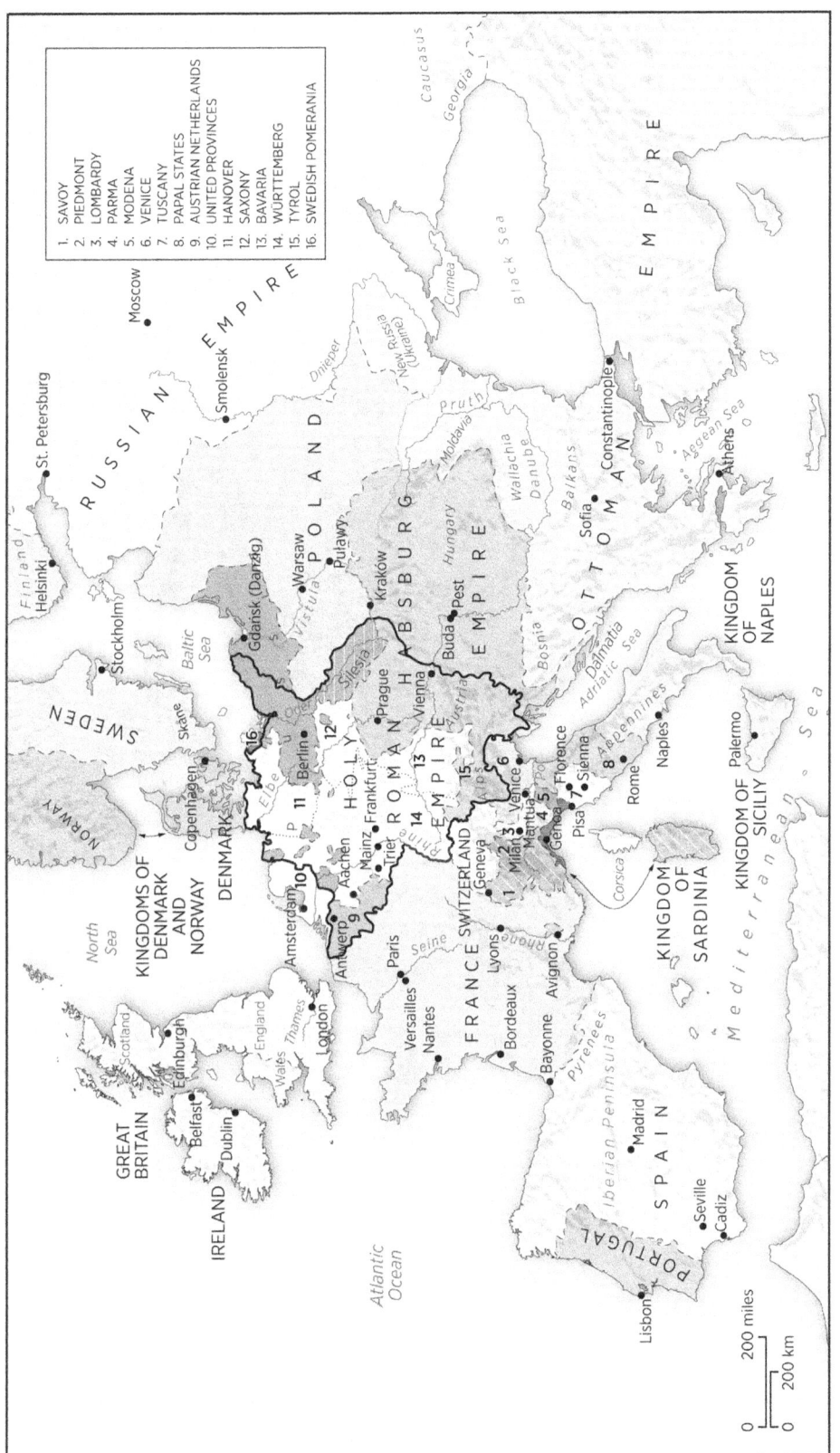

Europe on the Eve of the French Revolution, 1789

Europe at the Height of the Napoleonic Empire, 1812

Europe after the Congress of Vienna, 1815

Europe of the Congresses, 1814–24

Part One

WAR

War is nothing but a duel on a larger scale ... Each tries through physical force to compel the other to do his will ...
Carl von Clausewitz, *On War*

Napoleon revolutionized the world; filled with his name the four quarters of the globe; sailed beyond the seas of Europe; soared to the skies, and fell and perished at the extremity of the waves of the Atlantic.
François-René de Chateaubriand, *The Congress of Verona*

The present Confederacy may be considered as the Union of nearly the whole of Europe against the unbounded and faithless ambition of an individual. The great object of the Allies, whether in war or in negotiation, should be to keep together, and to drive back and confine the armies of France.
Lord Castlereagh to Lord Cathcart, 18 September 1813

During the battle our squares presented a shocking sight. Inside we were nearly suffocated by the smoke and smell from burnt cartridges. It was impossible to move a yard without treading upon a wounded comrade, or upon the bodies of the dead; and the loud groans of the wounded and dying were most appalling.
Captain Howell Rees Gronow, *Reminiscences*

This morning I went to visit the field of battle, which is a little beyond the village of Waterloo, on the plateau of Mont-Saint-Jean; but on arrival there the sight was too horrible to behold. I felt sick in the stomach and was obliged to return. The multitude of carcasses, the heaps of wounded men with mangled limbs unable to move, and perishing from not having their wounds dressed or from hunger, as the Allies were, of course, obliged to take their surgeons and wagons with them, formed a spectacle I shall never forget.

 Major W.E. Frye, *After Waterloo: Reminiscences of European Travel*

1

The European State System and the Napoleonic Wars

THE Congress of Vienna and the Congress System that dominated the European political scene from 1814 to 1823 were primarily reactions to the previous epoch. An understanding of the developments of this decade therefore demands some familiarity with what preceded it—both in terms of the geography and political structures of the *ancien régime* and of the rapid succession of national and international regimes that transpired in the maelstrom years of 1793 to 1813.

The European state system of the eighteenth century

The statesmen at Vienna were born into a world far different from our own. Europe on the eve of the French Revolution was not, as today, neatly divided into similar nation-states, but contained a myriad of different structures, ranging from small city-states to large multi-ethnic empires. The Europe of this period has been aptly described as divided into three zones: an eastern zone dominated by the large empires of Russia, the Austrian Habsburg domains and Ottoman Turkey, as well as the elective monarchy of Poland; a middle zone with the smaller principalities and city-states of Italy, Germany and Switzerland; and to the north and west, an outer ring of nascent national states, consisting of Sweden, Denmark, Prussia, the United Provinces (Holland), Great Britain and Ireland, France, Spain and Portugal. Even these latter states were not without imperial pretentions; several, in fact, possessed large colonial empires overseas.[1]

Though eighteenth-century Europe was not composed of parallel nation-state structures, neither was it organized along the lines of universal empire like ancient Rome. The empires of the European eastern zone were vast multi-ethnic states, but lacked any aspirations to universality. Each European state—whether republican city-state, national kingdom or multi-national empire—constituted an independent centre of sovereign political power. These states shared a common culture and a degree of economic interdependence. They exchanged diplomatic representatives, recognized the force of treaties between themselves and had evolved their own traditions of international law. Contemporaries were highly conscious of belonging to a 'society' of states or 'republic' of Europe. Historians today refer to this complex blend of cultural and economic interdependence and political independence as the 'European State System', out of which our own present-day system of kindred nation-states on a global scale has emerged.

Each of these autonomous political units was, of course, subject to both internal and external constraints. European society as a whole was aristocratic and corporatist: within each polity, a subject's rights and duties were largely defined by his or her membership in a hereditary 'estate' or 'order'. The eighteenth century was also, like our own, marked by its own peculiar patterns of national growth and international rivalry. Even before the outbreak of the French Revolution, the boundaries between states were often in a state of flux.

Eastern and Northern Europe

Russia

To the east was situated Europe's most populous country. Vast expanses of land and the possibility of escape had led landowners to impose serfdom on the peasantry at a time when the institution was dying out in Western Europe.[2] In the late seventeenth century, Peter the Great launched a broad programme of reform that recast Russia along Western lines and greatly enhanced her military strength. He forced the *boyars* (the old nobility) to shave their beards and wear Western clothes; he moved the capital westward to St Petersburg, a new city constructed on the Gulf of Finland; he seized church lands and subordinated the Russian Orthodox Church, transforming it into a mere department of state. Peter replaced the unruly palace musketeers (the *streltsy*) with a new professional army, introduced compulsory military recruitment for life, and imposed a new 'poll' tax on the hapless peasantry. He merged Russia's hereditary and service nobility, introducing the 'Table of Ranks' in 1722, which assigned personal status based on service to the state. Peter imported advisers from the West, sent Russians to study abroad, and founded military colleges and institutions of higher learning. In consequence, Russia extended her frontiers to the southwest at the expense of the Ottoman Turks and defeated Sweden in the Great Northern War (1700–21) to become the leading power on the Baltic.

Forty years after Peter's death, Catherine the Great seized power in a palace coup. During her 33-year reign, Russia's population soared from 23 to 37 million.[3] In exchange for absolute obedience to their monarch, the Russian aristocracy and gentry won control over local government and enjoyed unchallenged authority over their serfs. Catherine annexed territories from Poland, Sweden and Ottoman Turkey, including the fertile grasslands of 'New Russia' (the Ukraine). She extended Russia to the Black Sea and established a virtual protectorate over Georgia in the Caucasus. The Tsarina even dreamt of overthrowing the Ottomans and establishing a new Byzantine Empire in Constantinople.[4] Under her sceptre, the Russian military became the largest in Europe: by 1795, this 'colossus of the North' possessed a standing army of 279,000 infantry and 100,000 cavalry and Cossacks. Military reforms, based on tactics developed in the wars against the Ottomans in the Caucasus and Crimea, anticipated changes introduced elsewhere during the French Revolution.[5]

In short, Russia had emerged as a great power. Within the Russian state, the Tsars achieved absolute rule, untrammelled by the Russian Orthodox Church, local representative bodies, or even by the written law. 'I find in Russia only two estates' wrote one reformer, 'the slaves of the sovereign and the slaves of the landlord ... [T]here are no free men in Russia.'[6] The only restraint on Tsarist authority was the prospect of a palace coup. The great paradox was that Westernization had been initiated wholly from above. Western ideas touched only the upper echelons of society, widening the gulf between the governing classes and the vast majority of Russia's populace, still locked in serfdom.[7] Other Europeans viewed Russia's large armies, absolutist government and rapid expansion with a mixed sense of curiosity and alarm.

The Ottoman Empire

To the south, the territories of the Sultan stretched across North Africa, the Levant, Anatolia and even the Balkans in Europe, including Greece. Although the Ottomans ruled over Christian subjects, they were not Christians themselves, and in consequence they were not deemed by Europe's Christian rulers to be members of the European community. In the eighteenth century, the Ottoman Empire began to slip into what some have seen as a long decline: the legendary Janissary corps became a hereditary caste that blocked military reform; the artillery, engineers and navy fell technically behind Europe; government administration became less efficient; and North Africa and the Danubian Principalities of Moldavia and Wallachia (present-day Romania) grew virtually independent of Turkish control. Even in Bosnia and Turkey itself (Asia Minor), local chieftains sometimes defied the Sultan's authority. Russia took advantage of Turkish weaknesses during the Russo-Turkish War of 1768–74 and obtained important concessions, including de facto control of the Crimea and access to the Black Sea for Russian merchant ships.[8]

Scandinavia: Denmark and Sweden

Northwest of Russia, Scandinavia consists of a narrow extension of the North German plain (Denmark) and a larger peninsula cradling the Baltic Sea and stretching northward beyond the Arctic Circle (Norway, Sweden, Finland). Its population had reached approximately four million by the end of the eighteenth century. Control of this region had been contested between Denmark and Sweden for much of its history. Danish kings not only controlled the Sound—the narrow waterway connecting the Baltic to the North Sea—but also ruled over the German duchies of Schleswig and Holstein, and the Kingdom of Norway. In the late fourteenth century, all of Scandinavia fell under Danish rule, until the Swedes reasserted their independence in 1520. Sweden, which already possessed Finland, expanded by seizing the province of Skåne from Denmark and taking most of Pomerania on the southern Baltic coast. In the seventeenth century, Sweden swelled further in consequence of the battlefield triumphs of Gustavus Adolphus. She briefly became one of Europe's great powers and mistress of the Baltic, controlling its shores not only to the south but also to the east (Livonia, Estonia and Ingria). But in the Great Northern War (1700–1721), the Swedes faced a formidable coalition composed of Denmark, Russia and Poland. Swedish military power was pulverized by Peter the Great at Poltava in 1709. Russia occupied Finland, which she later returned; however she retained the Baltic provinces of Ingria, Estonia and Livonia; Hanover annexed Bremen; and Prussia seized Stettin (present-day Szczecin in Poland). The spectacular collapse of Swedish power abroad was accompanied by a resurgence of power by her nobility at home, known as the *Frihetstiden* or 'Era of Liberty' (1718–72). The warrior-king Charles XII died without heirs, and the *Riksdag* (or Estates) conditioned the succession to the crown on the new monarch's consent to an extraordinary diminution of royal power. In marked contrast, Danish rulers continued to exercise absolute power. Despite the loss of Skåne, they also continued to collect tolls on the traffic through the Sound.[9]

Poland and its partitions

Situated on the broad Northern Plain between Russia and the German states, Poland had long been one of Europe's largest states, with her origins reaching back to 966. It is worth examining her fate in some detail, not only as an object

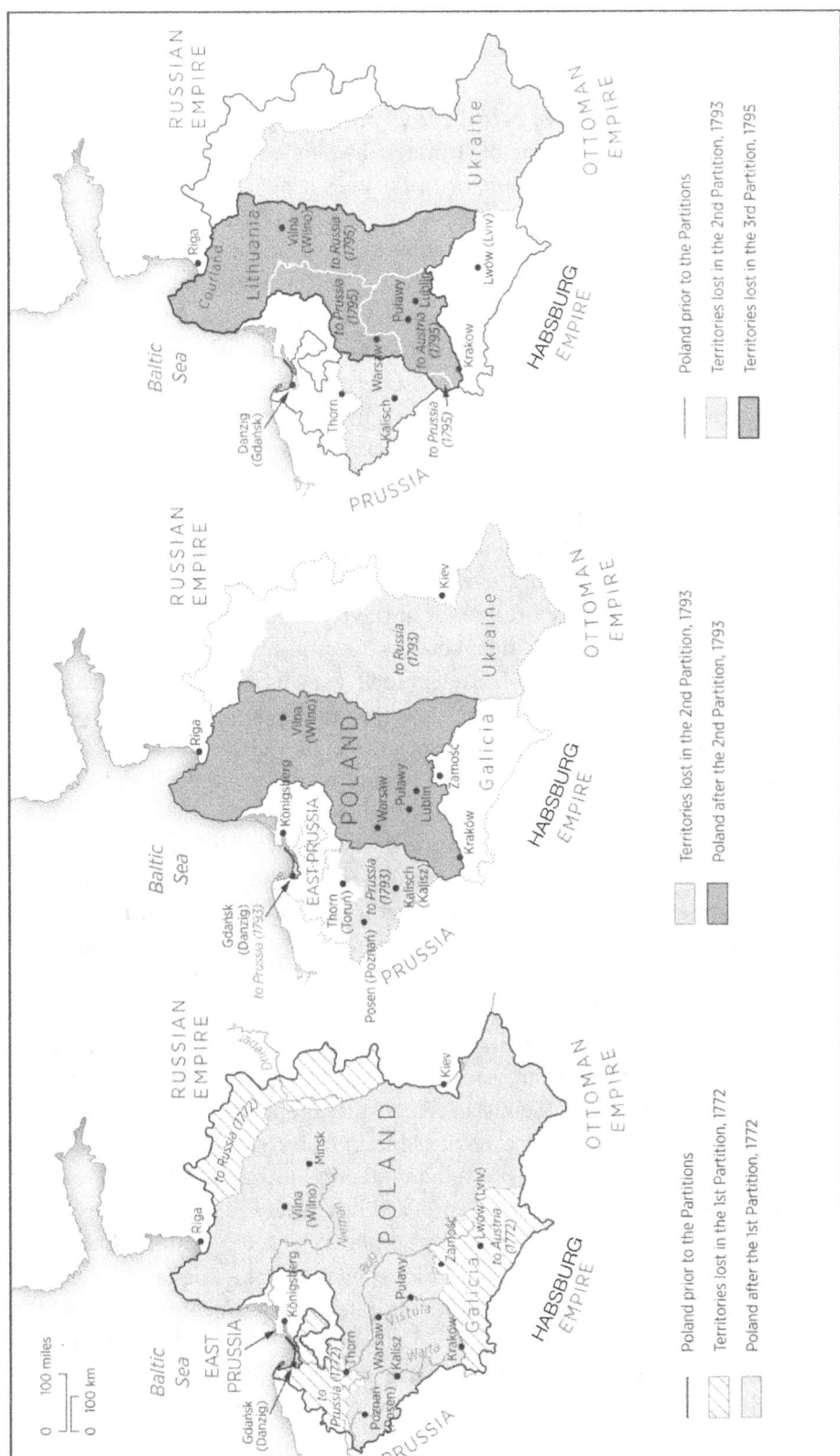

The Partitions of Poland

lesson in the realpolitik of late *ancien-régime* diplomacy, but also because her shadow would loom large over the later proceedings at Vienna. In 1569, Poland and Lithuania, including the Ukraine, had joined together to form an immense 'Commonwealth' (*Respublica*). Poland's capital then moved from Kraków (Cracow) to Warsaw, while the new Polish-Lithuanian Commonwealth became an elective monarchy with a Diet (*Sejm*) consisting of a Senate and 200 elected deputies, controlled by the Polish aristocracy (*szlachta*). The kings of the Commonwealth were elected by a colourful assembly of the entire nobility, gathered behind provincial banners in an open field. Foreign candidates were permitted, inviting the interference of other powers; indeed, different noble clans deliberately wooed foreign sovereigns as candidates.

In the seventeenth century, Poland's elected monarchs failed to curb the powers of the magnates in the *Sejm* or to obtain the powers needed for a centralized administration and larger royal army.[10] The *szlachta* even claimed the right to challenge royal measures by forming armed associations, known as *Konfederacy* ('Confederations'). In the early eighteenth century, a succession of Saxon kings preferred residence in their native Dresden to Warsaw. The Polish nobility benefited as their country's central government grew progressively weaker. The magnates basked in their 'golden freedoms'—exclusive rights to own land and distil alcohol, as well as exemption from land taxes, custom duties and even most grounds for arrest. They gloried in a mythical ancestry, claiming to be descendants of a race from the east, while Poland's peasantry remained mired in the toils of serfdom.[11]

In the late eighteenth century, Poland-Lithuania was still Europe's second largest state in area and third in population.[12] Yet Poland's size no longer reflected her power. The powerful Czartoryski family hoped to remedy their country's shortcomings by strengthening the powers of the Polish Crown. To overcome the opposition of the other magnates, they turned to Russia for support. In 1764, Catherine the Great procured the election of her handsome Polish favourite, Stanisław Poniatowski, whose mother was a Czartoryski. To Catherine's surprise, rather than acting as a Russian puppet, Poniatowski (now King Stanislaus Augustus) proposed the Czartoryski reforms, including creation of a responsible ministry and abolition of the notorious *liberum veto*, which allowed any deputy in the *Sejm* to veto legislation and to terminate the *Sejm*'s proceedings. These reforms were naturally opposed by Russia and Prussia, who hoped to keep Poland infirm.[13] Catherine demanded that the deputies of the *Sejm* accept a Russian guarantee of the political status quo, necessitating rejection of Poniatowski's proposed alterations. These events sparked a rebellion of Polish nobles, equally opposed to the King's reforms and Russian influence. Their revolt in turn triggered Russian intervention. Nor was this the end of this startling chain of events, for when Russian soldiers crossed into Ottoman territory to chase Polish recalcitrants, they unexpectedly provoked a new Russo-Turkish War: Russian forces swiftly defeated the Ottomans and overran their territories in the Balkans and the Crimea.

While the war in the east was still raging, Frederick the Great of Prussia took action to acquire a corridor along the Baltic to connect his territories in Pomerania with East Prussia: in fact, he reached an agreement with Russia and Austria that they all take slices of Polish territory. By each taking a share of the booty, Poland's three neighbours claimed to be acting on behalf of the European balance of power. Poland's military forces were insufficient to resist this combination, and the *Sejm* reluctantly ratified the loss of nearly one-third of Poland's territory and approximately four of her almost 11 million inhabitants in the First Partition.

In 1788, Russia was again drawn into conflict with Ottoman Turkey at a time when the rest of Europe was becoming preoccupied with events in France. King Stanislaus Augustus and the *Sejm* used these distractions to increase the size of the Polish army and to introduce a host of progressive reforms based on Enlightenment ideas, culminating in the Polish Constitution of 3 May 1791, which created a hereditary monarchy, confirmed the rights of the nobility, granted self-government to the towns and abolished the *liberum veto*. The adoption of the new constitution, however, quickly led to cataclysmic disaster. A group of conservative Polish nobles, sponsored by Catherine, opposed the changes and again invited Russian intervention. Having just concluded peace with Sweden and Turkey, Catherine launched a new invasion of Poland in 1792 on the pretext of crushing revolutionaries. Despite fierce resistance, the Poles were overwhelmed, the King yielded, and both Russia and Prussia took new slices of Poland in the Second Partition in 1793. Poland lost another four million of her inhabitants, while the deputies of the *Sejm* were coerced into endorsing the disastrous partition.

One year later, the Polish patriot Tadeusz Kościuszko—who had once fought bravely alongside George Washington for American independence—launched a popular insurrection against the occupying powers and even managed to defeat Russian forces at Racławice. Vastly outnumbered, the Poles were soon defeated, and Kościuszko's defiant gesture ended tragically in the total extinction of the Polish state by the Third Partition.

In three successive partitions—1772, 1793 and 1795—the ancient Kingdom of Poland was thus completely effaced from the map.[14] Her territories and population were entirely absorbed by Russia, Prussia and Austria. In 1797, the three partitioning powers signed a solemn treaty never to revive the Kingdom of Poland again. On the one hand, the partition of Poland distracted the eastern powers, preventing them from strangling the French Revolution in its infancy. On the other, the rape of Poland created an unfortunate legacy that was later to haunt—indeed to dominate—the statesmen at Vienna in 1814.

The Habsburgs and Europe's middle zone

The Holy Roman Empire and the German states

In Central Europe, Germany remained a patchwork of approximately 300 independent kingdoms, electorates, duchies, bishoprics and imperial cities, as well as hundreds of free imperial knights. The most important among these many polities were the larger states of Austria and Prussia and the German 'middle states' of Hanover (ruled by the kings of England), Saxony, Bavaria, Württemberg and Baden.

Since the sixteenth century an Austrian Habsburg had always been elected as the Holy Roman Emperor—titular sovereign of all the German states. But during the Thirty Years War (1618–48), the Habsburgs had failed to impose Catholicism on the Protestant German princes or to achieve the restitution of all the confiscated church lands; as a result, the German princes had become virtually independent of imperial authority.

The Habsburg Empire (Austria)

The real strength of the Habsburgs lay less in the prestige of the imperial title than in the value of their hereditary lands (*Erblande*).[15] They ruled over the heartland of Europe, with territories clustered in three main areas: Austria to the southwest (Upper and Lower Austria, Styria, Carinthia, Carniola and the Tyrol); Bohemia and Moravia to the northwest; and Hungary to the east (with Transylvania and Croatia/Slavonia). On the eve of the French Revolution, the Habsburgs also ruled over the Austrian Netherlands (present-day Belgium and Luxembourg), the Adriatic Principalities (including Istria and Trieste), Lombardy and Galicia (the name they gave to Southern Poland). Because most of these territories had been acquired through marriage not conquest, they were generally permitted to retain their own laws and institutions of governance; moreover, additional concessions had been granted to the nobles of Hungary, placing them in a privileged position within the empire.

In the early eighteenth century, the Habsburg Emperor Charles VI had been blessed with daughters but not sons. Determined to avoid a succession crisis, Charles made concessions to the other powers in exchange for their recognition of the 'Pragmatic Sanction', which bequeathed all of his dominions intact to his eldest daughter, Maria Theresa. Despite these arrangements, on his death in 1740 her succession was immediately disputed by Frederick the Great of Prussia. Without warning, Frederick occupied Silesia, one of the most economically advanced of all the Habsburg possessions. In eight years of war, Maria Theresa was able to prevent further losses but was never able to regain Silesia. Though Silesia was lost, Galicia was acquired from Poland in 1772.

By the time of the French Revolution, the Habsburgs held sway over almost two-thirds as many subjects as the kings of France. They did face one major disadvantage—their territories were decentralized, dispersed and encompassed a multitude of nationalities. Several unifying forces held these variegated dominions together—the spirit of *Kaisertreue* (loyalty to the emperor), the great landowning magnates, the German-speaking civilian bureaucracy and finally, the army. Maria Theresa and her son Joseph II, often regarded as 'enlightened' despots, attempted to consolidate further their conglomeration of diverse peoples, languages and traditions into a more uniform state. But when Joseph died suddenly in 1790, with the French Revolution raging in the background, his younger brother Leopold (previously considered an 'enlightened' ruler in Tuscany) abandoned the programme of reform from above.[16]

In foreign policy, the traditional enemy of the Habsburgs for centuries had been Bourbon France. But in the middle of the eighteenth century, under increasing pressure from the expansion of Prussia, Austrian minister Prince Kaunitz ventured a daring 'Diplomatic Revolution' by suddenly allying Austria with France against Prussia. It was this alliance that had led to the fatal marriage of Marie Antoinette, the daughter of Maria Theresa, with the Dauphin of France—the future Louis XVI.

Prussia

Through nearly continuous warfare in the seventeenth century, the rulers of the electorate of Brandenburg-Prussia had forged a powerful kingdom out of their disparate holdings on the Elbe, along the Pomeranian coast, and in the Rhineland. In exchange for the creation of a permanent standing army and greater powers of taxation, Prussia's rulers, the Hohenzollerns, granted their nobles almost absolute power over their serfs. They also established a highly efficient state bureaucracy, promoted religious toleration, and encouraged the growth of towns. An eminent German historian once characterized Prussia in this period as 'an autocratic, military kingdom, shaped by and for war and conquest, ... an aggregate of various, in part widely scattered lands and peoples, with considerable cultural and religious differences, further separated by significant social and economic barriers ... From these territories their carefully organized bureaucracy wrested the means for maintaining an army that in proportion to the population was far in excess of forces raised by other states'.[17]

The rising importance of Prussia can be judged from the sheer size of her standing army, which expanded exponentially: from a mere 8,000 in 1650; to 30,000 in 1688; to 43,000 in 1713; to 83,000 by 1740. Prussia's rulers further strove for great-power status by acquiring Pomerania from Sweden. A key turning point was reached in 1740 when Frederick the Great seized Silesia, not simply for its wealth but because it was contiguous with Prussia. Frederick's impetuous act of naked aggression led to two costly wars, but firmly established Prussia as a great power. With the additional shares she took of Poland, Prussia more than doubled in size between 1740 and 1795.

Switzerland

This small mountain country guarded the passes through the Alps connecting Italy, France and the German states. Three cantons (autonomous Swiss states) had formed the first Swiss Confederation in the thirteenth century; other cantons later joined during their struggle for independence from the Habsburgs. In the sixteenth century, the Swiss became bitterly divided by the Reformation. During the Thirty Years War (1618–48), Switzerland remained neutral, but Swiss mercenaries served in the armies of all the belligerents. The Treaty of Westphalia (1648) officially recognized the independence of the Swiss cantons from the jurisdiction of the Holy Roman Empire. In 1674, the Swiss Diet further declared Swiss neutrality in all European disputes. Although the Protestant cantons grew wealthier and more populous, the older Catholic cantons (including the original three) continued to dominate the Swiss Diet. Open warfare between Catholic and Protestant cantons finally broke out in the Villmergen Wars of 1656 and 1712. From 1712 to 1798, Swiss neutrality was respected by all the outside powers. During these same years, Switzerland grew more oligarchic: the rights of the dependencies (subject lands such as Vaud) were suppressed, power became more concentrated in a few wealthy families, and resident aliens and other foreigners lost their civic rights.[18]

The Italian states

South of Germany and Austria, jutting out into the Mediterranean Sea, lay the boot-shaped Italian peninsula. On the eve of the French Revolution, Italy was, like Germany, a patchwork of independent states or, as the Austrian foreign minister Metternich once quipped, no more than 'a geographical expression'. For centuries, Italy had been the playground of more powerful neighbours. After a series of wars in the early eighteenth century, the peninsula was parcelled out among the Habsburgs, the Bourbons, the Pope, and the House of Savoy. At Italy's southern tip, the Kingdoms of Naples and Sicily were, since 1734, ruled by the Neapolitan Bourbons—a new dynastic line established by children of the King of Spain (and therefore also cousins to the rulers of France). The centre of the Italian peninsula, from Rome in the southwest to Bologna and Ferrarra in the northeast, fell under the jurisdiction of the Pope. An Austrian Archduke ruled over the Grand Duchy of Tuscany, which included the proud cities of Florence, Pisa, Siena and Leghorn (Livorno). The Habsburgs also ruled directly over the Duchies of Milan and Mantua in Lombardy. Parma was ruled by another Spanish Bourbon, and Modena by the Este family. Finally, three city-state republics in Northern Italy—Venice, Genoa and Lucca—retained their independence, while the House of Savoy ruled over Piedmont, Savoy, Nice and the Kingdom of Sardinia.

Italy suffered from a shift in trade from the Mediterranean to the Atlantic; Italian industry also languished as her exports became primarily agricultural; her legal system remained a jumble of overlapping jurisdictions; the Church and nobility resisted attempts at reform; and Italians were severely struck by the great famine of 1763–64. Nonetheless Italy's population, already 16 million in 1750, continued to grow. Naples remained the third largest city in Europe. In the late eighteenth century, many Italians benefited from the peace that followed the rapprochement of Austria and France and from Enlightenment reforms. Piedmont's absolutist rulers increased their tax revenues, expanded their army, reformed the legal system, and centralized their bureaucracy in imitation of France. In Lombardy, the Austrian Habsburgs made the tax system more equitable and introduced a free trade in grain, thereby inducing noble landowners to improve their lands. In nearby Tuscany, Grand Duke Leopold abolished serfdom, prohibited torture, ended tax privileges, abolished guilds, suppressed the Inquisition and also established a free trade in grain. In Naples, Charles VII reigned for 25 years before becoming King of Spain in 1759. He left behind his eight-year-old son, Ferdinand IV, under the care of his minister Bernardo Tanucci. Tanucci suppressed the Jesuits and attempted to curb the feudal powers of the Neapolitan nobles; after his fall from power, Queen Maria Carolina and her favourite, John Acton, carried out similar policies with an emphasis on expanding foreign trade. Even the Pope, under pressure from reformers, banned the Jesuits in 1773.

By the end of the century, many Italian states had thus introduced important reforms. The demand for Mediterranean products, from olive oil and citrus fruits to wool and silk, was also on the rise. Italians nevertheless remained divided by geographic conditions, poor transportation routes, differences in dialect and local traditions. Since the days of Machiavelli, a few idealistic Italians had dreamt of unity for the peoples of the peninsula, but strong regional loyalties and the conflicting interests of France, Austria and the Papacy made the realization of any such vision seem remote.[19]

Western Europe

Spain

Turning our gaze to Western Europe, we are first struck by Spain, once the most powerful kingdom in Christendom. She provided a poignant reminder of the rise and fall of states. In the seventeenth century, she had engaged in a series of ruinous wars against France and had successively lost Portugal, Holland and the Franche-Comté. Habsburg Spain's predilection for endless war had resulted in severe inflation and a drastic debasement of her coinage; Spain's textile industry declined, her trade with her colonies dropped and even the former flow of bullion from the Americas slowed to a trickle. Even Spain's population shrank as a result of the plague.[20] By the beginning of the eighteenth century, Spain had not only lost her ascendancy but had degenerated into a battleground for the other powers. As a result of the War of Spanish Succession (1700–13), Spain came under the rule of a branch of the Bourbon family. Spain's most enlightened ruler, Charles III—the former King of Naples, who reigned in Madrid from 1759 to 1788—expelled the Jesuits, restrained the Inquisition, reformed the universities, encouraged new industries and ended the restrictions that had prevented Spanish ports outside of Seville and Cadiz from participating in colonial trade. But even Charles could not overcome the resistance of the privileged orders, the power of the Church, or the tensions between Spain's diverse geographic regions.[21] Spain still held onto her vast colonial possessions in the Americas, but even there she was slowly losing her grip.

Portugal

An independent kingdom since the reconquest of the Iberian Peninsula from the Moors, Portugal temporarily fell under the rule of the Spanish Habsburgs before regaining her independence in 1640. She controlled Brazil, trading posts on the African coast, Goa in India, Macao in China and the island of Timor. In the eighteenth century, Portugal's population was about two million. She benefitted from gold discoveries in Brazil and the market for her port wine, but suffered from the Lisbon earthquake of 1755. The Marquis of Pombal carried out Enlightenment reforms, reducing the power of the Church, the Jesuits and the nobles. During the Seven Years' War, Spain invaded Portugal, but the Portuguese were successfully defended by Britain, their traditional ally since the fourteenth century.

The United Provinces

The Dutch Republic, a federation of seven provinces, of which Holland was the largest, had also declined as a result of internecine warfare. Her provinces were separate oligarchies, loosely governed by an elected States General and dominated by wealthy Protestant merchants. A *Stadholder* served as admiral and Captain-General, posing an independent source of power. Dutch merchants were once the most prosperous in Europe—the French minister Colbert estimated that Dutch ships controlled three-quarters of the European carrying trade in the 1660s—but they gradually lost ground to their larger neighbours. The English challenged the Dutch in a series of wars in the late seventeenth century, when they seized much of the Dutch carrying trade and several of their colonies. In 1672, the Dutch Republic faced the nightmare of a war with the English at sea and the French on land. A French invasion was only halted by opening the dikes and granting extensive powers to the *Stadholder*, William of Orange. William strengthened the Dutch army, organized a series of international coalitions against Louis XIV and even seized the English throne in the Glorious Revolution of 1688. But high taxes, exorbitant wages, rising competition and the mercantilist policies of the other powers still made Dutch goods less competitive by the middle of the eighteenth century. Their exports of tobacco, fine cloth and linen, ceramics, canvas, herring, salt, timber and wine all fell. 'The root cause' of the collapse of Dutch overseas trade after 1720, a leading historian has written, 'was the expansion of industrial activity in the south Netherlands, Germany and Britain and the wave of industrial mercantilism which swept northern Europe'.[22] The Dutch became increasingly reliant on Britain and even invested their own capital outside the republic, preferring English funds. 'Holland follows England like a longboat follows in the wake of a warship to which it is tied', observed Frederick the Great.[23] In 1787, when a pro-French 'patriot' party seized power in Holland, Britain and Prussia successfully intervened to restore the *Stadholder* to his powers and to sever Dutch ties to France.

France

The eclipse of Spanish and Dutch power left France and Great Britain as the two most powerful states on the western seaboard. France had a population surpassed in Europe only by that of Russia; even as recently as 1750, their populations were roughly equal in size. In the course of the seventeenth century, under the threat of encirclement by the Habsburgs, French monarchs had greatly augmented their revenues, centralized control of their armies and promoted the doctrine of royal absolutism. Cardinal Richelieu had sent out *intendants* as the Crown's agents in the provinces, and Louis XIV subsequently subjugated the French nobility while maintaining their social privileges. Louis saw himself as performing God's will and even overturned the religious compromise of his ancestor, Henry IV, by expelling the Protestant Huguenots from France. With her large population and wealth, France became the model for other European states and, with a wartime army that may have exceeded 350,000 men in the 1690s, the greatest land power in Europe. Louis XIV attempted to deploy this unprecedented strength to extend France to her 'natural frontiers' on the north and east, but his policies were perceived as so aggressive that the other major European states, under the energetic leadership of William of Orange, formed a series of coalitions against him. Even then, the match was nearly equal. The memory of French aggression constituted a vital legacy that would play its part during the Napoleonic Wars and the Vienna Congress.

By the time of Louis XIV's death in 1715, more than three decades of almost continuous warfare had bankrupted the French state. France settled down to a period of much needed rest and relative tranquillity. She nonetheless continued to compete with England for maritime supremacy and took sides in most Continental disputes. By 1763, this led to the loss of most of her American and East Indian possessions. Some historians contend that engagement in Continental warfare while also competing with Britain beyond Europe's shores simply proved too much, even for Europe's most populous and prosperous state, leading to her decline in international influence. To take her revenge on Great Britain, France assisted the North American colonists in their war of independence 15 years later. The American colonists were victorious, but for his own country, the young French king—Louis XVI—succeeded only in racking up more debts. Nevertheless, with her robust industry and trade, central location, population of 29 million, advanced institutions of learning and vibrant culture, France still remained the foremost power on the Continent of Europe.

The British Isles

In eighteenth-century diplomatic parlance, the names of 'England' and 'Great Britain' were almost interchangeable,[24] and this usage accurately reflected England's domination of her sister kingdoms. England ruled directly over Scotland after the two kingdoms were merged by a 'Treaty of Union' at the beginning of the eighteenth century. Ireland retained its nominal independence and separate Parliament, but much of its land was held either by absentee Anglo-Irish landlords or by Scots-Irish Presbyterian landowners who resided in the northeast; Ireland's Catholic majority, subject to a series of 'penal laws', enjoyed no political rights. From 1714 onwards, the monarchs of England were also Electors (i.e., rulers) of Hanover, which gave England an interest and a voice in German affairs.

Great Britain's island location protected her from the ravages of Continental warfare. This was fortunate because her population and consequently her standing army were much smaller than those of France, Russia or the Austrian Habsburgs. In 1700, England and Scotland boasted a combined population of six million; by 1789, their population had increased to nine million.[25] Despite Britain's small size, her navy commanded supremacy on the open seas and she controlled an extensive overseas empire in North America, the West Indies and India. In foreign policy, her main interests were the acquisition of overseas territories of strategic or commercial value, and the maintenance of a 'balance of power' in Europe; historically, her greatest enemy was France.[26]

At home, the English Parliament had achieved supremacy over the monarch in the seventeenth century after a series of civil wars, while the British aristocracy had become the most open in Europe. In the early eighteenth century, England acquired the internal political stability she had lacked in the turbulent seventeenth century. Aristocracy, gentry and merchants cooperated with the Crown in the management of national affairs through a unique parliamentary system. Members of the aristocracy and wealthy merchants together dominated the 'unreformed' House of Commons, which represented both the counties and a limited number of towns and closed corporations known as 'boroughs'. The Prime Minister required the confidence of both the king and a majority of members in the House of Commons. Despite appearances, parliamentary elections were not as democratic as they are today. The ballot was not secret, and voters were usually under pressure to defer to their landlord's wishes. Even though the House of Commons was the scene of frequent and lively debates, its decisions were heavily influenced by the exercise of royal and ministerial patronage. A large number of placemen, accepting positions or benefits from the government, sat in the House of Commons, helping the government to retain its majority. The Prime Minister was thus assisted by the use of patronage to influence both elections and divisions (or votes) within the House itself.

Popular confidence in the British government and the public credit had made possible a miraculous 'Financial Revolution' in which the government raised seemingly endless sums of money by selling funds to the public. England also enjoyed the rule of law to a degree unparalleled in the rest of Europe. Foreign visitors, including a young Rhinelander, Clemens von Metternich, and a youthful Polish nobleman, Adam Jerzy Czartoryski, were spellbound as they witnessed—perhaps while sitting alongside the future Lord Castlereagh, then a student at St John's, Cambridge—the public trial of Warren Hastings, accused of misconduct while serving as Governor-General in India. Compared to the rest of Europe, England's press was also relatively free: its widely read pages were frequently filled with reports of the most recent parliamentary debate.

Indeed, Britain's unique combination of political stability, social mobility, technological expertise, overseas colonies, naval power and global commerce were leading her to revolutions in agriculture and manufacturing that would soon transform the entire world.

Shifting international rivalries

Such was the panorama of Europe on the eve of the French Revolution— the world into which the Congress statesmen were born. The interactions of these states naturally generated their own peculiar patterns of friendship and rivalry, just as between nations in our own time. For centuries, France's inveterate enemy had been Great Britain; since the seizure of Silesia, Austria's chief rival was Prussia. France was also the traditional ally of Poland, Sweden and Ottoman Turkey. Habsburg Austria and Bourbon France still basked in the halo of centuries of European splendour and grandeur, but astute observers recognized Russia, Prussia and Britain as the rising powers of the day. Poland, Sweden, Holland, Ottoman Turkey and Spain were irrefutably the declining powers.

The underlying cause of these changes may well have been, as historians often assert, alterations in the relative productive capacities of these societies. In any event, what political scientists now describe as the phenomenon of 'international anarchy'—the fact that states are subject to no central political authority or higher sovereign body and therefore must fend for themselves to ensure their own survival—would have been familiar enough to contemporaries studying the examples of Silesia and Poland.

Another major trend at the time, if slightly less obvious, was the geographic integration of Continental politics. At the beginning of the eighteenth century, the War of the Spanish Succession and the Great Northern War had been fought simultaneously by different actors in separate theatres, but by the time of the Seven Years' War (1756–63), these two theatres had merged.[27]

As the century drew to a close, traditional patterns of life, especially in the western zone, were being altered by the emergence of the Atlantic economy, improvements in agriculture and industry, the growing wealth and power of new social groups, the development of new ideas and the greater flow of information. These factors contributed to a series of revolutionary confrontations in Europe and her colonies that reached their climax in the great upheaval that began in France in 1789. Our focus will now turn to the impact of these revolutions, and especially of the French Revolution, on the structure and patterns of European international relations. The attempt to construct a 'Congress System' was largely a response to these events.

The challenge of the French Revolution

For more than a century, the government of France had thrived on the extension of credit. In imitation of Britain, her ministers had financed their most recent wars by borrowing. Suddenly, in the late 1780s the French Crown found itself in a dire financial crisis. Although France's economy was generally prosperous and the public debt was not out of proportion to the national income, the ministers were unable to tap into much of this wealth. Earlier compromises had exempted the nobles and even whole provinces from a host of taxes. The Crown had also sold off its rights to collect many future revenues to tax-farmers and office holders. Suddenly, in part because of the crisis in the Netherlands, the royal government was unable to obtain any more loans. To avert financial collapse, the Crown appealed to the nobility to surrender their fiscal privileges. Invited to a dazzling but improvised 'Assembly of Notables', the nobles refused to bail out the government and demanded that the Crown summon instead the Estates General, the traditional body representing the three great orders of French society—the clergy, nobility and commoners—which had not met since 1614. Both the fiscal crisis and mounting popular pressure forced Louis XVI to yield to the nobles' demand. The kingdom became further politicized by the election of deputies and the drawing up of detailed lists of grievances—*cahiers de doléances*—to instruct them. To make matters worse, these events coincided with a disastrous harvest, which was followed by an exceptionally cold winter.

Once the Estates General assembled at Versailles in May 1789, attention quickly turned from the dispute between the Crown and the nobility to a new disagreement between the privileged orders and the deputies of the Third Estate (represented by the bourgeoisie). This conflict had actually been gathering momentum for decades as the result of the circulation of the ideas of Locke, Voltaire, Montesquieu, Rousseau and their more vulgar popularizers, especially their attacks on hereditary privilege, the Catholic Church and absolute rule. Abbé Sieyès's stirring pamphlet, 'What is the Third Estate?' argued that commoners, as the sole class of 'productive and useful citizens', represented the true French nation, whereas the privileged orders—the clergy and nobles—constituted nothing more than an alien and parasitic class—'privileged persons, far from being useful to the nation, cannot but enfeeble and injure it'. The deputies of the Third Estate demanded an end to noble privileges and a national constitution. Their demands, inspired by Enlightenment philosophy, were backed by the agitation of the provincial peasantry and the urban crowds of Paris.[28]

The term 'revolutionary' was applied to events in France at an early stage. On 14 July 1789, fearing that the King might dismiss the Estates General, a group of Parisians stormed the Bastille in a search for arms. Louis XVI's resolve to use military force weakened and his government lost control over the Estates General at Versailles. Transforming themselves into a 'National Assembly', the deputies of the Third Estate and their allies among the privileged orders boldly passed the 'Declaration of the Rights of Man and the Citizen', abolished feudal and clerical privileges, confiscated church lands to pay off the debt, restricted royal power and adopted a written constitution. In October, a crowd of hungry Parisians marched to Versailles, entered the palace and hauled the royal family off to Paris.

These changes posed a direct challenge to the traditional institutions of European society. A revolution in France was especially shocking since France was widely regarded as the most advanced and powerful country in Europe: indeed, her political system had served as the blueprint for many of the other European states. Neither Louis XVI nor his Queen were genuinely committed to a sharing of power in the form of a constitutional monarchy, which was so very contrary to their upbringing. The Pope's condemnation of the changes brought by the Revolution rendered the King's position even more difficult. When the royal family attempted to escape in June 1791, they were recognized in the small town of Varennes and brought back to Paris as virtual prisoners of their own subjects. Events in France now appeared to pose a threat to every crowned head in Europe.

The Revolution became, in large part, a clash of ideas. The revolutionaries identified themselves with the ideals of the Enlightenment—faith in human reason, natural rights, social progress, egalitarianism and the 'General Will' of Rousseau's *Social Contract*. Almost every practice of French society, from the institution of monarchy and the privileges of the nobility to the Christian credo and the seven-day calendar, was brought under the scrutiny of human reason, as interpreted by the revolutionaries. Liberal sympathizers throughout Europe and America lent their support.

As early as 1790, Anglo-Irish politician Edmund Burke provided the counterpoint to revolutionary ideology with the publication of his *Reflections on the Revolution in France*. Burke attacked the notion of abstract rights, arguing that each society was in fact an organic growth, developed through a series of compromises fashioned over several generations to reconcile opposing interests. Therefore, no single generation had the right to repudiate it. In Burke's view, the social contract was 'a partnership not only between those who are living, but between those who are living, those who are dead, and those who are to be born'. Burke favoured limited, moderate reforms to address specific abuses and had even sided earlier with the American colonists against Britain, but he vehemently denounced the wholesale changes being introduced to French society by the revolutionaries in the name of abstract reason. He especially attacked their confiscation of church lands, abusive treatment of the French royal family and abolition of hereditary privilege, which he thought threatened the rights of property everywhere and would only lead to chaos. Burke saw the Revolution as the work of a small conspiratorial clique, acting for personal gain. Finally, he believed that religious faith was an essential adhesive for holding society together, and attacked the conspirators as atheists. Burke's arguments made a deep impression on the future Congress statesmen—Lord Castlereagh, who would represent Britain at Vienna in 1814, provided detailed summaries of Burke's book in letters to his step-grandfather. On the Continent, Burke's work was translated into German by none other than Friedrich von Gentz, future collaborator of Metternich and 'Secretary' at the Congresses. In Paris, Louis XVI pored over every page.

Hostile as they may have been to the Revolution, the other European powers were reluctant to intervene. Some even detected a benefit in an assumed weakening of France. In London, Prime Minister William Pitt told the House of Commons that he anticipated 15 years of peace. The Holy Roman Emperor, as the brother of the Queen of France, felt compelled to make a solemn warning at Pillnitz, but otherwise did nothing. Only at the end of April 1792 did war finally break out between France and the Habsburg Emperor. Even then, it was precipitated by French legislators who hoped to consolidate the gains of the Revolution through a successful war, rather than by any effort on the Emperor's part to tamper in French internal affairs.[29] The hapless French King supported the decision of the Legislative Assembly in the hope that the war would bring international relief to his plight. Europe became engulfed in a conflagration that would continue, with brief lapses, for more than 20 years. During this long contest, what was initially a war to defend the Revolution gradually transformed itself into a struggle over French hegemony in Europe.

We can think of this great conflict as consisting of five stages.[30] In the opening stage, revolutionary France withstood the onslaught of a coalition consisting of several major European powers. When the war first began, it seemed that the Austrians and their Prussian allies would quickly take

Paris. But the caution of their commanders and the concern of their governments with events in Poland allowed the French to repulse their forces and to occupy the Austrian Netherlands (present-day Belgium). Threats by the Duke of Brunswick, meant to protect the royal family, misfired and led to the fall of the monarchy on the night of 10 August 1792. A new legislature, the Convention, was elected by universal male suffrage just one month later. The Convention became racked by divisions between the 'Girondists', a group of deputies who had favoured the war, and the 'Mountain', led by Robespierre, Danton and Marat, who enjoyed strong support from the working class sections of Paris—both groups belonged to the famed Jacobin Club. Citizen Louis Capet (the dethroned Louis XVI) was placed on trial for treason against his own people, and condemned by the Convention after a tense roll call vote. On 21 January 1793, to the horror of foreign observers, the 39-year-old former king was executed by guillotine in the centre of Paris before a crowd of 50,000 spectators. The next month, France annexed the Austrian Netherlands (present-day Belgium). This was an affront to the British, who feared that possession of the Scheldt estuary would permit the French to launch an invasion fleet on the English coast.

The execution of the King and the annexation of Belgium led to an escalation of the war to include Great Britain, Holland and Spain; ironically, it was the French who declared war on these new adversaries rather than the reverse, just as they had previously taken the first step in declaring war on the Holy Roman Emperor. On 19 November 1792, the Convention publicly announced its intention to assist all peoples struggling for liberation from their kings—throwing down the gauntlet before the autocrats of Europe. Some historians have argued that with the collapse of traditional authority, a situation existed in France in which politics became a rhetorical contest between traditional liberalism and the new radical egalitarianism of Rousseau:

> Leadership passed to those who promised the greatest subservience to the people and the greatest equality. Once extreme notions of equality that denied individual differences dominated political discourse, the coming of the Terror seemed inevitable.[31]

The French Republic now became embroiled in a conflict against a coalition of powers as formidable as any ever faced by Louis XIV, and it seemed that the young republic might not survive. Surrounded by foreign enemies, the revolutionary leaders adopted a siege mentality, establishing a dictatorship far more tyrannical than the deposed monarchy had ever been. Food shortages and military setbacks were blamed on the imagined activities of foreign spies, priests and aristocrats. The Convention delegated temporary powers to a new executive authority, the Committee of Public Safety, created in April 1793. Members of the Paris sections marched on the Convention in June, demanding the arrest of the leading Girondists, who were executed soon afterwards. Republican leaders faced a civil war on three fronts—the *émigrés* along their borders, the royalist and Catholic provinces of the west (the Chouans and the Vendée), and Lyons and other cities to the east that sided with the Girondins.

This was the moment when revolutionary France descended into a nightmare of suspicion and paranoia. The radical followers of the Parisian journalist Hébert called for total war against France's internal and external enemies. The revolutionary government took drastic measures, implementing a 'Reign of Terror' and a new system of national conscription—the *levée en masse*—adopted by the Convention on 23 August 1793. The notorious 'Law of Suspects' (17 September 1793) allowed the arrest of anyone vaguely suspected of counter-revolutionary activity—including all those who 'by their conduct, relations, or language spoken or written, have shown themselves partisans of tyranny or federalism and enemies of liberty'.[32] The accused were tried before specially constituted revolutionary tribunals. The Convention also sent special 'representatives on mission' into the provinces with broad emergency powers. War was waged on Lyons to the east and the Vendée to the west. The 'General Maximum', enacted at the end of September, established maximum prices on basic commodities from tobacco, wine and shoes to paper, soap and meat. Violators of the economic decrees became subject to the Law of Suspects. In October 1793, Marie Antoinette was guillotined; in the same month, the Jacobin leader Saint-Just announced on the floor of the Convention that 'the provisional government of France is revolutionary until the peace'. The subsequent Law of 14 Frimaire awarded dictatorial powers to the Committee of Public Safety. Robespierre accused all the critics of the government, even those sitting in the Convention, of being counter-revolutionaries.[33] To European conservatives, this frenzy of mounting violence seemed to be a ghastly fulfilment of Burke's prophesies.

The guiding spirit of the Committee of Public Safety, Robespierre actually conceived of the Revolution in moral terms: 'Should all Europe declare against you, you are stronger than Europe! The French Republic is as invincible as reason; it is as immortal as truth. When liberty has made a conquest of such a country as France, no human power can drive her out.'[34] Fearing a foreign plot abetted by the Revolution's domestic enemies, he defended the revolutionary dictatorship in a speech before the Convention on 5 Nivose (Christmas Day, 1793): 'The aim of constitutional government is to preserve the Republic. The aim of revolutionary government is to found it. The Revolution is the war of liberty against its enemies.' Behind the veil of Robespierre's stern dictatorship stood a millenarian vision inherited from the Enlightenment:

> We wish to substitute in our country morality for egotism ... the empire of reason for the tyranny of custom ... the virtues and miracles of the Republic for the vices and puerilities of the monarchy ... We wish, in a word, to fulfil the course of nature, to accomplish the destiny of mankind, to make good the promises of philosophy, to absolve Providence from the long reign of tyranny and crime ... [I]n sealing our work with our blood, may we ourselves see at least the dawn of universal felicity gleam before us! That is our ambition. That is our aim.[35]

The revolutionary dictatorship culminated in the passage of the Law of 22 Prairial (10 June 1794), which deprived those appearing before the revolutionary tribunal even of the basic right to defend themselves. Talleyrand, the liberal cleric who had supported the Revolution in its early stages, fled in fear to America. Modern historians estimate that by the time the Terror was over, 300,000 had been arrested as suspects and as many as 40,000 had been executed. The Republicans further adopted a 'scorched earth' policy against the counter-revolutionary rebels in the Vendée to the west, killing hundreds of thousands of men, women and children.

By such coercive measures, the French were able to harness the energies of the entire nation in a way that had never been achieved before. French armies were enlarged by the active participation of all members of society, including those from the middle ranks once spared military service, ushering in a new age of 'total war'. Free of the social constraints of the *ancien régime*, the French introduced new battlefield tactics—a strengthening of artillery, greater reliance on skirmishers and snipers, promotion of talented officers of humble origin, and the granting of greater initiative to the rank and file. Massive frontal attacks by the new revolutionary armies brought heavy losses but overwhelmed the more disciplined lines of their opponents.[36] French generals were also encouraged to act more aggressively out of fear—17 were guillotined in 1793 and another 67 in 1794. 'Nothing illustrated better the violence of the French Revolution,' writes one historian, 'than the fact that its generals were more likely to die at the hands of their own government than as a result of enemy action.'[37] Of equal importance, the Eastern powers became distracted by the Third Partition of Poland. The French were thus able to regain control of both Belgium and the Rhineland. French troops next occupied Holland, where pro-French 'patriots' seized power, declared the creation of the 'Batavian Republic' and introduced reforms modelled after revolutionary France. The Batavian Republic allied with France against England while Prussia and Spain withdrew from the war.

The fact that these impressive victories were gained by the *gouvernement revolutionaire* at the cost of the victims of the Terror left behind a legacy still debated by historians two centuries later: were such convulsions the inevitable consequence of the overthrow of the *ancien régime*? Did the Terror foreshadow the even greater atrocities of the twentieth century?[38] While recent historians have generally railed against the Terror, at least one has noted that the French Revolutionaries 'fought to overturn not merely a distant colonial power, but an entire social order, and to do so with virtually all of Europe in arms against them. What is astonishing is not so much that they tried but that, in a very real sense, they succeeded.'[39]

Once the military situation had sufficiently improved, the organizers of the Terror were abruptly overthrown by members of the Convention fearful for their own safety. Robespierre and Saint Just themselves became victims of the guillotine. Under the new Constitution of the Year III (1795), the Convention was replaced by a bicameral legislature, elected by property-owning taxpayers on the basis of a limited franchise. A new executive was created consisting of five Directors, chosen by legislators. Talleyrand returned from America to Paris to become the Directory's foreign minister. By 1796, France was opposed only by her traditional enemies, Great Britain and Habsburg Austria. Austrian and French forces were evenly matched in Germany and Italy, and British sea power was unable to upset this balance.

The rise of Napoleon

In the next stage of the struggle—roughly from 1796 to 1802—an ambitious young general, Napoleon Bonaparte, broke the deadlock between France and the Continental powers. Born into the minor Corsican nobility in 1769, one year after the island of Corsica had been annexed by France, Bonaparte was blessed with a phenomenal memory, boundless energy, an extraordinary capacity for work and superior mathematical skill. Educated at French military academies in Brienne-le-Château and Paris, he trained as an artillery officer; at one time, he even dreamt of becoming a novelist. In 1793, he fought to take Corsica for the Jacobins but was driven off the island; he next directed a successful artillery assault on Toulon, then occupied by British troops; the same year, he became a protégé of Robespierre's brother, Augustin, after writing a Republican pamphlet. Briefly imprisoned after the fall of Robespierre, Napoleon successfully commanded the defence of the Convention in Paris in October 1795 from royalist attack (in Carlyle's words, with a 'whiff of grapeshot'). In consequence, Bonaparte—still only 27—was promoted to the command of the Army of Italy. Crossing the Alps and moving his troops in forced marches at lightning speed, he concentrated his forces at unexpected points to defeat the Austrians.[40]

Between 1796 and 1798, Bonaparte extended French power into Italy, Germany and Switzerland. The Revolution had already upset traditional political relationships within France by calling all authority into question: now, this same scepticism was projected outward. In the smaller states of the European 'middle zone', Napoleon copied the device of creating satellite republics from Holland; he used local 'patriots' sympathetic to the ideals of the Revolution to set up new pro-French governments in Bologna, Milan, Genoa and Switzerland. French forces had entered Savoy in 1792 to intimidate nearby Geneva; in March 1798, the French violated Swiss neutrality and declared the creation of a new Helvetic Republic (*la République helvétique*) made up of the Swiss cantons. After soundly defeating the Austrians, Bonaparte negotiated the Peace of Campo Formio (1797) in which the Austrians tacitly recognized recent French gains in exchange for their own acquisition of Venice. The arrangement thus displayed the same cynicism towards established frontiers that the eastern powers had already shown in their dismemberment of Poland. The crisis of political legitimacy that the Revolution had unleashed now extended beyond France's borders, throwing all existing governments and territorial arrangements into doubt.

By 1798, France was at war only with Britain. The British feared that the French might assist their republican sympathizers in Ireland, then seething with unrest from religious divisions and rule by an Anglo-Irish elite. Bonaparte sailed instead with a French army to Egypt to strike at the British passage to India. French activities in the Mediterranean excited the jealousies of Russia, which joined Britain and Austria in a 'Second Coalition'. Initially successful, the allies overturned French-sponsored republican governments in Italy and Switzerland. In Naples, Piedmont and elsewhere, this counter-revolution was often violent. Bonaparte received the news and returned forthwith to Paris, abandoning his army. In the French capital, he found support from politicians like Sieyès and Talleyrand, who was still the foreign minister. They hoped to use the rising star of Bonaparte to topple the increasingly unpopular Directory. After a successful *coup d'état*, Bonaparte awarded himself dictatorial powers in a new constitution—under the republican sounding title of 'First Consul'—thus completely frustrating the designs of his fellow conspirators. By then, the Russians had withdrawn from the Second Coalition. Napoleon defeated the Austrians, who again agreed to peace along lines similar to those of 1797.

Bonaparte now succeeded in winning over the active support of Tsar Paul of Russia, the estranged son of Catherine the Great. Paul was infuriated at

British demands to board foreign vessels in the Baltic in search of contraband. The Tsar organized a 'League' of Baltic powers against Britain to protect neutral shipping. But Paul's policies and impulsive conduct were so despised in Russia that he was murdered by a cabal of nobles, who smothered him in his bed, making short work of the League. Even so, this demonstration of foreign hostility severely shook the confidence of the British, who were powerless against France without a major Continental ally. When Prime Minister William Pitt resigned on a domestic question (King George III's stubborn refusal to honour Pitt's pledge to permit Catholics to sit in Parliament), the new British ministry concluded peace with France on relatively unfavourable terms, even consenting to return most of their recent colonial gains while permitting the French to retain their European conquests. The Peace of Amiens was signed in March 1802, and for the first time in a decade Europe was no longer at war.

Napoleon used this breathing space to inaugurate a whole series of great domestic reforms. His Civil Code secured some of the most important revolutionary gains, notably the abolition of feudalism, equality before the law and the opening of careers to talents. His Concordat with the Pope obtained papal recognition of the loss of the properties of the French Church. Above all else, Bonaparte was regarded as the saviour of the Revolution through the sheer fact that his military genius had prevented an allied invasion of France and the Bourbon restoration that would have been its inevitable aftermath. On the other hand, Bonaparte thwarted the democratic impulse of the Revolution. He strengthened his own central authority and the administrative apparatus necessary to enforce it; he robbed the popular assemblies of their powers and curtailed domestic criticism of his policies.

The birth of the Napoleonic Empire and the War of the Third Coalition

In the next phase of the contest, from 1802 to 1807, Napoleon grew increasingly despotic and transformed the recent extension of French power in Europe into a personal empire of unprecedented dimensions. Even before the negotiations at Amiens were concluded, Napoleon had made himself 'President' of the Cisalpine Republic and, in an attempt to appeal to Italian patriots, had changed its name to the 'Republic of Italy'. When peace with England was finally announced, Napoleon used this triumph to make himself 'First Consul for Life' of France. In September 1802, he annexed Piedmont and Elba to France; in February 1803, he abolished the Helvetic Republic and created a new Swiss Confederation, in which he asserted a right of interference as 'Mediator'.[41]

In the same month, the reconstruction of Germany along lines favourable to France was completed by the German Diet (an assembly of princes and rulers of the Holy Roman Empire). According to the terms of the peace with Austria, remaining church properties in Germany were secularized to compensate the leading German princes for their losses to France in the Rhineland. Napoleon wished to build up a following of client states in Germany, and he parcelled out the territories of the ecclesiastical principalities, the free cities and the imperial knights so as to gratify the larger states, especially Prussia, Bavaria, Baden and Württemberg. Talleyrand, now serving as Napoleon's foreign minister, played an active role in their distribution (extorting bribes in the process). The number of electors choosing the Holy Roman Emperor was increased, creating a Protestant majority and rendering future Habsburg possession of the imperial dignity insecure; in consequence, the Holy Roman Emperor declared himself hereditary Emperor of Austria in August 1804, paving the way for the complete destruction of the venerable Holy Roman Empire less than two years later.

Nor were Napoleon's ambitions confined to Europe. Napoleon acquired Louisiana from Spain and sent expeditions to Haiti and India. In all this Napoleon had committed no technical violation of the Peace of Amiens, but with these unexpected augmentations of French power, the British naturally refused to carry out those provisions of the treaty requiring them to evacuate the island Malta in the Mediterranean. War between France and Britain therefore resumed in May 1803. The British seized several French West Indian colonies and the French occupied Hanover—a possession of the King of England—but otherwise the two powers found themselves in much the same impasse as before.

This was the moment when Napoleon chose to make himself Emperor. After a failed attempt on his life, he sent agents into foreign territory to abduct the Duc d'Enghien, a harmless relative of the Bourbons, who was summarily executed in France in retaliation for royalist plots. Ostensibly to diminish any further threat of assassination, Bonaparte then decided to make his title hereditary, placing his brothers next in succession. On 2 December 1804, amidst great pomp and in the presence of the Pope, Napoleon crowned himself 'Emperor of the French' in the Cathedral of Notre Dame in Paris. To some, it seemed a complete betrayal of the Revolution; to others, a grotesque parody of the legitimate dynasty in exile. In May, Napoleon was crowned King of Italy in Milan Cathedral. From Milan, Napoleon proceeded to Genoa, where in early June he announced the annexation of the Ligurian Republic to France.

Napoleon could not harass the British without control of the seas, but the British were similarly hamstrung without a Continental ally. Fortunately for the British, French provocations served to unite Russia, Sweden and Austria with them. In November 1804, a Russian mission was sent to London to negotiate an alliance with Pitt, who was back in power. In the same month a joint declaration against French aggression was issued by Russia and Austria. Austria and Sweden entered the new coalition, though Prussia refused to commit herself and several of the smaller German states remained aligned with France. England acted as paymaster to the coalition, providing financial subsidies to the allies.

As soon as Napoleon learnt that a great 'Third Coalition' had formed against him, he abandoned his plans for the invasion of England. He moved his superbly organized *Grande Armée* of 200,000 men from Boulogne to the Rhine in two weeks, far more swiftly than the allies had ever thought possible. Napoleon had divided this army into several semi-autonomous corps, each with its own infantry, artillery, cavalry, engineers and experienced commanders, in order to give himself maximum flexibility. The allies, in contrast, were woefully unprepared. The advance troops of the Russian army began their long march only by the middle of September; a few days later, Napoleon's army was already crossing the Rhine. Napoleon, with the intention of cutting off the Austrians from the approaching Russians, deliberately crossed to the north and marched eastward before descending to the south. In October, he completely encircled Austrian forces, and subsequently occupied Vienna. His peace terms were so harsh, however, that the Austrians refused to surrender. At long last, Tsar Alexander and the main body of the Russian army advanced into Moravia, where they joined the survivors of the Austrian army in late November.

In early December 1805, Napoleon was able to tempt Alexander into battle at Austerlitz. Napoleon had spent time carefully studying the Pratzen Heights, where the battle would be fought, and then retreated—deliberately yielding this gently sloping hill to the allies. Napoleon feigned the appearance of a weak right flank in order to entrap his adversaries. Many of his own generals opposed the engagement, but the young new Tsar, Alexander I, was insistent—even mocking his leading general, Kutuzov, for failing to advance before the arrival of reinforcements.[42] The entire battlefield was covered in mist and the allies did not appreciate the full strength of the French army. The allies attacked the French right flank, not aware of French forces to the north. Just when the allied centre was dangerously denuded of troops, the sun broke through the clouds and the French charged, dividing the allied army in two and destroying the allied left flank exactly as Napoleon had intended. Napoleon was assisted by three of his most capable marshals—Soult, Bernadotte and Ney. The allies suffered heavy casualties, and the Tsar and the Emperor of Austria were fortunate to escape with their lives. This great French victory, fought one year after Napoleon's coronation, opened the way for the further expansion of his empire. After Austerlitz, the Prussians, who had been preparing to join Austria and Russia, abandoned all thoughts of joining the allied coalition; instead they signed a new treaty of defensive alliance with France. The Russians retreated into Poland, leaving the Austrians no choice but to sue for peace. Austria agreed to the loss of Venetia, Dalmatia and Istria. She also ceded the Tyrol to Bavaria and recognized the electors of Bavaria and Württemberg as kings.

Napoleon took this moment to depose the Neapolitan Bourbons, cousins to Louis XVIII. A French army was sent to Naples, which it occupied without resistance in February. The royal family fled to the island of Sicily, where they remained under British protection for the rest of the war. Napoleon proclaimed his own brother Joseph as the new Neapolitan King. Another French force occupied Ancona in the Papal States. French domination of the Italian peninsula was now complete, except for Rome itself. The irrepressible, expansionist tendencies of the Napoleonic Empire had become undeniably apparent. The only limit on French power seemed to be the sea, for the British Royal Navy had smashed the combined French and Spanish fleets at Trafalgar only six weeks before Austerlitz.

Napoleon next proceeded to subjugate Holland. To avoid offending Prussia, he did not annex Holland directly, but instead arranged for a 'Grand Committee' of Dutchmen to accept his younger brother Louis as their king in June 1806. The following month, Napoleon set about destroying the Holy Roman Empire by forming an association of smaller German states dependent upon France, to be known as the 'Confederation of the Rhine' (*Rheinbund*), from which both Austria and Prussia were excluded. Bavaria, Württemberg, Baden and 11 lesser states joined the new Confederation, formally allied to France and acknowledging Napoleon as its 'Protector'. The same states declared their independence from the Holy Roman Empire, which France also ceased to recognize. A few days later, the Holy Roman Emperor laid down his title and the 1,000-year-old empire came to an end.

The Prussians, still allied to the French, were willing to accept the creation of the Confederation of the Rhine and the destruction of the Holy Roman Empire, but they hoped in turn to create their own confederation of North German states. Napoleon refused to permit this. When Napoleon also offered to return Hanover to Britain, the King of Prussia became so incensed that he resolved on war. Repeating the earlier mistake of the Austrians, the Prussians acted before the Russians could come to their aid. King Frederick William demanded the withdrawal of all French troops behind the Rhine. Only two weeks after the Prussian ultimatum was sent, Napoleon crushed Prussian forces at Jena and Auerstadt. Absent from the war since 1795, the insistence of Prussia's aging generals on the tactics of the *ancien régime* against the greater versatility shown by the French helped to ensure a humiliating defeat.[43] In October 1806, French troops marched in triumph through the streets of Berlin. Yet the Prussians did not immediately surrender, and the remainder of their forces united with the Russian army. Meanwhile, Prussia's ally Saxony deserted her and turned to France. In December, Saxony joined the Confederation of the Rhine; at the same time, Frederick Augustus, the elector of Saxony, was elevated by Napoleon to the rank of king.

Fighting continued into 1807 as the French pushed to the east. In February, the French claimed a victory at Eylau in East Prussia, but the slaughter was so heavy that the French advance was checked. The next major confrontation took place in early June at Friedland. Ten days after the battle, mutual exhaustion led Napoleon and Alexander to meet on a raft in the middle of the Nieman River to negotiate an end to the war. Napoleon offered Alexander control of Europe east of the Vistula, including possible future acquisition of the European provinces of Turkey; Alexander offered to mediate between France and England and, if unsuccessful, to join Napoleon in a Continental boycott of British goods. The peace treaty was signed at Tilsit in July 1807. While offering Russia a generous compromise, Napoleon exacted unusually harsh terms from Prussia. She lost all of her possessions west of the Elbe River as well as all of her territories from the Third Partition of Poland—almost half of her existing population. Prussia also had to pay reparations and limit the size of her military. Napoleon incorporated Prussia's Polish territories into a new Duchy of Warsaw, a resurrection in miniature of the dismembered Polish state, designed to fire the imaginations of Polish patriots. Prussia's lands west of the Elbe were joined to those of several smaller German states to form the new kingdom of Westphalia, ruled by Napoleon's younger brother Jerome. The Peace of Tilsit marked the end of the third phase of the struggle between France and Europe. Single-handedly, Napoleon had defeated all of the powers of Europe except Great Britain. On their ruins he now endeavoured to construct a universal state.

The Napoleonic Empire at its height

The fourth stage of the contest, from 1807 to 1812, saw the Napoleonic Empire at its height. Weaknesses in the international system and the crisis of political legitimacy ushered in by the French Revolution had tempted Bonaparte to reorganize the whole of Europe. What had once been the most powerful member of the European state system had grown into a hegemonic power bringing most of Western and Central Europe under its aegis. The empire during this period can be envisaged as being composed of three concentric circles. The central circle was a vastly inflated France, which in 1807 included Belgium, the Rhineland and Northern Italy. This core was further enlarged: in

1809, by the Illyrian provinces (territories along the Adriatic taken from Austria and the Kingdom of Italy) and the remaining Papal States, including Rome; in 1810, by Holland and the North German coast up to Lübeck; and in 1811, by the canton of Valois, bringing the empire to its maximum extent. France then comprised 130 *départements*, all governed directly from Paris. Paris was the seat, too, of a new imperial court, established in imitation of the court life of the *ancien régime*.

Around this over-inflated France was a second circle of vassal states ruled by members of the Bonaparte family or otherwise dependent upon France. These included Italy, ruled by Napoleon's stepson, acting as viceroy; Holland, ruled by Louis Bonaparte from 1806 until its annexation by France in 1810; Naples, ruled by Joseph Bonaparte from 1806 until 1808 and afterwards by Napoleon's brother-in-law Murat; Westphalia, ruled by Jerome Bonaparte; Spain, ruled from 1808 onwards by Joseph; the Duchy of Warsaw, ruled by the King of Saxony; Switzerland, where Napoleon himself acted as 'Mediator'; and the Confederation of the Rhine, where Napoleon stood as 'Protector'.

France and her vassal states together composed what was known as the Grand Empire.[44] Throughout these territories, Napoleon introduced the same institutions that existed in France. By ending feudalism and serfdom, and by establishing civic equality and religious toleration, he hoped to win over the subjects of these new lands, thereby consolidating the gains made by his armies. At the same time, a centralized administration and a tightened system of censorship and surveillance were imposed to ensure the obedience of the potentially disloyal. The administrative reforms, the adoption of the Code Napoleon and the abolition of serfdom made the Napoleonic epoch as momentous an event in the history of these regions as the Revolution itself had been in France.

Finally, around the Grand Empire lay an outer circle of weakened but nonetheless independent powers—Austria, Prussia, and Russia—forced to ally with France and to participate as members in Napoleon's 'Continental System', an embargo on British colonial and manufactured goods that Napoleon hoped would disrupt Britain's economy and bring the island nation to her knees. At the beginning of this period, the Tsar—to the disgust of his nobles—acted in quasi-partnership with Napoleon, seeking his approval for annexing new territories from the Ottoman Empire; instead, Napoleon encouraged Alexander to seize Finland from Sweden (Britain's ally), which the Russians did early in 1808—an act of naked aggression largely aimed at protecting St Petersburg from invasion.

Inevitably, Napoleon over-reached himself. He lacked the inner sense of restraint that is the mark of truly great statesmanship. Even his foreign minister, Talleyrand, advised Napoleon that he was going too far. Although Napoleon's trail of conquests brought the benefits of the French Revolution to the rest of the Continent, his vision of a universal empire no longer suited Europeans in the early nineteenth century. Nor did Napoleon exercise his rule with impartiality; instead, following the example set by the earlier revolutionaries, he governed with a distinct bias towards France.[45] French generals were rewarded with titles and estates in the newly annexed territories or satellite states. Defeated powers not only suffered losses of territory, they were required to pay tribute in the form of reparations. Napoleon bled the rest of the Continent dry with his repeated requisitions, demands for the support of French armies of occupation and imposition of unequal trading terms. One historian has even called Napoleon's empire nothing more than a 'criminal enterprise' whose sole *raison d'être* was the looting of Europe.[46] In thus dominating Europe, Napoleon inadvertently awakened nationalistic sentiments in other peoples, which would play an important role in his downfall.

Napoleon's first serious difficulties arose in Spain. Spain's rulers had foolishly invited French troops across the Pyrenees to help them in a dispute with Portugal. Napoleon then used treachery to imprison both the King of Spain and his son. A group of hand-picked Spanish notables were hastily assembled at Bayonne, where they gratefully accepted a new constitution and dutifully elected Napoleon's brother Joseph as their new king. Napoleon's brother-in-law, the French general Joachim Murat, was put in Joseph's place on the throne of Naples.

Talleyrand resigned as foreign minister shortly after Tilsit; he later claimed to have been disgusted by Napoleon's usurpation in Spain.[47] Nevertheless, Talleyrand remained Napoleon's Grand Chamberlain and was sent to the magnificent assembly of German princes that Napoleon summoned to the town of Erfurt. The meeting was also attended by the Tsar, although the Emperor of Austria, as former Holy Roman Emperor, was pointedly excluded. In fact, Napoleon hoped to secure the Tsar's support in the event of a future conflict with Austria. At Erfurt, Talleyrand betrayed his master by counselling Alexander in late-night conversations to resist Napoleon. The former foreign minister told the Tsar that he considered those acquisitions up to the 'natural frontiers'—the Alps, the Pyrenees and the Rhine—as belonging to France, but he viewed all subsequent conquests as pure aggrandizements by Napoleon, threatening the equilibrium of Europe.

It was not only Talleyrand who reacted unfavourably to Napoleon's latest aggressions. The French Emperor had failed to take into account the potential reaction of Spanish public opinion to his machinations. The dethroning of the Spanish Bourbons unleashed a groundswell of discontent. By the time that 'King' Joseph reached Madrid, a national insurrection was underway. Rebel envoys were dispatched to London, where they received firm promises of support. A rebel army took control of the south, and in early July, even before Joseph entered Madrid, a French force was defeated by the rebels. Additional French forces poured into Spain, where Napoleon himself arrived in November 1808. By early December, the French Emperor had defeated the rebels in the field. His pursuit was cut short by the news that Austria was also preparing for war, just as British forces began pouring into Spain. The Peninsular War was left unfinished, to drag on for years, until the end of the empire itself.

In Germany, too, there were nationalistic stirrings in response to the Napoleonic adventure. Both Prussia and Austria called upon the German people to rise up against the yoke of French domination. In Prussia, far-reaching reforms, including mass conscription and the abolition of serfdom, were introduced in an attempt to mobilize the energies of the population. Austrian leaders—acting very much against the recommendations of Count Metternich, the young Austrian ambassador in Paris—thought to take advantage of Napoleon's involvement in Spain by declaring war on France in April 1809; at the same time, the Tyrol rose in revolt against Bavaria and peasant rebellions broke out in parts of Italy. To the bitter disappointment of the Austrians, neither the Prussians nor the Russians joined in their effort. The main Austrian army was defeated by Napoleon, whose army included both Saxon and Bavarian contingents, at Wagram in July 1809. Napoleon's triumph was so complete that he contemplated demanding the abdication of the Austrian Emperor and the dismemberment of Austria into its three principal components—Austria, Bohemia and Hungary. In the peace that followed, Austria was forced to cede Croatia and Carniola (which became part of the Illyrian provinces of the French Empire), Salzburg and the Inn district (annexed to Bavaria) and Galicia (divided between the Duchy of Warsaw and Russia). The Austrians further agreed to limit the size of their army. Napoleon also used this opportunity to annex Rome to the French Empire. When the Pope retaliated by excommunicating Napoleon, he was arrested and taken into French captivity, where he remained until 1814.

In the aftermath of the 1809 defeat, Austria entered into a new alliance with France. Her bonds with the French Empire were tightened in 1810 when Napoleon divorced Josephine and married Marie Louise, the daughter of the Austrian Emperor and a niece of Marie Antoinette. By this union with the oldest ruling house in Europe, Napoleon hoped to attain legitimacy for his new dynasty. The Austrians preferred to conclude this marriage rather than to see the French Emperor marry a Russian princess in her stead. Most fittingly, Prince Metternich's wife Eleanor, a granddaughter of the great Austrian diplomat Kaunitz, played a leading role in facilitating the transaction through her personal discussions with Napoleon. In 1811, Marie Louise bore the French Emperor a son and heir, given the illustrious title 'King of Rome'.

Napoleon thus managed to preserve his empire, despite the stirrings of 1808 and 1809, through his consummate military skill and the failure of his adversaries to coordinate their efforts. For the next three years his makeshift regime again seemed secure. Yet he still faced an unquelled rebellion in Spain, an unresolved war with England and the ill-concealed hostility of the rest of Europe. In the final stage of the struggle between France and Europe, these tensions would finally overwhelm Napoleon, causing his magnificent empire to collapse like a house of playing cards. This final phase, discussed in the next chapter, provides the immediate backdrop to the Congress of Vienna.

The plans of Czartoryski and Pitt for the reconstruction of Europe

Speculation on the means of avoiding international strife was scarcely new. Major wars had often been followed by the appearance of idealistic projects. Important schemes for a strictly regulated confederation of European states had been aired by, among others, Henry IV's minister the Duc de Sully in the early seventeenth century, and by the Abbé de Saint-Pierre in 1712.

In the memoirs that Sully published in 1638, he attributed his 'Grand Design' to Henry IV of France, but in fact the plan was clearly his own, formulated in response to the carnage of the French Wars of Religion and the Thirty Years War. One object of his plan was to weaken Habsburg power: Sully called for the complete divestiture of all Habsburg possessions in Europe outside of Spain and the redistribution of these territories among the remaining powers. Sully's design would have reduced Europe to 15 states of roughly equal size, consisting of six hereditary monarchies, five elective monarchies and four republics. Europe would thus be divided 'among a number of powers, who would have nothing to envy in one another on the grounds of equality and no reason to fear that the balance of power would be disturbed.'[48] The 15 states would further elect representatives to a 'General Council': larger states would have four representatives and lesser states, two. Each member state would be obliged to contribute soldiers and warships to an international army and navy, placed at the disposal of the council for use against aggressors and to quell internal unrest.

Three-quarters of a century later, Charles François Irénée Castel, the Abbé de Saint-Pierre, was witness to the devastation of the War of the Spanish Succession. He then served as one of the French plenipotentiaries sent to negotiate the Peace of Utrecht. Saint-Pierre published 'A Project for Settling Perpetual Peace', which he disingenuously claimed to be a mere restatement of Henry IV's earlier Grand Design.[49] 'Neither the balance of power nor treaties are sufficient to maintain peace', the Abbé solemnly warned, so 'the only way is a European union'. In 1714, an English translation outlined his plan in

12 crisp articles: the first set forth the agreement of the sovereigns of Europe to form 'a permanent and perpetual union between all subscribed sovereigns, and if possible all Christian sovereigns, to make peace unalterable'; the sovereigns were to be represented by deputies in a 'perpetual Congress'; the second article guaranteed the 'fundamental form' of each member state (whether hereditary monarchy, elective monarchy or republic); while the fourth provided a guarantee of all territorial possessions. Other articles defined the new Senate of Europe, which was to consist of 24 Senators or deputies, with each deputy representing one state (unlike Sully, Saint-Pierre gave each state equal representation). Member states were to contribute to the expenses of the union in proportion to their size and revenues. Most striking of all was Saint-Pierre's plan for the compulsory arbitration of disputes: no sovereign was to take up arms against another, unless the latter was found to be an 'enemy to European society'. If one sovereign had a complaint against another, the claim was to be submitted to the European Senate, which would mediate the dispute. If the mediation failed, the question was then to be submitted to a process of binding arbitration. Any sovereign who took up arms or failed to comply with the judgement of the Senate was to be deemed an 'enemy'.

The celebrated writer Jean-Jacques Rousseau later became custodian of Saint-Pierre's papers. In 1761, he published a famous summary of the plan— *Extrait du Projet de Paix Perpétuelle de Monsieur l'Abbé de Saint-Pierre*. Rousseau concurrently wrote a critique of the plan, although this was not published until 1782. Rousseau's summary called for the creation of a confederation empowered to give sanctions in order to regulate the conduct of European states:

> The confederation must embrace all the important powers in its membership; it must have a legislative body with the power to pass laws and ordinances binding on its members; it must have a coercive force capable of compelling every state to obey its common resolves whether in the way of command or prohibition; finally, it must be strong and firm enough to make it impossible for any member to withdraw at his own pleasure the moment he conceives his private interest to clash with that of the whole body.

Although Rousseau warmly praised Saint-Pierre's plan, he equally regretted that, in his own view, it could never be realized. Even so, Rousseau's publication brought the attention of all of Europe to Saint-Pierre's plan.[50]

In 1784, on the eve of the French Revolution, the German philosopher Immanuel Kant wrote that the destructiveness of wars would eventually lead states to form a universal federation to guarantee peace, much as individuals had joined together to form states to end civil strife. Kant repeated these arguments in 1795, at the height of the revolutionary conflict, in a celebrated essay entitled 'On Perpetual Peace':

> Each nation, for the sake of its own security, can and ought to demand of others that they should enter along with it into a constitution, similar to the civil one, within which the rights of each could be secured. This would mean establishing a federation of peoples. But a federation of this sort would not be the same thing as an international state ... A particular kind of union, which we might call a pacific federation (*foedus pacificum*), is required.[51]

Kant thought such a federation would eventually come about as the natural outcome of the conflicts between states and the dictates of human reason, but he realized that such changes were not to be achieved overnight. Clearly, what all these philosophical speculations had in common—from Sully to Kant—was their vision of some future federation or multilateral organization that would restrain state sovereignty to ensure lasting peace.[52]

The violence of the French Revolution and the bloodshed of the Napoleonic Wars seemed to fulfil Kant's prophesy of humankind's increasing destructiveness. These upheavals added a new urgency to the search for a more stable international order. How was the period of constant turbulence and flux ushered in by the Revolution of 1789 to be terminated? With so many rapid dislocations and transformations, which institutions and boundaries would prove durable?

Not surprisingly, statesmen joined the philosophers in reflecting on the means of ending the prevailing state of international anarchy.[53] Among them was Prince Adam Jerzy Czartoryski, the Polish companion of Tsar Alexander of Russia. At the age of 25, Czartoryski had been sent to St Petersburg at the time of the final partition of Poland as a virtual hostage to ensure the good behaviour of his family, permitting their continued ownership of their valuable estates.[54] At the Russian court, he was well treated and developed a close friendship with the Tsarina's grandson Alexander, then Grand Duke, who looked up to the slightly older Polish prince with admiration. Alexander secretly promised Czartoryski that he would one day amend the wrongs of the partitions by restoring Polish independence. When Alexander became Tsar in 1801, he felt this was not immediately possible, but during the early years of Alexander's reign, Czartoryski remained one of his most trusted advisers. As a member, along with three other young liberals, of the Tsar's 'Unofficial Committee', Czartoryski dreamt of transforming Russia as well as restoring Poland.[55]

In 1803 Czartoryski presented Alexander with a comprehensive memorandum on the future of Russian foreign policy, which bore a remarkable resemblance to the ruminations of the speculative philosophers on perpetual peace.[56] In his subsequent writings, Czartoryski explicitly compared his plan to Sully's seventeenth-century 'Grand Design'.[57]

A staunch Anglophile who had visited London as a young man with his father, Czartoryski began his memorandum by warning that to safeguard Europe from further French aggression, it would be necessary for Russia to ally with Great Britain. Yet Czartoryski believed that France, too, could be turned into an ally, once she realized that the other powers would not permit her to push beyond her natural frontiers. Czartoryski blamed the recent expansion of France on the almost universal dissatisfaction that had existed throughout Europe with the structures of the *ancien régime*; to contain her, Russia and Britain therefore needed to create a new order of stable states, especially in Central and Southern Europe, capable of withstanding French revolutionary propaganda and the military might of Napoleon. This could only be achieved, Czartoryski contended, by recasting Europe into states divided along ethnic lines, by granting liberal constitutions, and by forming regional federations.

Czartoryski's Polish identity gave him a profound awareness of the growing force of nationalism (in this context, the belief that each major ethnic group should have its own nation-state). 'Every individual nation', he wrote, 'has its own language, its mores, its habits, its manner of seeing and feeling'.[58] Naturally he desired, as part of his plan, to see Russia restore unity and autonomy to Poland. Even if the Tsar should choose to place a Russian prince on the Polish throne, Czartoryski insisted that the Poles would still feel eternal gratitude towards Russia for their national regeneration. The rebirth of Poland would also be in Russia's interest, he argued, since Poland would stand as a buffer between Russia, Austria and Prussia. In Italy, in place of Bonaparte's puppet 'Republic of Italy', Czartoryski proposed the creation of a strong and independent Northern Italian state, formed out of the union of Piedmont, Lombardy and Venice. In addition, he suggested that the various Italian states be associated in a regional federation for purposes of mutual defence. In Germany, Czartoryski likewise advocated the organization of a federation of smaller states, excluding both Prussia and Austria, modelled after the new United States of America. To the east, believing the decline of the Turkish Empire to be well advanced, he recommended the creation of both a Greek and a Slav state (the latter to be carved out of Ottoman Turkey and Hungary); these were to be united in a Balkan federation under special Russian protection. Within these new state boundaries, Czartoryski pleaded for the establishment of liberal constitutions giving full rein to the expression of public opinion and allowing increased popular participation in government. Czartoryski believed that the introduction of these changes would provide Europe with a new resilience, enabling it to overcome the French revolutionary threat.

The following year, Alexander opened the negotiations with Great Britain that would lead to the formation of the Third Coalition. Czartoryski was then serving as the Russian foreign minister. As principal advocate of the Anglo-Russian alliance, Czartoryski was entrusted with the delicate task of drawing up instructions for the special emissary sent to London in November 1804. He was thus provided with an ideal opportunity to communicate his ideas on European reconstruction to William Pitt, the British Prime Minister.[59]

The instructions began by emphasizing that France had succeeded in identifying her cause with 'liberty and prosperity' and that the time had come for the allies to deprive her of this important advantage by their own espousal of liberal constitutionalism. To this end, Czartoryski proposed a preliminary agreement between England and Russia to oppose the revival of former abuses by rulers restored with the help of allied arms, and to assure the subjects of liberated areas that they would receive their 'liberties on a solid basis'. Specifically, Czartoryski urged that the former King of Piedmont-Sardinia should be restored to his throne, but only on the understanding that he grant his subjects a 'free and wise' constitution. Switzerland and Holland were also to regain their national independence, provided that they too frame new constitutions in accordance with the wishes of their inhabitants. For the German states, Czartoryski proposed a federation without Austria or Prussia, as he had in his memorandum of 1803. In France itself, should the triumph of the coalition succeed in shaking the authority of Bonaparte, the people of France should also be free to choose 'any government' they might prefer, although a Bourbon restoration was to be hoped for.

In the final section of the instructions, Czartoryski proposed the formation of a new international league of states, under the direction of England and Russia, which would formulate new rules for international conduct and punish subsequent infractions with its combined might:

> When peace is made, a new treaty should be drawn up as a basis for the reciprocal relations of the European states. Such a treaty might secure the privileges of neutrality, bind the powers taking part in it never to begin a war until after exhausting every means of mediation by a third power, and lay down a sort of code of international law which, being sanctioned by the greater part of the European states, would, if violated by any one of them, bind the others to turn against the offender and make good the evil he has committed ...[60]

In this proposal, formalizing the ad hoc processes of coalition diplomacy, Czartoryski moved close to the vision of a federation of states earlier suggested by Sully, Saint-Pierre, Rousseau and Kant. It was a 'Grand Design' bold enough, Czartoryski hoped, to end the turbulence unleashed by the French Revolution.

It is worth noting that it is not simply on a theoretical level that we can trace the provenance of these ideas from the earlier philosophers down to Czartoryski and the other policy-makers of 1814. Frédéric-César de La Harpe, the Swiss tutor of Tsar Alexander I, was a follower of Rousseau, while Friedrich von Gentz, the future colleague of Metternich, had been a student of Kant's at Königsberg and even wrote his own lengthy article on 'perpetual peace' in 1800.[61] Czartoryski himself was probably influenced by Scipione Piattoli, an Italian priest living in Warsaw who had developed his own plan for a future European federation.[62]

In London, Pitt received the Russian overture enthusiastically. At a time when Britain was alone at war with France, Pitt could only look with favour upon a plan to form a new anti-French coalition.[63] Pitt disagreed, however, with many of Czartoryski's specific proposals for European reconstruction, and he drafted a set of counter-proposals, which he presented to Vorontsov, the Russian ambassador, in January 1805.[64] Pitt concerned himself far less than Czartoryski with European public opinion and much more with erecting new territorial barriers against French aggression. Pitt believed that the allies needed to restore ancient rights and to provide for the welfare of peoples to the greatest extent possible, but both of these considerations had to be subordinated to the still more important aim of 'the general security of Europe'. Pitt was especially concerned with what statesmen at the time considered 'the balance of power'. This was the age-old notion that the powers of Europe needed to exist in a balance, or equilibrium, in which no single power or group of powers was so strong that it would be tempted to conquer the rest. On these grounds, Pitt argued that certain nations, lacking in the requisite strength to defend themselves, could not be safely restored to their former stature, even if they should be liberated from the French yoke. In this class he placed Genoa, the Republic of Italy, Belgium and the Rhineland (mainly territories found in Europe's weaker 'middle zone'). Pitt proposed to distribute these territories to Austria, Prussia, Piedmont and Holland to form stronger protective barriers around France, whose preponderance now posed the chief threat to the European balance.

In the unlikely event that France could be driven back to her 'ancient limits' (the frontiers of the French monarchy before 1792), Pitt proposed the following arrangements: Piedmont and Holland should be enlarged to become barrier states on the French frontier; Austria should be made guardian of

Northern Italy; and Prussia should become guardian of the Low Countries and Northern Germany. To accomplish this, Pitt proposed the following specific territorial adjustments: Piedmont was to be strengthened through the addition of Parma, Placentia and part of Lombardy; Modena and Tuscany were to be given to Austrian archdukes; Austria was to acquire a portion of the Papal States and to retain Venetia; Belgium was to be divided between Prussia and Holland; and the Rhineland was to be annexed to Prussia. Austria would thus be compensated in Italy for Prussian gains in Germany.

Pitt agreed with Czartoryski that regional federations in Italy and Germany might offer these troubled areas means of additional security, and he further suggested that these federations should build and jointly garrison fortresses along the French frontier. He also agreed that while the restoration of the Bourbons in France would be highly desirable, it could not be a primary object of the alliance.

Finally, to provide 'solidity and permanence' to the new territorial settlement, Pitt proposed, in place of Czartoryski's plan for a pan-European federation, a union of the chief powers in which they mutually guaranteed one another's territories and rights:

> Much will undoubtedly be effected for the future repose of Europe by these territorial arrangements, which will furnish a more effectual barrier than has before existed against the ambition of France. But in order to render this security as complete as possible, it seems necessary, at the period of a general pacification, to form a Treaty to which all the principal powers of Europe should be parties, by which their respective rights and possessions, as they then have been established, shall be fixed and recognized; and they should all bind themselves mutually to protect and support each other, against any attempt to infringe them: It should re-establish a general and comprehensive system of public law in Europe, and provide, as far as possible, for repressing future attempts to disturb the general tranquillity; and above all, for restraining any projects of aggrandizement and ambition similar to those which have produced all the calamities inflicted on Europe since the disastrous era of the French Revolution.[65]

It seems quite likely that Pitt was influenced in these views by the writings of Gentz, or even by the Abbé de Pradt, whose *Prussia and its Neutrality* (1800) had specifically proposed uniting Belgium with Holland and strengthening Piedmont to create new barriers around France.[66] Some of Pitt's ideas might also have originated in the plan for territorial redistribution that Lord Grenville had drawn up during the negotiations for the Second Coalition in 1798.[67] Grenville's plan had contained several similar provisions, including a 'guarantee' of the possessions of the four great powers against future French aggression, pushing France back to her ancient limits, combining Holland and Belgium, and compensating Austria in Italy.[68]

The turmoil created by the French Revolution had thus led two of Europe's foremost statesmen—Czartoryski and Pitt—to agree on the need for a new territorial settlement and for some form of international federation to maintain it. They differed profoundly, however, on the character of each. Czartoryski's scheme was visionary and idealistic, perhaps even fanciful, as well as hostile to Austrian and Prussian interests. He especially depended on usurping France's role as the champion of popular liberties by espousing ethnic nationalism and liberal constitutionalism. Pitt's approach was more traditional, sympathetic to Austria and Prussia, concerned with such tangibles as the balance of military force among the great powers, and almost indifferent to the intangibles of public opinion and nationalism. In any event, the defeat of the Third Coalition meant that neither of these designs was to be adopted; instead, it was Napoleon's vision of a Grand Empire that was given its brief trial. But the proposals of Czartoryski and Pitt were not totally forgotten, and ten years later, when the Napoleonic experiment had failed, both Russian and British statesmen looked back to this exchange of ideas for guidance in the reconstruction of Europe. Despite their apparent futility at the time, the schemes of 1804–05 bore consequences of the greatest significance—from Czartoryski's proposal for a European federation sprang forth the Russian view of the Congress System and from Pitt's blueprint came the British-sponsored programme for territorial resettlement that was largely adopted in 1815.

2

The Collapse of the Napoleonic Empire, 1812–14

Napoleon's invasion of Russia and the Fourth Coalition

At the beginning of 1812, seven years after the exchange between Czartoryski and Pitt, French power was at its apparent height. Yet the final stage in the struggle between Revolutionary France and Europe was about to unfold. Fissures in the imposing edifice of Napoleon's *Grande Empire* were already visible. In Napoleon's eyes, growing acrimony with Russia, especially Russia's failure to enforce his 'Continental System'—a French-led boycott of British goods—overshadowed all his other difficulties. To prevent the gradual erosion of his authority, he resolved to set an example by invading the Russian colossus. At the head of an army of more than 600,000 men, composed of most of the nationalities of Europe, Napoleon crossed into Russia in June 1812. He had committed a monumental blunder that would destabilize his empire and lead to his own downfall less than two years later.

In an age before trains or mechanized transport, Napoleon's invasion was probably doomed once the Russians, initially outnumbered, refused to engage in decisive combat or to sue for peace in the summer months. Napoleon was still conducting a second war in distant Spain, while in Russia he was in command of an unwieldy multilingual force consisting of restive and distrustful Poles, Lithuanians, Germans and Austrians as well as French. Although he had stockpiled nearly two months of supplies, Napoleon had trouble moving them along the muddy and unpaved roads and had never intended to march any further east than Smolensk. After the Phyrric victory of Borodino, the French entered a deserted Moscow—soon destroyed by fires set by the Russians themselves. The invaders quickly discovered that they were stranded without provisions. Napoleon attempted to open negotiations with Tsar Alexander in early October, but received no answer. After losing a precious month awaiting a reply in Moscow, Napoleon finally realized he had no choice but to retreat. Rather than move south, he chose to retrace his steps westward. The unwieldy *Grande Armée* proved incapable of living off the occupied Russian territories. Shortages of food and water, the onset of winter, and harassment by Cossacks, soldiers and peasants decimated the retreating invasion force throughout November and December. Fewer than 40,000 survived the return to Germany. Recent historians have argued that this cataclysmic disaster was far from accidental—the Russian strategy was in fact to entice Napoleon's forces ever deeper into the vast expanses of Russia in order to weaken and destroy them.[1]

The annihilation of Napoleon's *Grande Armée* in Russia paved the way for the consolidation of a new anti-French alliance. Alexander experienced a profound religious crisis at the time of the invasion. Now he groomed himself for the part of Europe's liberator by surrounding himself with patriots of every conceivable national hue. He quickly resolved to carry the conflict across the Nieman River and back into Central Europe. The British offered financial subsidies to Russia and Sweden, which also joined the allies. But without the adherence of Prussia and Austria, the new coalition's prospects for success were slight.

From the Prussian vantage point, neither French nor Russian ascendancy in Central Europe could be viewed with equanimity. General Hans von Yorck, the Prussian commander in the field, acted on his own initiative in signing the Convention of Tauroggen, a secret armistice and pledge of neutrality with Russia. The Convention helped Alexander silence those Russian critics opposed to an extension of the war, while the subsequent Russian advance into East Prussia virtually forced the hand of the Prussian King, Frederick William III. The King initially accused Yorck of treason and made desperate overtures to Napoleon, but the latter's silence left him no alternative but to break with France and conclude a formal alliance with the Tsar.[2]

The signing of a Russo-Prussian treaty at Kalisch in February 1813 thus laid the cornerstone for the future destruction of French hegemony in Central Europe. The Prussians had at first sought the return of all their pre-1806 territories, including their Polish dominions, but the most that Alexander would concede was that Prussia should be restored to its pre-1806 'statistical, geographical, and financial' proportions. Prussia was guaranteed East Prussia but not Poland; instead, Alexander indicated that Prussia would receive compensation in Northern Germany—tacitly understood to mean Saxony—while he hinted that Russia would eventually acquire Prussia's former Polish territories, then still incorporated into Napoleon's puppet Duchy of Warsaw.[3]

The disposition of Austria at this juncture remained highly equivocal. The 1809 defeat had raised fresh doubts about Austria's ability to defend herself against French power. She was also now tied dynastically to France by the marriage of Marie Louise to Napoleon in 1810. The terms decided at Kalisch, moreover, could hardly have appealed to her. The Austrians strenuously opposed plans for Russian aggrandizement in Poland. They were equally outraged at clumsy Russian attempts to rally German nationalist sentiment against the authority of Francophile German princes. Finally, Austrian treaty obligations with France confined the size of the Austrian army to 150,000 men. Not surprisingly, the Austrian foreign minister, Prince Metternich, failed to rush to the allied standard. He proposed instead that Austria should act as mediator between the belligerents, thus making a bold attempt to play Russia off against France in order to clear Central Europe of both intruders. As early as December 1812, Metternich offered Austria's good offices to Napoleon for the arrangement of a general peace, and in February 1813, he dispatched emissaries with mediation proposals to both London and Prusso-Russian military headquarters.

In London, Metternich's mediation offer was quickly rebuffed. Lord Castlereagh, the new British Foreign Secretary, hoped for Austria to join the allies, not to cut Napoleon's losses through negotiation. He also saw no reason to let Austria interfere in Britain's disputes with France over British maritime rights. He therefore forwarded his own ruminations on war objectives to allied headquarters, along with instructions for the conclusion of subsidy treaties with Russia and Prussia. Castlereagh's thinking hearkened back to Pitt's design of 1805, employing 'great masses'—Prussia, Russia, and Austria—to keep France in check.

In the spring of 1813 these diplomatic manoeuvres were abruptly overtaken by military events. Throughout March and April, the allied armies continued their forward sweep, crossing the Elbe and occupying Dresden. The allies had now generally adopted the same military tactics as the French. Meanwhile, Napoleon was in Paris, calling up new classes of conscripts, moving National Guardsmen into regular units and welding together a new army. When he finally left Paris in mid-April, he once again commanded forces outnumbering those of his opponents, though a dangerous proportion of his troops were raw recruits and he lacked cavalry. Advancing into Saxony, Napoleon defeated the allies in early May, forcing an evacuation of Dresden and an allied re-crossing of the Elbe.

Even as the hostilities progressed, Metternich persisted in his mediation effort. Losses on the battlefield finally persuaded both Napoleon and the allies to yield to Austrian pressures for a short armistice in early June. The truce was detrimental to British interests to an extreme degree: first, Prussia and Russia consented to it without consulting London, despite prior pledges not to conclude a separate peace; secondly, it called for a cessation of hostilities in Germany but not in Spain, where the Duke of Wellington was still engaged in heavy fighting.

Metternich met with the Tsar at Castle Opočno in Bohemia in mid-June, after which Austrian, Russian and Prussian representatives signed a treaty at Reichenbach (present-day Dzierzoniow), stipulating a common set of territorial demands on France. Potential discord between Russia and Austria was avoided by adopting the vague formula that the Duchy of Warsaw would be dissolved and partitioned, without further elaboration.[4] (This ambiguity would cause future problems.) Since Britain had refused Austrian mediation, Metternich convinced the allies to confine their requirements to those points essential to a 'Continental Peace'—one that would settle outstanding Central European questions with France, while leaving Britain and her special interests (Spain, Naples and Holland) in the lurch. If Napoleon accepted these terms, the 'Continental Peace' was to be concluded and negotiations for a 'General Peace' would hopefully follow; should he refuse, Austria pledged to join the allies. Metternich next travelled to Dresden, where he met with Napoleon and after an exhausting audience obtained the French Emperor's consent both to an extension of the armistice until 10 August and to the opening of peace negotiations in Prague. British representatives remained excluded from the Prague talks, as British influence approached its nadir.

The sincerity of Metternich's mediation proposal has been the subject of much subsequent controversy. Metternich himself later told the allies that his offer had only been a sham to permit Austria time for rearmament, and as early as March, he attempted to conclude a convention with the Tsar and requested subsidies from Britain. Earlier generations of historians accepted Metternich at his word, observing that by 1813, Metternich already thought a stable peace with Napoleon was unattainable. Recent scholars have suggested that Metternich's efforts to restore peace were in fact genuine, since he truly desired to avoid the ravaging of Central Europe and hoped to maintain a viable balance between French and Russian power.

Whether genuine or disingenuous, Metternich's exclusion of Britain from Continental negotiations outraged British ministers, who feared that Austrian cunning might jeopardize Europe's deliverance from French oppression. News of the June armistice prompted Castlereagh to formulate a comprehensive list of British war aims, which he hastily transmitted to the Continent in early July. Again, he based his ideas on Pitt's plan of 1805. He pointed out that the only genuine security for the allies existed in their 'cordial union', and he patiently elaborated Britain's minimal requirements, including the return of Spain, Portugal and Naples to their 'legitimate sovereigns'; the fulfilment of British engagements to Sweden; the restoration of Austria and Prussia to their former sizes; the liberation of Holland; and the recovery of former Hanoverian territories. At the same time, Castlereagh finally accepted the Austrian offer of mediation. However, he stipulated that his acceptance should be communicated to Austria by the Tsar, and Alexander chose to withhold the news until the conclusion of the Prague negotiations.

Fortunately for the British, Napoleon spurned the outstretched hand at Prague. The collapse of his empire had occurred so swiftly that he had not yet adjusted—if ever he could—to the abandonment of his imperial vision; he would have had difficulty, in any event, in governing France without those foreign dependencies which had hitherto furnished him with extraordinary revenues, lands for distribution to his supporters and markets for French commerce; finally, Napoleon believed that the allied terms were only the thin end of the wedge and that any concessions would provoke still further demands. On their part, the ministers of the other powers—with the exception of Metternich—did little to facilitate the negotiations. At the stroke of midnight on 10 August, the talks terminated and a state of hostilities resumed. The armistice had largely redounded to the benefit of the allies: Austria was now in their camp and they had been able to reinforce their armies in greater numbers than the French.

The disturbing neglect of British interests exhibited by Russia and Prussia, as well as the entry of Austria into the alliance, prompted Castlereagh to send off a new 'Project of a Treaty of Alliance' in late September, outlining his grand conception of the ends and means of the European coalition. 'The present Confederacy', he wrote to his ambassador to the Tsar, 'may be considered as the Union of nearly the whole of Europe against the unbounded and faithless ambition of an individual. The great object of the Allies, whether in war or in negotiation, should be to keep together, and to drive back and confine the armies of France within the circle of their own immediate resources'. The negotiations at Prague had left a very bitter taste and Castlereagh admonished his own envoys to 'guard against a continental peace being made to our exclusion'. He proposed that the powers conclude a common treaty uniting themselves around a single set of mutual war aims. Like the later Treaty of Chaumont (March 1814), this proposal envisaged the perpetuation of the anti-French coalition into peacetime.

Castlereagh nearly exploded in anger when he learned that Metternich had forwarded a conciliatory reply to a French request for yet another peace conference only moments after the termination of the Prague talks. In a fit of indignation, he forwarded the message that Britain would not negotiate with the enemy before a real possibility for peace presented itself; under existing circumstances, no new discussions could be opened till Napoleon first accepted preliminary allied terms, and this goal could only be accomplished through force of arms.

Meanwhile, the accession of Austria to the coalition led the ministers of the three eastern powers (Russia, Prussia and Austria) to meet and reformulate their common war aims at Teplitz. They agreed, as before, that Austria and Prussia should be restored to their former size and status, and that Napoleon's twin creations, the Confederation of the Rhine and the Duchy of Warsaw, should be disbanded.[5] They reached no consensus, however, on how Germany and Poland were to be reconstructed. British representatives were again excluded from these discussions, and there were no references in the Teplitz agreements to either Holland or Spain. With their newfound superiority in numbers, the allies at last inflicted a decisive defeat on Napoleon at Leipzig in Saxony in late October 1813—known as the 'Battle of the Nations'.[6] Lord Aberdeen, the young British envoy to Austria, left a vivid description of the carnage after the battle:

> For three or four miles the ground is covered with bodies of men and horses, many not dead. Wretches unable to crawl, crying for water amidst heaps of putrefying bodies. Their screams are to be heard at an immense distance, and still ring in my ears. The living as well as the dead are stripped by the barbarous peasantry, who have not sufficient charity to put the miserable wretches out of their pain. Our victory is most complete. It must be owned that a victory is a fine thing, but one should be at a distance.[7]

The subsequent retreat of French soldiers across Germany and behind the Rhine, together with the defection of France's remaining allies among the smaller German states, marked the final eclipse of Napoleonic power in Germany. The way was now clear for an allied invasion of France. But before proceeding, the allied leaders were forced to consider whether, by crossing onto ancient French soil, they would arouse the dormant energies of its population. Would 1814 unleash a repetition of the French resurgence of 1792–93? Moreover, the most important of the previously stipulated allied war aims had been achieved: French influence had been removed from Germany, and sufficient liberated territory existed for the reconstruction of Prussia and Austria. Was there even a need to advance into France? Allied disagreements gave further pause for consideration. The King of Prussia insisted that an invasion of France could never succeed.[8] The Austrian minister, Metternich, was highly suspicious of Russian intentions in Central Europe and did not wish to proceed too far in dismantling French power: Napoleon remained a valuable piece on the diplomatic chessboard for future opposition to Russian schemes of aggrandizement. Finally, allied troops were exhausted and poorly equipped. Several allied generals favoured waiting at least until spring before continuing the campaign. Napoleon himself was counting on allied delays to give him time to organize new armies.

As the allied leaders pondered these questions, they proceeded from Leipzig to the former imperial capital of Frankfurt. Here, in answer to a French request for a renewal of negotiations, Metternich told a French envoy that the allies would be satisfied if Napoleon would agree to the reduction of France to her 'natural frontiers'—the Rhine, the Pyrenees and the Alps. Metternich, with Russian and British diplomats in attendance, even conceded that a discussion of British maritime rights might be included on the agenda of a future peace congress.

Once again, Napoleon failed to grasp at a most generous offer. An unenthusiastic reply to the Frankfurt proposals was transmitted in late November, accepting the suggested congress but not the attached conditions. Metternich acted as spokesman for the alliance in rejecting this response. On 4 December, the allies therefore issued a proclamation to the French people, promising France more territory than she had possessed before the Revolution, but reiterating their refusal to tolerate Napoleon's preponderance over the rest of the Continent. Allied leaders thus endeavoured to throw the onus for the continuation of the war directly onto Napoleon.[9]

Meanwhile, on the western edge of the Continent, Wellington's army crossed over the Pyrenees from Spain onto French soil almost in the same instant as the Battle of Leipzig. To the northwest, the advance of allied armies provoked Holland to explode in revolt. The British furnished the Prince of Orange (in England since April 1813) with funds, a small fleet and an expeditionary force, enabling him to return to his homeland in late November. To the south, an Austrian army occupied the Illyrian provinces and began advancing through the Kingdom of Italy, while King Murat of Naples betrayed Napoleon by entering into negotiations with Austrian envoys. To the east, Austrian troops poured into the cantons of the Swiss Confederation, which now declared independence from their French 'Mediator'. Signs of the collapse of Napoleon's empire were everywhere in evidence.

These startling events at last forced the hand of the intransigent French ruler. Napoleon appointed as his new foreign minister Armand de Caulaincourt—a soldier and moderate diplomat, who had served as ambassador to Russia and who had accompanied Napoleon on his retreat from Moscow in 1812. Caulaincourt immediately sent a conciliatory note to the allies accepting the Frankfurt offer of the 'natural frontiers'. But in their improved military position, the allies were now far from anxious to negotiate on this basis. They therefore returned a temporizing reply, explaining that they would first have to consult with the British government, which was inadequately represented at allied headquarters.

Castlereagh's mission to the Continent

The Frankfurt proposals were completely unacceptable to the British—especially the French retention of Antwerp and the negotiation of British maritime rights. As soon as news of the proposals reached London, Castlereagh sent a stream of bitter protests to his allies. The Tsar sent a high-ranking emissary, General Charles Pozzo di Borgo, to London in an attempt to explain Russian policy and to reach an agreement.[10] Fears that British objectives would be lost sight of in the forthcoming negotiations were so aroused that the cabinet took the momentous step of dispatching Castlereagh himself to the Continent. Such a voyage by a British Foreign Secretary in wartime was quite unprecedented, but its necessity had been painfully demonstrated by the course of events at Reichenbach, Prague, Teplitz and Frankfurt.

The importance of the written instructions for Castlereagh's mission, hammered out in a series of major cabinet discussions, would be difficult to exaggerate. Cabinet members realized that due to the tardiness of communications between Britain and the Continent, Castlereagh would be forced to act on his own initiative on most issues. Here was a last, great opportunity to set forth the fundamental principles to guide his conduct. Castlereagh himself played a dominant role in drawing them up, and by and large remained faithful to their spirit over the course of the next two years.

The instructions naturally focused on the redistribution of territories liberated from the former French Empire, to which Castlereagh applied Pitt's ideas of 1805. Britain's aim was to see 'a maritime as well as a military Balance of Power established amongst the Powers of Europe ...'. Her paramount concern was with the Low Countries. It was only from the Scheldt that the British imagined an invasion of Britain could be launched with any prospect of success, and it was French possession of the Scheldt that had first driven Britain to war with France in 1793. The instructions therefore insisted that Belgium must be separated from France and placed under Dutch rule. Holland would be further tied to Britain through a dynastic marriage alliance. Spain and Portugal must also be made independent of France and their former ruling families restored. In Northern Italy, Piedmont would be strengthened by the acquisition of Genoa. The instructions also proposed, as Pitt had initially suggested, that the coalition should continue into peacetime to guarantee the successful maintenance of the new territorial settlement. Under these conditions, Britain would agree to return most of the overseas colonies she had captured during the last two decades of warfare. But if these requirements could not be met, Britain threatened to retain these colonial acquisitions as compensation for her continuing insecurity.[11]

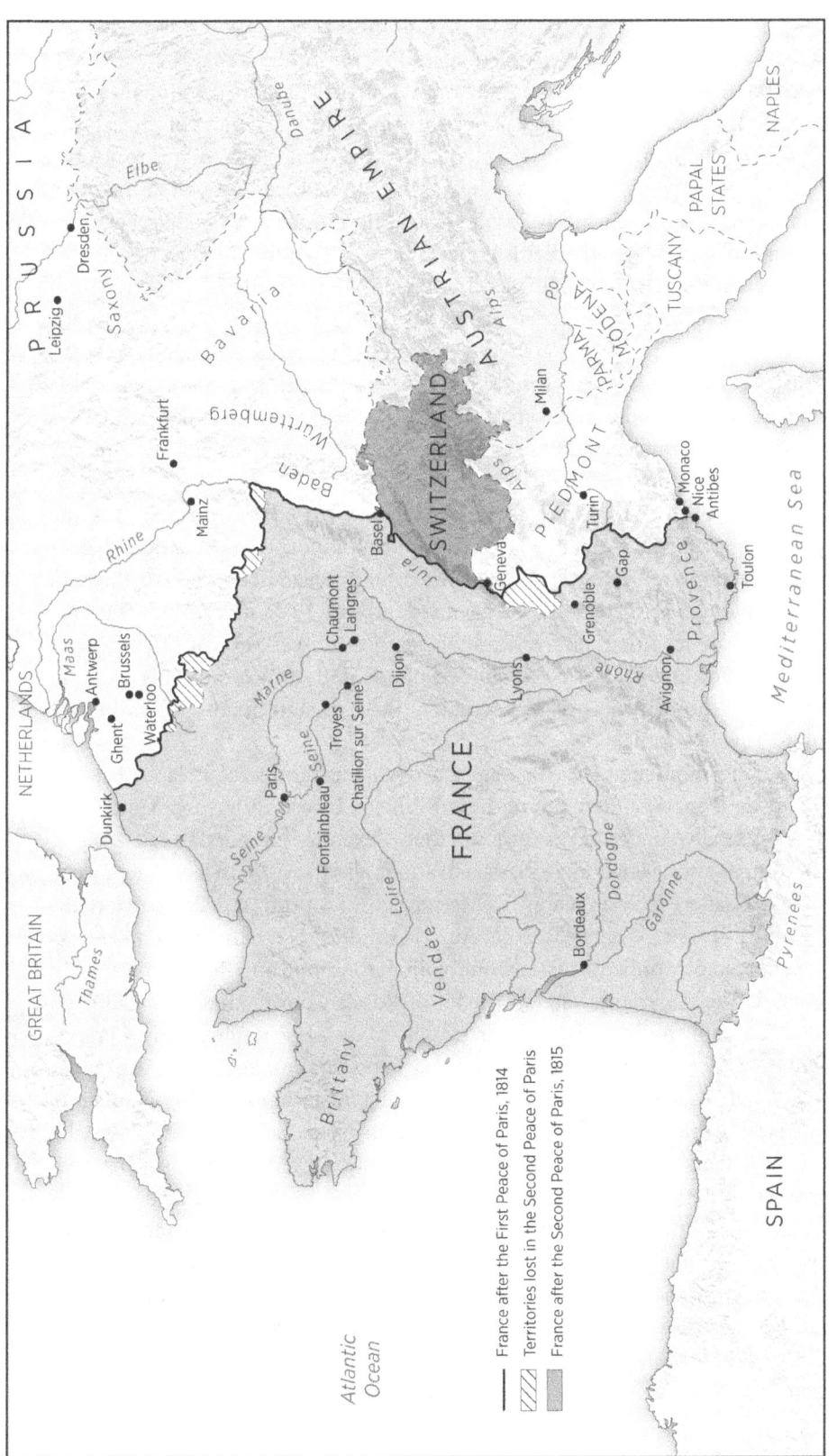

The Frontiers of France, 1814–15

One topic that was deliberately omitted from these instructions was the future of France itself. Like Czartoryski and Pitt in 1805, most of the cabinet favoured placing the self-proclaimed Louis XVIII on the French throne. The French Pretender, a younger brother of the unfortunate Louis XVI, had fled from France in the early days of the Revolution; since 1807 he had been living in England, where the British government gave him a modest pension to maintain his small court of exiles. The Prime Minister (the Earl of Liverpool) and several cabinet members toyed with the idea of sending one of the nephews of Louis XVIII to join Wellington's army, but Castlereagh firmly rejected this proposal just before setting sail for the Continent: as a young man, Castlereagh had visited revolutionary France and had become convinced that a Bourbon restoration could never successfully take place without the support of the French populace.[12]

Castlereagh arrived in Holland on 5 January 1814. He swiftly finalized the plans for a marriage alliance between the ruling houses of Britain and Holland. Despite an unusually severe winter, he proceeded southward through Germany and arrived in Basel, Switzerland, on 15 January. The Tsar had impetuously left for military headquarters on the very eve of Castlereagh's arrival, affording Metternich a golden opportunity to expound his views in private to the British Foreign Secretary. The two statesmen took an instant liking to one another.

At the moment of Castlereagh's arrival, the futures of Poland, Saxony, Hanover, Denmark, Belgium and the Rhineland were all in flux. Metternich was especially concerned at rumours that Alexander intended to take Poland for himself and to encourage Prussia to annex all of Saxony. In fact, only a week before Castlereagh's appearance, Metternich had promised Prince Hardenberg, the Prussian Chancellor, that Austria would agree to the Prussian annexation of Saxony only if Prussia would join her in opposing Russian designs in Poland. The Austrians were so fearful of Russian power that they had even slowed down the advance of their troops, to avoid being engaged in France while Russian forces remained to the rear in occupation of Central Europe.

While Metternich insisted on pursuing negotiations with Napoleon, Alexander thirsted for revenge for the French occupation of Moscow. The Russian Tsar yearned to march to Paris, where he could display his own magnanimity to the French people; he also had become highly suspicious of apparent Austrian pusillanimity. Moreover, Alexander had concocted his own scheme for the future government of France. Once in control of Paris, Alexander intended to topple Napoleon and replace him with another French general, Jean Bernadotte. Bernadotte had been a close friend of Napoleon's and in 1810 he had been chosen by the Swedes to become their Crown Prince. Alexander had met with Bernadotte for secret talks in 1812, when he apparently told Bernadotte that he might one day place him on the French throne. Soon thereafter, Sweden had joined the allies against Napoleon: Bernadotte, one of Napoleon's commanders at Austerlitz, thus played a prominent role in planning allied military strategy in 1813.[13]

By early 1814, four options were under allied consideration for the future government of France: (1) Napoleon might be left on the throne and France reduced to her ancient frontiers; (2) Napoleon might abdicate in favour of his infant son and a Regency under his wife, the Austrian-born Empress Marie Louise; (3) Bernadotte might be placed on the throne; or (4) the self-proclaimed Louis XVIII, living in exile in England, might be 'restored'. Not for an instant did the allied leaders ever consider turning France back into a democratic republic, since it was the republic, after all, that had plunged Europe into 20 years of war. The Regency was expected to favour Austria, just as Bernadotte would incline towards Russia, and one of Castlereagh's principal aims now became to discourage Metternich from attempting it.

At Basel, Castlereagh quickly agreed to join forces with Metternich in opposing Bernadotte's candidature. Both ministers dreaded a possible alliance between France and Russia, which the Tsar might use to dictate the resettlement of Central Europe. It was the first instance of cooperation between these two diplomats against Alexander—a pattern that was to be repeated many times over the course of the next eight years. It might be thought that Metternich made clever use of the French dynastic question to direct Castlereagh's animus against Russia. It had been primarily against Austrian attempts to reach a Continental peace with Napoleon, after all, that Castlereagh's mission had first been directed. Metternich indeed exploited Castlereagh's anxieties about the enigmatic character and policies of Alexander to win his support, not only on the French but also on the Polish and German questions. But Castlereagh did not leave the bargaining table empty-handed, since he obtained Austrian support on the two issues of greatest concern to Britain: the exclusion of maritime issues from any negotiations with France and the future independence of Belgium from French rule.[14]

Castlereagh and Metternich reached allied military headquarters together at Langres in eastern France in the third week of January. It was here that the small group of statesmen who would dominate European politics for the next eight years assembled for the very first time. It was a propitious moment, for the allied coalition was on the verge of dissolution. Austria had halted her military advance until Alexander's plans regarding France were made known. Alexander, on the other hand, refused to consider Napoleon's most recent offer to negotiate and threatened to continue his march alone. Castlereagh demanded formal meetings among the four chief ministers—both to resolve their differences and to concert on military strategy. He confronted the Tsar openly on the candidature of Bernadotte, though without much success, since Alexander disingenuously disavowed any intentions of raising the Swedish Crown Prince to the French throne. It was only when Metternich threatened to pull Austria out of the alliance that Alexander finally consented to participate in the ministerial discussions and to cooperate with the other allies.

A series of important ministerial conferences was thus inaugurated on 29 January. The allied ministers eventually hammered out the following compromise: they would accept Napoleon's request to open new negotiations, but they would not suspend hostilities during the talks. Moreover, they agreed to abandon their prior offer of France's natural frontiers as the basis for the talks. Instead, they now accepted the British view that France should lose both Belgium and the Rhineland and that British maritime rights should not be subject to discussion. They also agreed that France should exercise no influence over the distribution of territories outside her own borders. There was less agreement over the French dynastic question. The allies concluded that the question should be treated as a 'national one' for the French people to decide for themselves, but this determination was mainly to paper over their own differences. Castlereagh announced that Britain favoured negotiations with Napoleon as the *de facto* ruler of France, but if events in France ever called his authority into question, Britain reserved the right to withdraw from the talks. Over the future of Central Europe, no agreement could be reached at all. This final issue was left to fester, pending the defeat of France.[15]

The negotiations at Châtillon

Negotiations with the French opened on 5 February at Châtillon-sur-Seine. France was represented by its affable foreign minister, Caulaincourt, who genuinely desired peace. The allies were represented by high-ranking officials but not by their foreign ministers, which Caulaincourt astutely interpreted as an ominous sign. Castlereagh supervised the allied plenipotentiaries informally and constantly travelled back and forth to allied headquarters to confer with the other allied leaders.

The negotiations at Châtillon furnish a classic example of the dangers of negotiating with an enemy while still engaged in military operations. The demands of each side waxed and waned in accordance with the fortunes of combat. Metternich was probably the most sincere among the allies in his wish for a negotiated settlement. Napoleon and Castlereagh, in their own ways, also wanted peace, but on diametrically opposed terms: Castlereagh demanded the separation of Belgium from France whereas Napoleon insisted on France's natural frontiers. The Tsar agreed to the talks only with the greatest reluctance and secretly instructed his envoy to impede their progress. Against this motley background, what one envoy called the 'bad comedy' of Châtillon got under way.

At the second meeting of the plenipotentiaries, the allies demanded that France accept the 'ancient limits'—her pre-revolutionary frontiers. This was far less than the allies had offered Napoleon at Frankfurt, but with their armies advancing in all directions, the demand was hardly unexpected. Caulaincourt was too timorous to conclude peace on these terms without Napoleon's express approval and sent for additional instructions. Another problem was raised when Caulaincourt demanded to know what plans the allies had for Central Europe and which colonies England intended to return to France in the final settlement. Discussions were suspended altogether by the Russian envoy on 9 February. Castlereagh left Châtillon for allied headquarters at Troyes that same evening in disgust.

When he arrived back at Troyes, allied headquarters was astir with Alexander's newest proposal to occupy France and to summon a great 'Assembly of Notables' to determine France's political future. Alexander transparently planned to use his influence to pressure the delegates of this assembly to select Bernadotte as their new sovereign. When Castlereagh confronted the Tsar directly, he was told that British public opinion opposed further negotiations with the French and that even the Prince Regent was actively encouraging Napoleon's dethronement.

This crisis was soon overtaken by a second, when a letter arrived from Caulaincourt addressed to the Austrian Emperor. Caulaincourt at last offered the ancient limits, but only if the allies would agree to an immediate ceasefire. The Austrians favoured acceptance, but Alexander refused to renew the talks at Châtillon and threatened to advance to Paris on his own. Even on the morning of 14 February, Alexander still obstinately refused to consider a re-opening of the talks at Châtillon. Metternich again played his trump card, threatening to withdraw from the allied coalition in order to force the Tsar to cooperate with the other powers. The allies finally agreed to accept Caulaincourt's offer, but only on the condition that Napoleon immediately surrender all fortresses held by French garrisons behind allied lines.

Castlereagh himself rode to Châtillon on 17 February with these new allied terms in his hands. Caulaincourt was given the option of either accepting the allied proposal or of drafting a counter-offer. But a miraculous string of French victories, which had made the allies more conciliatory, worked precisely the opposite magic on Napoleon. Feeling the return of his old military prowess, he became completely intractable. No longer interested in the ancient limits, he instructed Caulaincourt to accept only the natural frontiers—including French control of both Belgium and the Rhineland. Once again, the negotiations were doomed.

Napoleon's unexpected battlefield successes forced the allied leaders to retreat from Troyes and sent a wave of fear through their ranks. The Austrians, with the approval of the Tsar, sent a desperate appeal for an armistice but the French Emperor again allowed the opportunity for a negotiated settlement to slip through his fingers. He offered the Austrians a separate peace on the Frankfurt basis, which they were obliged to reject. An important allied war council was held to assess the deteriorating military situation. When the Austrian generals advocated further retreat, the Tsar proposed detaching some of his Russian divisions from the Austrian army and placing them under Prussian command to the north. It was agreed that the Austrians should retreat to Langres, while additional forces would be given to the Prussians. Under the new allied strategy, Napoleon was to be confronted with two large armies. If he pushed eastward against the retreating Austrians the Prussians would advance on Paris. If he turned on the forces to the north the main allied army to the east would advance. New instructions were also forwarded to Châtillon, giving Caulaincourt a fixed time limit in which to accept or reject allied terms.

The Treaty of Chaumont

By mid-February, Castlereagh had come to appreciate that he had more to dread from allied disunity—what he called their ceaseless 'criminations and recriminations'—than from Napoleon's soldiers. His mind returned to his alliance proposal of September 1813, based on Pitt's earlier plan of 1805. Castlereagh's brilliant insight was to tie allied acceptance of his 'General Alliance' to a renewal of the financial subsidies that the British had regularly furnished to the allied armies on the basis of annual agreements. On 1 March 1814, at allied headquarters at Chaumont, he issued a circular inviting the other three powers to negotiate 'a treaty of Concert, Alliance and Subsidy'.[16]

The Treaty of Chaumont was negotiated and signed one week later. Sitting around a card table, the ministers joked that the stakes had never been higher. 'I am confident', Castlereagh wrote triumphantly to the British cabinet, 'this Treaty will have the most decisive and beneficial influence throughout the Confederacy in firmly cementing the union against France'.[17] In the event that Napoleon failed to accept the terms being offered at Châtillon, each of the four allies solemnly pledged to maintain 150,000 troops in the field till the conclusion of the war and not to sign a separate peace; Britain was further obliged to pay £5 million in subsidies for the following year, to be divided equally among the three other powers:

> The High Contracting Parties reciprocally engage not to negotiate separately with the common enemy, nor to sign peace, truce, nor convention,

but with common consent. They, moreover, engage not to lay down their arms until the object of the war, mutually understood and agreed upon, shall have been attained.[18]

The four powers further agreed 'to concert together on the conclusion of a peace with France, as to the means best adapted to guarantee to Europe, and to themselves reciprocally, the continuance of the peace'. In order 'to maintain the equilibrium of Europe, to secure the repose and independence of its States, and to prevent the invasions which during so many years have desolated the world', they agreed that even after the termination of the war, if any one of them were attacked by France over the course of the next 20 years, each of the others would furnish the immediate assistance of 60,000 troops. Finally, in several secret articles the treaty stipulated the future independence of Spain, Holland, Switzerland, Germany and Italy from France.

The treaty placed an especially heavy burden on Britain, since she pledged both to provide troops and to pay subsidies. On the other hand, in reality Russia and Austria each maintained more than 150,000 troops in the field, and while the obligation to pay subsidies was limited to one year, the obligation to maintain troops was indefinite. In signing the Treaty of Chaumont, Metternich abandoned his old weapon of threatening a separate peace. Had he refused to sign, however, Austria would have been estranged from both Russia and Britain. Metternich was not willing to be relegated to the sidelines, nor, at this point, to cast his lot with Bonaparte, who obstinately continued to refuse all reasonable offers of peace. Metternich may have also hoped that the treaty's palpable demonstration of allied solidarity would finally bring the French Emperor to his senses.

The Treaty of Chaumont constituted a decisive step in the development of the future Congress System. For here, as Czartoryski and Pitt had first proposed, the allies agreed to continue their wartime coalition into the subsequent peace. Scholars often see in this a tacit recognition of the importance of the balance of power, which had been disturbed by France. It was, in fact, a curious statement about the continuing disequilibrium of power in Europe. Remarkably, the treaty said nothing at all about the future government of France herself. Being unable to depose Napoleon and unable to persuade him to accept the ancient limits, the allies foresaw the extension into peacetime of an uneasy truce—the effectual conversion of Europe into two armed camps.

Almost simultaneously, Caulaincourt was given a final ultimatum at Châtillon to accept the ancient limits by 10 March. Napoleon never sent his erstwhile minister the requested new instructions. Caulaincourt managed to stave off a final rupture until 19 March, when the unhappy talks at Châtillon came to an end. Napoleon had lost his last chance to negotiate with the allies. Ten days later they would be at the gates of Paris.

The Bourbon restoration, March–April 1814

The system of Bonapartist authoritarianism that existed in 1814 was a far cry from the individual liberty and popular sovereignty promised by the first revolutionaries of 1789 or by Napoleon himself in his coronation oath of 1804. The legislative assemblies had atrophied and rarely met, the Senate was totally corrupted by the Emperor's powers of conferring *sénatoreries*, and Napoleon himself preferred to rule by decree (*senatus consulta*). The French Church was strictly regulated by the application of the so-called 'Organic Articles'; the 'Imperial University' permitted government control of secondary education; and prefects and police kept a careful watch on public activities and manifestations of opinion throughout the empire. Newspapers were strictly limited in number and placed under the complete control of the government. Critics like Madame de Staël had been exiled from Paris, their books censored or banned. In 1814, 320 political opponents languished in French prisons under a system of arbitrary arrest, a greater number than had been held by *lettres de cachet* under Louis XVI at the outbreak of the Revolution.[19]

Bonaparte had also betrayed the egalitarian promise of the Revolution by gradually reinstating a formal system of social hierarchy. The older aristocracy were not permitted to recover their former titles, but many were welcomed into the new imperial nobility, where they formed a curious amalgam with civilian bureaucrats and military officers. The most important of the new titles, awarded to marshals and senators, were endowed with generous grants of property taken from France's foreign conquests. The imperial nobility constituted only a fraction of a much larger elite of landowners, government-bondholders, important tradesmen and lawyers with landed income, known collectively as the 'notables' (*les notables*). By the electoral lists of 1810, the bulk of the 67,000 notables consisted of 24.5 per cent proprietors (including a large number of former nobility), 33.9 per cent administrators, 14.4 per cent in the liberal professions and 10.8 per cent tradesmen. The manufacturing and commercial bourgeoisie were less well represented.[20] The notables constituted a 'closed society'—a merger of the elites of the *ancien régime* with those who had gained from the changes of the Revolution. They were the main beneficiaries of the new regime, well illustrated by Napoleon's preference for indirect over direct taxation and by the wealth requirements introduced for eligibility into the electoral colleges or entry as an auditor in the Council of State.

Ironically, 'le menu people', the workers and peasants, for all their devotion to Napoleon, did not fare all that well under the empire. Indirect taxation and conscription struck at these groups with exceptional severity. After 1810, hired town labourers were required, as under the *ancien régime*, to keep *livrets*, or passbooks, in which their employment histories were recorded by their employers. Other regulations forbade combinations in restraint of trade by workers. On the other hand, bread prices in Paris were kept low through state intervention and an influx of foreign grain, and a shortage of manpower maintained high wages for town and rural labourers. The peasantry benefited from the abolition of feudal dues and tithes and a trickle of sales of *biens nationaux* (the church lands confiscated during the Revolution); they also saw Napoleon as the safeguard protecting them from a return to the *ancien régime*. Chaptal, the Minister of the Interior, thus observed:

> The ruinous system for the countryside combined with requisitions and conscription should have made the Emperor odious to the peasants, but such was not the case. They were among the warmest partisans, because he reassured them about the return of tithes, feudal rights, the restitution of property to *émigrés*, and the oppression of the lords.[21]

Towards the end of 1813, the adverse effects of a series of poor harvests had been compounded by the commercial consequences of the collapse of the empire. Unemployment and brigandage were on the rise, as in the early days of the Revolution. News of the overwhelming superiority of allied numbers fed the spirit of defeatism. The landed and commercial elites, whom Napoleon had worked most assiduously to win over to his regime, grew increasingly hostile. Napoleon convened the legislature in December 1813 in a desperate attempt to rally support against the invading armies. A committee of deputies was appointed to consider allied peace proposals. The deputies risked all by concluding that the allied demands were justified and that Napoleon must restore individual liberties if he expected Frenchmen to fight for him. The report was suppressed and the legislature disbanded—an ominous portent of Napoleon's faltering popularity.[22]

Nonetheless, Napoleon still remained very much in control of the French administrative and military machines. The efficiency with which his government called up 300,000 recruits in early 1813 in the aftermath of a major military disaster was not indicative of a regime on the brink of collapse. The levy of the autumn of 1813 was also spectacularly successful: 160,000 men from the classes of 1808 to 1814 were sought and 184,000 recruits were actually raised—a surplus of 24,000. A subsequent effort, however, to call up 150,000 from the class of 1815 was pursued less vigorously and achieved paltry results. The last levy of 1813, calling up 237,000 men from older classes, many of whom had already served several times, proved to be an abysmal failure, producing only 63,000 conscripts. A careful scrutiny of these levies, one French historian discovered, enables us to draw a 'political map' of France: the oldest provinces remained loyal to Napoleon, while those situated along the periphery—Flanders, Artois, Normandy, Maine, Anjou, Guyenne, Gascony, Bas-Languedoc and Provence—were either apathetic or openly hostile. Revenue collection serves as another litmus test of the viability of the Napoleonic regime. Taxes were of course unpopular, especially the *droits réunions* (taxes on alcoholic beverages), the salt tax (reinstated in 1806) and the monopoly on tobacco (recreated in 1810). In 1813, Napoleon was forced to double indirect taxes and to increase personal taxes and the land tax. The attempt proved far from effective: many of the new taxes simply went unpaid and by 1814, local officials no longer pressed for their collection.[23]

So long as the allies continued to negotiate with Napoleon's representatives at Châtillon, anyone declaring for Louis XVIII risked exile, imprisonment, or even death if a peace settlement were reached. While the allies searched for some public manifestation of French popular feeling, Napoleon's domestic adversaries awaited a positive signal from the allies before declaring themselves. By late March, the allied leaders thus found themselves in a formidable quandary. Their forces were approaching Paris in overwhelming strength. Yet Napoleon remained unwilling to agree to any terms that they could offer. And although Napoleon was growing increasingly unpopular, especially in the south and west, there were no visible signs of support for any rival form of government, least of all for the Bourbons. The collapse of the Châtillon negotiations to some degree cleared the way for allied cooperation with Napoleon's domestic opponents. The allies issued a proclamation to the French people blaming the rupture on Napoleon's own intransigence.[24] They had, in fact, grown quite desperate for some indication of anti-Bonapartist sentiment to latch onto.[25]

By 21 March, Napoleon had sustained a series of defeats and decided to move to the east to draw the allies away from Paris and to hamper their communications. The allies resolved to unite their armies into a single force to make the final drive on Paris. The Tsar and the King of Prussia advanced with the allied commanders, while Castlereagh, Metternich and the Prussian Chancellor Hardenberg remained with the Austrian Emperor at Dijon in eastern France. Late in the evening of 23 March, the allied commanders intercepted a letter from Napoleon to the Empress Marie Louise, in which the French Emperor stated his intention to draw the allied armies away from Paris; a second intercepted message reported rising discontent in the French capital. Based on these revelations, the Tsar persuaded the reluctant Austrians to hasten their advance on Paris. Napoleon failed to realize that the allies were moving westward and lost his opportunity to command the defence of the capital.

On the morning of 31 March, Paris capitulated to the allies. Under the terms of the surrender, French troops were permitted to leave the city. Most members of the governing council, which Napoleon had left in charge during his absence, had already fled. Only Talleyrand, out of favour with Napoleon, had stayed behind. Later that same day, Tsar Alexander, the King of Prussia, and the allied armies made their triumphal entry into the city, to the applause of large crowds. Napoleon, realizing his mistake, reached the outskirts of Paris just in time to learn of the city's capitulation. At nearby Fontainebleau, he busied himself with plans for regrouping his forces and liberating the capital. Meanwhile, Metternich, Castlereagh and the Austrian Emperor remained isolated from events in Dijon. At this critical moment, the fate of France therefore rested in the hands of the Tsar and Talleyrand, the two former conspirators at Erfurt.

Now came a period of intense political uncertainty. Alexander had long ago decided to consult the legally constituted representative bodies of France to determine the wishes of her people. The Tsar took up residence at Talleyrand's palatial home on the rue Saint-Florentin, where he held long discussions with his host on the future of France. A declaration was posted throughout Paris on the night of 31 March, announcing the allies' refusal to treat with Napoleon. The declaration invited the French Senate to designate a provisional government and to prepare a new constitution. News also reached Paris that Bordeaux, in the southwest, had declared itself for Louis XVIII on 12 March. Under the protection of the British army and with their connivance, the Bordelais royalists had at last provided the pretext that the allies so desperately needed to recall the Bourbons.

On 1 April, Parisian officials renounced their allegiance to Napoleon and declared for the King. Talleyrand's high status as Vice-Chancellor in the imperial government permitted him to preside over the handful of Senators still remaining in Paris, whom he assembled later that same day. The rump Senate quickly appointed a provisional government headed and controlled by Talleyrand. On 2 April, representatives of the Senate informed Alexander that Napoleon would be deposed.

At Fontainebleau, Napoleon was still planning to attack the allies and had even gathered as many as 60,000 troops. But when his generals started to defect and the Senate voted formally to depose him, Napoleon finally agreed to abdicate conditionally in favour of his son, the infant King of Rome. With the act of abdication in hand, Caulaincourt galloped straight to the Tsar's headquarters in Paris. Caulaincourt spent most of the night with Alexander, trying to convince the Tsar that the army and the common people were still steadfast in their loyalty to Napoleon, and that only by accepting the terms of the abdication and installing the Regency could further bloodshed be avoided.

The Tsar hesitated and wavered into the early morning hours. Finally, Talleyrand convinced the Russian autocrat that if a regency were established, Napoleon would be back in power within the year. The Tsar finally rejected Napoleon's offer.

Even now, Napoleon was still hoping to attack the allies in Paris, but his marshals tearfully informed him that they would no longer obey his orders. Napoleon had no choice but to sign an unconditional abdication on 6 April. Caulaincourt and the Tsar negotiated the Treaty of Fontainebleau, which permitted Napoleon to retain his imperial title. Napoleon was awarded sovereignty over Elba, a small island off the coast of Italy, and furnished with a small military establishment and an annual pension to be paid by the French government. The Empress Marie Louise was made ruler of several small duchies in Italy, and generous pensions were provided to Napoleon's stepson and other relatives. It was a strange act of magnanimity by the Tsar that the other allied leaders scarcely approved of and which they would later come to regret.[26]

Meanwhile, under Talleyrand's deft direction, the Senate announced that France was now a constitutional monarchy and that the people of France had recalled the Bourbons 'of their own free will'. Talleyrand had no intention of restoring the Bourbons without restraints, and the Senate announced that it would recognize the King only after he had sworn his allegiance to a new constitution. A document was drawn up, modelled after the French Constitution of 1791, which gave the restoration something of the character of a constitutional pact. Among its other features, this document established Senators with permanent seats in the legislature and hereditary revenues. Louis XVIII, suffering an attack of gout in England, was too ill to cross the Channel until the end of April. He had many liberal opinions—for example, he confirmed the sale of church lands during the Revolution—but he was quite uncompromising when it came to his own sovereignty. On his landing on French soil, he promptly scrapped the senatorial constitution in favour of his own grant of a *Charte* (or 'charter of privileges') to his subjects. The King's dissolution of the Senate and his disregard for its new constitution were widely viewed as checks on Russian policy, since Russian ministers had sat on the committee that had drafted the rejected constitution and Alexander had recommended its merits to Louis.

It may seem incredible that after 20 years of revolution and war, France had travelled full circle to a restoration of the Bourbon monarchy. Historians have offered many explanations for this astonishing turn of events. Talleyrand himself expressed the view that only the Bourbons could shut the Pandora's box of troubles that had been opened by the French Revolution since it was the Bourbons alone who could claim 'legitimacy'—a principled basis of authority that other parties could accept. In Talleyrand's argument, an obvious adaptation from Burke, the kings of France had rights analogous to those of property-owners. Bourbon rule was the natural order of things: when the king's rights could be successfully challenged, all other social relations inevitably fell apart. Many found Talleyrand—a political chameleon who had survived a succession of contrasting regimes—a strange spokesman for these views.

A second explanation for the return of the Bourbons focuses on the attempt of the allies to establish a European balance of power. They associated Napoleon with the boundless energies of the French Revolution. By removing Napoleon, they hoped to eliminate these energies and to return France to its former size and power. They naturally associated the Bourbons with the ancient limits. Louis XVIII could be presumed to respect the boundaries of his forbears. Expressed in more cynical terms, the allies expected the royal government to be embroiled in internal problems and to remain in perpetual gratitude to the other European powers for its very existence. Such a government would not be expected to pose a threat to the rest of Europe for decades to come.

The most obvious explanation for the return of the Bourbons, however, lays blame for these events squarely on Napoleon. Even at Châtillon, he might have concluded peace on honourable terms. When his insatiable ambition—or fatal insecurity—caused him to scorn all compromise, the allied leaders and the French populace had very few alternatives from which to choose. There was no allied consensus behind either the Tsar's favourite, Bernadotte, or a pro-Austrian regency under Napoleon's wife, Marie Louise. The instability and violence of the revolutionary epoch had further brought republican government into general disrepute. The restoration of the Bourbon monarchy therefore appeared to be the only viable solution, and a logical sequel to the imperial court and nobility created by Napoleon. Even Frenchmen could welcome the return of the Bourbons if they would at last bring peace.

The first Peace of Paris, May 1814

Europe rejoiced, for the decades of warfare appeared to be over. With the return of the royal family to the throne, the turbulent forces of the French Revolution seemed at last to have spent themselves. The first task facing the allies and the new French government was to negotiate a peace settlement. While ignoring his advice on domestic matters, Louis XVIII appreciated Talleyrand's high stature among the allied leaders and appointed him as foreign minister. It thus fell to Talleyrand to negotiate the peace. Discussions between Talleyrand, Castlereagh, Metternich, Hardenberg (representing Prussia) and

Nesselrode (representing Russia) began in early May. Spain also wished to participate in the negotiations as a 'great power', but she was kept at bay by deeming these conferences 'informal conversations'.[27]

One consequence of the allied installation of a French government of their own choosing was that the peace terms imposed on France were relatively lenient. The demands of British newspapers and the Prussian general staff for a punitive peace were largely ignored. The new French government strove to distance itself in every way from the transgressions of Napoleon. Talleyrand argued that allied concessions were needed to avoid compromising the new royal government in the eyes of French public opinion. The allies agreed that no financial indemnities would be demanded. This was in sharp contrast to Napoleon's own practice of demanding contributions from his defeated adversaries. The allies also permitted the French to keep the artworks that Napoleon had pillaged from the rest of Europe, again to reconcile the French populace. And even before the peace was negotiated, allied troops were evacuated from French soil, in exchange for the surrender of the French garrisons in the fortresses farther east.

The most urgent task facing the negotiators was, of course, to draw the new boundaries of France. At the beginning of 1814, to win allied support, Louis XVIII had announced his acceptance of the ancient limits. But when the time came for negotiating the treaty, Louis and Talleyrand pushed for additional territorial concessions, especially along the Belgian border. Castlereagh was infuriated and would brook no compromise on this point. The allies offered the French government moderate additions to the east, including part of Savoy and territories outside Geneva, giving France half a million more inhabitants than in 1792. Talleyrand was happy to accept these, even if taking properties that belonged to the House of Savoy plainly contradicted his new doctrine of 'legitimacy'. The border with Belgium, on the other hand, was moved back to the line of 1789.

The parties further agreed that Belgium would be united to Holland, that Antwerp would become a commercial port without fortifications and that the navigation of both the Rhine and the Scheldt would become free to all nations. The British accordingly achieved their most cherished war aims. In return, they agreed to return the colonies they had seized from France and Holland, except for a series of key strategic points that included Malta, the Cape in South Africa, Tobago and Mauritius. Thus, they secured the passage to India and their control of the Mediterranean and the Caribbean. Based upon the mounting anti-slavery campaign in London, Castlereagh also requested French abolition of the slave trade, which Britain had abolished in 1807. French royalists saw this demand, however, as a British ruse to prevent the French West Indies from becoming profitable, and categorically refused.

Although the abolitionists in the British House of Commons were outraged, Castlereagh felt he had no alternative but to acquiesce to French views.

The Peace of Paris was signed on 30 May between France and the four allies, joined by Spain, Portugal and Sweden. The public articles established the new frontiers of France and announced that Holland would increase in size, that Switzerland would be independent and that the states of Germany would be independent while united by a 'federative bond'. Its public articles further made known that the Austrian Habsburgs would possess several duchies in Italy, that the other Italian states would remain independent, that the navigation of the Rhine would be free and that most former French colonial possessions would be returned to France. The treaty proclaimed a complete amnesty for partisans of earlier political regimes—so that former Bonapartists would not be subject to punishment at the hands of vengeful royalists.

There were, in addition, a number of articles kept secret to avoid an adverse public reaction or the jealousy of the lesser powers. The first of these stated that the guiding principle in the reconstruction of the liberated territories would be the need to establish a satisfactory balance of power in Europe ('un système d'équilibre réel et durable en Europe').[28] France would have no voice in the future distribution of the confiscated territories now outside her borders, whose fate was to be determined solely by the four allied powers. It was further agreed that Belgium would be united to Holland, that Venice and Milan would be awarded to Austria, and that the independent city of Genoa would be given to Piedmont-Sardinia to compensate it for its loss of Savoy to France.

Finally, among the public articles of the treaty, the thirty-second announced that:

> All Powers engaged on either side of the present War, shall, within the space of two months, send Plenipotentiaries to Vienna for the purpose of regulating, in General Congress, the Arrangements which are to complete the provisions of the present Treaty.[29]

This stipulation, which was made generally known throughout Europe by newspaper announcements, provided the legal basis for the forthcoming Congress of Vienna.

Part Two

PEACE

And He shall judge among the nations and will settle disputes for many peoples. And they shall beat their swords into ploughshares and their spears into pruning hooks. Nation shall not lift up sword against nation, neither shall they learn war anymore.

Isaiah 2:4

The state of peace among men living side by side is not the natural state (*status naturalis*); the natural state is one of war. This does not always mean open hostilities, but at least an unceasing threat of war. A state of peace, therefore, must be established, for in order to be secured against hostility it is not sufficient that hostilities simply be not committed; and, unless this security is pledged to each by his neighbour (a thing that can occur only in a civil state), each may treat his neighbour, from whom he demands this security, as an enemy.

Immanuel Kant, On Perpetual Peace, 1795

[I]n order to render this security as complete as possible, it seems necessary, at the period of a general pacification, to form a Treaty to which all the principal powers of Europe should be parties, by which their respective rights and possessions, as they then have been established, shall be fixed and recognized; and they should all bind themselves mutually to protect and support each other, against any attempt to infringe them: It should re-establish a general and comprehensive system of public law in Europe, and provide, as far as possible, for repressing future attempts to disturb the general tranquillity; and above all, for restraining any projects of aggrandizement and ambition similar to those which have produced all the calamities inflicted on Europe since the disastrous era of the French Revolution.

William Pitt to Count Vorontsov, January 1805

The great military Powers of the Continent who have triumphed in the War...should recollect that they avowedly fought for their own liberties, and for those of the rest of the Europe, and not for an extension of their dominion...

With these principles in view, if the Allied Powers act liberally towards each other, and indulgently to other States, they may look forward to crown a glorious War by a solid and lasting Peace, and posterity will revere their Names, not only for having delivered, by their Arms, the World, from a Tyrant and a Conqueror, but for having restored, by Their Example, and by their Influence, the Reign of Moderation and Justice.
   Lord Castlereagh, 'Mémoire sur Pologne', 4 November 1814

Remember this: that the very Europe which has been brought to making the declaration I send you is intensely jealous of France, of the King, and of the House of Bourbon. These sentiments show themselves whenever the news is unfavourable.
   Prince Talleyrand to the Comte de Jaucourt, 16 March 1815

3

The Congress of Vienna, 1814–15

The decision to convene a congress

Although the frontiers of France had now been settled, the fate of an estimated 32 million people in unassigned territories beyond the borders of France was still to be determined. So, too, were the future arrangements for Switzerland and the German Confederation. Almost every frontier and country in Europe would be affected. Why, then, had the allied leaders gratuitously announced the summoning of a 'General Congress', inviting the interference of every lesser sovereign and would-be sovereign in Europe?

By inviting the other sovereigns of Europe to attend an assembly at Vienna, the allied statesmen were self-evidently appealing to accepted notions of public law. International congresses had first developed out of the European Church Councils of the Middle Ages. The pleas of international jurists like Hugo Grotius and Samuel Pufendorf for the rational deliberation of disputes had led to the frequent use of congresses at the close of major wars from the 1640s onwards—including the Congresses of Münster, Osnabrück, Nijmegen, Ryswijck, Utrecht, Cambrai, Soissons and Aix-la-Chapelle. The French Directory and Napoleon had similarly made use of congresses to legitimize French gains: for example, the Congress of Rastadt had been held to reorganize Germany in 1797. It was therefore quite natural that the allied leaders should seek to consummate their victory over France by holding a great European congress (even if somewhat unusual to convene the congress after the peace between the belligerents had been signed). After the upheavals of the past 20 years, it was clear to all that some such stabilizing and legitimizing influence was necessary.[1]

The particular idea of a gathering at Vienna was apparently first proposed by the Tsar shortly after the Battle of Leipzig. As early as January 1814, the allied leaders had agreed among themselves that France would have no voice in deciding the fate of territories outside her borders, and raised the possibility of a post-war conference. By then, too, the allied statesmen had already adopted the practice of acting in the name of 'Europe' rather than simply for themselves. Caulaincourt himself had proposed a two-tiered negotiation at Châtillon, in which the first tier would determine the territorial limits of France and the second, the distribution of all remaining territories.

Undoubtedly, the statesmen were equally actuated by narrower, more partisan motives: Alexander may have hoped to receive French support for his Polish designs; Metternich certainly wished to display the Habsburg monarchy to advantage and to play the role of grand mediator between Russia and Prussia. The proposed congress would also provide a convenient forum to resolve many of the issues involving the lesser powers, such as the form of future association of the German states, the fate of the minor German princelings deprived of their former autonomy, the future of Switzerland, the navigation of the Rhine and other European rivers, the possession of the Ionian Islands, the slave trade and the status of the German Jews (only recently granted rights of citizenship in much of Europe in consequence of the French Revolution). As Metternich observed:

> No great political insight is needed to see that this Congress could not be modelled on any that had [ever] taken place. Former assemblies that were called congresses met for the express purpose of settling a quarrel between two or more belligerent powers—the issue being a peace treaty. On this occasion, peace had already been made and the parties meet as friends who, though differing in their interests, wish to work together towards the conclusion and affirmation of the existing treaty.[2]

Whatever their reasons for summoning a congress, it is clear that the allied leaders mainly intended it as a ratifying instrument. They believed they could resolve their own differences and determine the main features of the territorial settlement before the other plenipotentiaries (delegates with full powers) ever assembled: the presence of the other delegates would chiefly serve to ratify and sanction their own decisions.

Preliminary negotiations in Paris and London, June–August 1814

While at Paris, the statesmen had already begun to tackle the issues surrounding the disposition of the liberated territories. The Prussian and Austrian ministers were aware of the Tsar's popularity among Parisians, as well as of the rumours that Alexander intended to keep all of Poland, including Kraków and Thorn (present-day Toruń). They wished to reach a common understanding before a new Russo-French alliance stood in their way. Hardenberg and Metternich differed, however, on the future of the key fortress of Mainz. Metternich especially feared any extension of Prussian power in the direction of Southern Germany, while the Prussians, already in occupation of Mainz, intended to keep it for themselves. Other problems of equal magnitude bedevilled Germany. What would be the future relations among the various German states? The former imperial nobility clamoured for a restoration of the Holy Roman Empire. The German middle states—such as Bavaria, Württemberg, Baden and Hanover—hoped for territorial gains that would bring them closer to the size of Prussia.

The allies faced difficulties that appeared to be just as insuperable in Italy. Joachim Murat, Napoleon's brother-in-law and a former French marshal, remained on the throne of Naples. The Neapolitan Bourbons, who had taken refuge in Sicily, longed to be restored on the mainland as their relatives had been in Paris and Madrid. But, in the final stages of the war, Metternich had signed a secret alliance with Murat in order to separate Naples from Napoleon. Now the alliance with Murat had become a painful embarrassment, deeply resented by Louis XVIII.

The Prussian Chancellor, Prince Hardenberg, confronted many of these problems in a long memorandum that he presented to the other allied ministers on 29 April. It was ambitiously entitled a 'Plan for the Future Arrangement of Europe'. Hardenberg called, first, for the creation of a German Confederation (*Bund*) to govern relations among the numerous German states. For the territorial settlement of Central Europe, he proposed giving Southern Poland, including Kraków, back to Austria, along with Salzburg, the Tyrol, and Breisgau on the Upper Rhine, and handing over most of Napoleon's new Duchy of Warsaw to Russia. Prussia would then make corresponding gains to the east, south and west. To the west, she would annex Westphalia and the Rhineland; to the east, she would annex Polish territory as far as the Warta River, including Posen (Poznań) and Thorn; finally, to the south, Prussia would acquire all of Saxony. Such annexations would, in Hardenberg's reckoning, have provided Prussia with a population about 600,000 greater than in 1805, an estimate plainly too low. Though Metternich hoped to cooperate with Hardenberg, he was unwilling to grant Prussia both Mainz and Saxony. Alexander rejected Hardenberg's plan outright for clashing with his own ideas on Poland. The allied ministers held several conferences in Paris to thrash out these problems, but soon reached a deadlock. By the end of May it was apparent they would have to continue their discussions in London, where the Tsar had agreed to visit the Prince Regent at the end of the war. At least there, the allied leaders would not have to worry about the interference of the French.[3]

During their short sojourn in Britain the allied sovereigns were exuberantly fêted by all around them. The climax was a great banquet at Guildhall, widely regarded as the most sumptuous feast ever held in Britain. By his conduct in London, the flamboyant Tsar nevertheless alienated the British cabinet. Playing to the crowds, Alexander chose to lodge with his sister Catherine at the Pulteney Hotel instead of with the English Prince Regent. He also visited members of the parliamentary opposition as well as the abolitionists William Wilberforce and Thomas Clarkson and the Quaker William Allen. Metternich, in contrast, kept a low profile.[4]

Against this backdrop, the allied ministers attempted further discussions on the territorial settlement. They made some progress on arrangements for the Netherlands, but they were unable to break the deadlock on the reconstruction of Central Europe. By mid-June, the four allied powers could only agree that the Congress should be summoned for 15 August, and that the eight powers that had signed the Peace of Paris (the four allies together with France, Portugal, Spain and Sweden) should serve as some form of preliminary committee.

The Congress had to be further delayed, however, so that Castlereagh could attend to parliamentary duties. The Tsar also insisted on his need to visit Russia. A new date for the Congress was set for late September. In the interim, Europe remained in a state of preparedness for war. France was evacuated by the allies but ringed by allied troops. Austria maintained a large army in Northern Italy, while Russian troops occupied Poland and much of Central Europe. The four allied powers signed a convention renewing the terms of the Chaumont Treaty, each pledging to keep 75,000 men on foot until the final peace was secured. Castlereagh informally agreed that Britain would continue paying the financial subsidies so desperately needed by the Continental allies.

The characters of the statesmen

Over 200 plenipotentiaries and heads of state gathered at Vienna in the autumn of 1814, but the truly important decisions would be the product of the small handful of men representing the five great powers—those same monarchs and ministers who had directed the final campaign against Napoleon, restored Louis XVIII, negotiated the Peace of Paris and summoned the Congress. Chief among these were Metternich for Austria, Castlereagh for Great Britain, Tsar Alexander for Russia, Hardenberg for Prussia and Talleyrand for France.[5] It is therefore worth interrupting our narrative to consider the backgrounds and characters of these five individuals in greater detail.

Collectively, they were the members of a privileged and landed aristocracy, nourished in their youths by the heady ideals of the Enlightenment. Prince Clemens Wenzel Lothar von Metternich (1773–1859), for example, came from a family possessing one of the most ancient noble pedigrees in the Rhineland.[6] The Metternichs owned large estates both in the Rhineland and to the east. Metternich's father had held high posts in the service of both the Archbishop of Trier and the Habsburg Emperor. Metternich himself was raised and educated by liberal Francophile tutors, and attended the University of Strasbourg in France and the University of Mainz. His elevated position in society was well illustrated when his father hired scores of carriages for his family to attend the coronation of Leopold II as Holy Roman Emperor in 1790, and two years later, when young Metternich, accompanied by Louise of Mecklenburg (the future Queen of Prussia) opened the formal ball at the coronation of the Emperor Francis. Young Metternich followed in his father's footsteps by entering into the service of the Habsburgs. He catapulted his fortunes by marrying Eleonore, granddaughter of the famed Austrian diplomat Prince Kaunitz, in 1795. With his father, Metternich attended the Congress of Rastadt (1797–99); afterwards, he served as imperial envoy to Dresden (1801–3), imperial ambassador to Berlin (1803–5) and finally, at Napoleon's personal request, as Austrian ambassador to France (1806–9). Thin and handsome with piercing blue eyes, Metternich often impressed others with his perfect manners and aristocratic bearing.

Prince Charles-Maurice de Talleyrand-Périgord (1754–1838) was similarly born into one of the most illustrious noble families of France, although they were no longer very rich.[7] Nineteen years older than Metternich, he was born in the same year as Louis XVI. Suffering from a mild physical disability (he was lame in one foot), he was pushed by his family into the clergy—despite being the eldest son—and placed under the protection of his uncle, the Archbishop of Reims. In the seminary of Saint-Sulpice, young Talleyrand avidly read works of Enlightenment *philosophes* as well as theology and developed something of a reputation as a sceptic; in the spring of 1778, he even went out of his way to meet one of his idols, the aging Voltaire—far from the favourite of most clerics. The following year, Talleyrand was ordained as a priest. In January 1789, on the strength of his father's deathbed request, Louis XVI nominated Talleyrand to become Bishop of Autun, despite his reputation as a reprobate. With more of a gift for administration than faith, Talleyrand was appointed Agent-General of the Clergy in 1780 to monitor the finances of the Church. French historian Emmanuel de Waresquiel suggests that it was during these five years as agent that Talleyrand learned 'not to go against an institution in which one occupies a leading role, but rather, to reform it from within, in small steps—knowing how to make concessions in order to save what is essential.'[8]

Talleyrand also helped to secure a government post for his older friend, the Comte de Mirabeau. A free-thinker and far from celibate, it was as a member of the First Estate that Talleyrand attended the Estates General in 1789. Here, he threw in his lot with those who favoured the transformation of the Estates into a unicameral National Assembly. Talleyrand also assisted in the secularization of Church properties and was one of the few bishops to take the oath to the Civil Constitution of the Clergy in the early days of the Revolution. On 14 July 1790, it was none other than Talleyrand who officiated at the great public ceremony held in honour of the fall of the Bastille—the *Fête de la Fédération*. As 'Bishop of the Revolution', Talleyrand stood alongside the Marquis de Lafayette (Commander of the National Guard) and the new constitutional monarch, Louis XVI. Shortly afterwards, Talleyrand abandoned the cassock altogether, adopting an alternative career as a politician and diplomat.

Prince Karl August von Hardenberg (1750–1822) likewise came from a wealthy and aristocratic family with estates in Hanover.[9] Biographers describe him as something of an epicurean. Educated at home by liberal tutors and in a private lyceum in Hanover, Hardenberg later studied mathematics and law at the Universities of Göttingen and Leipzig. Perhaps inspired by the example of Frederick the Great, Hardenberg epitomized the cosmopolitan German aristocrat who found satisfaction in public service. He initially entered the administration of his native Hanover, with its close English ties, but moved to the service of the Duke of Brunswick in 1782 after a marital scandal in London involving his wife and the Prince of Wales. In 1786, three years before the French Revolution, Hardenberg authored a memorandum for the Duke in favour of administrative reform. After another marital scandal, Hardenberg divorced in 1787 and remarried the next year. While the Revolution was unfolding in France, Hardenberg was searching for new state employment; he eventually obtained an appointment as the administrator of Ansbach and Bayreuth, then being absorbed into Prussia. With the outbreak of the war, Hardenberg was sent to rally support in the Rhineland for the King of Prussia. In 1794, Hardenberg rose to become the governor of Prussia's western Frankish provinces. He was later sent to negotiate Prussia's 1795 peace treaty with France. Frederick William III came to the throne in 1797 and immediately elevated Hardenberg to a position in his cabinet. In 1804, Hardenberg became Prussian foreign minister, but he was removed from his post in 1805, and again after Tilsit in 1807, at the express insistence of Napoleon. Appointed Prussian Chancellor in 1810 shortly after the removal of Baron vom Stein, Hardenberg followed liberal policies and became closely associated with the Prussian reformers of the period.

The pedigree of Robert Stewart, Lord Castlereagh (1769–1822), was of more recent vintage than these Continental aristocrats, but his family, too, was well-connected and counted among the largest landowners of County Down in Ireland.[10] His paternal grandfather had made a fortune in India; his father, a 'New Light' Presbyterian, numbered among the more important Irish Whigs; his English mother (who died in his first year) was the daughter of Lord Hertford; and perhaps most important of all, his famous step-grandfather, Lord Camden, was a prominent jurist and politician, and a close friend of William Pitt the Elder (the first Earl of Chatham). When the American Revolution broke out, both Camden and Castlereagh's father took the side of the revolutionaries. Young Castlereagh studied first with private tutors, then at a local academy and finally at St John's, Cambridge, where he was fed a steady diet of classical literature and utilitarian philosophy—all the while receiving informal instruction from Camden. He embarked on a career of parliamentary politics as soon as he came of age. His father expended so much of the family fortune on his son's election to the Irish House of Commons in the contest of 1790 that he had to forego plans for adding a new wing to the family home at Mount Stewart. The sacrifice proved to be a wise investment: with his family connections, industry, intelligence and talent, Castlereagh quickly rose to the highest governing circles and became adept at the necessary skills of electoral and parliamentary management. Like Metternich, he was tall and handsome, but those who did not know him well often described him as impenetrably cold.

In an age when monarchs saw themselves as members of the noble estate—*primus inter pares*—even Tsar Alexander (1777–1825) shared in the aristocratic upbringing and liberal education of the other Congress statesmen, albeit on a much more lavish scale—and with the daunting prospect of one day becoming an all-powerful autocrat.[11] The young prince grew up amidst the splendours and riches of the imperial court of his grandmother, Catherine the Great. At her command, he was educated alongside his younger brother Constantine by the Swiss liberal Frédéric-César de La Harpe, a republican and a disciple of Jean-Jacques Rousseau. As a boy, Alexander was taught to detest monarchical despotism and to admire constitutional government, by which he understood a *Rechtstaat* (a state governed by law, rather than by its ruler's whims). Alexander's life at Catherine's court alternated with visits to Gatchina, the palace of his estranged martinet father, the Grand Duke Paul, which was run like a Prussian military encampment. Alexander's enigmatic character can doubtless be traced to the extreme contrasts to which he was exposed in childhood: he grew adept at changing his views, chameleon-like, to correspond to those around him. The Empress intended that Alexander should succeed her, but she died before she could put her plan into effect. Alexander's paranoid father, Paul I, reigned only a short time before alienating ruling circles by his threatening conduct and his erratic foreign policy;

a conspiracy of nobles deposed and murdered him in 1801. Alexander was informed in advance of the conspiracy, but deluded himself into thinking his father's life would be spared. Many of his biographers speculate that, for the remainder of his life, Alexander suffered pangs of guilt for his father's death. In any event, his own early reign was characterized by the activities of the 'Unofficial Committee': a group of his young, liberal friends (led by Baron Pavel Stroganov and including Prince Adam Czartoryski), who proposed a series of domestic reforms for the Russian Empire, including a written constitution and the reform or abolition of serfdom. The young Tsar agreed with their ideas but often stepped back when it came to putting them into practice: a 'Charter to the Russian People' was approved but never promulgated; the body of nobles known as the Senate was granted the right to bring their objections to new laws to his attention, but this right was immediately withdrawn when they tried to exercise it; and few concrete steps were actually taken to help the serfs, for fear of precipitating a social revolution. An edict gave landowners the right to free their serfs, but few took advantage of it.[12]

Surely there is no better comment on the cosmopolitan and close-knit nature of the aristocratic social connections of this age than the romantic entanglements that ensnarled these same men at the Vienna Congress and which may have even sharpened their political antagonisms. Most remarkable of all were their relations with the daughters of the Duchess of Courland. Metternich was aggrieved for much of the Congress because one of the Duchess's daughters, the charming Duchess von Sagan, had broken off her amorous relations with him. The Tsar himself may have been a rival for Sagan's affections, or at least he tried to manipulate Sagan to wrest concessions from Metternich. Equally remarkable, Sagan's mother resided in Paris as Talleyrand's mistress, while Sagan's youngest half-sister, Dorothée, accompanied Talleyrand to the Congress to manage his household. This same young woman had once been in love with none other than Prince Adam Czartoryski, before being coerced into marrying Talleyrand's nephew. Czartoryski, in turn, had had a youthful affair with the Tsar's wife, the Empress Elizabeth, quite probably with the Tsar's encouragement. Historians suspect their relationship was briefly rekindled at the Congress. Meanwhile, the Tsar's own amorous attentions at the Congress were focused on Princess Katrina Bagration—not only the widow of one of his leading generals in the war against Napoleon, but also the woman who, a decade earlier, had borne Metternich his first child. Alexander's former Polish mistress, Maria Naryshkina, was also present at the Congress.[13] It is impossible to conceive of such goings-on at the more sombre summit conferences of our own day.

Equally incredible from today's perspective, nationality played relatively little role at the Vienna Congress, at least in terms of the loyalties of the statesmen. The principal statesmen were for the most part hardly nationals of the states they represented: Castlereagh grew up in Ireland, not England; Metternich was originally a Rhinelander, not an Austrian; Hardenberg was from Hanover, not Prussia; and the Russian Tsar was mainly assisted by Prince Czartoryski (a Pole), Count Nesselrode (a German), Baron vom Stein (a German) and Count Capodistrias (a Greek).

While all the chief statesmen had been born to nobility and riches, they were far from idle aristocrats: each minister had reached his high status through perseverance and talent. The same could even be said of the Tsar, who had managed to survive and master the dangerous game of palace politics. Each of the leading statesmen at Vienna had in fact encountered and overcome notable personal and political reverses. This was in part a by-product of the long struggle with Napoleon, in which everyone, at one time or another, was found on the losing side. But these experiences also contributed something to the acute sense of realism and pragmatism that these men generally shared, and which gave them strength.

Castlereagh, for example, as Chief Secretary of Ireland, had been given the arduous task of steering the unpopular Act of Union (uniting the Irish and British Parliaments) through the Irish House of Commons. He failed by a narrow margin on his first attempt, and only succeeded the following year after waging an all-out campaign in pamphlet warfare and using secret government funds to buy out Irish borough-owners (who owned seats in the House) with substantial bribes. The experience taught him lessons he did not forget: Castlereagh's 'dealings with men of parliamentary influence', the English diplomat Stratford Canning later wrote, 'while it lowered his estimate of public virtue ... placed him high in that commanding science, the knowledge of mankind'.[14]

Castlereagh and his mentor, William Pitt the Younger, had then resigned from office when King George III obstinately refused to honour pledges they had made to Catholics. From Ireland, Castlereagh moved to England in 1801, where most of the next 14 years were taken up in the contest against Napoleon. Castlereagh served in a variety of important posts—from President of the Board of Control (which oversaw the activities of the East India Company) to Secretary of State for War and Colonies. He was widely and unfairly blamed for British defeats on the Iberian Peninsula and the disaster on Walcheren Island in 1809; cabinet intrigues to oust him led to his notorious pistol duel with Foreign Secretary George Canning that same year and to his temporary retirement from office.

In Metternich's case, he witnessed the loss of the Austrian Netherlands and his family's Rhineland estates, Austria's humiliating defeats at the hands of Napoleon on battlefields from Lodi to Austerlitz, a series of ever more punitive treaties (Leoben, Campo Formio, Lunéville and Pressburg), and the dissolution of the thousand-year Holy Roman Empire. As Austrian ambassador to Berlin, he failed to persuade the Prussians to join the allied coalition against Napoleon before their defeat at Austerlitz. Metternich also suffered the rejection of his recommendation to avoid war in 1809, leading to Austria's defeat at Wagram. While this military disaster actually led to Metternich's promotion as foreign minister, the Austrian Empire tottered dangerously close to the brink of extinction. Metternich next engineered the Austrian marriage alliance with Napoleon, only to see the subsequent collapse of his pro-French policy; then he patiently delayed joining the new allied coalition, only to see Napoleon refuse all reasonable offers of compromise.

These earlier defeats and reversals may have made Metternich excessively cautious. On the one hand, like Talleyrand, he was a successful survivor; in his private correspondence he frequently described himself as supremely confident: 'I go forward as though I felt sure of being able to control the course of events. The least boastful man is obliged, in certain circumstances, to assume a self-confidence.'[15] He even regarded himself as a beacon of light in a turbulent age: 'People look on me as a kind of lantern to which they draw near in order to see their way through the almost complete darkness.' Contemporaries, however, sometimes judged his conduct as irresolute; the Tsar, for instance, complained that Metternich was 'no doubt a man of great intelligence, but the moment he sees the slightest difficulty, he hesitates, stops, looks all round for a way of escape, and then if he considers he can no longer avoid this obstacle, he plants all of his friends down in front of it.'[16] Castlereagh confided to his half-brother: 'our friend Metternich, with all his merits, prefers a complicated negotiation to a bold and rapid stroke.'[17] And according to Hardenberg, Metternich felt he could 'substitute ruse in place of courage of spirit and force.'[18] Henry Kissinger gives a more positive assessment of the same qualities—Metternich's policy was 'to keep all options open, to retain a maximum freedom of action.'[19]

The Tsar himself was no stranger to adversity: Alexander had endured the murder of his father, the defeats at Austerlitz and Friedland, the painful years of subservience to Napoleon, the shocking invasion of Russia and the burning of Moscow. In addition to these well-known disasters, Alexander was subjected to the constant intrigues and dissimulations of court life. As one historian has recently explained, it is quite impossible to understand Alexander's complex personality without an appreciation of these burdens:

> [H]is actions and even his ideas are incomprehensible unless one understands the context and the constraints within which a Russian monarch operated. Not just Alexander's father but also his grandfather, Peter III,

had been overthrown and murdered. So had the previous male monarch, Ivan VI. From his earliest days Alexander had been surrounded by court and political faction and intrigue. As emperor, he was the supreme source of honour, wealth and status. Most people to whom he spoke wanted to use him to advance their own interests or policies. They operated in patron-client networks which hid the truth from him and tried to reduce his independence. These networks spread across court, government and army, which were still essentially one community. The arrogant, ambitious and jealous men who peopled the networks were often very exhausting to manage. But the emperor had to manage them if he was to survive and if the army and bureaucracy were to function effectively. Faced with this Petersburg milieu, an emperor could be forgiven a large degree of suspicion, evasiveness and duplicity. Over the years a world-weary despair about human nature was almost bound to grow.[20]

As for Hardenberg, he had been mistreated by his wife, whom he eventually divorced; he had been compelled to migrate from one German state to another; and while in the Prussian service, he had experienced the defeat at Jena and the harsh terms imposed on Prussia at Tilsit; moreover, he was twice dismissed from high office at Napoleon's direct command. Hardenberg had also encountered severe setbacks in his attempts at reform in Prussia. In October 1810 a new law announced the abolition of the tax exemptions of the Prussian nobility, but after a firestorm of protests and bitter personal attacks, Hardenberg was forced to rescind the policy less than a year later. Indeed, some historians believe Hardenberg showed an alarming tendency to make concessions simply to cling to power.

This leaves Talleyrand: while this Frenchman was notorious for his ability to surmount the sharp vicissitudes of French domestic politics, even he was forced into exile during the Terror and had suffered partial disgrace and repeated humiliating verbal assaults from Napoleon. Thus it was that all five of the statesmen who would determine the fate of Europe at Vienna were individuals who had tasted the bitterness of defeat as well as the sweetness of victory—contributing to their hard-nosed pragmatism.

Finally, each of the principal statesmen at Vienna had been personally and profoundly touched by the events of the French Revolution. It can be said without exaggeration that their world views were forged in this common crucible. Talleyrand, of course, had been an active participant. A deputy to the Estates General, he had argued in favour of forming the National Assembly and had become known as the 'Bishop of the Revolution'. A follower of Mirabeau—whom Talleyrand had befriended before the Revolution—and an admirer of English constitutional monarchy, he was sent on a diplomatic mission to London in 1792. After the September Massacres he decided not to return to France and remained in London until 1794, when he was expelled. This was at the height of the Terror, and Talleyrand wisely chose to go into exile in America. He only returned to France in 1796. Shortly afterwards, he became foreign minister under the Directory and helped Napoleon to seize power in 1799. Talleyrand remained as Napoleon's foreign minister, lining his pockets with bribes and periodically urging greater moderation on his Emperor with scant success.

At Vienna, Talleyrand deliberately tried to distance himself from his revolutionary past. 'Among the illustrious persons with whom I have had the opportunity of making acquaintance since I have been here is Prince Talleyrand the Reverend', the young diplomat Stratford Canning recorded:

> He is the professor and protector of all that is sound in principle, pure in virtue, and venerable in establishment. He can't bear Jacobins, and wonders what people can mean by talking of anything but the indefeasible prerogatives of kings and the inalienable rights of nations. He quotes learned books about right and justice, looks back with horror on the Revolution, and calls Buonaparte a coward. Some little time ago he was inveighing with great vehemence against Jacobinism and Jacobins, when I took the liberty of saying to him—'*Votre altesse en a connu quelques uns.*' '*Oui*,' said he, '*je les ai tous connu—il n'y avait entre eux que l'égoïsme et l'intérêt personnel—pas le moindre sentiment pour la patrie!*' ['Your Highness knew a few of them.' 'Yes, I knew them all—they possessed only selfishness and personal interest, and not the least sentiment for their country!']²¹

Metternich and Castlereagh were far younger than Talleyrand when the French Revolution broke out, but the Revolution left a deep impression on both of them. Metternich was then a first-year student at the University of Strasbourg in France and witnessed the sacking of the town hall by a revolutionary crowd. The private tutor who had accompanied him to the university became a leading local Jacobin. Metternich nevertheless remained in Strasbourg for the rest of the year before transferring his studies to Mainz. At Mainz, he again came into contact with both the advocates and adversaries of revolutionary change. Meanwhile, his father had become the chief imperial official in the Austrian Netherlands—the first territory to be invaded by Revolutionary France. Criticized for failing to introduce needed reforms or to take adequate defensive measures against potential attack, Metternich's father was saddled with the blame for the fall of the Austrian Netherlands. Metternich's family then lost their ancient estates in the Rhineland to the advancing French armies. 'The French Revolution has reached that stage from which it seems to threaten ruin to all the States of Europe', Metternich wrote in defence of his father in 1794; 'The spread of general anarchy is its aim, and its means are enormous.'[22] Metternich subsequently took a dim view of revolution: 'Two elements are constantly at war in human society', he wrote, 'the positive and the negative, the conservative and the destructive.'[23] His most respected biographer, Heinrich von Srbik, believed that these formative experiences helped to shape Metternich's personality:

> [H]is political individuality is rooted in the thought and experience of the era of his birth and intellectual growth, in a world which was shattered by the most far-reaching event of modern history, the great Revolution and its consummator, heir and conqueror, Napoleon; [Metternich's] political existence was dedicated to the struggle against these destructive forces and their offspring, the two great trends of the nineteenth century, the national and the liberal.[24]

Young Castlereagh finished his studies at Cambridge and took a 'Grand Tour' of the Continent in 1791, precisely when the Revolution was turning more violent. He read a copy of Edmund Burke's counter-revolutionary *Reflections on the Revolution in France* just before his departure, and this greatly coloured his impressions. When he returned to Ireland, he quickly cast aside his youthful liberalism and allied with the British government against Irish radicalism. Ireland was then in the throes of revolution: the Society of United Irishmen, formed by Northern Presbyterian radicals and influenced by both the American and French Revolutions, hoped to unite Irishmen of all denominations and to sever ties with Britain; they were joined by impoverished Catholics in the rural South, already organized into anti-Protestant 'Defender' societies. In 1796, a minor disturbance took place on his father's own estates; Castlereagh helped to quell the unrest by administering oaths of loyalty to the Crown—he simply could not conceive that his father's tenants were genuinely disloyal. Castlereagh's step-uncle, the Second Earl Camden, was then made Lord Lieutenant of Ireland, and Castlereagh played an active role in assisting him in the suppression of the Irish Rebellion of 1797–98: Castlereagh received reports from government spies, arrested rebels and served in the highest decision-making circles in Dublin Castle. He favoured stern measures for the pacification of the northern province of Ulster, where General Lake instituted widespread beatings and house-burnings in 1797; Castlereagh may have even played some role in the enlistment of Protestant Orangemen as auxiliaries to combat the Catholic Defenders. Castlereagh remained, nonetheless, convinced that the lower orders were basically loyal. He believed that the rebel rank-and-file had been greatly misled by a small conspiratorial elite, which had imbibed foreign Jacobin ideas: 'It is a Jacobinical conspiracy throughout the kingdom, pursuing its object chiefly with Popish instruments.'[25] When his uncle was replaced by Lord Cornwallis, Castlereagh maintained his position in the government and supported Cornwallis' policy of pardoning the rank and file while arresting the revolutionary leadership:

> There seems an absolute necessity of giving pardon to such proportion of the Community as can with any degree of safety be taken back under the protection of the Laws ... Altho[ugh] it may be necessary to have the principals in the Rebellion still liable to punishment, yet we must be cautious not to make them too desperate else we shall fail in withdrawing the People from their influence.[26]

Castlereagh continued to see the Irish Rebellion in conspiratorial terms, but he also favoured limited reforms to improve local conditions. The Act of Union (joining Ireland and Britain) was, from his standpoint, one of these ameliorations. Castlereagh, along with his superiors Pitt and Cornwallis, believed this measure would enable Ireland to benefit by joining the British Empire, while it would also make it possible to permit Catholics, who would no longer be a majority under the Union, to sit in Parliament in Westminster (at least, this is what Castlereagh and Pitt had hoped would happen). In the aftermath of the Irish Rebellion, Castlereagh also recommended other reforms, such as reorganizing Ireland's Presbyterian congregations and reducing the tithes paid in support of the Protestant Church of Ireland. His aim was to restore a harmonious, hierarchical society in which the lower orders were firmly attached to as well as led by the propertied elite.

In the Tsar's case, the views of his Swiss tutor, La Harpe, made him sympathetic to many of the ideas of the French Revolution. His grandmother, Catherine II, read the French Constitution to him with approval (though she changed her attitude after the execution of Louis XVI). Czartoryski complained that Alexander was, in fact, a republican. In the early years of his reign—a decade after the outbreak of the Revolution—he still considered many schemes for reform, including the end of serfdom, with his 'Unofficial' Committee. After the agreement at Tilsit, Alexander turned back to the question of reform. He charged his minister Mikhail Speransky with the ambitious task of drafting a constitution, which would have created a series of local and provincial assemblies, capped by a national advisory assembly chosen by the Tsar from candidates recommended by the lower assemblies. The Tsar adopted Speransky's proposal to create a new council of state but not the rest of his plan; Speransky himself was ignominiously and unjustly dismissed in 1812 for suspected French sympathies.[27] Was the Tsar simply unwilling to place any real limits on his own prerogative?

The subsequent struggle with Napoleon led to the Tsar's increased religiosity, which, if not shared with the other allied leaders, was not uncommon among the Russian aristocracy and especially the Baltic Germans in the Russian Empire. Disillusioned with both French rationalism and the Russian Orthodox Church, these romantics were deeply influenced by German pietism and mysticism. Following Burke's reasoning to its logical conclusion, they yearned for a moral regeneration of society based upon Christian precepts.

Of these five men, Hardenberg—just slightly older than Talleyrand—had the most active experience in government service under the *ancien régime*. Like the Tsar, Hardenberg did not react to the Revolution by condemning all reform; instead, he saw administrative reform as the best alternative to revolutionary chaos, defining reform in his famous 'Riga Memorial' of 1807 as 'a revolution in a positive sense, one leading to the ennoblement of mankind ... Democratic principles in a monarchical government—this seems to me to be the appropriate form for the spirit of the age'.[28] Hardenberg wanted to weld Prussia together into a united, homogeneous state by eliminating all vestiges of feudalism and parochialism, while introducing free trade and uniform taxation; but he also hoped to preserve royal absolutism and his own power as Chancellor. Friedrich Meinecke, doyen of pre-war German historians, described Hardenberg as an individual full of contradictory impulses:

> Hardenberg's thought was eclectic. The traditions of enlightened absolutism, the philosophy of the Enlightenment itself, the liberal and democratic demands of the age, the models of the Napoleonic Empire and the kingdom of Westphalia, where the new rights of freedom and equality coexisted with a tautly centralized administration and a shadowy popular assembly—all these touched him, and he had learned from everything. He was the most cosmopolitan of the reformers, in the sense that he did not completely belong anywhere, spoke a variety of intellectual and political tongues, learned and relearned easily, but, to be sure, also found it easy to forget.[29]

Such flexibility would prove a useful trait for Hardenberg at Vienna.

A sixth Congress statesman also deserves some mention. By 1814, Hardenberg was experiencing a loss of hearing and so was accompanied to most of the meetings at Vienna by the junior Prussian plenipotentiary, the philosopher and statesman Wilhelm von Humboldt (1767–1835), brother to the famous naturalist.[30] In many ways, Humboldt's earlier life conformed to the pattern of the five other statesmen, although, more than the others, he was a true intellectual in politics. Humboldt's grandfather had been raised to the nobility for his service in the Prussian army; his father reached the rank of major and was rewarded for military service by an appointment as chamberlain at the royal court in Berlin; his mother had been a widow wealthy from a previous marriage. Humboldt and his brother were educated on their family estate outside Berlin by private tutors prominent in the Berlin Enlightenment; they later attended lectures by such luminaries as Christian Wilhelm von Dohm, an active spokesman for Jewish emancipation, and the philosopher Johann Jakob Engel. Humboldt visited Paris briefly in August 1789, at the very dawn of the French Revolution, and lived in the French capital again from 1797 until 1801. In Germany, he befriended Schiller, Goethe, the Schlegel brothers and Friedrich von Gentz; in Paris, he associated with Sieyès, Madame de Staël and Benjamin Constant. Humboldt was an even more passionate advocate of liberal reform than Hardenberg himself. His essay 'On the Limits of State Action', written in 1791 under the impact of the French Revolution (but only published after his death), argued that the whole purpose of the state should be to foster the liberty and cultural development of the individual. As Prussian minister of education from 1809 to 1810, Humboldt introduced free and universal education for all citizens and founded the University of Berlin. Later, he served as Prussian ambassador to Austria and as plenipotentiary to the Châtillon negotiations.

The principal negotiators at Vienna were thus cut from a common cloth but of a complex pattern—youthful privilege and wealth, an early exposure to and acceptance of liberal Enlightenment ideas, face-to-face confrontation with revolutionary upheavals in early manhood and, finally, participation in the long years of accommodation and struggle against their great contemporary Bonaparte, with all the checks and reverses that this entailed. Despite their long years of public service, they were also relatively young. They were a generation not likely to pose as the advocates either of universal reform or of wholesale reaction. The complexity of their prior experiences helps to account both for the subtlety of their aims and the endurance of their achievement.[31]

Diplomatic aims on the eve of the Congress

The principal task after the conclusion of the Peace of Paris was the distribution of the territories conquered by Napoleon but now outside French borders. In reshaping the boundaries of Europe, the statesmen faced the challenge of reconciling the changes of the revolutionary epoch with what had preceded it.

General approaches

In general, four quite different approaches to these problems were conceivable. The first approach would simply have been to restore Europe to its *status quo ante bellum*—a return to the *ancien régime*. This was, for example, the course recommended by many of the former German imperial knights, who had lost their independence under the Napoleonic reorganization of Germany and who now called for a restoration of their rights and the return of the Holy Roman Empire. Restoration was also the aim of the Neapolitan Bourbons, who desired the overthrow of Murat and their own return to Naples. The Pope likewise called for a reinstatement of papal power as it had once existed in Central Italy. In Spain, too, Ferdinand VII set about returning internal conditions to those that had prevailed before the Revolution, abolishing the Constitution of 1812 and reinstating the Spanish Inquisition. The same was true of Victor Emmanuel, King of Piedmont-Sardinia, who overturned all institutional changes initiated by the French since June 1800.[32] The French 'ultra-royalist' supporters of the Comte d'Artois, the younger brother of Louis XVIII, also would have preferred to go further in this direction. Talleyrand's formulation of the doctrine of 'legitimacy' gave some credence to these reactionary tendencies. Only by restoring old institutions and ways, it was argued, could the spell of the French Revolution be broken and stability regained. On the other hand, as a guide for territorial settlement, the doctrine of legitimacy raised some unique problems. At what date were territorial holdings to be considered 'legitimate'? If 1789 or even 1792 were chosen, for example, did that mean that Poland should be restored to her borders before the Second Partition?

A second approach might have been the naked aggrandizement of the four allied great powers—the chief victors in the late war whose armies still occupied most of Europe. Napoleon had accustomed Europe to such conduct over the past 15 years, and Humboldt spoke openly of the need for states to maximize their power. Such aggrandizement might take any one of several forms, based upon either the simple right of conquest, satisfying the solemn treaty obligations undertaken by the allies themselves in the course of the armed struggle, the notion of reimbursement for the costs of waging war against the Corsican usurper, or finally, the need to rationalize European frontiers in such a way as to create a durable European equilibrium or 'balance of power'.

Indeed, the goal of creating a durable balance of power in Europe constituted a closely related third approach, which Pitt had suggested as early as 1805 and which was explicitly identified in the secret articles of the Peace of Paris. This approach provided not only a rationale for territorial aggrandizement, but also a seemingly principled formula for the division of the spoils and the potential for creating a more stable Europe with the blessings of peace. The theory was that so long as the military strength of each of the five 'great powers' was sufficient to defend the possessor against the attacks of the other powers, the peace of Europe would be preserved—in the words of Friedrich von Gentz: 'What is usually termed a balance of power is that constitution subsisting among neighbouring states ... by virtue of which no one among them can injure the independence or the essential rights of another, without meeting with effectual resistance.'³³ Essentially, this was the programme of Castlereagh and Metternich, who hoped to fortify Central Europe in order to contain the two expansionist powers on its flanks: France and Russia. It almost goes without saying that this approach in general entailed sacrifices from the smaller powers on behalf of the greater.

A fourth approach, forward-looking but not without its advocates even at this time, would have been to redistribute territories on the basis of popular self-determination and nationality. This would have led to the restoration of an independent Poland, the preservation of Saxony, independence for the Italian city-states of Genoa and Milan, independence for Norway, a stronger federation of German states with greater popular participation and the independence of Belgium or its union with France. Such an approach was, after all, the implicit message of the French Revolution, even though it had been ruthlessly manipulated and shamelessly abused by none other than Napoleon himself. The allied powers themselves had dabbled in the use of nationalist sentiments in the course of the long armed struggle—the British had supported local patriots in Spain, Sicily and Holland; Austria had organized insurrections in the Tyrol; the Prussians had summoned up the forces of German nationalism; and Alexander had appealed to Russian patriotism and had bid with Napoleon for the support of the Poles. In France, the allied leaders had cautiously awaited a manifestation of popular feeling before imposing the Bourbons. This was, in fact, Czartoryski's preferred approach to European reconstruction, even now. But once the other allied leaders had become secure in their control of Europe, their attentions to nationalism rapidly diminished. Most of them had never felt wholly comfortable in any case with these volatile forces, so closely associated with the Revolution itself.

It would be a mistake, however, to categorize the negotiations of Vienna solely in terms of these over-arching ideologies. They provided the necessary frames of reference in which each power rationalized its objectives and couched its terms. The actual diplomacy at Vienna was more complex, defying glib characterization. It is only by relating these general approaches to the particular geopolitical tendencies of the powers and to the personal experiences and characteristics of their statesmen that one can hope to gain a true appreciation for the overall dynamic.

Specific aims

The individual aims of each of the powers on the eve of the Congress were relatively clear. The two 'acquisitive powers' were Russia and Prussia. Everyone knew that Alexander planned to create a new Polish kingdom of some kind under his own rule, and to give some or all of Saxony to Prussia, though the Tsar had kept the finer details of his plan shrouded in secrecy.[34] Hardenberg had made it equally clear that Prussia desired not only to be restored to her former proportions but also to consolidate her disconnected territories and to expand in all directions—especially by acquiring the contiguous Kingdom of Saxony and gaining control of the fortress of Mainz. This exterior goal carefully complemented Hardenberg's personal hopes for internal reform, transforming Prussia into a more uniform and homogeneous state. The Prussians further hoped to build a powerful German Confederation—a new association of sovereign German states—as a vehicle for weakening the authority of the German middle states and establishing Prussian control over Northern Germany.

Castlereagh had, for the most part, achieved Britain's principal objectives in the Peace of Paris. That treaty had already sanctioned the union of Belgium with Holland and the British retention of key strategic points around the globe to protect her maritime supremacy. The foundation had also been laid for the creation of a new *cordon sanitaire* of buffer states around France—the United Netherlands to the northwest and an enlarged Piedmont to the southeast. Britain's geographic separation from the mainland prevented her from having any other territorial aspirations (apart from the enlargement of Hanover, which Castlereagh readily relinquished). Castlereagh's primary goals at Vienna were therefore limited to achieving a strategic balance of power on the Continent that would establish a durable peace, favourable to Britain's political and commercial interests. Castlereagh proved to be far-sighted and the most 'European' of British Foreign Secretaries in the extraordinary lengths to which he was willing to go to achieve these ends. His own cabinet colleagues urged him to steer a more isolationist course. But Castlereagh was alarmed at the growth of Russian power, and he intended to act in concert with Austria and Prussia in opposition to the Tsar's Polish plans. He preferred to keep Poland divided among its neighbours rather than to see it resurrected as a Russian satellite. If Prussia could not be persuaded to cooperate, Castlereagh was even willing to contemplate a rival combination, somewhat daring in its very conception: Britain and Austria might ally with Bourbon France to halt the progress of the Russian juggernaut. But he remained cautious regarding French ambitions in Belgium and the Rhineland—'however discountenanced by the present French Government', he feared that such ambitions would 'infallibly revive whenever circumstances favour [their] execution'.[35]

Austria, like Britain, had achieved many of her objectives in the Peace of Paris—especially the creation of an Austrian sphere of influence in Northern Italy. But the fates of Galicia (Southern Poland), of former Habsburg lands held by Bavaria and of Tuscany were still unsettled. And unlike Britain, Austria did not enjoy the luxury of an island location. In the centre of Europe, she was surrounded by potential enemies: France in Italy, Prussia in Germany and Russia in Poland. Moreover, the defeat at Wagram in 1809, when Austria had faced Napoleon alone, greatly impressed Metternich with the dangers of relying on Austrian military power alone without allies. He therefore hoped to weave an intricate web of diplomatic entanglements that would ensure the integrity of her domains. The multi-ethnic character of the Austrian state made it especially susceptible to the evils of revolutionary nationalism, to which Metternich was inveterately opposed. His aims at Vienna were therefore clear: to obtain moderate territorial concessions from Russia and Bavaria; to create favourable spheres of influence in the territories surrounding the Habsburg realm; and to construct a new European order that would prove resistant both to internal revolutionary evils and to the demands of expansionist states such as France, Russia and Prussia. This meant he would impede the Tsar's plan to annex all of Poland and Prussia's to obtain both Saxony and Mainz. Metternich also faced the special problems of constructing a German Confederation, wooing the lesser German states and extricating Austria from her earlier pledge to Murat.

Talleyrand spent the late summer of 1814 drafting instructions to govern his conduct at Vienna, for the approval of Louis XVIII.[36] Here, he explained at length his doctrine of 'legitimacy', which he argued should guide the diplomats in their proceedings. Although France could obviously seek no territorial gains and had even agreed in the Peace of Paris to defer to the decisions of the allied powers, Talleyrand identified three specific objects he would pursue at the Congress: first and foremost, to elevate France back into the deliberations of the powers of the first rank; second, to restore the Neapolitan Bourbons to the throne of Naples in place of Murat; and third, to protect the King of Saxony from Prussia. Talleyrand's exposition of 'legitimacy' was calculated to make pleasurable reading for the French King; it provided a convenient excuse, too, for denying the allies the power to dispose of their conquests. Talleyrand's concern for Saxony doubtless reflected his belief that the emerging strength of Prussia posed a long-term danger to France (indeed, there was a slight incongruity in making the King of Saxony, elevated by Napoleon, into the darling of legitimacy). For the moment, Talleyrand's hands were tied by France's recent defeat and the collective memory of Napoleon's unparalleled usurpations. The best that Talleyrand could therefore do was to approach the Congress with a willingness to exploit to his advantage whatever opportunities might arise.

Finally, beneath the geopolitical interests of the leading states and the personalities of their statesmen lurked the harsh facts of military and economic power. For 'realists', this factor more than any other would explain the outcome in the negotiations to follow. This was an age when military might was still closely correlated with population. The relative strengths of the five major powers remain difficult to gauge with precision, but one historian has hazarded the following estimates of their land armies in the final years of the war and the first year of the peace:

	1812/1814	1816
Britain	250,000	255,000
France	600,000	132,000
Austria	250,000	220,000
Prussia	270,000	130,000
Russia	600,000	800,000[37]

From these numbers, we can sense the dormant but diminishing energy of France, the reasons behind the mounting anxiety over Russia, and the basis for the continuing rivalry between Austria and Prussia for the mastery of Germany. Meanwhile, Britain dwarfed the other powers in terms of naval might and financial resources.

The procedural question, September–October 1814

The Peace of Paris had stated merely that the plenipotentiaries in Vienna would decide on arrangements to 'complete the provisions' of the treaty. It was therefore with a mixed sense of excitement and confusion that delegates began to assemble in the Austrian capital in September 1814. Of course, as we have seen, the real intention of the allies in summoning all of Europe was merely to provide a forum in which to announce and legitimize their own decisions. But now that the Congress was upon them, it was not exactly clear how this outcome was to be achieved.

The formal opening of the Congress was postponed by the allies until 1 October, permitting Alexander time to visit Russia before arriving in Vienna. Even with this delay, the deadlock on the Polish-Saxon Question was so serious that no decisions on the territorial settlement had been reached when the sovereigns and plenipotentiaries began to assemble at Vienna in late September. There was now a real danger that the lesser states would interfere in the general settlement. Though France had renounced her right to any voice in the distribution of territories, allied indecision gave her a new opportunity to exert her influence. The attempt to use the name of Europe to legitimize their decisions thus threatened to backfire on the allies. Under these circumstances, the procedures to be adopted at the Congress suddenly became of critical importance, and the Congress of Vienna never really met at all in the sense originally intended.

Castlereagh, Metternich, Nesselrode and Hardenberg each arrived in Vienna by mid-September and preliminary talks between them commenced shortly thereafter. All still agreed, as Castlereagh reported to Liverpool, that 'the conduct of business must practically rest with the leading Powers'.[38] But the question that bedevilled them was how this was best to be achieved.[39]

Castlereagh versus Humboldt

Two views on the most advantageous mode of proceeding quickly emerged. Castlereagh argued that all the delegates should be immediately assembled for a general preliminary meeting. Here the six great powers (the four allies together with France and Spain) would propose that the general body invest its authority in a special commission made up of themselves. This commission would then draw up a set of proposals on the territorial settlement as well as determine how the Congress should proceed. As all the smaller powers were in one way or another dependent upon the great powers, Castlereagh believed the latter should be able to attain sufficient support at the plenary session through private lobbying. Within the commission of six, once agreement was reached by the four allies, France and Spain would simply be compelled to follow their lead: 'The advantage of this mode of proceeding is that you treat the plenipotentiaries as a body with early and becoming respect. You keep power by concert and management in your own hands, but without openly assuming authority to their exclusion.' This was the British model of deferential parliamentary politics *writ large*, and should not have been unexpected from one who, 15 years earlier, had been able to induce the Irish Parliament to vote itself out of existence.

A rival view was put forward by Wilhelm von Humboldt, the second Prussian plenipotentiary at the Congress, with the support of Metternich. Humboldt believed the Congress of Vienna could only be understood historically, as the product of the exceptional circumstances following the French Revolution and Napoleonic conquests. The complete disruption caused by these events had necessitated an unprecedented number of separate settlements among the various states of Europe. To avoid 'dangerous misunderstandings' and to prevent arrangements 'contrary to the general interest', representatives of all the states had been called together to conduct their multifarious negotiations in a single place. This 'marching in common step', Humboldt thought, was the closest that the states of Europe could ever reach to the ideal of a single 'European republic'. The conclusion of all these separate negotiations at the same time and place would to some extent provide the final arrangements with more force 'by the sanction, or at least by the common recognition, of them all'. Yet the negotiations taking place among each particular group of states remained separate and distinct:

> The Congress of Vienna is not a single negotiation, nor even a single set of negotiations bound together by a common purpose, but a complex of different negotiations that will lead to separate treaties having no other connection with one another except that each is connected to the general interest of Europe.

On these grounds, Humboldt argued that the distribution of territories was a question to be settled by the four allied powers alone, by right of conquest; similarly, the future of Germany was to be negotiated separately by the German states. In fact, Humboldt did not think it would be necessary for the plenipotentiaries to meet collectively at all, although he recognized that at the end of the Congress they might wish to acknowledge collectively all the decisions taken.[40]

A major objection to Castlereagh's proposal was the difficulty of determining which plenipotentiaries to recognize for Saxony and Naples. The four allied powers therefore resolved simply to take charge of the territorial settlement as if by right. Two committees would be formed to carry out this work: the first, charged with 'the great interests of Europe', would be composed of the six great powers; the second, charged with creating a new federal organization for Germany, was to be composed of the chief German states. Only after the redistribution of territories was first determined by the allies and then approved by France and Spain would it be communicated to the lesser states of Europe, who would at last be invited 'to make their opinions and wishes known'. Through this means, the ministers of the four allied courts believed they had at last resolved the thorny procedural question.[41]

Talleyrand confronts the allies

Talleyrand arrived in Vienna at the end of September and almost immediately learned of the allied plan for directing the business of the Congress. Curiously, but one month earlier, Talleyrand had proposed his own mode of proceeding to Castlereagh, transmitted through the British ambassador at Paris:

> He proposes in the first place that the congress shall not be held alternately in the apartments of different plenipotentiaries, but that a house be chosen and expressly fitted up for the negotiations ... He is desirous

that a regular protocol of each conference shall be drawn up and that one person shall be named by each great power, to whom that duty shall be entrusted.

In addition, Talleyrand had suggested the formation of two commissions: one on the affairs of Italy 'to protect the minor states of that country against the encroachments of Austrian ambition' and a second on Germany, to promote 'a preponderance ... equally unfavourable to the projects of Prussia'.[42] It seemed clear enough that in Talleyrand's thinking at that time, the decisions were still to remain firmly in the hands of the 'great powers'. Castlereagh had visited Talleyrand in Paris on his way to Vienna, and the two statesmen conferred for five hours; it is inconceivable that they did not reach some preliminary consensus on this threshold issue.[43]

Now that he was finally in Vienna, Talleyrand—accompanied by Labrador, the Spanish delegate—first officially met with the other ministers at Metternich's house on the afternoon of 30 September. The discussion quickly turned to the question of procedure. Talleyrand was handed an allied protocol; according to his report to Louis XVIII, when his eye spotted the term 'allies', he rebuked the other ministers by asking sarcastically whether they imagined they were still at war with France—'I repeated with some astonishment and even warmth, the word *allied powers* ... "allied", I said "and against whom? It is no longer against France; for peace has been made.... It is surely not against the King of France; he is a guarantee of the duration of that peace".'[44] The protocol was promptly withdrawn, but in its place the ministers handed Talleyrand their resolutions on the forms of the Congress. 'The visible aim of this plan', Talleyrand wrote to the French King, 'was to make the four powers, who called themselves allied, absolute masters of all the operations of the Congress'. Not surprisingly, Talleyrand adamantly opposed their proposals and brought forward all the arguments he could muster against the so-called 'right of conquest'. He told them

> that the idea of arranging everything before convening the Congress was a novel one to me; that they proposed to finish where I had thought it would be necessary to begin; that probably the power which it was proposed to confer upon the six powers could not be given to them except by the Congress ... I asked why the Congress could not be assembled at once, and what were the difficulties in the way?[45]

Talleyrand further announced that France would recognize nothing negotiated by the four powers since the signing of the Peace of Paris. On this discordant note, the meeting was adjourned. 'The intervention of Talleyrand

and Labrador has hopelessly upset all our plans', wrote Gentz, 'Talleyrand protested against the procedure we have adopted and soundly berated us for two hours. It was a scene I shall never forget'. Talleyrand published his protest, which led 13 of the smaller German states to hold a meeting to resist 'the usurpation of the great powers'.[46]

The ministers of the six powers reconvened on 5 October, when the allied ministers threatened to settle affairs by themselves; Talleyrand coldly responded that in this case he would leave their deliberations and await the formal opening of the Congress. His menacing tone—at least, according to his own reports—had a disturbing effect on the other ministers, who did not speak openly of excluding France again. However, they still could not come to any consensus on the proper mode of handling business at the Congress. Talleyrand himself proposed to postpone it, but to a definite date. A few days later, they met again and agreed to convene the Congress on 1 November, with a tacit understanding that even at this date it might be further postponed. On Talleyrand's insistence, they also announced its proceedings would conform to 'principles of public law'. Meanwhile, the allies had purchased additional time to continue their private discussions unhampered. It 'was evident', Castlereagh explained in his correspondence with the British cabinet,

> that a Congress never could exist as a deliberative assembly, with a power of decision by plurality of votes ... [A]s the business must take before Congress the form of a negotiation rather than of a decision upon a question put, the only course that could facilitate our formal proceedings was to give time for informal discussion in the first instance.[47]

Throughout October the allied powers remained deadlocked in the struggle over the future of Poland (discussed below). As the end of the month approached, however, the question of the opening of the Congress again needed to be considered. A meeting of the representatives of the eight signatories of the Peace of Paris was held on 30 October. Talleyrand offered a plan to form a 'General Committee' composed of representatives of all sovereign states. The General Committee would in turn create separate sub-committees to deal with the affairs of Poland, Saxony, Switzerland and Italy. His proposal was quickly rebuffed by the allies. Talleyrand accepted this rejection without demur, since he now realized he had more to gain from cooperation with Castlereagh and Metternich than by challenging the allies over procedural details.[48] The ministers adopted Talleyrand's clever suggestion that the credentials of all the plenipotentiaries present in Vienna should be examined and approved. Three of the powers were chosen by lot to take up this task, which proved to be a welcome diversion for the other representatives, reducing the general clamour for the Congress to begin.

Indefinite postponement

On 18 November the eight signatories of the Peace of Paris finally announced that the meeting of the Congress was postponed indefinitely. In fact, the Congress never met at all in the form of a plenary session of all the assembled delegates, as originally intended. The eight signatories of the Peace of Paris—the 'Committee of Eight'—met occasionally to serve as a formal directing body; a separate 'German Committee' (initially composed of delegates representing Austria, Prussia, Bavaria, Hanover and Württemberg) dealt with German affairs; while a handful of other special committees were formed to deal with such matters as the affairs of Switzerland.[49] The real business of the Congress, however, proceeded in the discussions of the ministers of the four allied powers, usually held at Metternich's Chancellery on the Ballhausplatz or across the road in Castlereagh's hired rooms at Minoritenplatz. It was a continuation of the same informal manner of transacting business that had been employed at Langres, Troyes, Chaumont, Paris and London.

The dispute over the procedures to be adopted at the Congress demonstrates precisely just how little regard was actually paid to the interests of the smaller powers. Even Castlereagh and Talleyrand, the two statesmen most anxious to consult the representatives of the lesser states, shared the assumption that they would defer to the great powers as a matter of course. The smaller states were feared only in combination with France (or, indeed, with any of the great powers, including Austria in Germany). But the law of conquest alone could not provide the allied leaders with the cloak of legitimacy they felt was necessary for the new international order to endure, and they were careful not to snub the other delegates too openly.

The social life of the Congress

At one level, the Congress of Vienna was about the territorial reconstruction of Europe. But at quite another it was a monarchical and aristocratic celebration of the end of the French Revolution and Napoleonic Wars—a joyous ritual cleansing. It is therefore quite impossible to speak of the Congress of Vienna without mentioning something of the social life and symbolic significance of the Congress. Two emperors, four kings, 11 ruling princes, more than 200 plenipotentiaries and a large number of uninvited emissaries were in attendance, many accompanied by large retinues of ministers, counsellors, relatives and servants. The former German imperial princes, the Jews of Frankfurt, the publishers of Europe and many other groups sent envoys. The city of Vienna—ordinarily with a population of about 200,000—swelled by more than one-third.[50] The picturesque central district—surrounded by a low wall and a wide grassy slope, or 'glacis'—was not large by modern standards, ensuring frequent contact of the sovereigns and their ministers with one another and with the general population. Even Metternich's suburban villa on the Rennweg, across from the Belvedere Palace, was just a brief walk from the city centre.

Although the Habsburg monarchy had been weakened by decades of war, the Austrian Emperor and Metternich were determined to demonstrate Habsburg strength by sparing no expense at the Congress. The principal sovereigns—the Tsar and the Kings of Prussia, Denmark, Bavaria and Württemberg—all stayed as the guests of the Austrian Emperor in the Hofburg, the ancient Habsburg palace at the heart of Vienna. A large feast was prepared for them each night, and 300 carriages with 1,400 horses were placed at the disposal of the honoured guests. As host to the Congress, Metternich also did a great deal of entertaining, providing dinners to several hundred people every Monday night at the Austrian Chancellery.

Though most of the plenipotentiaries and visitors never became involved in the secret negotiations that were settling the new frontiers of Europe, their festivities provided a splendid backdrop to the work of the diplomats. Lord High Steward (*Obersthofmeister*) Prince Trauttmansdorff helped to organize them, and the Empress of Austria also played an active role. There were almost daily parades, hunting parties, dinners, balls, concerts, operas and other entertainments. Several of these social events were especially memorable: the entry of the allied sovereigns into Vienna in September; the Festival of Peace held in the large park known as the Prater in October in celebration of the victory at Leipzig the previous year, followed that same evening by Metternich's 'Peace Ball' at his villa on the Rennweg; a masked ball, again at Metternich's villa, in early November; the 'Grand Carousel', a medieval jousting tournament held at the Spanish Riding School later in the month, in which all the participants appeared in medieval dress; a performance of the Seventh Symphony, conducted by Beethoven himself; the *tableaux vivants* in the grand ballroom of the Hofburg in which costumed actors and actresses, under the direction of the painter Isabey, depicted historical and mythological scenes; the funeral of the Prince de Ligne, an Austrian Field Marshal and the famous 'wit' of the Congress; a great sleigh ride and banquet held in January at Schönbrunn Palace; and a sombre memorial service held on 21 January in Stephansdom, the cathedral in the centre of Vienna, for Louis XVI of France on the anniversary of his execution. Of equal importance to the statesmen were countless dinners and soirées, especially those offered by the competing beauties in the Palm Palace, just around the corner from the Minoritenplatz—Wilhelmine, the Duchess von Sagan, and Princess Katrina Bagration. These often provided the venues for informal diplomatic encounters, especially between the allies and the French. The people of Vienna paid for most of these festivities through new taxes on the movement of goods. While innkeepers, landlords, merchants and musicians delighted in the presence of foreign guests, many Viennese found good reason to grumble.

The leading ministers, mostly men in their younger 40s, somehow found time to participate in these revelries. Metternich not only played frequent host but was deeply affected by his lingering infatuation for the Duchess von Sagan. In October and November, at the height of the crisis over Poland, the Austrian foreign minister was suffering almost unbearable pangs of grief from Sagan's rejections. After a full day of negotiating and playing the social host, Metternich frequently walked in the night air with his friend and colleague Friedrich von Gentz, the 'Secretary' of the Congress, as he divulged the details of his unhappy romance. Gentz, Talleyrand and others feared that Metternich was becoming distracted from his work.

One other aspect of the Congress deserves notice: the system of espionage conducted by the Austrian police. The Austrians had already constructed one of the most efficient networks of political police in Europe, and they immediately recognized the opportunities that the Congress afforded in this respect. Under the efficient direction of Baron Franz Hager von Altensteig, mail arriving in Vienna was opened, read and resealed, and the contents of wastebaskets and fireplaces were collected and summarized. Viennese of all social classes clandestinely entered into the pay of the police and filed their observations. A daily summary of the most interesting revelations was prepared each morning for the Emperor of Austria.[51]

The Polish Question and Alexander's diplomatic triumph, October–November 1814

The main issue confronting the allied statesmen at Vienna remained the reconstruction of Central Europe, especially Poland. Once one of the largest countries in Europe, we have seen that Poland had been partitioned by its immediate neighbours at the end of the eighteenth century. There was no little irony here, in that Prussia had once been a duchy under Polish suzerainty, a Polish army had occupied parts of Russia in the early seventeenth century, and as recently as 1683, a Polish king had saved Vienna from a Turkish siege. The final partitions of Poland took place in 1793 and 1795, during the French Revolution. Prussia received Warsaw, Danzig (Gdańsk) and Thorn (Toruń); Russia took all the territories east of the Niemen and Bug

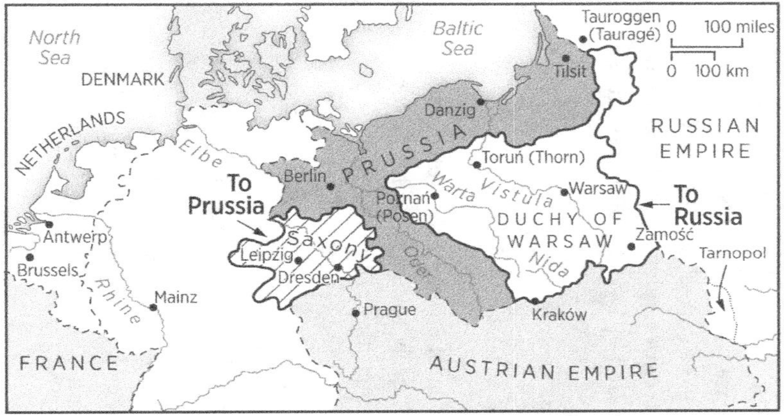

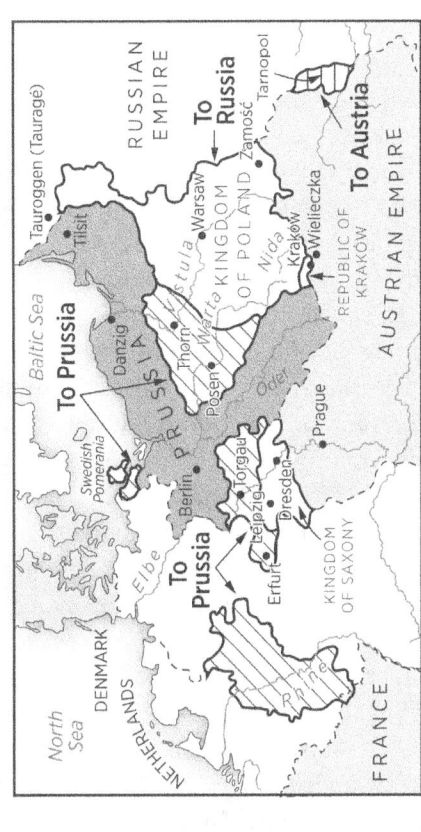

The 'Polish-Saxon' Question

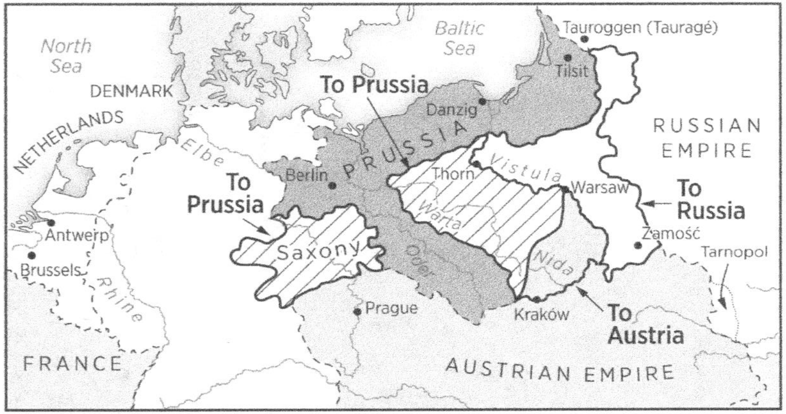

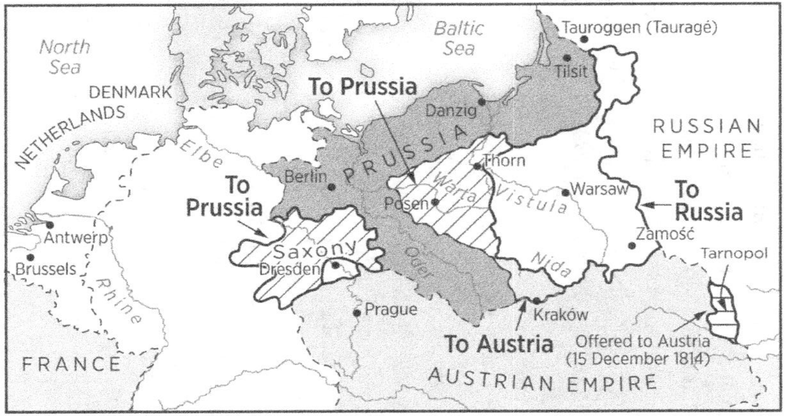

rivers; and Austria occupied the south, including the ancient Polish capital of Kraków.

The disappearance of Poland was therefore of recent memory, and the embittered Polish nobility still harboured hopes of resurrecting their ancient kingdom. As Crown Prince, Alexander had pledged to Czartoryski to one day restore the Polish kingdom, but as Tsar, he had so far failed to keep his promise. Napoleon had pandered to Polish sentiments by creating the nucleus of a new Poland in the form of the Duchy of Warsaw in 1807, made up of the Prussian share of the Polish partitions, with the cities of Warsaw, Thorn, Posen (Poznań) and Kalisch (Kalisz). He had also imposed the Napoleonic Code, granting personal freedom to the Polish serfs. In 1809, Napoleon further added territories taken from the Austrian share of the partitions, including Kraków and Zamość, so that the Duchy approached nearly the same size as that to which Prussia had been reduced.

At Tilsit, Alexander and Napoleon had made a secret agreement never to restore the Polish monarchy, but when the Tsar feared a French invasion in 1811, he attempted to rally the Poles to his side by openly offering them a Polish kingdom; distrustful of Russia, most Poles continued to side with Napoleon. The subsequent collapse of French power left the fate of the Duchy of Warsaw undecided: would it remain as the kernel of an independent Poland or be re-partitioned by the three eastern powers along the lines of 1795? Or would a third outcome ensue—the reconstitution of Poland under Russian tutelage? Throughout the final stages of the war, the three eastern powers had adopted various formulae that left the answer in doubt. But the fact that Russian forces occupied the area seemed to give Alexander a decisive edge in determining its fate (much as Poland's occupation by Soviet troops later gave Stalin a decisive voice in 1945).

The Tsar's Polish-Saxon plan

Alexander now toyed once again with the idea of reviving the Polish kingdom. He linked the resurrection of Poland closely to his plans for Saxony. Saxony and Poland were not contiguous: rather, they were narrowly separated by Silesia, the very territory that Frederick the Great had seized from Austria in 1740 to propel Prussia forward along the path to great-power status. Curiously, Poland and Saxony had been dynastically tied for much of the previous century. In 1697, the Elector of Saxony had been elected as King of Poland, for which prize he had renounced the Protestant faith of Saxony and converted to Catholicism. His hopes to unite Saxony and Poland failed when he became involved in a series of wars with Sweden. His son also reigned as both Elector of Saxony and King of Poland from 1733 until 1763; afterwards, the two territories again had independent rulers following the election of Poniatowski. The Polish Constitution of 3 May 1791 nevertheless stipulated that the Elector of Saxony should be Poniatowski's heir, and in 1807 Napoleon pointedly chose Frederick Augustus, the King of Saxony (only just elevated from his former status as elector), to serve as ruler of the newly created Duchy of Warsaw.

Alexander's plan called for the Russian annexation of the Duchy, which consisted of the Prussian and Austrian shares of the earlier partitions. To these, Alexander intended at some future date to add Russia's own Polish provinces—thereby completely reviving the moribund kingdom. Poland would be linked to Russia through a dynastic union in the Tsar's own person, but otherwise the Poles were to enjoy separate institutions of government, including their own written constitution and representative assembly.

At the same time, the Tsar had also promised to restore Prussia to her 1805 dimensions. But if Alexander were not to return Prussia's Polish provinces, how was Prussia to be restored to her former size? To compensate Prussia for her losses to the east, the Tsar proposed she annex Saxony to the west. He was in an exceptionally good position to suggest this exchange, since Russian troops occupied Saxony as well as Poland. The Tsar required only that the Saxon identity be preserved and that the Prussian union with Saxony be merely a dynastic one, similar to his own prospective union with Poland.

The Tsar believed that any gains Russia made in Poland were an amply deserved reward for her courageous role in the liberation of Europe. He also felt that Austria was entitled to little say in the distribution of territories recaptured from France before Austria had even entered the allied coalition. Some historians assert that the Tsar's plan was largely driven by motives of realpolitik: Alexander wished to provide security against future attacks from the west, which could only be achieved by Russian control of Thorn, Kraków and the lands between. To keep control of this vast territory, it would be best to harness Polish national feelings by the creation of a buffer state. Otherwise, the discontented Poles might always provide potential allies to those who, like Napoleon, sought to strike a blow at Russia herself.[52] The Tsar's strategy has even been favourably compared to the traditional Habsburg policy of giving special privileges to border regions like the Tyrol or Croatia to retain their allegiance.

As always, there was a strong element of ideological fervour behind the Tsar's plan. His proposal gave new hope to Poles dreaming of the resurrection of their nation in any shape or form—and was supported by such ardent Polish patriots as the aged Kościuszko. In the summer of 1814, with the Tsar's approval, Czartoryski met with a committee of prominent Polish reformers and grappled with, among other issues, improving the conditions of the

Polish peasantry. The Tsar himself remained reliant on Czartoryski for advice on Polish affairs, and on his way to Vienna Alexander even met with leading members of the Polish nobility at Czartoryski's estate in Puławy. There, the grandson of Catherine the Great enthusiastically toasted the Polish nation and promised to create a future Poland by uniting the Duchy of Warsaw with Russia's existing Polish provinces. He urged the Poles to establish institutions in the former Duchy similar to those in Russian Poland in order to facilitate their later reunification, although he also warned that Poland must remain dynastically linked to Russia not only in his own person but also under his successors.[53] To Czartoryski and a small inner circle of Polish notables, the Tsar further confided that he would resist all Austrian attempts to obstruct his Polish plans or to interfere with the new kingdom's internal organization. This partly explains the Tsar's hesitation in announcing his specific plans. The sincerity of his intentions was later borne out by his grant of a constitution to the Poles, which included a representative assembly, as early as November 1815, and which may have even been intended to serve as a model for the rest of his dominions.

Indeed, the Tsar's plans for Poland can be seen as part of his vision for the regeneration of Europe as a whole. The Tsar had already proposed a constitution for France (rejected, to be sure, by the Bourbon King); in preparation for the Congress of Vienna Czartoryski drew up fresh plans for the reorganization of Europe and the granting of liberal constitutions, hearkening back to his 'Grand Design' of 1803–4 and the diplomatic exchange with Pitt. The Prussian patriot Stein, the Tsar's former Swiss tutor La Harpe, and the Corfiote Capodistrias, along with Czartoryski himself, all accompanied the Tsar to Vienna as proponents of these liberal nationalist views. On the other hand, the Russian nobility and military mostly opposed Alexander's plans for Poland; so too, in fact, did Stein and Capodistrias, who believed that Poland did not possess a sufficiently robust 'third estate' to merit such autonomy.[54]

The other allied leaders also opposed Alexander's Polish plans, albeit for quite different reasons. Russia had already emerged as the foremost military power on the Continent, and Castlereagh, Metternich and Hardenberg feared any further increase in Russian strength.[55] They were especially apprehensive that Russian gains in Poland would leave Prussia's eastern border vulnerable, turning Prussia into a satellite of Russia, while also giving Russia control of the heights above the main invasion route to Vienna. 'How can you possibly contemplate placing Russia,' Talleyrand taunted Metternich, 'like a girdle around your principal and most valuable possessions, Hungary and Bohemia?'[56] The allied ministers likewise dreaded the effect that the creation of a new Polish kingdom might have in stimulating unrest among those Poles still remaining under Prussian or Austrian rule.[57] Castlereagh further feared that, without regaining their former Polish territories, Prussia and Austria would be driven apart by new disagreements over compensations to be found elsewhere, thereby impeding his own plans to strengthen Central Europe.[58]

Allied resistance to the Tsar's plans

It was not until 19 September that the Russian foreign minister Count Nesselrode finally unveiled the specific details of the Tsar's plan at an informal meeting with Metternich and Hardenberg: Russia would indeed swallow all of the Duchy of Warsaw, including both Thorn and Kraków. Metternich and Hardenberg vehemently objected, especially to the revival of the name of Poland, which would create immediate unrest among their own Polish subjects. If the Tsar carried through this plan, Metternich complained to Nesselrode, then Austria might as well 'consider Galicia as lost to us'.[59]

The Tsar and the King of Prussia made their grand entry into Vienna one week later, accompanied by troops and welcomed by the Emperor Francis on horseback. In separate audiences with Metternich and Castlereagh on 28 September, Alexander made official not only his territorial demands, but also his desire to resurrect the Polish royal title and to grant the Poles a constitution. He further announced his intention to add Russia's Polish provinces to the new kingdom at some future date. It was everything these ministers had dreaded.[60]

Castlereagh told the Tsar his proposal violated existing allied treaties, which stipulated that Austria should receive a portion of the Duchy of Warsaw. The Tsar responded that he was acting out of a genuine sense of 'moral duty' to the Polish people; moreover, British public opinion supported him. Britain might support a truly independent Poland, Castlereagh retorted, but could not regard the Tsar's plans in the same light. To this remark the 'Tsar frankly acknowledged that he was not prepared to make this extent of sacrifice on the part of his empire'. While the Tsar's intentions were undoubtedly sincere, Castlereagh pointed out that nothing would prevent the formal incorporation of Polish territories into Russia after his death. He further countered that the creation of an autonomous Poland within the Russian Empire would excite unrest among those millions of Poles still under Austrian and Prussian rule, and sow the seeds of future discord between the three eastern powers.[61]

The next day, Castlereagh had an even more candid discussion with Nesselrode. By insisting on the acquisition of the whole of Poland, he lamented bitterly, the Tsar was reviving that very system of hegemonic power which the allies had so recently combated in Napoleon. The Tsar's plan to annex all of Poland was 'not only dangerous but degrading' to Austria and Prussia, denying them even 'the semblance of a frontier' and forcing them into an 'undisguised state of military dependence upon Russia'. It threatened 'to revive the system we had all united to destroy, namely one colossal military power holding two other powerful states in a species of dependence and subjection'.[62] The British Foreign Secretary's objections could not have been more forcefully stated.

Thus, already in this initial skirmish, the battle lines were clearly drawn. The Tsar, prodded by Czartoryski and his own sense of honour, was occupying the moral high ground: the resurrection of Poland, even if under his own suzerainty, would best serve the interests of the Polish people. Even Czartoryski understood that there were limits to how far Alexander, as the Emperor of Russia, could go in satisfying Polish aspirations; he was already offering privileges to Poles that were denied to the majority of Russians. It is therefore hard to concur with Castlereagh that the sanctity of allied treaties somehow barred concessions to the Poles to remedy past injustices; this was akin to arguing that robbers had a moral obligation not to return their loot because such restitution would infringe their own agreement for the division of the spoils. Such specious reasoning was, however, merely a rhetorical device: Castlereagh's true concern was that Alexander's altruistic intentions would eventually come to naught, making the most critical aspect of his plan the fact that it would lead to a further accumulation of Russian power. Judging events from just 15 years later, Castlereagh's predictions proved to be regrettably prescient—Poles living under Austrian jurisdiction ultimately fared better than those in Russian 'Congress Poland'. But from the vantage point of 1814, there can be little doubt that it was the Tsar who was acting most sincerely as the champion of Polish interests.[63]

Although the Prussian ministers and generals were eager to obtain all of Saxony—after the Battle of Leipzig in 1813, Hardenberg had boldly hailed his master Frederick William III as the 'King of Prussia and Saxony'[64]—they shared their allies' concern that under the Tsar's proposed exchange their eastern frontier would become vulnerable. Despite the wavering of their monarch, Hardenberg and Humboldt therefore believed that greater cooperation with Metternich and Castlereagh was advisable. Indeed, Hardenberg was willing to go great lengths towards accommodating Austria. Not only their mutual interests in Poland but also in Germany bound them together. Here, the Prussians aimed at establishing joint control with Austria over the future German Confederation. If Prussia were unsuccessful in her bid to obtain new territories in Northern Germany, Hardenberg and Humboldt reasoned, she might still acquire comparable influence through her new powers in the Confederation. In particular, the Prussians advocated the formation within the Confederation of large administrative districts known as *Kreise* (or 'Circles', named after the regional administrative units of the late Holy Roman Empire). Through the creation of a large *Kreis* under Prussian control, the Prussian monarchy could find an alternative means for dominating Northern Germany. But to succeed, they needed the support of Austria.[65]

Though British interests were not directly at stake, Castlereagh quickly assumed a leading role in opposing the Tsar's plans. The situation was not unlike that at the beginning of 1814, when Castlereagh had taken charge of allied opposition to the Tsar's scheme to elevate Bernadotte to the throne of France. At an audience with King Frederick William, Castlereagh inveighed against Russian absorption of the Duchy of Warsaw, which he said would leave the Prussian monarch's 'provinces uncovered, and his state in obvious dependence upon another power'. Castlereagh advised the Prussians to employ all means short of war before submitting to the Russian demands. At a subsequent meeting with Hardenberg and Metternich, Castlereagh further elucidated the dangers of Austro-Prussian disunity. Hardenberg replied that Prussia could not risk the disfavour of Russia until she knew with certainty that England and Austria would guarantee her Saxony.[66]

It was not until 9 October—the night of one of the most magnificent balls of the entire Congress—that Hardenberg reached what he considered to be a suitable arrangement for the new German Confederation. Now he was at last able to present a firm offer to Metternich and Castlereagh in writing. Hardenberg began his proposal by pointing out that Russia, Bavaria and Württemberg had all made significant territorial gains—and that Austria, Holland and Hanover were also considerably larger than in 1805. Was not Prussia, he asked with a rhetorical flourish, which had made the greatest sacrifices to the allied cause, equally deserving? Then he came to the point of his note, which was to ask for Austrian and British approval of the complete union of Prussia and Saxony. Would Austria also help find an Italian kingdom for the deposed Saxon king? And would Austria abandon her efforts to place Mainz, the gateway to Northern Germany, under Bavarian sovereignty—so that Prussia would be left with *de facto* control? In exchange, Hardenberg promised Metternich and Castlereagh 'to enter with you into the most perfect accord on Poland'.[67]

Castlereagh, reading Hardenberg's note the next day, was absolutely delighted. He was thoroughly convinced that an Austro-Prussian *entente*, based on Prussian territorial expansion in Northern Germany, would be unassailable.[68] He admitted, on the other hand, that objections might be raised regarding the justice of dethroning Frederick Augustus, the King of Saxony. (Indeed, Talleyrand would later remark that the so-called treason of the King of Saxony was nothing more than a matter of dates, since each of the allied sovereigns had found himself at one time or another in league with

Napoleon.⁶⁹) Castlereagh, however, felt little remorse for the Saxon monarch. In his reply to Hardenberg, accompanied by a *note verbale*, Castlereagh readily accepted the Prussian terms. He pointed out that the allies were indisputably justified in seeking indemnities for risks undertaken and losses endured; at whose expense should they be indemnified, if not of those who had shared in French plunder, and who had refused to avail themselves of favourable opportunities to enlist in the allied cause? There was no one in Europe, concluded Castlereagh, less excusable than the Saxon king, who by every principle of international law had forfeited his rights. Castlereagh's expiations were doubtless aimed more at Metternich and the British cabinet, who received copies, than at Hardenberg himself.⁷⁰

Three days later, the Tsar called on Castlereagh at his apartments on the Minoritenplatz. The tone of their discussion began amicably enough, as the all-powerful Tsar and the British Foreign Secretary patiently rehashed their earlier arguments. Alexander maintained that his possession of Poland created no danger for Europe, since Russian troops would be withdrawn beyond the Niemen. The new Polish Kingdom would, he claimed, actually 'create a balance and a check upon Russian power'.⁷¹ Castlereagh answered that Russian annexation of the whole of the Duchy of Warsaw would not only violate the Tsar's treaty engagements—specifically, the Treaty of Reichenbach of June 1813, which had stated that Poland would be re-partitioned among the three powers—but it would also deprive Prussia and Austria of defensible borders. The Tsar repeated his prior assertion that he had a solemn 'moral duty' to the Polish nation. Castlereagh readily acknowledged the plight of the Poles, but again politely stated that he could see no fulfilment of a moral obligation when, in deference to Russian interests, the Tsar refused to create a truly independent Poland. Nor could Castlereagh see why the Tsar's obligations to the Poles existed on one side of the Warta River but not the other. Against these arguments the Tsar finally rested his case on the realities of military power: 'The Emperor', Castlereagh reported, 'insinuated that this question could only end in one way as he was in possession'. The British Foreign Secretary disclaimed all intention of dislodging the Russians by force, but told Alexander that he thought his aim was less to possess Poland as a conqueror than to govern her as a legitimate sovereign with the sanction of Europe. As their discussion ended, Castlereagh handed the Tsar a memorandum, chiefly drafted by his close assistant Edward Cooke, summarizing the British arguments. Britain had not opposed previous Russian gains in Scandinavia, Turkey or Persia, it stated, but if the Tsar now persisted in his demand to annex not some but all of the Duchy of Warsaw, this could only be perceived as the 'fourth instance of Russian aggrandizement within a few years'.⁷²

A week later, Castlereagh transmitted to the Tsar a copy of the treaty of 1797, in which the partitioning powers had pledged never to revive even the name of Poland.[73] The treaty had actually been furnished to him just two months earlier by Count Merveldt, the Austrian ambassador in London.[74] Castlereagh was using every arrow in his quiver to persuade the Tsar to modify or abandon his plan. While Castlereagh was taking these steps, entangling Britain ever more deeply in the web of Central European affairs, he received a stern missive from Lord Liverpool, the British Prime Minister, criticizing the Tsar's plans but also warning Castlereagh that a 'reconstituted Poland under the Tsar would be less unpopular in England than a new partition, and consequently, of Polish annihilation'. Indeed, when Czartoryski had been in London with the allied sovereigns the previous summer, he had actively courted British leaders, especially among the parliamentary opposition; he had then wisely made a further attempt to stir up British public opinion in favour of the Poles by sending General Józef Sierakowski to tour England and Scotland that very autumn, while the Congress was in session.[75] This public agitation was now helping his cause: Castlereagh could not let himself be seen, at least in the eyes of the British public, as the chief destroyer of Polish hopes.

Meanwhile, Metternich was playing a waiting game. He had received the approval of the Austrian Emperor for the transfer of Saxony to Prussia, yet he delayed in answering Hardenberg's earlier note. Some historians suggest that Metternich was waiting for decisive signs of support from Britain and France before transmitting his approval. He was certain to encounter vociferous domestic opposition from the army and other officials to the sacrifice of Saxony. He was, moreover, still engaged in tortuous negotiations over the shape of the future German Confederation. Indeed, the Polish and Saxon questions had become closely intertwined with the issue of German reorganization. On the one hand, the acquisition of all of Saxony might be less important to the Prussians if they could control Northern Germany through means of a federal *Kreis*. On the other, if Metternich gave his assent to the Prussian acquisition of Saxony, the Prussians would be more willing to make concessions on the new German Confederation in return. Yet, as the German nationalist historian Treitschke later pointed out, it is hard to see how Prussia could have obtained all of Saxony and also recovered much of its former Polish territory, despite explicit reassurances from Castlereagh and Metternich on just this point. Perhaps, as the work of historian Enno Kraehe suggests, the key to Austro-Prussian collaboration in these weeks lies less in Castlereagh's urgings and more in the common interests of Prussia and Austria in presenting a united front in their discussions over the future structure of the German Confederation.

The conspiracy of 23 October

The allied sovereigns were scheduled to visit Buda in Hungary from 24 to 29 October without their ministers, and Alexander looked to this occasion as a propitious moment to bypass the ministers and appeal directly to his fellow monarchs. Hardenberg therefore thought it quite essential to reach some sort of agreement with Austria before the sovereigns' departure. On 21 October, he wrote to Metternich, almost in a tone of desperation, begging for a response to his earlier, still unanswered offer.[76] Metternich finally sent his reply that night: Austria would indeed sanction Prussian incorporation of the whole of Saxony. For Austria's blessing, however, Prussia would have to cooperate in opposing the Tsar's Polish plans as well as meet Austrian demands regarding the rest of German reconstruction, including handing over control of the fortress of Mainz to Bavaria.[77] The price was high, but Hardenberg readily agreed to these terms.

As a result of this exchange of notes, Metternich and Hardenberg met at Castlereagh's apartments on 23 October—the very eve of the departure of the allied sovereigns. (The Tsar would later dub this meeting the 'Conspiracy of 23 October'.[78]) The three ministers now agreed on a joint strategy for opposing Russia. First, they would offer to support the creation of a truly independent Poland, separate from Russia. When this was inevitably rejected, they would propose a new partition in which Russia would receive a portion of the Duchy of Warsaw up to the line of the Vistula, including the city of Warsaw on the left bank—but still less than half the Polish territory the Tsar sought. The three statesmen were genuinely hopeful that their display of unity would persuade the Tsar to accept the Vistula frontier. If not, they would threaten to lay the entire proceedings on Poland before a plenary session of the Congress, leaving it to Europe to choose. This latter idea was almost certainly Castlereagh's, who of the three was the most inclined by experience to treat issues in a parliamentary way.[79]

Since Castlereagh had failed in his previous discussions with the Tsar, Metternich was now chosen to place the bell on the cat. On 24 October, at a long audience, Metternich informed Alexander that Austria, too, might resurrect a Polish kingdom in the south out of her own Polish territories—a suggestion that made the Tsar explode with anger. The Tsar accused Metternich of taking an insolent 'tone of revolt' and gave him such a verbal thrashing, Talleyrand wrote afterwards to Louis XVIII, that it would have been an extraordinary dressing-down even for one's servants.[80] Alexander stormed off to Buda, where he spent the next six days endeavouring to persuade the Emperor Francis to dismiss Metternich. The Austrian Emperor was more amused than perturbed: he advised the Tsar to play less at being his own minister, while he remained steadfast in his own support of Metternich.

Frederick William of Prussia, on the other hand, seems to have been swayed by the Tsar's insinuations and accusations.

In the meantime, Metternich remained busily engaged at hammering away at the Prussian position in the continuing sessions of the German Committee. He argued for a diminution of the powers that the Prussians had intended to confer on each German state heading a *Kreis*, and even questioned the utility of the proposed *Kreis* system at all. Hardenberg and Humboldt had no choice but to acquiesce as part of the price exacted for Austrian support on Saxony. Indeed, Hardenberg may have been having second thoughts about the terms of his collaboration even before the return of the sovereigns from Buda: he suggested that the three powers make a more generous offer to the Tsar of the Warta River, farther to the west, and that they insist only on Thorn for Prussia and Kraków for Austria.

The three allied sovereigns returned to Vienna on 29 October. The very next day, the Tsar sent Castlereagh a written response to his memorandum on Poland. In a cover letter, Alexander openly expressed his hurt feelings at the suspicions raised by his allies.[81] Russia had only acted defensively, not aggressively, the attached memorandum asserted, and her sole object throughout the last campaign had been to obtain a just equilibrium in Europe. Austria had already made substantial gains in Italy, superseding earlier agreements, while all the purported dangers to the defences of Austria and Prussia were purely 'imaginary'. Indeed, these powers had even acted as the allies of France at the time of the invasion of Russia in 1812, clearly extinguishing any obligations that Russia might otherwise have owed them under prior treaties. Czartoryski, the principal author of the Russian memorandum, addressed his father on 31 October with cautious optimism: 'Despite all these storms, I am not without hope that these matters will end quite well and that Poland will emerge in some form or other. We can be certain of the Emperor's sincerity; and that is most important.'[82]

The Tsar's reply was unexpected and scarcely welcome to Castlereagh, who now found himself in the awkward situation of having to contradict a foreign monarch in writing. His discomfiture was greatly increased by the fact that Hardenberg and Metternich had only just recently agreed to appoint him as neutral 'mediator' in the Polish dispute. Castlereagh therefore couched his reply with the greatest delicacy, reiterating the British position on the treaties and emphasizing the vulnerability of the proposed Austrian and Prussian frontiers.[83] He directed his response not against the Tsar, but against the anonymous 'writer' of the Russian memorandum. He began by repeating his now familiar refrain that a share of Poland had been solemnly promised to Austria at Reichenbach:

> Austria, being still at peace with France, bound herself to engage in the war, if her mediation failed to effect a peace upon certain principles

agreed upon with the Allies. In determining thus to hazard her existence in the field, Austria stipulated ... that she should receive a proportion of the Duchy of Warsaw, which had in part been constructed of Territories but recently wrested from her own Dominions ... There is no suggestion that Austria has, by any act, or consent on her part, released her Ally from the obligations of this covenant, or agreed to accept an equivalent.

He totally rejected the Russian contention that this pledge had been made contingent upon events ('purement éventuel'):

What has then deprived Austria of her rights to this specific object? It has been said the treaty was 'éventuel'. 'Eventuel' upon what? Not upon Austria fulfilling her engagements with good faith. Not upon there being the means of giving what was promised, but 'éventuel' upon the extraordinary principle, that, there being more than ample means to satisfy the treaty, a new right accrued to Russia, another party to the treaty, to decide according to her pleasure, whether Austria should obtain the object stipulated, or accept in lieu of it, what Russia deems an equivalent, at the opposite extremity of her dominions. It is a new position in public law ...[84]

The same treaty rights, Castlereagh continued, coupled with Austria's need for a secure frontier, accordingly trumped any 'balance-of-power' argument that her recent gains in Northern Italy had provided her with sufficient recompense:

[I]t is said, that ... Austria has received a full compensation in other quarters. This is not the question under the treaty. The question is, did the Emperor of Austria, upon due and fair notice, consent to receive it as such? Did he consent, in consideration of an extension of his former possessions in Italy from the Adige to the Ticino, to relinquish his right, under the treaty of Reichenbach, to be protected on the side of Poland? Did the several powers, who were parties to the peace of Paris, when assigning the Po as the Austrian boundary in Italy, suppose they were sanctioning an extension of territory on the side of Italy, in exchange for a military barrier between Russia and Austria, on the side of Poland?[85]

The severity of this clash of views is made all the more apparent by juxtaposing the internal documents generated in the course of preparing the exchanged memoranda. Czartoryski had been genuinely horrified at Castlereagh's earlier memorandum, which he had condemned as 'dishonourable and Satanic, Mephistophelean in matter and tone'.[86] In his private correspondence with the Tsar, Czartoryski held steadfastly to his view that European stability could be best secured by supporting the nationality principle.[87] In contrast, the three other allied powers focused on the tangible threat to Austrian and Prussian security that Russia's forward thrust into Poland would pose. Castlereagh pointedly sent to the British cabinet a copy of a detailed memorandum on security issues prepared by the Prussian General Knesebeck, who construed Russian territorial demands in Poland as serving only an *offensive* purpose.[88]

A rather mysterious attempt was also made, presumably by the Tsar, to bribe Metternich, whom the Emperor Francis had so resolutely refused to dismiss. An unknown person slipped a folded note into Metternich's hand at a masked ball at the Hofburg on the evening of 30 October. It stated that 'a person of the highest distinction' would pay him a large sum of money and secure the friendship of a 'woman of rank', which Metternich wished to have—implying Wilhelmine, the Duchess of Sagan, who was then attempting to gain custody of her illegitimate daughter in Russia, over whom the Tsar exercised some authority.[89] Metternich refused the offer, telling Wilhelmine angrily the next day that she would be 'quite astonished at what I have to tell you; as for me I am no longer astonished at anything, especially when it concerns that man.'[90]

Meanwhile, Metternich spent his time shoring up his position against internal opposition, taking the rare step of summoning an Austrian Council of State on the 31st. Here, he elaborated his notion that Austria might respond to Russian actions in the Duchy of Warsaw by creating her own 'Kingdom of Southern Poland' in Galicia. Metternich attempted to persuade his colleagues to agree to the Prussian suggestion of offering the Warta line to Russia, with the proviso that the Tsar relinquish his claims to the Polish royal title, but the most that they would sanction was an offer up to the Vistula, further east.

Collapse of the Triumvirate

The strategy adopted by Metternich, Castlereagh and Hardenberg had been one of uniform application of moral suasion to coax the Tsar to back down. Yet Castlereagh's deep involvement in Continental affairs was viewed with dark suspicion by his own countrymen, while Metternich's decision to surrender Saxony to Prussia was notoriously unpopular in his own court. The weakest link in the chain, however, proved to be Hardenberg. Badgered by Austria on the German Committee, threatened by a large Russian army in neighbouring Holstein and morally bound to Russia for the liberation of their own country just one year before, the Prussians were scarcely in a position to oppose the unequivocal wishes of the Tsar. King Frederick William III was especially sensitive to these facts.

The Tsar himself now launched a diplomatic offensive. On 5 November, less than a week after his return from Buda and the day after receiving Castlereagh's new memorandum, he held a long interview with his German advisor, Baron vom Stein. Alexander expressed his complete exasperation at the resistance he was encountering to his Polish plans. He found this shoddy treatment all the more remarkable, he told Stein, when he had risked his own life and embarked on a dangerous war to liberate Europe, and he had acquiesced to the enlargement of both Austria and Prussia. He further explained that he needed both Kraków and Thorn (Toruń) to protect his Polish possessions along the left bank of the Vistula. 'Everything,' he said, 'united against him. [Even] England, which had nothing to do with the matter, [had] appeared on the scene'. The Tsar ordered Stein to 'use [his] influence to lead Hardenberg to deal alone with Russia in this case and not to make common cause with Austria against him'.[91]

Later that same day, the Tsar and the King of Prussia summoned Hardenberg in what was to be one of the great turning points of the Congress. The Tsar openly accused the Prussian Chancellor of plotting against him, and the King of Prussia imperiously ordered Hardenberg to cease all opposition to Russian policy in Poland.[92] Stein reminded Hardenberg that Prussia was not in a position to resist Russian demands by force—Russia was ready to fight in Poland with 250,000 Russian and 38,000 Polish troops between the Vistula and the Warta, while Prussian and Austrian troops were dispersed throughout Germany.[93] The coalition so recently forged between Austria, Britain and Prussia—the 'Conspiracy of 23 October'—thus lay in ruins.

The close relationship between Russia and Prussia was reinforced by the turning over of the provisional occupation of Saxony to Prussia—a gesture first suggested by Stein and agreed to earlier—at just this juncture. The public announcement of this transfer by Prince Repnin, the Russian commander, on 10 November was intended to further cement Russo-Prussian ties.[94] Meanwhile, Austrian troops were ordered from Italy to Hungary, Galicia and Bohemia, where they could be positioned against Russia. Castlereagh and Metternich also began to think again about reaching towards France for support. Neither one was ready, however, to take the decisive step of aligning directly with their former enemy. Both remained hopeful that their accord with Prussia might still be salvaged, and their private talks with Hardenberg doggedly continued.[95] Metternich warned that Austria could not afford to give way on all three principal issues—Poland, Saxony and Mainz. He suggested that the King of Saxony be left with the nucleus of his kingdom, and that Mainz be made into a fortress of the new German Confederation, manned by an Austro-Bavarian garrison.

On 12 November, Metternich sent a formal note to Hardenberg conveying regret over Austro-Prussian differences, yet encouraging Hardenberg to solicit the Tsar's latest proposals, including how the latter would guarantee the security of Austria's Polish possessions. Metternich informed Hardenberg that Austria might still concede the 'Warta-Nida' line to Russia (giving the Tsar two-thirds of the Duchy of Warsaw, but returning Thorn to Prussia and Kraków to Austria) as well as submit to Alexander's creation of a constitutional monarchy in Poland, so long as the King of Saxony was left with the core of his dominions around Dresden.[96] On 23 November, the same day as the spectacular medieval jousting at the 'Grand Carousel', Hardenberg acted on behalf of all three powers in offering the Tsar the Warta-Nida line as well as their acquiescence to a Polish constitution.[97] Alexander consulted with Stein and Czartoryski, who urged that Prussia should obtain all of Saxony. Stein persuaded the Tsar to offer his allies not possession of Thorn and Kraków, but an assurance that these would become free cities under allied supervision rather than part of the new Russo-Polish kingdom.

Since Alexander had refused to confer control of Kraków on the Austrians, and since he also still insisted that Prussia obtain all of Saxony, his counter-offer was unacceptable to Austria. The attempt to persuade Alexander to reduce his ambitions in Central Europe without resort to force had failed. The Russians remained in occupation of the disputed territories (as the Tsar had so bluntly informed Castlereagh at the very start, they were in his 'possession'), and since none of the other powers was in a position to eject them, Alexander had to all appearances triumphed on the Polish Question.

The Saxon Question and the secret treaty of 3 January 1815

With Poland lost, the focus quickly shifted to Saxony—the other half of Alexander's reconstruction scheme. Hardenberg was quick to realize that his failure to sway the Tsar in Poland might have dangerous repercussions on the willingness of Metternich and Castlereagh to maintain their pledges on Saxony. He sent a *note verbale* to Metternich on 2 December, offering Austria control of Upper Silesia and providing for the Saxon King by moving him to Münster and Paderborn (in the very northwest corner of Germany next to the Netherlands, with a population of 350,000). Mainz, according to Hardenberg, should be controlled by an Austro-Prussian garrison in which Bavaria might also participate. Lastly, Hardenberg called on Austro-British support on the basis of Metternich's October promise of Saxony. He even sent Metternich a poem containing an emotional appeal to German nationalism.[98]

Metternich received Emperor Francis' permission to agree to the Russian acquisition of most of Poland, but even now the Austrians insisted that three conditions must be met: Austria should receive Kraków; internal political arrangements should limit Russian influence in Poland; and the Tsar must guarantee the security of Austria's Polish possessions. Metternich communicated these terms to Alexander on 5 December, as well as Austria's objections, under the new circumstances, to the Prussian acquisition of the whole of Saxony. Metternich's *volte face* was so complete that he chose this very moment—on 7 December, at a meeting with Hardenberg, Humboldt and the Hanoverian minister Count Münster—to jettison the *Kreis* system so cherished by the Prussians from the future German Confederation. (Never one to burn his bridges entirely, however, Metternich told the Prussians privately that they could still draw up two constitutions for the Confederation—one with and one without *Kreise*.)[99]

Castlereagh also was no longer willing to concede all of Saxony to Prussia. Although he told Hardenberg that the allies uniformly wished to see Prussia restored to her former power and dimensions, he considered the situation as now standing 'on different grounds' than before: 'the concert ... which was the basis of the understanding had avowedly failed through the conduct of his Sovereign; that under these circumstances, neither Austria nor Great Britain could espouse his claims in the manner they might otherwise have done'. No power would attempt to dislodge Prussia from Saxony by force, he assured Hardenberg, but—much as he had previously represented to the Tsar—such adverse possession could not, in itself, constitute 'good title'. Without the recognition of the other powers, Castlereagh warned, Prussia would 'remain in a state of disquietude and doubt, compelled to remain armed ...'.[100] Talleyrand smugly wrote to Louis XVIII that with the collapse of his prior policy, Castlereagh appeared to be 'lost', but the man who had bounced back from the defeat of the first bill for the Act of Union (1799), the fiasco at Walcheren and the duel with Canning (1809) was more resilient than this. The reasoning behind his change in posture, conveyed in his letter to Hardenberg, seems straightforward enough.

The unravelling of the 'Conspiracy of 23 October' culminated on 10 December, when Metternich sent Hardenberg a note officially retracting his previous offer of support on Saxony and begrudgingly awarding Prussia a mere one-fifth of that kingdom. Compensation to restore Prussia to her pre-1806 size would have to be found elsewhere—in Poland, Westphalia and the Rhineland.[101]

Hardenberg understandably felt betrayed. In Berlin, the Prussian occupation of Saxony had created the impression of a *fait accompli*. The incorporation of Saxony would have welded Prussia together into a compact mass; the territories offered to her now, in contrast, were dispersed across Germany. They would, moreover, place Prussia in direct contact with France as well as Russia, thrusting the initial burden of German defence exclusively onto her shoulders. Not only was this new offer, to Hardenberg's way of thinking, unfavourable, it was also undeserved. Had he not employed his best efforts to resist Russia? Were not Austria and Britain duty-bound, in consequence, to support Prussian claims to Saxony? For Hardenberg and Humboldt, the recent turn of events was almost too much to bear. Despite all of Prussia's sacrifices in the recent war, Prussia had failed to regain her former territories in Poland and was about to be cheated of contiguous territory in Saxony. The sharp contrast between what was being offered to her now and the high hopes of the previous spring in Paris was almost overwhelming.

Hardenberg summoned Stein, Czartoryski, Knesebeck and Humboldt for an immediate 'strategy session' in response to the Austrian retraction. He also sent an angry note to Metternich. Finally, he adopted the unusual and imprudent tactic of communicating to the Tsar several of Metternich's confidential notes in order to justify his own prior conduct.[102] This 'incorrect act', as Castlereagh reported to the British cabinet, resulted in nothing less than a 'diplomatic explosion'. In particular, the letters revealed that the Tsar had committed some double-dealing himself by making inconsistent claims to Hardenberg and Metternich. Alexander was infuriated, and it was only with the greatest difficulty that the Emperor Francis was able to dissuade him from challenging Metternich to a duel.

After consulting with Castlereagh and the Austrian Emperor, Metternich resolved to reveal some, although not the most damaging, of Hardenberg's own correspondence in order to exonerate himself, but without 'breaking the State Chancellor's neck'.[103] In some of these letters, Hardenberg had even hinted at fighting Russia a few years hence, after Prussia had recovered from the war, in order to win back her Polish possessions. The next morning, Metternich went to see Hardenberg, highly embarrassed about the situation, and obtained the Prussian Chancellor's permission to disclose additional papers to the Tsar.[104] According to Stein, Metternich also attempted to backpedal somewhat, maintaining that his letter of 10 December 'was not official but confidential, and that more of Saxony or Poland might still be demanded'.[105] When the Tsar confronted Metternich in person on the 13th, the latter accordingly produced several pieces of Hardenberg's correspondence, which were equally Russophobic in tone, further abetting Alexander's anger and sense of confusion.[106] The dearth of good humour was underscored by the death, on the same day, of the aged Prince de Ligne, Austrian Field Marshal and famous wit of the Congress, who coined its most memorable *bon mot*—'le Congrès danse beaucoup, mais il ne marche pas' ('the Congress dances, but it does not progress').[107]

The war scare

In the background, a vigorous pamphlet contest over the future of Saxony was being waged between Prussia and the smaller German states.[108] Each power also quietly began preparations for the almost unthinkable possibility of a renewal of the war.[109] As early as 27 November, Count Münster alerted the Prince Regent of England to this threat.[110] Castlereagh addressed the British cabinet on 5 December, weighing the prospects: 'Upon the existing state of affairs, extremely entangled in themselves, my opinion is, that it may unexpectedly assume a better aspect, but that it may equally lead to a total stagnation, and that it may, as Europe is more extensively armed than at any former period, suddenly end in war.'[111] Part of the problem was that none of the powers could long support the costs of remaining fully armed—'if we cannot agree upon some general system, the most likely case to occur is that of hostilities; and where all are armed, and none can long support the bur[d]en of their existing establishments, the chances are that the warfare will be early and general.'[112]

Rumours of an impending conflict even circulated Vienna. For example, a bitter exchange between Hardenberg and Humboldt on the one side and the Bavarian envoy Wrede on the other over the likelihood of a new war was reported by the Austrian police only one day after Castlereagh had written to his cabinet.[113] Even more ominously, on 11 December in Warsaw, Grand Duke Constantine issued a proclamation ordering the Polish army to prepare to defend themselves: 'His Majesty the Emperor Alexander, your powerful protector, calls on you ... to take up arms in the defence of your country and the preservation of your political existence.'[114] A Viennese bystander wrote to a friend in Paris on 14 December that the question of war or peace was now very much in doubt.[115] Jean Anstett, a prominent Russian diplomat, unknowingly confided to an Austrian police informant that if Russia's terms were not accepted, the Tsar himself thought war was likely.[116] According to another police report, Humboldt was brazenly hurling threats: 'Humboldt speaks of nothing but war and revolution ... Prussia will take Bohemia, Russia will take Galicia, and the Rhineland will rise up ... Humboldt's threats have produced a great sensation.'[117] Yet another police report alleged that, while the Prussians realized that most of the Saxon population was against them, they were counting on the support of the German nationalists in the *Tugendbund* (a German nationalist society disbanded in 1810).[118] The generals on each side furiously continued drawing up new plans and moving troops towards their borders.[119] Discontent was so rife that the Austrian delegation secretly circulated a new proposal among friendly German middle states that would have excluded both Prussia and pro-Russian Württemberg from the future German Confederation.[120] One spectator captured the conflicting emotions in a diary entry, hastily scrawled on 16 December: 'Austria fears that if she goes with France alone into the war, and France returns to the Rhine, she will have created a new burden. The longstanding opinion is that Austria should not let the war come, but with all the tension, the city speaks again of war.'[121]

In this febrile atmosphere, the allied ministers continued their efforts to reach a viable compromise through diplomacy. On 13 December, Metternich visited Hardenberg to recount the tale of his upsetting encounter with the Tsar. Perhaps because of the visible rise in tensions, the Tsar himself demonstrated a more conciliatory spirit when he visited the Emperor of Austria just two days after his violent attack on Metternich. Alexander still refused to concede Kraków—'which the Poles could not bear he should alienate as the tomb of their kings'[122]—but he offered to give Austria the Tarnopol district—a southern Polish province that Russia had acquired from Austria in 1809 with a population of 400,000. It was the first concession that the Tsar had offered from his original plan.

The Rhineland proposal

The Prussians, under intense Russian pressure, also now came up with a fresh offer after a series of 'brain-storming' sessions, held at the Tsar's prompting, between Stein, Czartoryski, Hardenberg, Humboldt and Knesebeck.[123] The idea that emerged was to award the King of Saxony a new kingdom on the left bank of the Rhine, carved out of Prussian territories, which would have a population of 700,000, as well as the fortress of Luxemburg and a seat on the tentative 'First Council' of the future German Confederation.[124] Their thinking was to keep Saxony intact and to deliver her to Prussia, but also to acknowledge the right of King Frederick Augustus to an equivalent kingdom of his own. Hardenberg anxiously called on Castlereagh on 19 December, and the next day Castlereagh met with Czartoryski, Hardenberg and Stein for a two-hour discussion in which they presented their imaginative Rhineland proposal as way of extricating them all from the current conundrum. The ministers handed Castlereagh a formal memorandum from Hardenberg encapsulating the novel solution, addressed to Britain and Russia, who, it was assumed, would act as intermediaries in conveying the proposal to Austria.[125] Castlereagh told the hopeful ministers, however, that he did not believe that either the King of Saxony, the Austrian and French ministers, or German public opinion would welcome their idea, and that even he did not find their arguments for the proposal sufficiently compelling to justify the transfer of King Frederick Augustus from Saxony to the Rhineland. Privately, Castlereagh's main concern was for British security: he feared that 'a weak prince' in the Rhineland would quickly become 'an instrument in the hands of France'.[126]

Castlereagh also took the occasion of this meeting with Hardenberg and Czartoryski to recommend the creation of a new 'Statistical Committee', composed of experts from all of the great powers, in order to reach greater consensus on the sizes of the populations in the disputed territories, since the conflicting estimates used by each side were greatly exacerbating their disputes. The Congress 'technocrats'—Münster, Dalberg, Clancarty, Hoffmann and Wessenberg—could focus on calculating these populations more accurately (or at least, take a more consistent and 'scientific' approach), so that the diplomats might then engage more comfortably in the business of swapping 'souls' to hammer out acceptable compromises and achieve a durable balance of power.[127] Castlereagh's suggestion was quickly adopted and, even more remarkably, after the briefest of hesitations, an invitation was extended to the French delegation to participate on the new committee. Nevertheless, the protocols of the Statistical Committee reveal that its sessions predictably continued to reflect the manifold divisions that existed among the powers.[128] Talleyrand, for example, wanted wealth and industry to be taken into account in the swapping of 'souls' and not just the sheer size of population, but his views were rejected. Czartoryski lambasted the committee for its estimate of the Duchy of Warsaw, which, he grumbled, 'diminished the population ceded to Prussia and augmented that kept by Russia, against all reason and truth'.[129]

Meanwhile, Metternich and Castlereagh found the latest concessions offered by Prussia and Russia, including the new Rhineland proposal, far from adequate.[130] In fact, they were already at work seeking to restore the European balance of power by enlisting the cooperation of France.[131] Talleyrand had long made it known that he opposed allied plans to unseat the King of Saxony, another distant relative of Louis XVIII, and Talleyrand's original instructions had even suggested that Frederick Augustus should be reinstated in Warsaw as well as retain his Saxon lands. Cloaked in the language of legitimacy, Talleyrand's chief concern was the threat to France posed by any increase in Prussian power.[132] Castlereagh had explained to Wellington before the Congress opened that he saw two possible approaches for resisting Russian pretentions: his own preference was to strengthen Central Europe by uniting Austria and Prussia; these 'limitrophe' Powers could be assisted by Holland and Hanover. But a second approach was also conceivable, if less desirable: Britain might ally with the 'South' (Austria and Bourbon France) against the 'North' (Russia and Prussia).[133] With the desertion of Prussia, this latter strategy now seemed to be the only feasible alternative. Metternich took the first step by sending Talleyrand a copy of the letter to Hardenberg in which he had withdrawn the offer of Saxony. The French foreign minister then smoothed the way for France's re-entry into the deliberations of the 'powers of the first rank' by his careful response, which emphasized that France's sole goal at the Congress was to promote the principles of legitimacy and equilibrium.[134]

The Tsar likewise tried new ways to surmount the impasse. First he sent Czartoryski to sound out Talleyrand, but this effort proved fruitless. The Tsar became so exasperated with Castlereagh's unwavering support for Austria that he next took the quite extraordinary step of sending a personal note to Count Lieven, the Russian ambassador in London, denouncing the British Foreign Secretary's conduct and authorizing Lieven to raise the matter directly with the British cabinet and the Prince Regent. After extolling the benefits of Anglo-Russian cooperation, which had previously accomplished the joyous deliverance of the Continent, the Tsar complained that,

> Lord Castlereagh, instead of supporting this natural tendency by his conduct, instead of fulfilling the functions of an impartial mediator, instead of seizing with alacrity an opportunity to renew former commercial and political ties with Russia, has preferred to adopt almost exclusively the interests of Austria and to foment the germs of distrust between all the cabinets of the Continent. It is essential to determine whether this system can be attributed without injustice to the British nation and cabinet, or whether we should admit that this minister is following a direction contrary to the intentions of the one and the general wishes of the other.[135]

The accompanying instructions to Lieven—drawn up by Czartoryski—pointed out that England was the only power to have actually profited from the calamities on the Continent, and that her present policy of cooperation with Austria appeared to be aimed at perpetuating discord among the Continental states so that she might continue to benefit from their disorder and devote her own resources to maintaining her domination of the seas and influence in the Western Hemisphere. In concert with Austria, Castlereagh was allegedly acting to repress the liberties and political energies that would otherwise lay a solid foundation for the future harmony and repose of the civilized world; instead, Castlereagh and the Austrians were imperiously compelling the sovereigns of Europe either 'to make slaves of their people or to have recourse to a foreign force to repress their spirit of independence—leaving them with a choice limited to these two forms of slavery'. Beyond this, they were challenging the right of Russia to keep her recent acquisitions and attributing designs of aggrandizement to the Tsar, of which he was wholly innocent. It was therefore absolutely essential for Lieven to take steps to check this dangerous policy, 'so pernicious to the well-being of Europe, to the true glory of Great Britain, and particularly to the legitimate interests of Russia'.[136]

At the request of the Tsar, formal talks on the Polish and Saxon Questions opened on 29 December. Talleyrand and other contemporaries suspected this mode of proceeding was adopted because the irate Tsar could no longer tolerate direct dealings with Metternich; several historians surmise the Tsar wished to have the allied powers formally ratify his acquisition of Poland.[137] The Tsar's Cypriote minister, Capodistrias, later claimed it was he who advised the Tsar to establish formal proceedings on the grounds that under the British parliamentary system they could not be bound by any secret or confidential understandings, which would be disavowed by later governments.[138] Metternich tried, in fact, to confine the talks to Austria and Russia on the Polish Question, but the Tsar insisted on the presence of Prussia and Britain, and that the discussions should embrace the fate of Saxony.[139] In a sense, it was with the formal meetings of this 'Committee of Four' that the official Congress at last began. Russia was represented by Count Andrei Razumovsky, the Russian ambassador to Vienna and one of the few ethnic Russians in the Tsar's entourage; he was assisted by Capodistrias. The other participants were the usual cast of characters—Castlereagh, Hardenberg and Metternich.

To Czartoryski's great chagrin, the Tsar had in the meantime refused to delineate the precise border between the new Polish kingdom and Russia's existing Polish provinces; the Tsar had also sent his younger brother, the unpopular Grand Duke Constantine, as his viceroy in Warsaw, over Czartoryski's strenuous objections. Czartoryski was equally disappointed at the Tsar's willingness to shed the Tarnopol district and part of the Wieliczka salt mines.[140] In a memorandum being prepared by the Russians for the final Polish settlement, Capodistrias further struck out the section promising future unification of Russia's Polish provinces with the new Polish Kingdom.[141] Was Alexander's support for Poland finally faltering?

The Prussians and Russians tendered their compromise offers at the first two sessions of the new committee: a Rhineland kingdom for the King of Saxony; Kraków and Thorn to become neutral cities; part of the Wieliczka salt mines and the Tarnopol district to be awarded to Austria; and a guarantee of Austria's Polish possessions. At their meeting on 30 December, Castlereagh reacted by pressing for the admission of France to the committee's deliberations, not as a matter of right—since she was clearly barred by the Peace of Paris—but on the grounds of expediency. At the same meeting, Metternich insisted not only on the admission of Talleyrand but also that the consent of the King of Saxony—who was still being held by the Prussians as an allied prisoner—must first be obtained before transferring him to any new territory.[142]

Hardenberg could scarcely endure this latest humiliation—this time, no less, at the hands of diplomatic colleagues who but six weeks before had argued that the King of Saxony had no moral claim to his throne. The Prussian Chancellor reacted to their tendentious claims in an angry and irrational outburst: Prussia would decide for herself whether the provisional occupation of Saxony by her troops would become permanent, and any refusal by the other powers to recognize Prussia's incorporation of these territories would be regarded as tantamount to a declaration of war! After expressing their shock at Hardenberg's conduct—in Castlereagh's words, 'a most alarming and unheard-of menace'—the other ministers reluctantly agreed that the permission of the King of Saxony should not, after all, be made a *sine qua non* to the arrangement.[143]

The Triple Alliance

Although Hardenberg's unexpected fit of temper did not break up the proceeding, this commotion, along with the simultaneous appearance of a comprehensive Russian memorandum on the final allocation of the Polish territories (which also included the Rhineland proposal, plans for the German Confederation and other details for the settlement of Central Europe),[144] provided the stimulus to what was surely the most surprising development of the entire Congress: the secret Triple Alliance of 3 January 1815. Precisely at this juncture, Castlereagh received the news that the British and the Americans had concluded the War of 1812 with the Treaty of Ghent, so that British troops were suddenly available for use on the Continent. Talleyrand had actually suggested an alliance between France, Austria and Britain just a few days earlier, which Castlereagh had at the time refused. But Hardenberg's rash words changed his mind. Castlereagh himself drew up a 'Treaty of Alliance' between the three powers on New Year's Day. In another remarkable touch of irony, Prince Razumovsky's beautiful palace at Vienna, the showcase for many of the Russian festivities at the Congress, accidentally caught fire and burnt to the ground during a gala New Year's Eve celebration just the previous night. Priceless sculptures from Canova and paintings by Raphael, Rubens and Van Dyck were lost. Half the Congress delegates came out to watch the early morning flames, including the Emperor Francis, Talleyrand and the Tsar, who found poor Razumovsky sobbing uncontrollably under a nearby tree. The same fateful night, Metternich made a final effort to win back his beloved Duchess von Sagan, sending her an expensive bejewelled bracelet with a painful declaration of his affections—all to no avail.[145]

Castlereagh's new pact was purely defensive in nature: in the event that any of its signatories were attacked in completing or enforcing the Peace of Paris, the other parties were obliged to come to its aid. Each power would contribute 150,000 troops and Britain would be allowed to substitute cash to meet her obligations. Several smaller states were to be invited to accede, including Holland, Hanover and Bavaria. Talleyrand wrote jubilantly to Louis XVIII that the allied coalition was now dissolved and France was 'no longer isolated from Europe'. Castlereagh made some rough calculations, optimistically concluding that the Russians and Prussians could muster 435,000 troops but that the Austrians, French, Anglo-Belgians, lesser German states and Piedmont could actually count on 535,000.[146] He hoped that the new defensive treaty would give Austria the confidence she needed to resist Prussian pretensions and consequently avoid conflict. He also believed that the treaty cleverly committed France to the defence of the new borders of the Netherlands. The specific terms were kept secret, but rumours of the existence of the agreement abounded. Castlereagh privately warned Humboldt that Britain would resist Prussia with 'her whole power and resources'.[147]

Historians remain fascinated with the treaty because it presented the remarkable spectacle of victorious allies separating into hostile camps over the division of the spoils, with some of them even allying with their former foe. After 20 years of war, how could Metternich, and especially Castlereagh, have contemplated an alliance with their arch-nemesis, France? It is therefore worth pausing to consider just how serious was the chance of war between the powers. They were, of course, still on a war footing, with hundreds of thousands of troops bivouacked across Europe. Count Merveldt, the bellicose Austrian ambassador in London, suggested shortly before the Congress began that Austria would prefer an immediate conflict, while she was still mobilized, to an uncertain future one.[148] On his visit to London in July, Czartoryski had asked Merveldt if he sincerely believed that Austria would take up arms against Russia for minor acquisitions in Poland when she had already made sufficient gains herself in Italy; Merveldt replied that he had no doubt that she would since Russia was already too powerful for the repose of Europe.[149] According to Talleyrand, Prince Schwarzenberg, the allied commander-in-chief in the 1814 campaign, likewise told the Tsar at the opening of the Congress that a war between them unfortunately seemed all but inevitable—if not at present, then within two years.[150] On 21 November, Castlereagh explained the Austrian viewpoint to the British cabinet:

> It is the deliberate opinion of many of their officers, and, I may add, ministers, that, rather than have the Russians at Craco[w] and the Prussians at Dresde[n], they had better risk a war with what they can get. Whether this is a sound opinion is another question; but, in point of fact, the war tone was much augmented amongst the Austrians immediately subsequent to the receipt of Prince Hardenberg's memorandum.[151]

By December, both sides were moving their troops into position for a possible confrontation, contributing to the war scare discussed earlier. On 5 December, Hardenberg sent a message to the military reformer General Gneisenau—Blücher's chief-of-staff and himself of Saxon origin—that 'it would be better to have a new war than that Prussia, after such glorious deeds and so many sacrifices, should come out of the affair badly.'[152] Stein's diary likewise contains references to gathering war clouds—'The Emperor Francis speaks loudly of war'.[153] The tone of Castlereagh's correspondence had not improved much three weeks later, when he wrote to Liverpool on 30 December that the Prussians were 'organizing their army for the field ... This may be all menace to sustain their negotiation, but they may also meditate some sudden effort, in conjunction with Russia, to coerce Austria and place themselves in a situation to dictate their own terms on all other points'.[154] Stein recorded in his diary on 31 December, with some dismay:

> The Austrians have collected an army in Bohemia [and] an army of Frenchmen would proceed from the Rhine to the Elbe. So Germany is to be abandoned to a new civil and French war in the interests of a supporter (*Anhänger*) of Napoleon's, and the question of whether it would be better to place him on the left bank of the Rhine or to tear up Saxony in order to give him a fragment. What blindness![155]

A letter from 5 January, which appears to be a report from Prince Schwarzenberg to the Austrian Emperor, also painted a most alarming picture: the Russians and Prussians were amassing the greater part of their troops along their borders with Austria, where they were constructing fortifications. The lesser German princes were alarmed and feared that the Prussians might employ force against them if they joined forces with Austria. Individual Prussian officers might even act on their own initiative (as General von Yorck had done in 1813), while the Austrian army was dangerously dispersed. The roads were in such poor condition that Schwarzenberg was apprehensive it would take longer to concentrate his troops than previously calculated. While he did not wish to overstep the bounds of his authority, he believed that conditions were worsening and that orders needed to be issued as soon as possible and that a response should be made to the requests of the lesser German states. Finally, he requested instructions on how to react if the Prussian commanders should attempt to exercise command over Saxon troops.[156] Schwarzenberg's trepidation, of course, can be interpreted in either of two ways: on the one hand, it shows his fear of war was genuine; on the other, it demonstrates that the Austrians did not feel very adequately prepared to fight it.

Indeed, as impressive as all this evidence in support of war at first appears, on closer scrutiny it consists of little more than outbursts of angry tempers, hyperbolic rumours, sabre-rattling for purposes of persuasion and cautionary troop movements. Many of these utterances were simply for emotional relief. In Castlereagh's case, he had to justify his deep involvement in Central

European affairs to the cabinet. On the other side of the equation, before leaving London for Vienna Castlereagh had remarked to Merveldt that no one could seriously consider that Austria would wage war on Russia, given the state of her army and her 'embarrassment' in Italy.[157] The Prussian envoy in London likewise regarded Austria as too weak financially to engage in any new war.[158] The Russians calculated that, if it came to a matter of force, the Austrians would be unable to resist them. According to Talleyrand, Metternich had been disappointed by reports of Austrian troop strength as recently as November—'with forces such as these, he believes the Austrian monarchy can do no better than resign itself to everything, and put up with everything!'[159] Talleyrand himself had written to Louis XVIII in October that even the mere 'hint at war' should suffice to prevent it.[160] In Paris, the royal government was terrified over the question of the reliability of its own troops—with good reason, it would turn out—surely one of the most effective deterrents to war.[161] And Liverpool and other members of the British cabinet had already instructed Castlereagh that Britain could not enter into another war over these issues. Liverpool argued that any war at present risked liberating the torrential forces of the Revolution, so that, even if a future war were likely, it would still be better to postpone it for a few years: 'It is unnecessary for me to point out to you the impossibility of His Royal Highness consenting to involve this country in hostilities for any of the objects which have hitherto been under discussion at Vienna.'[162] In announcing the new secret treaty to the British cabinet, Castlereagh therefore informed his colleagues that he had not actually committed Britain to anything beyond a possible payment of subsidies.[163] Moreover, it has already been seen that Castlereagh had assured the Tsar that no power would attempt to remove Russia from Poland by force, and that he had given similar assurances to Hardenberg with respect to Prussia in Saxony.

Nesselrode had thus presciently written to Pozzo di Borgo back in September that Austria 'would find the support of England and France of no more than negative use. We have Prussia and five hundred thousand men; hence she will only be able to use friendly representations against us; if they fail, there will be nothing to do but to give in.'[164] The Austrians were simply too infirm, the French royalists too timorous and the British too disinterested to actually engage in war over these issues. But were the Russians or Prussians any more willing? Russian support for Prussian objectives in Germany was already waning, and the Prussians themselves were unlikely to take on half the alliance alone. Despite his outburst in the 'Committee of the Four', Hardenberg had already come to terms with the sacrifice of much of Saxony a fortnight earlier—in his diary on 21 December, the Prussian Chancellor had scribbled: 'We are ready to cede a great part of Saxony' ('On est prêt à céder une grande partie de la Saxe').[165] It is therefore hardly surprising that a leading historian of the Congress concluded that 'scholarly opinion ... has generally discounted the likelihood of war, mainly on the grounds that all sides were exhausted and facing financial ruin'.[166]

Since there was little prospect that either Russia or Prussia would move beyond the borders of Poland or Saxony in a pre-emptive strike against their former allies—the only *casus foederis* under the new defensive alliance—it is, in fact, difficult to see just how the obligations under the new treaty would ever have been triggered. Even if the Prussians had turned their temporary occupation into a permanent annexation, this would not have given rise to any duty to act. What then, was the purpose of the enigmatic treaty? Did Castlereagh actually imagine that the Prussians might launch an attack? Or was the real aim of the treaty to pin down France in the Low Countries? Was it to guarantee Austria's Polish possessions in lieu of the guarantee sought from the Tsar? Was it to tie Britain, as Metternich hoped to do, to her Continental commitments? Was it, as noted earlier, to provide Austria with the courage to resist Prussian pretensions at the conference table? Or was it intended to serve as some sort of vague deterrent to both Prussia and Russia? Castlereagh's dispatches to London on the possibility of war must themselves be read as an attempt to justify his actions before a reluctant cabinet. The real significance of the new concert between Austria, Britain and France must lay in its stiffening of Austrian resistance and in the simple strengthening of ties between the three contracting parties.

Although the British ministers Liverpool, Bathurst and Vansittart (the Chancellor of the Exchequer) had all instructed Castlereagh to avoid risking British involvement in a war over the borders of Central Europe, when the treaty of 3 January actually arrived in London, Liverpool and Bathurst immediately approved it. Probably they felt they could not disavow Castlereagh's *fait accompli*, or at least they believed that the defence of Saxony would be more popular in Britain than support for the dismemberment of Poland would have been.[167] Not all of the British cabinet agreed, however, that Castlereagh had acted so judiciously by apparently risking involvement in a war over issues in which Britain had no immediate stake. Lord Mulgrave in particular demanded why, if the underlying purpose of the treaty had been to deter Prussia and Russia, its existence had deliberately been kept secret:

> I know not why it should have been made, or kept Secret as it was the consequence of open Measures on the part of Russia, & of the menacing attitude of Prussia and Russia. [I]f it were meant as a check to their Pretensions, it seems to me that it ought to have been avowed; kept secret it leads to nothing but action which we want to avoid, & in which [in] the

extremity of Circumstances we might have engaged without a previous Defensive Treaty ...[168]

This still seems an excellent question and only adds to the mystery behind the treaty.

Indeed, it remains uncertain to this day just how much the Russian and Prussian ministers really knew about this 'secret' alliance. The Prussians certainly suspected that such an arrangement might be coming—Hardenberg recorded in his diary on 16 December: 'There is supposed to have been a secret convention concluded between Austria, England, France and Bavaria on account of Poland and Saxony.'[169] But strangely, Hardenberg makes no mention at all of the treaty in his diary during the month of January, when rumour had become reality, and this despite the fact that he met Castlereagh alone on the evening of 4 January, the very day after the treaty was signed, for an extended 'confidential interview'.[170] Castlereagh reported that the Prussian cabinet had already decided against war three days earlier, immediately following Hardenberg's outburst—'I understand the point was considered on Sunday last in the Prussian Cabinet, and the opinions were in favour of a suitable modification of the Saxon question'.[171] In other words, *before* the secret treaty. And Hardenberg's diary reveals that he did in fact have a conference with several Prussian generals 'on military affairs' on 2 January. Moreover, over the course of the next week the two diplomats seem to have been, quite apart from their usual meetings, in almost constant contact: Castlereagh visited Hardenberg once on 6 January and twice on the 7th; on the 9th Castlereagh even showed Hardenberg a proposed declaration before submitting it to the other members of the 'Committee of Four'; on the 10th, Hardenberg dined with Castlereagh and Talleyrand at a diplomatic dinner; on the 13th, he met with Castlereagh and gave him an advance copy of a new proposal he intended to submit to the committee; on the 18th, he attended a ball given by Castlereagh's half-brother, Charles Stewart; and on the 23rd, Castlereagh visited him in the evening.[172] Yet nowhere does Hardenberg ever mention the treaty in his diary; nor do these many encounters seem, even with the backstage troop movements, indicative of hostile diplomats on the verge of war.

On the other hand, the treaty's existence was actively questioned at Castlereagh's private audience with the Tsar, on 7 January:

The Emperor went to other matters, and rather to my surprise, referred to reports that had reached him of an Alliance between Austria, France, Bavaria and Great Britain. Not feeling myself authorized to avow the Treaty, and not choosing to hold a language of too much disguise, I assured

His Imperial Majesty that acting upon pacifick principles ... he had nothing to fear from those Powers.[173]

Did Castlereagh's delphic response reassure the Tsar? Historian Sir Charles Webster concluded that Castlereagh thought the Tsar remained ignorant of the treaty.[174] Even after the treaty was signed, Talleyrand was still promoting a marriage alliance between Russia and France—improbable if the Tsar had actually confirmed his suspicions about the treaty. Later, the French royalists clumsily forgot to remove the secret treaty from the foreign ministry archives when Napoleon suddenly returned during the 'Hundred Days'.[175] Napoleon promptly sent a copy of the treaty to the Tsar, who scarcely reacted as if he had previously known its details: Capodistrias found him pacing the room in 'large steps' with his ears a bright red, in a state of near hysteria; Stein recorded in his diary that 'the Tsar was provoked by it; he was red and indignant, but he declared he would fight Napoleon with perseverance and energy all the same'. The Tsar angrily complained of the treaty in his instructions to Pozzo di Borgo, the Russian ambassador to the French court.[176] All this lay in the future, but it serves to show that the Triple Alliance probably did remain secret, reducing or negating altogether its value as a deterrent (as Mulgrave had pointed out). Perhaps the whole question is something of a 'red herring' since, even without direct knowledge of the treaty, the Russians and the Prussians were quite aware that their own actions were driving the other three powers together. It was, quite literally, the 'balance of power' in operation in the most classical sense.

Negotiating a final compromise

Returning to the four-power ministerial conference of 3 January—the same day that the three allies signed the new secret treaty—Metternich finally agreed to accept 'free city' status for Thorn and Kraków, virtually resolving what still remained of the Polish Question. These important cities would go neither to Russia, Austria nor Prussia but would become independent buffers. That evening, Castlereagh had an amicable exchange with the Tsar at a court ball, indicating an elevation of spirits.[177] We have already seen that the following night, Castlereagh met with Hardenberg for a prolonged tête-à-tête. When the Prussian Chancellor remarked that he believed the Saxon Question could still be resolved through negotiation so long as the consent of the Saxon King to the arrangements was not made a *sine qua non*, Castlereagh interpreted this as a sign of submission and wrote to Liverpool with some relief that he had 'every reason to believe that the alarm of war is over'.[178]

By 5 January, the tireless British Foreign Secretary had already drawn up a new plan for the reconstruction of Prussia, which he curiously seems to have refrained from sending to London.[179] It may be that this detailed proposal was inspired by his long conversation with Hardenberg the previous night. 'The data (*les données*)', his plan began,

> will suffice to show that even without joining all of the Kingdom of Saxony to Prussia ... there are sufficient means to restore her, as required by the Treaty of Kalisch, with the strength she had possessed before 1806, to assure to Hanover the districts intended by the treaty, to grant Saxe-Weimar an increase of 50,000 souls, and to indemnify the Grand Duchy of Darmstadt for its loss of Westphalia to Prussia.

Castlereagh based his laborious calculations on the work of the Statistical Committee. He averaged the disputed Prussian and Austrian estimates for Prussian losses in Poland and concluded that these amounted to 1,675,955 inhabitants. With additional Prussian losses to Hanover and other German states, Castlereagh calculated that Prussia was actually entitled to 2,657,835 more subjects. There was 'ample territory', he asserted, to indemnify Prussia this amount: the Rhineland and banks of the Moselle would provide her with one million new subjects; she could also obtain most of Westphalia, several districts south of the Meuse, part of the Duchy of Berg, and properties from the mediatized German princes; finally, she could take part of Saxony, including Torgau (but neither Leipzig nor Dresden), with a population of 695,235. 'It suffices from the foregoing that the means available incontestably exceeds the compensation required by the treaty.'[180] It almost seems as though Castlereagh had hoped to resolve the problem through his own sheer mastery of detail, just as when he had negotiated the dissolution of the Irish Parliament 14 years before.

At an audience with the Tsar on 7 January—the same meeting at which Alexander questioned the existence of the secret treaty—Castlereagh found the Russian autocrat to be in a remarkably conciliatory mood. Castlereagh patiently explained that the Rhineland proposal was unacceptable on strategic grounds: as an independent sovereign, Frederick Augustus would not be powerful enough to resist new acts of French aggression; only a larger state, such as Prussia or Holland, could be safely placed there. Castlereagh then used a map to demonstrate to the Tsar just how Prussia might, based on his new plan, be reconstructed to her former size with only the partial incorporation of Saxony. His words seem to have had some effect. At the meeting of the 'Committee of Four' on 9 January, Razumovsky announced that Prussia should be satisfied with only a part of Saxony; it was also agreed to admit the French into the committee's deliberations. It was obvious that Prussia was losing Russian support.

The new momentum towards a final settlement should thus be attributed at least as much to Alexander's acquiescence as to the perseverance of Castlereagh and Metternich. Historians have ascribed the Tsar's change of heart to a variety of motives. Some point to the possible effects of the vaguely known 'secret' treaty.[181] Others suspect that after having achieved his own goals in Poland, the Tsar simply lost interest in supporting Prussia. 'Russia', Castlereagh wrote to Lord Liverpool, 'will not encourage Prussia to resist, now [that] she has secured her own arrangement in Poland'.[182] In fact, at a meeting with the Tsar and Frederick William just before the ministerial conference of 30 December, Hardenberg was unable to secure a firm military commitment from the Tsar.[183] In effect, the Tsar preferred to impose new sacrifices on his ally, Prussia, over driving Austria into the arms of France. A third explanation for the Tsar's change of heart emphasizes the role of his sister, the Grand Duchess Catherine, who had just announced her engagement to the Prince Royal of Württemberg. The Tsar could scarcely pose as the champion of the German middle states if he forced Saxony out of existence. The Tsar may have also been affected by the anti-Russian sentiment revealed in the correspondence of Metternich and Hardenberg just a few weeks earlier. Yet another consideration was the fact that Castlereagh—always aware of the persuasive power of money—held out the possibility, promised at Chaumont, that Britain would pay Dutch bankers to cover Russia's outstanding loan if the Russians were cooperative.[184]

Was the Tsar also cooling towards his old friend, Prince Czartoryski, who would inform him only a few months later that he hoped that the Tsar's wife, the Empress Elizabeth, would seek a divorce so that he might marry her? While the Tsar had little passion for an arranged marriage he had entered at the age of 15, he told Czartoryski that divorce was out of the question on political as well as personal grounds: how would it look to his Russian subjects if he not only restored the Kingdom of Poland, but also sacrificed his wife to his leading Polish adviser?[185]

The most convincing explanation for the Tsar's new attitude, however, lies in his increasing religiosity. Many of the educated elite of Russia, especially the Baltic Germans, were strongly attracted to forms of 'awakened' Christianity, which emphasized a personal communion with God, an individual reading of the Bible and an ecumenical belief in the brotherhood of all true Christians. Alexander had undergone a profound religious conversion at the time of the French invasion and its after-shocks were still influencing his conduct. In 1812, he had been a zealous supporter of the new Russian Bible Society. At the very time that Moscow was being burned, Alexander was writing a detailed survey of mystical Christian literature for his sister Catherine, which encompassed all denominations, with the prominent exception of the Russian Orthodox.

After leaving London in July 1814, the Tsar spent time with his wife's family in Baden, where he met with Johann Heinrich Jung-Stilling and entered into a spiritual 'marriage' with Jung-Stilling and Roxanne Stourdza. When the Tsar returned to Russia, his friend Prince Alexander Golitsyn (the founder of the Russian Bible Society and Procurator of the Holy Synod) noticed a marked change in his demeanour; the Tsar confided that he was reading a chapter of the New Testament every day. During the early months of the Congress of Vienna, Jung-Stilling published a journal in which he developed the theme that the Tsar was acting as God's instrument and performing his work. Jung-Stilling saw the 'trinity' of allied sovereigns—Catholic, Protestant and Orthodox—as symbolic of the triumph of Christianity over the secularism of the French Revolution. By December 1814, Austrian police agents observed that the Tsar was spending fewer hours with the beautiful Princess Bagration and much more time with Roxanne Stourdza—one of his Empress's ladies-in-waiting, a follower of the prophetess Baroness Julie von Krüdener, and the spiritual 'wife' of the German Pietist Johann Heinrich Jung-Stilling. Stourdza, Krüdener, Jung-Stilling and other 'awakened' Christians convinced Alexander that he had a divine mission to fulfil as the spiritual liberator of Europe. Against these weighty concerns, Prussian demands for the whole of Saxony no doubt paled into insignificance.[186] On 31 December, while Castlereagh was drafting the Triple Alliance and Razumovsky's palace was being consumed by flames, the Tsar was thus engaged in writing a message of Christian brotherhood to his fellow sovereigns, which would later serve as the basis for his 'Holy Alliance' (discussed in Chapter 4, below).[187] The Tsar was ready to act again as Europe's saviour, even if it meant leaving the Prussians in the lurch.

Although conditions finally seemed ripe for the settlement of Central Europe, the denouement still took several weeks longer to reach. With no real prospect for success, Hardenberg and Humboldt stubbornly submitted a new 'Projet' at the very first meeting of the new 'Committee of Five' (the four allied courts plus France), again demanding all of Saxony and proposing the transfer of the Saxon king to the Rhineland.[188] Did the Prussians repeat these stale claims simply as an opening gambit, a bargaining posture?[189] Or did they think they could pressure the King of Saxony himself, still in their custody—like Persephone in Hades—to succumb to their demands? Metternich began preparing a counter-proposal, which Castlereagh hoped would be framed upon 'principles so liberal and advantageous to Prussia as to induce that Court to acquiesce in the general wishes', but the Austrians, especially Schwarzenberg and Stadion, with the encouragement of Talleyrand, began pressing Metternich to greatly reduce Prussian gains in Saxony.[190]

Castlereagh now revealed his great skill as a negotiator by opposing both extremes. His efforts provide a remarkable picture of 'balance-of-power' diplomacy in action. Still believing in the need to strengthen Prussia in Northern Germany, the British Foreign Secretary insisted that the Prussians should be awarded two-fifths of Saxony as well as territories along the Elbe and the Rhine. Castlereagh even insisted, over Austrian objections, that the fortresses of Erfurt and Torgau must be handed over to Prussia. To Metternich's appeal for stronger frontiers, Castlereagh—who had previously been so focused on the theme of the defensibility of frontiers during the Polish crisis—answered that if Russia and Prussia united against Austria 'such a combination could only be resisted by a counter-alliance, and it was to France and Great Britain she must look for support in such a crisis, and not to a solitary fortress the more or less beyond her own frontier'.[191] Meanwhile, Talleyrand was stirring up so much trouble among the Austrians that Castlereagh finally told the French that Britain would not help them in Naples until the future of Saxony was decided.

Castlereagh also took steps to convey his objections to the Rhineland transfer more forcefully to the Prussians. On 23 January, he again spent the evening with Hardenberg: 'He thinks that the King of Saxony', Hardenberg jotted in his diary, 'will be more dangerous to us on the Left Bank of the Rhine than in Saxony'. Castlereagh further informed Hardenberg of the vociferous opposition Metternich was encountering in his own court—the Austrians were already 'envious', Hardenberg noted, of Prussia's acquisition of Erfurt and Torgau.[192]

To find a way out of the imbroglio, the Austrians (Gentz and Wessenberg) came up with the idea of returning part of the Tarnopol district to Russia, so that Russia could in turn give a larger slice of Poland to Prussia, which would then need less of Saxony. The British, French and Hanoverians (Clancarty, Münster and Dalberg—all active members of the Statistical Committee) developed a different alternative: Prussia would be given Torgau and Erfurt and 900,000 'souls'. It was this last idea that became the basis for the Austrian counter-proposal, presented to the Committee of Five on 28 January.[193]

The Prussians were willing to give up the Saxon capital of Dresden but they were determined to make a last stand to acquire Leipzig, scene of the decisive victory over Napoleon the previous year. Castlereagh could dissuade neither Hardenberg nor the Prussian King in private interviews. The dispute was only resolved when the Tsar, still in a conciliatory mood, consented, at Castlereagh's urging, to make further concessions in Poland, returning both Posen and Thorn to Prussia:

> The Emperor was very reasonable and promised to do what in delicacy he could, and as some means of assisting the negotiation, he placed Thorn and its rayon at my disposal, to make such use of with Prussia as I might

think fit. Thorn being a position on the Vistula to which Prussia had always attached considerable importance, I lost no time in communicating to Prince Hardenberg the Emperor's intentions. The following day, he told me that with the aid of Thorn he had overcome the King's reluctance to leave Leipsick with Saxony.[194]

Under Castlereagh's direction, Hanover and Holland, both client states of Britain, turned over additional slices of territory to Prussia—'uniting these with the slender means otherwise available, a fund was created which might operate a salutary reduction in favour of Saxony'.[195] At the same time, Hanover was given East Frisia to the west and the university town of Göttingen to the south.

The fruits of the labours of the Statistical Committee greatly assisted in this final push. Populations of districts were added and subtracted in a somewhat mechanical fashion to attain the desired results, and a final agreement on the reconstruction of Central Europe was at long last reached on 6 February 1815, just before Castlereagh's departure for London, where he was needed to defend Liverpool's government in Parliament. The Prussian King's disappointment was so palpable that Castlereagh considered his final interview with him his most 'painful' encounter at the Congress.[196] Although the Prussians did not receive all of Saxony and their territories remained dispersed, they obtained a large arc of territory stretching across Northern Germany from the Rhineland to Pomerania. The lands they gained in the west were, in truth, far more valuable than those they had yielded in the east. Their position in the Rhineland made them part of the new barrier of states around France, much as Pitt and Castlereagh had always intended. Meanwhile, Russia annexed most of the Duchy of Warsaw, but made several other last-minute concessions, sacrificing not only Posen and Thorn, but also the ancient royal capital of Kraków, which became a free city.

The negotiations over the new boundaries of Central Europe highlighted the determination of the great powers to reach major decisions by themselves without consulting the lesser states and with little concern for the wishes of the subject populations actually involved. The Saxons had expressed their desire to remain united under their sovereign Frederick Augustus and the other smaller German states had rallied in their support, but this hardly seemed to enter into the calculations of the diplomats, except to add rhetorical support to positions they had already adopted for other reasons. Nowhere was this more dramatically demonstrated than in the workings of the Statistical Committee, where each 'soul' was accorded equal weight. Europe's 'middle zone' became a vast fund for compensating the great powers, upon whom the peace of Europe ultimately depended. 'Souls' were distributed from this fund with scant regard for history or tradition in order to preserve an imagined balance of power, to the maximum extent compatible with the powers' other objectives. The Congress statesmen were familiar with such concepts as dynastic rivalry, proportionality and even grasps at hegemonic power, but they had far less appreciation for the emerging power of nationalism, which they tended largely to dismiss. Even so, Castlereagh was careful to issue a public statement recommending that the eastern powers respect the language and traditions of the Polish people, and explaining that Britain would have preferred a complete restoration of an independent Polish state; although this expression of sentiments may have been sincerely felt, its patent purpose was to stave off future criticism of his actions in Parliament.[197]

Other questions at the Congress

With the Polish-Saxon Question finally out of the way, the other pieces of the puzzle fell quickly into place. Separate committees had been working all along on such diverse issues as the formation of the new German Confederation and approval of the new Swiss constitution. Other issues included the future of Tuscany, the transfers of Genoa and Norway, the treatment of German Jews, the abolition of the slave trade, the navigation of international rivers and the formulation of a set of rules to govern questions of diplomatic precedence. The decisions of the Congress left almost no part of Europe untouched.

The German Confederation (Bund)

Perhaps the most important of these other issues was the creation of a new form of association for the German states, replacing both the ancient Holy Roman Empire, which had dissolved in 1806, and Napoleon's makeshift Confederation of the Rhine (*Rheinbund*). As a result of the French Revolution and the Napoleonic Wars, the number of separate polities in Germany had been drastically reduced from about 300 in the last days of the *ancien régime* to 39, including Austria, Prussia, the middle states and four free cities. The new Confederation was intended to preserve the independence of the German states while enabling them to provide for their common defence against aggressors such as France. It was also expected to become a forum in which the larger German states—Austria and Prussia—might assert their leadership over Germany as a whole. German nationalists hoped that it would provide the first step towards the creation of a united Germany.

In September 1814, Hardenberg had originally drawn up 41 articles for the new federal constitution (*Bundesakte*), creating seven *Kreise* (administrative districts), a council of *Kreis* chiefs and a federal diet (*Bundesversammlung* or assembly) in which all the German states and mediatized princes would participate.[198] Each *Kreis* was to be led by one of the larger states, which would direct its military. Behind this democratic façade, Hardenberg intended that Prussia and Austria should jointly control the new Confederation and merely consult with the lesser German states. Metternich pared down Hardenberg's original plan to 12 articles, which Austria and Prussia jointly submitted to the German Committee in October—at the height of their cooperation over the Polish-Saxon Question. The new draft gave Austria presidency of the Confederation. Two of the German middle states on the Committee—Bavaria and Württemberg—strenuously objected to any measures that might reduce their own sovereignty. Meanwhile, the smaller German states, excluded from the Committee, began holding their own meetings on 14 October—the same day as the first meeting of the German Committee itself—and even submitted a written protest on 16 November.[199] In mid-November, the meetings of the German Committee were suddenly suspended altogether because of the impasse on Saxony. We have already seen that Metternich jettisoned the *Kreis* system in his communications with Hardenberg in December. The sessions of the German Committee finally resumed early in 1815, when the committee was reconstituted on a wider basis to include more of the German smaller states.

After the resolution of the Polish-Saxon Question, Metternich spent most of his time working on the German Committee. In late May, he submitted a new proposal for the organization of the Confederation, which became the basis for all subsequent discussions. The German Confederation that eventually emerged was a pale substitute for the former Holy Roman Empire. Its primary purpose was the defence of its member states, especially from French aggression. Each member state promised to submit disputes with other members to mediation rather than to resort to arms. Article XIII, a key provision of the new federal constitution, promised that each member state would eventually grant its own constitution based on 'Estates' (*landständische Verfassung*). A federal diet was created, over which Austria enjoyed a permanent presidency.

While some German patriots had hoped that the new Confederation would serve as the voice of the German nation, Metternich had structured the federal organization to represent Germany's independent rulers. The middle states—in particular, Bavaria, Baden and Württemberg in Southern Germany—were given a disproportionate influence in the new body, making it even more likely to protect states' rights and unlikely to develop into a truly representative national assembly. It was delegated to the new Federal Diet itself to work out further details, such as the creation of a federal army and a set of fundamental laws. The Act of Confederation could not be amended without the unanimous approval of all the states, a virtual impossibility. Most of this suited Metternich perfectly.

Italy and the problem of Murat

In the first months of the Congress, the reconstruction of Italy took a back seat to Central European affairs.[200] Twenty years earlier, many Italian intellectuals had welcomed the French Revolution as a natural sequel to Enlightenment reforms, but the turmoil in Paris had caused their rulers to halt their own reform efforts abruptly and to seek closer ties with the Church. Napoleon, a Corsican, was especially attuned to Italian affairs. It was in Italy that he catapulted his fortunes forward by defeating the Austrians; in 1797, he terminated the venerable Venetian Republic and handed its remains over to Austria; it was to Milan that he returned in May 1805 to crown himself as King of Italy, only a few months after his imperial coronation in Paris.

By 1809, Napoleonic Italy consisted of five main regions: (1) Piedmont, the area around Rome, and the Illyrian provinces (present-day Croatia), all of which had been incorporated directly into France; (2) the Kingdom of Italy—comprising Venetia, Lombardy and the northern Adriatic coastline—which was governed by a viceroy, Prince Eugène de Beauharnais, Napoleon's stepson by his first wife, Josephine; (3) the Kingdom of Naples, which was ruled by Napoleon's brother Joseph and later by Joachim Murat—one of Napoleon's bravest marshals, who also happened to be married to his sister, Caroline; (4) the island of Sardinia, to which the King of Sardinia-Piedmont had retreated; and (5) Sicily, where the King of Naples had similarly taken shelter under the protection of the British fleet. Napoleon introduced typical French reforms on the mainland, including the abolition of feudalism and tithes, the confiscation of Church lands, a more efficient administration and the institution of civil marriage, but he accompanied these measures with new taxes, military conscription and enforcement of the Continental System, making French rule highly unpopular. In Naples, both Joseph and Murat rebuffed Napoleon's frequent admonitions, some of which reveal the French Emperor in a harsh and unflattering light—'I see with pleasure that you have burned an insurgent village', he instructed his brother. 'I suppose that you allowed the soldiers to pillage it. That is the way in which villages that revolt should be treated.'[201]

As Napoleon's grip on Europe loosened, the task of clearing French troops from Italy fell to the Austrians. Seeing the writing on the wall, Murat had already entered into secret negotiations with them the previous summer; a consummate opportunist to the end, he was also in active negotiations with Napoleon as late as mid-December 1813, seeking to increase his share of Italy in the unlikely event that the French Emperor somehow extricated himself from his troubles. Murat adamantly refused, however, to obey Napoleon's order to send his own troops north of the Po to help stave off the allied invasion. Murat finally deserted his brother-in-law altogether in a hastily concluded defensive alliance with Austria in early January 1814. Metternich leapt at the chance of securing Murat's support for the approaching campaign against Eugène: in exchange for the assistance of 30,000 Neapolitan troops and a renunciation of all claims to Sicily, the Austrians guaranteed Murat's throne in Naples and even promised incremental territorial gains from the Papal States.[202]

In the meantime a liberal Whig officer, Lord William Bentinck, had been sent by the British government to Sicily in 1811 to console and advise the Neapolitan King, Ferdinand IV. Bentinck persuaded Ferdinand to accept a liberal Sicilian constitution based on the British model. Early in March 1814, Bentinck sailed north with an expeditionary force of 6,000 troops and landed at Leghorn (Livorno) with the intention of liberating the mainland from the French yoke. Bentinck dramatically issued proclamations inviting Italians to rise up against their oppressors. From Leghorn, he marched his small force to Genoa.[203] Without prior authorization from Castlereagh or any other senior minister, Bentinck promised the Genoese their independence. While Murat was advancing on Eugène from the south and Bentinck was approaching from the west, an even larger Austrian force was marching from the east. Eugène finally surrendered to the Austrians in mid-April after receiving news of his stepfather's abdication in Paris.

To bring Austria into the coalition, the allies had previously offered her the return of Venetia, to which Lombardy had been added in the summer of 1813. This was confirmed in the first Peace of Paris, in which Lombardy-Venetia was ceded to Austria. Piedmont surrendered part of Savoy to Geneva but was strengthened as a 'buffer state' on the borders of France by the acquisition of Genoa and Nice, in accordance with Pitt's plan of 1805. Although the territorial reconstruction of Northern Italy was thus settled, the fate of much of Central Italy remained unresolved when the statesmen gathered at Vienna the following September. Metternich's chief concern was to establish an Austrian sphere of influence in Italy by keeping France, her principal rival, out of the peninsula. Italian nationalism was of far less concern to him than the exclusion of France. He therefore rejected out of hand Talleyrand's proposal to form an Italian Committee similar to the German one.

Of equal importance, the powers at Vienna still faced the problem of what to do about Murat. Since he occupied a throne formerly belonging to the Neapolitan Bourbons, cousins to Louis XVIII, his removal became Talleyrand's paramount objective at the Congress. Talleyrand suspected

Metternich of being overly sympathetic to Murat since the Austrian statesman had once been Caroline Bonaparte's lover. To shore up his position Murat sent his own representative to the Congress and shrewdly conveyed a long memorandum in justification of his conduct to both Castlereagh and the leaders of the British parliamentary opposition.

In fact, at the time of Louis XVIII's restoration Castlereagh was still ambivalent about the future of Naples. Meeting with Castlereagh in Paris, William A'Court, the British envoy to the Bourbon King (then in Sicily), asked if he could give assurances to Ferdinand IV that he would be restored in Naples. 'Most assuredly not', Castlereagh immediately retorted,

> Gain time, evade the question as much as possible, but be careful not to drop a word that may induce the Sicilian Govt. to believe there is any intention of dispossessing Murat. The question is one of considerable difficulty. Austria is bound to support Murat, as far as treaties can bind a Nation. Russia would have been in the same predicament but for an accident, & tho' we ourselves have not formally acceded to this Treaty, yet we have so far acknowledged Murat's title to have acted in concert with him.[204]

By the time of the Vienna Congress, however, both Metternich and Castlereagh had come to the conclusion that Murat, as a remnant of the Napoleonic Empire, had to be replaced. The Russians were not actively involved, but they, too, favoured the claims of the old royal family.[205] Even though the allied ministers were thus in general agreement on the necessity of dislodging Murat, the real issue was how this could best be achieved. Both Castlereagh and Metternich strenuously opposed the use of French troops to perform the task. Castlereagh hoped to avoid a conflict altogether, or at least to do without any allied declaration against Murat, which would have had to be defended in Parliament. Always sensitive to the allure of money, Castlereagh proposed instead that the allies offer Murat a generous financial reward for his peaceful abdication.[206] Unfortunately, Murat refused all such enticements.

At the Congress, Castlereagh and Metternich eventually decided to bypass Talleyrand altogether on this question and to correspond directly with Paris to obtain Louis XVIII's consent to Austrian acquisitions in Northern and Central Italy in return for an Austrian engagement to depose Murat themselves and to restore the Neapolitan Bourbons.[207] This understanding included the French King's agreement to permit Marie Louise—as the daughter of the Austrian Emperor as well as the wife of Napoleon—to remain as the Duchess of Parma during her lifetime. Castlereagh also insisted, as we have seen, that the French adhere to his Saxon policy.

The British Foreign Secretary accordingly believed that he had settled all outstanding Italian issues when he met with Louis XVIII in Paris on his way home from Vienna in late February 1815. In the event, the problem of Naples solved itself when Napoleon returned to France during the Hundred Days (see the next chapter). Castlereagh was suddenly again willing to tolerate Murat, but the latter, already suspicious of the allied powers and overestimating the strength of Italian nationalism, seized on Napoleon's sudden reappearance to march northwards and declare himself as 'King of Italy'. His appeal for a war of national liberation went largely unheeded, and his army was quickly defeated by the Austrians. Murat fled, while the Bourbons were restored in Naples after making a secret pledge to the Austrians not to introduce a constitution. Murat went into hiding in Corsica and returned to Calabria in southern Naples six months later in a misguided attempt to reconquer his kingdom. He was captured and executed on the orders of Ferdinand IV.[208]

Elsewhere in Italy, the transfer of Genoa became a controversial subject in the British House of Commons because of the pledge that Lord Bentinck had made to the Genoese. No other issue arising out of the Vienna Settlement quite so thoroughly infuriated the British Whigs. In the subsequent debate in Parliament on 20 March 1815, Castlereagh justified his handing over of Genoa to the House of Savoy as a necessary step towards restoring the equilibrium of Europe.

Further to the east, Austria agreed to return the Legations of Ravenna, Bologna and Ferrara to the Pope. Austria achieved complete ascendancy over the rest of Central Italy: the Austrian Emperor's brother was restored as Grand Duke of Tuscany and his grandson was installed in Modena. The final piece of the puzzle concerned, once again, Marie Louise, and her claim to a life interest in the Duchy of Parma, Piacenza and Guastalla—which Louis XVIII had reluctantly agreed to accept. Another Bourbon, Maria Louisa, sister to the King of Spain (better known by her Napoleonic title, the Queen of Etruria) was a rival claimant. The powers carved the Duchy of Lucca out of Tuscany, in which they awarded Maria Louisa a life interest; Parma would then revert back to her line on the death of Marie Louise, at which time Lucca would be returned to Tuscany. The allied leaders thus cut a pragmatic deal applying the wisdom of Solomon to reconcile competing rights and pledges. Their settlement also had the intended end result that Italy was placed firmly under Austrian tutelage.[209]

Switzerland

In the initial stages of the French Revolution the tradition of Swiss neutrality had been respected. But, after concluding peace with Austria in 1797, French armies had entered Geneva and the Vaud. Early in 1798, the French occupied the central canton of Berne and took control of the entire Swiss Confederation. A French-sponsored constitution created a more unified Swiss state, governed by a French-style Directory and two councils with deputies from each canton; the Tsar's former tutor, Frédéric César de La Harpe, served as one of the Directors. In 1799, Switzerland became a battleground when Austrian and Russian troops crossed her frontiers. In 1803, Napoleon then replaced the Swiss Constitution with a new 'Act of Mediation', creating a weaker federal system whose capital and chief executive (or *Landammann*) circulated successively among the leading cantons. French intervention nonetheless ended the subjection of dependencies (like the Vaud) to the older cantons, eliminated special privileges, created equality before the law and introduced a system of universal education.

In November 1813, after the Battle of Leipzig, an extraordinary Swiss Diet assembled in Berne: it abolished Napoleon's Act of Mediation and restored Swiss neutrality. The allies ignored the declaration and 200,000 Austrian and Russian troops poured into Switzerland in late December on their way to France. In a declaration to the Swiss people, the Austrians and Russians called for a new Swiss constitution. They wanted to break Swiss ties with France, while the Tsar seems to have hoped to establish greater Russian influence—perhaps using Switzerland as a social laboratory to test his ideas for the rest of post-Napoleonic Europe. Three young and very able diplomats—Capodistrias (a Greek from Corfu) for Russia, Ludwig Lebzeltern for Austria and Stratford Canning (a cousin of George Canning) for Britain—were sent to guide the Swiss in choosing their destiny. A new Swiss Diet, now representing 19 cantons, met in April 1814 and remained in session until completing the new constitution. The new Swiss Act of Confederation created a federal militia and a federal diet; only the new Swiss Diet could enter into foreign alliances or declare war. Most other governing powers, however, were left to the cantons. Each of the cantons preserved its own form of government, while also exercising one vote in the Federal Diet. According to Stratford Canning, Capodistrias 'sided generally with the new cantons, whereas the old ones expected sympathy and countenance from me'. While Berne and other older cantons hoped to reinstate their traditional powers over former dependencies, such as the Vaud and Argovy, in fact all the cantons remained equal in status.[210]

Meanwhile, the allied powers stipulated in the Peace of Paris that Geneva should be joined to the Swiss Confederation. At the Congress of Vienna both the Swiss Federal Diet and several cantons sent their own representatives: Vaud, for example, was represented by the Tsar's old tutor La Harpe and Geneva by Charles Pictet de Rochemont and François d'Invernois. In the autumn of 1814, most remaining Swiss issues were territorial ones: whether part of the Pays de Gex should be attached to Geneva; whether Switzerland should obtain the Versoix corridor to connect Geneva to the rest of the Confederation; and whether the Valtelline should be returned to Switzerland. The Swiss also desired allied approval for their new Act of Confederation and sought formal recognition of the inviolability of their territories and neutrality. At the Vienna Congress, a specially constituted Swiss Committee—whose members numbered Stein, Humboldt, Sir Charles Stewart, Stratford Canning, Wessenberg, Dalberg and Capodistrias—began its sessions in mid-November. The committee's recommendations were only slightly modified when they were finally submitted to the chief ministers of the five powers on 9 February (only three days after the Polish-Saxon settlement). It was agreed that Geneva, Neuchâtel and Valais should become new cantons; the Basel Bishopric and the city of Biel were handed over to the canton of Berne; Switzerland also obtained the Versoix corridor and part of the Pays de Gex, but was denied the Valtelline. Capodistrias negotiated further concessions for Geneva in Savoy, and a final agreement for the territorial settlement of Switzerland was finally signed on 20 March 1815. Switzerland was enlarged to twenty-two cantons and its borders strengthened—creating a sturdier 'buffer' to the southeast of France. The new Swiss Act of Confederation was actually incorporated into the Vienna Final Act, an action that some historians have argued was an infringement of their sovereignty, but also the price they had to pay for international recognition of their neutrality. An international declaration of Swiss neutrality was itself delayed because circumstances suddenly required the allies to march through Switzerland one last time during the Hundred Days, but on 20 November 1815, the allied powers issued a declaration in Paris recognizing the independence, neutrality and inviolability of the Swiss Confederation—a pronouncement that historian Sir Charles Webster has described as 'one of the most important results of the period'.[211]

Scandinavia

In the summer of 1814, before the Congress met, there was also great uncertainty surrounding Scandinavia. The situation here was as complex and labyrinthine as anywhere else in Europe. For seven centuries, Finland had belonged to Sweden, while Norway had been an autonomous kingdom under the Danish sceptre almost as long. During the Napoleonic wars, Denmark had been neutral in 1807 when George Canning—then British Foreign Secretary—had ordered the bombardment of Copenhagen and seizure of the Danish fleet to prevent its falling into French hands. This act of aggression drove the Danes straight into Napoleon's embrace. Denmark's rival, Sweden, remained allied with Britain and Russia, and in consequence suffered the occupation of Swedish Pomerania by French troops. The Swedes remained loyal to the British even after Tsar Alexander concluded the Peace of Tilsit with Napoleon. On the basis of the new French alliance, the Tsar ordered the invasion of Finland early in 1808, ostensibly to comply with Napoleon's demand to close Swedish ports to British trade, but with the underlying motive of obtaining a territorial shield for his own capital at St Petersburg. The King of Sweden, expecting an invasion from the Danes and harbouring his own designs on Norway, had left eastern Finland dangerously denuded of troops and the province was successfully overcome.[212]

The Tsar precipitated a series of changes in Scandinavia by his seizure of Finland. The loss of both Swedish Pomerania and Finland led to a military and aristocratic coup in Stockholm: King Gustav IV Adolf was deposed in March 1809 and replaced by his uncle, Charles XIII, who had no legitimate heirs.[213] In July, the Swedish *Riksdag* (Diet of the four estates) chose a popular Danish prince, Christian August, as heir to their throne, partly in the belief that he might win Norway; the prince, on the other hand, secretly looked to uniting all of Scandinavia under Danish rule as in the fourteenth century. The Swedes next concluded peace with Russia in September 1809, formally acknowledging the loss of Finland. Alexander (under the influence of Speransky and Czartoryski) in fact granted the Finns far greater autonomy than they had ever enjoyed under the Swedes, establishing a precedent for his own later conduct in Poland. The Swedes shortly thereafter concluded peace with both Denmark and France. The situation was further transformed when the recently elected Crown Prince died suddenly in a riding accident in May 1810.[214] The Swedish *Riksdag* reassembled to select a new heir to the throne. The leading contenders appeared to be the son of the deposed king, the older brother of the dead prince, and the King of Denmark. At the last minute, an unexpected candidate was unanimously chosen—Napoleon's marshal, Jean Bernadotte, who had commanded local French forces in the region. Many thought he had acted kindly and presumed he had the support of Napoleon; others preferred an outsider over a return to the deposed royal family; the lower classes thought Bernadotte might end aristocratic privileges; the nobles thought a skilled military commander might help them recapture Finland.

Bernadotte quickly realized that Sweden did not have the resources to regain Finland and focused his energies on obtaining Norway instead. He refused to assist Napoleon in his invasion of Russia, and met with the Tsar at Åbo (in Southern Finland) in August 1812, at the height of the French invasion of Russia. Alexander not only dangled the distant prospect of placing Bernadotte on the French throne, but he also promised Russian assistance in obtaining Norway for Sweden. Six months later, the situation had dramatically reversed itself: Napoleon's *Grande Armée* was destroyed and Sweden and Prussia had enlisted in the allied coalition. In the Treaty of Stockholm, the British promised to help Sweden obtain Norway, to reward her with the former French Caribbean island of Guadaloupe, and to provide her with a subsidy; in return, Sweden was to place an army of 30,000 men in the field against Napoleon. After the allied victory at Leipzig, Bernadotte concentrated on defeating the Danes, still aligned with the French, whom he vanquished at Bornhöved in December 1813. In the Treaty of Kiel (January 1814), the Danes agreed to transfer Norway to Sweden and to enter the allied coalition against France; they were promised Swedish Pomerania and the neighbouring island of Rügen as compensation, as well as the return of all their colonial possessions by Britain, except Heligoland.

Many Norwegians, however, were hostile to Swedish rule. Both history and geography seemed to dictate against it since they were separated from the Swedes by mountains and closer to the Danes by water. The Norwegians reacted to the proposed transfer by declaring their independence: 112 delegates gathered at Eidsvoll, drafted a constitution and elected Prince Christian, heir to the Danish throne, as their sovereign on 17 May 1814. The British government refused to recognize the Norwegian government or to assist the Norwegians in any way. Nevertheless, the British had their own misgivings about the conduct of Bernadotte during the invasion of France. The imbroglio in Norway even became a topic of debate in the British House of Commons. The British government strove to convince Prince Christian to resign and the Norwegians to submit to Sweden, but with scant success. Russia, with troops in neighbouring Holstein, also insisted on performance of the Treaty of Kiel. A brief armed conflict actually ensued between Sweden and Norway in the summer of 1814. Just before the assembling of the Congress of Vienna, an agreement was seemingly reached: Bernadotte consented to the Eidsvoll Constitution, preserving Norway's separate institutions and limiting the association of the two countries to a dynastic union. On 4 November 1814, at the height of the Polish-Saxon conflict in Vienna, a special Norwegian assembly (*Storting*) recognized Charles XIII of Sweden as their King. Bernadotte nonetheless remained resentful of the actions of Prince Christian and used these as a pretext to delay full execution of the terms of the Treaty of Kiel. Britain, about to compensate Sweden for the island of Guadeloupe (which had been returned to France rather than to Sweden), decided to withhold payment until Bernadotte performed all of Sweden's obligations under the treaty.[215] This was how matters still stood in 1815 when the Congress ended.

All of the recent territorial exchanges in Scandinavia were confirmed at Vienna and included in the final settlement: Lauenberg passed from Hanover to Prussia, which in turn transferred it to Denmark in exchange for Swedish

Pomerania and the island of Rügen; Sweden had lost Finland to Russia but received Norway from Denmark under the terms of the Treaty of Kiel; finally, Sweden was supposed to surrender Rügen to Denmark in order for the Danes to complete their exchange with Prussia. The Tsar was especially satisfied since he had secured increased protection for his capital, while he calculated that the prize of Norway would be sufficient to keep the Swedes from challenging the new arrangements.[216] The greatest losers were the Danes, who received only Lauenberg for their sacrifice of Norway and Heligoland. The Finns and Norwegians hardly entered into the equation (although the Tsar had paid more attention to Finnish nationalism than the Swedes ever had). Once again, we witness a swapping of 'souls' in the interests of treaty obligations and the diplomats' understanding of their own needs, defended by invoking the requirements of European equilibrium.

The rights of German Jews

The rights of German Jews also came to the attention of the Congress.[217] Perhaps nowhere else did the statesmen better reveal themselves as the true heirs of the Enlightenment. For centuries, European Jews had been confined to separate communities, subject to their own laws and limited in their contacts with outsiders. During the Enlightenment, ancient prejudices against Jews were suddenly challenged. In 1781, the Prussian theologian, Christian Wilhelm von Dohm, a friend of the Jewish thinker Moses Mendelssohn, published 'On the Improvement of the Civil Status of the Jews', criticizing Christian prejudices and urging the admission of Jews to full citizenship. A few months later, Joseph II of Austria issued a toleration edict, admitting Jews to state schools and ending age-old restrictions. Ten years after that, the National Assembly abolished all Jewish disabilities in France. When Napoleon created the Confederation of the Rhine, he also extended full rights of citizenship to its Jews. In 1809, Wilhelm von Humboldt, a frequent guest at the lively Jewish salons of Berlin, drafted a lengthy memorandum in favour of extending full rights of citizenship to the Jews of Prussia. Hardenberg personally persuaded King Frederick William to issue an edict of toleration in March 1812. Meanwhile, the Jewish financier Rothschild successfully negotiated the granting of full civil rights to the Jews of Frankfurt in 1811. Bavaria followed suit in 1812, while one of the secret articles of the Peace of Paris established complete freedom of conscience throughout the Netherlands.

The defeat of Napoleon led several of the German states to attempt to renege on these obligations: Frankfurt and the Hanseatic cities of Bremen, Lübeck and Hamburg all threatened to repudiate Jewish rights. Their Jewish communities therefore sent delegates to the Congress—Jacob Baruch and

J. Gumprecht represented the Jews of Frankfurt, while a respected Christian jurist, Dr Carl August Buchholz, was sent by the Jews of Bremen, Lübeck and Hamburg. The Austrian police intended to deport Baruch and Gumprecht, who mistakenly entered Vienna without diplomatic visas, but Metternich personally intervened on their behalf. Not only Humboldt, Hardenberg, Gentz and Metternich but also Castlereagh, Talleyrand and Nesselrode were all strong advocates of Jewish emancipation, and the Tsar had granted Russian Jews limited rights in 1804. Besides sharing Enlightenment views on religious toleration, these statesmen frequented Jewish salons for after-dinner conversation at Vienna during the Congress, and were indebted to Europe's leading Jewish bankers—the Rothschilds in London and Frankfurt and the Herz family in Vienna. It was chiefly the smaller states—Frankfurt, the Hanseatic towns, Bavaria, Darmstadt and Saxony—that stood in the way of Jewish rights. In addition to anti-Semitic prejudices, they feared the new federal constitution would restrict states' rights; therefore they opposed any constitutional provisions protecting Jewish liberties.

Jewish rights eventually became the subject of discussion in the German Committee. Article 2 of the initial Austro-Prussian draft for the federal constitution had contained a provision 'to safeguard internally the constitutional rights of every class,' language aimed in part at protecting Jewish citizens. In December 1814, at the height of the Saxon crisis, the Austrians submitted a new draft, which expressly indicated that 'toleration of the Jews' was to be incorporated into the constitution. On this issue at least, Austrians and Prussians could still agree. On 4 January Hardenberg even took the time to address the Prussian envoy in Hamburg on Jewish rights, instructing him that the city's plans to renew restrictions on Jews were inconsistent with the Prussian royal edict of 1812, with the views of the powers at Vienna and with the spirit of the times.[218] Meanwhile, within the German Committee the Austrian draft met with opposition from the smaller states. A new draft, submitted by Hardenberg and Humboldt in April, proposed unrestricted freedom of religion throughout the German Confederation: 'the three Christian denominations shall enjoy equal rights in the German states, and adherents of the Jewish faith insofar as they assume the duties of citizenship, shall be accorded corresponding rights'. This was revised again in early May to state that Jews should receive 'insofar as they assume performance of the duties of citizenship, corresponding rights' and that where this conflicted with existing provisions in various state constitutions, the Confederation should work to remove these inconsistencies. Bavaria proposed that the issue be referred to the new Federal Diet rather than being placed in the Federal Constitution itself. At the session of 31 May, Austria and Prussia insisted that the issue was a constitutional one, but permitted a weakening of the language. Finally, on

17 June 1815, the very eve of Waterloo, the German states adopted the following formula: 'The [Federal] Diet shall consider the means of effecting, in the most uniform manner, an amelioration in the civil state of those who profess the Jewish religion in Germany ... [U]ntil then, [they] shall enjoy the rights heretofore accorded them in several states.'[219]

This was intended to protect the Jewish communities until the new Federal Diet could itself resolve the issue. However, the delegate from Bremen, a vocal opponent of Jewish rights, revised this language, deliberately changing the final sentence from '*in* several states' to '*by* several states'. His purpose was to establish a basis for the later argument that the provision did not apply to emancipation measures introduced by France. Gentz, Metternich and Hardenberg nonetheless all thought the issue had been favourably disposed. 'Metternich, Wessenberg, Hardenberg and I', Humboldt wrote his wife, 'maintained the cause as well as we could'. Metternich assured the Jewish deputies that there was, moreover, a second guarantee of their rights in Article 80, which confirmed 'the well-acquainted rights of every class of inhabitants' in Frankfurt. 'By this disposition', Metternich wrote to the Jewish representative Baruch on 9 June, 'the Jewish community of Frankfurt-am-Main will find satisfaction, as the legal compact which they had previously made is fully confirmed'. To Buchholz, Metternich further explained that the powers intended that 'the liberties and rights' already conferred on the Jews of Germany should be 'preserved intact'.

Despite Metternich's well-meaning assurances, there was an unhappy, post-Congress sequel—the Jews of Bremen and Lübeck were expelled from their communities, while Frankfurt reimposed its traditional restrictions. These steps drew the bitter criticism of Hardenberg. Castlereagh, who knew about religious bias, was similarly outraged and instructed the British envoy 'to encourage the general adoption of a liberal system of toleration with respect to the individuals of the Jewish persuasion throughout Germany, in order that they may not be deprived of those indulgences they have lately enjoyed'.[220]

This was not the first time that rights of conscience had been negotiated at an international congress, since the rights of Catholics and Protestants had frequently appeared in treaties during the century of religious wars. But it was the first time that the rights of Jewish communities were specifically protected by international agreement, as unsatisfactory as the final outcome may have proved to be. Again, this example provides a good demonstration of how the new international order was meant to operate. Here, the representatives of the great powers negotiated measures with concerned lesser states in order to arrive at measures they expected them to follow; but there was no mechanism for enforcement of such internal matters, which were left to the future Confederation.

The slave trade

Another moral issue in which the statesmen of Vienna—in particular, Castlereagh—acquitted themselves with some dignity was that of the slave trade. It is worth contrasting their conduct with the handling of this issue by Revolutionary France and Napoleon. In October 1789, the French National Assembly had refused to seat a group of mulattoes from the West Indies; it similarly failed to halt the slave trade after hearing conflicting testimony from the abolitionist *Société des Amis des Noirs* and the white colonists and merchants who profited from the trade. The French Legislative Assembly later granted rights of citizenship to free people of colour, but conspicuously failed to extend these rights to slaves on the sugar plantations of the French West Indies. Inspired by the bold rhetoric of the 'Declaration of the Rights of Man', the slaves of Saint Domingue (Haiti) revolted against their masters in August 1791. When the British and Spanish, assisted by French plantation owners, threatened to take the island, commissioners sent by the French Legislative Assembly at last freed the slaves. In 1794, the French Convention outlawed slavery in all the colonies and granted full rights of citizenship to all men, regardless of race. In Haiti, General Toussaint l'Ouverture, a freed slave, led the island's forces successfully against British and Spanish troops; l'Ouverture issued a constitution permanently abolishing slavery and establishing himself as governor for life. None other than Napoleon ordered the reconquest of the island: l'Ouverture was duped into surrendering, sent to France, and died in a cold prison cell in the French Alps. Napoleon restored slavery in Guadeloupe in 1802 and was preparing to do the same in Haiti, but suspicions of his plans sparked another rebellion. Haiti declared its independence in 1803, although Napoleon was able to restore slavery in the other French colonies.[221]

In Britain, Evangelical Protestants had adopted the abolition of the slave trade as their *cause célèbre* even before the French Revolution. Due to their efforts, the slave trade, although not slavery itself, was abolished throughout the British Empire in 1807. Meanwhile, Britain had used her mastery of the seas to acquire the colonies of both France and Holland, as well as to eliminate the slave trade, *de facto*, north of the equator. In May 1814, William Wilberforce, leader of the 'Saints' in Parliament, secured passage of a resolution in the Commons opposing the return of any colonial possessions to France without first obtaining French abolition of the slave trade. While Louis XVIII and Talleyrand were personally sympathetic to the anti-slavery cause, they argued that French planters were jealous of England and demanded the right to 'restock' their plantations with slaves; hence, the trade could not be ended immediately without losing the planters' support for the restored Bourbon dynasty.[222] In the Peace of Paris, Castlereagh reluctantly agreed to the return of colonies to France without abolition. Places where the slave trade had been unknown for years shockingly saw it reinstated. The Evangelical 'Saints' were furious, and when Castlereagh triumphantly laid the peace treaty before Parliament, Wilberforce bitterly denounced it: 'I cannot but conceive I behold in my hand the death warrant of a multitude of innocent victims, men, women, and children, whom I had fondly indulged the hope of having myself rescued from destruction.'[223]

Against this background, Castlereagh was instructed to spare no efforts at Vienna in securing abolition of the hideous trade. Both the Tsar, who had spent time with Wilberforce in London, and the Pope were in support of these efforts. Of the colonial powers, Holland, Sweden and Denmark readily agreed to abolition, but France, Spain and Portugal—whose rulers ironically all owed a debt to the British for their restoration—were firmly opposed. Castlereagh realized that any international prohibition would be utterly meaningless without some mechanism for its enforcement—and who could better enforce the prohibition than the British Royal Navy? France, Spain and Portugal viewed this demand as nothing more than a ploy to maintain British naval supremacy by furnishing the British with a standing pretext for boarding every vessel on the open seas.

At Vienna, Castlereagh's specific objectives with respect to the slave trade were to secure its abolition north of the equator; to shorten the time preceding its abolition by France, Spain and Portugal; and, lastly, to obtain the 'right of visit' in order to be able to search suspicious vessels in African waters.[224] Castlereagh even considered an economic boycott of colonial produce from the slave-trading states (a curious anticipation of the 'fair trade' movement of our own day) and suggested the formation of an international committee, to extend beyond the life of the Vienna Congress itself, to supervise the issue.[225] This 'sort of permanent European Congress' was to consist of ambassadorial conferences in both London and Paris.[226]

Castlereagh coupled his own efforts at Vienna with simultaneous approaches through his envoys in Paris and Madrid. Wellington obtained Louis XVIII's assent to an immediate cessation of the slave trade north of the equator. Based on a casual comment by Talleyrand, the eager British government even offered France possession of the island of Trinidad if the French would immediately abolish the slave trade, but their offer was refused.[227]

Talleyrand well understood Castlereagh's need for an agreement on the slave trade to silence his critics in Parliament, and he used this as another bargaining chip to dislodge Murat from Naples. Talleyrand called for the 'Committee of the Eight' (the eight signatories of the Peace of Paris) to form a committee to deal with the slave trade in December 1814. Spain and Portugal opposed his suggestion, hoping to limit all consideration of the trade to the colonial powers, where they would constitute a majority. Castlereagh insisted, however, that the slave trade was an issue of general interest. A committee was finally formed at Vienna in January 1815. Castlereagh circulated a number of memoranda, partly with an eye to producing them later in the House of Commons. The powers accepted his proposal for the appointment of a permanent committee to oversee the abolition. Finally, on 8 February 1815, two days after the Central European settlement was reached, the powers issued a joint démarche condemning the slave trade as repugnant to the 'spirit of the age'.[228]

Again, the treatment of the slave-trade issue furnishes us with an example of how the new international order was intended to operate: the great powers were supposed to negotiate among themselves to reach a collective decision and then to impose this decision both on themselves and on the outside community of lesser powers. Even at the height of the Saxon crisis, Castlereagh apparently met with the Tsar, the Emperor of Austria and the King of Prussia to discuss the slave trade. But, as was the case for Jewish rights, the new system failed to secure the results intended. The most that Castlereagh could actually achieve was a commitment from France to eliminate the trade within five years and from Spain and Portugal within eight.[229] Castlereagh, who had paid bribes to overturn the Irish House of Commons and subsidies to the allies to overthrow Napoleon, was not above offering compensation in these discussions. For the concessions he obtained towards abolition of the trade, Britain nobly agreed to pay Portugal £300,000 and Spain £400,000.

Rivers and precedence

Several other issues were also successfully tackled at Vienna, including free navigation of the Rhine and other major European rivers and the creation of a uniform system of rank between different types of representatives (such as ambassador and *chargé d'affaires*) for purposes of diplomatic protocol. These agreements again provided an instructive demonstration of what could be achieved through conference diplomacy, honest negotiation and a willingness to compromise.

The question of a general guarantee

It will be recalled that back in 1804, echoing Sully and the Abbé Saint-Pierre, Czartoryski had idealistically called for the creation of a league of states to prevent future wars:

> When peace is made, a new treaty should be drawn up as a basis for the reciprocal relations of the European states. Such a treaty might ... bind the

powers never to begin a war until after exhausting every means of mediation by a third power, and lay down a code of international law which ... would, if violated by any one of them, bind the others to turn against the offender.

Pitt had been of the same opinion, recommending the conclusion of 'a treaty to which all the principal powers of Europe should be parties, by which their respective rights and possessions, as they then have been established, shall be fixed and recognised; and they should all bind themselves mutually to protect and support each other against any attempt to infringe them'.[230] The turmoil of the French Revolution and the Napoleonic Wars had thus led these two statesmen—Alexander's childhood friend and Castlereagh's mentor—to conclude that Europe should establish a formal system of collective security.[231]

The final territorial settlement in 1815 so closely resembled Pitt's plan of 1805 that Castlereagh included a copy of that document when he presented the terms of the settlement to Parliament: Austria was made the guardian of Northern Italy, Prussia was thrust forward to the Rhine to secure Northern Germany and a ring of buffer states was placed around the girth of France, with the United Netherlands to the northeast and Piedmont to the south. The main difference between Pitt's scheme and the final settlement was only to be found further to the east, where Russia had created a new Kingdom of Poland under her aegis.

Before leaving for London at the end of February, Castlereagh therefore put forward a very ambitious proposal, hearkening back to the original ideas of Czartoryski and Pitt: that of a general guarantee of the final territorial settlement by the five great powers, to be upheld by force:

> the best alliance that could be formed in the present state of Europe was that the Powers who had made the peace should by a public declaration at the close of the Congress announce to Europe whatever difference of opinion may have existed in the details, their determination to uphold and support the arrangement agreed upon; and further, their determination to unite their influence, and if necessary, their arms, against the Power that should attempt to disturb it.[232]

From the description of the previous disputes it might well seem as though the great powers had forgotten the travails of 20 years of revolution and war, but such was not the case. The Tsar, who was already contemplating his own league of Christian brotherhood, warmly embraced Castlereagh's idea of a general guarantee, and Gentz actually completed the first draft of the declaration by 13 February, in which each of the great powers pledged to oppose any attempt to overthrow the 'established order'. The Tsar was reportedly moved to tears when Gentz's draft was read to him. Castlereagh sent a circular letter to the members of the British diplomatic service announcing that the Congress would crown its labours with the guarantee —'there is every prospect of the Congress terminating with a general accord and guarantee between the Great Powers of Europe, with a determination to support the arrangement agreed upon, and to turn the general influence, and, if necessary, the general arms, against the Power that shall first attempt to disturb the Continental peace'.[233]

If a general guarantee of all European borders had been issued and enforced, it would indeed have marked the dawn of a new epoch in world history, but the project was frustrated when the statesmen began to consider whether to extend their guarantee to the European possessions of the Ottoman Empire. Metternich hoped for this, and Castlereagh specifically raised the issue of Turkey with the Tsar—perhaps at the instigation of the Ottoman government itself. The Russians would only consent to such a broadening of the guarantee, however, after they first resolved all their outstanding differences with the Turks, and the Sultan rejected this proposal outright. Historian Paul Schroeder argues that the Russians deliberately raised the possibility of a European guarantee with the Ottoman Turks at Constantinople (Istanbul), in order to ensure its rejection.[234] In fact, Castlereagh was still urging the Turks to resolve all issues with Russia in order to salvage his guarantee proposal, just hours before his departure from Vienna. Gentz later wrote that the Ottomans rejected the offer because they did not want to place Britain in the position of mediator between themselves and Russia.[235] Despite the failure to conclude a guarantee before Castlereagh's departure, the notion of a general guarantee continued to hold great appeal, especially for the Tsar. A Russian diplomatic 'circular' (an identical message sent to several courts) was sent in May, as the Tsar himself prepared to leave Vienna, again announcing that 'the Cabinets intend to establish the inviolability of the acts of the Congress by reciprocal guarantees'.[236]

Did the common desire to end the cycle of wars and obtain world peace provide sufficient motivation for the powers to put aside their differences? While the powers contemplated the possibility of a general guarantee, it is worth noting that they failed to conclude one before the return of Napoleon. Was the guarantee something that they might have eventually negotiated, or would the Turkish obstacle have always barred this outcome? And, just as important, how would such a guarantee have operated alongside the recently concluded secret alliance of 3 January 1815 (which Holland, Hanover and Bavaria had also joined)?

Originally, there was no plan to consolidate all of the separate agreements reached at Vienna into a single document. This reflects Humboldt's earlier vision of the Congress as nothing more than a series of simultaneous negotiations, coincidentally proceeding at the same place. But on 10 February 1815, after the main contours of Central Europe were finally resolved, the great powers did at least agree to merge the multitude of separate agreements into a single, unified treaty.[237] Though the Congress itself had never met in plenary session, they hoped to enhance the legitimacy of their decisions through this device. In order to obtain protection for its own special interests as part of a *quid pro quo*, each state would subscribe to the settlement in its entirety, effectively creating a new system of public law for Europe.[238] This was, perhaps, the next best thing to a general guarantee, the primary difference being the absence of a specific provision or mechanism for its enforcement.

A final treaty was eventually drawn up by early June, consisting of 121 articles. The treaty was so lengthy that it took 26 copyists an entire day to make one duplicate. During the week of 19 June, copies of the 'Final Act' (so named by Gentz) were circulated and signed by the representatives of the signatories of the Peace of Paris—with the exception of Spain, which protested against its losses in the treaty. Metternich and Talleyrand were still in Vienna, but the Tsar, the King of Prussia, Castlereagh, Wellington, Hardenberg and Humboldt had all long since left. The lesser powers of Europe were next invited to accede, creating what one historian has described as a 'general instrument' that would serve as the 'basis for the international life of Europe for nearly fifty years'.

Assessments of the settlement

In February 1815—after resolution of the principal territorial disputes—Gentz gave this assessment of the Congress:

> The grand phrases of 'reconstruction of social order', 'regeneration of the political system of Europe', 'a lasting peace founded on a just division of strength', &c., &c., were uttered to tranquillise the people, and to give an air of dignity and grandeur to this grand assembly; but the real purpose of the Congress was to divide amongst the conquerors the spoils taken from the vanquished. The comprehension of this truth enables us to foresee that the discussions of this Congress would be difficult, painful, and often stormy.[239]

Political caricaturists of the day ridiculed the scene of allied victors embarking on a war over a division of their spoils, while a Whig opponent told the British House of Commons that 'the Congress of Vienna seems, indeed, to have adopted every part of the French system, except that they have transferred the dictatorship of Europe from an individual to a triumvirate'. According to many of these critics, the Congress statesmen ignored the traditional rights of smaller states and the popular aspirations of nationalities like the Poles, Belgians, Norwegians, Italians and Germans; in so doing, they set the stage for revolutions and conflicts later in the century. Such sentiments were echoed as recently as 1995, when one historian—Pamela Pilbeam—wrote that the powers partitioned Europe much as they had Poland, and that at Vienna 'the only visible principle behind their actions were those of an opportunistic balancing act, to ensure that none acquired appreciably more than the other'. In *The Rites of Peace: The Fall of Napoleon and the Congress of Vienna* (2007), Adam Zamoyski likewise observes that the allied statesmen did not establish any new form of 'legitimacy', but simply 'decided to reorganize and run Europe by accord between themselves, without reference to the minor powers, let alone public opinion'.[240] Zamoyski further criticizes the Congress statesmen—in support of Pilbeam—for ignoring the rising force of nationalism: 'there was certainly no lack of awareness of the strength of national feeling in Germany, Poland and Italy, and by failing to take it into account in their arrangements the architects of the settlement defeated their own purpose and sowed the seeds of untold problems in the future'.

Most modern scholars, however, give the Vienna settlement high marks. Edward Vose Gulick, for example, saw the settlement as the perfect realization of balance-of-power principles, aimed less at stability than at the survival of the individual great powers and thoroughly imbued with a late eighteenth-century spirit of rationalism and moderation.

Henry Kissinger argues that, in the aftermath of the French Revolution and Napoleon, the great powers faced a collapsing world order and were groping towards a new definition of their international role. The Congress statesmen erected a system based on constraints to ensure peace and stability: a restored balance of power inhibited each power's capacity to upset the new international order, while a consensus of shared values reduced each power's desire to do so. The result, according to Kissinger, was an unparalleled success: the longest period of peace that Europe has ever known.

Historian Paul Schroeder similarly salutes the Vienna statesmen for their forbearance. He argues that alleged nationalist demands, which they are sometimes accused of ignoring, more often than not were the claims of particularist groups, such as the German imperial knights. Moreover, no peace settlement, he argues, should be made responsible for achieving greater social justice within states; instead, the Vienna settlement must be judged on the basis of its impact on the international system—in his words, how well it 'reconciled great-power demands for influence'.[241] Schroeder believes the work of the Vienna Congress comes off well in comparison to other post-war settlements. He largely attributes its success to the willingness of the statesmen to confront structural problems in the international system openly, such as historic state rights versus the needs of the international community and the security needs of both great and small powers. The previous 20 years of struggle had, according to Schroeder, provided an invaluable education in which statesmen had learned the wisdom of accepting limits. Contradicting Pilbeam, Schroeder finds that the Congress statesmen exhibited an impressive devotion to normative notions of public law. Schroeder rejects the view that the settlement reflected a pure 'balance of power' and rewrites the definition of 'a just equilibrium', which he argues was used by European leaders at the time to include mutual restraint and deference to public law—in other words, stability in a larger sense. Schroeder even goes so far as to incorporate Talleyrand's appeal to 'legitimacy' into the contemporary definition of equilibrium.[242] He offers the lenient treatment of defeated France and the Tsar's concessions on the Polish frontier as examples of this spirit. In contrast, he points out that the attempt to apply balance-of-power principles to the negotiations over the Polish-Saxon Question largely failed.[243] Schroeder credits this diplomatic revolution chiefly to the efforts of Britain and Russia, two hegemonic states that agreed to work within a moral framework, even respecting the rights of smaller states. In this sense, he sees the Congress of Vienna itself as truly revolutionary:

> 1815 is the one and only time in European history when statesmen sat down to construct a peaceful international system after a great war and succeeded ... This astonishing accomplishment in international politics ... made possible much of the structural change and progress in nineteenth century European society.[244]

Political scientists have now also jumped into the fray in evaluating the Congress. Typically, their purpose is to compare the Vienna settlement with other post-war arrangements. In *The States System of Europe, 1640–1990: Peacemaking and the Conditions of International Stability* (1994), Andreas Osiander points out that the French Revolution challenged institutions not only within but also between states: 'If the thinking that had triumphed in the French Revolution had a basic message, it was that every custom, every social construct could be challenged. The international system, just as much as the domestic organization of the actors that made it up, was such a construct.'[245] According to Osiander, this crisis of legitimacy led to a search for new principles by the Congress statesmen in order to provide a framework for European reconstruction:

> Even if the old set-up was partially retained or restored, it could not be simply for the sake of custom. In order to have a consensus on, or

legitimacy for, anything, thenceforth it had to be in the name of some abstract concept. This is the chief reason why, by 1815, the variegated pattern of pre-revolutionary constitutional forms had given way to a considerably more standardized international landscape, which was shaped to a much greater extent than before by abstract theorizing. It is the abstract nature of this thinking that is its most striking feature ... This also explains why everybody was constantly talking about 'principle(s)', and why people were so fond of the equally abstract expression 'system'.[246]

Osiander sees the emergence at Vienna of what he calls the 'great power principle': the great powers simply arrogated to themselves the right to redraw the borders of Europe and subsequently guaranteed the neutrality of Switzerland, Prussian gains in Saxony, the new frontiers of Poland and the incorporation of Belgium into Holland. 'Great-power relations had their ups and downs', Osiander writes, 'but the international system enjoyed an unprecedented degree of stability for the next hundred years, warranting a general presumption throughout the system that the great powers ... knew best and would act wisely'.[247]

In *After Victory: Institutions, Strategic Restraint and the Rebuilding of Order after Major Wars* (2000), G. John Ikenberry similarly emphasizes, as his title suggests, what he sees as a masterful exercise of restraint by the statesmen at Vienna:

> The political order that emerged from the Vienna settlement combined elements of the old European logic of balance with new legal-institutional arrangements meant to manage and restrain power. Its most important departure from previous peace agreements was that it sought to cope with problems of menacing states and strategic rivalry by tying states together through treaty and a jointly managed security consultation process.[248]

Following Schroeder, Ikenberry attributes this 'strategic restraint' largely to the influence of Britain and Russia as 'hegemonic powers' that attempted to 'to lock in a favourable post-war order and to use institutional arrangements to build legitimacy and conserve power'. John Vasquez, another theorist of international relations, concurs. Vasquez points to two key features of the settlement: first, the Congress statesmen created 'rules of the game' that states could follow in their future relations; and secondly, through the skilful use of conference diplomacy, bargaining games and compensation systems, the Congress 'was able to establish a territorial settlement that all the major states could live with and which the new French regime could accept'. By resolving outstanding territorial issues in a comprehensive way, Vazquez argues, the Congress statesmen went a long way towards establishing the stability of the succeeding century.[249]

Adam Zamoyski finds several flaws in the arguments of these Congress apologists. First, he claims there was no subsequent century of peace, since 'even in the absence of a general war, there was plenty of fighting going on'. Secondly, Zamoyski asserts that the Vienna settlement did not actually last that long. Because the Congress statesmen ignored the forces of nationalism, the settlement had to be revised as early as 1830, when Belgium received independence from Holland and fresh revolts swept across Europe.

Historian Alan Sked criticizes Schroeder and the 'strategic restraint' school from a different standpoint. He argues that the diplomacy at Vienna did not actually differ that much from what had gone on in the preceding century. Sked takes a 'realist' approach not dissimilar to the judgement of Gentz in 1815, contending that each of the great powers at Vienna primarily acted to maximize its own power: 'Everyone at the time regarded—and rightly regarded—the settlement as a carve-up of Europe in the interests of the great powers. If Talleyrand invoked the principle of legitimacy, it was merely to strengthen the case for the Bourbons, whose own rights and claim to be restored could not even be taken for granted.'[250] Despite all the rhetoric, argues Sked, each power was willing to discard its professed principles whenever these stood in the way of its ambitions. Britain and Russia, in his view, did not act as 'hegemons' at all: rather, all five of the great powers practiced traditional balance-of-power politics. Concessions were made to France because the powers did not want to render the regime they had just themselves imposed too unpopular; even so, the settlement was greatly resented by Frenchmen of all political persuasions. Nor was Austria subordinated by either Russia or Britain: in fact, Sked believes the Congress was a triumph for Metternich.

The late Enno Kraehe—who examined the intricate diplomacy of the Congress as closely as any modern scholar—occupied a middle ground in these controversies. In characterizing Metternich's arguments, Kraehe thus wrote:

> [O]n the highest plane of international politics, where no court existed to weigh competing briefs, so long as the mores of humanity were not flagrantly abused, all parties would be guided by interests, expecting legal arguments to provide only a veneer of civility to veil the strength of the victor and soften the blow to the ones who yielded. In this case, if Alexander tired before the Prussians did, as surely he must, his dignity would suffer less by acknowledging ostensibly superior logic and moral principles than by appearing to submit to force.[251]

In other words, Kraehe concludes that the Vienna statesmen were guided by their own perceptions of state interests, but that they expressed their views, somewhat Habermas-like, in the language of universal principles to disguise and even soften the raw exercise of power and coercion. And, on occasion, the way in which such principles were expressed might even take on a life of its own, restraining the actors and influencing the outcome. As Castlereagh revealingly remarked in describing Hardenberg's change of course in a letter to Lord Liverpool: 'I did not feel myself called upon to combat the reasoning, which was the *mere vehicle* on the part of P[rin]ce Hardenberg of disclosing this change of policy' (emphasis added).[252] Thus even Castlereagh did not take the rhetoric too seriously when it provided a mere fig leaf covering interests. Accordingly, Castlereagh himself could argue with dexterity either for or against the rights of the King of Saxony.

It may be, however, that the best way to approach the Vienna Congress is through an application of what international-relations theorists describe as a 'levels-of-analysis' approach. This is the notion that a complex event can be viewed from more than one perspective (typically that of sub-system, system and environment).[253] Historians, closely tied to their primary sources as they investigate the unfolding of events, tend to focus on the first 'level of analysis': the declared and undeclared intentions of the individual actors and their ensuing behaviour—in other words, what did Alexander, Castlereagh, Hardenberg, Metternich and Talleyrand desire to achieve at the Congress? Historians next consider the reasonable options facing each of these statesmen and the choices they made. How did their pursuit of these particular objectives culminate in the final settlement? This historical approach is, in the main, the method that has been adopted in this chapter. We have seen that Castlereagh's aims, enumerated in his instructions of December 1813, were rooted in Pitt's plan of 1805: to ring France with buffer states, to unite Belgium with Holland, to strengthen Prussia, to unite the German states in a federation and to give Austria control of Northern Italy. All of these objectives were eventually achieved either in the treaties with France or in the Vienna Final Act. Alexander, following the line adumbrated by Czartoryski as early as 1804, wanted to raise up a reunified Poland under Russian suzerainty—remedying the wrongs, as best he could, of the earlier partitions. He also favoured Prussian acquisition of Saxony, the spread of consultative assemblies across Europe and a general guarantee of the final settlement. King Frederick William of Prussia and Hardenberg hoped to expand their kingdom by acquiring contiguous territories in Saxony, but only partially realized their goal. Metternich wished to maintain Austrian control of Northern Italy, establish Austrian leadership of the new German Confederation and cooperate with Castlereagh in opposing the Tsar's Polish-Saxon plan. Talleyrand entered the negotiations with the aim of restoring France to the first rank of powers, preserving her frontiers, restoring the Neapolitan Bourbons and protecting the King of Saxony. He was largely successful (although, as we shall see in the next chapter, the frontiers of France would be further reduced after the Hundred Days).

We can thus view the outcome of the negotiations simply as the result of the triumphs and errors of the diplomats as their competing ambitions collided and their strategies interacted. Castlereagh, for instance, developed a close working relationship with Metternich shortly after he arrived at allied headquarters early in 1814, when the two cooperated against the Tsar's ambitious scheme to summon a popular assembly in Paris and to place Bernadotte on the French throne. These same two ministers cooperated again at Vienna nine months later, this time in concert with Hardenberg in order to defeat Alexander's Polish-Saxon scheme. The Prussian King proved unwilling, however, to defy the Tsar, whose demands for Poland were reluctantly conceded. The ministers' attention then turned to Prussian claims on Saxony. Here, the joint pressure exerted by Austria, Britain and France, combined with the Tsar's own religiosity, limited Prussian ambitions and brought about fresh concessions and a series of compromises. By early February 1815, the allied powers at last arrived at a consensus on the reconstruction of Central Europe. All the other pieces of the puzzle then quickly fell into place.

It is equally clear that these diplomats personally abhorred the threat posed by the French Revolution and disdained both popular nationalism and the interference of the lesser powers in decisions of world politics. It is therefore not surprising that the deliberations of these statesmen at Vienna gave little if any consideration to the claims of subject nationalities and lesser states. From the perspective of these outsiders, as Pilbeam and Zamoyski charge, the settlement was therefore less than equitable. Was it 'unfair' for the great powers to seize and redistribute the territories of Genoa, Poland, Belgium, Northern Italy and Saxony without considering the desires of the local inhabitants? Or were such sacrifices genuinely required to maintain the general peace?

To this level of analysis also belong those debates, once common fare among historians, over which diplomatic virtuoso deserves the *palme d'or* for the best performance at the conference. Was it Talleyrand, who brought France back to the conference table? Was it Castlereagh, who often took the lead and negotiated many of the final compromises? Was it Alexander, who prevailed on Poland and subsequently made concessions on his own terms? Or was it Metternich, who skilfully appeared to take a back seat so that other diplomats might achieve his objectives for him?

At the next level of analysis, individual personalities and views are pushed aside in favour of the geographic, strategic, economic and political concerns affecting each of the leading states. We step back from the canvas for a broader view. From this perspective, the personal weaknesses and strengths of the statesmen, their individual beliefs and their negotiating strategies were far less important than overriding geopolitical realities. Here, we can see that both Britain and Austria were largely satiated powers. Britain required a stable peace on the Continent in order to concentrate her efforts on maintaining her command of the seas, expanding her commerce and controlling her vast overseas empire. Austria—a sprawling multi-ethnic empire united by dynastic ties and nestled in the heart of Europe—sought buffer states separating her from France and Russia, a predominant voice in Germany and Italy and Continental stability. With the signing of the First Peace of Paris, these two powers had achieved their primary territorial objectives: the incorporation of Belgium into Holland for Britain and control over Northern Italy for Austria. By September 1814, their common goal was therefore to preserve the existing balance (or more properly, distribution) of power on the Continent. This coincidence of interests may very well have underpinned the personal friendship that blossomed between Castlereagh and Metternich, and their cooperation at the Congress was at least as important as the more recently anointed role of Britain and Russia as 'hegemons'. In contrast, Russia, Prussia and France were the acquisitive powers: Russia was in the process of extending her control across the flat plains of Europe by taking the lion's share of Poland in the west and by establishing a sphere of influence over parts of the Ottoman Empire to the south; Prussia required an enlargement and consolidation of her territories in order to re-establish her great power status; and France wished to restore her position as a great power and to extend, wherever possible, her borders towards her natural frontiers.

It could be further argued that the interplay of these national interests, dictated by geography and strategic necessity, provide a sufficient explanation for the dance of alliances at the Congress and the contours of the final settlement. Simply put, Austria and Britain acted together, in later stages with French assistance, to restrain Russia and Prussia. But Russia had the advantage of the largest army in Europe—in occupation of both Poland and Saxony when the Congress began. While Britain had command of the seas, served as paymaster to the coalition (through its subsidies to the allied powers), possessed an expeditionary army on the Continent and enjoyed the good will of lesser states such as Holland, her influence was necessarily weakened by her distance and the smaller size of her army by Continental standards. Castlereagh was further constrained by isolationist sentiment in the cabinet and in Parliament—itself a reflection of the 'asymmetry of motivation' between Russia and Britain with regard to the distribution of territories in Poland and Germany. Russian 'hard power' was thus opposed mainly by the 'soft power' of persuasion. Given these factors, it is not surprising that Russia was able to dictate the arrangement in Central Europe to meet her own needs. Britain and Austria were more successful in drawing in the reins on Prussia, which was weaker militarily. The smaller states and subject nationalities, totally lacking in military power, were virtually ignored.

At the final level of analysis, we consider the international system as a whole. It seems clear enough that the Vienna Congress marked a decisive step in the evolution of the modern state system. Even before 1789, changes to the map of Europe, such as the invasion of Silesia and the extinction of Poland, were far from unknown. But to a far greater degree than previously, the French Revolution and the conquests of Napoleon had cast all existing boundaries and governments into doubt, creating a crisis of legitimacy and escalating by tenfold the degree of anarchy in the international system. As Kissinger, Schroeder, Osiander and others maintain, the mutual endorsement of the territorial settlement at Vienna by all five of the major powers was intended to fill this vacuum and to restore stability to the international system as a whole. After Vienna, states were once again expected to honour their written agreements.

Even more remarkable than the professed allegiance of the allied leaders to new diplomatic principles was the sheer simplification of the map. On the eve of the French Revolution, the disorganization and weakness of the European 'middle zone' had posed a fertile area for the rivalries and expansion of the great powers. The French Republic and Napoleon began reorganizing and reshaping the diverse constitutional forms of this European 'middle zone', and the Congress statesmen continued their work.[254] Like the *ancien régime* in France itself, all existing borders and governments had suddenly been brought into question. The loss of sovereignty by smaller, independent polities was an inevitable concomitant of this process. Even at the time, Gentz hypothesized that the disappearance of the smaller states actually contributed to international stability.[255] The Vienna settlement went a long way towards the rationalization and simplification of the European 'middle zone', although the final steps in this process were to be carried out later in the century. In fact, the enlargement of Piedmont and Prussia, undertaken at Vienna for security reasons, contributed greatly to the later unification of Italy and Germany. Alexis de Tocqueville's insight that the French Revolution promoted processes of centralization and standardization first commenced under the *ancien régime* would therefore seem to apply with equal force to the international system itself.

All of this refers, of course, to the territorial settlement and says nothing at all about the celebrated 'Congress System'. This latter system arose not out of the territorial reconstruction of Europe, but out of a surprising series of subsequent events, as we shall see in the next chapter.

4

The Birth of the Congress System, 1815–18

The Hundred Days, March–June 1815

On the morning of 7 March, Metternich was suddenly awakened from his slumber by startling news: Napoleon was missing from Elba. The allied powers immediately suspended the homeward march of their troops. No one yet knew where Napoleon was or his true intentions, but his escape cast a dark shadow on all the preceding work of the Congress.[1]

In fact, the exiled emperor had made the ultimate gamble. Landing in the south of France, he issued stirring declarations to the army and the French populace. In contrast to Bourbon assertions of dynastic legitimacy, Napoleon claimed to rest his title on the general will. Many in France were ready to welcome his return—peasants who feared the revival of feudal rights or the loss of purchased lands to the returning *émigrés*, workers hard hit by unemployment caused by a flood of English manufactures, former officers and soldiers dismissed or on half-pay and imperial civil servants supplanted by royalists. Avoiding royalist Provence, Napoleon marched his small force directly northeast to the mountain districts. A crucial test occurred outside Grenoble, where his small band faced French regulars for the first time. Napoleon's men advanced and at the critical moment opened their formation to reveal the presence of the Emperor. The government battalion refused to fire and, in a rush of enthusiasm, the two forces merged together with outstretched arms.

Once it became known that Napoleon had returned to France, the allied leaders at Vienna issued a joint manifesto, dated 13 March, declaring that Bonaparte had violated the Treaty of Fontainebleau. As the 'enemy and disturber of the peace of the world', he had placed himself beyond the pale of civil and social relations and drawn upon himself the 'public vengeance'. Convinced that the French would rally around their legitimate sovereign, the allies promised to lend Louis XVIII whatever assistance he might need. They also drew up plans to amass an overwhelming force of more than half a million men, should Napoleon succeed in France. In London, Castlereagh could not bring himself to believe that Napoleon would be accepted by the French, and secretly offered to place British troops in Belgium directly under French command—a pledge to maintain the French monarchy more resolute than any undertaken in the previous two decades of war.

All of these decisions were taken before it was known that Napoleon would triumphantly succeed in regaining the French throne. The allied leaders envisaged acting as mere auxiliaries to Louis XVIII in suppressing a local uprising. But the royalists proved absolutely powerless before Napoleon's advance: troops continually defected before a shot was fired. On the night of 19 March, Louis ignominiously fled the Tuileries without a word of warning to his ministers or the diplomatic corps. Unable to secure Dunkirk, he retreated to the Belgian interior at Ghent, at least indicating that he would not return to exile in Britain. Not a drop of blood had been shed in his defence. The next evening, Napoleon reoccupied his throne as if the Bourbon restoration had never occurred.

In the face of this new challenge, the alliance stood remarkably firm. As Gentz observed, Napoleon's return was not at the worst of times: the allies had fortuitously resolved their major differences, while their armies had not disbanded.[2] The statesmen at Vienna therefore determined to resist Bonaparte at all costs, and for this purpose agreed to renew the commitments previously undertaken at Chaumont. A new formal treaty of alliance against Napoleon and his supporters was concluded on 27 March (backdated to 25 March), in which each power pledged to furnish 150,000 troops to maintain the Peace of Paris and to prevent Napoleon from ever occupying the French throne. They would not put down their arms until all possibility of Napoleon's return to power was removed. News of Napoleon's triumph in Paris was still unknown to them, and Louis XVIII was made a party to the treaty. His adherence was, in fact, a source of potential embarrassment to the British government in Parliament, and Castlereagh insisted on adding a formal reservation that Britain was under no duty to support the Bourbons. News of Napoleon's return to the Tuileries reached Vienna on 28 March, only one day after the new treaty was signed.

In France, the army and many of the lower classes appear to have been genuine enough in their support of the restored imperial regime, though modern historians generally concur that the 'notables'—those wealthy landowners, stockholders, tradesmen and professionals whom Napoleon was most eager to woo—held aloof. For the most part, they deplored his return, which they rightly feared would bring war in its wake. Reports from the *départements* show that the local prefects and mayors either lacked enthusiasm or were openly antagonistic. Napoleon had no choice but to attempt to consolidate his control by posing as a democrat; he openly bid for the support of the former French Jacobins, previously ostracized by the royalists, and appointed several former revolutionaries as ministers, including Carnot, Maret and Fouché. Indeed, he could do little else, since many of his former officials refused to serve. Not to be outdone by Louis XVIII's *Charte*, Napoleon further announced that he would summon a great national assembly of representatives, or *Champ de Mai*, to draft a new French constitution. He immediately abolished feudal titles, confiscated the wealth of the royal family and ended the slave trade. Nonetheless, he feared veering too far to the left and privately swore he would never become the head of a *jacquerie*.

Napoleon launched a diplomatic offensive, making separate appeals to each of the allied leaders. He addressed the Emperor Francis in intimate terms as his father-in-law, and sent the Tsar copies of the secret alliance of 3 January 1815 between Britain, Austria and royalist France. Whatever Alexander had earlier known of the treaty, he flew into a rage when he was finally presented with a copy. But after two decades of aggression, Napoleon's protestations of peace fell on deaf ears. Once it was clear that the allies would not tolerate Napoleon's return passively, the fate of Europe hinged on the outcome of the race between allied troop movements and French rearmament. Napoleon began preparations for war even before reaching the Tuileries. Relying on the efforts of Davout and Carnot, he hoped to mobilize French resources as in 1793.

Although the allies appeared to have overwhelming numbers at their disposal, the threat posed by Napoleon was a real one. Allied leaders feared he might succeed in galvanizing the French nation and win the support of the dispossessed peoples of Europe—the Poles, Belgians, Italians and Saxons—while straining the fragile ties of the alliance beyond the breaking point. Moreover, it would be months before the Austrians and Russians would be able to cross into the eastern frontier of France. Napoleon believed that if he could knock out British and Prussian forces before the more slowly moving Austrians and Russians arrived on the scene, he might be able to achieve a negotiated peace.

The return of Napoleon also spawned new divisions among the allies with respect to the future of France. Castlereagh fixed the blame for his return on the French army and remained devoted to the Bourbon cause, though for parliamentary reasons he could not disclose his sentiments openly. The Tsar, on the other hand, held the incompetence of Louis and his ministers responsible, and Metternich and Talleyrand once again began to consider alternatives to the Bourbon dynasty. Except for the English, wrote Gentz, 'it is seen by all that the Bourbons are incapable of ruling.'[3] As in 1814, more than one alternative existed. There was the possibility of a regency under Marie Louise in the name of Napoleon's son, or of a constitutional monarchy under a new ruler such as the Duc d'Orléans. Alexander wavered hesitantly between the regency and the Duc d'Orléans until mid-April, when he finally opted for the latter.

Napoleon's Minister of Police, the former Jacobin and regicide Joseph Fouché, became a natural focal point for these intrigues. Fouché was able to use his own agents to open direct channels of communication with Talleyrand and Metternich. Metternich sent a secret agent to Fouché in early April, with the message that the allies would consider only three options for France: Louis XVIII, the Duc d'Orléans or the regency. His message was intercepted by Napoleon, who nonetheless refused to remove his minister of police. News of the mission had been shared by Metternich with the Russians and Prussians, but concealed from the British.

Castlereagh repeatedly told the Austrian envoy in London that the British government opposed both the regency and the Duc d'Orléans, and would prefer a return of the legitimate sovereign, although they would not make this a *sine qua non* for peace. To counter his allies' schemes to establish a rival dynasty, Castlereagh drew up ambitious plans for French constitutional reform. His reform programme consisted of four steps, each more damaging to the king's pride than the last: first, the dismissal of the king's favourite, the Comte de Blacas; second, the appointment of Talleyrand as the head of the French cabinet; third, the appointment of the regicide Fouché as a royal minister; and finally and most remarkable of all, the transformation of France into a constitutional monarchy on the British model by shifting political power from the king to his ministers. Louis must, Castlereagh cautioned, 'maintain his political authority by using the active political characters that have sprung up during the Revolution'. The king must further 'abstract himself as much as possible from all personal and party preferences ... and declare his determination to govern by responsible ministers'.[4] Of course, Louis would retire from the political arena only in appearance, since he could still use royal patronage to manage the assembly.

Meanwhile, on 23 April Napoleon had issued his own new constitution, the 'Additional Act'. Drafted chiefly by the liberal Benjamin Constant, it granted Frenchmen a free press, freedom of worship, and a legislature with two chambers. The new constitution, clearly borrowed from the Bourbon *Charte*, was to be submitted to a plebiscite. Its sudden appearance before the proposed *Champ de Mai* robbed the *départemental* colleges of their ostensible purpose for meeting. Napoleon also announced immediate elections to the new Chamber of Representatives so that these could be held before the gathering of the *Champ de Mai*, scheduled for 26 May.

The situation for the allies and the royalist exiles at Ghent was markedly tense as they waited to see if Napoleon could succeed in igniting a spark to the French national spirit. Wellington expected nothing less than an outbreak of a new round of democratic revolutions once the national representatives assembled. Castlereagh reacted by calling on Louis to convoke the French Chambers behind allied lines even before Napoleon was defeated. The royalists at Ghent wisely rejected this fantastic proposal since they clearly could not hold elections in France. But in reality, the ceremony of the *Champ de Mai*, postponed until 1 June, was reduced to nothing more than an ostentatious patriotic display and review of troops, which came and went without materially affecting the situation.

Ten days later, Napoleon secretly left Paris to take command of the 128,000 troops of the *Armée du Nord*. On 15 June, he surprised Prussian forces at Charleroi; the next day, he defeated the Prussians at Ligny, while the left flank of his army fought inconclusively against Anglo-Dutch forces under Wellington's command. Napoleon marched his forces forward, hoping to drive a wedge between Wellington and the Prussians. The French right flank, around 32,000 strong, was sent under the command of Grouchy to pursue the Prussians. Grouchy marched too far east, however, leaving the Prussians between himself and Napoleon. Meanwhile, Napoleon advanced with 70,000 men and superior artillery against Wellington's lesser army of 60,000, which had retreated to a strong defensive position near the Belgian village of Waterloo. Wellington had already studied the topography of the battlefield, much as Napoleon himself had done at Austerlitz ten years before. Not only would the French be advancing uphill, but there were folds and creases on the cornfields and hills where Wellington could conceal some of his troops, as well as fortified farmhouses like Hougoumont and La Haye Sainte, which could serve as advanced posts, disrupting French advances. Finally, Wellington knew that the Prussians would be returning to join him against the French.

In the late morning of 18 June, Napoleon began his effort to annihilate Wellington's army. But Wellington's troops refused to budge despite repeated French assaults, while heavy rain the day before had left the ground muddy and rendered the French artillery less effective. A massive cavalry attack, led by Marshal Ney, was resisted by the British infantry, who formed themselves into squares protected by walls of bayonets along their perimeters. By afternoon, the Prussian army started to arrive and it became clear that Napoleon would soon be outnumbered. Nevertheless, he had so clearly gambled on an early victory in the Netherlands that he refused to abandon his offensive. The French attempted a series of massive infantry charges up the hill, all of which foundered. Finally, around six o'clock, French forces took the farmhouse at La Sainte Haye. Some military historians conjecture that a well-timed assault might then have turned around the entire battle, but this failed to materialize. Meanwhile, the Prussians began appearing in greater numbers. As the sun was setting, Napoleon at last ordered his best fighting force, the veterans of the Imperial Guard, to take the offensive. Despite their well-disciplined advance, they were cut down by heavy British fire, and their retreat signalled the final rout of the French. As night fell, most of Napoleon's *Armée du Nord* lay in tatters. The bodies of 40,000 dead and wounded from both sides cluttered a battlefield of no more than two square miles.[5]

Contemporaries were anticipating the defeat of Napoleon from the sheer weight of allied numbers, but they did not foresee that he would meet with precipitate disaster before the alliance had gathered in its full strength. Wellington's triumph provided the allies with the same moral and psychological advantages that an early victory might have bestowed on Napoleon. Unwilling to be left outside the gates of Paris as he had been in 1814, Napoleon rushed back to the capital, where he drew up plans to use Grouchy's troops, survivors from Waterloo and the Paris garrison to repel the invaders. The recently elected Chambers, however, would have none of this. Hoping for more generous terms from the allies without Napoleon, they demanded his abdication. Sensing the hopelessness of his situation, Napoleon reluctantly abdicated for a second time. The Chambers, with its large number of former revolutionaries, sent out separate sets of emissaries (which included both Benjamin Constant and Lafayette) to the allied sovereigns beyond the Rhine and to the allied commanders. Arguing that Napoleon was no longer in power, they demanded an immediate armistice and the right to choose their own form of government. But Wellington and the allied statesmen looked on all talk of a cease-fire with suspicion while Napoleon was still at large.

Metternich and Castlereagh proposed that Louis XVIII move to the south of France to re-establish his government outside the zone of allied occupation, but Louis chose instead to accept an invitation from Wellington to follow in the rear of the latter's advancing forces, thus ignominiously re-entering his realm in the baggage train of a foreign army. Wellington, moreover, refused all suggestion of compromise with the representatives of the French Chambers, and bluntly told the emissaries that their only hope for peace was an unconditional restoration of the legitimate king. Back at allied headquarters across the Rhine, the victory at Waterloo was received ecstatically, giving the British a decisive voice in the French dynastic question. Metternich suddenly committed himself wholly for the Bourbons. The Tsar was less enthusiastic but recognized that the situation was now largely beyond his control.

In Paris, Fouché took control of a new provisional government appointed by the Chambers. In direct negotiations with Wellington, he arranged for the withdrawal of the French army from Paris, the dissolution of the Chambers and the restoration of the king, thus playing a role analogous to that of Talleyrand in 1814. Talleyrand, who had previously delayed responding to the King's summons to Ghent, now also suddenly appeared on the scene. Louis XVIII re-entered Paris amidst general rejoicing on 8 July, about a hundred days after his flight. To please his foreign allies, Louis XVIII agreed to appoint Talleyrand and Fouché as his chief ministers, only to dismiss them a few months later. Napoleon surrendered to the British, who carried him away to the distant island of St Helena, where he was to die in 1821. Some historians suspect his death was the result of arsenic poisoning by a French royalist agent.

The second Peace of Paris and the Quadruple Alliance, July–December 1815

Although the Napoleonic adventure was finally over, the Hundred Days had palpably demonstrated the continuing fragility of the international system. The allied sovereigns and their ministers uniformly detected the evil genius of the French Revolution behind this latest crisis—'The force that cemented the union between the four cabinets', Capodistrias would later write, 'was the fear inspired by the Revolution personified by the man on St. Helena'.[6] To shore up the Bourbons in France and to stabilize Europe, the allies developed an ambitious set of new safeguards and institutions, often referred to by historians as the 'Congress System' since their predominant feature was the use of periodic summit conferences, or 'Congresses', to cope with international problems. In brief, the new allied formula consisted of: (1) the occupation of France by allied troops; (2) new territorial losses and the payment of reparations by France; (3) an extension of the Treaty of Chaumont in the form of a new agreement, the 'Quadruple Alliance' of 20 November 1815; and (4) the use of the Paris 'ambassadorial conference' to supervise France, as well as similar ambassadorial conferences in other European capitals to deal with other issues, such as the slave trade, as they arose. Beyond all this, there was an assertion of moral principles sponsored by the Tsar in the form of the 'Holy Alliance' of September 1815. Metternich would have liked to have added a common European centre for reporting and sharing counter-revolutionary police intelligence, but he never succeeded in this.

It would be a mistake to presume that this 'Congress System' necessarily grew out of the Congress of Vienna itself. Of course, that earlier convocation might easily be seen as the first in a series of similar meetings. But the reality was that the Congress System, much as its inauguration may have been influenced by the final success of the Vienna Congress, was primarily a response to the Hundred Days. The foundations of the celebrated Congress System are to be found in the documents that accompanied the signature of the Second Peace of Paris, and not in the Vienna Final Act.

As is so often the case in peace negotiations, the objects of the war were re-defined retrospectively in the months following its termination. These were now expanded to include, not merely the removal of Bonaparte, but the creation of a stable government in France. For example, in the Russian memorandum that Nesselrode submitted to the ministerial conference on 28 July, drawn up with the assistance of Castlereagh and Wellington, it was asserted that the recent alliance had three aims: first, to deliver France from Bonaparte; second, to return France to the internal and external conditions established by the Peace of Paris; and third, to guarantee to France and Europe the maintenance of the Peace of Paris and the decisions of the Vienna Congress. Metternich concurred with this assessment: for him the alliance had two objects: to combat Napoleon's usurpation, and 'to place a government in France on a solid basis in order to offer a guarantee of tranquillity to France and to Europe'. Metternich pointed to 'the urgent necessity of putting a brake to those principles subversive to the social order upon which Buonaparte had based his usurpation'. Indeed, Metternich announced that 'it is time at last to give a name to the evil that we are combating in France: *Armed Jacobinism*, which alone could hope to derive a real advantage from a new upset in the political relations of the powers'. The allies, he concluded, therefore had the right to ask that France adopt a form of government and institutions comparable to those of the other powers, and which, by a just balancing of powers, would assure their stability. They also had a right to demand 'that France submit to momentary measures of internal policing [by the presence of a foreign force] that will offer the royal government a just support and a pledge of repose to Europe'.[7] On 11 August, Wellington defined the object of the war even more succinctly—in an echo of Bonaparte's famous phrase—as 'put[ting] an end to the French Revolution'.[8]

The Congress System was assigned a similar set of aims. In light of the differences in interpretation that subsequently arose, it is instructive to keep the events of the Hundred Days firmly in mind. Was the peacetime extension of the alliance intended to stifle the forces of revolution, or mainly to preserve the existing European equilibrium? Was the system directed solely against France, or against revolution in general? From the perspective of 1815 there was scarcely any distinction between the two. The greatest threat to Europe was perceived to come from France, and this menace arose from the power of the Revolution. France and the European revolution were seen as virtually inseparable.

The Drafting of the Quadruple Alliance

All this becomes quite clear from the earlier drafts of what became the Quadruple Alliance of November 1815. The first proposal was prepared by Capodistrias and presented by the Russians to the other allied powers in October.[9] Its preamble expressed the desires of the allied sovereigns to maintain the monarchy in France and the 'constitutional order' on which it was based. The first article stated that the contracting parties promised to uphold the existing treaty settlement, and that 'these measures had as their unalterable principle to procure for France the necessary time and means for affirming the Royal Authority on the basis of legitimacy and on the salutary maxims consecrated by the Constitutional Charter'.[10] The second article specifically proposed that the allied signatories would provide direct assistance to the King to maintain 'the monarchy and the constitutional order' against the return of any member of the Bonaparte family or against any other attempt, 'in consequence of the delirium of revolutionary passions', to introduce into France an order which would 'menace anew the security of Europe'.[11] The sixth and final article stated that, in order to facilitate the execution of the treaties and to provide for 'the system of reciprocal guaranties', the signatories would renew their conferences 'at fixed periods' (á des epoques determinées). In other words, the purpose of this alliance was to maintain the Bourbons, with or without popular support, as the best bulwark against revolution.

Castlereagh objected to much of this rhetoric, which would have been difficult to defend in Parliament. He wrote to Liverpool that the Russian draft bore 'on the face of it too strong and undisguised a complexion of interference, on the part of the Allied Sovereigns in the internal concerns of France, without sufficiently connecting such interference with the policy which a due attention to the immediate security of their own dominions prescribed', and furthermore that it 'appeared to make the Allies too much umpires in all constitutional struggles in France by professing a determination to support with all their efforts both the monarch and the charter'.[12] In other words, it was too obviously counter-revolutionary and royalist in intent. Just as Castlereagh had aimed at minimal goals to hold the alliance together during the Napoleonic Wars, he now desired to circumscribe its future operation to a system of cooperation that would come into effect only when a power's own security was directly at stake. Important differences in the British and Russian interpretations of the alliance were already emerging. In the alternative draft that Castlereagh put forward, many of the Russian references to the monarchical and constitutional order in France were deleted.[13] What is hard to overlook, however, is that many of these references remained by implication. For example, where the preamble of the Tsar's project had stated that the object of the coalition was the affirmation of the French monarchy and the existing constitutional order, Castlereagh transformed this into the following more ambiguous phrase: 'the re-establishment in France of the order of things which the recent attempt by Napoleon Bonaparte had temporarily subverted'. But to the allied ministers, this could scarcely have implied much change in meaning. Indeed, Capodistrias and Razumovsky specifically criticized Castlereagh's reference to the 'order of things' (*l'ordre des choses*) as too 'vague' and without any impact on public opinion, and therefore counselled the Tsar to 'support our draft (*redaction*)'.[14] They feared that such ambiguity would create the fatal impression that the powers were not united in support of the 'legitimacy of the throne and the constitutional charter (*Charte*)'. They urged that the treaty announce allied support for these institutions with greater precision—'These arrangements are essentially founded on the restoration of monarchy in France'.[15]

Again, borrowing from the Russian proposal, Castlereagh proposed three *casus feoderis*—those circumstances in which alliance members would be called upon to act—which in fact became the basis for the subsequent alliance: (1) the protection of existing treaties; (2) the perpetual exclusion of Bonaparte and his family from the throne of France; and (3) the protection of the general tranquillity and their respective peoples against other forms of revolutionary disturbance *arising out of France*.

This last point was, of course, the most ambiguous one and the greatest source of later controversy. In its original form, Castlereagh would have included the King of France in allied discussions arising under this heading. Thus Castlereagh's own proposed second article stated:

> As the same revolutionary principles that supported the last criminal usurpation might again, under other forms, tear at France and threaten the repose of other states, the High Contracting Parties ... pledge that in the case of such a terrible event re-occurring anew, they will concert among themselves and with the legitimate sovereign.[16]

The situation of March 1815, when Castlereagh had thought the allies might act as auxiliaries to the King of France, provided the obvious inspiration for this passage. Nevertheless the phrase 'legitimate sovereign' raised some eyebrows in London. Bathurst underlined the term in pencil and scribbled above it 'Louis XVIII or his heirs and successors'. In the adjacent margin he added: 'The right of the people to choose their King will become the subject of debate in Parliament if the legitimate sovereign remains in the Treaty'.[17] The version finally adopted by the four powers on 20 November made use of Castlereagh's precise phrasing but replaced 'le Souverain légitime' with the simpler 'Sa Majesté Très Chrétienne' (the traditional appellation for the King of France).

Castlereagh himself summarized the course of these negotiations in a letter to his half-brother:

> The Treaty of Alliance and Wellington's Instructions are translated by Gent[z] from a draft of mine. Capo d'Istria, whom I like very much as a minister and man of business, had prepared a Project for the former from the outline you carried to England, but these gentlemen, who have no Parliament to watch them, never hit the tone upon such matters. I consider the nuances of an alliance against France and not against the King to be one of the most difficult to seize, that can be stated, and I rather flatter myself that I have got the whole thing on right grounds.[18]

There was an element of irony in all this since, as recently as May 1815, it was Alexander who had proposed convening a national assembly to give the French people a voice in determining their future form of government, while it was Castlereagh who had remained committed to the ancient dynasty. Despite the British public disclaimer to Article VIII of the Treaty of 25 March 1815, no group of men had done more to promote the royalist cause than Castlereagh, Wellington and the British cabinet. The lesson was not lost on the other allies: British political discourse required the idiom of non-interference but British actions bespoke otherwise.

As a result of these negotiations, the final form of Article VI of the Quadruple Alliance—furnishing the foundation of the Congress System—became the following:

> To facilitate and to secure the execution of the present Treaty, and to consolidate the connections which at the present moment so closely unite the Four Sovereigns for the happiness of the World, the High Contracting Parties have agreed to renew their meetings at fixed periods, either under the immediate auspices of the Sovereigns themselves, or by their respective Ministers, for the purpose of consulting upon their common interests, and for the consideration of the measures which at each of those periods shall be considered the most salutary for the repose and prosperity of Nations and for the maintenance of the peace of Europe.[19]

Article II of the same treaty also contained the following provision, equally important, pledging allied consultation in the event of a new revolution in France:

> And if the same revolutionary principles, which had supported the last criminal usurpation, might again, under other forms, convulse France and

thereby endanger the repose of other states, the High Contracting Parties, solemnly admitting their duty to redouble their watchfulness in these circumstances, for the tranquillity and interests of their peoples, engage, in case so unfortunate an event should again occur, to concert amongst themselves, and with His Most Christian Majesty [the King of France], the measures that they may judge necessary for the safety of their respective states, and for the general tranquillity of Europe.[20]

On the same day that the treaty was concluded, the allied ministers sent a confidential note bearing their combined signatures to the French foreign minister, informing him of the existence of the treaty, the object of which was to 'bind the destinies of France to the common interest of Europe'—'the allied cabinets consider the stability of the order of things happily established in that country as one of the essential bases of a solid and durable tranquillity. It is towards this object that their united efforts are constantly directed. It is their sincere desire to maintain and consolidate the result of these efforts, which has dictated all the stipulations of the new treaty'. The allied powers had consequently taken measures to protect 'the future internal repose of France' and to prevent 'dangers to royal authority'.[21]

Other counter-revolutionary measures

The instructions furnished by the allies to Wellington as supreme commander of the allied force of occupation likewise leave little doubt as to the goals of the coalition. Among the two stated objects of the allied occupation, the second was 'to protect Europe not only against a direct attack from France, but against the no less formidable danger of being disturbed and obliged to recur to arms in consequence of the revolutionary convulsions of which there is reason to fear [France] may still be exposed'. Wellington was quite frankly instructed to support Louis against any future revolutionary upheaval: 'The deep interest which the Allies have in sustaining the lawful Sovereign on the Throne of France has induced Our Royal Masters ... to give a distinct Assurance to the King of France of their determination to support him with their Arms against any Revolutionary Convulsions'. Moreover, it was left to the Duke's own discretion to determine 'when and how their troops shall be directed to act' since there were such a 'variety of shapes in which the revolutionary spirit [might] display itself in France'.[22] The counter-revolutionary intentions of the allies could not have been pronounced more blatantly than this.

The new 'ambassadorial conference' likewise had as its goal the strengthening of the royal government. The conference was composed of the ambassadors of the allied powers in Paris and met weekly under Wellington's direction to discuss the internal state of France. Every significant step taken by the French royal government was supposed to be submitted for their approval.[23]

Meanwhile, the French government took steps to punish those 'traitors' most responsible for the Hundred Days. This was precisely what the allied leaders expected the French government to do. Castlereagh himself personally drew attention to 'the necessity of urging the Government of Louis 18, without further delay, to adopt some measure of vigour against the most criminal of traitors'. Most of the participants were exonerated, but a list of the worst culprits was produced. One of these, Marshal Michel Ney—whose betrayal had led to the final collapse of the royal government in March 1815—failed to flee Paris and allowed himself to be captured. A brave and popular war hero, Ney was publicly tried in the Chamber of Peers; he advanced the somewhat novel legal argument that he was protected by the terms of the military capitulation of Paris, which had stipulated that residents of the capital would be immune from prosecution for acts performed during the Hundred Days. Despite the entreaties of Ney's wife, the Duke of Wellington refused to intercede on Ney's behalf. The Marshal was convicted by the Peers and executed in December. While the royal government might have preferred his earlier escape, it would not pardon him.

The final guarantee of the King's stability lay in the structure of the new international system. The periodic reunions of the allied cabinets and the allied force of occupation applied a new external pressure to redress any imbalance of forces within France and to combat her perceived revolutionary tendencies. Castlereagh thus instructed Sir Charles Stuart, the British ambassador in Paris and a member of the new ambassadorial conference,

> that anything that menaces the dynasty of the Bourbons, the regular order of the Succession, or the Constitutional Settlement, upon the faith of which the King has resumed the Throne, you will protest against as compromising, in the view of Your Court and of the whole Alliance, not only the internal tranquillity of France, but the general repose and security of Europe.[24]

One question naturally arises: would these same strictures also apply to the outbreak of revolutions outside of France? Would such revolutions also be seen as endangering the general tranquillity and thereby provide grounds for the mobilization of the coalition? This was one of the key issues facing the future. The fact that British statesmen would not commit themselves in advance was taken by other allied leaders as more of a peculiarity of the

British political system than as a harbinger of any real differences in outlook. It was, after all, Castlereagh himself who had raised a cloud of dust over this question. By his policy of dissimulation towards France during the Hundred Days, he had conveyed a tacit message to the Continental powers they were not soon to forget.

The terms of the peace

At the same time that the allies were working out the terms of their renewed alliance, they were also negotiating the Second Peace of Paris with France. The allied ministers were in unanimous agreement that the new treaty had to be less lenient than the peace of May 1814. Feelings ran so high that Prussian troops in Paris had to be stopped from blowing up the Jena Bridge.[25] In late September, the allies decreed that the stolen works of art that the French had previously kept ought to be returned.[26] The famous bronze horses from ancient Constantinople were packed and returned to St Mark's in Venice; the Roman sculptor Canova came to Paris to oversee the return of treasures to the Vatican; the ancient marble statue of Laocoon and his writhing sons was sent back to Rome; and additional sculptures, paintings and manuscripts were returned to Antwerp, Amsterdam, Berlin, Florence and other cities across Europe.

The allied sovereigns and their ministers, as well as the representatives of many lesser states, arrived in Paris to help negotiate the new peace treaty. There were also a great many other foreign visitors on the scene. In a very real sense, the negotiations at Paris actually constituted the next great European Congress. There were angry calls for the partial dismemberment of France: the Prussians proposed new French cessions to Bavaria and the Netherlands, and a transfer of Luxembourg and Mainz from these other countries to themselves; the Spanish claimed the Basque provinces; the Netherlands desired more of Flanders; from London, even the British cabinet demanded that France should be permanently weakened. The Hanoverian minister, Count Münster, tried to obtain additional territory for Hanover and even persuaded the English Prince Regent of the justice of his claims.

Such territorial demands were firmly resisted by Castlereagh, Wellington and the Tsar. 'I leave you to judge what prospect we shall have of forcing the King to assign away for ever all the great places of the Monarchy', Casteregh wrote to the cabinet, 'I am confident he had better leave the Country'.[27] Here, in contrast to earlier disputes, the British Foreign Secretary and the Russian Emperor acted together. Castlereagh approached the Tsar and approved a Russian memorandum on the proposed peace terms before it was circulated to the other powers. He also sent his half-brother, Lord Charles Stewart, to London in late August to explain his policy to the cabinet.[28] Castlereagh believed that a temporary allied occupation offered France's neighbours better security than any permanent territorial cessions, which would only plant the seeds for future conflict:

> The more I reflect upon it, the more I deprecate this system of scratching such a Power. We may hold her down and pare her nails so that many years shall pass away before they can wound us ... but this system of being pledged to a continental war for objects that France may any day reclaim from the particular states that hold them ... is, I am sure, a bad British policy.[29]

In the end, France lost some territory in the Netherlands, along the German border and in Savoy, sacrificing the gains of the peace treaty of 1814 and bringing her back to the boundaries of 1790. The Versoix corridor was awarded to Switzerland, and Monaco became an enclave surrounded by Piedmont.

In 1814 France had also escaped all demands for reparations, but she was not so fortunate this second time. An indemnity of 700 million francs was imposed for the costs of the recent war; France was also asked to agree to compensate private claimants; new defensive fortifications were to be built in the Netherlands; and an allied occupation force of 150,000 men was to remain in France for a period of three to five years. Finally, the treaty contained a clause on the slave trade, affirming the clause in the Vienna Final Act.

On 20 September, the allies presented these new peace terms to France in a virtual ultimatum. The preamble to the proposed treaty stated that the allies had, by their 'united efforts', preserved both France and Europe from Napoleon and 'the Revolutionary system reproduced in France'. Repeating his stratagem from the opening phase of the Vienna Congress, Talleyrand refused all cessions whatsoever, pretending that the new allied demands were contrary to international law since Louis XVIII had never been a belligerent. France could not, he argued, be forced to pay for the acts of a usurper. The allies, however, responded that their conditions were reasonable and that their sole concern was 'the safety of the adjoining states'. Meanwhile, Talleyrand had grown increasingly unpopular in France. The Tsar had also become irreconcilably opposed to the wily French foreign minister ever since learning all the details of the secret treaty of 3 January 1815. On 25 September, Talleyrand submitted his resignation to Louis XVIII and, to his surprise, the King accepted.

Talleyrand was replaced by Armand-Emmanuel du Plessis, the Duc de Richelieu (1766–1822), a genial descendant of the famous cardinal. As a young nobleman, Richelieu had personally witnessed the Parisian crowd breaking into the royal apartments at Versailles in October 1789; shortly afterwards, Richelieu had been sent by Marie Antoinette on a special mission to seek assistance from her brother in Vienna. As an *émigré*, Richelieu later served in the Russian army until Alexander appointed him as Governor of Novorossiya ('New Russia'), an area including Odessa and the Crimea, in 1803. Just as Napoleon had once chosen Caulaincourt as his foreign minister to appease the Tsar, Louis XVIII now selected Richelieu to help repair Franco-Russian relations. He was, as Talleyrand quipped derisively, the Frenchman most knowledgeable about the Crimea. Richelieu reluctantly accepted the allied peace terms, and the Second Peace of Paris was signed on 20 November 1815, the same day as the Quadruple Alliance.

The Holy Alliance, September 1815

To this new international system was appended the 'Holy Alliance', signed in Paris by the two Emperors and the King of Prussia on 26 September 1815. The name itself was taken up mockingly by radicals, especially in Britain, as an epithet for the Congress System itself, while Castlereagh disdainfully referred to this capstone as a 'piece of sublime mysticism and nonsense', and Metternich largely shared his view.[30] But both these men were Enlightenment rationalists and the Tsar may have better embodied the religious yearnings of the new romantic age. Alexander considered this solemn pact as one more step towards the fulfilment of his earlier liberal programme of 1805.

As early as July 1812, the Tsar had written to the Prince Regent of England expressing his view that there was less need for treaties than for generous sentiments uniting all peoples 'as brothers impressed with providing all the mutual help they need'. Alexander further spoke of the need to end the prevailing 'egoism of individuals and states'.[31] The Treaty of Kalisch in February 1813 contained language that the day would soon come 'when treaties will no longer be truces but will be observed with a religious faith ...'. In the summer of 1814, the German mystic Franz von Baader sent the Tsar, the Emperor of Austria and the King of Prussia each a copy of his tract entitled *Ueber das durch die französische Revolution herbeigeführte Bedürfnis einer neuen und innergern Verbindung der Religion mit Politik* ['On the need created by the French Revolution for a new and closer bond between religion and politics']; this called for the creation of a new federation based on Christian principles. It has already been seen that on 31 December 1814, while Castlereagh was drafting his secret treaty with Austria and France, the Tsar was actually working on an appeal to the allies for a new association based upon the ideals of Christian brotherhood. The future peace of Europe, he said, must rest on the same foundation that had secured victory during the war—the union of the allied sovereigns:

> Penetrated equally with the immutable principles of the Christian religion common to all, it is on this unique foundation of the political order, as well as of the social order, that the sovereigns [must] associate among themselves in order to purify their maxims of state and to guarantee the relations between the peoples that Providence has entrusted to them.[32]

The Tsar told Castlereagh that he had been particularly inspired by the latter's suggestion to conclude some kind of general guarantee at Vienna.[33]

Nine months later—after the defeat of Napoleon at Waterloo—the task of drafting the text of the Holy Alliance finally fell on the shoulders of Alexander Stourdza, a Greco-Romanian Orthodox intellectual acting as secretary to Alexander's minister, Capodistrias. Stourdza was a follower of Baader as well as a member of the Russian Bible Society, and the brother of Roxanne Stourdza, the Tsar's spiritual 'wife'. He went with the Tsar to Heidelberg two days before the Battle of Waterloo, where he met Madame de Krüdener for the first time; he then accompanied the Tsar and Capodistrias to Paris for the negotiations of the new peace treaty, and even wrote a letter used by the Tsar to oppose the plans of some of the allies for the dismemberment of France.[34] According to Stourdza's later account, the Tsar wrote down a brief list of points to include in the Holy Alliance in his own hand and gave these notes to Capodistrias, who in turn passed the assignment on to Stourdza. Stourdza's text included references to the fraternity of peoples as well as of monarchs. The goal of the new treaty, Stourdza wrote, was quite simply the 'entry of Christian charity into the sphere of politics'.[35] It reflected the thinking of the Tsar and Capodistrias—and even of Czartoryski—in conceiving of an alliance of liberal Christian states, each endowed with their own national assemblies.

Metternich's alterations

The Tsar initially called on Metternich to inform him of the treaty but otherwise refused to enter into specifics, which he felt could only be properly discussed with his fellow sovereigns. But when the Tsar afterwards provided a copy of the proposed treaty to the Emperor of Austria, Francis naturally gave it to his foreign minister to review. Metternich instantly recognized the treaty as an attempt to combine 'religious and political-liberal elements'; he also considered many of its expressions of religious sentiment as highly unsuitable to an international agreement. The Austrian Emperor and King of Prussia agreed and authorized Metternich to negotiate with the Tsar on their behalf.

An original draft, found in the archives in Vienna by a Swiss historian in 1928, reveals just how Metternich subtly revised the text in order to transform it from an alliance of Christian peoples into a more conservative league of monarchs. The preamble to the original Russian draft had called for the powers to change their methods to create a new order of things based upon the 'sublime truths' of Christianity. Metternich eliminated all reference to the need for a change in existing policy. In the rest of the preamble, the text had the sovereigns announce their determination to regulate their future conduct, both in the internal administration of their own states and in their relations with other governments, in accordance with Christian precepts of justice, charity and peace. Metternich left these sentences untouched.

Metternich made the most significant changes to the first article of the proposed 'treaty'. The original Russian draft had stated that 'in conformity with the words of Holy Scriptures, which command all men to consider each other as brothers, *the subjects of the three contracting parties* shall remain united by bonds of true fraternity, and, considering themselves as fellow countrymen, shall lend each other support and assistance on every occasion'. In place of this fraternity of peoples, Metternich substituted a unity of thrones. His new text read: 'in conformity with the words of the Holy Scriptures, which command all men to consider each other as brothers, *the three contracting Monarchs* will remain united by the bonds of a true and indissoluble fraternity, and, considering each other as fellow countrymen, shall, on every occasion and in every place, lend each other aid and assistance'. This same article, in the original text, had concluded by stating that the separate armies of the contracting powers would now consider themselves as members of the same army, 'called upon to protect religion, peace and justice'. In place of this, Metternich substituted references to monarchical paternalism: the monarchs 'shall be considered by their subjects and armies *as fathers*; and, regarding themselves towards their subjects and armies *as fathers of families*, they will lead them, in the same spirit of fraternity with which they are animated, to protect religion, peace, and justice'.[36]

To reinforce this new paternalistic imagery, Metternich made several minor changes to the two remaining articles. In the second article, Stourdza and the Tsar had written that the sole animating principle between governments or their subjects should be one of rendering 'reciprocal service': that they should all consider themselves as the 'members of *the same nation*, under the denomination of the Christian nation'; and that the three allied monarchs should 'consider themselves as delegates from Providence for governing three provinces of *the same nation*'. The emphasis was thus on peoples and rulers as members of a unified Christendom. Metternich changed this metaphor from three provinces of the same nation to 'three branches of the same family'.

The remainder of the second article simply acknowledged the sovereignty of Christ; this was left virtually untouched by Metternich—the three sovereigns 'confessing that the Christian world, of which they and their people form a part, has in reality no other Sovereign but Him to whom alone power really belongs …'. The three sovereigns consequently recommended to their peoples 'as the sole means of enjoying the peace that arises from a good conscience, and which alone is durable, to strengthen themselves every day in the principles and in the exercise of the duties which the Divine Saviour has taught to mankind'.

The third and final article of the Holy Alliance invited other parties to join in the agreement. The Russian draft had initially extended this invitation to all 'states', but Metternich changed this to all 'powers', perhaps suggesting some limitations on membership.[37]

By substituting just a few phrases, Metternich had skilfully altered the entire character of the proposed treaty: what the Tsar had intended as an alliance of rulers and peoples became a federation of monarchs; the appeal to all peoples to help one another became a reciprocal accord between monarchs to furnish assistance to one another, perhaps even against their own subjects. The Tsar accepted these changes to obtain the concurrence of the Emperor of Austria, and even with these changes the treaty still retained much of its original ecumenical Christian flavour.

The unveiling of the Alliance

The early victory at Waterloo had deprived the Russians of the opportunity to display their military strength. On the 10 September, the allied leaders attended the Tsar's magnificent review of 160,000 Russian troops, including 28,000 cavalry and 540 pieces of field artillery, held on the Plain of Vertus near Chalons. A 'Te Deum' was celebrated with seven altars. The Tsar was assisted by the mystic, Madame de Krüdener. Two weeks later, the Holy Alliance was unveiled. Castlereagh described how, as the Tsar gave him a copy of the alliance, he enthusiastically 'developed his whole plan of universal peace'.[38] Alexander published the treaty three months later on Christmas Day in St Petersburg, and ordered it to be read aloud in churches across Russia in March 1816.[39] The Austrian Emperor and the King of Prussia acceded to the treaty, as did most of the other countries of Europe, including even democratic Switzerland; only the Prince Regent of England and the Pope stood aloof, while the Ottoman Sultan, as a Muslim, was perforce excluded.

Castlereagh and Metternich remained wholly unsympathetic. Castlereagh had grown up in an Ireland torn by denominational strife, and the cold logic of 'New Light' Presbyterianism made him impervious to the nebulous, emotion-laden appeals of mystical religion that the Tsar found so inspirational. Castlereagh and Metternich both recognized, however, that the proposed pact might provide a useful tool for curbing Russian expansionism. The Emperor Francis 'felt great repugnance to be a party to such an act, and yet was more apprehensive of refusing'. Castlereagh reported to the British cabinet, 'it was quite clear [the Tsar's] mind was affected; that peace and goodwill was at present the idea that engrossed his thoughts'. Therefore, Metternich and the Austrian Emperor were 'unwilling to thwart him in a conception which, however wild, might save him and the rest of the world much trouble so long as it should last'. For the same reasons, Castlereagh recommended to the cabinet that the Prince Regent might also become a party:

> The fact is, that the Emperor's mind is not completely sound. Last year there was but too much reason to fear that its impulse would be to conquest and dominion. The general belief now is that he is disposed to found his own glory upon a principle of peace and benevolence ... It is, at all events, wise to profit from his disposition as far as it will carry us: and this is particularly the feeling of Austria and Prussia ...[40]

The cabinet, however, decided that the Prince Regent could not sign the treaty himself, so instead the Prince wrote a letter to the Tsar expressing his personal concurrence with its principles.

Within the Russian camp, Capodistrias' assistant, Alexander Stourdza, launched a vigorous defence of the new treaty and its principles in two essays in late 1815: 'Considérations sur l'acte d'alliance fraternelle et chrétienne du 14/26 septembre 1815' [Considerations on the act of fraternal and Christian alliance of 26 September 1815] and 'De la Sainte-Alliance' [On the Holy Alliance]. In these works, Stourdza identified Napoleon as heir to the French Revolution; his fall was the climax to a period of unprecedented disorder, commencing in 1789, which had been caused by the 'principle of subversion of every social and religious institution'. In these circumstances, there was an urgent need for the restoration of order in public life, which could only be achieved by adopting principles 'too long relegated to the sphere of domestic life'. Following the reasoning of Baader, Stourdza argued that Christianity provided the necessary 'corrective to our evils and our errors'. He discerned in Christian teachings the 'sole means to consolidate human institutions and remedy their perfections'.[41] The Holy Alliance rested on the belief that government should be founded on 'conscience, religion, morality and experience'. The alliance, once its true principles were better known, could not be violated without 'awakening the conscience' of each monarch and his people. Stourdza's reasoning was strangely reminiscent of Robespierre's speech

20 years earlier, with its clarion call to replace selfish egotism with a new morality.

The Tsar and the ecumenical Christian party who sponsored the Holy Alliance were far from lunatics, even if their vision of a Christian Europe as an antidote to the perceived evils of the French Revolution was uncongenial to Castlereagh, Metternich and most of us today. Their answer to the challenge posed by the French Revolution to the international system was clear enough: the creation of a new European federation, based on fraternal feelings and guided by Christian precepts, was the only true means for establishing perpetual peace. It was part of the same intellectual current that had inspired Chateaubriand to publish his *Genius of Christianity* [*Génie du Christianisme*] in 1802, and the German romantic poet Novalis (1772–1801) to write *Christendom or Europe* [*Die Christenheit oder Europa*] in 1799 (though first published posthumously only in 1826). Novalis had identified the source of the crisis in Europe in the conflict between two competing sets of values: the older values of tradition, hierarchy and obedience, and the new revolutionary values of freedom and universality. Only a third force, he believed, could bring these conflicting forces into balance—that of religion:

> It is impossible for secular forces to put themselves into equilibrium; only a third element, which is both secular and superworldly, can solve the problem ... Christendom must come alive again and be effective, and, without regard to national boundaries, again form a visible Church ... From the holy womb of a venerable European Council shall Christendom arise, and the task of awakening will be prosecuted according to a comprehensive divine plan. Then no one will protest any longer against Christian and secular compulsion, for the essence of the Church will be carried out under its guidance as a peaceful and formal state process.

Tsar Alexander, Alexander Stourdza, Franz Baader and Madame de Krüdener never read these words, but they shared the poet's sentiments. Just what role their very public pronouncement of Christian moral principles would play in the unfolding of actual events, however, was less obvious.

The allied occupation of France, 1815–18

In the aftermath of the second Peace of Paris, France was now occupied. The continued presence of allied troops in the north of France was intended not only to restrain French aggression, but also to provide for the King's personal safety during the critical period when the bonds of loyalty and deference were re-cemented, uniting the legitimate monarch with his subjects. The existence of such a force in March 1815 might have averted all the calamities of the Hundred Days and the bloodletting of Waterloo: 'It is quite obvious if 80 or 100,000 men had been placed in the fortresses between Valenciennes and Givet, when Napoleon landed at Cannes', wrote Castlereagh, 'the King need never have quitted Paris and the countenance alone of such a force would, in all probability, have secured to His Majesty the fidelity of such a proportion of the troops of the line of France, aided by the National Guards, as would have enabled Him to suppress the rebellion without the necessity of calling for the interference of foreign powers'.[42] The allies would not so err twice.

The allies unanimously approved the Tsar's suggestion that the Duke of Wellington be appointed as commander-in-chief of the occupation force. Wellington was also placed in charge of overseeing the construction of a string of barrier fortresses in the Netherlands, intended to provide additional security against France after the allied withdrawal.[43] Each of the great powers contributed 30,000 troops to the occupation force, while five lesser German powers (Bavaria, Württemberg, Denmark, Hanover and Saxony) formed a fifth contingent of equal number—bringing the total to 150,000 men. A special demilitarized zone was established between the French and allied army, to prevent incidents between troops. The Second Peace of Paris stipulated that the occupation would have a duration of up to five years, but Article V provided for an early termination: 'if ... the Allied Sovereigns, after having, in concert with His Majesty the King of France, maturely examined their reciprocal situation and interests, and the progress which [has] been made in France in the re-establishment of order and tranquillity, shall agree that the motives that led them to that measure have ceased to exist'.

Wellington established his headquarters in the northeast at Cambrai. In administering the occupation, Wellington kept in close touch with Louis XVIII and his ministers. The French government was also subject to the supervision of the allied ambassadors in Paris. The occupation force quickly became unpopular in France, even among the royalists. French opinion sought to reduce the force as quickly as possible and to eliminate it altogether at the first opportunity. The Duc de Richelieu sought the cooperation of the allies in ending the occupation to boost support for the King. As early as 1816, Richelieu requested an initial reduction in the number of allied troops to lessen the financial burden on France. Wellington at first opposed any reduction in the size of the occupation force, fearing that it would become unable to obtain subsistence from an unwilling populace or to suppress unrest. But he was gradually persuaded to alter his views by Madame de Staël and the weight of French public opinion. In 1817, Wellington agreed to a reduction of 30,000 men; in 1818, he was finally won over to an early withdrawal when he realized that a prolonged occupation would only render the King unpopular.

Nonetheless, the troops could not leave before the payment of reparations by France for damages caused during the Hundred Days. France owed both an indemnity of 700 million francs (£28 million) and an undefined amount of reparations based on actual damages. Demands for reparations had in fact been submitted only after the Peace of Paris had been concluded. The claims were predictably high, reaching 1,200 million francs, and the French refused to pay this astronomical sum. Castlereagh and the Tsar agreed that payment of these claims was certainly much more than the French government could afford. At the Tsar's suggestion, Wellington was chosen to judge how much compensation each of the allied powers was entitled to receive. Wellington reduced the total bill to less than one-quarter of the original demand. Of the allied powers, the Prussians alone objected, for it was mainly Prussia and the other German states that now saw their claims diminished.[44] To expedite the withdrawal of the troops, the English banker Sir Alexander Baring offered to lend the French monarchy the money it needed to pay off its debts. Baring raised one loan in London to settle the indemnity and a second with Dutch bankers to settle the payment of reparations once they had been fixed. Louis XVIII and the French government gratefully accepted the loans to relieve France of the burden of occupation. The French ultra-royalists made a surprising, clandestine eleventh-hour effort to prevent the troop withdrawal on the grounds of their nation's instability. They sent none other than the Baron de Vitrolles, who in 1814 had borne secret messages to the allies that had proved instrumental to the first Bourbon restoration. The alarming reports he carried in 1818, however, were contemptuously dismissed by the allied leaders.

The Congress of Aix-la-Chapelle, 1818

In the autumn of 1818, the proposed removal of allied troops provided the occasion for the first reunion of allied leaders since 1815. With the first great peacetime summit conference of paramount powers, an audacious experiment in international cooperation was now launched. In effect, the great powers would debate and resolve all issues amongst themselves and then hand down their verdicts to the rest of Europe. To avoid the hostility of other states, their collective hegemony was to be concealed behind a mask of seeming restraint.

Initially, there was some disagreement over the legal basis for convening the Congress. Metternich was the first to propose the rendezvous, perhaps thinking that by seizing the initiative he could limit the reunion to the four allies and keep control firmly in the hands of Austria and England. The Tsar's minister Capodistrias urged instead the inclusion of both France and Spain, who he anticipated would act as the allies of Russia. The Tsar himself wished to refer the question to the ambassadors in Paris, but Metternich asserted that the meeting should consist solely of the members of the Quadruple Alliance in its *intégrité primitive*, that is, 'in all its simplicity'. Pozzo di Borgo, the Russian ambassador in Paris, complained that Metternich intended nothing less than the 'political excommunication' of France and Spain in order 'to paralyze the actions of Russia'. From London, Castlereagh wrote that the 'real question is whether a General Congress is desirable or not'. He preferred the reunion to be viewed, not as 'supplementary to the Congress of Vienna', but as a 'special conference' on the basis of Article VI of the Quadruple Alliance, which called for meetings of the allied sovereigns at 'fixed periods' to discuss topics of mutual concern. The allies should focus on France but might also use this occasion to treat other issues, 'in order to give to their progress that useful impulse which has never failed to result from the immediate superintendance of the sovereigns when assembled together'. Nor should their discussions impede particular negotiations with the lesser powers, who, Castlereagh believed, might be consulted whenever specific matters concerned them.[45]

Castlereagh's message arrived too late for the Continental powers, who had already decided to meet on the narrower basis of Article V of the Second Peace of Paris, which simply stated that after three years the allies might concert with France for an early termination of the occupation. This narrower basis eliminated the problem of having to explain why the lesser powers remained uninvited. The ministers officially termed the gathering a '*réunion*' or '*entrevue*' (interview) rather than a 'Congress', again to avoid following the precedent set at Vienna of inviting the lesser powers to the scene of their deliberations; but in their private correspondence, the diplomats continued to refer to the assembly as a 'Congress', as do most historians. The ambassadorial conference in Paris issued a circular in late May announcing the allied decision to exclude the rest of Europe, even those German middle states with occupation troops.[46] Since the secondary states would not be participating, it was necessary to hold the reunion on allied territory. Several places were considered, but the spa town of Aix-la-Chapelle (Aachen), under Prussian rule since 1815, was chosen for its proximity to Wellington's army in the northeast of France. There may have also been some thought that the presence of the allies at Aix might dampen the nationalistic enthusiasm recently shown by German students. Fittingly, Aix had served as the location of Charlemagne's coronation 1,000 years before.

Even before the Congress began its labours, there were the typical efforts at side agreements in a flurry of *pourparlers*: Capodistrias met Metternich and Hardenberg at Carlsbad (present-day Karlovy Vary); Metternich and

Hardenberg attended the Diet of the German Confederation together on their way to Aix; and Castlereagh had originally planned to meet Metternich at Spa before the discussions at Aix got underway.[47]

The sovereigns began arriving in Aix in late September, just before the leaves began changing their colours. The Tsar was accompanied by Capodistrias, Nesselrode, Count Lieven and (over the loud objections of Castlereagh and Metternich) Pozzo di Borgo; Emperor Francis of Austria brought Metternich, Gentz and the ambassadors Lebzeltern and Zichy; King Frederick William III of Prussia took along his brother Charles as well as Hardenberg, Humboldt, the conservative Prince Wittgenstein and Count Bernstorff (only just raised, to Humboldt's distress, from his position as Danish ambassador in Berlin to the office of Prussian foreign minister); for France, the Duc de Richelieu attended with Caraman, Rayvenal and Mounier; finally, Castlereagh came with his half-brother, Lord Stewart, while the Duke of Wellington attended the Congress as the commander of the occupation forces. Several important financiers also found their way to Aix, including Alexander Baring, David Parish, Pierre César Labouchère of the Hope banking firm in Amsterdam, and two of the Rothschild brothers. So, too, did the Welsh social reformer Robert Owen, Thomas Clarkson for the anti-slavery movement, and Louis Way, an advocate for Jewish emancipation. The celebrated artist Sir Thomas Lawrence travelled to Aix to paint a series of grand portraits of the illustrious sovereigns; once there, Lawrence held his sittings for the monarchs in the town hall. The Italian soprano Angelica Catalani came to entertain the distinguished visitors; Carl von Clausewitz (the author of *On War*) was also there, as commander of the local garrison.[48]

The Emperor of Austria was greeted warmly by the Catholic inhabitants of the Rhineland; some saw his reception as a popular condemnation of the transfer of this Catholic territory to Protestant Prussia. The last of the Holy Roman Emperors paid a hushed visit to the gold and silver casket of the first (Charlemagne) in Aachen Cathedral, where he was surrounded by friendly priests as he knelt in prayer.

Something of the festive atmosphere of Vienna, though on a much smaller scale, prevailed at the reunion at Aix. The conference participants attended the customary dinners, concerts and balls, although on many evenings they just preferred to play the popular card game whist. There were balloon ascents, trips to the town's famous thermal springs, a ball on the Emperor Francis' name day and a celebration commemorating the victorious Battle of Leipzig, which Richelieu studiously avoided. The highlight of the conference was a grand review of allied troops in late October at Valenciennes. The King of Prussia and the Tsar made a brief excursion to Paris to visit Louis XVIII. Metternich threw himself into a new love affair with the Countess Lieven, the charming 34-year-old wife of the Russian ambassador in London. There was also a new presence on the scene—foreign correspondents sent to Aix by the leading London journals—thus providing something of a landmark in the history of the press.

France and the scope of the Alliance

As well as approving the withdrawal of their troops, the allies had to determine the terms of their future relationship with their former adversary. Richelieu had requested that France be permitted to join the alliance, transforming it into a pentarchy of great powers. Louis XVIII boldly instructed his minister to either join the alliance or destroy it.[49] But could France be permitted to join a confederation the chief object of which was to restrain her? Or could the nature of the alliance be altered, reshaping the coalition of former wartime allies into a broader association of great powers for the supervision of a peaceful Europe (a problem somewhat analogous to the expansion of NATO at the end of the Cold War)? This was the fundamental question confronted at Aix.

In a preliminary memorandum prepared for the British cabinet, Castlereagh argued that the purpose of the Quadruple Alliance was strictly to watch over France, so she could hardly be admitted to it. But he was also concerned that France, if spurned, might attempt to construct her own rival league of lesser states. To preserve the alliance without isolating France, Castlereagh therefore proposed that France should be invited to participate in all future periodic reunions convened under Article VI of the Quadruple Alliance. This 'expedient', he explained to the British cabinet, would 'give France her concert but keep our security'.[50]

When Castlereagh first met the Tsar at Aix-la-Chapelle on 27 September he was pleasantly surprised to find Alexander in complete agreement with him on the necessity of preserving the Quadruple Alliance. Nine-tenths of France, the Tsar told the British Foreign Secretary, were 'either corrupted by bad principles or violent party sentiments, and the remainder had little experience or ability in conducting a government, especially one of a constitutional description'. France was therefore 'still subject to a violent malady'. Under these circumstances, the Quadruple Alliance was Europe's only safeguard, and any attempt to dissolve it would constitute nothing less than a 'criminal' act. Alexander further denied the rumours that he maintained his large army for war or conquest, professing his sole aim to be the preservation of the new European system—'I have as much territory as I can desire, and more than I can well manage ... I consider my army as the army of Europe, and as such alone shall it be employed'.[51] At an audience with Metternich on

29 September, the Tsar reiterated the point that all outside speculation of dissension within the alliance was groundless.[52]

The Congress began the first of its 47 official sessions on 30 September. The allied ministers typically met in the mornings, while the Tsar passed his time with Frederick William III and the Emperor Francis. The ministers recorded the decisions reached at each conference session in a document referred to as a 'protocol'—derived from the Latin term for papers glued into a book. Each protocol was simply a register of minutes of the conference, customarily signed by the ministers present. The protocol recorded the decisions taken, but not the arguments advanced in debate. Ministers also sometimes attached various memoranda, declarations or other documents to the protocol. The same procedure had been followed by the various committees at Vienna, and would be carried on by the other congresses that followed.[53]

At the conference of 1 October, the allied ministers signed a protocol agreeing to the evacuation of the occupation force from France.[54] The alleged purpose of the Congress was thus settled at the outset. The discussions then turned to the more vexed question of the admission of France into the alliance. Metternich somewhat mystically opined that since the Quadruple Alliance (and the earlier Treaty of Chaumont) had applied principles of morality to France, the admission of France would undermine its foundations by mixing conservatism with innovation.[55] Castlereagh likewise opposed French entry into the allied coalition and circulated among the delegates an edited version of the memorandum he had prepared for the British cabinet.[56] Beyond the conference walls, Richelieu's entreaties to the Tsar to admit France into the alliance met with a harsh refusal—'How can you make such a proposition to me', the Tsar asked his old friend, 'after admitting that the internal state of France is still precarious?'[57] Without the support of the Tsar, Richelieu's bid to bring France into the Quadruple Alliance was doomed to failure. On 12 October the allied ministers unanimously agreed to preserve the Quadruple Alliance intact without France.[58] They would also maintain their continuing duties under the Treaty of Chaumont. The decision constituted a disappointing setback not only for Richelieu and Louis XVIII, but also for Pozzo di Borgo and Capodistrias, who had favoured a broader coalition of powers in which France and Spain would serve as the allies of Russia and provide a counterpoise to the Anglo-Austrian bloc.

The Russian Alliance proposal

Although the allies had accepted Castlereagh's reasoning with respect to the membership of the Quadruple Alliance, the Tsar now authorized his ministers to introduce a far-reaching proposal for the creation of a complementary league of all European states. The Tsar had several discussions beforehand with Castlereagh, who wrote to the cabinet that

> both the Tsar and his minister, Count Capo d'Istria, were, in conversation, disposed to push their ideas very far indeed, in the sense of all the Powers of Europe being bound together in a common League, guaranteeing to each other the existing order of things, in Thrones as well as in Territories, all being bound to march, if requisite, against the first Power that offended, either by her ambition, or by her Revolutionary transgressions.[59]

In fact, the Russian Chancellery had been preparing this ambitious project for many months, and on 14 October Capodistrias finally unveiled his lengthy memorandum to the allied council.[60]

The proposal began by asking how, with the evacuation of France, the allies might strengthen those moral ties protecting the French monarchy from revolution and thereby enable Europe to maintain the general peace and the treaties of 1815. The evils of the revolutionary period were ascribed both to selfishness ('egoism') and to 'partial or exclusive political combinations', by which was meant the propensity of states under the *ancien régime* to look after their own selfish interests instead of towards the common good. The memorandum then drew a distinction between the Quadruple Alliance, composed of the four allied powers, and a broader 'general alliance', which, it claimed, consisted of all the signatories of the Vienna Final Act and had as its purpose a guarantee of the *status quo* in thrones as well as territories. This general alliance both 'fixed the state of possession' and guaranteed 'the inviolability of territories as well as their legitimate representatives, or, in other terms, the principle of legitimacy'. According to the Russian memorandum, the existence of this new European system was nothing less than the 'work of Providence'.

It is worth emphasizing that the Russian memorandum did not equate this 'general alliance' with the Holy Alliance, which it described as 'moral' in nature; rather, this other alliance rested on the Vienna Final Act and the treaties of November 1815 collectively. The memorandum concluded by calling on the allied cabinets to draft a protocol specifying those events that would lead to a mobilization of their forces—i.e., the *casus foederis* of their continuing alliance. It also called for a separate declaration by the allied powers to the rest of Europe, proclaiming the existence of this broader 'general alliance', based on the solidarity of all legitimate sovereigns and guaranteeing to all states their existing territories and governments.

Against the spectre of revolutionary violence, the Tsar and Capodistrias thus hoped to erect the bulwark of a confederated Europe—a realization, in concrete form, of the spiritual precepts of the Holy Alliance. This was to be accompanied by the introduction of constitutional reforms, turning each member state into a *Rechtstaat* and transforming Europe as a whole into a federation of peaceful states, immune from revolution. In this way, Europeans would finally succeed in attaining the highest aspirations of the eighteenth-century philosophers for perpetual peace, but in a form permeated with the spirit of Christian fellowship. The Tsar's sweeping proposal was fitting from a ruler who claimed to be acting neither for his own glory, nor even for Russia, 'but in the interest of the entire universe'.[61] As one historian has rightly noted, the proposal announced at Aix was to be the fulfilment of the Russian programme of 1804: 'The grand idea of Czartoryski and Pitt would at last be realized'.[62] The Russians even suggested the creation of a common army and navy to enforce the new *Pax Europaea*.

For five long days, the allied ministers heatedly debated the Russian propositions.[63] Metternich saw advantages to the Russian proposal quite beyond their own intentions:

> the feeling of security that would follow such a transaction; [t]he moral impossibility for the Emperor Alexander to attempt any extension of his frontiers; [t]he strength which the civil party in the Prussian government would acquire over the military party, who aim only at disturbing the possessions of their neighbours; [t]he effect which such an act would produce on the minds of people and parties ...

The only disadvantage the Austrian foreign minister could foresee was the opposition of Britain: 'Ought the continental courts to reject the proposition of the Emperor Alexander because England cannot be one of its contracting parties? Ought they to conclude the treaty despite the exclusion of England?'[64]

Castlereagh, of course, argued tenaciously in favour of a narrower conception of the alliance. With Wellington's support, he affirmed that Britain would act to maintain the post-war territorial boundaries, to enforce the existing engagements against France, and even to attend the reunions held under Article VI of the Quadruple Alliance, but he told the other ministers that she would not undertake any new commitments beyond these existing obligations. He readily admitted that all European states now adhered to the Treaties of Paris and the Vienna Final Act—'the great Charte by which the territorial system of Europe, unhinged by the events of War and Revolution, has been again restored to order'. Yet, though Europe was presently 'under the protection of a moral guarantee of the highest nature', Castlereagh insisted that this was not technically an 'alliance in the strict sense of the word', since it afforded no special security or guarantee to any particular area.[65] Moreover, a universal alliance, such as the Tsar was now proposing, could never succeed in practice. Such a scheme would keep all of Europe fettered to the status quo by protecting all existing rulers, even the most unjust, without any regard to their actions:

> The idea of an 'Alliance Solidaire', by which each State shall be bound to support the state of succession, government, and possession within all other States from violence and attack, upon condition of receiving for itself a similar guarantee, must be understood as morally implying the previous establishment of such a system of general government as may secure and enforce upon all kings and nations an internal system of peace and justice. Till the mode of constructing such a system shall be devised the consequence is inadmissible, as nothing would be more immoral or more prejudicial to the character of government generally than the idea that their force was collectively to be prostituted to the support of established power without any consideration of the extent to which it was abused.[66]

The argument that Castlereagh raises here is an important one, transcending the particular circumstances of 1818. Would the Tsar's system—in effect, a novel proposal for world government—have necessarily frozen all state governments and borders in place, the bad along with the good? Was the guarantee of the status quo an essential condition of the Russian plan, based upon the belief that European rulers would willingly surrender some degree of their sovereignty *if* they thought that their own thrones and borders could thereby be preserved? Could the Tsar's proposal have been modified to permit some changes through peaceful channels—such as domestic reforms introduced from above by each nation's sovereign, like the French *Charte*, the Polish Constitution, or the constitution promised by the King of Prussia—coupled with an agreement to submit international disputes to the mediation or arbitration of the great powers (or to an even larger federation of member states), just as the philosophers of perpetual peace had originally proposed? Were European rulers anxious enough, in fact, to yield some of their sovereignty to an external tribunal of great powers in exchange for the protection of the latter from the threat of revolution, even without the security that an express guarantee of borders and thrones would have provided? In other words, was Europe ready, in response to the French Revolution, to accept an unprecedented degree of international cooperation—really, the first step towards the creation of a supra-national state? Or would the creation of such a federation, dominated by a massive Russian army, have proved top-heavy (more of a post-Napoleonic 'Warsaw Pact' than a genuine federation of independent states)?

Castlereagh contended that the most to be achieved in terms of international association was his own proposal, whereby: (1) all the states of Europe were parties to the Vienna Final Act; (2) the four allied powers had agreed, as members of the Quadruple Alliance, to collaborate in the event of French aggression; and (3) the five great powers would cooperate by interposing their good offices from time to time to settle disputes among nations. Apart from Castlereagh's theoretical objections was the simple fact that Britain remained protected by her insular location. The Continental powers, having more to fear from France and revolutionary upheaval generally, were more willing to overlook the potential problem of freezing imperfect arrangements in place for a modicum of security.

Even if Castlereagh had thought an extended alliance possible, however, his hands were tied. He no longer enjoyed the same latitude he had possessed when Britain was at war. The British cabinet, in closer proximity to Aix than Vienna, sent an incessant stream of instruction and advice. His former rival George Canning, now a cabinet member, objected strongly to any public announcement of future meetings by the allies, whether under Article VI of the Quadruple Alliance or any other basis. The proper policy for England towards Europe, Canning told the cabinet, was to interfere only in extreme emergencies, and then with decisive force.[67] Castlereagh was instructed that no specific pledge concerning periodic reunions could be brought before Parliament in the present public mood; he could therefore fix a date for the next reunion, but he could not approve any attempt by the allies to proclaim a succession of meetings as part of any permanent system. Yet Bathurst also admitted that 'the objection which I am now stating is not to the system, but to the expediency of declaring it in a circular letter'. Not surprisingly, Richelieu wrote to Louis XVIII from Aix that Castlereagh quite frankly lived in fear of Parliament: 'Every treaty or convention concerning the interests of the continent, it seems to Lord Castlereagh, will excite an opposition [in Britain] the violence and force of which he has little doubt ... His pusillanimity deprives Europe of the strongest guarantee she could have obtained for her future.'[68]

In the face of such adamant British opposition, the Tsar finally dropped his ambitious alliance proposal. The absence of British participation would have been a fatal defect to his system. This left in place Castlereagh's suggestion that France should be made a party to future allied convocations. Castlereagh explained his reasoning, which was adopted by the allies, to the British cabinet in these terms: the Quadruple Alliance of November 1815 consisted of two parts—Articles I to IV established a military alliance in case of a renewal of the war with France—'though existing as an eventual engagement, [it] may be looked upon as practically in abeyance, unless some act on the part of France, falling within the *casus foederis*, shall call it into activity'. The other part of the alliance, found in Article VI, provided for 'a Concert of Peace between the Four Powers, for the purpose of consulting upon their common Interests, and for the Maintenance of the Peace of Europe'. It was 'supposed to remain in full activity, throughout the period of Peace and Repose, as the means of [their] consolidation and conservation'.[69] It was to the latter concert that France was to be invited.

The allied ministers next agreed to draft a series of critical documents implementing their decisions. These included a protocol renewing the Quadruple Alliance without France, the specific terms of which were to be kept from Richelieu. The new protocol would be kept secret 'in order not to produce unnecessary Alarm in Europe, as well as Irritation in France'. It would define how, if one of the parties to the treaty believed a *casus foederis* had arisen, it was to bring this to the attention of the other parties; and, if new disturbances occurred in France, where and how the powers should assemble their forces to reduce unnecessary delay. The allies would also draft a second protocol, containing their invitation to France to join in the allied reunions held under Article VI of the Quadruple Alliance, and announcing to the rest of Europe the possibility of future reunions but without providing any fixed schedule. This second protocol, to be signed by Richelieu as well as the allied ministers, would of necessity be made public:

> It's object will be publicity. [Richelieu] must be enabled to explain to the Chambers and to France, the Relations in which the King is now to be placed to the other Principal States. It is also felt that the other Powers in Europe are entitled to know the nature of the Concert which has been established with France, and to be, as far as possible, assured that it is not only not of a description to prejudice their Rights, but that it forms a wise and salutary Provision for the maintenance of the existing settlement of Europe, which must be the first wish, as well as the paramount Interests of all.[70]

While Castlereagh admitted that it would probably prove necessary to lay this second document before Parliament, he hoped its deliberate designation as a conference protocol rather than as a treaty would obviate the need for any parliamentary debate or vote:

> I have thought it material to call Your Lordship's Attention to this distinction, because I apprehend that, if this principle is adhered to, it will not be necessary to call for the opinion of Parliament upon the Measure. It may be deemed right to the Prince Regent to carry the latter Document to

the knowledge of Parliament—at all counts, to accede to it's production if called for. Where the purpose is only to establish a Mode of deliberation to the decision of which the Crown is the competent Authority and where no previous Engagement is taken, binding the Crown to any other act than that of consulting to an end, which the Parliament has already sanctioned, there does not appear any Matter, upon which Parliament could possibly pronounce, at least nothing on which Ministers could becomingly ask for it's sanctions.[71]

These protocols were initially drafted by Capodistrias, but Castlereagh found them so verbose and 'otherwise objectionable' that they were rewritten by Gentz.[72] In deference to the British cabinet, no reference was made to specified periods for meetings or even to when the next assembly would take place. The proposed protocol reiterated that in the event of a revolutionary disturbance in France, the monarchs or their ministers would meet as required by the Quadruple Alliance.[73]

At the height of the discussions on the future of the alliance, the Tsar and the King of Prussia left the town of Aix for a short visit to the French King in Paris. Richelieu was astute enough to warn Louis XVIII to avoid even hinting at any desire for a special relationship with Russia: 'it is important to abstain from all that could give the Tsar any suspicion that we seek to establish a special concert between France and Russia ... He should remain persuaded that, content with our position, we have no other view than to join the other four powers to maintain an order of things founded on Christian morality and the true interests of peoples'.[74]

Castlereagh's interview with the Tsar

Shortly after the Tsar's return to Aix, he held an important audience with Castlereagh. The latter still found some of the terms of the proposed allied protocol objectionable, since they 'went unnecessarily to pronounce upon the internal affairs of France'. The Tsar and the British Foreign Secretary reviewed the protocol paragraph by paragraph. As for the section that spoke of any future revolutionary menace coming from France, Castlereagh proposed, 'for our Parliamentary convenience to alter the phrase' and to refer to the Quadruple Alliance generally.[75]

Castlereagh also defended his previous rejection of the more comprehensive Russian alliance proposal, tactfully attributing his unwillingess to accede to the Tsar's wishes to his own government's parliamentary difficulties. This certainly furnished a useful pretext for dodging the Tsar, but it also risked creating some degree of ambiguity (similar to his actions during the

Hundred Days). Did it mean that he had tacitly accepted the Russian propositions, even though he could not avow his support openly?

That the Tsar may have reached this conclusion seems evident enough, even from the report that Castlereagh himself sent to his cabinet colleagues back home. His discussion with the Tsar had turned to the Quadruple Alliance, and especially to the third article requiring the allied powers to 'concert' in the event of a new revolution in France:

> I found the Emperor's mind at first very loose [on] this part of our engagements, and under the impression that, an event occurring in France, it would give rise to the *casus foederis*, but upon a little discussion, [he] admitted that it must depend upon the nature of the event, and I think I succeeded in making him feel that it could only be judged of at this time, and that the question must be decided upon prudential considerations.[75]

Castlereagh explained to the Tsar that Britain's parliamentary system would not permit her ministers to enter into binding commitments in advance, and that acceptance of the Tsar's suggested '*alliance solidaire*' might even place his government's majority in Parliament at risk:

> This part of the interview enabled me to make the Emperor feel that in our system we could never put our decision on any other ground than on our own security, as combined with that of Europe; That we could never suffer a supposed engagement to the King of France to decide the question, without losing all our means of being of use to the cause, and that in order to render us useful as Allies, [the Emperor] must take us subject to our own modes of acting ... The Emperor entered very much into these considerations, and expressed his thanks to me, more than once, for having attracted His attention to views of our joint interests, with which his mind was very little familiar.[75]

Castlereagh deliberately played on the difficulties of his current parliamentary situation to explain his rejection of the Russian proposal:

> I told the Emperor that it was my duty to give him a correct picture of the strength and weakness of our system; That it would be for H[is] I[mperial] M[ajest]y's wisdom to draw from it the utmost resource, for the common cause of peace and order, of which it was susceptible, but, to do this, the publick mind must be managed; The nation must not be alarmed with the apprehension of war, when the danger was not at hand. The Allies

might always, under these reserves, depend on the Prince Regent and His Government for doing their utmost, in the spirit of their engagements.

I thought it material, towards the close of my audience, to speak fairly to the Emperor of the critical situation in which not only the Government, but the cause, might be placed by any proceeding here which might unnecessarily awaken contest at home; That we had a new Parliament, and a nation as intensely bent on peace and economy, now, as they had been, some years since, on war and exertion; That it was neither the same nation, nor the same Parliament now; That it would become so again, at least in a great degree, if the exigency called it forth, but that to put at issue now any new policy of eventual exertion would be to run the hazard of losing the sanction already obtained from Parliament, in favour of our continental engagements.[75]

The British Foreign Secretary referred to his need to obtain cabinet approval, but reassured the Tsar that while there might be differences in management, there was no genuine disagreement on substance:

[I]n time of war ... I had never shrunk from personal responsibility, and had, under the instructions I had received, endeavoured to avoid the inconvenient delay of frequent references, home, but that in time of peace, it was a very different case; My colleagues were entitled to see their way, and not to be embarked hastily in Parliamentary difficulties, upon the result of which it was impossible to calculate. In short, I told [him] fairly, that we could not finally sign upon our own judgement, without being assured also of the sentiments of the Government at home, whose views I was persuaded would be met with the more cordiality and consideration by H[is] I[mperial] M[ajest]y, as we were all agreed upon the substance, and it was only a question of management.[75]

The Emperor Alexander replied that he would do everything in his power to maintain the incumbent ministers in office:

The Emperor spoke very kindly of the Government, of his sense of their past exertions, and of his persuasion, that anything which affected their strength, or lowered their character in the eyes of Parliament or of the nation would essentially compromise the present continental system, of which they were known to be the authors and sincere supporters, and that he would accommodate to their convenience to the utmost, but that we must not forget what was due, both to ourselves and to France, whose exclusion, if it results from a point of form, would be most unwise, and the terms of whose introduction ought to be so managed, as not to have the aspect of being dictated by her to those powers, who were better entitled to give her the law....

I concluded my interview by explaining to the Emperor that any proceeding by treaty was inadmissible, as exposing the Government to a new vote, under disadvantageous circumstances; that the proceeding by protocol must bind us to nothing beyond existing engagements, and that, in it's form and phraseology, it must not bring too prominently into view the disputable Points.

The Emperor said he had derived satisfaction from the explanation I had given him, that he should apply himself, without delay, to see how he could combine his own views with ours, and that he hoped to be enabled to see me, the next day but one, that is, tomorrow ...[75]

The conversation between Castlereagh and the Tsar on this occasion thus took on the tone of a pleasant exchange between two old friends collaborating on the steps to be adopted to strengthen the European alliance without requiring a new vote in the British Parliament. It also seems clear from this report where the source of future ambiguity lay. Castlereagh had explained that the British could not commit themselves in advance, but they could be counted upon to act when the critical moment arrived; all that he was requesting from his allies was a concession in form to avoid embarrassment in Parliament; or, as he put it tersely, 'we were all agreed upon the substance, and it was only a question of management'. The Tsar seems to have taken this explanation as an indication that the British were, in fact, in concurrence with his own construction of the alliance. That the Russians drew the conclusion that the much sought-after guarantee was now in place is amply demonstrated by the following Russian summary, or 'de-briefing':

Whether this solid guarantee is explicitly legislated or not, whether diplomatic acts announce it as a positive or only [as] a virtual obligation, this guarantee is nonetheless sacred in the eyes of the Emperor. His Majesty finds this guarantee as the generating principle, in the sense taken literally in the [Holy Alliance] of 26 September 1815, and especially in the nature of the motives that have dictated this agreement and which have been greeted by all European governments with the most imposing unanimity.[76]

Meanwhile, with the main issues respecting the structure of the alliance seemingly resolved, the documents intended to memorialize the new arrangements were completed by 4 November. On that day, Wellington was authorized by the allies to transmit these important papers to Richelieu. The French minister presented his response to the allied ministers on the 12th.[77] Three days later, the allied ministers again read the note to Richelieu, his response, the protocol, and the declaration at their conference session and proceeded to sign the documents.[78] The public declaration on behalf of all five cabinets was issued from Aix later that same day. This announcement now became the public face of the alliance:

> The intimate union established among the monarchs, who are joint parties to this system, by their own principles, no less than by the interests of their people, offers to Europe the most sacred pledge of its future tranquillity ... The Sovereigns, in forming this august union, have regarded as its fundamental basis their invariable resolution never to depart, either among themselves, or in their relations with other states, from the strictest observation of the principles of the right of nations; principles, which, in their application to a state of permanent peace, can alone effectually guarantee the independence of each government, and the stability of the general association ...

The sovereigns declared that they would adhere to these principles in their own face-to-face meetings as well as in those of their ministers. They further pledged to discuss matters affecting the lesser states on their invitation and with their participation. The Congress System, if limited in scope, had become an established fact of European life.

On the same day that this declaration was published, the allied military committee, presided over by the Duke of Wellington, finalized its secret contingency arrangements in the event of a renewed contest with France: within two months of the occurrence of any *casus foederis*, British soldiers were to be ready at Brussels, the Prussians at Cologne (Köln), and the Austrians at Stuttgart; a month afterwards, the Russians were to be assembled at Mainz.

The allied ministers at Aix also agreed to terminate the special supervisory role of the allied ambassadorial conference in Paris over the French government. France was now a fully fledged member of the alliance, but the Quadruple Alliance remained quietly in the background to deal with any resurgence of her former revolutionary energies.

A guarantee of borders, not thrones?

Just when it seemed that the debate on the scope of the alliance was over, the Russian ministers introduced a modified version of their original plan—this time seeking a guarantee of territories but not of thrones. The idea seems to have originated in a memorandum drafted by the Prussian official Ancillon (a relative of Gentz's) and communicated to the Russian Court in 1816. It is unclear whether Hardenberg was caught by surprise. On the one hand, he recorded in his diary that the proposal appeared to come 'from a paper originating out of our cabinet'; on the other, Castlereagh reported that Hardenberg had given him the plan before the conference.[79] In any event, the Prussians remained extremely concerned over their ability to withstand the initial blows of a French attack, especially since the German Confederation had failed to finalize its plans for a federal army before the evacuation of allied troops from France.[80] Perhaps the Prussian generals, unknown to Hardenberg, had raised the issue of a territorial guarantee with their Russian counterparts.[81] One historian, for example, found Ancillon's original 11-page treaty of guarantee (*Garantievertrag*) in the Prussian State Archives, bundled with other documents from the Congress of Aix-la-Chapelle.[82] In the Austrian archives, there is likewise a Russian communication, dated 22 November 1818, transmitting a copy of Ancillon's proposal for reciprocal guarantees.[83]

Another researcher found a copy of a similar treaty in the Russian archives, also in a folio marked 'Aix-la-Chapelle, 1818'. The provisions of this draft treaty bore an uncanny resemblance to the 'Grand Design' of Sully and the proposals of the Abbé Saint-Pierre. The document complained of the shortcomings of the allied declaration of 15 November, and urged the need for a more 'explicit' guarantee of borders, based on 'a definition of mutual obligations':

> 1st. The conduct of the nations will be guided by a rule binding upon each and all: an engagement to remain within the present territorial limits fixed in Europe by the last treaties, and an intention not to attempt to expand these same, unless with the approval of the Alliance or in the case of voluntary agreements.
>
> 2d. They mutually guarantee the respective territories as fixed by these treaties and promise to make common cause against any state seeking to trouble the general peace. This clause shall become immediately effective.[84]

There was no comparable provision, however, for a guarantee of thrones. Like the later Covenant of the League of Nations (1919), this proposal called for action by the future federation against 'aggressors'—here defined as those who sought to change existing borders without the prior approval of the alliance. Certainly this more limited guarantee would have eliminated Castlereagh's objection to keeping 'legitimate' but manifestly unjust rulers in power. Metternich might have accepted this more limited form of guarantee, which could have been used to restrain Russia, Prussia or France, but

Castlereagh feared that, even in this more limited form, the guarantee would still provide a standing pretext for Russian interference in Central Europe.

According to Castlereagh, Metternich was initially embarrassed by this new proposal, which he considered 'as growing out of an exaggerated spirit of alarm on the part of Prussia' and a 'romantick feeling' on the part of the Tsar, who frequently referred to the guarantee that the allies had discussed at Vienna but had never concluded—'the idea contained in which he has often wished to realize, namely, to make a general Alliance against the Power that should first break the peace'. Castlereagh endeavoured to persuade Metternich to resist the scheme. Among other arguments, he raised the objection that the proposal would give the German states a confusing new choice of appealing either to the German Confederation or to Europe as a whole. Nevertheless, Castlereagh feared that the Austrian foreign minister still saw the proposed guarantee as an 'antidote' to the 'spirit of military conquest of the Prussian army'. He soon learned that Metternich had in fact come to an understanding with Hardenberg in favour of the proposed guarantee, but also 'not to admit any system of guarantee embracing all states' and 'not to agree to any which should not save the Germanic Confederacy from having its states interfered with or withdrawn'. Hardenberg and the King of Prussia then paid a visit to the Tsar, in which they expressed their fears over 'the exposed position in which Prussia was placed' and proposed that the German Confederation should be included in the guarantee as a single entity, rather than as individual states.[85]

The allied statesmen thus reduced Ancillon's original proposal to a reciprocal guarantee of the borders of the four Continental powers (Austria, France, Prussia and Russia), joined by the Netherlands and the German Confederation. The rest of Europe simply lay outside its scope. Castlereagh told Metternich that even in this narrower form 'it was utterly impossible for England to make herself a party to all the questions and possible wars with which such a combination might have to deal—that the insular position of England was such as to destroy all principle of reciprocity'.[86] Yet the ministers of the five great powers apparently agreed to the proposal: even Castlereagh gave his consent, despite his personal reservations, since Britain would be excused 'from the onerous part of the obligation'. Castlereagh warned Hardenberg that Prussia's chief security was still to be found in the Quadruple Alliance, while he recommended to the British cabinet that they should consider adhering to the new guarantee since the other powers were only requesting 'the general concurrence and good offices' of the Prince Regent. Castlereagh thought the plan might even provide some degree of protection against Russian power—'If the Emperor should court such a system as a pledge to Europe of his pacifick intentions, as a sort of guarantee against himself, embracing even the dominions of the Porte [Ottoman Turkey] in Europe, ought Europe to refuse it, if it is reduced within practicable limits?' Such a limited guarantee might even give Britain greater rights of interference on the Continent, if her future interests so demanded.[87] The details of the new guarantee however, could not be worked out before the Tsar's departure from Aix, and in the end nothing ever came out of this proposal, just like those that had preceded it.[88] According to Gentz, this was principally because of British opposition. The Prussians further floated the idea of placing an allied army of observation in the Netherlands with Wellington at its head, an idea actually first suggested by the British before the Congress; but this, too, was rejected as more likely to provoke the French than to protect the allies.[89]

The Spanish-American colonies

Despite the pre-Congress announcement from Paris ostensibly limiting the scope of the discussions at Aix, the ministers of the great powers dealt with a host of other issues besides the evacuation of France. The allies saw their reunion as an important opportunity for addressing all matters of mutual concern, ranging across Europe and even stretching beyond the Atlantic Ocean to the shores of the Americas. In the heyday of great-power cooperation, the Congress of Aix-la-Chapelle provides the most vivid demonstration of how the Congress statesmen intended the new system to operate. As at Vienna four years earlier, the great powers—including Bourbon France—discussed issues amongst themselves and made determinations affecting the rest of Europe. With overwhelming military power at their disposal, the five great powers formed a pentarchy capable of imposing their will on the entire Continent whenever they could reach their own consensus.

The most important of the subsidiary issues facing the statesmen at Aix by far was that of formulating a response to Spain's urgent entreaties for assistance in crushing the rebellions then spreading like wild fire through her colonies in South America. Here was an opportunity for the allies not merely to theorize about the virtues of allied cooperation, but actually to put them into practice. Dmitri Tatishchev, the Russian ambassador in Madrid, had originally hoped to invite a Spanish plenipotentiary to participate in the Congress precisely on these grounds, but found himself stymied by Britain. It was Castlereagh, however, who raised the issue of the Spanish American colonies before the assembled ministers on 23 October.[90]

Earlier Spanish attempts to obtain assistance

A decade earlier, as Secretary of State for War and Colonies, Castlereagh had been among those who had encouraged the same colonists to declare their independence from French-dominated Spain.[91] Following the example of Spain herself, the colonists had established local juntas during the French occupation with which British merchants, cut off from Continental Europe by Napoleon, had developed a thriving trade. In 1814, Ferdinand VII had disappointed the colonists and British merchants alike by attempting to re-impose Spain's old navigation laws restraining colonial trade. Indeed, the restored monarchy's commercial policies had helped to trigger a new wave of rebellion. Now, the question was whether or not to help the Spaniards restore colonial rule.

In August 1817, a year before the conferences at Aix, Castlereagh had informed the government in Madrid that five prerequisites needed to be met before Britain could agree to act as mediator in the dispute: (1) Spain had to sign a treaty abolishing the slave trade; (2) Spain should offer a general amnesty to all the insurgents; (3) South Americans should enjoy the same legal rights as the King's subjects in Spain; (4) South America should be granted the benefits of free commerce—enabling the British to continue their trade—with 'a fair preference' given to Spanish goods; and finally, (5) Spain should acknowledge that any proposed mediation could not 'assume an armed character' but must be 'confined within the bounds of good offices'.[92] In other words, the British would mediate but would not intervene militarily to help Ferdinand suppress the rebellions.

Commercial considerations weighed especially heavily on the British. Only a month before leaving for Aix-la-Chapelle, Castlereagh confided to the Austrian ambassador in London that he would take no steps that might injure British trade with South America: after spending millions in the Peninsular Wars to restore the Spanish Bourbons, Castlereagh asked rhetorically, 'How could I present to Parliament a clause that would place our commerce in that part of the world into other hands?'[93]

After being refused by the British, the Spanish ministers had turned to Paris and St Petersburg. They complained loudly that the British mediation, by excluding the possibility of armed intervention, would simply be scorned by the rebels. Richelieu had responded favourably, but requested more information about the terms that Spain was actually willing to offer to the colonists. In June 1818, the Spanish government sent a circular note to France and the allies offering four points as the basis for a settlement: a general amnesty for the rebels; equality of honours and offices for *creoles* (those of Spanish blood born in the Americas) and *peninsulares* (those born in Spain); Ferdinand VII would adopt those measures recommended by the allies; and trade with the colonies would be governed by liberal principles.[94] In the meantime, another crisis had arisen in South America. In the summer of 1817, a force from Brazil had invaded territory in the La Plata region (Buenos Aires and Uruguay), which was claimed by both Portugal and Spain. The two Iberian kingdoms sought allied mediation, even though the question would become moot if the colonists secured their independence. Richelieu considered the possibility of helping Spain or, if Spanish rule could not be restored, of establishing new Bourbon monarchies across the Atlantic.[95]

Thus, by 1818, the battle lines were clearly drawn and the fate of much of the 'New World' hung in the balance: South American colonists were asserting their independence; the King of Spain sought moral and military assistance from his fellow European rulers; Russia and France were sympathetic to his pleas; and Britain, which controlled the sea routes, was opposed to armed intervention by the allies on both moral and commercial grounds.

The discussions at Aix

At Aix, Castlereagh told the allied ministers that 'in no case would England take an active part in steps against the insurgents, even if the most suitable propositions were made by Spain'. He then read the prior communications between London and Madrid to the assembled delegates and emphasized, as the Russian minister Nesselrode reported to the Tsar, that 'England believes herself obliged to declare that in no case can her intervention be hostile to the insurgents; at the same time, she cannot give them any guarantee of Spain's good faith in fulfilling the engagements that she entered with them or in maintaining concessions she accorded them'. Nesselrode observed that 'Lord Castlereagh mixed his explanation with so many details regarding his parliamentary position as to give the impression that this concern alone served as the basis for his reasoning'. In a separate report, Capodistrias concurred in Nesselrode's appraisal: 'The long narrative of the British plenipotentiary tended to give the feeling at the conference that in this matter his government consulted above all else its own parliamentary convenience.'[96] It was the same complaint that Richelieu had earlier voiced to Louis XVIII.

At a second conference on South America, held the very next day, Castlereagh proposed that the five powers should collectively address Madrid, offering joint mediation on the basis of their 'good offices', but without armed support. He advised the Spanish government to grant those South American provinces still firmly under Spanish rule the same concessions that were being offered to those in open revolt. The British Foreign Secretary especially feared that if allied force were applied on Spain's behalf, the alliance would bear moral responsibility for all measures, no matter how punitive or mistaken, that the Spanish government later enacted.

The diplomats' attention turned to whether it was actually necessary for the allies to avow publicly in advance that their intervention would be unarmed and pacific when it was precisely armed intervention that Spain sought. The

Russians and French feared that any such declaration would actually encourage the insurgents to persevere in their rebellion. Capodistrias agreed that the allied powers should not intervene militarily, but he felt that by their silence the allies might at least induce some uneasiness among the rebels, which could have a beneficial effect. Castlereagh repeated his earlier arguments, with Metternich's support, while the Prussians silently aligned themselves with Britain and Austria. Richelieu insisted that he could not agree to a resolution so prejudicial against Spain without first discussing it with that court, and he greatly regretted that Castlereagh had so emphatically opposed Madrid's request to send a delegate to Aix. Capodistrias suggested that the allies address a collective note to Madrid, asking the Spanish government for its own views and for an explanation of how they planned to pacify the colonies.

The long debate ultimately produced no concrete result, other than an instruction to Gentz to draft an exposé identifying the main points of agreement and disagreement.[97] Castlereagh, at least, was satisfied: 'The conferences which have taken place on the question of the Spanish colonies have been productive of the most essential advantage', he told the cabinet with marked delight.

> It seems admitted that the five Powers distinctly understand each other to the extent that force is not to be employed, and that this important fact is to be made clear, not only to each other but to the Government of Spain. It seems also understood that they can neither proceed with any hope of success, nor with any attention to character and justice, unless Spain as a preliminary act shall be prepared to give its faithful provinces the same measure of advantage which it proposes, through mediation, to offer to those in revolt.[98]

Castlereagh was able to browbeat the other ministers at Aix because of the vital importance of sea power in influencing events across the Atlantic. His aim was not to help the rebels but to persuade Spain to make reasonable concessions. If this failed, Castlereagh would have preferred to see the erection of pro-British constitutional monarchies in South America over the rise of democratic republics friendlier to the United States.[99] Ten days later Castlereagh addressed Metternich on the same subject, reiterating his arguments.[100] Rumours that the United States might recognize the independence of Buenos Aires arrived while the ministers were still at Aix. To Castlereagh's surprise, the Russians and French urged that Wellington be sent to Madrid on behalf of the five great powers, to preside over an ambassadorial conference on Spanish America that even a representative from the United States might attend.[101] Capodistrias and Nesselrode further proposed that the allies impose economic sanctions on the rebellious colonies, but Castlereagh objected to this measure, which would have been highly detrimental to British commerce.[102]

Wellington and Castlereagh resolved to clarify British views on Latin America at their final audiences with the Tsar, but only if the Russian Emperor raised the topic first. Wellington was unsuccessful, but Castlereagh found his opening even as the Tsar's horses were being hitched to his carriage. For his part, Alexander promised the British Foreign Secretary to stop his diplomatic agents from raising false expectations in Madrid.[103] Thus, in the end the Continental powers agreed to toe the British line—offering Wellington as a mediator, but only if the Spanish would first accept all five conditions previously stipulated by the British government. In fact, Wellington declined to serve, partly on the grounds that the insurgents could not be properly represented.[104]

It has been argued by some historians that the New World was deliberately excluded from the operations of the Congress System. Paul Schroeder adduces that the two world hegemons, Britain and Russia, each wanted to preserve its own special 'sphere of influence'—the Ottoman Empire for Russia and the Americas for Britain. In reality, the extension of the alliance into both spheres was carefully considered. At Aix, the powers might well have intervened in Latin America if the Spanish had promptly accepted the British conditions. London's consent to any allied intervention in the Americas was certainly a necessary prerequisite due to her overwhelming naval power. The British did not intend to sacrifice their commercial interests in Latin America either to Spain—if allied intervention was successful—or to the United States—if it were not. Actions against the South American rebels would also have been overwhelmingly unpopular in Parliament. In fact, many of those helping the rebels were British, including Lord Cochrane, commander of the rebel Chilean fleet. But Castlereagh was willing to permit mediation under certain circumscribed conditions. Indeed, discussions on these issues continued in ambassadorial conferences well after the meetings in Aix ended. The mediation between Spain and Portugal was moved to Paris, while the question of mediation between Spain and her colonies continued to be debated by Castlereagh and the allied ambassadors in London. The Tsar even sent Capodistrias on a special mission to Paris and London not long after the Congress of Aix-la-Chapelle in a fresh effort to resolve these thorny issues.[105]

Other issues at Aix

Other matters considered at Aix included enforcement of the Treaty of Kiel against Sweden, execution of the terms of the Vienna Settlement with respect to the territorial exchanges between the German states of Bavaria and Baden, suppression of the Barbary pirates, the treatment of Napoleon on St Helena, complaints against the Prince of Monaco, the claims of Hesse, and further discussions on the slave trade, the emancipation of the German Jews and issues of diplomatic etiquette.[106] It is worth looking at a few of these subjects in closer detail. The allied ministers were also becoming increasingly alarmed at events in Germany, discussed in the next chapter.

The suppression of the slave trade and the Barbary pirates

At Aix the British continued to press for the 'right of visit' to suppress the slave trade, as they had at Vienna. Thomas Clarkson, one of the original founders of the British Committee for the Abolition of the Slave Trade in 1787, even travelled to Aix-la-Chapelle. Castlereagh had previously requested a statement by the allied powers, addressed to Portugal, urging abolition of the slave trade, as well as a convention for a mutual right of limited search. At Aix, the allied ministers signed the letter to Portugal, but they remained suspicious of the British demand for a 'right of visit', even if it were made reciprocal. The French simply would not allow their ships to be searched by the British Royal Navy.[107]

Meanwhile, the Barbary pirates on the coasts of North Africa continued to raid shipping in the Mediterranean, taking captives to be sold into horrifying conditions of slavery. Discussions for the suppression of the pirates were held at Vienna and continued in an ambassadorial conference in London in 1816.[108] They posed less of a danger to ships flying the British flag after Lord Exmouth bombarded the city of Algiers that same year. At Aix, Tsar Alexander suggested the formation of a European 'maritime league' to suppress the Barbary pirates. He even tried to combine the problems of piracy and slavery by proposing that the slave trade be declared to be a form of piracy, that all Christian states establish a new international anti-slavery organization with an independent judicial court in Africa and its own fleet and, finally, that all nations should recognize the 'right of visit' vested in this new international agency. In London, the British Admiralty frowned on the idea of yielding its supremacy in the Mediterranean to any international force. Fortunately for the British, there was no need to respond immediately to the Tsar since he did not plan to implement his proposal for five years, when Portugal was finally scheduled to join in the prohibition of the slave trade. Consequently, no agreement was reached at Aix regarding either the creation of an international maritime league or the elusive 'right of visit'. But the discussions continued even after the Congress was over since these issues were also referred to the ambassadorial conference in London.[109]

The Jews of Germany

Despite the best efforts of the diplomats at the Congress of Vienna, Frankfurt and the Hansa towns of Northern Germany had rescinded the rights earlier extended to their Jewish citizens. In 1817, the Prussian government borrowed a large sum from the Rothschilds to meet its financial obligations. In exchange for the loan, the Rothschilds asked for Prussian support in the German Federal Diet on the issue of Jewish rights. Friedrich von Gentz was also receiving substantial personal loans from the Rothschilds. Two of the Rothschild brothers attended the Congress at Aix-la-Chapelle, where Gentz introduced them to Metternich.[110] Lewis Way, a nephew of Castlereagh's assistant Edward Cooke, hoped to convert Jews to Christianity; he was also a strong advocate for Jewish rights. Way had visited Prussia and Russia the previous year, when he had been received by the Tsar. At Alexander's invitation, Way also attended the Congress of Aix-la-Chapelle. With the enthusiastic support of the Tsar, Metternich and Gentz, a special protocol of the Congress re-affirmed the rights of German Jews already included in the Vienna Final Act.[111] Again, however, these measures would largely prove ineffectual. In Frankfurt, the anti-Semitic 'Hep' riots occurred in August 1819, and Jews remained second-class citizens until as late as 1864.[112]

The imprisonment of Bonaparte

The treatment of Napoleon as a prisoner on St Helena was yet another topic discussed at Aix. British reports, as well as the appeals of Napoleon's mother to the Tsar and of Napoleon's brother to Metternich, were read before the allied ministers, who unanimously approved of British conduct. The allies remained suspicious of possible schemes to rescue Bonaparte and as a result of their discussions at Aix, Napoleon's communications with the outside world were further curtailed.

Enforcement of the Treaty of Kiel

Under the Treaty of Kiel, Denmark had given Norway to Sweden, but Bernadotte still refused to fulfil Sweden's promise to pay compensation to Denmark. There was also the problem that Bernadotte was refusing to assume the Norwegian debt. At Aix, Castlereagh persuaded the Tsar to place greater pressure on Sweden. The four allied powers recognized their right and 'even their obligation' to intervene in Scandinavia. They sent the Austrian ambassador, Count de Ficquelmont, to Stockholm with identical notes in protest, finally compelling Sweden to fulfil its obligations under the treaty.[113]

* * *

The Congress of Aix-la-Chapelle, largely overlooked by historians today, marked not only the commencement of the Congress System, but also its apogee. The Congress of Vienna had focused on negotiating a territorial settlement; later Congresses would be summoned in direct response to specific crises. There were no corresponding necessities at Aix: the evacuation of allied troops provided a mere pretext for the assembly, but could easily have been accomplished without it. The true aim of Aix was to solidify and perpetuate the post-war system of allied cooperation and conference diplomacy.

Writing to his wife, Metternich said he had 'never seen a prettier little Congress'.[114] Gentz extolled the display of allied unity at Aix as the principal means of salvation for a continent still under siege by the dark forces of the revolution:

> All European countries, without exception, are tormented by a burning fever, the companion or forerunner of the most violent convulsions which the civilized world has seen since the fall of the Roman Empire. It is a struggle, it is war to the death between old and new principles, and between the old and a new social order ... If, in this dreadful crisis, the principal sovereigns of Europe were disunited in principles and intentions ... we should be all carried away in a very few years. But happily, such are not the dispositions of the princes who are protectors and preservers of public order; their intimate union, calm and constant in its action, is the counterpoise to the disorder which turbulent spirits try to bring into human affairs ... Now, this truly sacred union, of which the Holy Alliance is but an imperfect symbol, was never manifested in a more reassuring manner than at the time of the conferences at Aix-la-Chapelle ... Sovereigns and ministers understood what was required. They felt keenly the need of mutual confidence and more direct agreement than that which treaties could establish; they sacrificed secondary interests, which under less serious circumstances, might have divided them, to the paramount interest of uniting to defend the trust which Providence had confided to them, and put aside every other consideration, to preserve authority in the shipwreck by saving the people from their own follies ... Thus it is that the Congress of Aix-la-Chapelle has fulfilled its high mission. The general impression it has made in Europe is its best witness ... [I]t has everywhere encouraged the friends of order and peace, and terrified innovators and the factious.[115]

While the Tsar may have believed that the allied powers had consolidated a broader agreement at Aix, in Castlereagh's view the main benefits of the new European alliance were found less in its solemn guarantees than in the simple advantages afforded by continuing the practice of face-to-face diplomacy. After the invention of the telegraph, telephone, television, mobile phone and Internet, it is almost impossible for us today to imagine the nearly complete absence of direct contact and the dearth of information between statesmen that existed two centuries ago. By meeting in person, Castlereagh felt the ministers were able to remove misunderstandings and to harmonize their interests. Coming directly from Aix, he wrote to the cabinet enthusiastically:

> At all events, it is satisfactory to observe how little embarrassment and how much solid good grow out of these reunions, which sound so terrible at a distance. It really appears to me to be a new discovery in the European Government, at once extinguishing the cobwebs into which diplomacy obscures the horizon, bringing the whole bearing of the system into its true light, and giving to the great Powers the efficiency and almost the simplicity of a single state.[116]

A younger politician (and future Prime Minister) would later recall how Castlereagh had once explained to him that 'one of the great difficulties' in ordinary diplomacy was

> the want of an habitual confidential and free intercourse between the Ministers of the Great Powers *as a body*; and that many pretensions might be modified, asperities removed, and causes of irritation anticipated and met, by bringing the respective parties into unrestricted communications common to them all, and embracing in confidential and united discussions all the great points in which they were severally interested.[117]

This all makes perfect sense, especially when we consider that Castlereagh was above all a pragmatic politician who preferred private negotiation, removed from the scrutiny of the public or of competing powers. Congresses like Aix-la-Chapelle not only reduced the tendency of statesmen to demonize their opponents, they also vastly increased the opportunities for direct bargaining. Only the face-to-face contact that the new Congress System afforded could allow for the kind of horse-trading at the international level that had once enabled the young Castlereagh to win over the Irish House of Commons—what Sir Harold Nicolson would later call the British 'shopkeeper' approach to diplomacy. Even where final resolutions were not reached at Aix, several of the key discussions continued in ambassadorial conferences. The Congress System was in full swing.

Part Three

DIPLOMACY

The art of negotiation with princes is so important that the fate of the greatest states often depends upon the good or bad conduct of negotiations and the capabilities of the negotiators.
    François de Callières, *On the Manner of Negotiating with Princes*, 1716

At all events, it is satisfactory to observe how little embarrassment and how much solid good grow out of these reunions, which sound so terrible at a distance. It really appears to me to be a new discovery in the European Government.
    Lord Castlereagh to Lord Liverpool, 20 October 1818

If we are successful, everyone will wish to share our success with us … If we fail, our closest allies at the time will assure us that they were never of our way of thinking. Such is the way with all human undertakings that offer serious chances of danger and success.
    Prince Metternich to Prince Esterhazy, 2 February 1821

The precise aim of [all] malcontents is one and the same. It is the overthrow of everything legal … The principle which monarchs must oppose to their plan of universal destruction is the preservation of everything legal.
    Prince Metternich to Tsar Alexander, May 1821

The sole aim of the alliance is that for which it was formed: to combat revolution.
    Tsar Alexander to the Comte de La Ferronnays, 27 October 1822

5

The Alliance in Operation, 1819–20

Central Europe and the Carlsbad Decrees

After 1815, the principal goal of European statesmen shifted from defeating Bonaparte to combating the threat of social revolution. In the minds of the conservative ruling class, a great upheaval was being planned by a conspiracy of secret Jacobin societies, spread throughout Europe and governed by a mysterious central directory. Such convictions, as fantastic as they may appear to us today, seem to have been genuinely held. The proliferation of secret revolutionary societies in Italy, France, Spain and the rest of Europe gave them a semblance of reality. In this atmosphere, concessions to liberalism, especially the creation of new representative assemblies, were anathema.

Metternich's reform proposals

To Metternich, the preservation of the existing social hierarchy, the maintenance of the authority of legitimate sovereigns and the rule of law were virtually indistinguishable. Even so, Metternich was not opposed to every change or reform. But his notion of reform was one that improved the efficiency of established authority, not its representativeness. Rulers might govern more effectively by being better informed about their subjects' wishes, but not by alienating their sovereign authority. In multi-ethnic Austria in particular, recognition of the representative principle might have led to a dissolution of the monarchy. At the same time, Metternich often found himself frustrated by the random and inefficient methods of governing the Austrian Empire, which he feared would ultimately weaken Habsburg power. Like other statesmen of his day, he had been favourably impressed by the efficiency of Napoleonic despotism. Just as Speransky in Russia and Stein and Hardenberg in Prussia had proposed reforms based on the Napoleonic model, Metternich submitted a series of proposals for administrative reform in 1811 and 1817 (that is, both during and after the Napoleonic epoch), which would have reorganized and regularized the system of imperial government.

Under Metternich's suggested scheme, a council of state, or *Staatsrat*, would have advised the Emperor; this council might have even been expanded to include representatives from the provincial diets. Metternich further proposed that, prior to making some decisions, the Emperor might also consult a separate council of his key ministers, composed of the heads of the various government departments (*Hofstellen*). In domestic politics, Metternich thus stood as the advocate of monarchical absolutism tempered by the recommendations of a centralized state council. Some historians have gone so far as to suggest that the implementation of these proposals would have promoted federalism and greater flexibility within the Austrian Empire, although this view remains controversial. Historian Alan Sked argues convincingly that Metternich simply wanted to replace the Emperor's method of receiving advice from conflicting written memoranda with a deliberative council in which proposals were discussed orally and final decisions were reached for recommendation to the Emperor. In the event, Metternich's plans for internal reform simply gathered dust in the Emperor's desk drawer. Metternich's failure to secure moderate administrative reform in Austria may have added to his hostility to constitutional reform in the rest of Germany, but it seems more likely that he opposed these changes out of his existing fears that they would play into the hands of the revolutionary party.[1]

Structure of the German Confederation

As a result of the Napoleonic Wars and the Congress of Vienna, the number of separate polities in Germany had been reduced to 39 (including Austria). Of these, only seven had populations greater than one million.[2] It has already been seen that the Act of Confederation inaugurated the German Confederation (*Bund*) as a replacement for the former Holy Roman Empire. The authors of the Confederation hoped that the German states would look to each other for support, instead of aligning with the great powers and inviting continuous wars; the primary purpose of the new Confederation was to erect a common defence against French aggression. Each member state further promised to grant a constitution (*landständische Verfassung*); the original intent behind this provision had been to consolidate new governments and to bind subjects more closely to their rulers. While some patriots had hoped that the new diet, or assembly of the Confederation (*Bundesversammlung*), would serve as the voice of the German nation, Metternich and the other statesmen at Vienna structured the federal organization to represent Germany's independent rulers, not its people. The middle states—such as Bavaria, Baden and Württemberg in Southern Germany—were given a disproportionate influence in the Diet, making it likely to protect states' rights, while the Act of Confederation could not be amended without the unanimous approval of all the member states.[3]

At the state level, the middle states of Germany were struggling to organize viable governments, defeat the claims of the older estates and mediatized princes for special privileges, and strengthen the loyalties of their subjects. Bavaria, the largest of the middle states, had nourished an ambitious programme for territorial expansion, but this unravelled when the Bavarians were forced to return Salzburg to Austria. Austria promised to support Bavarian territorial claims against Baden, but these were overruled by the mediation of the great powers in the aftermath of the Congress of Aix-la-Chapelle. While the peaceful resolution of the dispute has been heralded as a victory for the new Congress System, these quarrels made it quite impossible for the middle states to cooperate as a 'Third Germany' counteracting the influence of Austria and Prussia.

German nationalism and the *Burschenschaften*

Notwithstanding the weaknesses of the Confederation and of the resistance of the restored German state governments, embers of German nationalism and liberalism yet burned. Students and professors who had earlier enlisted in the struggle to liberate Germany from French rule continued to call for greater national unity—'above all', wrote one prominent student leader to his father in 1818, 'we want Germany to be considered one land and the German people one people'.[4] Enlightened members of the state bureaucracies, men such as Hardenberg and Humboldt, also continued their efforts to achieve some measure of modernization and political reform. In many German states, educated jurists, academics and civil servants (*Bildungsbürgertum*) eclipsed the commercial classes (*Besitzbürgertum*) in importance. In the absence of a more developed middle class, these professors, students, lawyers and state bureaucrats became the chief repositories of German liberal thought.

Universities were the principal breeding grounds of German nationalism because it was at these institutions of higher learning that new and bold ideas could most freely be discussed. An embryonic national spirit was fostered by the fact that universities were attended by students and scholars from all over Germany, not only from those states where they were located. Students organized themselves into *Burschenschaften*, fraternal associations without regard for provincial origin, which replaced the duelling and drinking clubs of the previous century. The first *Burschenschaft* was formed at Jena in 1815; other universities in Southern and Central Germany quickly followed suit by forming their own branches. Members idealistically adopted *Ehre, Freiheit und Vaterland* ('Honour, Freedom and Fatherland') as their motto. There was also a seamy underside to the movement, with elements of xenophobia and even anti-Semitism.[5]

As a demonstration of their solidarity, more than 500 *Burschenshaft* members gathered in 1817 at the Wartburg, where Martin Luther had translated the Bible into German three centuries before. The students joyously commemorated both the German Reformation and the allied victory over Napoleon at Leipzig in 1813. They marched from the town marketplace to a nearby castle, where they feasted and listened to patriotic speeches. Next they proceeded to church where they heard a stirring sermon, followed by outdoor gymnastic exercises. As night fell, the students stood around a triumphant bonfire, burning symbols of political repression, such as a corporal's cane and reactionary tracts—including works by Ancillon and Schmalz, conservative advisors to the King of Prussia—just as Luther had once burned papal bulls. Metternich, Gentz, Stourdza and other European conservatives were aghast. They felt that a revolution in Germany might be even more dangerous than the one in France. George Rose, the English ambassador in Berlin, described the student activities at the Wartburg in lurid terms as 'a scandalous scene of revolutionary effervescence'.[6]

The following year, despite criticism from both the Austrian and Prussian governments, the liberal Grand Duke Karl August of Saxe-Weimar permitted student representatives from 14 universities to meet at Jena in October 1818 to form the General German Student Organization (*Allgemeine deutsche Burschenschaft*). Gentz was unabashedly appalled:

> The *allgemeine Burschenschaften* is based expressly and essentially upon the idea of German unity, and to be sure, not merely an idealistic or literary unity, but rather a true political unity. It is also revolutionary in the highest and most frightful sense of the word ... [T]he unity towards which these Jacobins have been striving continuously for six years cannot be realized without the most turbulent of revolutions, without the overthrow of Europe.

The real battle for the future of Germany, however, was not being waged at the universities but between liberals and conservatives within the state bureaucracies. Article XIII of the Act of Confederation had called for new constitutions, but were these to include assemblies based on national systems of representation or traditional estates (*altständische Verfassung*)?

By 1819, most of the Southern states—Bavaria, Baden, Württemberg, Hesse-Darmstadt and Nassau—had promulgated constitutions loosely modelled after the French *Charte*, in part to eliminate traditional privileges and in part to preserve their own sovereignty vis-à-vis the Confederation. These new constitutions had also established freedom of the press, religious toleration and equality before the law.[7]

The Prussian reform movement

Even in Prussia, the forces of movement and reaction were locked in mortal combat. Here, as in so many other parts of Europe, the kingdom stood at a genuine fork in the road, which had the potential of becoming a major turning point. In the aftermath of the Prussian defeat at Jena in 1806, Prussia had inaugurated a series of major reforms—the abolition of serfdom and guilds, the creation of municipal governments and the formation of a popular militia as a reserve force (*Landwehr*). Hardenberg had announced financial reforms in October 1810, abolishing noble tax exemptions. The same royal decrees promised the creation of representative bodies for the provinces and for the nation as a whole. Widespread criticism had followed, causing Hardenberg to summon a handpicked 'Assembly of Notables'. But, as Calonne had discovered in France, these notables turned out to be anything but compliant and demanded the summoning of traditional estates. Hardenberg had Marwitz, the leader of the aristocratic opposition, briefly imprisoned, but he also succumbed to noble demands by resurrecting their tax exemptions in the royal edict in September 1811, and consequently imposing a new poll tax on commoners. The Prussian Assembly of Notables was dismissed, but the promise of a future representative assembly was reiterated and a provisional national assembly was actually convened (by using members from a national commission examining the state debt). A further pledge to create a representative body was made in a joint Russo-Prussian declaration to the German people in 1813, at the height of the war of liberation. As the crowning achievement of the Prussian reform movement, King Frederick William III issued a royal edict on 22 May 1815 ('Verordnung über die zu bildende Repräsentation des Volks'), promising his subjects a constitution with a national representative assembly. The edict was published on 8 July 1815, as allied armies marched into Paris. Even at this high-water mark, however, important qualifications were contained in the King's promise: the provincial estates were to be restored before the national assembly was formed; the new national assembly was to be elected 'out of the provincial estates'; and the assembly was to be merely advisory.[8]

The King of Prussia did not rush to fulfil his pledge. At least one historian has argued that Frederick William concluded he had already reformed quite enough.[9] In May 1816, the King reduced the reach of earlier reforms by limiting the number of peasants who could free themselves from their lord's control. In April 1817, the King sent a reminder to Hardenberg that the new national assembly had never been intended to be more than advisory.[10] Implementation of the constitutional promise was further delayed when the government sent agents into the provinces to collect the opinions of leading citizens in 1817. Meanwhile, an important confrontation between Prussian reformers and conservatives occurred when the latter attempted to reduce the size of the *Landwehr*, fearing that its middle-class officers might provide the nucleus for a future insurrection. Their efforts failed when a leading reformer and war hero, Hermann von Boyen, threatened to resign if their measures were adopted.[11] The opponents of reform were gaining in strength, but they were still unable to tip the balance.

Frederick William grew increasingly reliant on the opinions of a conservative coterie at court—composed of Prince Ludwig Wilhelm Wittgenstein, Johann Peter Friedrich von Ancillon (Gentz's relative, a former tutor to the Prussian Crown Prince and the author of the guarantee treaty that had been discussed at Aix), Theodor Schmalz (a law professor at the University of Berlin who had written tracts against the *Tugendbund* and who had mocked the demand for a constitution) and Duke Charles of Mecklenburg (the brother of the deceased queen). These court conservatives applied almost continuous pressure on the Prussian King throughout the course of 1818. When liberals from the Rhineland presented Hardenberg with a petition urging progress towards the promised constitution, the King interpreted their action as a challenge to his authority.[12] When Hardenberg spoke a month later to the Federal Diet in Frankfurt on the same subject, the King was deeply offended that the Chancellor had not obtained prior royal approval for his speech.

At the Congress of Aix-la-Chapelle, Metternich joined the voices of the conservatives in Berlin—warning the timorous Frederick William of the existence of revolutionary conspiracies even within the Prussian state bureaucracy itself. Metternich supplied Wittgenstein with two memoranda for the King: the first bitterly condemned the plan to introduce a constitution with a representative assembly, a foolhardy experiment that Metternich predicted would culminate in revolution. Metternich argued that because of the diversity of Prussian territories, the King should establish provincial assemblies but not a national one. The second memorandum called for measures to censor the press and to control the universities. The Tsar simultaneously circulated a memorandum at Aix-la-Chapelle, authored by his protégé Alexander Stourdza, also calling for stricter press censorship to prevent a revolutionary outbreak in the German states.[13]

Against the onslaught of these conservative forces, Frederick William held surprisingly steadfast to his plans for introducing a national constitution. Perhaps he acted out of obstinacy, or the simple belief that his own solemn pledge could not be lightly discarded.[14] Humboldt went to London as Prussian ambassador in 1817 but requested to return to Berlin in 1818 because of his wife's illness. In January 1819, the King therefore offered the liberal Humboldt appointment as head of a commission to draft the constitution. Humboldt at first refused, knowing that Hardenberg was already preparing his own proposal. But in the end Humboldt acquiesced to the King's request. In late February, he produced a document proposing a constitution with communal, district and provincial assemblies, and a national assembly of representatives elected directly by citizens on the basis of a narrow franchise. Humboldt saw the creation of the new assemblies as a means of educating and invigorating the Prussian body politic. He wished to couple the creation of the Prussian national assembly with a new cabinet system in which ministers—such as himself—bore direct responsibility for their own departments. A few months later, Hardenberg presented the King with his competing ideas for constitutional reform. Like Humboldt, the Chancellor called for the creation of communal, district and provincial assemblies, as well as a national assembly. However, Hardenberg proposed that the latter's members be nominated by the provincial assemblies rather than being elected directly. Whichever plan was chosen, the introduction of a new constitution to Prussia, despite Metternich's dire prognostications, seemed imminent. The King appointed yet another committee to compare the plans.[15]

That spring, the newly elected assemblies of Baden and Bavaria were convened for the first time. Not surprisingly, these new bodies encountered initial growing pains as members adjusted to new roles. This experience further militated against the adoption of a representative system in Prussia, especially when, in late March, the King of Bavaria secretly wrote to Frederick William that he would revoke the Bavarian constitution if he had the opportunity.

The assassination of Kotzebue

It was precisely at this delicate juncture, on 23 March 1819, that Karl Sand, a theology student at the University of Jena, murdered August von Kotzebue, a conservative publicist in Russian pay.[16] Sand had been invited into Kotzebue's home; suddenly, in the middle of their conversation, he stabbed Kotzebue with a knife and then tried to take his own life. The unfortunate deed seemed to confirm earlier accusations that the liberal student associations were revolutionary organizations. Frederick William ordered all Prussian students at Jena to return home immediately and directed his foreign minister, Count

Bernstorff, to cooperate with Austria on measures for restraining the universities. Gentz was in a frenzy, in part because, as a writer, he feared sharing Kotzebue's fate. Metternich, then touring Italy with the Austrian Emperor, could not imagine that students or professors could make very effective revolutionaries, but he believed that the German universities might be planting the seeds for future discord by training a whole generation of revolutionaries. He also shared Gentz's view that Kotzebue's assassination had created the right moment for introducing counter-revolutionary measures, especially since the Tsar had been personally insulted. 'A true misfortune will produce some good', Metternich wrote to Gentz, 'since poor old Kotzebue represents an *argumentum ad hominem* which even the liberal Duke of Weimar cannot defend'.[17] Here, at last, was Metternich's opportunity to teach the more liberal middle states a lesson.

In fact, other German rulers quickly followed the example of Prussia by withdrawing their students from Jena, forcing the Duke of Weimar himself to request the Federal Diet in Frankfurt to consider a uniform code of academic discipline throughout the German states. Austria proposed new restraints on academic freedom and demanded that no German state be permitted to hire a professor who had been dismissed elsewhere for political reasons. When this proposal languished in the Diet, Metternich devised a new strategy to bypass Confederation mechanisms altogether.

As his first step, Metternich conferred with the King of Prussia at Teplitz in late July, where the latter was vacationing with Wittgenstein and Bernstorff. This was the same spot where, only six years earlier, they had cemented ties for the final coalition against Napoleon. The shaken monarch now confided to Metternich that 'everything you foresaw has occurred'. Metternich told Frederick William that Prussia was in imminent danger and had to take rapid steps to combat all revolutionary tendencies. He also again advised that a representative constitution was incompatible with the monarchy. Deeply affected by Metternich's revelations, the King summoned Hardenberg to Teplitz and ordered him to work with Bernstorff and Wittgenstein in conjunction with Metternich to develop a written statement on the suppression of seditious activities and on the future Prussian constitution. Hardenberg was thus forced to bind himself in writing to Austria on the issue of Prussian domestic arrangements. Hardenberg showed Metternich a summary of some of his ideas rather than his full constitutional plans ('Ideen zu einer landständischen Verfassung in Preussen'), omitting such details as his intended bill of rights. One of his biographers regards it as a 'tragic development' that the Prussian Chancellor was still striving for a peaceful dualism with Austria; the German historian Treitschke once contended that Hardenberg was acting to win back the confidence of his sovereign. At the same time, Hardenberg ordered the arrest of several leading German nationalists—the so-called 'prosecution of the demagogues' (*Demagogenverfolgung*)—including Jahn and Arndt, popular leaders in the earlier 'War of Liberation' against Napoleon. An Austro-Prussian convention, signed at Teplitz on 1 August 1819, further agreed that stricter controls were needed over the universities, that Prussia would not introduce a new constitution until her state finances were in order and, finally, that Prussia would not introduce representative institutions 'incompatible with her geography and internal administration'.[18]

If Metternich thought that he had succeeded in quashing all prospects for the Prussian constitution, however, he was very much mistaken. Terrified as Frederick William was of revolution, he hesitated to abandon his earlier constitutional pledge. Shortly after the meetings at Teplitz, Hardenberg submitted a revised draft for the constitution, based in part on the promises he had made to Metternich. On 23 August 1819, the King then issued a new order forming yet another committee for the final drafting of the constitution, which was scheduled to hold its first session in October. More remarkable still, the King appointed Hardenberg, Humboldt and Ancillon as members.[19]

The Carlsbad Decrees

Meanwhile, Metternich met with representatives from Prussia and seven other German states, who had been specially invited to the spa town of Carlsbad in Bohemia (on Austrian territory, not far from Bavaria). Now that he had acquired Prussian support, he encountered little difficulty in obtaining the approval of the principal middle states for repressive measures, and they quickly agreed to the censorship of all publications with fewer than 20 pages, the proscription of the *Burschenschaften*, the appointment of state inspectors to oversee teachers and students at the universities and the creation of a Central Investigation Committee at Mainz to investigate suspected revolutionary activities.[20] Although the informal gathering of representatives at Carlsbad had no legal authority as such, the so-called 'Carlsbad Decrees' were subsequently adopted without discussion by the Federal Diet in Frankfurt on 20 September. Enforcement of the decrees was left up to the individual states, although one state could bring forward a complaint and demand Federal execution against another state whose actions were too lax.

Metternich's aims in Germany were not, however, confined to the passage of repressive legislation; they equally encompassed the defeat of the Prussian reform movement, the subordination of the middle states and the prevention of unwarranted interference by Russia. To achieve these ends, the institutions of the Confederation, including the structure of the Federal army and the interpretation of the controversial Article XIII, were finalized during a series of conferences at Vienna from late November 1819 until May 1820. Gentz submitted a detailed memorandum arguing that *landständische*, or 'estate', constitutions were different from representative ones: the latter, Gentz believed, were based on ministerial responsibility and popular sovereignty, and therefore quite incompatible with sovereign monarchies; *landständische* constitutions, in contrast, were based on the representation of traditional corporate estates (as under the *ancien régime*).[21] In interpreting Article XIII, the delegates consented to Metternich's view that member states could only adopt constitutions based upon principles of monarchical sovereignty (meaning that no ruler could transfer any of his sovereign power to a representative assembly). In the changed post-war atmosphere, the representatives of the Southern German states feared that Austria and Prussia might even demand that they rescind their existing constitutions; this never happened, but all of the German states readily agreed to permit Federal intervention in the event that they were threatened with revolutionary activity. The results of these decisions were memorialized in an amended version of the Vienna Final Act.[22]

Collapse of the Prussian reform movement

Back in Berlin, Humboldt and Hardenberg were busy squabbling over the status of ministers on the council of state. Humboldt wished for ministers to have true responsibility over their departments, thus paving the way for Prussia's transformation into a constitutional monarchy, but Hardenberg was unwilling to reduce his own powers as Chancellor. Humboldt further weakened his position by criticizing the Carlsbad Decrees, a policy that was the King's own. Hardenberg finally demanded that the King dismiss Humboldt or accept his own resignation. On 31 December 1819, Humboldt and Boyen were dismissed.[23] This proved a hollow victory for Hardenberg, who now faced only opponents of reform among the King's advisors. In the end, the promised constitution was never delivered in Hardenberg's lifetime; in 1823, Prussia created a system of provincial estates without a national assembly, just as Metternich had recommended. The failure to achieve a constitution has been attributed to the antagonisms separating Hardenberg and Humboldt and to the secret collaboration of Metternich and Wittgenstein; yet it is difficult to imagine how further reforms could have been instituted, given the paranoia of the King and the ruling classes in these years. The significance of these events can scarcely be exaggerated. The German historian Friedrich Meinecke saw it as one of the great turning points in German history. Had the reformers succeeded, Prussia might have evolved into a peaceful constitutional monarchy, avoiding much of the bloodshed of the next century.

Reactions of the allies

Meanwhile, Metternich was hoping to secure approval of the Carlsbad Decrees by both Britain and Russia. As signatories to the Vienna Final Act, they retained some right to express their views on German affairs, and Metternich hoped to enlist their support to increase the pressure on the German middle states. While 'Great Britain could not condemn constitutions or recommend eliminating the liberty of the press', Metternich told the British ambassador at Vienna, she could still support energetic measures, even 'despotic ones', in times of revolutionary danger when 'the dagger is pointed at the breast of every sovereign, and the seat of every principle of justice'. Metternich was just as concerned to secure the approval of the Tsar, whom he feared might take the side of the German constitutionalists and pose as a champion of the middle states—especially Württemberg, ruled by the Tsar's brother-in-law King William.[24] In fact, the repressive legislation at Carlsbad had already been proposed by Alexander Stourdza. Historian Stella Ghervas points out that several scholars once presumed that Stourdza's writings had even provided the main inspiration for the decrees, when in fact he was merely a precursor.[25]

In London, Castlereagh was generally supportive, confessing to the Austrian envoy that 'we are always happy to see evil germs destroyed, without the power to give our approbation openly'. Austrian policy had already been subjected to vituperative criticism in the press and Parliament, and Castlereagh did not wish to invite further attacks by openly associating the British government with the Carlsbad measures, much as he acknowledged their necessity. Nor did he think that such cooperation fell within the proper province of the alliance. Castlereagh warned Metternich that he was mistaken in seeking the Tsar's approval, which would be construed as an open invitation to meddle in German internal affairs.[26]

Castlereagh's prescience was amply confirmed when the Tsar's minister Capodistrias circulated a memorandum among the allied powers attacking the Carlsbad Decrees and proposing that each German state should instead enact its own counter-revolutionary legislation, based upon its own peculiar needs. This was followed in early December 1819 by a proposal that Russia and Britain should prepare a joint statement on the conferences then proceeding at Vienna.[27] Castlereagh responded that, as signatories of the Vienna Final Act, Russia and Britain undoubtedly had the right to intervene if the constitution of the German Confederation were violated, but this seemed unlikely to occur. The German states were harmoniously cooperating in working out the details of the Confederation, and Castlereagh concluded that it would be best for the non-German powers not to interfere. The British declaration was sufficient, on this occasion, to deter Russian action and to let Metternich complete his revision of the Confederation unhampered.[28] It illustrated, once again, two very different conceptions of the alliance: the Russian view that the alliance provided a framework for the supervision of Europe, and the British view that its application—or at least its visible application—should be strictly curtailed.

Peterloo and the Six Acts

In the years after Waterloo, political unrest was not confined to the Continent of Europe. Immediately upon Castlereagh's return to London in 1815, he witnessed rioting in the streets protesting the Corn Bill, which artificially propped up wheat prices by restricting imports. In 1816, backbenchers in the House of Commons rejected the government's attempt to renew the Property Tax. Economic recovery was rendered even more difficult by a natural disaster: in April 1815, while Napoleon was still in the Tuileries, Mount Tambora had exploded in far-off Indonesia. Dust in the atmosphere led to the cold summer of 1816 and massive crop failures.[29] Over the next few years, Britain became the scene of widespread discontent, fuelled by a combination of economic, social and ideological factors—a robust tradition of popular radicalism, the new ideas of the revolutionary epoch, the expansion of the press, the delicate equilibrium of the new industrial economy and the economic recession that followed the Napoleonic Wars.[30]

To the extent that the suppression of political unrest became the chief concern of the European alliance in these years, Castlereagh's views of this domestic agitation also merit some examination. One of the highlights of popular radicalism in Britain was the demonstration at St Peter's Fields in Manchester on 16 August 1819. This public assembly of thousands of men, women and children was dispersed by a charge of yeomanry cavalry ordered by the local magistrates. The incident became known to contemporaries as the 'Manchester Massacre' or 'Peterloo'. The liberal and radical press was outraged, and Whig leaders exchanged letters strongly critical of the magistrates. But at a Special Session of Parliament held in November and December the actions of the magistrates were upheld and the 'Six Acts' were enacted—a series of repressive measures bridling the press and limiting public gatherings.[31]

While Castlereagh's precise role in the cabinet deliberations is unknown, it is certain to have been an important one. In the Ireland of his youth, Castlereagh had personally confronted one of the most important revolutions in its history. He always took the view, however, that the common people were largely loyal and obedient. The revolutionary rank-and-file were being misled by their leaders, who had themselves been seduced by French ideas.

As Leader of the House of Commons in 1819, it fell on Castlereagh's shoulders to present the government's case. On 29 November, Castlereagh introduced the Six Acts. Moving the first reading of the Seditious Meetings Prevention Bill, he presented all the government bills to the House as a single package. In this important debate, he most clearly expressed his ideas on the reasons for the unrest of 1819. His analysis consisted of three contentions: that the discontent was not caused by economic difficulties; that it was instead the work of agitators motivated by Jacobin principles; and that the proposed measures of repression would be sufficient to restore order, since the common people were fundamentally loyal. His arguments were thus not too different from what Metternich himself might have presented.

His parliamentary opponents, the Whigs, pointed to the fact that disaffection was found only in the manufacturing districts—how, then, could one doubt that it was based on economic grievances? Going one step further, Whig leaders blamed the pressure of taxes: 'The nation was over-taxed, and that was the root of the evil.'

In the debate, Castlereagh at first denied the existence of economic distress, altogether; later, he admitted it might exist but insisted that its degree was greatly exaggerated and that it was unconnected to political disaffection since 'the most disaffected' were not the most distressed.[32] The true origins of the unrest were not to be found in the economy, he told the House, but in the ideas of the French Revolution now being propagated by a small band of itinerant agitators who were travelling from country to country and endeavouring to delude the common people. 'How long were the prosperity and tranquillity of the country to be put in danger in this manner?' Usually known for his coolness and reserve, Castlereagh spoke with great emotion, imploring the House 'for God's sake, to look their difficulties in the face ... Wicked and dangerous men ought to be deprived of the power of keeping the country in continual agitation.'[33] He feared there was now 'a spirit of disaffection bordering on rebellion.'[34]

Castlereagh believed that the root of the evil was to be found in the murderous doctrines of Jacobinism, and he told the members of the House, 'when they looked to the scenes around them—when they saw what was passing both at home and abroad—when they considered what theories of government were afloat, not only here but elsewhere, they were bound to create a fence around the constitution ...'. The legislation that he was proposing would not deprive freeborn Britons of their customary rights, he contended, for the measures only prevented those abuses introduced from France:

He had no wish to prevent [the people] from assembling, when deliberation was really the object which they had in view; he had no wish to put an end to those meetings which were the peculiar boast of England, which, till modern times, had been productive of so much benefit and advantage. In latter times, however, these meetings had been of a different kind, and seemed, from the manner in which they were conducted, to have been borrowed from another country …. [T]he tumultuous meetings which had become common, which were marked with a character wholly different from that of peaceful deliberation, which had never been known in this country till of late years, which were quite an innovation upon all its habits, customs, and prejudices … were borrowed from the worst days of France ….[35]

Castlereagh referred to the practice of attending public assemblies armed or in martial array, which he believed was also borrowed 'from the worst of times of the French Revolution' and could only lead to open rebellion, 'and that which was its never-failing concomitant, military despotism'.

The radical reformers had pointed to the presence of women and children among the crowds at Manchester as proof of their peaceful intentions, but according to Castlereagh the attendance of women at mass meetings was just another example of imitation of the French Revolution. Castlereagh urged that the proposed measures, limiting the license of the press and the right of public assembly, be made permanent. The agitators were so malicious, he argued, that they would take advantage of any loopholes in the law. 'They had already seen with what cunning, wicked and evil-disposed men often availed themselves of the expiration of a law or the circumstance of parliament not sitting, to resume their old practices ….' Under pressure from independent members, however, Castlereagh and the government had to abandon this aspect of their original programme. Nonetheless, they succeeded in enacting the Six Acts for a temporary period.

It is worth reflecting on this repressive legislation and the arguments used in the debate when evaluating British foreign policy during these years. On the one hand, popular unrest in Britain hampered the ability of a government dependent upon parliamentary support from cooperating more actively with the Continental powers. On the other, it helped create an underlying bond of sympathy among the ruling elites of Europe in pursuit of many of the same objectives.[36] We can see why Castlereagh told the Tsar that they were 'agreed upon the substance' and differed only in 'management', and why he confided to the Austrians that his government was 'always happy to see evil germs destroyed without the power to give [their] approbation openly'. *The Times* and other London dailies were not slow in drawing the obvious parallels between the Six Acts and the Carlsbad Decrees.

In one respect, matters were far worse than the ministers had even imagined. Through an informer, a plot was discovered to murder the entire cabinet while they were dining at the house of Lord Harrowby, the President of the Council, as the opening salvo of a popular revolution. The conspirators, led by the radical politician Arthur Thistlewood, were arrested in February 1820 at their hideaway on Cato Street; apparently, they had competed for the privilege of cutting Castlereagh's throat.[37]

The revolution in Spain and Castlereagh's State Paper of 5 May 1820

Post-war events in Germany and Britain had merely posed the threat of revolution. At the beginning of 1820, the worst nightmare of the allied statesmen was realized when an actual revolution erupted in Spain. To understand the origins of the revolt, it is necessary to return briefly to the dark days of the Napoleonic Wars when King Ferdinand VII of Spain—a Bourbon—was being held captive in France. The common people of Spain rose up in rebellion, but the upper classes and senior army officers were initially hesitant, both because they abhorred mob violence and because Ferdinand's ostensible abdication had lent the new Bonapartist regime some semblance of legitimacy. Local notables eventually assumed leadership of the revolt, forming revolutionary committees known as juntas in each province and inviting British intervention. The provincial juntas quickly organized a Central Junta, which was succeeded by the regency that convened a Cortes (or Spanish parliament) in September 1810.

The following year, an extraordinary Cortes assembled at Cadiz to draft a new constitution. The Spanish Constitution of 1812 recognized Ferdinand as monarch but announced that sovereignty resided in the nation. Conservative patriots had hoped for an upper chamber to represent the interests of the aristocracy, similar to the British House of Lords, but the extraordinary Cortes was dominated by the more radical spirit of the urban crowd in Cadiz. The new constitution was therefore closer to the French republican model than to the British: it abolished noble, clerical and provincial privileges, granted equal civil status to Spaniards in the Americas, guaranteed a free press and individual liberties, eliminated feudal dues and established a unicameral legislature based upon universal manhood suffrage in which Crown officials could not sit. A council of state was created to advise the king, local government was transferred to elected municipalities and a new progressive income tax was introduced.[38] Conservatives believed the new constitution was fatally unsuited to the social realities of Spain. When the Cortes further abolished the Inquisition and launched an attack on Church property, the Spanish clergy were driven into opposition against the constitutionalists. The Cortes also failed to reach any reconciliation with Spain's colonies in the Americas.[39]

Restoration of Ferdinand VII, the 'Desired'

At the time of Ferdinand's restoration in March 1814, liberals and conservatives alike looked to the King for support. The nobles desired a restoration of their privileges; the army, compensation for its successful struggle against the French. But Ferdinand returned to the throne at a difficult moment. Spain's trade and population were both declining. The country had 184,000 men under arms, which it could scarcely afford. The King himself lacked political training, having been shunted aside by his father and subsequently isolated by Napoleon. Almost immediately, Ferdinand quashed the constitution and restored his own absolute power. Leading liberals were arrested while the building where the Cortes had once met was sacked by an unruly mob. Collaborators with the French, known as *afrancesados*, were exiled. All newspapers except the official gazette were prohibited, while the Inquisition and the Jesuits were reinstated. The intensity of the reaction took many Spanish liberals by complete surprise. Membership in secret Masonic lodges mushroomed, especially in the army where officers had been exposed to French liberal ideas. Unrest in the military increased when large numbers of officers were retired without pay in peacetime reductions. The return of conscription in 1817 was another cause of discontent. The government tottered on the brink of bankruptcy, while the country was in economic shambles from the long years of war and the truncation of ties with its colonies.[40]

It was especially the latter, emphasizes historian Charles Esdaile, that lay at the heart of the problem: 'Bankrupt and exhausted, Spain could only restore her situation through victory in America. However, precisely because Spain was bankrupt and exhausted, this was not a practical possibility.'[41] Even as recently as 1810, more than half of Spain's entire revenues had been derived from the colonies.[42] The Catalan textile industry, for instance, had been highly dependent upon the American market.[43] But during the French occupation the colonies had achieved virtual autonomy and had developed a new robust commerce with Britain and the United States. Ferdinand's attempt to restore Spanish royal power in the Americas and to re-impose traditional restrictions on colonial trade provoked its leaders to demand formal independence. Ferdinand vacillated between listening to his civilian advisors, who recommended a political compromise, and the Ministry of War, which advocated the use of force. An army of 10,000 men was sent to Venezuela to subdue the colonists; they enjoyed initial success but were unable to capitalize on their early victories. The tide began to turn in 1818: José de San Martín defeated the Spaniards in Chile that April, while Simón Bolívar triumphed in Colombia the following year. Ferdinand had hoped for armed intervention against the rebels by the great powers at Aix-la-Chapelle, but to no avail.

In 1819, the Spanish government gathered a new expeditionary force at the port of Cadiz, to sail to America in a fleet of antiquated ships obligingly provided by Russia. The expedition was quarantined at port because of an outbreak of yellow fever. This fortuitous event gave time for a revolutionary fermentation to spread amongst the troops.

The *Pronunciamento* of 1820 and its aftermath

Ironically, those garrisons intended to suppress the independence of Latin America raised the banner of revolt in Spain itself. Cadiz had never been sympathetic to the restoration, and agents from Argentina actually assisted in stimulating discontent among the troops.[44] With the government in a state of post-war retrenchment, younger officers were without possibility of promotion.[45] On 1 January, 1820, a regimental commander, Major Rafael de Riego y Nunez—apparently with the connivance of liberal merchants in Cadiz—proclaimed the Constitution of 1812 at the town of Cabezas de San Juan.[46] His cohort, Colonel Quiroga, took the town of San Fernando and the Isle of Leon in the harbour of Cadiz the next day. Riego failed to take Cadiz and marched to Málaga and Córdoba for fresh recruits, but found meagre support. 'Nothing is more remarkable in this insurrection', wrote Sir Henry Wellesley, the British ambassador in Madrid and a younger brother of the Duke of Wellington, 'than the apathy of the people, who ... look to the quarrel to be one between the King and the army, with which they have no concern.'[47]

In the ensuing weeks, Wellesley continued to believe that the insurrection would dissipate and that the rebels had made a strategic error by proclaiming the Constitution of 1812, 'which in most parts of the country is to the full as unpopular as the prevailing system which it is the professed object of the insurgents to reform.'[48] But Ferdinand's government was paralysed by fear of the unreliability of its own troops, while Riego was marching through Andalusia. By the end of January, Wellesley was reporting that, 'with regard [to] the public feeling, with the exception of persons immediately about the Court, nine out of ten of the inhabitants wish well to the insurgents.'[49] The army did almost nothing to halt the insurrection, which spread to Corunna by the end of February.[50] 'It is to be lamented', wrote Wellesley, 'that the King did not take the resolution of going in person to Andalusia, taking with him those Generals who had distinguished themselves in the last war, and who are known to be popular in the army. A decided measure of this kind taken at an early period would probably have crushed the insurrection at once.'[51]

By the beginning of March, a disheartened Wellesley predicted that if some measures were not taken soon to appease the rebels, the insurrection would spread to the capital itself. Soon afterwards, news was received of

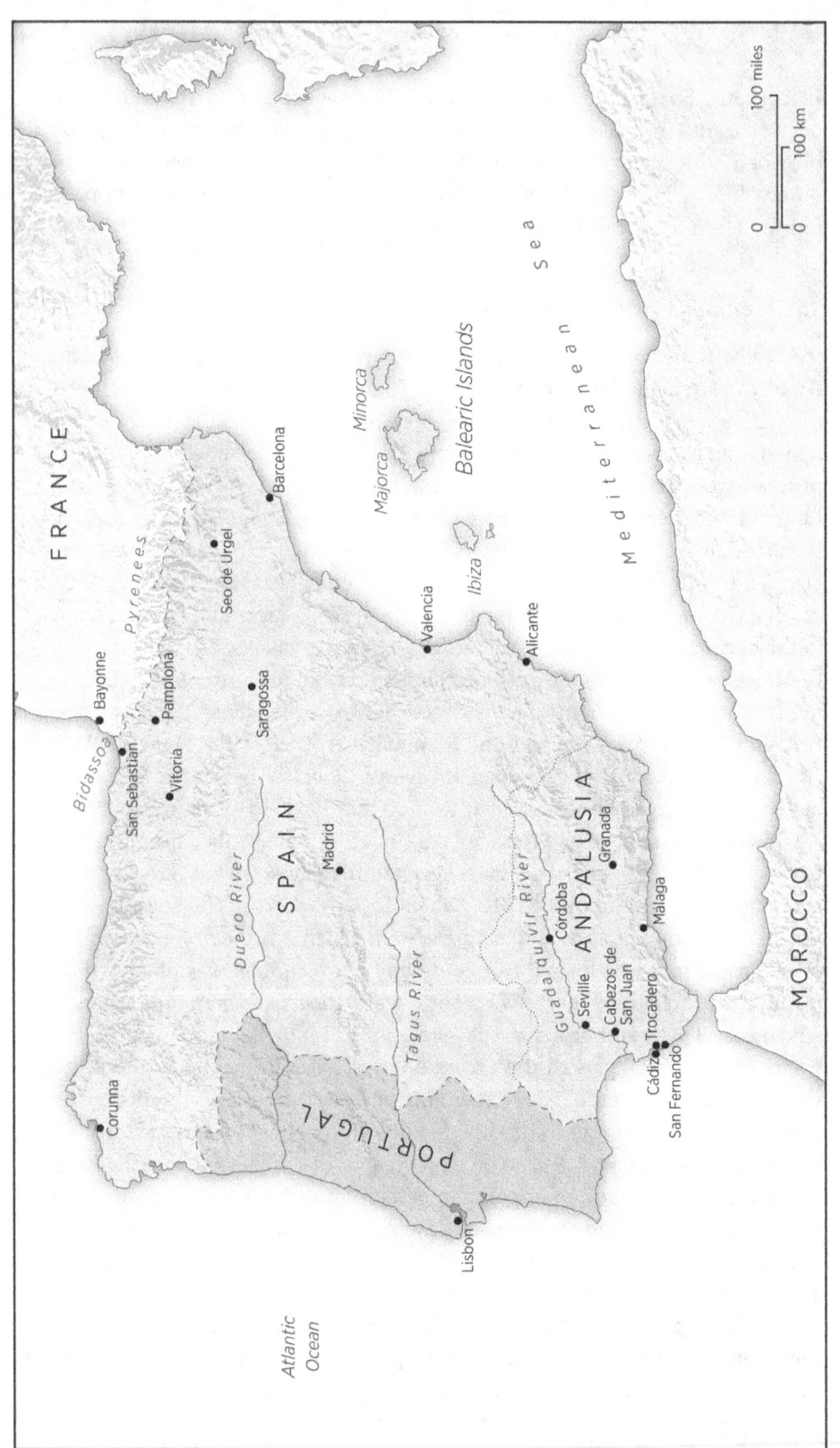

Spain at the Time of the Revolution of 1820

revolutionary outbreaks in Barcelona, Saragossa and Pamplona, and of the defection of the commander of the royal army.[52] Crowds ominously gathered in the streets of Madrid. Ferdinand announced a summoning of the ancient Cortes, but even this news, according to the British ambassador, 'was received by the public and by the officers and troops of the garrison with strong expressions of discontent and disappointment, and from the reports which reached the palace there was every reason to apprehend a general insurrection throughout the city in the course of the night'. Ferdinand became convinced that only his acceptance of the Constitution of 1812 could avert a revolutionary upheaval, and he announced his assent on 7 March.[53]

Riego and the other junior officers responsible for the insurrection had proclaimed the Constitution of 1812 as a symbol of resistance to absolute rule. Now that the King had agreed to their demands, the liberals were suddenly returned to power. Ferdinand appointed a new council of state composed of moderate reformers. Not only the institutions but many of the same men whom Ferdinand had dismissed in 1814 were reinstated. Revolutionary clubs formed in Madrid and other cities, while an unrestricted press began to demand even more far-reaching changes. 'It would seem that the mischievous publications issuing daily from the press have kept the public mind in a continued state of ferment', reported Wellesley. 'These publications are read and commented upon in clubs which have been established in different quarters of the town, and which are numerously attended.'[54] Less than five years after Waterloo, a major European power had again fallen victim to the revolution.

Allied reactions

With respect to the allied powers, the crisis in Spain drove their already divergent conceptions of the alliance even further apart. When news of the revolt in Spain first reached Vienna, Metternich feared similar outbreaks across Europe. When these failed to materialize, he adopted a policy of deliberate inaction. The Tsar, with almost equal predictability, was eager to take the offensive. Alexander began soliciting allied opinions on Spanish developments as early as 15 March, calling for the powers to discuss the issue 'confidentially' even before he knew the unrest had spread to Madrid.[55]

As Spain's immediate neighbour, France was the power most directly affected by these events. Moreover, in February, only one month after Riego's *pronunciamento*, the Duc de Berri was assassinated. He was the son of the Comte d'Artois, nephew to both Louis XVI and Louis XVIII, and in the direct line of succession to the throne. The revolutionary movement thus appeared to be on the ascendant. In England in these same months Thistlewood was organizing his conspiracy to murder the entire British cabinet. The Tsar thus began to worry for the future safety of France after the death of Louis XVIII. In Paris, the liberal Décazes ministry, only just installed in November 1819, fell from power, and Richelieu was re-appointed to his old post.[56]

Anxiety mounted, reflected in the French press, that the revolution might spread from Spain across the Pyrenees to France. Permanent officials at the French foreign ministry, such as the Comte de Rayvenal, urged Richelieu to restore France's great power status by playing an active role in Spain. Richelieu proposed sending a special envoy, the Marquis de La Tour du Pin, to Madrid, bearing a message from Louis XVIII to Ferdinand VII in favour of establishing a French-style *Charte*. This attempt to exert family influence was foiled by none other than Sir Charles Stuart, the British ambassador in Paris. Stuart sent news of the project to Wellesley in Madrid, who in turn informed the Spanish government. Spaniards criticized the plan as an unwarranted interference in their internal affairs, and the proposed French mission never took place.[57]

In the meantime, the Tsar instructed his ministers to send a circular to the other allied courts inviting them to participate in a joint remonstrance against the Spanish revolution. The circular proposed that the powers consider direct military intervention, and even offered the use of Russian troops. Alexander had not entirely forsaken his prior liberal sentiments, however, and continued to believe that the allies should encourage a modicum of constitutional reform in Spain by introducing a *Charte* along French lines.[58] Not surprisingly, both Metternich and Castlereagh resisted the Tsar's plans for allied intervention in the Iberian Peninsula. The Austrian foreign minister nonetheless wished to avoid an open confrontation with Alexander, for he half-suspected the proposal was a trap. Capodistrias had proposed armed intervention, Metternich conjectured, knowing full well that the other powers were bound to reject the scheme. This would then enable Capodistrias to discredit the alliance in the Tsar's eyes. Metternich was therefore doubly cautious in praising the spirit of the Russian proposal, even while rejecting it on practical grounds. Relying on advice offered by Wellington, Metternich contended that foreign arms simply could not succeed in suppressing a revolt in Spain. History had demonstrated that 'foreign action has never either arrested or controlled the effects of a revolution.'[59]

Metternich looked chiefly to Castlereagh to restrain the Tsar, much as he had relied on Castlereagh's support during the 1814 campaign, at the Vienna Congress, and at Aix-la-Chapelle. True to form, the British responded to the Russian proposals with two incisive memoranda—Wellington's report of 16 April and Castlereagh's 'State Paper' of 5 May 1820. In the former, Wellington furnished the perspective of a military expert, based upon his personal experiences in Spain. Nowhere, the Duke concluded, were the conditions for foreign intervention less favourable: 'There is no country in which foreigners are so much disliked', he wrote, 'especially the French'.[60]

Castlereagh's State Paper of 5 May 1820

Castlereagh's State Paper provided a penetrating analysis of the origins of the alliance and the obligations of its members, and became known as one of the classic formulations of nineteenth-century British foreign policy. As one historian has written, it was 'the first statement of general principles to which English diplomacy had ever committed itself'.[61] In a sense, it was an extension of his reasoning at Aix-la-Chapelle. His purposes in drafting this exegesis, he informed the Prince Regent, were to silence 'calumnies' on British policy towards Spain, to respond to recent proposals from St Petersburg and Berlin, and to 'recall the attention of the Allied Cabinets to the true and correct principles of the alliance, and to the necessity of not generalizing them, so as to render the concert an embarrassment, especially to a Government constituted like that of [Britain]'. Castlereagh also needed to politely refuse yet another overture from the Tsar for a treaty of general guarantee.[62]

In the text of the State Paper itself, Castlereagh explained that the alliance had never been intended as a 'Union for the government of the World, or for the superintendence of the internal affairs of the other states'. Such a uniformity of conduct could never be achieved because each of the member states had its own distinct geographical position, strategic concerns, political system, economic interests and cultural traditions. Indeed, any attempt to extend the alliance beyond its original conception was, in his view, 'more likely to impair or even destroy its real utility'. The alliance should only be invoked when the common danger was so great that the powers would cooperate in the general interest. This had happened during the recent war, when the alliance had been directed against 'the revolutionary power, more particularly in its military character actual and existent within France ... and not against the democratic principles, then as now, but too generally spread throughout Europe'. According to the State Paper, it was not the social insurrection in France that had united the allied powers, but the danger that France had posed to their own security by her military power and repeated acts of aggrandizement. Only when a similar threat to the European balance of power again arose, Castlereagh argued, would the treaty obligations of the alliance come to the fore. Spain constituted no such threat to Europe on account of her internal weakness, small army and geographical isolation—'there is no portion of Europe of equal magnitude, in which such a revolution could have happened, less likely to menace other states with that direct and imminent danger which has always been regarded, at least in this country, as alone constituting the case which would justify external interference.'[63]

Castlereagh admitted that the alliance might, from time to time, expand the scope of its operations—but he cautioned that such exceptions were never to be performed as a 'matter of course'. Intervention in the internal affairs of other states could not be reduced to a uniform 'system'. Any attempt to do so would be repugnant to a constitutional state like Great Britain. Since the precise interests of the allies in such questions could never be determined beforehand as a matter of general principle, it would be best to treat such situations on a case-by-case basis. In the case of Spain, Ferdinand's repressive policies were held in general contempt by the British public. British ministers, unlike the Tsar, had to be sensitive to public opinion. Castlereagh also contended, as he had in France in 1814, that it would be useless for foreign powers to employ armed force to restore a fallen monarch's powers, since just as soon as they withdrew their troops the restored regime would be likely to collapse. Finally, Castlereagh advised the allies to refrain from giving any advice, or even from holding a conference on Spanish affairs, since these steps, if not backed by force, would do more harm than good. Castlereagh believed there was no justification for foreign intervention in Spain, unless the royal family were threatened or Portugal were attacked.

A letter that Castlereagh sent to his half-brother Lord Stewart a few months earlier sheds further light on the reasoning behind the State Paper. In the early years of the war against France, Castlereagh wrote, Pitt had made an egregious error by defining his nation's goals too broadly, opening the country to dissension that later hampered the war effort. For Britain to participate on the Continent, the connection with the national interest must be palpable and beyond reproach. 'This is our compass and by this we must steer; and our Allies on the Continent may be assured that they will deceive themselves if they suppose that we could for six months act with them unless the mind of the nation was in the cause. They must not, therefore, press us to place ourselves on any ground John Bull will not maintain....'[64] It was the same argument he had made to the Tsar at Aix, but a curious one from a politician who was often contemptuous of public opinion.

Metternich seized upon these British objections as posing an insurmountable obstacle to the Tsar's proposals. A conference without Britain would simply publicize the divisions within the alliance. Instead of a formal reunion, Metternich therefore recommended an ambassadorial conference at Vienna to concert on measures. The Austrian foreign minister did at least make one concession to Alexander's *amour propre*, by finally agreeing to his earlier request for joint instructions to the allied ambassadors at Paris in the event of the sudden death of Louis XVIII. Metternich further agreed that the

Austrian Emperor should meet with the Tsar that coming summer to consult on possible additional counter-revolutionary measures.⁶⁵

The allied powers thus failed to act in Spain because of British opposition, French hesitation and Austrian distrust of Russia. The resulting policy of non-intervention accorded well with Britain's commercial interests, since Ferdinand's efforts to re-impose mercantilist restrictions on Latin American trade would have been highly detrimental to British merchants had they succeeded. The Spanish Revolution was momentarily left to run its course, while the appearance of allied unity was preserved intact. The focus of the alliance was now squarely on the threat of revolution, but the statesmen of the pentarchy were not altogether agreed on how the enormous resources of the alliance should be brought to bear on this problem.

The Neapolitan Revolution and Metternich's dilemma

A major turning point in the history of the alliance was reached when another revolution occurred, this time in Naples. This event ultimately led to an open rift between Britain and the three eastern courts. From the outset, the Neapolitan Revolution raised different questions from the Spanish one. Metternich believed that Austria's position in both Italy and Germany depended upon the swift suffocation of insurrection in those areas. Of equal significance, he deemed it essential that Russia not ally with the constitutionalists. Rivalry between France and Austria for predominance in Italy and the insistence of Britain that reliance on the alliance be avoided added two further complications. Metternich's dilemma was twofold: first, how to retain a free hand for Austria in Naples while enlisting allied support; and second, how to preserve Austrian friendship with Britain while also meeting Russian demands for a formal congress.

The outbreak of revolution in Naples

The Napoleonic episode, for all its drawbacks, had brought many aspects of enlightened government to Italy. Old privileges and administrative chaos had been swept aside by centralized governments. In Naples, Murat had abolished feudalism, created a modern army, consolidated direct taxes into a single land tax, and sold off Church lands. The French occupation had also inadvertently introduced Sicilians to the benefits of independence from the mainland. When the Neapolitan Bourbons were restored, King Ferdinand IV proclaimed a full amnesty, confirmed new property rights, kept most of the French innovations in centralized administration and allowed public officials and army officers to retain their posts. After Murat landed in

Italy in the 1820s

Calabria in late 1815, there was a brief period of reaction under the Prince of Canosa, who was appointed as minister of police, but Canosa was quickly dismissed at Metternich's insistence. Sicily and Naples were then unified as the Kingdom of the Two Sicilies in 1816. Two advocates of enlightened rule, Luigi de' Medici and Donato Tommasi, were appointed as the ministers of finance and justice. At the same time, Austrian troops remained stationed in the kingdom at local expense until 1818. The kingdom also owed debts for the costs of Murat's final campaigns and for bribes paid to Metternich and Talleyrand to facilitate the return of the Bourbon dynasty. The decision to preserve French methods of administration further contributed to the need for high taxes. To meet these continuing costs, de' Medici dismissed state employees, dropped public projects and reduced army pay. Tensions were increased by the general economic recession, competition with new sources of foreign grain, and a rise of brigandage in the countryside. Neapolitans thus experienced an economic crisis accompanied by mounting rural poverty. A commercial treaty with Britain, concluded in 1816, actually gave preference to British over Neapolitan shipping. A new Concordat with the Papacy, concluded in 1818, restored the ecclesiastical courts. Middle-class intellectuals, frustrated at the absence of a constitution and the slow pace of change, were driven underground by rigid censorship and a lack of effective outlets for protest or dissent. Liberal Muratist army officers, professionals, artisans and even lower clergy joined together in a loose network of secret societies, originally organized to resist the French, known as the *Carbonari* (or 'charcoal-burners'). Although banned in 1816, the *Carbonari* reputedly had thousands of members.[66]

Rosario Macchariali and Pietro Serra, two former Jacobins living in Salerno, organized a clandestine summit meeting of *Carbonari* members from different provinces at Pompeii in 1817. Subsequently an assembly of *Carbonari* delegates from around the kingdom was convened at Salerno in January 1818. They agreed to adopt the Spanish Constitution of 1812 and to launch coordinated uprisings in Salerno, Naples, Foggia and Bari. The royal government, alarmed at reports of the proliferation of *Carbonari* lodges, made arrests in Salerno in 1818. Two leading Muratist generals, Guglielmo Pepe and Pietro Colletta, were sent to reorganize the local militias of the provinces of Avellino, Basilicata and Capitanata with its capital at Foggia. Pepe and Colletta deliberately enrolled *Carbonari* members in these forces, in part to help eradicate banditry but mainly with an eye to preparing a future revolt.[67] Pepe in fact planned to seize the Austrian Emperor and Metternich during their visit to southern Naples in 1819, but his plan fell through when their route was changed.[68]

According to William A'Court, the British envoy in Naples, the kingdom was thrown into a state of ferment by news of the revolution in Spain.[69]

Pepe made new plans for a rebellion, to be launched on 24 June 1820, but again his scheme did not go quite as expected and he returned to the capital city on 27 June. To his surprise, on 2 July, in the town of Nola, just east of the city of Naples, a cavalry regiment commanded by two junior officers, Michele Morelli and Giuseppe Salvati, defected and demanded a new constitution. From Nola, Morelli and Salvati marched to Avellino. They were joined by the priest Luigi Minichini (a *Carbonari* leader who had helped to organize the uprising) as well as by another disaffected regiment and a crowd of 200 additional *Carbonari* members.[70] By the time that they entered Avellino, Morelli had more than a thousand men under his command; in the excitement, they were joined by the commander of the local garrison, increasing their numbers still further. In Naples, the commander of the royal army recommended that Pepe be sent to suppress the uprising, but the ministers, perhaps suspecting Pepe's loyalty, chose another Muratist, General Corrascosa, instead. As news spread by semaphore telegraph (sending signals with flags), other towns joined in the uprising while the soldiers sent to suppress it turned back. Foggia, the chief town in the region, along with its regiment of cavalry declared for the Spanish Constitution on 3 July. The *Carbonari* in Foggia had printed proclamations and tri-colour banners ready for the event. 'Everything, it seems,' observes one historian, 'had been carefully prepared in advance'.[71]

Meanwhile, Pepe had secretly left the capital on the evening of 5 July to join the rebels.[72] From Avellino, Morelli marched to Salerno on the same day. The insurrection finally reached the capital itself by 6 July.[73] Ferdinand made vague promises of a constitution, but, as in Spain, these pledges were inadequate to silence the crowds. Naples 'is in a state of anarchy and confusion beyond belief', A'Court bemoaned: 'No act of violence, however, has yet actually been committed, but we are on a mine, which may explode in an instant'.[74] Without further resistance, the King capitulated by naming his son, the Duke of Calabria, as Prince Vicar-General. The very next day, the Prince Vicar-General proclaimed the Spanish Constitution of 1812, giving a semblance of legitimacy to the uprising.[75] A provisional government was formed with Generals Carrascosa and Colletta and respected Muratist reformer Giuseppe Zurlo as members. On 9 July, Pepe returned to the capital; armed *Carbonari* paraded through the streets of Naples in triumph, carrying the Spanish Constitution in a hackney chair. Four days later the King swore to the constitution in a public ceremony as canons fired into the air.[76]

Thus, in the course of a single week, Naples was transformed from a seemingly stable monarchy into a revolutionary state.[77] Metternich, Castlereagh and Richelieu were all equally shocked, since they had considered Bourbon Naples to be the very epitome of good government.[78] A'Court could only explain the revolution as the product of a conspiracy of Muratist army officers with the *Carbonari*, towards which the lower classes remained apathetic.[79]

Metternich had found no signs of unrest when he had toured Naples in 1819. He now attributed the uprising to the activities of the 'sects' and the intrigues of French agents. He predicted anarchy would soon spread throughout the kingdom and feared that Naples might act as a lightning bolt, triggering a surge of national sentiment throughout Italy. However, Metternich's initial fears proved illusory. Naples remained relatively tranquil.[80] General Pepe took charge of the revolutionary army, while moderate aristocratic and bourgeois elements assumed the reins of government. The Austrian *chargé* at Naples depicted events in a favourable light as a popular movement in which constitutional ideas had happily taken root: 'the clergy, the nobility, the military, the bourgeoisie, and above all, the judicial order are inbred with them'. The government continued to collect taxes and pay its debts. Although the *Carbonari* gained strength in the army and the political clubs, the government pursued a conciliatory foreign policy. The new foreign minister, the Duke of Campochiaro, made every effort to appease the allied powers, even going so far as to suppress a newspaper critical of Austria.[81]

Unfortunately, the Neapolitan moderates (generally, Muratists) proved unable to repress the enthusiastic excesses of the political clubs and the radical press, while the city of Palermo in Sicily rebelled against Neapolitan rule just a few weeks later, placing new strains on the constitutional regime.[82] The dynamic was not dissimilar to historian François Furet's depiction of earlier events in France, with growing pressure towards the left. The *Carbonari* formed their own general assembly, posing a rival centre of power until a national parliament was elected and assembled at the beginning of October. By late August, A'Court was already complaining that the ministry was 'deplorably weak' and held in great contempt by the *Carbonari*.[83] General Pepe, according to the British diplomat, had submitted to the authority of the *Carbonari* to retain his command.[84] In A'Court's view, the influence of the *Carbonari* threatened the very survival of the kingdom:

> The existence of these formidable sects renders the business much more complicated than in Spain, and much more difficult to be brought to a successful issue. How can any government go on, if there exists an occult power infinitely more strong than that of executive government, and having objects and interests totally unconnected with those of the Nation?[85]

The royal family was now, according to the British envoy, 'entirely in the hands and at the mercy of the *Carbonari*' and consequently in the gravest danger.[86] The King secretly confided to the allied ambassadors that he was terrified for his life and sought their assistance to escape from Naples, but they advised that they had no authority to remove him, and that his personal escape, even if it succeeded, would leave the rest of his family in a 'dreadful situation'.[87] A'Court dreaded the consequences of any attempt at foreign invasion—'The resistance might be great, and the whole country become the theatre of bloodshed and pillage'. Yet he feared that misfortunes might be greater still if the kingdom remained at the mercy of the 'sects'. He had no hesitation in writing, 'that the great mass of the Nation is decidedly in favor of a Constitution'.[88]

The allied response

Metternich was determined to crush the Neapolitan Revolution from its inception.[89] We have seen that Ferdinand of Naples had signed a secret treaty with the Austrians at the time of his restoration in 1815, in which he had pledged not to alter the kingdom's domestic institutions without Austrian consent. His proclamation of the Spanish Constitution had been a violation of these terms. Of far greater importance, Austria could hardly succeed in censoring the press and the academies in Germany and Northern Italy if she tolerated a fully fledged revolution in neighbouring Naples. Indeed, the whole security of Metternich's system seemed to be at stake. A successful revolution in Naples might unleash a chain reaction throughout Southern and Central Europe. And, if constitutional changes were countenanced in Italy and Germany, how could the Habsburgs resist such innovations in their own dominions? Since royal absolutism was the glue that held the polyglot Habsburg Empire together, Metternich anticipated that the spread of representative institutions to Austria might even lead to her own demise. Facing such dangers, Austria had to look to her own interests first, though she also counted on the support of the allies. Metternich's diplomacy therefore aimed at securing a free hand for Austria in Naples, coupled with an absolute uniformity in language and conduct by the five powers. Of course, he hoped that royalists in Naples might spontaneously overthrow the new order; but in the event that the revolution was not toppled by local elements, Austrian intervention was inevitable. Unfortunately, Austria had less than 20,000 troops in Lombardy-Venetia and needed time to reinforce her divisions.[90] Eighty-five thousand Austrian troops were ordered to assemble there.[91] Metternich also wanted to secure the support of the other allied powers, since he was loath to commit Austria while Russia remained free to interfere in Central Europe and while France might still emerge as the champion of the smaller Italian states. As early as 26 July, Metternich therefore suggested to the other powers that, since the Emperors of Austria and Russia had already decided to meet late in the summer to discuss Spanish matters, the allied ambassadors at Vienna might join them at Pest to deliberate over Naples. Metternich's greatest challenge lay in persuading the Tsar. Only a few weeks earlier, Metternich had been playing Castlereagh's tune with respect to Spain—that foreign intervention could never succeed against internal unrest—now, he was cautiously urging precisely the opposite for Naples.[92]

Castlereagh, as astonished as Metternich by news of the revolt, wrote to his half-brother, Charles Stewart, on 29 July:

> [We] cannot but witness with increased surprise and grief the forcible subversion of the Govt. of Naples. The Neapolitan Army had no grievance whatever, as an army, to complain of; unlike that of Spain it was well cloathed and regularly paid; it nevertheless constituted the principal if not the sole agency by which the state has been overthrown; not on account of any reproach, which those who have brought this change pretend to impute to the government of their Sovereign, as a justification or an explanation of their conduct, but from a wild desire of effectuating some theoretical reform in the Constitution of the country, which in the precipitancy of the convulsion which has taken place has ended in a blind adoption of the Spanish Constitution of 1812 with all its imperfections.... [93]

Castlereagh held several conferences with the Austrian ambassador, Prince Paul Esterhazy, and told Stewart to assure Metternich that Britain considered the event in an entirely different light from the revolution in Spain. He well understood that the Neapolitan insurrection threatened existing institutions throughout Italy and naturally gave rise to apprehensions in Austria for the security of her Italian possessions. The British Foreign Secretary advised the Austrians to act quickly in reinforcing Lombardy-Venetia, in moving troops to the neighbouring independent states, and in entering Naples itself. 'If Austria thinks fit to set her shoulder to the wheel', Castlereagh told the Austrian ambassador, 'there can be little doubt of her competence to overrun the Kingdom of Naples and dissolve the rebel army.'[94] But he also cautioned that the principles of the State Paper of 5 May 1820 must be respected: Austria could act unilaterally, on the basis of self-defence, but Britain could not be associated in any way, shape or form with the suppression. 'The question should be treated as *special* rather than general; as *Italian* rather than European; and in consequence, as falling under the jurisdiction (*dominion*) of Austria rather than the alliance.'[95]

In effect, Castlereagh offered Metternich the same behind-the-scenes support he had afforded in Germany: 'Up to the present stage of our proceedings the view taken at Vienna of the Neapolitan Revolution corresponds exactly with what I always thought it must be', he wrote to Stewart.

> The change ... was such as satisfied me that the Court of Vienna would not delay for a moment to pour a large and commanding Military Force into their Italian Dominions—That they would as little hesitate to take under their immediate protection such Italian States, and especially Tuscany and Lucca, as might with them dread the conflagration—That they would be prepared, if called upon, to defend the Papal States, & that in this imposing attitude, they would watch and ascertain the actual state of affairs at Naples, communicate with their Allies, and thus be prepared to act upon that system which sound policy and their own immediate safety might dictate.[96]

Wellington went even further, offering the gratuitous advice that 80,000 soldiers should be more than enough to defeat the revolutionaries. Secret instructions were also issued to the British naval squadron in the Mediterranean to 'to provide ... for the security of the royal family, and if necessary receive them on board'.[97]

Queen Caroline

In truth, Castlereagh found his own hands tied by a dire domestic crisis. The death of George III on 29 January 1820 and the accession of George IV had brought the latter's uneasy relationship with his estranged wife, Queen Caroline, to the breaking point. The King first insisted upon a divorce; when he could not get his way, he compelled his ministers to bring forward a 'Bill of Pains and Penalties' against her. After several years of living abroad, Caroline returned to Britain to defend her privileges. Assisted by the radical London politician Alderman Wood and the Whig leader Henry Brougham, the Queen received widespread popular support. Her landing was accompanied by 'arguably the largest movement of the common people during the early nineteenth century'.[98] She was placed on trial in the House of Lords in August 1820, precisely when the allied leaders were discussing how best to respond to events in Naples. Castlereagh played a special role in the case, since his agents on the Continent had been collecting information about the Queen's activities for years.[99] The bill against the Queen caused a popular outcry, and Castlereagh and the ministry were forced to bear the brunt of this discontent. Canning resigned from office and Robert Peel refused an offer to take his place.[100] The Tory government was on the verge of dissolution and remained in power only because George IV refused to appoint the Whigs, who had taken up the Queen's cause.

With the same fervour with which they defended the Queen, the Whigs, the radicals and a great number of London newspapers welcomed the revolution in Naples. The events in Naples, said the liberal *Morning Chronicle*, 'will be received by the friends of freedom and humanity with exultation. It is gratifying to learn that another portion of the human race are delivered from despotism, and rapturous that the glorious object has been attained without the loss of a single life'.[101] In these circumstances, reported the Austrian ambassador to Metternich, it was essential to avoid any discussion of Naples in Parliament. The extent of the danger, from the Austrian perspective, was reinforced when several Whig Peers denounced the activities of the 'Holy Alliance' in the House of Lords.

While Castlereagh encouraged the Austrians to exert their influence unilaterally in Italy, French and Russian leaders had exactly the opposite reaction. Neither government desired to remain a passive spectator while Austria acted independently. The French wanted to demonstrate their return to great power status and were intensely jealous of Austrian designs. The Tsar believed that action by the alliance offered the best panacea against the further spread of the revolutionary movement. Moreover, there were prominent parties in both France and Russia that favoured modifying the constitution of Naples along the lines of the French *Charte*, rather than permitting Naples to return to unmitigated absolutism.[102]

New Congress proposals

Throughout August and September, the chancelleries of Europe struggled over what form action in Naples should take. On 10 August, the French circulated a formal proposal to the other members of the pentarchy. The restoration of Ferdinand in Naples had been the principal goal of the French six years before at Vienna. Because of their dynastic ties with Naples, the French claimed it was especially appropriate for them to bring the current crisis to the attention of Europe.[103] They readily acknowledged that Naples, unlike Spain, required foreign intervention, and that Austria was the power in the best position to act. But they called for moral force to accompany this exercise of physical force. Based on the agreements concluded at Aix-la-Chapelle, the French therefore demanded a reunion of the five allied cabinets 'dans toutes les formes' (in effect, with all the formalities) to deal with the insurrection. Private correspondence between the French ministers reveals that among their underlying motives was the desire to prevent the Austrians from increasing their dominion over Italy or the British from turning the Mediterranean into a British lake by creating a protectorate over Sicily. A congress would afford the French an opportunity to avert military measures, or alternatively, to exert some control over the future reconstruction of Naples. Richelieu and Etienne Pasquier, the former Napoleonic official who had become the French foreign minister, equally feared a barrage of domestic criticism if they stood idly by while Austrian troops marched into Naples. They were further encouraged to seize the initiative by Pozzo di Borgo, the ambitious Russian ambassador in Paris.[104]

Castlereagh rejected the French congress proposal just as soon as it was received. Action in the name of the alliance was precisely the thing he sought to avoid. To accommodate the British, Metternich responded to the French invitation by reiterating his original suggestion that the allied governments should refuse to recognize the new Neapolitan government and that a conference of ministers, rather than a formal congress, should convene at Vienna to establish a European counter-revolutionary 'information centre' and to discuss the instructions to be sent to the allied diplomats at Naples. Such a forum would, of course, have been exceptionally advantageous for Metternich, who could be expected to exercise his well-known ascendancy over his 'harem'—the Viennese diplomatic corps.

News soon arrived in Vienna, however, that the Tsar had rejected Metternich's original July proposal. Since the Tsar was travelling west to attend the opening of the new Polish Diet, he desired to meet the Emperor of Austria and the King of Prussia in the early autumn. The Russians also proposed a full-dress reunion of the cabinets at the same time and place. Curiously, they recommended that the four signatories of the Quadruple Alliance meet without France. Shortly after issuing these instructions, the Tsar and his ministers in Warsaw received the French congress proposal. Although the Russians chastised the French for their suspicions of Austria, they warmly greeted the suggestion of a formal reunion. Meanwhile, the incorrigible Metternich was still endeavouring to reach a compromise by repeating, on 28 August, his offer to hold an informal ambassadorial conference on Naples at Vienna.[105]

Metternich's efforts were intended to mollify the British, who remained adamantly opposed to summoning a congress of any kind. 'With all the respect and attachment which I feel for the system of the Alliance, as regulated by the transactions of Aix-la-Chapelle', Castlereagh wrote to Stewart in Vienna on 16 September, 'I should much question the prudence, or, in truth, the efficacy of any formal exercise of its forms and provisions on the present occasion'. Castlereagh believed that the present troubles lay entirely outside the *casus foederis* of the alliance, based upon the treaties of 1815 and 1818. New dangers had arisen, not from any infractions of the treaties, but from the 'internal convulsions' of an independent state. Reflecting on the unfortunate effects of formal allied conferences and declarations on the first French revolutionaries—again demonstrating how very much the revolutionary paradigm remained foremost in the minds of the allied leaders—Castlereagh recommended that the allies conduct themselves in a manner less conducive to 'misrepresentation and excitement'. At the very least, he expected that if the other allies insisted on meeting, they should limit their discussion to the peculiar case of Naples and refrain from all 'general declarations' or 'universal pledges'.[106]

Moreover, Britain could not, he instructed Stewart, participate in a hostile league against Naples under any circumstances. First, such an engagement would have to be approved by the British Parliament, which was unlikely to occur. Second, the British squadron in the Bay of Naples, sent to protect the royal family, could not safely remain at anchor there if Britain and Naples were in a state of war. Third, British support for intervention would endanger British property and trade. Lastly, if intervention were conducted under the aegis of the alliance, the Austrian expeditionary force would need to be directed by a council of allied ministers, a hopeless impracticality. For all of these reasons, Castlereagh concluded that the wisest course for Austria—and for Europe as a whole—would be, as he had repeatedly recommended, for the Austrians to act unilaterally in Naples. The 'local interests which Austria had in the question ... render her interference both more natural, more justifiable and less odious than if the particular case was to be avowedly taken up in the face of European abstract, and consequently more controversial, grounds by powers less directly threatened'.[107] This was a direct slap in the face of Russia. Castlereagh even offered to assist the Austrians by protecting Ferdinand and the royal family with the British naval squadron at Naples while the rebellion was being crushed. There can be little doubt, then, that Castlereagh wholly supported the counter-revolutionary enterprise. But he thought it would be more efficacious if its actions remained subtle—even covert. In this sense, his recommendations for Naples in 1820 echoed his policy towards the restoration of the Bourbons in France in 1814–15. There was, as at Aix, an agreement on the 'substance' but not on its 'management'.

Almost at the same time that Castlereagh's letter reached Vienna, Metternich received the Russian response to his latest attempt to substitute an ambassadorial conference for a formal reunion. The Tsar was unrelenting: the evils facing Europe were so grave that a firm demonstration of allied unity was indispensable; the allied cabinets must meet in their full panoply and concurrently with the allied sovereigns, at Troppau in late October.[108] Thus, despite Metternich's agile manoeuvres to reconcile what he appropriately termed the 'impossibilities of Britain' with the 'modes of Russia', he was finally forced to choose.[109] Since 1814, he had consistently relied on Castlereagh to restrain the Tsar. But now, for the first time, he hesitated to continue along this familiar path. His anxieties over Russian expansionism had finally been eclipsed by the greater danger of revolution. Not only did the Tsar offer Austria more tangible support, but Metternich feared that the mercurial Alexander, if rebuffed, might once again pose as the patron saint of liberal constitutionalism, encouraging revolution everywhere.[110] 'Of all the evils,' he observed, 'the greatest would be to see the Emperor Alexander abandon the moral tie that unites us and set himself up again as the power protecting the spirit of innovation.' Moreover, Metternich was reluctant to send Austrian troops to Naples with an unfriendly colossus at her back. The dangers to be expected from alienating his good friends, the British, were negligible by comparison, and with the domestic crisis in Britain, Metternich was not even sure that Liverpool and Castlereagh would survive in office. The Austrian foreign minister finally resolved his dilemma by submitting to the Tsar's demand for a full-blown congress.[111]

The British, as Castlereagh had warned, refused to participate, although the British Foreign Secretary admitted that 'under the transactions of Aix-la-Chapelle, it may perhaps be difficult to refuse, to *any one* of the signing powers, the right of convening such a reunion, if it should feel that there is matter to deliberate upon falling within the understood principle[s] and sphere of these transactions'.[112] The greatest surprise came not from Warsaw or London, but from Paris. For, after having first proposed the congress, the French suddenly announced that they would follow England's lead and merely send observers without powers to the allied reunion. Thus, the French turned down their own invitation. The reasoning behind this somewhat bizarre turn of events appears to have been as follows: with Britain abstaining, Richelieu and Pasquier concluded that all the anticipated benefits of allied unanimity were lost. They were therefore reluctant to pose as the collaborators of the autocratic eastern powers when the British claimed they could not do so because of their constitutional form of government, which the two western powers ostensibly shared. The French ministers were equally disinclined to leave a British squadron at anchor as the only neutral force in the Bay of Naples. Privately, the French were greatly perturbed by British intransigence: 'I have believed for a long time', Richelieu complained to Capodistrias, 'that Lord Castlereagh is determined to nullify every act of the grand alliance not directed against France.' [113]

Despite their pretence of neutrality, the French still hoped to throw obstacles in the way of Austria. In lieu of action within the framework of the alliance, they secretly sounded out the Russian minister Capodistrias on an alternative approach. Rather than give a free hand to Austria, they proposed a Franco-Russian mediation between Austria and the current government of Naples. The mediating powers could assist the Neapolitans in establishing a wise and moderate constitution, avoiding the necessity for foreign intervention altogether. The proposal found a friendly ear in Capodistrias and would, in fact, play a prominent role at the coming congress. It resonated with the liberal side of Russian foreign policy ever since Czartoryski's proposals of 1804—expressing the same hope for moderate constitutions and national assemblies in order to harness popular energies as the best alternative to revolution.[114]

Revolution in Portugal

While the allies were thus engaged in debate over the best means of handling the revolution in Naples, yet another insurrection occurred in Portugal. Little wonder that the ruling elites of Europe thought they were being besieged on all sides by revolutionary forces—the continuing after-shocks of the great upheaval in Paris, already 30 years old. The royal family of Portugal had, with British protection, sailed to Brazil during the Napoleonic Wars and still had not returned. The British had obtained favourable trading privileges for their help: the Anglo-Brazilian commercial treaty of 1810 imposed higher duties on goods entering Brazil from Portugal than from Britain. On the advice of Talleyrand at the Congress of Vienna, the Portuguese had raised Brazil to the status of an independent kingdom at the end of 1815. The Portuguese revolutionaries of 1820 sought not only liberal reforms, but also a reduction of British influence and the return of their monarch and his court from Rio de Janiero to Lisbon. They feared Portugal was becoming subservient to her own colony.[115] As in Spain and Naples, the Portuguese army initiated the revolt and the Spanish Constitution of 1812 was declared. Portugal, however, was party to a century-old treaty with Britain, which protected her territorial integrity. The British sphere of influence and the efficacy of British sea power in Portugal were so widely recognized that there was never the remotest possibility of intervention by any other power. Castlereagh warned the King of Portugal, still residing in Brazil, that he should not pin his hopes on assistance from either the 'Holy Alliance' or Britain, and Metternich later delivered a similar lecture to Portuguese royalists soliciting his support. The outbreak of the Portuguese Revolution (*Revolução Liberal*) nonetheless underscored the dangers facing Europe and added to the panic of the allied sovereigns.[116]

Britain declines the Congress

This development had no impact whatsoever on the British decision with respect to the coming congress. Castlereagh had already written to his half-brother in Vienna of his surprise that Austria had accepted Russia's invitation for a conference at Troppau with all the formalities ('dans tous les formes convenables'). An 'avowed and formal European Conference is more likely to embarrass than assist us'. Austria must 'take' the power to act in Naples, he warned, but Britain could not 'give it': 'The difference being that in the one case, the responsibility is where it ought to be, with them—in the other it is *Joint*, which embarrasses us, without essentially assisting them.'[117] When Count Lieven, the Russian ambassador in London, pressed Castlereagh to send a formal representative to Troppau, his efforts were therefore rewarded with quite the contrary effect. On 12 October, the British cabinet officially announced it would send no plenipotentiary, though Stewart would be permitted to attend as an observer. The latter was instructed to heed the principles of the State Paper of 5 May 1820, and his functions were strictly curtailed to reporting events and to ensuring that the terms of the treaties of 1814 and 1815 were meticulously observed.[118]

The British ministers especially feared that pronouncements from Troppau would have to be defended in Parliament, and Castlereagh again warned the other powers that the appearance of allied unity could only be preserved if such declarations of general principles were studiously avoided. The Tsar's conception of the alliance, Castlereagh frankly told Lieven, 'aims at a perfection, which we do not believe applicable to this century or to mankind. We cannot follow him along this path. It is a vain hope, a beautiful phantom, which England above all cannot pursue. All speculative policy is outside her powers.'[119] He likewise informed Prince Esterhazy, the Austrian ambassador, that 'if it is desired to extend the alliance so as to include all objects, present and future, foreseen and unforeseen, it would change its character to such an extent and carry us so far that we should see in it an additional motive for adhering to our course at the risk of seeing the alliance move away from us without our having quit it.'[120]

What Castlereagh feared most was that if the revolution in Naples were suppressed in the name of the alliance, the British government would, as an alliance member, share the blame under a theory of joint liability—'Such a league would render the British Government both morally and in a Parliamentary sense responsible for all the future acts of the league'. This would bring the intervention under the scrutiny of Parliament, handing the opposition a golden opportunity to tug and tear at Britain's ties with her Continental allies:

> Such a league would most certainly be disapproved by our Parliament; and even could it be sustained, it is obvious that, from that moment, every act of the Austrian army in the kingdom of Naples would fall as much under the immediate cognizance and jurisdiction of the British Parliament, and be canvassed as freely and fully, as if it were the act of a British army and commander-in-chief. The objections to such a system in a Government such as ours are insuperable.[121]

Moreover, this was at a moment when the British ministers could scarcely brook such criticism. The government's situation in Parliament was far worse than it had been when Castlereagh had pleasantly conversed with the Tsar at Aix-la-Chapelle. The government's highly unpopular bill against the Queen was being debated in the House of Lords just as Castlereagh had to face the question of British participation at Troppau. Castlereagh continued to recommend in the strongest terms that Austria act unilaterally in Naples rather than as an agent of the European alliance. In his view, the three eastern powers were stretching the fabric of the alliance beyond its original purpose and intent. It could not be used as an instrument for systematic interference in the internal affairs of other states, especially when facing mere 'domestic upsets' that posed no real threat to the equilibrium of Europe.

The Russian perspective

At the opposite end of Europe, Capodistrias was preparing a 'position paper' for the Tsar shortly before the new Congress assembled, which addressed the proper role of the alliance in Naples from the Russian vantage point. According to Capodistrias, the allies were unanimously agreed on the most important issue: 'the pressing necessity of making common cause against the revolution, that enemy of all peoples and all governments'. But there were two contrasting views—or 'systems of conduct'—on the best manner of proceeding: 'One is the *system of expediency* ("*le système des convenances*"). The other—the *system of duty* ("*le système du devoir*").' The British 'system of expediency' was based on the assumption that 'the treaties do not impose any obligation on the allied powers to combat the revolution today, because the revolution has not chosen France as its theatre'. The Russian 'system of duty', based on the 'spirit of the existing transactions, especially the treaties of Paris in 1815 and the acts at Aix-la-Chapelle in 1818', took a very different view. According to the Russian system, 'in whatever country the revolution chooses to destroy the order of things established by the general alliance, the allied courts must arm themselves against the revolution and seek to overcome it'. Under the British system of expediency, many questions arose regarding the proper form of the Congress. Such issues did not arise under the Russian system: 'In adopting *duty* as its principle, no question or doubt can remain on these ... aspects, because all questions are judged and all doubts are resolved by a double authority: that of the treaties and of experience.'[122]

Capodistrias foresaw the obstacles in the way of obtaining an agreement at Troppau, but he believed that a firm demonstration of allied unity was indispensable for the triumph of order over revolution. He urged the Tsar to persuade his allies that unity was required by the existing treaties. If the British could not be persuaded that these obligations applied to revolutions outside of France, then the other allied leaders might still be. If that effort failed, however, Capodistrias went one step further. To remove all future ambiguity, he recommended cutting the Gordian Knot—the Tsar should simply propose a *new alliance*, aimed squarely against revolution in general terms: 'Let us define in the most positive way the new obligations that we will contract to unite us against the revolution and to destroy its disastrous influence. Let us sign a new treaty that will bind us to these precise obligations.'[123] Capodistrias cited the example of the Treaty of 25 March 1815, in which the allied powers had stipulated a *casus foederis et belli* against France, when she had been invaded by 'the revolution personified' in Napoleon. He recommended to the Tsar that the deliberations at Troppau should therefore consider 'a system of general conduct founded on right', and provide a 'definition of this system in clear terms'.[124] In short, either the existing treaties of 1815 to 1818 were already aimed at defeating revolution wherever it arose, or the allied powers should conclude new engagements that would unequivocally do so. Capodistrias saw the primary challenge of the coming Congress in this task of establishing a system of general counter-revolutionary principles, placing him at direct loggerheads with Castlereagh.

Capodistrias presented these ideas to the Tsar while they were together at Warsaw, where Alexander was present to open the second session of the Polish *Sejm*, or Parliament, in mid-September. The Tsar's old friend, Prince Czartoryski, had become gradually disillusioned with the Tsar's behaviour, although a leading historian sympathetically concludes that Alexander was actually caught in an 'impossible balancing act' between Russian and Polish opinion. The Tsar was still taking affirmative steps to join Russia's existing Polish provinces with the new 'Congress Poland', abolished serfdom in the Baltic state of Livonia in 1819, and had secretly entrusted his minister Novosiltsev to draw up a constitution for the Russian Empire as a whole based on the Polish Constitution.[125] In October 1819, at Warsaw, Novosiltsev submitted his first draft; a year later, again at Warsaw, Novosiltsev presented the Tsar with two copies—one in Russian and one in French—of a written constitution with 191 articles. It provided for a sharing of legislative power between the Tsar and a new assembly ('General Diet'), to be composed of two chambers. Russian subjects would henceforth enjoy liberty of the press, freedom of religion and rights for the accused.[126] This was a pivotal moment—a potential turning point—in Russian, no less than in Prussian, Spanish or French history.

At the same time, the Tsar had appointed his unpopular brother, Constantine, as the commander-in-chief of the Polish army and permitted him to exercise arbitrary powers in contradiction to the new Polish constitution, despite the loud protests of Czartoryski and the entire Polish

Administrative Council. The Tsar was deeply offended in 1817 when the deputies of the Polish *Sejm* forwarded a series of 'Observations' critical of the government. In May 1819, Russian authorities imposed strict censorship in Poland after local newspapers condemned a decree by the Grand Duke Constantine ordering the arrest of anyone found jeering in a public theatre. Czartoryski, then travelling in the west with his young wife, complained to the Tsar, but Alexander supported his brother and even threatened to rescind Polish rights. When a sovereign grants his people 'liberal or constitutional principles', the Tsar explained to the Austrian ambassador in reference to the Polish case, he must equally provide 'repression in proportion' to ensure his subjects do not 'abuse' their rights or 'pass a certain line'.[127] In August 1820, Czartoryski urged the Tsar to protect the Polish Constitution and to support Greek Christians in Turkey, but his entreaties again fell on deaf ears. When the Tsar opened the *Sejm* in September, he lectured its members on the 'evil spirit' then unfurling across the Continent. Despite the complaints of the Polish deputies, the Tsar refused to lift the new censorship; on leaving Warsaw, he even secretly authorized his brother to override the Polish Constitution if he felt such a step were necessary.[128] In his closing speech to the *Sejm*, the Tsar asked the deputies to examine their own consciences to judge whether their discussions had helped Poland or whether they had in fact fallen victim to the 'seductions too common in these days'.[129] It was in this decidedly irritable state of mind that the Emperor and Autocrat of All the Russias stepped into the imperial carriage and made his way to Troppau to collaborate with the other allied leaders.

6

Rift and Reunion, 1820–22

The Congress of Troppau and the Principles of Intervention, October–December 1820

In late October, the sovereigns and their ministers trundled in their carriages into Troppau (present-day Opava), a small provincial town in Austrian Silesia on the foothills of the Carpathians. The town's chief advantage lay in the freedom it afforded from all distractions. Its location within the Austrian Empire meant that Metternich could play host to the conference and pursue his favourite practice of reading everyone else's mail. The reunion was not a formal 'Congress' from the British perspective, but for the three eastern courts it was nothing less. The Tsar was accompanied by his younger brother Nicholas, Nesselrode, Capodistrias, Vorontsov, Stroganov, and Golovkin, the ambassador to Austria. The Emperor of Austria attended with Metternich, Gentz, Zichy and Lebzeltern, the ambassador to Russia. Britain, officially just a spectator, sent Lord Stewart, while the French observers were the ambassador to Austria, the Marquis de Caraman, and the ambassador to Russia, the Comte de La Ferronnays. The Prussians were represented by Hardenberg, Bernstorff, the Crown Prince and General Krusemarck. The King of Prussia arrived a fortnight later with Prince Wittgenstein.[1] With the sovereigns and their retinues, more than 400 guests were suddenly added to a town whose population ordinarily numbered only 1,200. Castlereagh, Richelieu and Pasquier were conspicuously absent.

Metternich's duel with Capodistrias

The contest between Capodistrias and Metternich for the conscience of the Tsar occupied centre stage for most of the Congress. Born on Corfu while that island was still under Venetian rule, Count John Capodistrias (1776–1831) had attended the University of Padua from 1794 to 1797, the final years of the Venetian Republic. He developed contacts with other Greeks and became acquainted with the chief works of ancient and Enlightenment philosophy. He returned to Corfu to find his family under persecution from French authorities. In 1799, Russia and Turkey cooperated in driving the French from Corfu, and the young Capodistrias helped to write a new constitution and became Secretary of State to the new Ionian Islands. The French recaptured the island in 1807, and Capodistrias entered Russian diplomatic service soon thereafter. A member of the Russian delegation at the Congress of Vienna, Capodistrias had attained parity with Nesselrode as joint foreign minister by 1816. Each man represented a different facet of the Tsar's complex personality. Capodistrias shared Alexander's devotion to the welfare of humanity above the interests of a single state. Contemporaries saw Capodistrias as something of a philosopher, holding liberal and constitutional ideas. He abhorred revolutions, but he felt that European stability could never be successfully maintained by a blind return to the absolutism of the *ancien régime*. States could best be immunized from revolutionary infection by the spread of moderate constitutions like the French *Charte*. To ensure their conservative character, it was better for new institutions to be promulgated from above than below. Like Czartoryski, Capodistrias also harboured special loyalties—in his case, to Eastern Orthodox Christianity and the cause of his fellow Greeks. Western scholars have tended to minimize or ignore this religious dimension, but Capodistrias was not simply 'liberal' in the Western sense: like his secretary Alexander Stourdza, he saw the need for a new approach, one which united rulers and peoples under Christian principles.[2]

Metternich detested Capodistrias and arrived at Troppau geared up for battle. Since the beginning of the year, Stewart had noticed his greater seriousness of purpose: 'Metternich is an altered man from what he was at Aix-la-Chapelle and a far different one from what he was at the Vienna Congress. His labo[u]r is incessant now. He has laid aside all trivial pursuits—neither play, women or conviviality engross; ... his whole Mind and time are devoted to his *Cabinet du Travail*.'[3]

On 20 October Metternich had his first audience with the Tsar at Troppau. Alexander was disturbed by the opposition he had just encountered in Warsaw, as well as by the reports that Metternich had forwarded to him of a widespread revolutionary conspiracy with its headquarters in Paris. Similarly to the King of Prussia a year earlier at Teplitz, the Tsar reproached himself for not having listened more carefully to Metternich in the past.[4] '[A]ll our faculties', the Russian Emperor afterwards told Stewart, 'should be directed to counteract and oppose that fatal spirit which was making such rapid progress in Europe'.⁵ Yet, as always, the Tsar remained of two minds, and he also told La Ferronnays, the French ambassador, that the best way to combat the secret societies might be to anticipate popular strivings 'by granting a portion of that freedom which the revolutionaries were attempting to seize by force'.⁶ And so, as the allied statesmen began their labours, the overarching question was: did the Russian Emperor now favour a programme of repression, or was he still an advocate of liberal reform?

The opening session

Encouraged by the Tsar's apparent demeanour, Metternich opened the first formal session of the conference just three days later. The delegates decided to record their proceedings in a simple conference journal instead of using signed protocols, in order not to embarrass the British. Metternich launched the discussion by reading his own memorandum, which condemned the Neapolitan Revolution, affirmed the treaties of 1814 and 1815, asserted the right of intervention by threatened states and, finally, sought allied 'moral support' for Austrian intervention in Naples. Austria's sole aim, Metternich declared, was the liberation of the King and the restoration of his full authority; she would seek no territory or benefit for herself. Naples would be temporarily occupied for a transitional period, but any changes introduced after the King's restoration would be left up to his own discretion.⁷

The Prussians appeared to subscribe wholeheartedly to these views.⁸ The same assent, however, was not so readily extended by France or Russia. La Ferronnays questioned why the allies could interfere in Italy but not in Spain. The Russian delegates simply remained mute. Afterwards, the Tsar instructed Nesselrode and Capodistrias to visit Metternich before the next conference session to find out just what 'moral support' the Austrians sought.

Austro-Russian parleys

The two Russian ministers called on Metternich on the evening of 26 October. They understood his basic plan for intervention but said they could not pronounce judgement until they knew more of his specific ideas. Metternich willingly explained the nature of the 'moral cooperation' he sought. According to the subsequent Russian report, he spoke 'for a long time' of the serious crisis that Europe faced; though the proposed plan of intervention was pregnant with danger, he felt he could not abandon it 'without seeing the Italian Peninsula and the rest of the European Continent fall prey to the radical sects'. In prescient words—which might have applied with equal force to the coalition forces invading Saddam Hussein's Iraq two centuries later—Metternich told

Nesselrode and Capodistrias that the expedition would 'not [be] dangerous in itself. We can arrive in Naples without difficulty. But what do we do when we are there? That is when the real difficulties and great perils begin'. The solution to the problem, Metternich ingeniously asserted, lay with the King of Naples himself. His letters to the Emperor of Austria revealed that he was a 'captive' and that none of the acts he had sanctioned since the outbreak of the revolution had been expressions of his own free will. The allies would thus present themselves as surrogates acting on his behalf: Ferdinand's 'action will be legal, and it is he who wants to provide for the security of his kingdom'. The King would serve, in reality, as the instrument of the allies.

Nesselrode voiced the objection that in the eyes of his subjects, the Neapolitan King would be seen as taking recourse to foreign arms to rule over them. If Ferdinand was presently a creature of the radical sects, he would later become one of the Austrian army. These were not suitable elements, Nesselrode concluded, for the reconstruction of the monarchy.

Capodistrias was even more scathing in his criticism: any revelation of the King's secret communications with the allies would expose his moral turpitude: Ferdinand had taken a solemn oath sanctioning changes demanded by a large number of his subjects, and now he would punish those same subjects. Indeed, how could the allies publicize such communications without also revealing the deplorable 'moral nullity' of the sovereign whom they were about to make the arbiter of the destinies of his people? It was not skilful diplomacy that was needed, Capodistrias declared, but 'a policy based on principles of equity and above all of pure morality and conscience'. Metternich terminated the discussion by asking the Russian ministers if they would not at least 'recognize the principle we have established? Do you agree that when the interior relations of a state take an offensive character towards neighbouring states, there is a right to ... act efficaciously to contain the contagion?'[9]

The following evening, the two ministers called on Metternich again. The Austrian foreign minister now had a chest cold, so Lebzeltern remained to read various documents aloud. These included the latest despatches from London, which insisted that Austria must act unilaterally in Naples. Metternich next presented a draft of his latest memorandum. Many of the ideas it contained had been expressed in conversation the evening before. He viewed the business in Naples as but 'one episode in a larger drama'. What specific 'moral support' did Austria actually seek? For a start, she asked that the allies make a common reply to the note received from the Neapolitan constitutional government on 1 October, to demonstrate their unanimity.

Capodistrias and Nesselrode agreed that the issue of Naples itself was, in fact, of only secondary significance—of far greater importance was the unity of the allied cabinets. Here, the Russians posed a sensitive question: while all agreed that the two constitutional states, Britain and France, had been generally supportive, it was clear that much uncertainty lay ahead. In France, would Richelieu's ministry remain in power after the next elections? In Britain, would the Tory government survive the current domestic crisis? And, if the Tories fell, would the new Whig government be 'neutral and well-intentioned', or would it actually prove friendly to the revolutionaries? In these circumstances, the real issue before them was how the allies might attain their goal without being surprised along the way by complications arising from Great Britain or France. Metternich agreed that the most important point was that all the allied powers had recognized the necessity of building 'a dam to resist the torrent of revolutions'. Beyond this, he indicated he had disclosed all his best ideas and that Austria would proceed with the occupation of Naples, but he earnestly invited the Russians to present their own views. What 'system of conduct' would they recommend? Since by then it was already midnight, their discussion ended.[10]

Capodistrias' 'System of Conduct'

The next official session of the Congress was held at Metternich's rented house on the afternoon of 29 October. Not only the eastern powers but also the British and French 'observers' were in attendance. Metternich read several of the most recent despatches received, including a letter from the King of Naples himself. Hardenberg submitted Prussian comments on the earlier Austrian memorandum and expressed his desire for an allied declaration against revolution; but he also conveyed Prussia's willingness to defer to the views of the other allied courts.[11] In truth, the Prussian Chancellor was greatly distracted by the constitutional conflict still proceeding in Berlin.

Nesselrode made a short statement at the same session, but the official Russian response to Metternich's proposals came in the form of a memorandum, circulated on 2 November and discussed by the ministers of the three eastern powers throughout the course of the following week. Not surprisingly, Capodistrias' lengthy memorandum was quite at odds with Metternich's proposed course of action, but it was quite consistent with his own earlier advice to the Tsar. Its preamble articulated a general right of intervention based on the treaties of 1814 and 1815 and the agreements at Aix-la-Chapelle, and drew an explicit analogy between the current situation in Naples and that of France during the 'Hundred Days' of 1815. Once again, said Capodistrias, the allies had a 'moral duty' to set things right. He then proposed an allied 'System of Conduct' resting on three broad principles: (1) states disturbed by revolution no longer belonged to the European alliance; (2) 'revolutionized states' that threatened others, either by their example or conduct, required the intervention of the allied powers 'to protect the states thus corrupted against the progress of the evil and Europe against its contagion'; and finally (3) any such counter-revolutionary intervention must be based on existing treaties and must respect current territorial divisions. The Russians thus agreed with Metternich that Europe was under siege by the dark forces of revolution and that a firm showing of allied unity was the best way to combat these evils. But Metternich had proposed intervention by Austria as an endangered state, acting with the moral support of her allies; Capodistrias urged intervention by the alliance on the grounds of general principles, with Austria acting as their agent. This elevation of the right of intervention to a matter of principle, as the participants well knew, directly contradicted all of Castlereagh's previous admonishments.[12]

Far worse from Metternich's perspective was the specific application that Capodistrias now made of these principles to Naples. The aim of the allies, he said, should be to provide Naples with the 'dual freedoms' of political liberty and national independence. The allied powers should begin by making a joint proclamation to the people of Naples: this should demand that they liberate the King, quash all revolutionary legislation, suppress the sects, and establish 'an order of things which would guarantee the realization of a wish authentically national' ('un ordre de choses qui garantirait la réalisation d'un voeu authentiquement national'). Though vague, this final formula implied that the Neapolitans should convene some sort of national representative body (much as the Tsar had recommended for France in 1814, Poland in 1815 and Spain in 1820). If the Neapolitans accepted these terms, Capodistrias concluded, then the allies could offer to mediate between Ferdinand and his subjects. If they refused, then Austria should occupy the country on behalf of the allies.

In short, Capodistrias wished to see the Neapolitan Revolution destroyed no less than Metternich, but he preferred for this to be accomplished through friendly mediation and the erection of a moderate constitution, rather than by Austrian bayonets. Moreover, if Austria did march into Naples, he desired that she should act as the agent of the alliance and thereby be subject to the supervision and interference of the other powers.[13] In his diary, Hardenberg wrote approvingly that the Russian memorandum had 'much that is good and not mystical'.[14]

On 5 November, the Russian ministers submitted an explanation of their conduct to the Tsar for his approval. In two remarkable internal memoranda, of which Capodistrias appears to have been the principal author, they listed a number of specific objectives for the Congress: (1) an act explaining that any government that submits to or sanctions a revolution is 'excluded from the European alliance', thereby giving the allies the right to intervene to bring that state 'back into the alliance' if it shows hostility to other states by either 'its example or influence'; (2) an allied communiqué to the Neapolitans asking them to introduce reforms, establishing 'on the one part the inviolability of the legitimate power' of the King and, on the other, the need for 'wise institutions conforming to the needs and wishes of the Sicilian nation' (in effect, a constitutional government); (3) an agreement that allied intervention in Naples should follow the same principles as the earlier occupation of France in 1815–18, with the Austrian army acting 'under the name of the army of Europe' and a conference of allied ministers negotiating with the Neapolitan government; (4) after the restoration of royal authority in Naples, an application by the allies of the same principles to the revolutionary states of Spain and Portugal; and finally (5) the allied courts should meet again in 12 to 18 months to conclude 'a pact of solidarity between the governments of Europe', which would guarantee to each 'the double advantage[s] of political independence and interior security', providing happiness to their people and stability to their institutions. Instead of replying to the note from Naples, Capodistrias further proposed that the allies invite the King to send one or two representatives to Troppau to concert with the allies 'on how to liberate the King from the influence of the sects and reconstruct the monarchy'.[15] The objectives thus reiterated many of the common themes of Russian policy since 1814.[16]

Behind the scenes, the energetic Capodistrias laboured at undermining Metternich's programme through secret collaboration with the French. At Warsaw, he had favourably received the French proposal for Franco-Russian mediation. Although his ideas had not yet been fully accepted by the Tsar, he had sent a message to Paris recommending that Louis XVIII—as head of the House of Bourbon and the first monarch in Europe to have 'voluntarily accepted a constitution'—offer to mediate between Europe on the one side and the two revolutionary states of Naples and Spain on the other. Moderate liberals and representatives hand-picked by each king could then hammer out a consensus under French supervision. Capodistrias further informed the French ministers that the Tsar was inclined to accept this proposal, but only if the other allied cabinets would also agree. Both Richelieu and Pasquier were delighted and hastily sent messages to Troppau in support of these propositions.[17] Meanwhile, a second initiative for moderate constitutional reform and French mediation had originated among the moderates in Naples, who sent Prince Cariati as their representative to sound out opinions in Paris. Finally, the French chargé d'affaires in Naples was also working towards the same end. It appeared that this active constitutional offensive might finally halt the Austrian war machine. The decision to intervene was therefore neither a straightforward nor an easy one.[18]

Metternich parries the thrust

The situation was serious enough for Metternich to appeal directly to the Tsar. If Russia would not lend her support quickly and without conditions, he boldly announced, Austria would act unilaterally—even at the cost of dissolving the alliance itself. Metternich also brought Alexander additional alleged proofs of the activities of the secret societies and of French intrigues in Italy. A written response to Capodistrias was swiftly prepared by Gentz and presented by Metternich at the next conference. It argued that Capodistrias had failed to interpret correctly the treaties of 1814 and 1815, which did not strictly require intervention. The Austrians further asserted that it was inappropriate for the allies to discuss the future government of Naples since this could only be determined by the King of Naples himself. The allies especially could not require that a representative assembly of the Neapolitan people be convened to ascertain the 'authentic national' will, since such a requirement would constitute an unreasonable interference in Naples' internal affairs. Moreover, the genuine national will was to be found not in popular assemblies, but in the royal sovereign, chosen by Providence as the sole 'legitimate interpreter' of the 'national wishes'. Indeed, it was hardly fitting for the absolute monarchs of Russia and Austria to require the summoning of representative bodies in other states. Instead, the scope of allied intervention should be narrowly tailored to the restoration of legitimate power: 'Austria prejudices in no way the use which the royal power, once re-established, will consider it ought to make of its incontestable faculty to take into consideration the real needs of its people. The allies ... can give advice ... but cannot infringe upon the rights of legitimate authority.'[19]

On 7 and 8 November, the ministers of the three eastern courts met again at Metternich's rooms, where the Austrian foreign minister read the latest correspondence from Naples, including a letter from the King showing that he still feared for his life. Ferdinand confirmed that everything he had done since July had been under the threat of force. Metternich, Capodistrias, Nesselrode and Hardenberg continued their negotiations two days later at Bernstorff's, who was suffering from an attack of gout. The ministers discussed endlessly how to apply their general counter-revolutionary principles to the specific case of Naples. The Russians proposed to serve as mediators, but their offer was rebuffed.

That evening, after Capodistrias and Nesselrode had left, Metternich came up with one of his master strokes. Capodistrias had suggested that the King of Naples send an envoy to Troppau—Metternich would propose instead that the allied powers invite the King of Naples himself to meet with them. On the one hand, the invitation would unmask the rebels in Naples, who claimed to be acting with the King's consent. Either they would refuse to let Ferdinand leave the country, revealing that he was in fact their prisoner, or they would allow him to leave, in which case he could be expected to denounce the revolution as soon as he was safely out of their grip. The very debate, moreover, was certain to sharpen the antagonisms between the Neapolitan moderates and radicals. The proposed invitation also served a second and more devious purpose—the frustration of all the mediation projects being put forward by Capodistrias and the French. The King of Naples himself would perform the role of mediator between the powers of Europe and his wayward subjects. What need could there be for Louis XVIII or any other mediator when His Sicilian Majesty was ready to perform this task? Lastly, the King's departure from Naples would rob France and Britain of any pretext that their neutrality was necessary in order to protect the life of the King.[20]

In the meantime, Capodistrias had also been at work at his drafting table. On the 14th, he presented a sketch for the basis of future allied conduct—'Bases d'une Transaction'—which included general principles for intervention similar to those in his earlier 'System of Conduct', coupled with a proposal that an effort be made at a friendly reconciliation with Naples without military action.[21] Here, then, lay the chief difference between the two men. Both equally deplored the Neapolitan Revolution, but Capodistrias wanted to provide the Neapolitans with an opportunity to avoid military intervention through mediation and to replace the revolutionary regime with a liberal constitutional state; Metternich preferred simply to crush the revolution and restore the full plenitude of royal power.

The mutiny of the Semenovsky

The cogency of Metternich's arguments was fortuitously strengthened by external events. On 14 November, news reached Troppau of a mutiny of the elite Semenovsky Regiment at St Petersburg, which had demanded the dismissal of its commanding officer.[22] To grasp the significance of this event, it is necessary to understand something of the exalted position that the Semenovsky Regiment held in the imperial army, and indeed in Russian society generally. A century earlier, Peter the Great had organized two prestigious regiments of imperial guards—the Preobrazhensky and the Semenovsky—to replace the mutinous *streltsy*. Both regiments had fought with distinction against the Swedes at Poltava. Later Tsars and Tsarinas had often chosen to be depicted in the uniforms of these regiments in their portraits. Only the most talented from the highest ranks of the nobility had once served in these regiments. The Semenovsky Regiment had played a key role in Catherine's palace coup against her husband, Peter III, and as a young Grand Duke,

Alexander had held his very first commission as an officer of the Semenovsky. The conspirators had deliberately waited until the regiment was on duty to strike against Paul I, and Alexander was wearing a uniform of the Semenovsky on the day he received news of Napoleon's invasion.[23]

Paul I had opened up the regiment to commoners, but its officers continued to come from the best noble families, and under its popular commanding officer, General Potemkin, it had remained a bastion of comfort, even for non-commissioned men. The Tsar typically received a report from 'his' illustrious regiment each evening. In July 1819, the Tsar's youngest brother, the Grand Duke Michael Pavlovich, was appointed commander of the brigade and was shocked to learn of the special privileges still enjoyed by the Semenovksy Regiment. The Grand Duke Michael and Count Alexis Arakcheev replaced Potemkin with Colonel F.E. Schwartz, a harsh disciplinarian. Schwartz constantly flew into a rage at daily inspections, spat on his men and even violated army regulations by ordering corporal punishment for minor infractions committed by soldiers decorated for their bravery in the Napoleonic Wars. On the evening of 17 October 1820, the enlisted men of the First Company informed their commander that they would no longer obey Schwartz's orders. A French envoy, the Comte de Gabriac, reporting to Le Ferronays, blamed the regiment's mild insubordination

> on the fatal military mania of the imperial family, the deplorable heritage of Paul I and Peter III ... which has nothing in common with the real spirit of war, but which continually torments the soldiers with drills, censures of their behaviour, and inspections of their barracks, encouraged by commanders ever more difficult and demanding, like the cruel Schwartz.

Schwartz fled the scene, but the general in command of the imperial guards assembled the company and ordered the men to march to the Peter and Paul Fortress for imprisonment. When the other companies of the regiment objected, they, too, were imprisoned. This was the shocking news that was now rushed to the Tsar at Troppau by special messenger.[24]

Stewart wrote to his brother that the Tsar was 'visibly affected at this incident'. Alexander told his allies that he blamed the mutiny on the recently introduced system of education, which had permitted the guards to form their own classes and 'gave facilities to discontented spirits to cabal and seduce'.[25] But in fact, the Tsar could not bring himself to believe that insubordination in this famous regiment had been caused either by harsh conditions, the conduct of Schwartz, or even by the actions of his own soldiers. Instead, he attributed the mutiny to the activity of foreign revolutionaries—the mythical 'Secret Committee', which both Metternich and Alexander believed was orchestrating events from Paris. In a private letter sent to his minister Count Arakcheev, the Tsar revealed his true feelings:

> Since I am accustomed to speaking to you confidentially, I can say nothing will convince me, whatever people may say, that this action was planned by our soldiers or arose solely from their harsh treatment ... I think the incitement came from outside the army ... I blame the secret societies which, according to the evidence both you and I possess, are much displeased with our alliance and our work at Troppau. It would appear as if the object of the insurrection was to intimidate us ... to force me to abandon my work at Troppau and to make me return speedily to St. Petersburg. But through the will of God, we have avoided this and snuffed out the evil at birth.[26]

The impact: Metternich's triumph

By now, the Tsar had experienced difficulties with the Polish *Sejm* in Warsaw; there had also been unrest in the German states, uprisings in Latin America, Spain and Portugal, the assassination of the Duc de Berri in France, mass demonstrations and the Cato Street conspiracy in Britain, the rebellion in Naples and, finally, his own beloved Semenovksy Regiment had mutinied. Moreover, he was being subjected to increasingly conservative pressures emanating from Russia. For years, Lebzeltern's reports from St Petersburg had described the opposition of the Russian serf owners to reforms that might threaten the institution of serfdom, while the Tsar's close friend Prince Alexander Golitsyn had grown hostile to liberal reformers, whom he suspected of harbouring atheistic views; finally, the romantic nationalist historian Nikolai Karamzin was writing that Russians should reject the cosmopolitan values of the West, especially liberal constitutionalism, in favour of their own traditions of paternal Tsarist autocracy.[27] Under the impact of these events, the Tsar fell increasingly under Metternich's spell and became quite willing to dispense with Capodistrias' programme for moderate constitutional reform. This indeed marked a momentous turning point in Alexander's outlook and in the history of the alliance as a whole. The Tsar's liberal policies and even his romantic vision of Christian ecumenicalism became increasingly captive to his fears of revolution and to Metternich's enchantment.

To ensure that the issue of mediation would never rear its head again, Metternich also deliberately planted the idea of a French mediation with one of the French delegates, the Marquis de Caraman, in a form in which it was certain to be rejected. The incident offers an illuminating demonstration of Metternich's consummate skill—or deviousness—in the conduct of diplomacy.

Caraman was completely ignorant of the French mediation proposal, which had been conveyed in secret instructions to his rival, the Comte de la Ferronnays. On 7 November, he privately discussed the possibility of French mediation with Metternich, who seemed to welcome the idea. Richelieu and Pasquier were elated with Caraman's report and instructed him to offer the 'good offices' of Louis XVIII, but to avoid the word 'mediation'. La Ferronnays realized, however, that the proposal was being raised at the worst possible moment, since Metternich was using it to support his allegations to the Tsar that the French were intentionally sabotaging the alliance in order to place themselves at the head of a league of constitutional states. Once Caraman learned of the invitation to Ferdinand he, too, realized that he had been duped. But the damage was already done: the Tsar expressed outrage at the prospect of mediation between legitimate rulers and revolutionaries and delivered a vigorous reprimand to La Ferronnays (as French ambassador to Russia). Caraman was also publicly humiliated when his proposal was formally discussed and rejected at the conference session of 7 December. Thus, the two-headed hydra of Franco-Russian mediation and constitutional reform in Naples was, to all appearances, soundly slain by Metternich.[28]

Metternich consents to general principles

With respect to the form under which the intervention should take place, Alexander remained insistent that military action should occur only under the auspices of the alliance and not as a purely unilateral act. Though certain to antagonize Castlereagh, Metternich was willing to concede this much to consolidate his triumph over Capodistrias and the French. The notion of establishing general principles for intervention, moreover, was hardly uncongenial to him. Metternich therefore reversed his earlier critique of Capodistrias' interpretation of the treaties and suddenly embraced the Russian view that they imposed a moral duty on the signatories to suppress revolutions in other states.[29]

The *Protocole préliminaire*

The result of this concession was the high-water mark of counter-revolution in the history of Europe—the famous *Protocole préliminaire* (or 'preliminary protocol'), drafted by Capodistrias and negotiated and signed by the three eastern courts at the session of 19 November. Ironically, it was the same day of the year on which, exactly 28 years before, the French Convention had promised to support peoples against kings. The new protocol was the exact antithesis, but it adopted the same moral fervour as the earlier Girondin decree. Its first section set forth three propositions strongly redolent of Capodistrias' earlier 'System of Conduct' and his 'Bases of a Transaction':

(1) States belonging to the European alliance, which have experienced changes in the form of their internal government (*regime intérieur*) from revolution, with consequences that threaten other states, *ipso facto* cease to be part of the alliance and shall remain excluded from it until their situation provides guarantees of legal order and stability.
(2) The allied powers do not limit themselves simply to announcing this exclusion; but, faithful to the principles that they have proclaimed and to the respect owed to the authority of every legitimate government, they refuse to extend their recognition to changes brought about by such illegal methods.
(3) When states where such changes have occurred cause other countries to fear immediate danger because of their proximity, and when the allied powers are able to exercise effective and beneficial action towards them, then, in order to return them to the alliance, the allied powers will employ: first, friendly representations; and second, measures of coercion, wherever such coercion is required.[30]

With these words, the great alliance, whose goal had once been the general peace and cooperation of nations, now became shackled to the task of counter-revolution. While fear of revolution had first given rise to the Congress System, it now became its exclusive concern. It is equally obvious that these principles cleverly provided a rationale for allied intervention in Naples while excusing inaction in Spain.

The *Protocole* went on to say that since Naples had undergone revolutionary changes, the powers were determined to take affirmative steps to liberate the King of Naples and the nation—restoring royal authority on a solid basis and assuring the nation 'its tranquillity and happiness' (which was all that remained of Capodistrias' earlier paean to the 'authentic wishes of the nation'). For this purpose, the *Protocole* said, the kingdom would be occupied by an Austrian army acting in the name of the allied powers. Attached to the protocol was the invitation to the King of Naples to meet with the allied sovereigns.

Initial British objections

While the British and French observers had attended the earlier official sessions of the conference, the drafting of the *Protocole préliminaire* took place entirely beyond their ken.[31] As Stewart wrote to his brother, when they visited

Metternich's lodgings, they found the conference doors shut. On 19 November, after a long and splendid dinner presented by the Austrian Emperor, Stewart, Caraman and La Ferronnays finally met again with the ministers of the eastern courts for a formal session of the Congress. Metternich produced the *Protocole préliminaire*, already bearing the signatures of Metternich, Hardenberg, Bernstorff, Nesselrode and Capodistrias. The eastern powers also announced that an invitation was being extended to King Ferdinand to meet with the allied sovereigns at Laibach, several hundred miles to the south, in January.[32] Stewart's indignation knew no bounds, for the protocol violated every British stricture regarding the scope of the alliance. The manner in which it was drawn up and communicated further betrayed a total lack of regard for British interests. Metternich later tried to explain all this away by telling Stewart that his main concern had been to keep the French delegates out of the discussions and to prevent their intriguing with Capodistrias. Metternich even disclosed the secret instructions that the three eastern courts had sent to their envoys in London in the event that a change in the British government resulted in the release of Bonaparte.[33]

None of these palliatives could compensate for the shoddy treatment that the British had received. Even before receiving the *Protocole préliminaire*, Castlereagh suspected Metternich of buckling under Russian pressure. A cabinet memorandum, sent to Stewart on 4 December, warned that any general principle of allied intervention proclaimed from Troppau would dangerously mislead the monarchs of Europe into thinking that they could always retain their thrones through foreign support. Castlereagh, who like the others had lived through the execution of Louis XVI, greatly feared that the secret appeals of the King to the allies at Troppau were only courting disaster:

> I cannot but lament ... this hazardous mission and especially at the present moment, from which nothing but danger to the King's person and to his authority can, as I apprehend, be expected to result. It is impossible not to tremble, when one adverts to the number of letters now in existence, any one of which might prove fatal to a Sovereign, if by any imprudence it should fall into improper hands. This, amongst other considerations, ought to induce our Allies gravely to weigh how far they can venture on the responsibility of systematically encouraging all the Crowned Heads of Europe to expect aid from them in those perilous situations in which they either are, or may find themselves involved.[34]

This fatal delusion, the British Foreign Secretary warned, would discourage rulers from either maintaining power by their own means or accommodating themselves to necessary changes in their systems of government.[35]

Castlereagh berated Esterhazy, the Austrian ambassador, commenting bitterly that the 'right which the [allied] monarchs claim to judge and condemn the actions of other states establishes a precedent that is dangerous to the liberties of the world'.[36] He sardonically remarked to Lieven how singular it was for the eastern powers to be scrapping the alliance in favour of such discredited doctrines as divine right and passive obedience.[37]

A more formal protest to the *Protocole préliminaire* was forwarded to Stewart at Troppau less than two weeks later. The right claimed by the three eastern courts, Castlereagh contended, was in direct violation of international law. Britain herself would be excluded from the alliance by the principles of the protocol, since her own political system was the product of the Glorious Revolution and the Act of Settlement. 'The extreme right of interference between nation and nation', he continued, could 'never be properly made a matter of stipulation or be assumed as the attribute of the Alliance'. The promulgation of such principles was more likely to promote than to discourage Jacobinism by arousing popular distrust. No improved order of things could be expected to result from threatening nations with foreign intervention or by imposing unpopular governments. The logic of Castlereagh's arguments and the emotional force with which they were conveyed drove home the message that they were a sincere expression of his views.[38]

Yet Castlereagh also confided to Lieven, the Russian ambassador, that it was less the aims of the eastern courts than their public announcement that he opposed. He continued to share their abhorrence at the progress of the revolutionary movement.[39] While this remark may have weakened the force of his criticism, it indicated his hope that an open breach in the alliance might still be avoided. It further shows Castlereagh's continuing concern with parliamentary management—a theme he had emphasized to the other allied leaders in discussions on the Hundred Days, at Aix-la-Chapelle in 1818, with regard to the Carlsbad Decrees, and most famously, in his State Paper of 5 May 1820.

Even before Castlereagh's response was received, Stewart's initial reaction was so severe that the three eastern courts realized they might have to abandon the protocol. Metternich still aimed, however, at committing Russia in a formal treaty against revolution, decisively separating Alexander from the liberal movement. The unity of the two courts that Metternich regarded as the most 'free in thought and action'—Austria and Russia—would more than compensate for the dissension of England. As Stewart explained to his half-brother, '900,000 Russians in his rear and the mystified character of the minister at the helm leads Prince Metternich to consider all points and objects as secondary to that of committing Russia in the eyes of Europe against liberal and revolutionary doctrines, and to the embarking her in a common cause with Austria against constitutional Italy and Germany'.[40]

The Act of Guarantee

To accompany the earlier protocol, Metternich had also instructed Gentz to draft an 'Act of Guarantee', something he had considered even before the Congress of Troppau. At least one historian has seen the guarantee as the natural outcome of the proposed *Protocole préliminaire*: having lost British support, there was no longer any bar to the conclusion of the guarantee long sought by the Continental powers.[41] A guarantee of thrones and territories had been anxiously sought by the Russians at both Vienna and Aix-la-Chapelle and was even included in the Russian ministers' confidential memorandum to the Tsar of just a few weeks earlier. With a harsh condemnation of the protocol expected from London, the guarantee seemed likely to take its place. Indeed, the first three principles of the guarantee did not differ appreciably from those of the protocol, except that Gentz drew a new distinction between changes introduced by legitimate authority and genuinely 'revolutionary' states:

(1) Every revolution brought about by usurped power or in a manifestly illegal fashion, and even more so, every revolution conceived and executed by criminal means, becomes *ipso facto*, whatever its character, its course, or its effects, the object of a just and legitimate intervention by foreign powers.
(2) Revolutions conceived and executed by the legitimate powers of the state justify foreign intervention only in cases where they expose the primary interests of neighbouring states or the whole of civilized society to evident danger by their character, their course or their effects.
(3) When a revolution combines these two characteristics—both an illegal origin and a dangerous and hostile tendency towards other states—the right of intervention attains its maximum force.[42]

Under this new typology, Britain's Glorious Revolution was distinguishable from the Spanish and Neapolitan Revolutions: it had been carried out by a legitimate power rather than through criminal means, and it had not exposed neighbouring states to danger (although neither the Irish nor Louis XIV would have agreed). In the tumultuous times since the French Revolution, however, no real benefit could ever hope to accrue from revolutionary changes, since the very example of a successful revolution would in itself have a destabilizing effect on others. Where a revolution was not caused or confirmed by legitimate authority, and where it further posed a threat to neighbouring states, intervention became a moral duty. On this basis, the allied powers would effectively guarantee the legitimate sovereign and the fundamental institutions of every state in Europe. The language of the guarantee provided, however, that the allied powers would not interfere in instances where a legitimate sovereign had granted limited reforms—such as the French *Charte*. This preserved one avenue for social change and improvement, but no other changes would be countenanced. Even where a legitimate sovereign subsequently sanctioned an illegal change—such as had seemingly occurred at Naples—that state would not be excused from allied intervention unless the powers themselves agreed that the change was consistent with the peace and tranquillity of Europe.

While the guarantee asserted that intervention against revolutionary regimes was always justified, the form that it might take would be contingent upon specific circumstances. In some cases, the allied powers might suppress a revolutionary government for posing a danger to neighbouring states, even though this new government had been approved by the legitimate monarch; in other cases, the powers might not intervene at all.[43]

The proposed guarantee demonstrated the extent to which Metternich was now willing to abandon his earlier partnership with Britain. The act deliberately borrowed language from prior Russian proposals, while it also struggled with the problem of balancing demands for political legitimacy with the broader need for a stable international order. Both the guarantee and the earlier protocol were attempts to provide that surety of thrones which the Tsar had requested but which the allied powers had refused to grant at Vienna and Aix-la-Chapelle. But with all pretence of internal constitutional reform dropped, the high-flown rhetoric of the guarantee was trenchantly criticized by none other than Capodistrias himself when it was finally presented by Metternich and Gentz at the conference session of 28 November. If the guarantee was based on the treaties of 1814 and 1815, as the Austrians claimed, Capodistrias queried why it was needed at all. Why not adopt a simple protocol, elucidating the terms of the existing agreements, as Russia had advocated at Aix-la-Chapelle? On the other hand, if the act created new rights, then it was unlikely that constitutional states such as England, France and the Netherlands would be willing to sign it. Encountering this unanticipated assault, Metternich abruptly abandoned the guarantee. It never even came before the British and the French, who would most certainly have rejected it.[44]

The Troppau Circular

The result was that the only significant public document to issue from Troppau grappling with general intervention principles was the circular that the three eastern powers finalized at the conference session of 7 December and sent to their diplomatic missions just afterwards, while still waiting to receive official responses to the *Protocole préliminaire* from London and Paris. The 'Troppau Circular' repeated much of the earlier protocol's inflated phraseology and could hardly have made pleasant reading for the members of the British cabinet.

The circular began by declaring that the powers, who had so recently cooperated in delivering Europe from Napoleon, would now 'put a curb on a force no less tyrannical and no less detestable, that of revolution and crime'. The three eastern courts claimed the right to adopt common measures of safety and precaution against the dangers posed by revolutionary states—especially when those states attempted to propagate revolution beyond their own borders. While the powers had no aims of territorial aggrandizement and would not oppose wise and judicious reforms adopted by legitimate sovereigns of their own free will, they were resolute in their determination to deliver Europe from the curse of revolution. Since the dangers arising from the Neapolitan Revolution clearly posed a threat to other states, the powers declared that they would apply these principles to that unhappy kingdom. The circular explained that the King of Naples had been invited to meet the allies at Laibach, where he would be free of all constraints and would act as mediator between his 'erring people and the states whose tranquillity they threatened'.

The Troppau Circular concluded by stating that its principles were based on the treaties of 1814 and 1815 and that the decisions reached at Troppau were being conveyed to Britain and France so that those governments might take them under their 'consideration'.[45] Castlereagh accepted none of its propositions, and when the circular was later leaked to the London press, he was forced to repudiate it publicly.

Plans for reform in Naples and for papal mediation

While the ministers at Troppau were thrashing out the general principles of intervention, Metternich also busied himself with the critical task of determining the future organization of the government of Naples. He had initially objected to Capodistrias' plans for constitutional reform on the grounds that the allied powers had no business meddling in that kingdom's internal affairs beyond the restoration of its legitimate monarch, but now that Alexander had converted to the cause of legitimacy, Metternich was suddenly willing to put forward his own agenda for domestic reform. Once Ferdinand was safely out of the hands of the revolutionaries, Metternich proposed he should revoke all of the changes that had occurred since the outbreak of the revolution.

First and foremost, the King was to reassert his own absolute power and to reject all forms of representative assembly. But Europe was also entitled to some form of assurance for the future stability of Naples. It would therefore be necessary, Metternich stated, for Ferdinand to consult the needs of his people and to strengthen his administration by the creation of advisory bodies, much as Metternich had proposed for Austria in 1817. A conference of allied ambassadors should guide the King through the delicate period of transition. Eventually, the King should create an advisory Senate, composed of separate Neapolitan and Sicilian sections, while provincial bodies composed of the chief landowners should administer the countryside. Finally, and most startlingly, Metternich proposed that Ferdinand confirm these new arrangements by granting a 'pragmatic sanction', to be guaranteed by the allied powers, binding the King and his heirs to the new system in perpetuity. The newly reorganized government of Naples would provide a model for the other Italian states, which Metternich hoped to see widely imitated. These ideas were to be refined further at Laibach. None of these purely administrative reforms, however, addressed the kingdom's deeper economic and social needs.[46]

Meanwhile, French policy at Troppau had fallen into a state of some confusion. Although Pasquier, the French foreign minister, resolved to reject the *Protocole préliminaire* as early as 1 December, he waited until the middle of the month before sending instructions to Troppau, so that France might be seen as following Britain's lead. The eastern courts readily forgave Castlereagh for rejecting the protocol since he was obviously constrained by domestic politics, but they accepted no such excuse from the French.

This same pattern of hesitation was repeated with respect to the invitation to Ferdinand: Louis XVIII sent a separate invitation to the King of Naples to repair to Laibach, but it was not forwarded in time to accompany the invitation from Troppau, and in fact was not delivered before Ferdinand actually left Naples. Thus, when Caraman and La Ferronnays complained to the other ministers that most of the difficulties in the negotiation could be traced to the three eastern powers' habit of meeting in private to reach all the principal decisions, Metternich and Capodistrias retorted that the French themselves were to blame for sending a delegation so lacking in authority that it was powerless to act without reference to Paris.[47]

At the session of 7 December, Capodistrias made a last clever bid for mediation—this time by proposing that if the Neapolitans should refuse to let Ferdinand leave the kingdom, the Pope should come forward to mediate between Naples and the allied powers. Metternich again displayed his mastery of diplomatic tactics by warmly embracing the proposal rather than rejecting it. He enthusiastically suggested that a letter of invitation be sent to Rome at once. In subsequent discussions with Capodistrias, the Austrian foreign minister objected to the use of the term 'mediator' in the invitation, and subtly altered its contents so that the Pope was requested to add his spiritual support to the moral support of the allies and the material assistance of Austria. To add insult to injury, the Austrian diplomat Lebzeltern was chosen to carry the invitation to Rome. Metternich told Lebzeltern that the appeal to the Pope was nonsensical and that Austria had only agreed to the proposition to humour the Tsar; Lebzeltern was further instructed to ensure that the offer was rejected in Rome. At the same time, Lebzeltern was to conduct secret talks in Rome to obtain permission for the passage of Austrian troops through the Papal States on their way to Naples. Once again, Capodistrias was hopelessly outmanoeuvred.[48]

Metternich's 'Profession of Faith'

By mid-December, Metternich was spending his evenings at Troppau in long tea-drinking sessions with the Tsar. The tenor of their conversations can be surmised from Metternich's 'Profession of Faith', a document specially prepared for the Tsar with the approval of the Austrian Emperor, and purportedly representing Metternich's political credo. Crudely fashioned to win Alexander's approval for his policies, it nevertheless provides an interesting glimpse into how this generation continued to cope with the upheavals of their age. Europe was in turmoil, the 'Profession' began, with all customs, laws, religion and morality brought into doubt and disrepute. To what could this breakdown in order be attributed? After briefly tracing the history of the world from Roman times, Metternich focused on the invention of printing, the Reformation and the rapid growth of human knowledge. One of the consequences of these astounding improvements had been the appearance of what Metternich identified as the 'presumptuous man'—one who believes that each person should act as his own guide, make up his own laws and substitute his own judgement for received tradition and established authority. The invention of the printing press especially compounded the evil by accelerating the circulation of such presumptuous ideas. The weaknesses of governments and the presumptuousness of a small group of talented men had finally led to the outbreak of the French Revolution. The despotism of Bonaparte helped to disseminate the evil by displacing local laws, institutions and customs across Europe. The revolutionary spirit had spread from France to Germany, Italy and Spain, where it was kept alive by secret societies whose rallying cry was the demand for a constitution. The middle classes were especially prone to infection with these ideas—they pretended to speak for the common folk to justify their own ambitions when, in fact, the great mass of people remained indifferent.

In the face of these challenges, Metternich called upon the legitimate monarchs of Europe to fulfil their sacred duties by restoring order and tranquillity. The present moment demanded strong government, stability and the maintenance of existing laws and institutions, not experimentation with untried reforms that excited popular passions. As a remedy to these evils, Metternich prescribed repression against the secret societies and the press, caution in approaching reform, strict observance of religion, sound state finances, and most important of all, solidarity among legitimate sovereigns. 'To every great state determined to survive the storm, there still remain many chances of salvation, and a strong union between states on the principles we have announced will overcome the storm itself.'[49]

While Metternich's 'Profession of Faith' expressed some sincerely held convictions, it is not too far-fetched to suppose that the 'presumptuous man' it identified was none other than his principal antagonist at Troppau, Capodistrias. Despite all these Herculean labours to win over the heart and mind of the Tsar, it appears that even as late as the week before Christmas Alexander's 'conversion' was less than complete. The Russian ruler still told Stewart that he hoped the display of allied unity at Troppau would be sufficient to persuade the Neapolitans to end their revolution and reform their government, avoiding the need for military intervention at the eleventh hour.

Reactions in Naples

All eyes were therefore focused on Naples and how that country would react. The Neapolitan Parliament had begun its session at the beginning of October. At first, its deputies had hoped for a reconciliation with Austria, but they were dismayed when only Spain and Switzerland recognized their authority and Austria began amassing troops. The deputies optimistically held out hopes that 'truth and justice' would prevail at Troppau, since the allies had seemingly acknowledged constitutionalism in Germany and Spain.[50] The invitation from Troppau to King Ferdinand was received on 6 December. A final French proposal for mediation had already been rejected earlier that same week.

After receiving the allied invitation, Ferdinand initially approached the diplomatic corps in Naples for help in drafting a message to Parliament. A'Court and his colleagues complained that they were probably 'the most unfit persons in the Kingdom to assist at such a discussion' and advised Ferdinand to summon his own ministers instead.[51] The moderates—led by the King's own son, the Duke of Campochiaro, and the finance minister Giuseppe Zurlo—seized the occasion to try to push through constitutional reforms to strengthen the royal prerogative and to win the approbation of the allies.

They successfully persuaded the King to make concessions in order to win the assembly's approval for his departure. On 7 December, the King sent a message to the assembly that if he were permitted to proceed to Laibach, he would do all in his power to persuade the allied sovereigns not to intervene in Naples; he further submitted an elaborate programme of constitutional reform which included introduction of a royal veto, a Chamber of Peers, ministerial responsibility to the Crown and guarantees of individual liberties. The same proclamation was sent to the provinces in an endeavour to win their support. The *Carbonari* in the capital city responded by organizing hostile street demonstrations. The assembly became so intimidated that it rejected the King's message and declared the Spanish Constitution inviolate. Ferdinand was forced to dismiss the Zurlo ministry and to take a solemn oath against altering the existing constitution in any way. On the strength of this promise, the assembly granted the King permission to leave. On the afternoon of 13 December, the British ship *Vengeur*, commanded by the same Captain Maitland who had carried Napoleon off to St Helena in 1815, set sail from the Bay of Naples with the King and the Duc di Gallo aboard.[52] Like Capodistrias, A'Court feared the effect of the King's anticipated disavowal of so many solemn oaths.[53]

The royal party landed in Leghorn and reached Florence by 23 December, where they were greeted by the Comte de Blacas—recently named as the chief plenipotentiary of the French delegation at Laibach and as ambassador to Naples—and by the Austrian diplomat Lebzeltern, then on his way to Rome with the allied invitation to the Pope. Lebzeltern recommended that Ferdinand repudiate his oath at once, even before he met the allies; Blacas cautioned against taking this action, fearing that such a sudden revocation would make the King appear as either deceptive or cowardly. A compromise was adopted in which Ferdinand addressed a confidential letter to the Emperor of Austria, denouncing the Neapolitan Constitution and explaining that he had been forced against his conscience to take an oath upholding it.

Back in Naples, the moderate ministry fell and the radicals assumed the reins of government. Despite their efforts to organize resistance, the country was rapidly plunging into chaos under the pressure of the impending invasion. The new government placed two of the leading moderates, including the Duke of Campochiaro, on trial for treason.[54] Metternich was absolutely elated at this turn of events. Had the Neapolitan moderates pushed through their reform programme, Capodistrias and the French might have found some basis for urging conciliation; now, the Neapolitans themselves had provided the best demonstration of their unsuitability to constitutional rule. As the sovereigns and ministers departed from Troppau for Christmas, all that remained to be done was to receive the King of Naples at Laibach and to issue orders for the Austrian army to commence its march.⁵⁵

The Congress of Laibach and the Piedmontese insurrection, January–May 1821

After welcoming in the New Year at Vienna, the allied leaders proceeded to Laibach (present-day Llubljana), a picturesque town in Austrian Slovenia. Metternich continued to play his favourite role as Congress host. The Congress of Laibach was attended by much the same personnel as Troppau, except for Hardenberg, who returned to Berlin to take up his losing battle for a Prussian constitution. The British and French remained mainly as observers, but the Comte de Blacas now took charge of the French delegation, while Robert Gordon, chargé d'affaires at Vienna, represented Britain during Stewart's increasingly frequent absences. Prince Alvaro Ruffo, Neapolitan ambassador to Vienna and an admirer of Metternich, was appointed as the plenipotentiary for Naples.⁵⁶

At Metternich's suggestion, the allies had agreed to invite to Laibach not only the King of Naples but also representatives from the principal Italian states—Piedmont (Sardinia), Tuscany, Modena and the Holy See (the Papacy). The presence of the Italian courts was intended to strengthen the legitimacy of Austrian operations in Naples. Their attendance also made it possible to deliberate on common measures of administrative reform and repression. Naturally, it was not intended that these new delegates should participate in the proceedings until after the allied powers had reached their own decisions. Some suspected that Metternich might propose an Italian Confederation, although this was not part of his plan. While Metternich believed that approval of the Austrian occupation of Naples by the lesser Italian states would keep French mediation schemes at bay, the French government hoped for precisely the opposite—that the presence of these states might offer them fresh opportunities for restricting Austrian influence.

At Troppau, Metternich had successfully established his sway over the Tsar, thwarted Capodistrias, defeated Franco-Russian attempts at mediation, and obtained freedom for Ferdinand. With Austrian control of operations in Naples now secure, his main concerns at Laibach were preparing the way for an Austrian victory over the Neapolitans, securing the support of France and the Italian states, and finalizing plans for the reconstruction of the Neapolitan government. The 'essential object for Austria after the close of the Troppau Conferences', explained Stewart to his half-brother, 'was to repair her rejection of the French mediation and to secure the aid of France'.⁵⁷

French policy in disarray

The government in Paris, not fully appreciating the new warmth of feeling between Austria and Russia, issued additional instructions for Laibach at the end of December in support of papal mediation. These instructions also specified that in the event of hostilities France would follow Britain's example by remaining neutral. All three French delegates, arriving at Laibach on 8 January, shared the opinion that these new orders had been largely superseded by events: Metternich would welcome the abstention of France, La Ferronnays wrote to Pasquier, since he would present this to the Tsar as further evidence of French sympathy for the revolutionaries; Caraman sensed the hopelessness of expecting moderation from the King of Naples. Blacas was even more emphatic: papal mediation was now a chimera; France could no longer forestall armed intervention, but she might still play an effective role by having her representative on the allied commission that would regulate the future occupation; this final opportunity would be lost if France refused all association with the allied operation. Blacas pointedly asked for permission to return to Rome, feeling his presence at Laibach had become useless. Privately, he regretted that France had not taken an early lead in supporting a fellow Bourbon monarch against revolution.[58]

After reviewing the latest reports from Troppau, Pasquier and Richelieu retracted their new instructions even before receiving these trenchant criticisms from their emissaries. Pasquier might even have been willing to sever French ties with the alliance, but Richelieu was determined to preserve the fragile links forged at Aix-la-Chapelle. The ministers were also reluctant to risk alienating the independent Italian courts. An entirely new set of instructions, issued on 9 January, gave Blacas full authority to concur in any act adopted by the three eastern allies and approved by the Italian states—even extending to armed intervention in Naples. The government in Paris approved the future appointment of a French commissioner to help administer the occupation.[59]

Why, throughout this period, did French policy continually appear to be in such disarray? The underlying reason for French vacillation lay in the fact that France could not, as a constitutional state and after the occupation of 1815–18, wholly side with the autocratic eastern powers; and yet, as a Continental monarchy, and after struggling to attain parity within the alliance, she also could not desert it.[60]

The conference sessions and the fictitious conference journal

By the time the sovereigns and their ministers reconvened in Laibach, Capodistrias' reputation had sunk so low that Metternich recorded with glee that the Corfiote 'writhes like a devil in holy water'. But the Tsar was still determined, as the British envoy Robert Gordon reported, to obtain 'a justification of the reasons which have called upon him to act a principal part in the measures to be taken against Naples; and, as if impressed with a notion that great odium will be attached to the interference of Russia in this question, he seems anxious to prove to Europe that [he] has not been motiv[at]ed by choice, but in conformity with the obligations imposed upon him by treaties, and the principles of the alliance'. [61]

The early Congress sessions

As at Troppau, most of the important business continued to be conducted in private conferences between the ministers of the three eastern powers. The British had few objections to this mode of proceeding since they wished to avoid all association with odious measures of repression. The French, however, were highly offended at their continuing exclusion from the councils of Europe. On 11 January, Blacas and Caraman went to Metternich's residence in protest and won a partial victory: the first plenary session of the Congress—with both the French and British in attendance—was held the very next day.[62]

After the conference on 12 January there was another lull in the official sessions while Metternich, Capodistrias, Nesselrode and Bernstorff continued to meet privately with Prince Ruffo of Naples. At an interview between Metternich and Alexander on 13 January, some of the most important decisions of the Congress were taken. The Tsar and the Austrian foreign minister agreed that the King of Naples should submit a letter to the allied powers requesting their assistance, that the allies should then provide an official reply and that letters conveying the allies' determination should be sent by the King to his son, the Prince Vicar-General, then acting as Regent in Naples.[63]

Meanwhile, Blacas received his new instructions from Paris on 18 January, furnishing him with full powers to accede to all the resolutions of the allies. He went directly to Metternich to complain of the continuing neglect of France and even threatened to raise the matter directly with the Emperors Francis and Alexander.[64] His protest led to another assembly of all five courts on the following day and to the formal presentation of Prince Ruffo as the Neapolitan plenipotentiary. As at Troppau, Capodistrias proposed that the deliberations should be recorded each day in a conference protocol, signed by each minister. The French and British delegates again objected to this procedure, leading to the adoption of the same expedient as before: the results of each session were to be inscribed in a simple conference journal.[65] The delegates then examined the letters drafted by the three eastern courts, which were to be exchanged between the allies and Naples. After this, the meeting was adjourned.

When the ministers reconvened two days later, on 21 January, Blacas declared the letters proposed by the eastern powers to be unacceptable to France—particularly where they drew specific comparisons between Naples and France during the Hundred Days, doubtless inserted by Capodistrias. Blacas and Capodistrias fell into an acrimonious debate over the degree of cooperation required of France under the engagements undertaken at Aix-la-Chapelle. Their dispute was only resolved by Metternich's explanation that any threatened power had the right to appeal to the allies, but that each of the allied powers could then respond based upon its own peculiar circumstances—perhaps offering moral or material support, or even eschewing any involvement altogether. This ingenious solution was actually an adroit paraphrasing of an argument once used by Capodistrias himself and also employed by Castlereagh to oppose abstract principles of intervention. The cantankerous session ended with Capodistrias suggesting that the French plenipotentiaries should try their own hand at revising the controversial letters.[66]

The fictitious journal

By the time the ministers reassembled the next day, Caraman had reduced the exchange of letters to an imaginary narrative to be included in the instructions to Naples. Were it to be presented in this form, Blacas announced, the French would be able to accede along with the other courts. The eastern courts were extremely pleased with this novel solution. Capodistrias was assigned the task of drafting the proposed instructions and submitted the fruits of his labours on 23 January. But his draft contained language from the spurned *Protocole préliminaire*, which was offensive to both Britain and France. Gordon, the British delegate, protested vehemently, while Blacas announced that France could not agree to the instructions in that shape. Metternich finally broke the deadlock by proposing that Gentz redraft the papers in the form of a fictitious congress journal.[67]

Within a day, the prodigious Gentz had produced the journal, reporting six imaginary sessions from 11 to 22 January, with the controversial letters annexed. Gentz's ruse fooled not only contemporary diplomats but also most subsequent historians. The fictitious journal described how Ruffo had supposedly been admitted as a plenipotentiary and had read a message to the allies from the King of Naples, conveying his gratitude and asking the allies for permission to act as 'conciliator' of his people. It then reported how Metternich had solemnly replied on behalf of the allies, informing Ruffo of their willingness to assist Ferdinand but also of their determination not to recognize changes achieved 'by criminal means'. Ferdinand was called upon to make the supreme sacrifice by violating his oath and renouncing the constitution. Finally, the journal recorded how Ruffo next responded to the allies by presenting the King's submission, including a letter to his son intended for publication in Naples. None of these events had actually occurred, although the enclosed letter was meant to be used. The letter justified Ferdinand's violation of his oath as a necessary step in order to spare his subjects the miseries of war. It also referred to the necessity of providing the allies with guarantees for the future stability of the kingdom. It failed, of course, to make any mention of the imminent occupation of Naples by foreign troops.[68]

To accompany this first letter from the King to his son, a second letter was prepared which the Prince Regent in Naples was instructed to keep secret or to publicize at his own discretion. This second letter announced the pacific and amicable intentions of the allies in sending an Austrian army to Naples to restore order. Yet a third letter was sent to the Prince, which he was instructed to keep secret. It recommended that he appoint a Council of Regency and leave the capital post-haste at the head of his guards, ostensibly to take command of the army. Once safely out of Naples, the Prince was to take refuge in the fortress of Gaeta to await further events. Finally, new instructions were also issued to the allied diplomats at Naples: they were to try to persuade the Prince to overthrow the constitution and to welcome the Austrians peacefully to avoid bloodshed. Metternich doubted this last initiative would succeed, but agreed to it to placate Alexander.[69]

Stewart's outrage

The allied powers reviewed Gentz's journal at a plenary session on 25 January. Stewart, who now participated in the Congress for the first time, was shocked to find Metternich up to his old tricks in trying to associate Britain publicly with the eastern powers in repressive acts. The proposed letters were sprinkled with references to the 'allied sovereigns', which implicated a degree of British consent that would have been impossible to defend in Parliament. Stewart therefore insisted that a formal British disclaimer be entered into the conference journal.[70] To some extent his opposition was more nominal than real. Writing privately to A'Court in Naples, Stewart expressed the view that the British could hardly be held liable for expressions used by the King of Naples in addressing his own son, and that A'Court should enlighten the Neapolitans on the true state of British opinion. 'The nicety of the question', in Stewart's view, was that 'Great Britain should not appear to be included and yet not to withdraw from a moral and intimate understanding with the other powers'.[71]

Of greater importance than Stewart's histrionics at the conference of 25 January was the decision of Blacas, exercising the wider latitude bestowed by his most recent instructions, to accede to the conference protocol in the form of a *note verbale*. The French delegation not only pronounced their agreement with the latest allied resolutions, but also ordered the French chargé d'affaires in Naples to conform to the instructions about to be sent to the envoys of the eastern courts. Such adhesion was not difficult for Blacas, who later wrote that 'if the revolt was not punished at Naples, if the liberals were able to hold on to some hope of safety or protection, all of Italy might follow the example of Spain and Portugal'. It seemed vital to strangle the revolution in its infancy at Naples, while cooperation with the eastern powers also guaranteed a place for France in the decision-making of the coming months.[72]

The Italian states

At the sessions of 26 and 28 January, the four Italian courts at the Congress were finally invited to participate formally by approving the protocol and its attached letters. Only Cardinal Spina, the representative of the Pope, showed signs of resistance by his continuing insistence on papal neutrality (Spina was concerned with Austrian plans to march through papal territories on the way to Naples). On 30 January, the Duc di Gallo—the representative of the constitutional regime in Naples, who had been kept waiting all this time outside Laibach at Görz—was at last permitted to attend the Congress. At a preliminary audience with Ferdinand, Gallo advised his sovereign to protest against the proceedings at Laibach and to return at once to Naples as the protector of his subjects. The King told Gallo frankly that he intended to submit to the allied demands. Gallo arrived at the Congress deliberations just when Stewart and Pozzo di Borgo were engaged in a fierce altercation over whether Gallo should be informed of the British disclaimer. The conference chamber suddenly hushed when Gallo was announced. Ruffo, who was there, stepped into the next room to avoid embarrassment. Metternich read the allied resolution to occupy Naples, and Gallo humbly promised to do all he could to convince his countrymen to respond to allied wishes. To Metternich's delight, Gallo then surprisingly denounced the current government in Naples himself.[73]

In the background, preparations for the Austrian expedition to Naples continued apace. Metternich conveyed copies of their marching orders to the other delegates, and on 29 January, Metternich, Capodistrias, Nesselrode, Bernstorff and Blacas discussed the financing of the expedition. The Neapolitans would, of course, be required to pay for all of the costs once the expeditionary force had crossed the Po River, but a question arose over whether they would also be forced to bear the costs of the Austrian mobilization in prior months. It seemed unlikely that they could support this additional burden, so Metternich made a virtue out of necessity by magnanimously announcing that if the Neapolitans welcomed the occupiers without resistance, they would be relieved of this added cost. Even the expenses of the occupation itself were far greater than the Neapolitans could afford, and Austria therefore offered a loan to Naples for this purpose, to be raised by the Rothschilds and to be guaranteed by Russia and Prussia.[74]

The Austrian expedition to Naples

Sixty thousand Austrian troops crossed the Po River on their way to Naples on 6 February. At Laibach, the allied leaders finalized their plans for the reconstruction of the Neapolitan government. In the elaborate charade that Metternich had designed, the 'initiative' lay with the King of Naples to propose a new form of government, while the principal states of Italy and the allied powers had the right to review and approve the King's plans.[75] For the first time, however, the allies came up against the true character of the ruler whose authority they had done so much to uphold—the Achilles' heel of any system of legitimacy based on hereditary rule. Gentz painted a memorable if lamentable picture of this central figure:

> The King has arrived here without having with him a single man capable of giving advice or transacting business. He has never himself had the least taste for work; he has now so lost the habit of it that it is difficult to engage him to read a dispatch that consists of more than one page ... Like all weak men, he conceives of nothing but extremes; he passes in turn from imprudence to the most fearful reserve, from terror to temerity.[76]

The King made no better impression on Stewart, who warned Castlereagh at the end of January that 'One of the greatest difficulties of all which it is apprehended will now have to be contended with is to operate upon the King's mind to force him to go forward again to Naples. He has not in his own inclination the least disposition for this step, and would much rather go and hunt wild boars near Vienna. He is growing more weak and timid daily'.[77] Back in Naples, A'Court held the same view: 'I believe the Allied Powers had very little idea of the sort of people they had to deal with, or the sort of Govt. this was, when they decided upon sending special plenipotentiaries to Naples. An old proverb says, you cannot build palaces with mud. This will be clearly demonstrated'.[78]

When Ferdinand and Ruffo first submitted their plans to the allies in private, the ministers were sorely disappointed. Ruffo's plan, reported Gordon, was

> so little consonant with the spirit of the times, and contained in so large a proportion all the defects of the ancient government ... that he was requested by all parties to remodel his plan ... Reproducing his ideas they were again objected to upon the same grounds, and even Austria was placed in the singular position of advocating the cause of liberty against the despotic principles upon which Prince Ruffo, in the name of his King, had wished to ground his new system.[79]

Blacas and the ministers of the three eastern courts each drew up their own plans for Naples. Metternich proposed his familiar programme of a royal advisory council (*Consulta*) and a council of state for each realm of the 'Kingdom of the Two Sicilies' (Naples and Sicily). Provincial assemblies were to be appointed by the King, each of which would nominate candidates to the council of state, from whom the King would ultimately choose its members. Capodistrias urged that the *Consulta* should have independent authority, but was successfully opposed by Metternich on the grounds that this might too closely approach a representative system. Even Metternich's modest proposals were only forced upon the King and Ruffo with the utmost difficulty, and Metternich finally had to threaten to withdraw all Austrian support to bring Ferdinand to his senses. Plans for the reconstruction of Naples were finally presented at a plenary session of the Congress, including the four Italian courts, on 20 February. The other Italian states were almost as reluctant to approve of these measures as the King of Naples was to accept them, since their collaboration might someday require them to adopt analogous measures. They affirmed the proposed arrangements on 21 February, while Russia, Austria and Prussia bestowed their approval on the very next day.[80] '[T]he Allies consider it as essential to the safety of other governments in Italy' reported the British observer, 'not to appear to sanction self-constituted reforms by conceding a single article of those which have sprung from unlawful authority.'[81]

French and British reactions

By this time, the French delegates were again in a state of confusion. Only a few days after announcing their adherence to the allies in late January, they received fresh instructions from Paris to avoid committing France to taking any part in new hostilities in Italy. Richelieu and Pasquier were concerned that the French army might become disaffected if it engaged in a campaign against the Neapolitans.[82] Pasquier chastised the delegates and practically threatened to disavow them for their adherence to the conference protocol of 25 January. Blacas took the personally humiliating step of registering a declaration in the conference journal on 2 February, establishing that if circumstances required coercive measures, France would not participate in them. When the issue of approving prospective arrangements for the Kingdom of Naples therefore arose in late February, the French plenipotentiaries simply declared they could give no opinion whatsoever.[83] La Ferronnays was intrepid enough to ask Metternich, before all the other delegates, whether the formal communication of plans by Ruffo to the allies meant that the King had made a binding commitment to them, and whether the allies would henceforth exercise a right to intervene in Naples if the King altered those arrangements. After a long and stony silence, Metternich replied affirmatively.[84]

The vacillating conduct of France at the Congress was a source of some discomfiture, not only for Metternich but also for the Tsar. Alexander nevertheless told the French delegates that, on the basis of the principles established at Troppau and Laibach, he was ready to support French intervention against the revolutionary government in Spain along lines similar to the Austrian mission in Naples—a prospect that Richelieu and Pasquier found somewhat chilling.

An even ruder shock for the eastern courts was the ferocity of British opposition. The invitation to Ferdinand from Troppau had triggered a wave of hostile speculation in the British press, which now considered an invasion as all but inevitable. For example, on 4 January 1821, *The Times* considered why the allied powers might wish to attack Naples, despite the fact that no violence had occurred and life and liberty were respected: 'Freedom which is not stained with blood, but is allied to peace, prosperity, and reason, becomes to sickly minds the more formidable and odious; just so far as to the rest of mankind it is an object lovely and inestimable.' The Whig journal, *The Morning Chronicle*, hinted on the same day that armed intervention in Naples might lead to a general conflagration: 'The Sovereigns having determined on putting down the revolutionary principle, as they term it, when they think they are able to do so, will never want a pretext for acting ... But their hollow and hypocritical pretexts cannot blind the people of Europe. Who knows but the wicked aggression which they are now planning, may, contrary to their intentions, turn out beneficial to the world?'

A few weeks later, several English newspapers printed an excerpt from Metternich's vehicle, the *Oesterreichische Beobachter*, containing an abstract of the 'Troppau Circular'. Additional excerpts were printed in *The Morning Chronicle* on 15 January, accompanied by this bitter lament:

> Alas! for England, the classic land of liberty! Low indeed have we fallen, if we join the banners of the Holy Alliance in this unholy Crusade against Reform. But it cannot be; Englishmen will never prove themselves so unworthy of the proud distinction achieved for them by their ancestors, as to approve of principles distinctly condemning the Revolution of 1688. The Ministers who attempt to involve this country in the guilt of this project of the Holy Alliance, will become an object of scorn and detestation to their contemporaries and to posterity.[85]

The Times on the same day wrote that, if the Austrians dared to invade Naples, it would largely be the fault of the British ministers for having failed to oppose their designs at Troppau.

In the face of these public attacks, Castlereagh felt obliged to issue a diplomatic protest to the Troppau Circular. Its immediate publication brought the rift in the alliance out into the open: 'The system of measures proposed ... would be in direct repugnance to the fundamental laws of this country... [We] do not regard the Alliance as entitled, under existing Treaties, to assume ... any such general powers.' Nonetheless, Castlereagh's critique was fashioned on as narrow grounds as possible: he objected to the form of the proposed intervention in Naples, but not to the fact of intervention itself. As in his earlier unpublicized statements at Aix-la-Chapelle, in the State Paper of 5 May 1820, and in his criticism of the *Protocole préliminaire*, Castlereagh argued that the alliance could not be extended to become an instrument of systematic repression. But his new, public protest also made a point of strenuously condemning the Neapolitan revolutionaries, and while it announced that Britain had no reason to interfere, it recognized 'that other European States, and especially Austria and the Italian Powers, might feel themselves differently circumstanced'.[86]

These nuances were insufficient to silence the cries of the British radicals, independent members of Parliament and Whigs. *The Morning Chronicle* called for British intervention to assist the beleaguered Neapolitans, or at least to defend the island of Sicily, as early as 15 February. Six days later, Sir James Mackintosh moved in Parliament for an investigation into the government's conduct on this question. After fierce debate, the motion was defeated by 194 to 125.[87] The debate coincided with news of the Austrian march. The government's defence turned on its lack of complicity with the eastern powers. To the disgust of Esterhazy, the Austrian ambassador in London—and later of Metternich—no one in England defended the invasion itself.[88]

Quite apart from this wave of hostile public opinion, Castlereagh was having his own inner doubts about the direction in which the autocratic eastern powers were taking the Congress System. He complained to Stewart, his half-brother and close confidant, on 13 March:

> [O]ur Allies will still deceive themselves upon the political attitude of this Government. They idly persevere in attributing the line we have taken, and must steadily continue to take, to the temporary difficulties in which the Government have been placed, instead of imputing them exclusively to those principles which in our system must be immutable, and which, if the three Courts persevere much longer in the open promulgation of their *ultra* doctrines, will ere long work a separation which it is the wish of us all to avoid.[89]

Back in Laibach, the Congress statesmen held a special meeting to discuss Castlereagh's protest. Metternich proposed publishing the Troppau Circular alongside the British response. Capodistrias accused Castlereagh of 'bad faith' in launching an unnecessary general attack on principles sanctioned by treaties to which the British had adhered. Gordon retorted that the eastern courts were to blame for announcing principles against which Britain had previously objected.[90] The Congress held what was supposed to be its last official session on 26 February and announced that it would reconvene in September 1822 at Florence. The allied sovereigns and ministers decided to remain at Laibach for another month while they awaited the results of the Austrian expeditionary force.[91] These came sooner than expected: on 7 March, General Pepe attempted to boost Neapolitan morale by leading his forces into the Papal States to attack the Austrians at Rieti. They were instantly crushed. Within two weeks, the Neapolitans signed an armistice and Austrian troops were marching peacefully into the kingdom.[92]

Alexander and divine favour

A long letter that the Tsar sent to his friend Prince Golitsyn at this time provides remarkable insight into the intensity of the Russian Emperor's religious feelings and the degree to which he had strayed from his earlier liberalism. He began by condemning those malefactors responsible for revolutions across Europe, whose efforts he believed to be directed against Christianity itself: 'In a word, they have only put into practice the doctrines preached by Voltaire, Mirabeau, Condorcet ....' An 'inner voice' told Alexander that these evils were the 'work of the enemy', and he wrote of his Christian duty to combat this 'infernal work' with all the means that divine Providence had placed at his disposal. The danger was even greater now than it had been under the despotism of Napoleon.

With detailed references to the Book of Judith—who had overcome a hostile army through her trust in God—and St Paul's Epistle to the Romans, the Tsar explained how profoundly moved he had been by the miraculous salvation of the King of Naples. All had gravely doubted the odds of the King's deliverance out of the hands of the revolutionaries. Ferdinand had not freely acceded to their demands, his secret correspondence with the Emperor of Austria had revealed. 'In one of these secret letters', the Tsar told Golitsyn,

> was a phrase that struck me. It said that [the King] was in the power of his enemies and at their dagger point, without the help of anyone; nevertheless his confidence in God had not weakened, for what was impossible for man was not impossible for God, and placing all his faith in Him alone, he had kept alive the hope that he would not be abandoned. When I read that passage, something inside told me that his hope would not be disappointed, that God would surely not abandon him.

Then, despite all the obstacles, Ferdinand was actually able to reach the allies in Laibach—'God had blessed our intentions', Alexander concluded, 'because they were pure and because they were based on faith in Him alone'.

The Tsar also explained to Golitsyn that at Troppau the allied powers had made a solemn pact that 'none of them would invade another or extend their boundaries, or change the current state of territorial possession, as guaranteed by the treaties ... No extension of territory in Europe is possible ... because the powers of Europe have decided not to tolerate any changes in the present state of possession'. The Tsar finally revealed that he was surrendering his own will to God—'I abandon myself completely to His direction, to His determinations ... I can only follow with complete abandon ... My unique resource is the Lord'. The King of Prussia and the Emperor of Austria, the Tsar observed, were similarly 'religious to the bottom of their hearts and recognize the omnipotence of the Lord'. His policy henceforth would be based on the Holy Alliance—especially the intimacy between the three cabinets who had been the first to adhere to it. This alliance 'resists all attempts raised against it—all the liberal revolutionaries, radical levellers, and Carbonari of all the corners of the world—because there is no illusion about this: there is a general conspiracy behind all these societies—they hear and communicate all—I have the proofs in my hand'.[93] With thoughts such as these swirling around the Emperor's head, there was very little that Metternich really had to do to keep him in line.[94]

Revolution in Piedmont

While the news from Naples was encouraging, the allies were soon in for another shock. On 14 March, the first reports filtered in of the outbreak of a revolution in Piedmont, the second largest of the independent Italian states.

At almost the same time, they received news of an insurrection in the Danubian Principalities of the Ottoman Empire, described more fully in the next section. It seemed that the forces of revolution were again in the ascendant.

Back in 1814, the ruler of Piedmont, King Victor Emmanuel, had adopted far more reactionary policies than Ferdinand of Naples. The King himself refused to wear clothing styles adapted since the French Revolution. While there was no outright persecution of collaborators with the French, there was an extensive purge of office-holders: an edict employed the old Royal Almanac of 1798 as the basis for all appointments, stripping a whole generation of magistrates of power. The restored regime abolished the Napoleonic codes, opposed constitutionalism and handed control of education over to the Jesuits (only recently reinstated by the Pope). At the same time, the monarchy returned greater autonomy to local governments, virtually ensuring a resurgence of corruption and local rivalries. The administration of justice also became more arbitrary: the modern practice of using oral testimony in public trials was abandoned in favour of the secret inquisitorial methods of the *ancien régime*, while salaries to judges were replaced by the older system of fees paid by litigants. The appointment of inexperienced officials based solely on their royalist sympathies led to new inefficiencies in administration, while censorship drove opposition underground. The royal government arbitrarily interfered in the enforcement of private contracts to such a degree that Piedmont was unable to obtain loans from British bankers. The negative impact of these changes was compounded by an economic recession, heightened by the subsistence crisis of 1816–17. After 1818, the King relented somewhat and experimented with a measure of reform, including the appointment of Prospero Balbo (the father of Cesare) as Minister of the Interior in 1819.[95]

Younger Piedmontese aristocrats such as Cesare Balbo joined junior army officers and middle-class members of the secret societies (the *Carbonari* and *Federati*) in aspiring for a written constitution and the expulsion of the Austrians from Italy. These Piedmontese liberals looked to establish links with Italian nationalists in Austrian-controlled Lombardy. They hoped to win Victor Emmanuel's favour by offering him the prospect of acquiring Lombardy-Venetia to create a strong Northern Italian state. While historians have frequently praised Austrian rule in Lombardy-Venetia for its efficiency in comparison with other Italian governments at this time, Italian nationalists still found grounds for dissatisfaction: German was being imposed as the official language, Austrians and Slavs filled the civil service, Austrian products were given preference over local ones and there was a strict censorship. Revolutionary activity was made into a capital crime (though rarely enforced).

The revolution in Naples greatly stimulated activity among reformers and revolutionaries throughout the north of Italy. Piedmontese and

Lombards began planning for a general insurrection while Austrian forces were still bogged down in Naples. In October 1820, one of the leading Lombard patriots, Silvio Pellico, former editor of the short-lived liberal journal *Il Conciliatore*, was arrested. In January 1821, student demonstrations at the University of Turin were forcibly repressed. Piedmontese liberals nevertheless pushed ahead with their plans. They especially looked to the heir-apparent, Charles Albert (Carlo Alberto), the Prince of Carignan—French-educated and frequently expressing liberal opinions—as their potential leader. A group of younger nobles and army officers, led by Count Santorre di Santarosa, finally decided to take action while Victor Emmanuel was away from his capital of Turin. Their plan was to seize Turin and demand that the King grant the Spanish Constitution of 1812 and declare war on Austria. Charles Albert was informed of their intentions but wavered over whether or not to lend his support.[96]

On 9 March, the leaders of the conspiracy, aware of the Prince's hesitations, decided to postpone the revolt. However, the garrison of Alessandria, the kingdom's chief fortress, rebelled that same night, proclaiming the Spanish Constitution and hoisting the tricolour in support of Italian unity and independence. News of the Austrian victory over the Neapolitans at Rieti a few days earlier was still unknown. The insurrection quickly spread to Turin, Genoa and Savoy. Victor Emmanuel abdicated in favour of his brother Charles Felix (Carlo Felice). Since the latter was away in Modena, none other than Charles Albert became Regent: he publicly declared for the Spanish Constitution the very next day. This was the only way, he later argued, to preserve order and avoid a massacre; in any case, he was already looking for a means of escape. Only five days later the new monarch, Charles Felix, issued a proclamation from Modena denouncing the revolution. The new King ordered Charles Albert to leave Turin and join loyal troops at Novara. On the night of 21 March, Charles Albert abdicated the Regency, urged his compatriots to submit, and proceeded to Novara, where he was further ordered to leave the country for Tuscany. Meanwhile, Charles Felix submitted a request for Austrian assistance.[97]

The danger that the Piedmontese Revolution might have posed to Austria seems difficult to exaggerate—especially during the brief period before the victory at Rieti was known. The Austrian army was still engaged in Naples and there were few additional Austrian troops available in Italy: what if the Neapolitans were successful and Lombardy-Venetia also rose up in revolt? Metternich, the Tsar and the Emperor Francis held a long conference at Laibach the same evening that they received news of the Piedmontese revolt. They quickly resolved to send troops from other parts of Austria to Northern Italy to boost troop levels to 60,000. In addition, the Tsar agreed to order 90,000 Russian troops to Italy to assist the Austrians. Here were the fruits of the new spirit of cooperation between the eastern powers. The Tsar's firm determination lifted up everyone's spirits at Laibach completely.[98]

Castlereagh consents to Russian intervention

Although Castlereagh had been preaching for two years against any extension of the alliance, in this particular instance he adopted an approach more analogous to that of the eastern courts. With Austria already in Naples, the power in closest proximity to Piedmont—whose interests were the most directly threatened—was France. But the British would not have been pleased to see French troops return to Italy. It was only two years since an allied occupation force had left France herself.

Castlereagh therefore wrote to Gordon on 5 April that

> I cannot hesitate to admit that if a foreign force must needs enter Piedmont, I had infinitely rather see a Russian than a French army destined to undertake that service. Neither a French nor an Austrian Occupation can well take place without exciting an immediate jealousy between these two powers. A Russian occupation would bear upon the face of it a more temporary character, but though comparatively less objectionable perhaps than either of the others, and more especially than a French occupation, which I regard from the nature & composition of their Army as altogether inadmissible. It could not but be productive of the most serious Evils & must inevitably give rise to a great fermentation of sentiment both in France & Germany.[99]

Like British actions during the Hundred Days, this statement is most revealing. Castlereagh was continuing to play something of a double game. On the one hand, ever since his State Paper of 5 May 1820, he had been arguing that the operations of the alliance should be limited to intervention against France in its 'military' capacity. When convulsions in other states occurred, Castlereagh had generally been quite confident that some neighbouring power, such as Austria, could quell them. But in the unlikely event that local power was inadequate, he, too, seems to have looked to the gears of the great European coalition to be set into motion to crush it. There was no way in which Russia could claim that her own security was directly endangered by events in Piedmont; she could only justify acting in Italy as an agent of the alliance because of the threat posed by revolution generally. The fact that Castlereagh lent his support to such foreign intervention in his correspondence to Gordon, in effect countenancing counter-revolutionary activity in the name of the alliance, did not mean, however, that he was ready to admit such approbation openly on the floor of the House of Commons.

Castlereagh hoped most of all that the Piedmontese Revolution would extinguish itself without any resort to foreign arms, especially after the Austrian success in Naples; then any Russian force sent to Italy could be quickly disbanded, especially since 'the presence of such a force, if not indispensably required, must press severely upon the resources of the countries through which it must pass, & which it is ultimately destined to occupy'. In fact, the Piedmontese insurrection collapsed almost as suddenly as it had arisen. The combined effect of the flight of Charles Albert, the defeat of the Neapolitans and the reinforcement of Austrian forces in Lombardy together doomed the rebels. Desperately attempting to seize the initiative, their dwindling forces attacked Novara on 8 April. They were quickly defeated by loyal regiments of the Piedmontese royal army. The leaders of the rebellion fled the country, while the cities of Turin and Genoa were recaptured by the royalists. According to historian Michael Broers, the revolutionaries 'found no significant means of popular support'.[100] At the request of Charles Felix, Austrian troops entered the kingdom to help suppress any smouldering embers of unrest.

By May 1821, as the allied leaders finally departed from Laibach, Metternich had ample grounds for satisfaction. He had won his duel with Capodistrias for the soul of the Tsar and he had maintained the Austrian 'sphere of influence' in Italy without French interference. Both the Neapolitan and Piedmontese Revolutions had been suppressed. Austrian forces were in occupation of both kingdoms and Italy was again quiescent. Moreover, Alexander had promised to keep 123,000 troops along the Austrian border, ready to assist when needed, until the next Congress, planned for the following year. Despite the estrangement of Britain and France, the Congress System thus seemed to be performing its most essential purpose: cooperation between the allied sovereigns to crush the revolutionary movement. Metternich's tortuous policy at Troppau and Laibach appeared to be completely triumphant. Even Napoleon was no longer a threat, since the former French Emperor had died in isolation on the remote island of St Helena on the 5th of the same month.

The Greek Revolution, the Hanover interview and the threat of a Russo-Turkish war, 1821–22

But these were scarcely times for complacency. The next crisis to occupy the attention of the allied leaders was already visible on the horizon as the Laibach Congress was coming to an end. Taking place outside the boundaries of Christian Europe and the Holy Alliance, uprisings among Greek Orthodox Christians in the Ottoman Empire would provide the occasion for a *rapprochement* between Britain and Austria, while they would severely test Metternich's hold upon Alexander.

The Danubian Principalities and Greece in the 1820s

Challenges to Ottoman rule

The Ottoman Turks had ruled over much of the Balkan Peninsula since the fourteenth century. The once mighty Byzantine, Bulgarian and Serbian Empires had crumbled and their territories had been incorporated into the Ottoman Empire as mere provinces.[101] Only the Ionian Islands, where Capodistrias was born, had remained under the Christian rule of Venice, succeeded in turn by Russia, France and eventually Britain. The Danubian Principalities of Moldavia and Wallachia (present-day Romania and Moldova[102]) recognized the Sultan as suzerain and paid an annual tribute to Constantinople, but kept their own aristocracy, the boyars. By the eighteenth century, the Sultan was treating their rulers, the *hospodars* (*voyvodas*), as officials to be appointed and dismissed at will. The *hospodars* headed elaborate courts and had ample opportunities for self-enrichment. They came from the Phanariot class—well-educated and wealthy Greek or hellenized families, living in the Phanar (or 'lighthouse') neighbourhood of Constantinople.[103]

Despite its vast extent, the Ottoman Empire never became a tightly unified, homogenous state. Each religious group remained organized as a separate community, or *millet* ('nation'), led by its own religious officials and following its own laws and traditions.[104] Many historians—although no longer all—would contend that by the late eighteenth century the Ottoman Empire was showing increasing signs of frailty. Trade had shifted from this region to transatlantic routes. The Janissaries—renowned infantry fighters, once recruited by a compulsory levy (*devşirme*) on Christian boys from the Balkans—had become an entrenched caste with a variety of roles. Fearing the loss of their privileges, the Janissaries obstinately refused to adopt Western methods of fighting and posed a major obstacle to reform. Finally, effective control over large portions of the empire had fallen into the hands of local notables, the *ayans* (*âyân*).[105]

Under these conditions, Ottoman forces had met with defeat from the armies of Catherine the Great. The Sultan reluctantly concluded the Treaty of Kutchuk Kainardji in 1774, ceding territory to Russia along the Black Sea and recognizing Russia as the protector of Orthodox Christians in Moldavia, Wallachia and the Aegean Islands, entitled to make representations on their behalf. The Sultan further agreed to the independence of the Crimea and to obtain Russian approval before appointing the *hospodars* of the Danubian Principalities. The same treaty granted Russia the right to establish consulates throughout the Ottoman Empire and permitted Russian subjects free navigation through the Straits of the Bosporus and the Dardanelles, thus allowing Russian merchants to establish commercial links between the Black Sea and the Mediterranean. Soon, there was a flourishing export trade shipping Russian wheat to Western Europe.[106]

Less than 20 years after this humiliating defeat, Sultan Selim III attempted to play the role of an enlightened despot by announcing the creation of an Ottoman 'New Order'—strengthening control over provincial governorships, creating new secular schools, improving methods of tax collection and, most important of all, creating a new infantry corps organized along French lines and equipped with modern weapons. Selim's 'New Order' corps (*Nizam-I Cedid*) was to form the nucleus of a modern army that would eventually replace the Janissaries. But the Janissaries struck first by deposing and murdering Selim in 1807. After a brief interlude under the reactionary Mustafa IV, Mahmud II ascended the Divan as Sultan in 1808. His accession took place only a few months after Alexander had met with Napoleon at Tilsit, where the two emperors had discussed the possible partition of the Ottoman Empire. Meanwhile, warfare between Turkey and Russia had resumed at the end of 1806. Despite Russian victories, the Sultan stubbornly refused to yield to the Tsar's demands. In 1811, with rapidly deteriorating relations with France, Alexander opened peace negotiations with the Ottomans. The Treaty of Bucharest, signed by Russia and Turkey in May 1812, awarded Bessarabia (the territory along the Black Sea between the Dniester River and the Pruth, previously part of Moldavia) to Russia, and granted limited autonomy to Serbia, where a revolt by Christian Serbs had erupted. The same treaty confirmed the Sultan's suzerainty over the Danubian Principalities and promised the return of 'conquered' territories. The Sultan interpreted the latter concession as a Russian pledge to evacuate the Trans-Caucasus, but the Russian negotiators had no intention of returning any territories that had voluntarily placed themselves under Russian protection.[107]

When French troops reached Moscow later that same year, Mahmud regretted that he had perhaps yielded too much. Napoleon's invasion of Russia at least gave the Sultan the opportunity he needed to crush Serb rebels with impunity. Elsewhere, too, Ottoman power seemed to be resurgent: in Mesopotamia, Halet Effendi restored direct Ottoman rule in Baghdad with ruthless efficiency; in Egypt, Mehemet Ali, an independent-minded Albanian governor, created a Westernized army along the lines earlier proposed by Selim for Turkey. Although Ottoman Turkey was not a party to the Vienna settlement, the Sultan had an observer at the Congress, the Phanariot Ioannis Mavroyeni, and Ottoman interests were jealously guarded by Britain and Austria, both of which dreaded further Russian expansion.

Mahmud saw the root of his problems in the rise of overmighty subjects in the provinces—the *ayans*. When he ascended the Divan in 1808, an *ayan* had temporarily seized control in Constantinople and had summoned other notables to reorganize the empire.[108] Several of the *ayans* later refused to assist him in the war with Russia. Throughout his long reign, Mahmud acted to overcome such effrontery by eliminating powerful local rulers.[109] A major challenge to his authority came from Ali Pasha of Janina, another shrewd Albanian, on the western side of the Balkans (Ioánnina in present-day Greece). Ali Pasha conducted himself as a virtually independent ruler, establishing separate diplomatic relations with several European courts and turning Janina into a favourite meeting place for Greek merchants. In 1820, the Sultan dismissed Ali from the governorship of Epirus and summoned him to Constantinople, but Ali astutely refused to obey. An Ottoman army laid siege to Janina, while Ali Pasha called on Greek Christians to join him in a war of liberation against the Turks. Ali's call went unheeded, and Ottoman forces took Janina that summer. The aging Pasha retreated to a fortified island, where he remained until being betrayed and killed in January 1822.[110]

The Greek revolt

Despite centuries of Turkish rule, Greek Orthodox Christians had never abandoned their separate ethnic identity or memories of a more glorious past. Methods of Turkish administration encouraged this, since the Greeks largely remained under the daily rule of their own church and village leaders.[111] Indeed, the Peloponnese (the southern peninsula of Greece, below the Gulf of Corinth) enjoyed a virtually autonomous administration. The Orthodox Church retained control over education as well as religion and became the chief repository of Greek culture and tradition. Even the peasantry maintained their separate cultural identity, not only through language and religion, but also through epic poetry and popular ballads.[112] In the mountains, Greek bandits known as *klephts* preyed on both Ottoman authorities and the Greek mercantile elite. To protect against the bandits, the Ottomans permitted the organization of local militia bands, known as the *armatoloi* (or as the *kapoi* in the Peloponnese), but there were frequent interchanges between these armed groups.[113]

Educated Greeks enjoyed something of a privileged position among Christians within the Ottoman Empire. The Phanariots assisted in administration. Greek merchants dominated commerce and served as intermediaries between Western Europe and the Ottoman Turks. Overseas communities of Greeks in Vienna, London, Paris and Odessa served as vital commercial contacts. Greeks were also held in high repute as shipbuilders, shipowners and sailors. When French shipping was reduced during the Napoleonic Wars, Greek merchants took up much of the Mediterranean carrying trade.[114] At the same time, a number of Greek scholars, living either in the Ottoman Empire or in exile in other parts of Europe, embarked on new studies of the Greek language, literature and history just on the eve of the French Revolution.

From Paris, Adamantios Korais published his 'Library of Greek Literature' and helped to forge the modern Greek language out of ancient and spoken dialects. A revival of interest in classical Greek civilization throughout the rest of Europe also had a direct impact upon educated Greeks.[115]

This regeneration of national consciousness occurred precisely as new doctrines of nationalism were being disseminated by foreign intellectuals. Language, religion, tradition and historical association were all seen as factors binding together a people, such as the Greeks, into a common nation. Some Greeks became infected with these new ideas on their sojourns abroad. Foreign travellers to Greece—such as Richard Church, Chateaubriand and Lord Byron—helped spread these enthusiasms.[116] Greek students, professors, writers, lawyers, merchants and even priests began thinking about replacing the Ottoman regime with an independent Greek state.[117] Rhigas Pheraios published his 'Map of Greece', linking modern Greece to the Greeks of antiquity; he also issued a proposed constitution and a series of revolutionary proclamations based on the French Declaration of the Rights of Man. Rhigas called for the creation of a new Byzantine state in the Balkans; captured by the Austrians, this early Greek patriot was handed over to Turkish authorities and executed in 1798.[118]

Sixteen years later, three Greek immigrants in Odessa formed the *Philiki Hetairia*, or 'Society of Friends'. The professed aim of this secret organization was to overthrow the Ottoman Empire in Europe and to create a new Byzantine state with Constantinople as its capital. The society had some initial difficulties proselytizing members. In 1817, members of the *Hetairia* approached the influential Russian minister from Corfu—Count Capodistrias. To their disappointment, Capodistrias advised them to limit their activities to educational and cultural pursuits. The Tsar was also informed of the existence of the society but took no steps to suppress it or even to inform Ottoman authorities. The following year, the *Hetairia* moved its headquarters from Odessa to the Greek quarter of Constantinople and gained the support of the Bishop of Patras, several Greek officers in the Russian army and an increasing number of Greek merchants. The society also developed a system of secret, self-contained cells (groups with limited knowledge of one another), which quickly spread among the Greeks of the Danubian Principalities and the Peloponnese. By 1820, the organization counted over a thousand members. Like other clandestine societies of the day, its members shared secret rituals, oaths and practices. Several of the Russian consuls in the Balkans were Greeks who lent their active support, while the society continued to attract new members by feigning official Russian sponsorship.[119]

Once again, an envoy was sent to St Petersburg to offer leadership of the society to Capodistrias. When the Russian foreign minister refused a second time, they approached instead his friend Prince Alexander Ypsilantis, an aide-de-camp to the Tsar.[120] A Phanariot relative of Stourdza's, Ypsilantis' father and grandfather had both been *hospodars*; the Greek patriot Rhigas had even once served as his grandfather's secretary.[121] His father had been deposed as *hospodar* of Moldavia for aiding the Serbian revolt and had found refuge on Russian soil.[122] Ypsilantis himself had lost an arm on the battlefield at Dresden in the service of the Tsar and had attended the Congress of Vienna with Capodistrias and Stourdza as part of the Russian delegation. Appointed as the leader of the *Hetairia* on 24 April 1820, Ypsilantis continued to encourage the notion that the conspirators enjoyed the secret support of the Tsar, while fresh efforts were made to ally with both the Serbs and the Romanians. Ypsilantis and the other leaders of the *Hetairia* decided to launch their rebellion in the Peloponnese and Epirus, but changed their plans when the new *hospodar* of Moldavia, the young Michael Sutzo, joined their movement in November. Ypsilantis was more familiar with the Principalities at any rate, where Russia enjoyed special treaty rights. When a messenger from the *Hetairia* was captured with secret documents in February, Ypsilantis resolved to act at once.[123] On 6 March 1821, while Ottoman troops were still engaged in their campaign against Ali Pasha, Ypsilantis crossed the Pruth River in a Russian uniform, entered the Danubian Principalities, and rode to Jassy; the next day, he boldly issued a proclamation declaring their independence. He hoped his actions would precipitate the outbreak of similar Christian uprisings throughout the Ottoman Empire. He also sent a stirring message directly to the Tsar, asking him to take the lead in liberating the Orthodox Christians of Europe and restoring Christianity to Constantinople: 'Save us, Your Majesty! Save our religion from those who would persecute it, return us to our temples and our altars where the divine light once spread ….'[124]

The Phanariot regime in Moldavia was friendly to Ypsilantis and the Greek boyars were sympathetic, but the Romanian boyars and peasants remained indifferent or hostile. Support among Greeks swelled because Ypsilantis deliberately encouraged the belief that he was acting on the Tsar's orders. Sutzo joined the rebels, and several Turkish garrisons in Moldavia were massacred. Ottoman authorities feared a Greek revolt in Constantinople itself.

Although neither Capodistrias nor the Tsar seems to have had advance knowledge of the revolt, several of the commanders of the Russian Second Army—a force of 80,000 men in Southern Russia, whose primary role was to resist the Ottoman Turks—almost certainly did.[125] The Tsar received news of the rebellion while still at Laibach and firmly under Metternich's spell. Although he felt a deep empathy for the sufferings of fellow Orthodox Christians, he could not countenance an open rebellion against a legitimate sovereign: 'There is no doubt', he wrote to his friend Prince Golitsyn, 'that the impulse behind this insurrectional movement could only have been given by the central committee in Paris, with the intention of making a diversion to help Naples and to prevent us from destroying one of the synagogues of Satan, established solely to propagate and spread his anti-Christian doctrine'. Ypsilantis had 'openly admitted', wrote the Tsar, that he belonged to 'a secret society' whose goal was the liberation of Greece, and Alexander reasoned that 'all these secret societies are directed by the central committee in Paris' and have as their actual aim the paralysis of 'the Christian principles professed by the Holy Alliance'.[126] These views are all the more incredible when we consider that the Tsar was personally acquainted with Ypsilantis.

At a meeting with Metternich and the Emperor Francis, the Tsar agreed to condemn the uprising, which Metternich equated with the revolutions in Italy.[127] Capodistrias was ordered to send a message from Laibach to Ypsilantis, stating that the Tsar would offer neither 'direct nor indirect assistance', that Ypsilantis should immediately terminate the revolt, and that he was stripped of his military commission.[128] The Russian ambassador at Constantinople, Baron Gregory Stroganov, was instructed to inform the Porte of the 'surprise, pain and indignation with which the Tsar had learned that Prince Ypsilantis was at the head of the insurgents'; Stroganov was furnished with a copy of the letter to Ypsilantis and was further instructed to offer every assistance to the Sultan in suppressing the revolt.[129] The rebels learned to their dismay that, far from intervening on their behalf, the Tsar had openly condemned their actions. With Russian consent, the Sultan was free to send his troops into the Principalities.[130]

The situation was further exacerbated by a nearly simultaneous revolt among the Romanian peasantry, seeking social change rather than national liberation. In January 1821, Tudor Vladimirescu, a Romanian militia leader, had issued a revolutionary bulletin calling on peasants to rise up against oppressive boyars and Phanariot Greeks. Vladimirescu reached Bucharest at the beginning of April with a force of 65,000 followers. Ypsilantis reached the outskirts of the city two weeks later with a smaller force. The two armies had no supplies and were forced to live off the land, alienating the local peasantry. On 13 May, Ottoman troops entered Moldavia. The Wallachian government and both rebel armies quickly fled Bucharest for the mountains. Vladimirescu was kidnapped by members of the *Hetairia* and murdered on 8 June for negotiating with the Ottomans.[131] Sutzo had already fled to Russia in April. With the death of Vladimirescu, peasants began deserting the rebel armies en masse. The Sultan's army easily defeated Ypsilantis' dwindling forces within a fortnight. Ypsilantis fled to Hungary, where he was promptly arrested by Austrian authorities and spent the last seven years of his life in captivity.[132] Thousands of other refugees, helped by officers of the Second

Army, flooded into Russian Bessarabia. Stroganov was instructed that Russia refused to expel those Christian refugees who had sought asylum.[133]

Although Ypsilantis' uprising failed utterly, it unleashed a second and more formidable insurrection in the Peloponnese. By early April, with the encouragement of Bishop Germanos of Patras and Ypsilantis' brother Demetrios, the revolt had spread to the armed bands of *klephts* and militia throughout the peninsula and the neighbouring Aegean islands. The Greek rebels benefitted from control of the sea by their merchant ships. Greek passions were inflamed, and as many as 15,000 Muslims were slaughtered by Greek militia leaders and their peasant followers at Kalavryta, Mesolonghi and elsewhere.[134] These atrocities led in turn to acts of retaliation by the Turks.[135] The Sultan suspected that Orthodox Christians throughout his domains were engaged in a far-flung conspiracy, and he was outraged that the most favoured non-Muslim *millet*, the Greeks, had attacked Muslims. Mahmud sought a declaration of holy war from Muslim religious leaders but was refused.[136]

The head of the Greek Orthodox Church, Patriarch Grigorios V, publicly anathematized Ypsilantis and the *Philiki Hetairia* in a show of allegiance to the Sultan.[137] Despite the Patriarch's forthright condemnation of the revolt, Mahmud still suspected him of collaboration. Moreover, as Patriarch, Grigorios was responsible for the conduct of his flock and in the Sultan's eyes he had failed miserably in the discharge of this duty. According to European reports, on Easter Sunday armed soldiers burst into the church in Constantinople where the aged Patriarch was officiating, put ropes around his neck and those of several bishops, pulled them in their robes to the gates of the quarter, and hanged them. Eyewitness accounts record that the Patriarch's death was excruciatingly slow and painful. On the orders of the Sultan, Grigorios' body was left hanging for three days before being dragged through the market and tossed into the sea.[138] Angry mobs attacked and looted Christian churches throughout Asia Minor in gruesome revenge for the atrocities in Greece. Leading Phanariots were executed. The Sultan ordered Russian ships passing through the Straits to be detained, effectively halting the Russian grain trade.

The Russian ultimatum: The 'four points'

These outrages fairly cried out for a response from Orthodox Russia. The Tsar and Capodistrias were already in Warsaw on their homeward journey when they received the first reports of the murder of the Patriarch.[139] Stourdza argued that the sufferings of Greek Christians under the Turkish yoke justified action, while he carefully distinguished the Greek insurgents from the revolutionaries in France, Italy and Spain to justify this conclusion.[140] Back in Constantinople, Stroganov proposed a joint allied remonstrance protesting the execution of the Patriarch but found himself opposed by the British ambassador, Percy Smythe, the sixth Viscount Strangford.[141] Stroganov therefore acted on his own in presenting several notes to the Ottoman government—known in diplomatic parlance as the 'Porte', or gate, after the entry to the palace of the Grand Vizier. These were presented in late May and early June. Stroganov objected not only to the treatment of Orthodox Christians but also to the detention of Russian merchant ships and to the continuing occupation of the Principalities by Ottoman troops after Ypsilantis' defeat, in violation of the Treaties of Kutchuk Kainardji and Bucharest. He threatened to withdraw from his post unless the Porte changed its policies, and promptly moved from the city to his summer residence in nearby Buyukderi.[142]

From St Petersburg, fresh instructions were issued to Stroganov. These rejected the toppling of Ottoman rule in Europe, which would have had the unwelcome effect of encouraging the revolutionary movement rather than stifling it. The Ottomans were to be reassured, Stroganov was told, that Russian intentions were both 'pacific' (in demanding only the simple execution of the treaties) and 'conservative' (in recognizing that the survival of the Ottomans remained necessary to 'the maintenance of peace in Europe').[143] For its part, the Porte continued to demand the extradition of the refugees in Russia. The British ambassador, Lord Strangford, had some of Stroganov's despatches intercepted in Odessa and shared them with the anxious Ottoman ministers to demonstrate that the Tsar was far less belligerent than his envoy.[144] This led the Grand Vizier to complain of Stroganov's conduct directly to St Petersburg in an effort to have him recalled.[145]

The Tsar, however, was beginning to question whether the Ottomans were genuinely acting to suppress a revolution or whether they were not in fact waging a more general war on their Christian population.[146] Even before the Grand Vizier's protest was received, Capodistrias forwarded new instructions to Stroganov to deliver an ultimatum to the Porte consisting of four demands: (1) the Sultan must withdraw his troops from the Principalities; (2) the Sultan must distinguish between 'guilty' and 'innocent' Christians in suppressing the unrest; (3) the Sultan must guarantee the future protection of Christians in his domains; and (4) churches destroyed in the course of the revolt must be rebuilt at the Sultan's expense. The Russian ultimatum rebuked the Ottomans for the execution of the Patriarch and massacre of Christians and warned that it might soon become quite impossible for Christian states to engage in diplomatic intercourse with the Sultan—how could Christendom 'remain an unmoved witness to the extermination of a Christian people'? It further suggested that the method of ruling the Danubian Principalities should be altered, and that Russia should be made the 'Protector' of Christians throughout the Ottoman domains, much as she already was in the Principalities. Finally, the Sultan's ministers were warned that if they failed to provide a satisfactory reply within eight days, the Russian ambassador would be withdrawn—a possible prelude to war. What became known as the 'Four Points' were delivered on 18 July 1821.[147]

Would Mahmud accede to the Russian demands? Eight days later, the Russian 'dragomans' (or official interpreters), the Franchini brothers, went to the Porte to collect the Ottoman reply but were told to return in three hours. One immediately set sail to inform Stroganov, while the second suddenly fell ill just after his brother's departure. Receipt of a response was delayed by this accidental circumstance until the ninth day, but on the basis of this technicality, Stroganov immediately asked for his passports before even reading the reply.[148] The Turkish response would have been unacceptable in any event. The British and Austrian ambassadors employed all their efforts to prevent the infuriated Ottoman officials from imprisoning or harming Stroganov, which would have made war inevitable. The Russian envoy was permitted to embark safely for Odessa on 10 August.[149]

The Russians had also sent copies of their ultimatum to the other allied courts and invited them to communicate their views.[150] Alexander appealed directly to the Emperor of Austria by harshly condemning Turkish atrocities— 'incited by acts of the Turkish Government, Muslim fanaticism demands and obtains new victims each day'. The Tsar could envisage only two possible outcomes, both 'equally deplorable': if the Ottomans triumphed, they would destroy a Christian nation; if they succumbed, then 'a new source (*foyer*) of disorder' would be created, which 'will spew out (*vomira*)' new misfortunes across Europe. While the Tsar did not doubt that the Paris revolutionaries had deliberately planned the revolt to stir up trouble for the alliance, he was confident that the solidarity of the allied courts, already so successful against the revolutionaries in Italy, would also prevail further east. Despite repeated provocations, he told the Emperor Francis, Russia had refrained from taking up arms in defence of her incontestable rights. Nevertheless, he was awaiting responses from his allies with a 'just impatience'. The Russians claimed that Christian states had no positive duties towards the Sultan beyond fulfilling their treaty engagements to preserve the peace. The Tsar therefore pressed the Emperor Francis to learn what Austria's position would be in the event that a war were forced upon Russia by these continuing outrages. Because the consequences of such a war would affect all the powers, Alexander was desirous of establishing a 'concert' in advance.[151]

The Russians similarly made a direct approach to France: the Tsar told La Ferronnays that France should make Russia, not Turkey, her ally.[152] The French were not unreceptive. Pasquier, the French foreign minister, wrote to La Ferronnays that if Russia went to war with the Ottomans, France would not want to undermine her future potential as an ally by raising objections; indeed, France was ready to sacrifice her own interests in the east to maintain her friendship with Russia, although this resolve was to be carefully concealed from Austria.[153]

These events brought the Greek revolt into the immediate focus of the great powers. Until now, neither Metternich nor Castlereagh had displayed much concern over the tragic fate of thousands of Christians and Muslims—'three or four hundred thousand are hanged, slaughtered or impaled', reflected Metternich, 'it hardly matters'.[154] But the prospect of a new Russo-Turkish War, which might lead to the collapse of the Ottoman Empire in Europe, was something to which they could scarcely remain indifferent.[155] The constellation of interests was consequently very different than in Italy just a few months before. At the time of the revolution in Naples, Metternich had been willing to sacrifice Austrian ties with Britain as the price to be paid for Russian support. However, he was far from anxious to see Russian troops intervene in Turkey, which would encourage Balkan nationalism, or to see European Turkey, with its extended border along Austria's southeastern flank and control of the Danubian delta, become a Russian possession or protectorate. 'We should regard as a *casus belli* any Russian territorial expansion in the Levant that would extend her contact with us', he had previously instructed one of his ambassadors: 'The preservation of Turkey stands, therefore, in the forefront of our interests.'[156] The Austrian Chancellor therefore now faced the unenviable task of explaining to the Tsar just how it was that Austrian intervention in Italy was justified, whereas Russian intervention in the Balkans was not.

Luckily for Metternich, Alexander was himself torn in competing directions. On the one hand, the execution of the Patriarch, burning of churches and slaughtering of Balkan Christians were deliberate affronts to Orthodox Christianity, practically inviting Russia to intervene. Capodistrias was thus presented with the perfect opportunity for steering his master towards a war for Greek independence and the realization of long-standing Russian ambitions in Turkey. On the other hand, Alexander opposed all revolutionary change and wished only to act in strict unison with his allies in accordance with his vision of a European federation.

Under these circumstances, Castlereagh, isolated from the eastern courts by his condemnation of the Troppau Circular, now veered back to his more traditional policy of cooperation with Austria. No less than Metternich, he deplored the possibility of a Russo-Turkish War. As so often in the past, the two men coordinated their efforts to tame the Tsar and prevent Russian aggrandizement. They also shared a second task, equally problematic: wresting reasonable concessions from the Sultan. (It should be mentioned that Castlereagh became the second Marquess of Londonderry in April 1821, but following the convention of most historians we continue to use his earlier title.)

Metternich approached the problem, typically enough, by praising the Tsar's lofty ideals while condemning their proposed application. The Greek revolt, he had already told the Tsar at Laibach, was the work of the secret revolutionary 'Directory' in Paris. There was nothing the conspirators would rather see more than the Tsar embroiled in a war in Turkey, so that they would be free to launch a general uprising in Europe.[157] Metternich also tried to discredit Capodistrias by sending copies of alleged proofs of his clandestine connections to the Greek rebels.[158] The Corfiote by necessity had divided loyalties, and Metternich intended to exploit his dilemma to the full. Castlereagh took the unusual step of personally addressing the Tsar from London (based upon the latter's invitation to do so at Aix-la-Chapelle): the Greek uprising, asserted the British Foreign Secretary, was analogous to the revolutions in the West and provided yet another example of 'that organized spirit of insurrection which is systematically propagating itself throughout Europe'. If events in Greece seemed more violent than elsewhere, it was simply because 'passions and prejudices, and above all ... religious animosities' had lent these disturbances their 'odious and afflicting colours'—a description reminiscent of his depiction of the Irish Rebellion 25 years earlier. Epitomizing views to be held by the British Foreign Office for much of the next century, Castlereagh admitted that

> Turkey, with all its barbarisms, constitutes in the system of Europe what may be regarded as a necessary evil. It is an excrescence which can scarcely be looked upon as forming any part of its healthful organization; and yet for that very reason, any attempt to introduce order by external interference into its jarring elements, or to assimilate it to the mass, might expose the whole frame of our general system to hazard.[159]

Since the actual security of Russia was not the least bit threatened by these regrettable events, Castlereagh appealed to the Tsar to show forbearance while these commotions resolved themselves without outside interference. It might be supposed that the appeals of Metternich and Castlereagh were examples of the sheerest hypocrisy, but it seems far more likely that they genuinely believed in the existence of some sort of European conspiracy and had simply harnessed their convictions to pragmatic ends.

Six weeks later, Castlereagh—who had no lack of experience with denominational strife—instructed Sir Charles Bagot, the British ambassador at St Petersburg, to draw the Tsar's attention to the fact

> that the horrors of a fanatical spirit of religious persecution are not exclusively to be attributed to the Turks, but are found to prevail under perhaps not less aggravating circumstances on the side of the Greeks; In short, that

> the Christian subjects of the Porte, prostituting the sacred emblem of their religion, commit as many deeds of blood, and push their resentments, as well as their views of extermination, quite as far under the Cross, as the Turks do under the Crescent.[160]

Castlereagh continued to tar the Greek uprising and the other European revolutions with the same brush. His object was transparently to expunge all thoughts of intervention from the Tsar's mind:

> I quite concur with Prince Metternich in regarding a Turkish War, in support of the present Greek Insurrection, arising as it undoubtedly has done out of a Revolutionary organization, and fomented as it undoubtedly is by Revolutionary agents, as one of the most serious and alarming dangers to which the European System could be exposed; and I feel the strongest confidence, however pressed by difficulties, that it is a snare into which the Emperor is not likely to fall. And I cannot conceive any course more likely to prove fatal to the Christian population of Turkey than the entrance of Foreign Troops, avowedly for their Support. Such a determination once taken would in all probability prove the signal for a general and undistinguishing massacre of the Christians throughout Turkey. From this calamity no military protection by any foreign state could shield them.[160]

Prussia and France also responded to the earlier Russian solicitation. Perhaps chafing from Austrian domination of the German Confederation, the Prussians were determined to pursue an independent course. Bernstorff emphasized the importance of assigning priority to the needs of the alliance.[161] The French ministers appeared intent on using the crisis to recover their lost influence in Continental affairs. Alone among the great powers, France seemed willing to countenance independent Russian action in Turkey. As at Troppau, there were even attempts to establish a separate Franco-Russian entente.

In the summer of 1821, Alexander still thought only of acting with the approval of his allies. Yet his conscience continued to struggle with the worsening plight of fellow Orthodox Christians. The Porte had failed to satisfy the demands of his July ultimatum, and the Tsar's sentiments were being further stirred by Capodistrias and the 'war party' in St Petersburg. Capodistrias reported every Turkish atrocity and adroitly argued that action by Russia in Turkey would be analogous to that of Austria in Naples. His own personal views are best revealed in the lengthy letter he sent to Bishop Ignatios on 28 July, intended for circulation among the Greek rebel leaders. Capodistrias advised them to maintain possession of the Peloponnese and the Greek islands, to establish a strong but representative government and to dissociate themselves from the revolutionary governments of Europe. He further hinted at the continuing prospects for Russian intervention, asserting that it was only by 'force of arms' that the Ottoman Turks could be restrained.[162] According to the French ambassador, Capodistrias asked him rhetorically whether the Tsar 'should ignore the opinion of his [own] people, the general cry of the Russian nation?' The Tsar's ambition, La Ferronnays reported to Paris, was 'wholly religious; it is less on the Turkish Empire than on the religion of Mohammed that he declares war, and it is as the avenger of Christians that he has sworn to push the persecutors of the religion of Jesus Christ back into Asia'.[163] Pozzo di Borgo recommended that in the event war did erupt, Russia should take advantage of the opportunity to conquer Constantinople and to eliminate Turkish rule from Europe.[164]

In late July, the Tsar received an unofficial memoir from the Prussian foreign ministry, written by the conservative bureaucrat Ancillon. This paper, too, predicted the collapse of the Ottoman Empire in Europe. According to Ancillon, the Greek uprising was directed against Ottoman despotism, which constituted not a legitimate government, but rather the absence of one. Ottoman rule over Christian subjects represented the sheer exercise of force over a conquered people rather than any form of legitimate authority ('c'est une puissance, ce n'est pas une autorité'). To such power, submission was due only until the subjects were capable of breaking free. For Ancillon, as for Stourdza, this circumstance sharply differentiated the Greek uprising from the revolutions of Christian Europe. The allies were not bound by any principle of legitimacy with respect to the Sultan's rule over the Balkan Christians; on the other hand, they were subject to 'humanitarian' principles. The murderous excesses of the Ottomans threatened the very survival of the Greek people and therefore gave rise to a humanitarian duty on the part of the Christian states of the Holy Alliance. Of all the powers, Russia alone had treaty rights justifying intervention.[165] Ancillon called upon Alexander to seize the initiative by issuing a declaration; if the Porte failed to meet his demands, Ancillon urged a conference of the allied powers and action by the Holy Alliance. His words reportedly left a deep impression on the Tsar. When the Russian Emperor secretly met the mystical Madame de Krüdener that September at St Petersburg, she likewise prophesied the fall of the Ottoman Empire, declaring it to be Alexander's destiny to liberate Jerusalem and the Holy Places from Muslim rule, just as he had once freed Paris.[166]

The Tsar thus found himself besieged on all sides, from millenarian mystics and bellicose generals to the general public, for a war of vengeance and liberation.[167] In late August 1821, he held a critical private audience with Capodistrias. Rehearsing the arguments supplied by Metternich and Castlereagh,

Alexander asserted that despite all appearances the revolution in Greece was the work of the secret European 'directing committee' in Paris—'If we reply to the Turks with war, the Paris directing committee will triumph and no government will be left standing'.[168] Capodistrias disagreed, but he argued that even if this were the case, Russia should still intervene on behalf of those blameless Christians being so indiscriminately slaughtered. Attempting to view events from the Tsar's own perspective, Capodistrias repeated Ancillon's argument that Russia should simply act on behalf of the alliance.[169] The Tsar rejected this reasoning, but offered his minister another chance to re-formulate his proposal. A few days later, Alexander instructed both Capodistrias and Nesselrode to prepare their own separate plans for negotiations with the Porte. Once again, the Tsar appeared to be vacillating. Would there be war or peace? Capodistrias lamented the loss of time, since Turkish troops were continuing to massacre his countrymen while the Tsar temporized.[170] In his next memorandum, he reminded the Russian Emperor that he had both 'religious and political duties' to fulfil: the Ottomans, Capodistrias said, were now 'in a state of hostility' against the 'Christian world'. Because Russia also had obligations towards her European allies, Capodistrias concluded that she should obtain their 'moral or material' support for a restoration of order in the East. His recommendation remained the same. Russia should intervene on her own, but act as the nominal agent of the alliance.[171]

From Vienna, both the Emperor Francis and Metternich reassured the Tsar that Austria would support Russia's just grievances, although they drew the line at any support for the Greek rebels. The Austrian Chancellor suggested his favourite device—an ambassadorial conference at Vienna (much as he had proposed during the early stages of the Neapolitan crisis). The conference would take over all negotiations with the Porte and act as a 'foyer of deliberation', instructing the allied diplomats at Constantinople. Metternich's proposal was swiftly rebuffed, as might have been expected, in St Petersburg.[172]

Meanwhile, a special appeal was also made by the Tsar to Great Britain. On 10 September, an official answer was given to Castlereagh's earlier letter. The Tsar pointed out that the Ottoman Empire was not protected by the Vienna Final Act, that horrendous atrocities had been committed and that his own patience was wearing thin. Although Alexander agreed that the uprising could be attributed to the 'revolutionary spirit of the century', he nonetheless saw the Ottoman government as far from blameless: the vast majority of Christians in the Principalities were loyal to the Sultan, yet Muslim troops had 'spread desolation and death'. It was true that the entry of foreign troops might encourage the revolutionaries and would make the intervening power responsible for any atrocities subsequently committed by Greek Christians, but he feared that abandoning them to Muslim fury might have consequences that were graver still.[173] The Tsar informed the British ambassador in St Petersburg that the Russian public was clamouring for war and he needed to know what Britain's reaction would be if he took steps to intervene.

A renewed demand, based on the 'Four Points', was accordingly submitted to the Porte.[174] At Constantinople, Strangford floated the idea of a joint proclamation calling for the Greeks to surrender to the allies rather than to the Porte, but this, too, was rejected.[175] Only the approach of winter prevented Russia from embarking upon immediate preparations for war.

Instructions sent by Castlereagh to his envoy at Vienna at the beginning of October reveal this statesman's most intimate thoughts. He believed that the withdrawal of Stroganov might actually encourage the Porte to make concessions; he was equally confident that the Tsar would ultimately refrain from war, with the result that the Greek revolt would eventually collapse:

> However much it is to be regretted that the barbarous horrors which are committed on both sides cannot, from their very nature, be made to cease by some decisive act of authority, yet it is obvious if the fanaticism on one side and the hopes of successful revolt on the other shall not be excited by the expectation of external interference, that the power of the gov[ernmen]t must e'er long prevail over the desultory efforts of the insurgents, and the country be restored to that species of tranquillity, which we can alone expect ever to find under the heavy pressure of the Turkish yoke, operating upon the very defective materials which the Greeks furnish for the construction of a more mild or rational system of gov[ernmen]t.

While Capodistrias was anxious for the Tsar to take action, Castlereagh counselled delay: 'You will represent ... the importance of gaining time, because in all such cases, time is the greatest pacificator—the evil against which we contend is not accessible to reason.'[176] At the same time, he hoped the threatening posture of Russia would make it easier for Britain and Austria to obtain concessions from the Sultan.

The Hanover interview

In the face of these perils, the idea of a personal meeting between Castlereagh and Metternich seems to have occurred to both statesmen almost simultaneously. Castlereagh was already on his way to the German state of Hanover with George IV when he sent an invitation to Metternich to meet him there. Metternich made the same proposal to the British chargé d'affaires in Vienna. The two ministers met for ten days in mid-October 1821, for what was to be their last encounter. Bernstorff from Prussia and Count Lieven from Russia were also invited, but Bernstorff never showed up and Lieven, who first went to St Petersburg to consult with the Tsar, almost came too late. At Castlereagh's request, Countess Dorothea Lieven conveniently arrived before her husband to renew her romantic liaison with Metternich. Much time was spent discussing British domestic politics, since George IV was intent on dismissing Lord Liverpool and replacing him with Castlereagh; it took all the combined efforts of Metternich and Countess Lieven to reconcile the British monarch to the idea of retaining his Prime Minister.[177]

The primary focus of the meeting remained the unfurling crisis in the Sultan's domains. Castlereagh and Metternich quickly developed a common strategy, although they agreed not to cooperate too openly for fear of offending the Tsar.[178] Metternich would make Austrian support contingent upon a series of unlikely conditions, whereas Castlereagh would leave undefined how Britain might react; they further decided to convene a congress the following year. Once again, this diplomatic duo acted together to restrain the Tsar—using Alexander's well-known predilection for collaboration in the name of Europe. The meeting actually ended with the arrival of Count Lieven, bearing the glad tidings from St Petersburg that the Tsar still favoured allied solidarity over the pursuit of unilateral action in Greece.[179]

Still, nothing could be taken for granted. Castlereagh had already written on 28 October (the day before Lieven's arrival) to Bagot in St Petersburg, in a letter intended for the Tsar. He confessed his personal sympathies for the Greek Christians under the 'Turkish yoke', but pointed out that statesmen must be guided by the dictates of reason, not the heart. A statesman's highest aim was to provide for peace and security, and these valuable possessions were not to be gambled away in risky ventures to improve the lot of humanity. He could not speculate on what might result from a Russo-Turkish war, but he would not favour a new form of government for the Greeks at the cost of confusion and destruction in Turkey, placing the European alliance itself at risk. Finally, Castlereagh politely asserted that the Tsar was quite mistaken in believing that the European possessions of the Ottoman Empire lay outside the borders of the Vienna settlement.[180]

Metternich similarly sent a steady stream of communications to St Petersburg. Austria would support the Russian demand that the Sultan evacuate the Danubian Principalities, he reaffirmed, but she would not condone the use of foreign arms to assist the Greeks. Metternich continued to insist on the importance of separating 'legitimate' treaty issues—principally the demand for the evacuation of the Principalities—from all other questions; he then cleverly maintained that the Turks had already agreed to the evacuation and were guilty merely of justifiable delay.[181]

These Anglo-Austrian efforts to forestall Russian intervention were rendered all the more difficult by the continuing obstinacy of the Porte, which had every reason to avoid a potentially disastrous war and yet refused to make meaningful concessions. Having recently appeased the Russians on the issues of the Danubian delta, the autonomy of Serbia and the control of the Trans-Caucasus, the Sultan no longer trusted Russian promises and had no intention of withdrawing his troops from the Principalities before the Greek rebels were thoroughly crushed. Indeed, Mahmud continued to suspect the Russians and Greeks of being in secret collaboration. In September and October, the Ottoman government at last made some conciliatory gestures—offering to withdraw from the Principalities if the Russians promised not to enter with their own troops.[182] But the situation changed for the worse when a new Turkish foreign minister (or 'Reis Effendi'), who eschewed all compromise, was appointed.

Meanwhile, the Greeks continued to enjoy mastery of the sea and the Turks were distracted by their final campaign against Ali Pasha.[183] The worst Greek massacre of Turks took place in October at Tripoli (or Tripolitsa) in the Peloponnese, where thousands of Muslim and Jewish residents of the town were slain.[184] Fresh Turkish massacres of Christians followed in Smyrna and Constantinople in November, while the Ottoman Government reiterated its demand that Russia turn over Michael Sutzo and other refugees. That same month, Russian army observers reported the presence of 25,000 Ottoman troops in Moldavia; in December, they feared as many as 350,000 Ottoman troops were ready to march—misinformation deliberately spread by the Ottomans themselves to deter Russian intervention, but which paradoxically led some Russian military analysts to mistakenly conclude that the Porte was preparing to launch an offensive to regain Bessarabia from Russia.[185] Capodistrias blamed Castlereagh and Metternich—England's 'commercial selfishness' and Austria's 'restless jealousy'—for the Sultan's truculence since, he claimed, Mahmud now felt assured that the allies would not intervene.[186] The Ottomans finally captured Ali Pasha in January 1822. In the same month, a republican constitution for Greece was declared at Epidauros, though the Greeks remained divided between three leaders—Alexander Mavrocordatos, George Kondouriotis and Theodore Kolokotrones.[187]

When the Austrians advised the Porte that it should adopt a less belligerent approach or all of Europe would soon ally with the Greeks, they were arrogantly told that all Christian subjects in the Ottoman Empire would be dead long before any Russian troops could save them.[188] Under conditions such as these, the Tsar grew increasingly frustrated at the lack of concrete action. His ministers asked the Austrians to assemble a *corps d'observation*, much as Russia had done for Austria in Piedmont.[189] The Tsar wrote to Count

Lieven in London, complaining that the allies should help Russia, just as Russia had assisted the rest of Europe, most recently, in Italy.[190] Nesselrode informed the Austrian ambassador that if the Turks did not meet Russia's legitimate demands by March 1822, Russia would have no other recourse but war.[191] When the Ottoman government announced at the end of February that it still would not remove its troops from the Principalities, allied leaders became convinced that armed conflict was inevitable.

Once again, it was Alexander who pulled back from the abyss at the very last moment, giving way out of a genuine sense of attachment to the European alliance and fear of revolution. Castlereagh and Metternich had long been deluging him with alleged proofs of the ties between the Greeks and the revolutionary movement. In late December, Castlereagh sent another long despatch to Bagot in St Petersburg, depicting the progress of the revolution from South America to Spain and culminating in Greece: 'the insurrection throughout European Turkey, in its organization, in its objects, in its agency, and in its external relations, is in no respect distinguishable from the movements which have preceded it in Spain, Portugal, and Italy...'[192] Castlereagh even proposed that the Tsar consider intervening against the Greeks rather than the reverse, though he realized this might not be possible for religious reasons. Bagot wisely refrained from showing this part of his instructions to the Tsar, but utilized most of Castlereagh's other arguments.[193] This reasoning seems to have had some impact on the Tsar: 'I am sensible of the danger which surrounds us all,' Alexander told Bagot, 'when I look to the state of France ... when I see the state of Spain and Portugal, when I see, as I do see, the state of the whole world, I am well aware that the smallest spark which falls upon such combustible materials may kindle a flame which all our efforts may perhaps hereafter be insufficient to extinguish.'[194]

Even more importantly, the Tsar was continuing to experience deep religious emotions. In the winter of 1821–22, while Capodistrias was speaking for the Russian foreign ministry, Alexander was frantically searching Scriptures for guidance on whether or not to embark on war. Finally, sometime in mid-February, he reached an answer. Fortunately for Europe, it seemed that God desired Russia to resolve the problem peacefully.[195]

The Tatishchev mission

Alexander nonetheless wished to reach some understanding with the other great powers for the protection of the Greeks. Capodistrias suggested that the allies submit a collective demand to the Porte for a redress of Russian grievances, arrange a mutual withdrawal of their diplomatic legations and even plan joint military operations in the event that the Sultan failed to meet their requirements. He recommended that Stroganov be sent to London and Count Peter Tolstoy to Vienna for the purpose of negotiating these arrangements. The Tsar also solicited the advice of Nesselrode, who recommended that Count Dmitri Tatishchev be sent to Vienna instead of Tolstoy and that they rely on Count Lieven, already in London. Capodistrias rightly interpreted the Tsar's selection of Nesselrode's nominees as an ominous portent of his own loss of influence.[196]

Rather than attacking Turkey, the Tsar thus dispatched a confidential envoy to Vienna.[197] Tatishchev arrived on 5 March 1822 and held a series of conferences with Metternich that lasted until late April. The Russians originally proposed that Austria support their demands for immediate evacuation of the Danubian Principalities and for Russo-Turkish talks on the future of Greece. The Tsar also still sought the right to act as the 'Protector' of the Greek Christians. Metternich continued to support the first of these demands but not the others. How could the allies, he contended (with the help of Gentz), dictate to a legitimate sovereign how to treat his subjects in rebellion? Since the Sultan had already agreed to evacuate the Principalities just as soon as they were pacified, Metternich deftly argued that the Russians had nothing more to demand there either, since the Sultan clearly could not fulfil his pledge while those provinces were still in open rebellion.[198]

When Tatishchev demanded that Austria at least offer to sever diplomatic relations with the Porte if Russia were compelled, by the Sultan's intransigence, to go to war, Metternich consented, but only if the other allies would do the same—a totally meaningless gesture since there was not the slightest chance that the British would ever take such a step.[199] On 19 April, Tatishchev and Metternich signed a final agreement acknowledging that the Porte had conceded its duty to evacuate the Principalities when it was safe to do so. Metternich also composed a long letter to the Tsar, again separating the specific treaty issues from the more 'general' question of the future of the Greeks. He proposed two ways for the allies to proceed—either to postpone all further discussions till the forthcoming congress on Italy, or to establish an ambassadorial conference at Vienna.[200]

Capodistrias was infuriated by the results of the Tatishchev mission: just a few weeks earlier he had advised the Tsar that only a show of force would ever lead the Porte to observe its treaty obligations. If Russia accepted Metternich's latest proposals, Capodistrias feared, the Sultan would simply use this extra time for the continued devastation of Greece.[201]

While Metternich was conferring with Tatishchev, similar discussions were being conducted in London between Castlereagh and Lieven. Like Metternich, Castlereagh warned the Russians that they should not go beyond the 'Four Points' in their demands, and he categorically refused any suspension of diplomatic relations with the Porte. He even sent a letter to Bagot in St Petersburg, again intended for the Tsar, in which he openly addressed the rumours that the Russian 'war party' planned to establish an autonomous Greek state.[202] Fortunately, the Ottomans suddenly felt pressured by the outbreak of a war with Persia, and they miraculously began their evacuation of the Danubian Principalities on 13 May. The fall of the pro-Russian Richelieu government in Paris in December 1821 then made the Tsar more reluctant to embark on a new war in the East. The arrival of Tatishchev with signed agreements from Metternich, combined with the news conveyed by Strangford that the Sultan was ready to evacuate the Principalities, again persuaded Alexander to refrain from war.

Six weeks later, Tatishchev was sent back to Vienna to participate in an ambassadorial conference to prepare the groundwork for the coming congress.[203] In his instructions to Tatishchev, the Tsar noted with some satisfaction that the allied powers had recognized Russia's right to use arms against the Turks even though they had also expressed their keen desire to preserve the peace. In the new negotiations, Tatishchev was therefore assigned two specific goals: (1) to secure the Ottoman withdrawal from the Principalities; and (2) to persuade the Sultan to send plenipotentiaries to meet with Russian envoys to restore Russo-Turkish diplomatic relations. Beyond this, Russia claimed to seek no new rights. This retreat from Russia's original objectives caused Metternich to boast of his ascendancy over St Petersburg: 'The work which Peter the Great began and his successors continued has been shaken to its foundations.'[204] Capodistrias remained in the Tsar's service, but removed himself from all involvement in the Greek Question. Stourdza, the spokesman for the Holy Alliance, had already been suspended from Tsar's service several months earlier.[205]

The threat of war in Turkey and of a possible schism between Russia and her European allies was thus averted, at least temporarily. Whether this was because of Alexander's solicitude for the alliance, the diplomatic skill of Metternich and Castlereagh, continuing fears of a revolutionary conflagration, cabinet changes in France, or the deus ex machina of the Turkish war with Persia, the allied leaders could breathe a collective sigh of relief—even as the tragic massacres in Greece continued unabated.

Ironically, some of the worst bloodletting of the Greek War for Independence coincided with the Turkish withdrawal from the Danubian Principalities. A Greek rebel force from Samos landed on the island of Chios (Scio) in early March. Later that month, an Ottoman fleet surrounded Chios and Turkish troops enslaved or slaughtered the island's Greek inhabitants, inspiring the artist Delacroix to paint one of his most moving tableaux.[206] Castlereagh and Metternich were shocked but unwavering in their policies. In Britain,

France and Russia, the Greek cause gained in popularity. In June 1822, Castlereagh was forced to defend his position in Parliament, but fear of future Russian domination of the Mediterranean through the Black Sea remained just as powerful a force in the British popular imagination as Philhellenic enthusiasm for the Greeks.[207] While Castlereagh argued on the floor of the House of Commons that the British bore no culpability for the crimes committed by the Porte, he harshly reprimanded the Ottoman ministers in his confidential instructions to Lord Strangford.[208] In fact, Castlereagh was preparing to recognize the Greeks as belligerents, just as he had done with the Latin American rebels (and as Canning would later do with the Greeks).[209]

Assessments

Did the handling of the Greek crisis in these years constitute yet another triumph for the Congress System? In fact, the allied leaders had been unable to restrain either the Greeks or the Ottoman Turks, and their solitary success seems to have been in persuading the Tsar not to intervene in the conflict. Unlike the earlier revolutions in Latin America, Spain, Italy and Portugal, the Greek insurrection posed the additional complication of religion. This cut across existing constitutional alignments and traditional geopolitical concerns. Russia, the mainstay of the system, had strong incentives to act more independently in the East. The chief stumbling block was that, much as the Tsar and those around him sympathized with the Greeks as Christians, the Tsar also continued to detest revolutions and to crave great-power solidarity. According to historian Matthew Anderson, on this occasion the Tsar exhibited 'a width of view and a freedom from merely national and selfish considerations which could be matched by no other European ruler of the period'.[210] Likewise, historian Paul Schroeder points to this as a clear 'instance where a state has foregone concrete material advantages for the sake of moral principle'.[211] The 'moral principle' was, of course, simply that of preserving the existing socio-political order from the threat of revolution. Political scientist Matthew Rendall makes the point that Russia under Alexander I was no longer expansionist. The Tsar acted with restraint in part because of his concern that the Russian conquest of Turkey would unite the other great powers against him; of equal importance, he remained in genuine dread of revolution.[212] Indeed, an official Russian study later in the 1820s concluded that Alexander's restraint had been due to his wish to preserve friendly relations with his allies, his contempt for revolutionaries, and his solicitude for 'guarantees of the general peace'.[213]

According to Edward Ingram, a distinguished historian of British imperialism, the Eastern Question remained the new system's Achilles' heel.[214]

In 1815, the great powers could not agree on whether to include the Ottoman Empire in a general guarantee. As a league of Christian states, the Holy Alliance also excluded it (adding to the Sultan's suspicions). The Ottoman Empire thus lay astride the border between the areas that Ingram defines as the 'core' and 'periphery'. In the core, Ingram argues, a new equilibrium was established. Violence was exported to the periphery, where it continued to hold sway for the rest of the century. Ingram's dichotomy may be overdrawn: the guarantee of Europe was a loose one and the Tsar no doubt thought action justified in Turkey no less than in Naples. It was the strategic interests of Austria and Britain that blocked his advance, not any legalistic recognition of the territorial limits of the Vienna settlement. Even if the Tsar was not actually convinced by the arguments of Castlereagh and Metternich, he still preferred not to act without their sanction. He seems to have been dominated by a genuine fear of revolutionary conspiracy, as ironic as this may appear, since he personally knew Ypsilantis and the conditions of the Greek Christians under Ottoman rule. The Tsar seems to have hovered at the 'tipping point', and tottered backwards and forwards over the issue of intervention. According to German historian Eberhard Schütz, whenever the Tsar was finally ready to abandon the Greek insurgents to their fate, the Sultan's excessive persecutions always led him back from the brink.[215] Two years later, in 1824, the Tsar would actually adopt the opposite course and begin preparations for intervention; even later in the decade, his younger brother and successor, Nicholas I, would actually take action. But in 1821–22, the system held fast despite the tempest.

7

The Twilight of the Congress System, 1822–23

The Congress of Verona

The last of the great European peacetime congresses was held in 'fair Verona', where Capulet once fought Montague. Like the fabled strife between these ancient noble houses, the final gathering of allied sovereigns and ministers displayed greater division than unity.

Doceañistas and *exaltados* in Spain

While the diplomats of the allied powers had been focused on events in Italy and the Ottoman Empire, the constitutional regime in Spain had survived unchecked. As in Naples, the liberals were divided into two camps: the *doceañistas* and *exaltados*. The *doceañistas*, or 'Men of 1812' (later known as *moderados*), were members of the property-owning and professional classes.[1] Authors of the Constitution of 1812, some of them had been temporarily imprisoned by Ferdinand VII or had fled the country in 1814; they now favoured such moderate reforms as a restricted franchise, the addition of an upper chamber to the Cortes, a bridling of the free press and the protection of property.[2] The *doceañistas* were also notoriously anti-clerical: they abolished the Inquisition, reduced the tithe and sold off monastic lands.[3] The *exaltados* were younger men of similar background—junior army officers and members of the local juntas—who took credit for the Revolution of 1820. They appealed to lower-class sentiment in the towns and cities, especially in Galicia and the south. The *exaltados* remained committed to the unicameral Cortes as the embodiment of the sovereignty of the people. Curiously, neither group was willing to abandon the goal of restoring Spain's rule over South America or of restricting colonial trade, although the new government announced its preference for a political compromise over a military solution and sent new commissioners to negotiate with the rebels. A six-month cease-fire was declared, only to be followed in June by another victory for Bolívar, the 'Liberator'.[4] Making matters worse, in January 1821, Mexico joined the ranks of the other colonies in the struggle for independence.

In Spain, apprehensions of counter-revolutionary intervention by the allied powers added to the general malaise. When the King of Naples was summoned to Laibach by the allies, the Spanish government took immediate alarm and considered convoking an extraordinary Cortes to organize the national defence. The Spanish foreign minister, Evaristo Pérez de Castro, informed Sir Henry Wellesley, the British ambassador, that he viewed the acceptance of the allied invitation by the Neapolitan monarch as 'highly disgraceful'. 'Putting the best colour upon the proceedings of the allied sovereigns', Castro told Wellesley, 'he could view them in no other light than as an unjustifiable interference in the rights which all nations possess of regulating their own system of government, and as directly attacking the fundamental principles of the Spanish Constitution, which, he repeatedly observed, had been described by Prince Metternich as *"Un Code d'Anarchie"* [a code of anarchy].'[5] Wellesley reassured Castro that the political changes in Spain were viewed quite differently from those in Naples, although his palliative words were nearly sabotaged when a letter was received by the Prussian ambassador from Laibach, disclosing 'the intention of the three sovereigns of Austria, Prussia and Russia, as soon as the affairs of Naples [were] settled, to occupy themselves with those of Spain and Portugal'.[6] Wellesley was able to persuade the other diplomats not to convey this inflammatory message to the Spaniards, while his own dispatches to London frequently reiterated his conviction that, in the event of foreign intervention, all recent progress towards greater moderation would be lost to 'the feeling, whether right or wrong, that it is the first duty of a Spaniard to resist foreign interference'.[7]

In the meantime, a formal protest against intervention was prepared for the allied courts by the Spanish government. As in Naples, the same rumours that were undermining the position of the moderate liberals were bolstering the King's spirits and encouraging his obstinacy: 'I believe that the King and his secret councillors are impressed with the conviction that, the affairs of Naples once settled, the sovereigns will turn their attention to Spain ....'[8] The mood of the Spanish ministers was somewhat lifted by the arrival of Castlereagh's condemnation of the Troppau Circular, but they questioned his caveat that a country nonetheless had the right to interfere in the internal affairs of another if its 'immediate security or essential interests' were somehow threatened—this loophole, they pointed out with perspicacity, might allow Austria to interfere in Naples, France in Spain, or Prussia in the Netherlands.[9]

In early February 1821, hostile crowds, urged on by the *exaltados*, gathered before the royal palace in Madrid. They shouted insults at Ferdinand as he returned in his carriage, leading to a violent clash when an escort from his bodyguard assaulted members of the militia in the crowd. The ministers, who had taken no additional steps to protect their sovereign, blamed the guards for the incident and insisted that Ferdinand should be separated from his bodyguard.[10] When the King lamented to Wellesley that he feared for his life, the British diplomat responded somewhat disparagingly that he was in no real danger and that most of his problems could in fact be attributed to 'ill-advised plots' to overturn the new constitutional order, in which he was 'always suspected of being more or less implicated'. Through a confidential intermediary, Wellesley received a secret list of alleged 'reforms' to which the King would willingly acquiesce. These included the restoration of his own sovereign power, the creation of a new Cortes based upon Spain's traditional estates, the abolition of the leading political parties, a requirement that no law should pass the Cortes 'without the previous knowledge of the King'; and lastly, 'the introduction of a sufficient foreign force to maintain the tranquillity of the kingdom'. These proposals, Wellesley sadly concluded, demonstrated all too plainly that the Spanish monarch had 'a very erroneous notion, both of his own situation and of the modifications of the Constitution to which the people might be willing to submit'. In fact, Wellesley advised Ferdinand to destroy the incriminating paper immediately.[11]

In March 1821 the King opened the new Cortes with a pledge to maintain the Constitution of 1812. Against his ministers' advice, Ferdinand added several sentences at the end of his prepared speech, referring to the insults he had received a month earlier, complaining of the failure of the ministers to uphold his royal dignity and appealing to the Cortes to strengthen the executive power. The ministers were shocked and considered whether to submit their resignations, when they found themselves suddenly dismissed by the King.[12] Taking into account Ferdinand's deceptive behaviour and the means at the ministers' disposal, Wellesley marvelled at their admirable 'moderation and forbearance' in their acceptance of their fate: 'They were, in point of character, talent and influence, the leading members of the Cortes, the fittest persons in the country for the situations which they occupied ... If the King had [played] straight with his ministers ... much progress might have been made.'[13] In response to the King's impromptu remarks, the liberal Cortes charged him to take steps to strengthen not only his own safety, but also that of all the political institutions of the country, including the Constitution itself. Ironically, the envoys of the three eastern courts at last received their new instructions, making it clear that, at least for the time being, they had no intentions of interfering in Spain.[14] Meanwhile, the King selected Eusebio de

Bardají, another *doceañista*, to form a new ministry.[15] In April, reports were received in Madrid of the collapse of the government in Piedmont and of the success of the Austrian expedition to Naples, ominously leaving the two new revolutionary states on the Iberian Peninsula in complete isolation. The discouraging news led to a few minor public demonstrations, which were speedily suppressed.

By the summer of 1821, the initial alliance between the *doceañistas* and *exaltados* had completely unravelled. Since Riego's *pronunciamento*, Ferdinand had appointed two successive *doceañista* governments, both of which had failed to reward the junior army officers who had spearheaded the revolution.[16] Dwindling revenues had even forced the *doceañistas* to order the dissolution of the army intended for the Americas, where the revolution had begun.[17] The dismissal of Riego from his post, spreading unemployment, the mounting costs of the war in America and the reimposition of former taxes triggered popular demonstrations in the capital in September; this was followed by a resumption of agitation by the *exaltados* in the provinces.[18] Whole areas of the country were withdrawn from the authority of Madrid.[19] The anti-clerical acts of the *doceañistas* had equally outraged the Spanish clergy, who helped organize small guerrilla bands of counter-revolutionaries, especially in the rural areas of the north. Thousands of peasants rallied against the regime, particularly where the secular purchasers of church lands raised their tenants' rents. 'Neither Moderates nor Radicals (*exaltados*) had the support of the country', writes one historian, 'for the great mass of people remained loyal to their monarch and their priests.'[20] To make matters worse, yellow fever broke out in Catalonia.[21] The *doceañistas* were thus besieged on all sides.

The unrest of 1821 led the ministers to announce an extraordinary session of the Cortes, as well as to reintroduce the unpopular practice of conscription. When new elections were held at the end of 1821, the *exaltados* obtained a majority in the Cortes, which promptly elected Riego as its president.[22] The Constitution of 1812, however, left the prerogative of appointments in the hands of the King, so Ferdinand defied the majority in the Cortes by choosing yet another *doceañista*, the moderate playwright Francisco Martínez de la Rosa, to form a government.[23] Even now, the support of the Crown might have enabled the ministers to overcome many difficulties, but after witnessing the course of events in Naples and Piedmont, Ferdinand VII looked increasingly to foreign intervention and grew ever less cooperative. He deliberately tried to foment division among the liberals, realizing that chaos in Madrid would make allied intervention that much more likely.[24] At the same time, the Cortes blindly continued its rejection of a compromise peace with the American colonists, while its persistent attacks on the Church fed the fires of counter-revolution.

The Revolution takes a radical turn

In July 1822, the royal guards at Madrid—elite regiments with aristocratic officers—mutinied against the constitutional regime in the name of the King. The ministers and the commander of the constitutional army were imprisoned in the palace, where they agreed to the demands of the royalist insurgents. Other army regiments, just outside Madrid, were ready to intervene on the King's behalf. But the pusillanimous Ferdinand fatally hesitated by failing to lead the guards out of Madrid and placing himself at the forefront of the counter-revolution. The militia and artillery regiments rallied to the constitutional order, and after several days of street fighting, the uprising of the guards was quelled by Riego and his friend Colonel Evaristo de San Miguel.[25]

The main effect of the 'July Days' was the resignation of Martínez de la Rosa. Control of the government thus passed into the hands of the *exaltados*, and Ferdinand VII became their virtual prisoner. San Miguel formed a new government in which he served as both Prime Minister and foreign minister, while other leading posts were filled with the army officers who had initiated the Revolution of 1820.[26] The Spanish Revolution thus passed into its radical phase, much as Metternich had always predicted. 'Spain,' observed the French writer and statesman Chateaubriand, 'now exhibited a servile copy of our revolutionary course: clubs, motions, assassination and destruction.'[27] Radicalism also bred counter-revolution. The Spanish royalists in the northeast, led by the Archbishop of Tarragona and the Marquis of Mataflorida, enrolled thousands of peasants in an 'Army of the Faith' and declared a regency on Ferdinand's behalf at Seo de Urgel in Catalonia. The Urgel regency appealed directly to the allied powers for help.[28]

Franco-Spanish relations

As in 1820, of greatest importance was the impact of these developments on France, Spain's immediate neighbour and linked by dynastic ties to Spain's ruling family.[29] Already in August 1821, the Richelieu ministry had begun to concentrate troops along the Spanish border, forming a *cordon sanitaire* to halt the spread of yellow fever from Barcelona; later the same contingent was openly renamed a *corps d'observation* to prevent the spread of revolutionary contagion.[30] Spain lodged an official complaint against these menacing troop movements, causing the French government to send assurances that their actions were not intended as inimical. Then in December 1821, the Richelieu ministry fell. It was replaced by a new ultra-royalist ministry, supported by the Comte d'Artois and pledged to a more ambitious foreign policy.[31] The new French foreign minister, Mathieu de Montmorency, had once been a liberal noble and supporter of the Abbé Sièyes, but he was shocked by the Terror into becoming a religious conservative and 'Grand Master' of the royalist *Chevaliers de la Foi*. Montmorency was especially eager to take action in Spain.[32] Besides strengthening the position of the ultra-royalists in France, a successful expedition would also avenge Napoleon's losses in Spain during the Peninsular Wars.

The King of Spain had already requested help from the allied sovereigns at Laibach but, with the exception of the Tsar, his pleas had fallen on deaf ears. In February 1822, Ferdinand VII secretly appealed to his uncle, the King of Naples, to seek assistance from the allied sovereigns on his behalf. The Spanish monarch specifically requested 6,000 troops from Louis XVIII. The French government replied in March that they could only support an indigenous movement arising spontaneously in Spain, since Britain's well-known opposition prevented them from taking any greater initiative. In April, Montmorency suggested to the allies that an ambassadorial conference might be established in Paris to discuss whatever measures could be taken to assist Ferdinand. In June, he further recommended that the powers discuss what support they would be willing to provide to France if she were compelled to intervene in Spain, either because the King's life was in danger or because the Spanish constitutionalists had declared war.[33]

The French also set a parallel policy in motion by sending secret terms to Madrid: Louis XVIII offered to mediate the dispute between Ferdinand and his subjects, even holding out the prospect of direct intervention if the King of Spain would grant his subjects a *Charte* on the French model. There was an obvious similarity between this proposition and earlier French initiatives in Naples.[34] The French offer reached Madrid too late to prevent the rising of the royal guards, and Ferdinand would probably not have agreed to it before he had attempted the abortive coup in any event. After the 'July Days', however, Ferdinand had no choice but to negotiate for foreign help, and he promised the French to convoke the Cortes in its traditional form in exchange for their support.[35]

Russian initiatives and Metternich's prowess

Ferdinand's plea through the King of Naples had also stung the conscience of the Tsar. To cover his retreat in Turkey, the Russian Emperor redirected his energies towards the west. In late April, he revived his proposal for the formation of a European army. A new Russian memorandum circulated the chancelleries of Europe: it invoked the Troppau Protocol and the declaration from Laibach calling for the assistance of monarchs in distress. Under this reinvigorated scheme, each of the allied powers was to provide an armed contingent: the Russian force would march to Spain by way of Austria, Lombardy, Piedmont and France. The Russian Emperor also wished the allied powers to draw up specific plans for the number of troops they would contribute, where their troops would assemble and what routes they would take on their march.[36]

As always, Metternich suspected the chicanery of Pozzo di Borgo and Capodistrias behind these grandiose designs: Pozzo, he imagined, was attempting to compensate for his loss of influence in Paris since the fall of Richelieu, while Capodistrias was hoping to expose the alliance as a sham in order to free Russian policy in the east from its restraining force.[37] Metternich was therefore careful to praise the idealism of the Tsar's proposal even while objecting to its application on the grounds of practicality; privately, he denounced Alexander's scheme as 'absolute nonsense'. All the allies really needed to do in Spain, Metternich contended, was to lend their moral support to the 'healthy' part of the Spanish nation.[38]

The incident neatly illustrates something of Metternich's technical virtuosity as a diplomat. If Castlereagh's strength in diplomacy was his frank acknowledgement of conflicting interests and his willingness to roll up his shirt sleeves to engage in hard bargaining behind the scenes (whether by offering financial succours or territorial concessions), Metternich's two great talents were surely his keen perception of the psychological needs of both allies and adversaries and his capacity to adapt: he could, for example, identify what would appeal most to the Tsar and trim his message accordingly. Metternich often preferred to work through others and frequently sent out multiple and even inconsistent messages addressed to different audiences to attain his goals. A French historian has marvelled at his system of 'correspondance à trois étages' (three-tiered correspondence): the first letter was sent to his envoy at a foreign court with the understanding that it would be disclosed; a second was transmitted to the same envoy with instructions on how to use the first, meant to be confidentially conveyed to the court to which he was accredited as a token of the envoy's sincerity; finally, Metternich sent his true instructions, which were to be kept secret. In May 1822, he thus sent a message to Lebzeltern, the Austrian ambassador in St Petersburg, to be shared with the Russian ministers, in which he argued that it would be difficult to persuade the other allies to join a European army, the very formation of which might endanger the safety of the King of Spain; a second letter, supposedly intended for the Tsar alone, emphasized the risks that England would break from the alliance and that disturbances would erupt in France; finally, Metternich wrote to Lebzeltern privately that he believed the proposed intervention in Spain was actually an intrigue hatched by Pozzo and Capodistrias to separate the Tsar from the allies in order to regain their influence.[39]

When Metternich rejected the Tsar's ideas for intervention on the grounds of the insurmountable obstacles facing an allied march on Spain, Alexander suggested as an alternative that an allied (in effect, Russian) force be stationed in Piedmont, ready to intervene in France in the case of a revolutionary outbreak, or to march across France to Spain if events so required. Moreover, this new plan would conveniently require Russian forces to cross only territories under Austrian control. At the very least, Alexander insisted that the Spanish Question should be discussed at the next reunion of the allied powers, which, as had already been agreed upon at Laibach, was to be held in Florence in September. The events of 1822 now catapulted the Spanish crisis to the very top of the European agenda, and Metternich could hardly object to Russian and French demands that it be discussed.[40]

Plans for the Congress

With the scheduled date of the allied reunion approaching, Metternich wrote to Castlereagh requesting that he personally attend to perform his customary role of restraining the Tsar. The two statesmen had already discussed possible British participation at the conference when they had met in Hanover. To spare Castlereagh any embarrassment from involvement in Italian affairs, Metternich proposed that the conference be divided into two distinct phases: the first, which Castlereagh could attend in Vienna, would focus on the Turkish problem; the second, to take place in Florence, would deal with the Austrian occupation of Naples and Piedmont. The Spanish Question was to be added to the deliberations in Vienna.[41]

The British cabinet, reluctant to see Castlereagh leave for the Continent, only approved the mission on 25 July. Castlereagh's official instructions with respect to Spain, written largely by himself, were brief: Britain would honour her treaty commitments to Portugal, protect the safety of Ferdinand VII and follow a policy of 'rigid abstinence from any interference in the internal affairs of that country'.[42] Castlereagh planned to travel to Vienna by way of Paris, so that he could reach a prior understanding with the French government. Any consensus reached by Britain, France and Austria on Spain would effectively bind Russia.

The death of Castlereagh

On 12 August 1822, Castlereagh, overwhelmed with work and in a state of severe depression, suddenly committed suicide. This event dramatically altered the prospects for the coming conference as well as for the European alliance as a whole. For years, Castlereagh had been beset by occasional bouts of depression, which he sometimes referred to as attacks of 'blue devils'. Conflicts between the King and the cabinet, especially over the handling of the Queen Caroline crisis, had added greatly to his stress. Castlereagh may have also been under some emotional strain from the false allegations of a blackmailer. Finally, it has recently been suggested that Castlereagh was suffering from the tertiary stage of syphilis, contracted decades earlier when he was a student at Cambridge. Close friends began noticing periodic fits of paranoia. At an audience with George IV on 9 August, Castlereagh broke down completely. Later the same day, Castlereagh saw Wellington. After several minutes of conversation, the Duke candidly told him: 'From what you have said, I am bound to warn you that you cannot be in your right mind.' Over the next three days, Castlereagh remained under the care of his wife and doctor. He fell into a fever as his condition worsened. Fearing that he might be suicidal, they concealed his pistols and razors and kept him under constant surveillance. On the morning of the 12th, Castlereagh was left alone for a few moments and found a small penknife, which he promptly struck into his throat. When his doctor returned, Castlereagh fell into his arms murmuring "tis all over". So ended this 'most European' of British foreign secretaries, and Britain's closest tie to the Continental powers. 'I can imagine only too well how sad you must be', Countess Lieven wrote to Metternich from London. 'Besides mourning [Castlereagh] as a friend, you have to mourn him as a minister—perhaps the only man in England who understood European politics, and whose principles as well as his inclinations urged him towards friendship with Austria.'[43]

Castlereagh's successor at the Foreign Office, George Canning, had previously served as Foreign Secretary until 1809, when he and Castlereagh had quarrelled, jointly resigned from the cabinet and fought a famous duel with pistols. The remarkable clash of two cabinet ministers, at a time when the country was at war, was enough to bring down the Portland government. Castlereagh had returned to office as Foreign Secretary in 1812, but Canning had remained in opposition, only finally returning to government service as ambassador to Portugal (1814–16) and President of the Board of Control (1816–20). He resigned from the cabinet again over the Queen Caroline affair, and was about to embark for India as the new Governor-General when he received the news of Castlereagh's suicide. Although the Prime Minister, the Earl of Liverpool, never faltered in Canning's support, it was only after some hesitation on the part of George IV and the rest of the cabinet that Canning was finally offered Castlereagh's entire 'heritage'—both leadership of the House of Commons and the Foreign Office.[44]

Canning never developed the close personal ties with foreign leaders that Castlereagh had enjoyed in the final years of the war. He consequently viewed the Congress System more as a loathsome fetter binding England to despotic states than as a useful instrument of policy. In 1818, a fellow cabinet member had informed Castlereagh that Canning held the 'system of periodical meetings of the four great powers with a view to the general concerns of Europe' to be a 'very questionable policy'.[45] Indeed, after Castlereagh's State Paper of 5 May 1820, Canning exclaimed to his cousin, 'We shall have no more congresses, thank God!'[46] In Canning's view, each state had to attain its own unique blend of liberty and order, and this balance could not be imposed on nations such as Naples, Piedmont or Spain by an external coalition of despotic states. In his eyes, the original goal of the alliance—the containment of French aggression—had been perverted by the autocratic powers, and he was only too happy to see this new 'Areopagus' (or world tribunal) destroyed. Canning's general hostility to the alliance system as well as his personal antipathy to Metternich meant that the Austrian Chancellor could no longer find freedom of action by oscillating between Russia and Britain.[47]

Wellington's mission

Since the arrangements for the impending conference had been designed especially to accommodate Britain, since the cabinet had already given its approval, and since the Turkish question, the slave trade and the future of Latin America were all on the agenda to be discussed, Canning consented on this one occasion to British participation in another European congress. The Duke of Wellington, as the government member most familiar with the diplomats of Europe, was appointed to take Castlereagh's place as British plenipotentiary even before Canning took office. Wellington's departure was delayed, however, by a bout of influenza, and it was not until 20 September that the Duke finally arrived in Paris.[48]

There, Wellington met with the new head of the French government, the Comte de Villèle. Already Minister of Finance, Villèle was named as President of the Council on 4 September, shortly after Montmorency's departure for Vienna. More circumspect than Montmorency, Villèle showed a greater willingness to wait upon events. He feared that French intervention in Spain would strain his government's finances, endanger the loyalty of the army and risk a calamitous defeat. Such a rash adventure was also certain to be opposed by Britain. Wellington informed him that 100,000 men would be needed to topple the constitutionalists in Spain.[49] Villèle explained that France had already amassed a force of that magnitude along the border. Although some in the French government favoured seizing the initiative to rescue Ferdinand VII, Villèle himself opposed such action unless provoked by a violation of French territory, the overthrow of Ferdinand, or some act directly hostile to

France. He even admitted to Wellington that, while 'the *morale* of the French army was very much improved', it still could not be entirely relied upon. French soldiers would certainly not enter Spain, he insisted, as the mere tools of the alliance; nor would France permit foreign troops on her own soil, effectively throwing cold water over the Tsar's plans. Villèle intended above all to maintain France's freedom of action.[50]

After these discussions, Wellington was cautiously optimistic that his own reputation on Spanish military matters, Britain's opposition, and the cooperation of Villèle and Metternich would effectively forestall any plans for intervention in Spain. After the receipt of Wellington's reports, Canning likewise feared interference in Spain less from France than from the three eastern courts, who might attempt to cloak their actions in the mantle of the alliance. Canning found any such scheme so 'objectionable ... in principle' and so 'impracticable in execution', that he instructed Wellington to refuse any association with it, 'come what may'. Where Castlereagh had condemned allied interference in the internal affairs of other states with a blink and a grin, Canning meant serious business; but he was not willing to commit British forces to oppose either France or the three eastern courts, so long as they confined their action to Spain herself.[51]

The last of the congresses

Meanwhile, the plenipotentiaries of the Continental powers had been patiently waiting in Vienna for Wellington's arrival since early September. Metternich's chief objective was to ward off intervention in Spain in order to prevent the fissures in the alliance from widening. He temporized by playing the French and Russians off against each other: to the Tsar, he prophesied the dangers of a French expedition across the Pyrenees, which might lead to a revolution in Paris; to the French, he warned of the threat of invasion by Cossack hordes, who might revoke the French *Charte* on their return from Madrid. Metternich hoped such duplicity would incite Russian objections to French action and French opposition to Russian proposals, thereby reducing all plans for armed intervention to a complete nullity. He preferred to limit allied involvement to a pledge of moral support to the royalists at Urgel; he may have even thought that the royalists could succeed, as in Piedmont. But he could not openly ally with Britain against intervention since this might shake Alexander's confidence in the alliance.[52] The Austrian Chancellor— the exalted position to which Metternich had been elevated after Laibach— still needed to keep the Tsar in check on both the Turkish and Italian questions, including the issue of when Austrian troops should be withdrawn from Naples and Piedmont.

To hold the alliance together, Metternich joined with Nesselrode and Montmorency in mid-September to make a special appeal to Castlereagh's half-brother, Charles Stewart, now the third Marquess of Londonderry. They requested that Sir William A'Court be delayed from taking up his new post as British ambassador to Spain, and even intimated that the allies might issue a joint declaration to the Spanish government.[53] At Verona one month later—just before the arrival of Montmorency and Wellington—Metternich confidentially proposed to the foreign ministers of Russia and Prussia that the three eastern courts ought to exert leadership at the Congress by acting in concert to destroy the constitutional regime in Spain through moral action, including a possible rupture of diplomatic relations. This new overture remained concealed from both Britain and France.[54]

In the meantime, instructions to the French delegation at the Congress had been drafted by Villèle and approved by Louis XVIII after Montmorency's departure. The French plenipotentiaries were directed to avoid commitment on the Spanish Question and focus attention instead on the evacuation of Austrian troops from Naples and Piedmont.[55] Villèle listed a number of conditions that might lead to war with Spain—including violations of French territory, threats to the security of the Spanish royal family, and insults to the French minister in Madrid—but France alone was to judge the necessity of either withdrawing her ambassador or sending in troops. Montmorency was also to ascertain the extent to which the other allies would assist France if she were obliged to act in Spain, especially if she were opposed by Britain; he was even directed to negotiate a *traité eventuel* to that end.[56]

Notwithstanding these instructions, Montmorency continued to strive for French intervention across the Pyrenees with the moral support of the allies, which he saw as analogous to the Austrian incursions in Naples and Piedmont. Villèle actually viewed these situations as dissimilar, explaining to his foreign minister that Austria had resolved on intervention in Naples before the reunion at Laibach, whereas France had not yet reached any determination on Spain. Villèle even thought Russian assistance would do more harm than good, by stirring up popular passions against the presence of foreign troops on French soil.[57]

Wellington finally reached Vienna on the evening of 29 September, just as the other delegates were loading their carriages for the Italian Congress. The location of the latter had been moved by Metternich from Florence to Verona, where the police could exercise better control.[58] Because of Wellington's late arrival, the Vienna conference had resolved almost nothing, and the fate of Spain was left to be decided at Verona. The Duke hoped to delay the departure of the sovereigns and conducted a series of hasty interviews over the next two days. Just before Wellington's appearance, Lord Strangford's account of his last meeting with Ottoman officials at Constantinople had already outraged the Tsar.[59] Wellington added greatly to Alexander's indignation when he bluntly informed him that the French would not welcome Russian troops on their soil.

Wellington stayed in Vienna until he received authorization from Canning to follow the other plenipotentiaries; Montmorency already had permission from Villèle to proceed to Verona, but only if Wellington also did so. When these two plenipotentiaries finally arrived in Verona two weeks later, they found themselves in the midst of an august assembly truly worthy of the last of the great European congresses.[60]

Congress splendours

The social life of the Verona Congress far surpassed that of Aix-la-Chapelle, Troppau, Laibach or anything else Europe had witnessed since the halcyon days of the Vienna Congress itself.[61] The monarchs of Russia, Austria and Prussia and numerous other German and Italian potentates were all in attendance, along with thousands of ministers, courtiers, servants and other guests. The Tsar's chief advisors included Nesselrode, Pozzo di Borgo, Tatishchev, Lieven and Stroganov; Metternich had the services of Gentz, Lebzeltern, Esterhazy and Zichy; Wellington was accompanied by Stewart (Londonderry), Strangford and Robert Gordon; the King of Prussia arrived late but was represented by Bernstorff, Hatzfeldt (Prussian ambassador to Vienna), Wittgenstein and Hardenberg (the latter would die in Italy before the end of the Congress).[62] The French delegation included, in addition to Montmorency, the ambassadors to Austria and Russia—Caraman and La Ferronnays—as well as the curly-haired ambassador to Britain, the celebrated ultra-royalist writer François-René de Chateaubriand (1768–1848).

Like so many of his generation, Chateaubriand had initially been sympathetic to the ideals of the French Revolution, but he later fought as a counter-revolutionary and went into exile. He returned to France in 1800 and published a lively defence of Catholicism, which became a seminal work of the new Romantic movement. Chateaubriand entered government service under Napoleon, but turned against the Emperor after the murder of the Duc d'Enghien; he was later banished from Paris for his critical writings. He made a tour of Greece and the Holy Land under the patronage of the Tsar's wife, the Empress Elizabeth. In 1814, he published an influential pamphlet, *Of Buonaparte and the Bourbons*, which contributed to the return of Louis XVIII. After the Restoration, Chateaubriand became a prominent ultra-royalist journalist and politician, ambassador to Prussia and, finally, ambassador to Britain. Summoned from London to attend the Congress, he met Villèle in Paris and carried the official royal instructions to Verona. He was rightly suspected of being sent by Villèle to watch over Montmorency's shoulder.[63] Unknown to Villèle, Chateaubriand was contemptuous of the Vienna settlement and thought it essential for the stability of the monarchy to achieve greater glory, quite possibly in Spain.[64]

The Rothschilds, who had helped finance the Austrian expedition to Naples, had three family members present at the Congress and even paid all of Metternich's expenses.[65] Also present was the French financier Gabriel Julian Ouvrard, who proposed lending money to the Urgel regency.[66] Bernadotte's son Oscar, the Crown Prince of Sweden, arrived from Stockholm, to the consternation of the Legitimists. Notable women attending the Congress included the Archduchess Marie Louise (Napoleon's former Empress, now pregnant with the child of her secret husband, Count Neipperg), Countess Tolstoy, Countess Lieven, Countess Volkonsky and Lady Londonderry (the wife of Castlereagh's half-brother). Count Charles of Spain sought recognition as the envoy of the Urgel regency but was only admitted as an unofficial observer, while the representatives of the Greek provisional government were turned away at Ancona.[67]

The Roman ruins of Verona provided a magnificent backdrop to the proceedings, and the city became so crowded that special passes were required for entry. 'All the greatness of the modern world was assembled at Verona', wrote Chateaubriand, 'amidst the wrecks of ancient greatness left by the Romans'.[68] Among the highlights of the Congress was the performance of *La Santa Alleanze* ('The Holy Alliance'), a new piece for ballet, choir and orchestra expressly written for the occasion by the highly acclaimed composer Gioachino Rossini. On 22 November, Rossini conducted his new work before 23,000 guests in Verona's ancient open-air amphitheatre. There was also the usual fare of balls, operas, concerts, banquets and soirées, even including a horse race.

As always, the real business of the Congress was transacted in the private conferences of the ministers of the five powers. An official in the foreign ministry, Baron Charles Joseph Edmond Sain de Boislecomte (1796–1863), served as secretary to the French delegation at the Congress; at the request of La Ferronnays, he kept a detailed journal—*Résumé historique du Congrès de Verone*—which survives as one of the best records of the Congress deliberations.[69] 'From the first day of his arrival', noted Boislecomte, 'Prince Metternich proposed to reduce the negotiations to simple conversations between the heads of the five cabinets'.[70] Most of these discussions took place at Metternich's apartments in the Palazzo Cappellari. 'The sittings of the Congress were irregular', Chateaubriand later recalled, 'held whenever communications were made on the part of the different courts. These communications were heard; copies of them were presented to the plenipotentiaries, who, after the lapse of a day or two, replied to them by notes, which were afterwards annexed to the minutes'.[71]

In March 1815 the allied ministers had been unanimous in their determination to overthrow Napoleon. At Laibach six years later, the three eastern powers had agreed that Austria should intervene in the Italian states in the name of the European alliance—the British had then objected to the form, but not to the fact, of intervention. But now, in 1822, the allies were in a complete quandary over the fate of Spain, which lay at the western extremity of Europe, far from the eastern powers and within the orbit of France and Britain. Was any action on the part of the allies required at all? If so, should it be moral or military? If military intervention proved necessary, should it be Russian or French? If France acted, should she act unilaterally, or at the behest of and under the supervision of the allied powers? Would Britain actively oppose armed intervention in Spain? And how would Portugal and Spain's rebelling colonies in the Americas be affected by these events? These were the pressing issues to be resolved by the Congress statesmen.

In his chronicle, Boislecomte drew a most illuminating contrast: at Troppau, Metternich had opened the conference forcefully by presenting his own memorandum; at Verona, he claimed such writings and official forms were better relegated to the past. In 1820, Metternich had wanted to resolve issues; now, according to Boislecomte, he wished only to elude them.[72] Nor did Wellington, Boislecomte added, appear to welcome the Congress any more than did Metternich, or at least, the Duke hoped that no concrete outcome would ensue, which might have to be defended in Parliament.[73]

Montmorency's three questions

The chief ministers of the European pentarchy—Metternich, Wellington, Montmorency, Bernstorff and Nesselrode—held the first informal meeting of the Congress ('une réunion confidentielle') on Sunday night, 20 October.[74] Metternich again presided. At Vienna, he had already inquired as to French intentions vis-à-vis Spain, and Montmorency now responded by reading aloud two memoranda. The first of these traced relations between France and Spain since the outbreak of the Spanish Revolution; the second asserted that the turmoil in Spain posed a threat to all of Europe, but most especially to France. Montmorency claimed the new Spanish government had already committed numerous provocations. Circumstances might therefore force France to recall her ambassador from Madrid, leading the Spanish Cortes to declare war on France. 'Dangers could be foreseen', the French foreign minister cautioned his colleagues with some apprehension: 'War was possible, perhaps even likely. Such a war could only be considered as defensive.'[75]

France, he further declared, 'is called upon, as the allies recognize, to take the initiative with appropriate measures to eliminate the danger. She believes that the principles of the alliance ... authorize her to claim from the [other] great courts that moral support (*appui moral*) which guarantees to each of them the force of all, and even to invoke their material assistance (*sécours matériel*) if circumstances render it necessary'.[76]

Perhaps, mused Montmorency, the recall of the allied ambassadors from Madrid would sufficiently demonstrate their solidarity to cause the Spanish rebels to reflect more soberly on their situation—boosting 'monarchical elements', encouraging a reform of the Spanish Constitution, and even vanquishing the revolution.[77] But, in the event that France was compelled to engage in a defensive war against Spain, she needed to know whether she could count on the support of her allies. Montmorency then posed three questions:

(1) If France recalled her ambassador from Madrid, would the other allies adopt similar measures?
(2) If war broke out between France and Spain, would the other allies lend France their moral support (*appui moral*)?
(3) If France requested help in the event of war, what material assistance (*sécours matériel*) would the other allies make available to her?[78]

Once he had finished, Montmorency handed out copies of his second memorandum—containing the three questions—for the ministers to show to their sovereigns.[79] In all this, he was clearly violating Villèle's directive to limit discussion of the Spanish Question. Historians still debate whether Montmorency was deliberately attempting to commit France in a fashion that Villèle could not easily disavow, or whether he had fallen into a clever trap set by Metternich, who wanted to bring French policy under allied control. Or perhaps it was just that, as Montmorency himself claimed, it was impossible to discern what support the allies would furnish to France without first raising the question.[80] Before the meeting adjourned, the delegates considered, in addition, an urgent appeal from the royalists at Urgel for armed support.[81]

The Congress of Verona now entered its critical phase. A familiar problem arose: how could the allied ministers reconcile the conflicting demands of Russian activism and British non-interventionism? And, if intervention did occur, should a pan-European or French expeditionary force be deployed? It was less than five years since an allied force of occupation had left French soil. Could the French be entrusted with such a delicate task without reawakening those ambitions that had previously plunged Europe into 20 years of war?

If successful, would the French encourage Ferdinand VII to issue a *Charte* in Madrid, placing a French constitutional model under the gaze of the restored monarchies of Austrian-dominated Italy? Would the French also attempt to reconquer Spain's lost colonies? Or would French intervention end disastrously with the Spanish massacre of French troops, much as Wellington feared? On the other hand, were the other powers ready to watch a large Russian force tramp across Europe? The allied ministers decided that they would submit their responses to the French questions in ten days.

So long as the Tsar insisted on a pan-European expedition, Metternich's ploy of using French resistance to such a force had a reasonable chance of success. But after learning of Villèle's opposition, followed by Montmorency's three questions, the Tsar abandoned his original plan to march across France. Instead, he offered to send 150,000 troops through Germany to Piedmont, where they could wait upon events—holding the 'Jacobins' in check in France as well as providing a supply of fresh reinforcements if needed by the French in Spain.[82] This was, in fact, the same plan he had proffered the previous spring. The French remained suspicious, nonetheless: '[T]he question is reduced', remarked Boislecomte in his journal, 'to knowing at what point the Emperor Alexander will order his troops to march. The first movement they make, even in Russia, will forcibly determine war... The [French] cabinet sees that, in accepting their help, they implicitly accept their passage through France'.[83]

On 23 October, the Emperor of Austria held an audience with Chateaubriand. In seeming contradiction to his own Chancellor's policies, Francis called upon the French to quench the flames of revolution in Spain. The Prussians, however, protested that the French were far too incompetent to undertake such a mission—their 'soldiers are like children, without experience, and [their] officers cannot be counted upon'. Wellington also persisted in his view that war should be avoided, while Metternich continued to rely on British opposition to check the Tsar, shrewdly observing to the French delegates that it was only by 'continued friction that roughness could be smoothed' and that England's opposition was needed to wear down Russia's zeal.[84] With such a divergence of opinions, it is scarcely surprising that Boislecomte concluded that France would be unable to combat the Spaniards without first securing 'the consent of Europe'.[85]

Metternich summoned the allied ministers to the Palazzo Cappellari on 24 October to read parts of a dispatch he had recently received from the Austrian envoy at Madrid. It stated that a military incursion into Spain would be repugnant to the national pride and had scant chance of success. Memories of the bloodstained Peninsular War were still recent, the report continued, making the French the absolute worst choice for such an expedition.

Metternich refrained from reading other passages from the same dispatch, which indicated that a firm demonstration of moral support by the allies might nonetheless be sufficient to inspire Spanish royalists to rise up and restore the King's full powers.[86] Two days later, Wellington offered Montmorency Britain's 'good offices' to mediate between France and Spain.[87]

The Tsar's vacillation

Despite intense lobbying from both Metternich and Wellington, the Tsar remained adamant that some action had to be taken to extinguish the revolutionary embers flickering in Spain before they ignited all of Europe. The once peace-loving Tsar was now the foremost advocate of war.[88] Since the other powers had only just persuaded Alexander not to intervene in Turkey, they had to tread carefully in Spain lest the Tsar deduce the alliance itself was a sham. As we have seen, shortly after 20 October the Tsar in fact reconciled himself to French unilateral action across the Pyrenees.

On 24 October, before the ministerial gathering at Metternich's, Montmorency had gone directly to the Tsar to explain his conduct. 'I have made great sacrifices to maintain the peace', Alexander responded wistfully, yet 'I am the object of suspicion in Europe. Your position is less delicate. They believe I nourish ambitions in Turkey, but they cannot suspect you of wishing to conquer Spain. You are on excellent grounds to place yourself on the defensive.'[89] The Russian Emperor, according to Boislecomte, considered that war was 'already declared' and counselled Montmorency to follow 'moral and religious principles' in his policies.[90] Alexander further vowed not to act before receiving a formal invitation from France: 'It is for *you* to decide what to do. This is a question to be handled by you. I will not act except upon your request.'[91]

The Tsar emphasized the urgency of the situation in a conversation with the French ambassador La Ferronnays three days later: 'I will not leave Verona without finishing this business—it is too dangerous to do nothing. If the revolutionaries saw us separate without reaching a determination, they would be convinced our union is broken. The sole aim of the alliance is that for which it was formed: to combat revolution.'[92] But the Russian Emperor also reaffirmed his promise not to send unsolicited troops into France—'not a single foreign soldier would enter France except at the request of her government'.[93] On 29 October, Pozzo di Borgo was sent to concert with the French representatives; Montmorency told him that Russian troops were not immediately needed.[94] The Tsar was left with the option of assembling his forces along his own frontiers while waiting for a signal from France to commence the march across Europe. Montmorency was further reassured at another audience with the

Tsar on 7 November.⁹⁵ Russian troops, he reported to Villèle, 'would never pass through France except in accordance with our desire and after our formal requisition'.⁹⁶ Villèle nevertheless remained steadfastly opposed to Russian assistance: 'What would we do with 100,000 Russians in the present state of things?'⁹⁷

The motives that had reconciled the Tsar to French unilateral action remain somewhat obscure.⁹⁸ The Tsar told the envoy from Rome, Cardinal Spina, that he was bent on war because only an application of force could successfully overturn the revolution in Spain, as it had in Naples.⁹⁹ But the Tsar was also aware that objections to the deployment of a 'European' force—a thin guise for what would primarily be a Russian one—were being raised on all sides. If he allowed the French to form the vanguard of the allied expedition, he could still prepare an auxiliary force in the rear—much as he had done when the Austrians had entered Piedmont.

It does not appear, however, that Metternich had failed to persuade the Tsar of the grave risks connected with French intervention. If anything, the Austrian Chancellor had succeeded only too well, for it seems that the Tsar believed that a French campaign in Spain would most likely end by toppling the Bourbon monarchy in France, much as Metternich alleged. Such a fiasco would then provide a new opportunity for an allied army to march into Paris. For years, Metternich had been brainwashing Alexander with alleged proofs that the revolutionary movement was a monolithic conspiracy, masterminded by a mysterious directing committee in Paris (which Metternich half-believed himself), so the Tsar's eccentric eagerness to return to France, the *fons et origo* of revolution, should have come as no surprise.¹⁰⁰

The evidence in favour of this interpretation of the Tsar's conduct is almost overwhelming. After speaking to Tatishchev and Pozzo di Borgo, Lebzeltern reported to Metternich on 25 October that '[t]he Emperor would like to let France be ensconced in Spain, convinced that she will take false measures. Her armies defeated, still in Spain, the revolution will erupt in France, and Austria will be obliged to accept Russian intervention in the west'.¹⁰¹ Boislecomte recorded an exchange between the Tsar and Metternich, most likely based upon the same report, attributing these words to the Russian autocrat: 'I believe France is strong ... but the morale of her troops does not permit her to undertake a war of this nature, and it would be wise for her to abstain from it'.¹⁰² On 28 October, Metternich divulged to Londonderry (Stewart) that the Tsar's greatest ambition was still to take action in Paris: 'The Emperor of Russia ... would desire that France should pour her *Gangrené* troops into Spain, in order that he might bring his 200,000 or 300,000 Russians into France'.¹⁰³

Such professions were not just relayed through Metternich. On 5 November, Wellington wrote to Canning that '[t]he Tsar of Russia is more than ever anxious for war, and I know that a few days ago he had not given up the notion of an operation by the Russian army ….'[104] A week later, the Tsar advised Wellington that an allied—not a French—army should occupy Spain once military operations were over.[105] And on 27 November, just as Wellington was preparing to depart from Verona, Alexander confided to him that he did not believe that French intervention in Spain could ever succeed:

> He then talked about the French army, and repeated his conviction that it was neither in a state of discipline or of efficiency to effect any purpose; and he did not think less ill of the government! I asked him then, 'To what will all this come? Does your Majesty expect that if there should be a war the French government can stand it?' 'No; but if it should not, we have the means of setting it all to rights!'[106]

Remarkably, this candid confession was offered at precisely the same moment in which the Tsar's ministers were tirelessly urging the French to undertake the very mission he so castigated. His phrase, 'the means of setting it all to rights', was a thinly veiled reference to allied intervention in Paris. Ironically, such fantastic notions may have provided the true impetus behind the Tsar's *volte face* and sudden acquiescence to French unilateral action in Spain.

The Tsar was hardly alone in holding such opinions. Villèle himself had told Montmorency that he did not wish to see foreign troops on French soil, precisely because this would have such an injurious effect on public opinion that it might precipitate a new revolution in France instead of suppressing the one in Spain.[107] Metternich had likewise complained to the Tsar as recently as 15 November that if France ventured into Spain, her government might collapse.[108] And across the Channel, Canning was haunted by identical fears: 'a beaten or baffled French army, flowing back upon France, would infallibly set France on revolution—a new "Illiad of woes" for Europe'.[109] Perhaps these shared views were not so very far-fetched: only seven years later, the proud Bourbons would in fact be driven from the throne.

Metternich's new proposals

Still hoping to avoid military intervention without offending the Tsar, Metternich devised a new stratagem. On 28 October, at a four-hour interview with Montmorency, he raised the question of how the allies ought to communicate the results of their deliberations to the Spanish government. Metternich additionally told the French foreign minister that he wanted to know which specific events the French would consider as provocations to war, especially since France should not undertake military action before exhausting her other remedies, such as issuing a declaration or withdrawing her ambassador.[110]

According to Metternich, everything suddenly became clear to him in the course of this discussion—it was one of his more inspired moments, comparable to the evening when he had thought of inviting the King of Naples to Laibach.[111] Metternich suggested to Montmorency four ways of transmitting allied views to Spain: (1) a collective declaration to the Spanish government, announcing that the allied powers would withdraw their diplomatic representatives (their 'legations') from Madrid; (2) a 'special declaration' issued separately by each power; (3) the withdrawal of the French ambassador alone, as Russia had done at the Porte; and finally (4) letting Britain speak to the Spanish government 'in the name of Europe'. Each of these approaches would help to fortify the Spanish royalists while weakening the position of the revolutionaries.[112]

The idea of an allied declaration, accompanied by the recall of the allied diplomats from Madrid, was in reality nothing new: it had been hinted at in the approach to Londonderry in Vienna; it had been suggested again by Metternich in his secret overture to the eastern powers on 15 October; and most recently, it was among those options mentioned by Montmorency in his three questions. What was novel was the way in which Metternich, a master procrastinator, now put these proposals to work as another means of delaying action. French opposition and the passage of time could then be counted upon to bury the Tsar's projects without earning his enmity. Metternich ironically insisted that to 'save time', each power should begin drafting its instructions for Madrid at once, while still finalizing its response to Montmorency's three questions.[113] The Austrian Chancellor presented these options to Montmorency as a fait accompli agreed to by the other powers, when in fact his proposal was totally unknown to either Britain or Russia.[114]

The allied responses to Montmorency's three questions

The five cabinet ministers reassembled on the evening of Wednesday, 30 October, for another 'conférence générale' to disclose their responses to Montmorency. As expected, Nesselrode announced that Russia would support France by recalling her ambassador from Madrid and providing both moral and material assistance. This reply was everything that the French could have hoped for. Austria and Prussia promised to recall their ambassadors and to lend their moral support; they also agreed to furnish material assistance, but wrapped this last part of their offer in such conditions and qualifications as to make it a worthless pledge.[115]

Finally, it was Wellington's turn to read his response. Metternich had tried to sweeten the bitter medicine beforehand by informing the British delegates that much of the overblown rhetoric in the allied responses had been deliberately inserted to appease the Tsar, but Wellington's dismay was still palpable.[116] The Duke harangued the ministers for more than an hour, telling them that the British were generally opposed to foreign intervention; that the contemplated rupture of Franco-Spanish relations was more likely to lead to war than peace; and that conditions in Spain could only be improved by the Spaniards themselves, not by foreign arms. Wellington further apprised the ministers that the British could not hypothesize in advance how they might react to the outbreak of war without knowing the precise circumstances that precipitated the conflict. Any other approach, Wellington somewhat tactlessly asserted, 'would be not only premature and unjust, but would probably be unavailing'.[117] Wellington found the argument that Spain, in her present state of anarchy, posed any kind of threat to France or to any other allied power to be quite ludicrous. Finally, he predicted that a French expedition without British support would almost certainly fail, placing Louis XVIII in the humiliating position of having to beg for the assistance of the other powers.[118]

Wellington's response was jarring to France and Russia, although it must have come as no surprise to Metternich since Wellington had explained his views earlier in the day to Gentz, who was translating his note from English to French.[119] To make matters worse, the beginning of Wellington's response almost seemed to parody the Russian one: both began inauspiciously with the same phrase.[120]

Britain was thus once again openly at odds with the other members of the alliance. As an insular power, she did not share the same anxieties as her Continental allies; as a constitutional monarchy, she was more subject to popular pressures and less hostile to constitutional change. Perhaps of even greater importance, British strategic interests dictated against allowing either France or Russia to occupy Spain.

A short discussion followed. Montmorency disputed most of Wellington's points and even gave specific examples of the provocations— mainly hostile speeches in the Cortes and critical articles in the Spanish newspapers—that France had been forced to endure. Wellington repeated his claim that France and the other allies had little to fear from Spain. Before the meeting adjourned, Metternich outlined the agenda intended for the next day: the allies would officially submit the responses they had just read; then they would discuss both the *casus foederis* and the steps to be taken to communicate their decisions to the Spanish government.[121]

The formal congress: the *casus foederis* and communication to Spain

After the acrimony of the ministerial conference, Wellington undertook a series of private visits to explain and justify the British perspective.[122] The Tsar had been deeply offended by Wellington's choice of language, especially his characterization of allied plans as premature and unjust. Alexander was further stirred by the presence at Verona of the Italian sovereigns, who feared that if the revolution in Spain were not crushed, it would return to Italy. According to Boislecomte, Metternich had to visit the Russian Emperor several times just to cool his temper.[123]

At the Tsar's insistence, the first formal session of the Congress was convened the very next evening with all 13 of the allied plenipotentiaries present.[124] Gentz was also there, fulfilling his traditional role as Congress secretary. Metternich opened the meeting by reading a new memorandum that he and Gentz had only just composed. He then officially received the allied responses to Montmorency's questions.[125] Disagreements quickly arose over which documents to attach to the conference protocol. Wellington desired to insert his objections so that his participation could later be defended in Parliament. The other powers, however, preferred to issue no protocol at all rather than to advertise their differences.[126]

The ministers next tackled the question that Metternich had so ingeniously posed to Montmorency: how could they best convey their disapprobation to the Spanish government? In the new memorandum, Metternich contended that to assist France, the allies required a more precise definition of the *casus foederis*. Moreover, the captivity of Ferdinand, whom Metternich referred to as 'the sole authentic and legitimate organ between his country and foreign states', raised the whole issue of future relations between the allies and Spain. The options that Metternich now presented to his colleagues had been ostensibly reduced to three but were, in truth, still four: (1) either one collective or five separate allied declarations; (2) a protest by the four allied powers on behalf of France; or (3) mediation by one of the powers, presumably Britain, on behalf of the allies.[127] La Ferronnays and Pozzo di Borgo both insisted on separate declarations.[128] Nesselrode informed the ministers that his master, the Tsar, likewise desired that they conclude a treaty identifying the *casus foederis* for allied action in Spain; such a solemn act would reaffirm the vitality of the alliance.[129]

At Wellington's request, a special conference of the five cabinet ministers was summoned on the evening of 1 November. Wellington vigorously protested against all premeditated plans for foreign interference in Spain and appealed to the other ministers to respect Britain's 'peculiar situation' as a parliamentary state. Metternich proposed British mediation—doubtless as a sop to Wellington—which was summarily rejected by Montmorency. The Austrian Chancellor finally concluded that the powers should present separate notes based on similar principles and aims to the government at Madrid. With the exception of Wellington, all of the ministers readily acknowledged the wisdom of this course.[130]

Behind the scenes, the British and Russians were actively jockeying for the support of France. Wellington and Strangford encouraged the French delegation to resist the cry for war, while the Russian delegates—Nesselrode, Tatishchev and Pozzo di Borgo—positively pressed the French to act.[131] According to Boislecomte, Wellington repeatedly called on Montmorency to warn him of the problems the French would face. Strangford was even more aggressive, informing the French that Wellington's support was necessary because of his exalted status in Spain; that the whole problem could be reduced to the sheer fact that the Tsar had an army of 800,000 troops and felt compelled to use at least 100,000 of them somewhere; and finally, that England had prevented Russia from intervening in Turkey and could halt France in Spain, too.[132] The Russian delegates spoke 'with no less heat'.[133] Nesselrode, Pozzo di Borgo and Tatishchev chided the French delegates for being seduced by the British, and promised Russian support if Britain entered the contest on the side of the Spanish constitutionalists. 'I can have a signed engagement within a quarter of an hour', Nesselrode reportedly told La Ferronnays; 'rely on us to oppose England and Austria', boasted Pozzo di Borgo.[134]

All of the allied plenipotentiaries were present at the next plenary session of the Congress, held at Metternich's apartment on Saturday afternoon, 2 November. Pozzo di Borgo had persuaded Montmorency that Wellington's protest could not go unanswered because it might later be produced in the British Parliament. The primary purpose of the meeting was therefore to hear the French rejoinder to the allied responses. In a preliminary conversation before the meeting officially got underway, Wellington, Nesselrode and several other delegates listened to Montmorency read aloud his intended reply, which was harshly critical of Britain. Wellington offered to retract his prior statement, but only if the others would do the same. Nesselrode, however, argued that since these documents had been submitted to the Congress, they should not be withdrawn. One historian has suggested that the Russians feared this was simply another of Metternich's ruses to further delay the proceedings. 'Energetic discussions filled all corners of the room', recorded Boislecomte, 'demonstrating that spirits were still too divided and that nothing was ready for general discussion'. Their quarrelling became so animated that the delegates decided to cancel the meeting rather than to call the formal session to order. Instead, the four Continental powers resolved to pursue their negotiations privately and to postpone the next Congress session until greater progress was made.[135]

Interim negotiations by the Continental powers

Matters were clearly not going well for the British at Verona. Even at Troppau and Laibach, Londonderry observed, Britain had acted in partnership with France, but now she stood in isolation.[136] The four Continental powers set to work defining those conditions that would lead to war and drafting their declarations for Madrid.[137] By 4 November, they decided to send instructions to their own diplomatic envoys in Madrid rather than issue declarations directly to the Spanish government.[138] Two days later, the Russians peremptorily announced to the other powers that they would withdraw their ambassador from Madrid.[139]

For the British, it was almost like a return to those dark days when they had been ignored in negotiations with Napoleon, although occasional attempts were made to consult with them and gauge their reactions. Wellington notified the Continental powers that, despite his many objections, he still wished to act separately from them 'as little as possible'.[140] Three Russian delegates—Nesselrode, Tatishchev and Lieven—called upon Londonderry on 7 November to request that A'Court be instructed not to openly contradict the other members of the diplomatic corps in Madrid.[141]

Dissension within the French delegation led the four French plenipotentiaries to hold a private conclave on the very next day. La Ferronnays demanded the meeting so that they might speak at Verona with a more consistent voice. Should they actively encourage the outbreak of a war with Spain? In preparation for their discussion, La Ferronnays ordered Boislecomte to draw up a balance sheet of arguments for and against war.[142] When the votes were finally cast, La Ferronnays and Chateaubriand were in favour of war with Spain, but Caraman (the French ambassador to Vienna and an admirer of Metternich) was opposed. So, surprisingly, was the head of the delegation, Montmorency. Boislecomte surmises the French foreign minister did not wish to openly flout his instructions from Villèle. The outcome of the consultation was therefore indecisive, and Montmorency omitted all mention of this 'war council' in his correspondence with Paris.[143]

On the same day, Montmorency also had interviews with both the Tsar and Metternich. The Russian Emperor approved of what he saw of the proposed French instructions, but he warned Montmorency that the Spanish Revolution was becoming ever more threatening and could only be reversed by force of arms. The Tsar thus exhorted the French to take immediate action.[144] With Metternich, Montmorency discussed possible *casus foederis*, which would trigger action by the alliance. The Austrian Chancellor felt the drafts of the diplomatic instructions were now advanced enough for the delegates to begin focusing their energies on this other task, and he explained to Montmorency his own views on which affronts would clearly constitute *casus foederis*. Such provocations included a declaration of war on France or any attempt to dethrone or execute Ferdinand. Other actions that might endanger Franco-Spanish relations, however, were less obvious and could not be so easily foreseen. These latter, Metternich argued, should be referred to the ambassadorial conference in Paris. Although this step would hand more power over to Pozzo di Borgo than Metternich would have liked, it would at least furnish the allies with some mechanism for exercising supervision over French actions in Spain.[145]

While struggling with these issues, the delegates continued to receive news from Spain where, from their perspective, matters seemed to be going from bad to worse. The Austrian and French envoys in Madrid both sent reports to Verona describing the proliferation of secret societies, especially the *comuneros*.[146] The Verona delegates further used this interval to convene a special session on 9 November on the 'Eastern Question' and to conduct talks on Italian affairs.[147]

Genesis of the *procès-verbal* of 19 November 1822

For nearly a fortnight, the Continental powers continued to revise and exchange drafts of their instructions for Madrid. Their chief ministers assembled on 10 November to review the Russian and Prussian drafts, which Montmorency thought too harsh. Montmorency afterwards submitted his own proposed instructions to Metternich, who made several alterations. The text of the Austrian instructions was shared with the French delegates on 12 November. Montmorency next gave a copy of his proposed instructions to Wellington, who harboured such grave doubts that he immediately wrote to the British ambassador in Paris, instructing him to alert Villèle that his orders were not being obeyed at the Congress.[148]

Montmorency sent his proposed treaty for the *casus foederis* to Metternich two days later, on 14 November; the two statesmen met the next day to craft a compromise bridging their minor differences.[149] In consequence, the chief ministers of the four courts—Montmorency, Metternich, Nesselrode and Bernstorff—held another joint meeting on Sunday evening, 17 November. Here, Montmorency unveiled the three situations that France would deem as *casus foederis*, precipitating immediate war and entitling France to the assistance of her allies: (1) any Spanish attack on France; (2) any attempt by Spain to provoke revolution in France; and (3) any attack on the Spanish royal family or attempt to overthrow the reigning dynasty. These cases deviated only slightly from those specified in Villèle's instructions of 15 October and Metternich's note of 8 November. Montmorency then denominated three additional situations as 'casus belli'. These lesser offences would result in the immediate rupture of French diplomatic relations with Spain and probable war, but they would not necessarily entitle France to the assistance of her allies: (1) any menace or threat to the Spanish royal family; (2) any insults to France or to the French ambassador; and (3) any threats to French subjects in Spain.

Nesselrode immediately proposed 'reciprocity' among the allies with respect to Montmorency's three *casus foederis*, so that any one of them could request a collective consultation. This would give Russia the power to initiate action, even though she was not directly threatened by events in Spain. La Ferronnays objected, since Russia was not placed in any evident danger, but Montmorency accepted this new gloss without demur.[150]

Over the next three days the ministers shaped Montmorency's conditions into the form of a conference protocol, stipulating those specific events that would trigger an immediate conflict. At Metternich's suggestion, the potential instances of *casus belli* were left unspecified and the four powers agreed in such instances merely to refer the matter to the ambassadorial conference in Paris (just as Metternich had first proposed to Montmorency on 8 November). The instructions to be sent to the ambassadors in Madrid were drafted in such provocative tones as to make a breach with the Spanish constitutionalists almost inevitable. After condemning the revolution for plunging Spain into chaos and threatening Europe, each asked the Spanish government to restore Ferdinand's absolute power and threatened to break off diplomatic relations if it failed to do so.[151]

During these same weeks Wellington had continued to hold separate discussions with Montmorency, Metternich and the Tsar; he still clung to the hope that war could be averted. On 19 November, the allied ministers called on Wellington and presented him with their *procès-verbal*, which he instantly and vehemently rejected. It was the same day of the year as the *Protocol préliminaire* at Troppau and the earlier Girondin decree. On 20 November, Metternich, Montmorency, Nesselrode, Bernstorff and Wellington assembled again for a more formal session of the Congress.[152] Wellington realized that he had been used by Metternich as a means of persuading the Tsar to abandon his proposal for a European army. Once the Tsar had renounced this idea, Metternich had accepted the rest of Russian policy *in toto*, including identification of the *casus foederis*, the rupture of diplomatic relations with Spain and even the promise of conditional support for France. Indeed, having removed Capodistrias, who left the Tsar's service in mid-August, Metternich found himself deferring to Russian interests to maintain his influence over the Tsar.[153]

Wellington was outraged at both the language of the proposed conference 'protocol'—the new appellation for the same document he had been shown the evening before—and the instructions for the diplomatic corps in Madrid, which he thought more likely to provoke war than to prevent it, and which seemed to be deliberately calculated to endanger the very safety of the Spanish royal family. The only concession that Wellington could extract from the other powers, however, was an agreement that the proposed protocol should be redesignated as a simple *procès-verbal*—a totally meaningless gesture since it was, by any name, in reality a treaty between the Continental powers. Since it was equally evident that Wellington could not be swayed, the other ministers prepared to send their parallel instructions to Madrid without the adhesion of Britain.[154]

Metternich's apparent victory

At the final session of the Congress on the Spanish Question, held the very next day, Wellington submitted a scathing remonstrance, denouncing the decisions of the Continental powers.[155] A further complication loomed on the horizon: Montmorency had emphasized all along that he was drafting 'conditional' instructions for Madrid on his own authority and that these would ultimately have to be approved by his government in Paris. It was uncertain whether Villèle, known to oppose the war, would actually agree. On the morning of 22 November, Montmorency left Verona for Paris, carrying his proposed instructions. The instructions of the three eastern powers were also forwarded to Paris, in an effort to have them issued simultaneously with France in a flawless display of Continental solidarity. Regardless of the action taken by Villèle, however, the instructions of the eastern powers were to be sent on to Madrid.

Metternich gloated over another apparent victory. He wrote to the Austrian ambassador in Paris that his ultimate objective had always been to obtain allied support for the royalists at Urgel while breaking off diplomatic relations with the revolutionaries in Madrid; based on the agreements reached at Verona, he confidently believed that all support from France, material as well as moral, would now be channelled through the Spanish royalists and be subject to allied supervision.[156]

Other issues at Verona

Although the Spanish Revolution provided the central theme of the Congress, it was not its sole topic: the allied powers continued to act as the arbiters of Europe. The Eastern Question, for instance, remained of vital concern, and the Russians raised the problem of Turkish harassment of their commercial shipping from the Black Sea into the Mediterranean. At Vienna, there was even an explosive session in which the Russians accused Lord Strangford of betraying their interests. At Verona, the allies agreed to support Russian demands and to return the problem to British mediation at Constantinople. Even Strangford seems to have regained the Tsar's favour.[157]

With respect to Italian affairs, Metternich hoped to establish a central investigation committee similar to the one in Mainz for the German states. This might have been just the first step towards the formation of an Italian League (*Lega Italica*), a confederation of Italian states under Austrian leadership like the German Confederation, but Metternich's plan was strangled in its infancy by the joint opposition of France, the Papacy and the other secondary Italian states, who also turned the Tsar against it. The French were further able to preserve Charles Albert's hereditary rights to the throne of Piedmont, to secure a phased withdrawal of Austrian troops from Piedmont and to obtain a reduction of the Austrian occupation force in Naples. Some of the attention of the Congress was also devoted to reviewing plans that the secondary Italian states submitted to the allies for protecting themselves from revolutionary unrest.[158]

With British participation at the Congress, the issue of the slave trade was revived. Wellington delivered a blistering memorandum on 24 November, attacking the inhumanity of the trade and demanding the elusive right of visitation, but he was rebuffed by a French reply, authored by Chateaubriand. The Congress thus took no concrete steps towards eliminating the trade, still seen primarily as an English concern, beyond issuing a platitudinous declaration condemning its continuation.[159]

Finally, with respect to the rebellious Spanish colonies, Wellington announced that in order to preserve her commerce, suppress piracy and protect her subjects, Britain was giving *de facto* recognition to those Latin American states that had clearly established independent governments. The other powers protested against this step as undermining the unity of the alliance and infringing the legitimate rights of Ferdinand VII, but they were otherwise powerless to stop it. Chateaubriand was determined to prevent Britain and the United States from obtaining exclusive commercial relations with Latin America to the detriment of France, and he was already thinking that French intervention in Spain might be followed by a new congress in which the problems of Spain and her colonies could be settled together. In fact, he even contemplated the creation of a new generation of independent Bourbon monarchies in the Americas.[160]

Most of the attending sovereigns did not leave Verona till mid-December, when they proceeded to Venice for a week of further entertainment before returning to their own capitals. On 14 December, the three eastern courts issued the 'Verona Circular'. Drafted by Gentz, this public document praised allied solidarity and exorcised the revolutionaries—'those who conspire against the legal authority [of the monarchs] and the simplicity [of the people] to plunge both into a common abyss of destruction'.[161] The circular was a patent attempt to dispel rumours and to present a façade of allied unity to conceal the reality of schism.

Meanwhile, Wellington had already left Verona for Paris on 29 November. Relying on Villèle's earlier views, he still hoped that war in Spain might be averted; but he was less sanguine than before, knowing that the provocative instructions of the eastern courts would be sent to Madrid in any event. The ambassadorial conference in Paris, headed by Pozzo di Borgo, reviewed the notes from Verona and gave the French government three days to react before sending the incendiary instructions to Madrid.

The French expedition to Spain

Metternich's triumph at Verona, if it ever existed, was short-lived. Villèle remained as determined as ever to preserve French independence of action. Moreover, just after Montmorency's arrival in Paris, the Urgel regency was overthrown by the Spanish constitutional army.[162] General Mina captured the town and set it ablaze. Villèle used the rout of the regency and the continuing opposition of Britain to postpone sending new instructions to the French chargé d'affaires in Madrid, the Comte de La Garde. Although he requested that the other allies do the same, the three eastern powers refused to countenance any further delay.

In London, Canning pondered whether to offer British mediation between France and Spain. On the one hand, he needed to protect British commerce with Latin America and therefore had to prevent Spain from reasserting her stifling grip over colonial trade; on the other, he wanted the Spanish constitutionalists to reform their constitution in order to forestall a French invasion. By December, Canning actually decided to defer recognition of the independence of the Latin American states in order to play a more decisive role by proffering British mediation to maintain the peace. Hoping that Villèle would succeed in delaying the transmission of the hostile allied instructions, Canning authorized Wellington, who arrived in Paris on 9 December, to tender Britain's 'good offices' between Spain and France. Wellington made this offer with some reluctance and it was, as he expected, curtly refused.[163]

Chateaubriand returned to Paris on 20 December. At a tumultuous meeting of the council of ministers held in the presence of the King on Christmas Day, Villèle refused to break off French diplomatic relations with Spain.

Both Villèle and Montmorency brought letters of resignation in their back pockets. While all of the ministers concurred with Montmorency, Louis XVIII ultimately sided with his more cautious chief minister. The King's decision led to Montmorency's prompt resignation. Villèle repudiated Montmorency's policy of cooperation with the eastern powers in his instructions to La Garde. He justified France's defensive measures, urged a reform of the Spanish constitution and even threatened that France might at some future date withdraw her legation. The diplomatic envoys of Russia, Austria and Prussia thus withdrew from Madrid, while both the French and British ambassadors remained in place.[164]

Subsequent pressures from the French ultra-royalists forced Villèle to seize the initiative in Spain. Chateaubriand was appointed as France's new foreign minister. In his view, glory—not liberty—was the French popular ideal.[165] We have seen that Chateaubriand bitterly resented the Vienna settlement and feared for the survival of the Bourbon monarchy if some great foreign-policy or military success were not accomplished. He imagined that Spain offered the perfect opportunity for both. Even from Verona, Chateaubriand had sent Villèle unmistakable signs of his eagerness for war:

> It is for you, my dear friend, to see whether you ought not to seize an occasion that may never occur again to return France to the rank of the military powers, to hoist again the white cockade in a short war, almost without danger, to which the opinion of the royalists and of the army at this moment forcibly propels you. There is no question about the occupation of the Peninsula; it is confined to a rapid movement, which should restore power to real Spaniards, and spare you future perplexities ... To destroy a hearth (*foyer*) of Jacobinism, to replace a Bourbon on the throne by the arms of a Bourbon, are results that outweigh considerations of a secondary nature.[166]

Although La Garde remained in Madrid, he had been instructed to advise the Spanish government to reform the Constitution of 1812. The Spanish *exaltados* responded on 10 January, rejecting this advice and gratuitously insulting the French. On the 18th, La Garde was therefore ordered to quit his post. One week later, Louis XVIII formally requested the French Chamber of Deputies to authorize French military intervention in Spain: 'A hundred thousand Frenchmen, commanded by a Prince of my family ... are ready to march ... to conserve the throne of Spain to a descendant of Henri IV, to preserve that fine kingdom from ruin, and to reconcile her with Europe ... Let Ferdinand be free to give to his people the institutions they cannot hold but from him.'[167] So, it seemed that there would be war between France and Spain after all.

A bitter debate nonetheless ensued in the French Chambers for several weeks. From across the English Channel, Canning sent a stream of angry protests, objecting both to foreign interference in the internal affairs of a sovereign country and to the existence of a *pacte de famille*—a dynastic alliance between the Bourbon powers. Not only Canning, but also the British public at large took great umbrage at Louis XVIII's astonishing declaration to the French Chambers—especially his pronouncement that new institutions could only be granted by the monarch (held 'but from him'). This new attempt to spread Legitimist doctrine across the Pyrenees, Canning told the French, seemed to 'strike at the roots of the British Constitution'. In the House of Commons, the British Foreign Secretary openly denounced the French King's speech. He made vague references that 'Britain was fully prepared to meet the new emergency' and even hinted that French action might force the British to intervene, presumably in defence of Spanish sovereignty. Such conduct by Castlereagh would have been unimaginable. But even from Canning, this public bluster was pure bluff. Canning was simply trying to deter French action; privately, he informed the cabinet that the country was in no condition to wage war and that British naval superiority could not be effectively deployed in Spain.[168] Canning even launched two new diplomatic initiatives in his frantic efforts to preserve the peace: Fitzroy-Somerset was sent to Madrid to persuade the Spanish government to make timely concessions to avoid invasion and Canning suggested to Metternich and Bernstorff that they might use the ambassadorial conference in Paris to discourage French actions. Both these endeavours brought equally dismal results.[169]

Ironically, the parliamentary debates of March 1823 were almost as savage in their criticism of British conduct at the Congress of Verona as they were of the Continental allies: why had Wellington not taken a more positive stand in defence of the Spanish constitutionalists against the 'League of Kings'? Was Canning's 'come what may' instruction to Wellington an effective protest, or had it simply handed a *carte blanche* to the reactionary allied sovereigns? If Canning was willing to bluff in order to deter France in 1823, why had he not threatened war at the Congress of Verona, when such a step might have been truly effective?

In reality, Canning was not ready to defend ideologies of any variety, whether liberal constitutionalist or counter-revolutionary. His primary concerns remained commercial and strategic. On 31 March 1823, he informed the French government that Britain would not act against a French expedition in Spain unless one of three contingencies occurred: Portugal was attacked, the French attempted to help Spain regain control of her American colonies, or the French established more than a temporary occupation of Spain. These conditions alone could trigger conflict between Britain and France;

otherwise, Canning judged the interests at stake for Britain to be insufficient to justify a war. In marked contrast to Castlereagh, Canning published this statement in the London press only five days later.[170] Apart from this, Canning was following the policy previously laid down by his predecessor—there was no grand departure. And indeed, seeking to emphasize this continuity, Canning actually now published Castlereagh's State Paper of 5 May 1820, hitherto unknown to the public. On 30 April 1823, Canning won a great victory when the Commons approved, by a majority of 372 to 20, his policy of neutrality. But if there was no departure from Castlereagh in general strategy, the differences in tone and procedure were in themselves significant.[171]

Six weeks earlier, on 15 March, the Duc d'Angoulême—the son of the Comte d'Artois and husband to the only surviving child of Louis XVI and Marie Antoinette—had assumed command of a French army of 100,000 men stationed along the Pyrenees. He was assisted by the more experienced General Guillemot, a veteran of the Napoleonic Wars, as well as by several other former Napoleonic marshals. The French campaign in Spain was launched a few weeks later. The 'Hundred Thousand Sons of Saint Louis', led by a combination of royalists and officers who had served in Napoleon's campaigns, crossed the Bidassoa River into Spain on 7 April. Despite Wellington's dour prognostications, the French proved spectacularly successful. Welcomed by many Basques and Catalans, the French were surrounded by sympathizers and advanced rapidly to Madrid, where the Count d'Abisbal agreed to surrender the city. Their initial advance has been described as more of a promenade than a military contest. The invaders were helped by the fact that rather than forcibly requisitioning supplies from the countryside, everything was promptly paid for by the French financier Ouvrard. The constitutionalists retreated southward, dragging Ferdinand with them first to Seville and then to the city of Cadiz in Andalusia. Spanish liberals across the country sought refuge in other towns and fortified cities, including Corunna, Pamplona, San Sebastian, Alicante, Granada and Barcelona. Angoulême proclaimed a regency in Ferdinand's name from the capital on 25 May. The main body of French troops marched south to Cadiz, where the Cortes was sitting and Ferdinand was held captive. At the end of August, they seized the fortress of Trocadero after a bayonet charge from the seaward side; next, the French army turned the guns of Trocadero onto the city of Cadiz, which surrendered at the end of September. The Cortes extracted an oath of loyalty from the King, released Ferdinand to the French and promptly dissolved itself. Angoulême returned to France in triumph in November, leaving behind a force of 45,000 French troops, which were gradually withdrawn over the next four years. Chateaubriand and the ultra-royalists rejoiced at the thought that they had succeeded where the great Napoleon had failed.[172]

By such means, the absolute powers of Ferdinand VII were fully restored. Like his uncle the King of Naples, Ferdinand immediately revoked the Constitution of 1812 and repealed all the acts of the *Trienio Liberal*. When it came time to reforming the kingdom, however, Angoulême found all his ideas stubbornly rejected. Ferdinand refused to listen to either Angoulême's appeals for clemency or his recommendations for a moderate constitution. Instead, the Spanish monarch publicly promised his subjects 'holocausts of piety'. This new policy of repression was orchestrated by the stern Minister of Justice, Tadeo Francisco de Calomarde. The unfortunate Colonel Riego was captured, hanged and quartered; his body parts were gruesomely displayed in different parts of Spain as a solemn warning to would-be revolutionaries. Riego's wife and children fled to England, where sympathizers raised a subscription on their behalf. The Duc d'Angoulême personally refused all credit for this policy of bloody repression. Pozzo di Borgo visited Madrid but was equally unsuccessful in curbing Ferdinand's appetite for vengeance and beat a hasty retreat to Paris. The ambassadorial conferences in Paris and Madrid each sent a stream of good advice, most of which was ignored.[173]

In the House of Commons, Canning had boldly declared his hope that the constitutionalists in Spain and not the French invaders would emerge as the victors of the struggle. When the French nonetheless prevailed, Canning took further steps to ensure the independence of Spain's former colonies in the Americas. With France in occupation of Spain, would she also help Ferdinand subdue the colonists? In August 1823, Canning told the American ambassador that he expected that as soon as the war in Spain was over, 'a proposal will be made for a Congress, or some less formal concert and consultation, specially upon the affairs of Spanish America'.[174] Chateaubriand and Villèle did indeed intend to propose a congress to settle the problem of the Spanish colonies, and they even had embryonic plans to send Spanish Bourbon princes to Mexico and Peru with French funds and naval support. Canning acted to pre-empt these schemes in early October by entering into a series of discussions with the French ambassador in London, Prince Jules de Polignac, a staunch ultra-royalist. Canning told Polignac that Britain would not permit foreign interference of any kind between Spain and her colonies, and that the British would also refuse to enter into any 'joint deliberation' on the Spanish colonies—whether congress or conference—in which they enjoyed no more than an 'equal footing' with the other, less interested European powers. Afterwards, Canning drew up a record of their discussion, persuaded Polignac to sign it and circulated the resulting memorandum among the chanceleries of Europe. In the United States, President James Monroe had in the meantime issued his 'Monroe Doctrine', a solemn warning to France and

Spain against any attempt to re-capture Spain's former colonies once the latter had achieved *de facto* independence. Thus, although royal power was restored on the Iberian Peninsula, it was never extended again over the liberated colonies across the Atlantic.[175]

In December 1823, the King of Spain nonetheless issued his own invitations to a 'conference' in Paris to adjudicate 'differences' between Spain and her colonies. But after the 'Polignac Memorandum' and the 'Monroe Doctrine', Ferdinand's invitation had no appeal. Chateaubriand remained hopeful that Britain might accept the Spanish proposal, but Canning rejected it outright in the reply he sent on 30 January 1824. To clinch the argument, Canning laid the Polignac Memorandum and his own reply to Ferdinand's invitation before Parliament. Though the Paris ambassadorial conference could no longer obstruct the independence of the Americas, it met for periodic sessions in 1824 and 1825, as much to monitor progress within Spain as to give guidance on relations with her former colonies and remaining colony of Cuba.[176] Most of this advice, as we have seen, was scorned by Ferdinand. In December 1824, Canning finally granted full recognition to three of the new South American states. Two years later, in December 1826, he would also send British troops to Portugal to prevent incursions by opponents of the Portuguese constitutional government armed by Spain. In his most memorable speech, announcing to the members of the House of Commons the embarkation of British troops, Canning boasted that he had 'called the New World into existence, to redress the balance of the Old'.[177]

* * *

The unilateral action of France in restoring Ferdinand VII of Spain has long been regarded as delivering the deathblow to the Congress System. Austria had previously intervened in Italy, but she had acted in the name of the alliance; the Congress of Vienna, moreover, had firmly placed the Italian states under Austrian tutelage. Villèle and Chateaubriand, on the other hand, had deliberately rejected Montmorency's policy of collaboration and spurned the chance for France to act as the agent of the allies. France refused to act with the eastern powers even in so mundane a matter as the recall of her ambassador, and Britain had equally refused to acknowledge the right of either France or of the alliance as a whole to intervene on the Iberian Peninsula. Britain and the United States had then acted in cooperation to safeguard the independence of Spain's former colonies from French or Russian interference. Britain also opposed the handling of this issue by the European alliance, except on her own terms, much as she had done ever since it was first raised at the Congress of Aix-la-Chapelle.

The end of the Congress System

The Congress at Verona did, in fact, turn out to be the last of the great reunions arising directly out of the treaties of November 1815. It accentuated the divisions of the allies rather than resolving them.[178] As the memory of the great Revolution of 1789 and the conquests of Napoleon receded, the willingness of European leaders to sacrifice national interests for the general cause gradually eroded. Britain was now openly opposed to allied counter-revolutionary intervention, while France was again flexing its muscles with little apparent restraint.

'The issue of Verona', Canning wrote jubilantly in January 1823, 'has split the one and indivisible alliance into three parts as distinct as the Constitutions of England, France and Muscovy ... and so things are getting back to a wholesome state for us all. Every nation for itself, and God for us all. Only bid your Emperor be quiet, for the time for Areopagus, and the like of that, is gone by'.[179] The French envoy to Naples echoed these views:

> The fear of revolutions is the common sentiment which, for the past eight years, has held the great powers united and Europe in peace. A peril, once it is past, is quickly forgotten, and this fear will be greatly enfeebled once the Peninsula will have been restored and pacified. Then the politics of the interests, of the ambitions of one power versus the other, the old politics, if you wish, will resume all its rights.

Baron de Vitrolles, the French ultra-royalist, predicted that Verona would be 'the last of the European congresses: the sovereigns are estranged—divided, dissatisfied—looking after ... their personal interests and individual defense'.[180] Even Metternich thought it unlikely that another congress would be summoned for some time and admonished Gentz that greater care should be taken in future to reach a preliminary consensus through conferences '[b]efore talking about congresses'.[181] Of course, contemporaries did not know for certain that the end of the Congress System had already been reached.[182] The grandiose system expired, not with a bang, but a whimper.

In less than a year after the French excursion into Spain, Louis XVIII was dead. The allied leaders had long anticipated his demise with trepidation, but in the actual event no secret instructions proved necessary. Louis' younger brother, the ultra-royalist Comte d'Artois, ascended the throne as Charles X without incident.

Further to the east, the Tsar was growing increasingly restive in the last years of his reign. He became ever more reliant on Metternich for advice on foreign affairs and on the stern Arakcheev for management of the

Russian interior, especially the new and oppressive system of military colonies, in which regiments were settled alongside peasant villages so that soldiers could help raise crops—an experiment in human engineering perhaps best described as a blend of the militarism of the Tsar's youth at Gatchina with the utopian vision of the socialist Robert Owen.[183]

During the late 1820s, the powers fell into the practice of using ambassadorial conferences in place of full-dress congresses attended by sovereigns and their foreign ministers. Nonetheless, the pentarchy of great powers continued to cooperate. After the French expedition to Spain, the Greek Christians in revolt in the Ottoman dominions again provided the main focus of their attention. Canning, like Castlereagh, at first tried to remain aloof from the dispute. He recognized the Greek rebels as belligerents in March 1823, but only to protect British shipping in the Mediterranean.[184] By September of the same year, Strangford had obtained the agreement of the Sultan to all of the points desired by the Russians, even including assurances for an improved governance of Greece. But before the year's end, the famous poet Lord Byron had moved from Venice to Greece and raised a substantial loan in London for the Greek rebels. His death in Missolonghi in April 1824 set in motion a tidal wave of popular Philhellenic sentiment in Britain and across the continent.[185]

The Tsar's Congress proposal

Just as the autumn months sometimes give way to the return of warmer weather during an 'Indian Summer', so it was with the Congress System. The vision of the Congress System had still not quite vanished. We have seen how Ferdinand of Spain, with the help of Chateaubriand and Villèle, attempted to revive it in December 1823. The same was true in the east. Disappointed by the lack of progress in Greece, the Tsar issued a circular in January 1824, inviting the allies to convene a new congress on the 'Eastern Question'. Alexander further proposed the formation of three new principalities in Greece, over which he would act as protector, as he did for the Danubian Principalities. Russia would thus act with the sanction of the alliance, as Austria had in Naples and France had in Spain.

Metternich and Canning both opposed the Tsar's new plans. Metternich, however, was willing to countenance another congress as a means of delay; Canning remained opposed to it in principle. After Strangford's successful negotiations with the Porte, the Tsar was urged to reopen diplomatic relations, but he deliberately delayed sending an ambassador back to Constantinople. Canning reluctantly agreed to let Britain participate in a conference and even conceded that the negotiations should take place in

St Petersburg. But when the Tsar's circular was leaked to the Paris press, it made him seem so transparently ambitious, at least in the eyes of the British public, that it became quite impossible—or so Canning claimed—for Britain to cooperate.[186] The Greeks themselves complained of the Tsar's plans, which would have left them nominally under the jurisdiction of the Ottoman Empire. Canning offered Britain's 'good offices' as an impartial mediator between the Greeks and Turks, but bluntly retracted his approval of Alexander's congress proposal. The British government could not, Canning told the Austrian ambassador, participate in the charade of a congress merely so that the Tsar could save face.[187] Alexander was so infuriated that his ambassador in London, Count Lieven, did not dare to raise the Greek Question with Canning for the next nine months.[188] The British Foreign Secretary thus seemed to be striking out on his own course in the east as in the west: recognizing the Greeks as belligerents, corresponding with the Greek rebel government and rejecting the Tsar's congress proposal.

An ambassadorial conference at St Petersburg actually held two sessions in June and July of 1824, in which the British ambassador, Sir Charles Bagot, mistakenly participated.[189] Meanwhile, the Turkish campaign against the rebels was faltering. In desperation, the Sultan invited Mehemet Ali, the Pasha of Egypt, to send his son Ibrahim to reconquer Greece. Ibrahim sailed with the Egyptian navy and landed a well-trained force on the Peloponnese in February 1825. The same month, the allied conferences at St Petersburg resumed without the participation of Britain. Metternich, copying the stratagem he and Castlereagh had employed at Vienna towards Poland, declared Austria to be in favour of a genuinely independent Greece. In April 1825, the four powers signed a protocol calling for an end to the fighting, but they could agree to little else and by May their talks were suspended. The Tsar grew increasingly resentful at what he rightfully regarded as a lack of reciprocity from the other allied courts. In August 1825, a new Russian circular complained that the allied powers had been using the conferences solely as a means of paralyzing Russia.[190] The Russians also discovered to their dismay that Ibrahim had reached an agreement with the Sultan to enslave or murder all of the Greek Christians in order to depopulate the Peloponnese, which he planned to repopulate with Muslims and place under his own sceptre. At the end of the same eventful month, Countess Lieven was given confidential instructions in St Petersburg to advise Canning that the Tsar was ready to enter into bilateral negotiations with Britain on Greece. In September, a delegation from the Greek insurgents arrived in London, seeking British mediation, while in October, the Lievens met privately with Canning, informing him of the Tsar's secret offer to enter into negotiations and of Ibrahim's plans to rid the Peloponnese of its Christian population.[191]

By this time, the Russian Emperor had finally resolved on the war he had so long avoided. In mid-September, he left St Petersburg to meet with army leaders in the Crimea to plan his spring campaign. But in December 1825, while visiting Taganrog on the Sea of Azov, Tsar Alexander suddenly died under mysterious circumstances (inspiring a popular legend that he had actually retreated to a monastery). Two years earlier, his brother Constantine had renounced his rights to the throne in order to marry a woman of lower social status, although this was not publicly known. While the Tsar had clamped down on reform, liberal military officers, especially those who had served in France, still longed for change in Russia. Arakcheev actually had evidence of a planned coup against Alexander, but he was distracted and distraught by the murder of his own mistress by members of her household staff. Constantine's exclusion from the throne then precipitated the 'Decembrist' revolt by the liberal regiments of the imperial guard. A number of the Decembrist leaders had actually been among those former officers of the Semenovsky Regiment dispersed to other regiments. The new revolt was quickly quelled. Constantine's younger brother Nicholas thus came to the throne after suppressing unrest among his own officers, a bloody prelude to a generally repressive reign.

Gradually, the founders of the Congress System were thus passing from the scene. At the beginning of 1822, Castlereagh, Alexander, Metternich, Louis XVIII and Hardenberg were all still alive and active—three years later, all save Metternich were gone. Four events in particular were major setbacks to the Congress System: (1) the death of Castlereagh and advent of Canning; (2) the unilateral French expedition to Spain; (3) the rejection of both Franco-Spanish initiatives for a congress on Latin America and of the Tsar's proposal for a congress on Greece; and (4) the death of the Tsar. By the end of 1825, the Congress System was truly dead.

When Nicholas acceded to the throne, Canning sent Wellington on a mission to St Petersburg, not only to congratulate the new Tsar, but more importantly to negotiate an accord on the Greek Question. Canning was motivated by the rising tide of Philhellenic sentiment in Britain, the opportunity to separate Russia from Austria and the shocking news of Ibrahim Pasha's plan to depopulate the Peloponnese. Canning at last became willing to placate the rising tide of British Philhellenism by taking more active steps on behalf of the Greek rebels. Russia and Britain agreed to cooperate on behalf of Greek independence, and France joined their partnership in the Treaty of London (July 1827). The two westernmost constitutional states were thus able to find common ground with autocratic Russia, while the two German powers—Austria and Prussia—stood detached from these events. Sultan Mahmud, who had finally taken steps against the Janissaries in 1826, refused to meet allied demands, and the combined British, French and Russian fleets destroyed the

Turkish-Egyptian fleet at the Battle of Navarino (October 1827). Russia then declared war on the Ottoman Empire, while the three parties to the Treaty of London (Britain, Russia and France) withdrew their ambassadors from Constantinople. After these catastrophic events, the Porte accepted allied peace terms at the London Conference, and the Russians consented to the creation of an independent Greek state. In 1831, the first President of independent Greece—none other than Alexander's former minister, Capodistrias—was assassinated. In consequence, the ambassadorial conference in London, presided over by Lord Palmerston, the new British Foreign Secretary (a former Canningite Tory turned Whig) went into action. It magically transformed Greece into a monarchy and offered her throne to a Bavarian prince. What is most significant is that all of these changes took place under the aegis of ambassadorial conferences rather than a full-fledged congress.[192]

Revolution in France

In July 1830, almost exactly 15 years after the Battle of Waterloo, the long awaited revolution in France finally occurred. Charles X—the former Comte d'Artois—had shown far less caution than his elder brother, Louis XVIII, by passing a series of unpopular laws aimed at providing compensation for properties lost during the Revolution of 1789. To curb the popular outrage, Charles and his chief minister, Prince Jules de Polignac, then dismissed the French Chambers, dissolved the National Guard of Paris and issued a series of royal ordinances bridling the press. Metternich applauded these measures, which he compared favourably to the Carlsbad Decrees, and further rejoiced that the French King had finally thrown down the gauntlet against liberalism. The outcome, however, remained in doubt. Citizens took to the streets, the army deserted the King and the French Chambers, refusing to disband, declared for Charles' younger cousin, Louis Philippe, the Duc d'Orléans—a situation that Metternich now compared to the Glorious Revolution in England in 1688. To avoid bloodshed, Charles abdicated and went into exile, while his cousin Louis Philippe took the throne. Rather than 'King of France', Louis Philippe styled himself as the 'King of Frenchmen'—emphasizing that his sovereignty was derived from the people and not based on claims of divine right.

A revolution had thus occurred in France, the precise circumstance under which, pursuant to Article VI of the Quadruple Alliance, the four allies were obliged to confer. But the mighty alliance, which had once parcelled out territories, intervened in sovereign states and dictated the destinies of Europe, was now practically a dead letter. 'The four Great Powers were in fact bound by the Treaty of November 20th, 1815', writes the historian Sir Charles Webster, 'which had been reaffirmed at Aix-la-Chapelle in 1818, to consider together with the King of France if a revolution broke out in his dominions what measures should be taken ... It is surprising how little notice they took of this engagement. It is hardly mentioned in the discussions of the continental ministers'.[193]

No less a figure than Wellington—the former commander of allied forces in occupied France, the victor over Napoleon at Waterloo and an active participant at the Congresses of Vienna, Aix-la-Chapelle and Verona—was then the Prime Minister. The 'Iron Duke' decided that there was no time to consult with the other courts and that Louis Philippe should be immediately recognized.[194] The Russian minister Nesselrode was blissfully enjoying the waters in the spa town of Carlsbad, while Metternich was nearby on his estate at Königswart. In a letter to the Emperor Francis, Metternich specifically noted the obligations still existing under the Quadruple Alliance and informed his sovereign that he planned to meet with Nesselrode to discuss the latest developments in Paris. Francis also had not forgotten his duties under the treaty and responded: 'There must be unity in our principles, our plans, and our mode of carrying them out, and to effect this, a basis of union between the great powers must be re-established.'[195] The Austrian and Russian ministers met face-to-face the very next day. Metternich found Nesselrode quite astonished at the events in France, but the Russian foreign minister also acknowledged that the fall of the Bourbons was the result of processes long at work. The two ministers signed a short note, known as the *chiffon de Carlsbad*, in which Austria and Russia agreed 'not in any way to interfere in the internal disputes of France, but ... to permit no violation on the part of the French government either of the material interests of Europe, as established and guaranteed by general transactions, or of the internal peace of the various states composing it'.[196] Metternich recommended that they take no further steps until they reached an understanding with Prussia, even suggesting that Berlin might serve 'as the centre at which the concert would have been arranged'. Nesselrode replied that Tsar Nicholas would not permit a single drop of Russian blood to be shed to save France from her errors: Russia would therefore rigorously abstain from all interference in France. This was where their joint efforts ended—the British and Prussians never even entered into the discussion.

Not only did the Revolutions of 1830 signal the final dissolution of the Congress System; they also changed the map of Europe yet again. The French-speaking, Catholic Belgians had never been happy at being placed under Dutch rule in the United Netherlands—a creation of the First Peace of Paris. Riots began in Brussels almost as soon as news was received of the successful revolution in Paris. Dutch attempts to use force led the discontent to spread, and the Belgian States General declared Belgian independence and summoned a national assembly to draft a constitution. In 1831, the King of the Netherlands attempted to reconquer his lost Southern provinces, but the advance of his forces was halted when a French army intervened and a cease-fire was declared. The powers referred the problem to an ambassadorial conference in London, again presided over by Palmerston. Metternich admitted that Vienna was too distant to serve as the conference centre, and Tsar Nicholas would not even consider a conference in 'revolutionary' Paris. None other than the wily Talleyrand—who had astutely sided with the Orléanists—was sent to London as the special emissary of France.[197] Although the Congress System was now obviously gone, the powers thus continued to collaborate on a variety of issues. The French proposed a partition of Belgium between France, Holland, Prussia and a tiny free city-state around Antwerp. Rather than see any of the Belgian provinces joined to France, the London conference eventually reached a solution by offering the Belgians their own state and promising the future neutrality of Belgium in European disputes. The independence of Greece and Belgium were the first chinks in the armour of the Vienna Settlement. Farther to the east, the Poles also rose up in revolt in 1830, led by Tsar Alexander's old friend Prince Czartoryski. Unlike Greece and Belgium, however, the tragic Polish uprising was crushed mercilessly: 'Congress Poland' lost her autonomy and became a mere province of Russia. So Castlereagh proved to be right after all about the fate of Poland under Russian suzerainty. The unrest in Poland was accompanied by a series of rebellions in the Russian military colonies, leading that experiment to be abandoned as well.

Popular discontent also continued to simmer in Britain. The Earl of Liverpool had died in 1827. When Canning succeeded him, the Tory Party divided between his followers and those of Wellington. Canning died a few months later and Wellington, as we have seen, assumed the Premiership. The victory of Daniel O'Connell, a Catholic, in an Irish by-election precipitated a new crisis and, to his credit, Wellington passed Catholic Emancipation—the measure previously urged by Pitt, Castlereagh, Canning and Wellington ever since the Act of Union in 1800—which finally permitted Catholic members to sit in Parliament. But Wellington opposed further parliamentary reform and his government lost its majority in the House of Commons. A liberal Whig majority was elected, resulting—after a two-year struggle—in the passage of the Reform Bill of 1832. Led by Earl Grey, many of the Whigs in the new cabinet had once been among Castlereagh's fiercest critics. As constitutional states, Britain and France found it increasingly difficult to act in concert with the autocratic states of the east. Metternich still hoped for some degree of cooperation between the great powers and for the formation of a common conference centre at Vienna for the struggle against revolution, as well as for the management of the Eastern Question. The British, however, preferred to see London established as the permanent conference centre of Europe. When a fresh crisis arose in Spain in the early 1830s, the three autocratic eastern powers formed an alliance at Münchengrätz; the British then launched a rival 'Quadruple Alliance' consisting of the constitutional monarchies of Britain, France, Spain and Portugal. Two surviving members of the Secret Alliance of 3 January 1815, Metternich and Talleyrand (now acting as ambassador to Britain), thus affixed their signatures to opposing treaties.

By the mid-1830s, the former Congress System—the attempt to have all of the great powers of Europe act in collaboration and march in common step—had therefore been replaced by two hostile alliances and the new practice of resorting to occasional ambassadorial conferences to deal with individual crises as they arose. The two alliances confronted each other on the Iberian Peninsula, where Britain and France backed liberal regimes in Lisbon and Madrid, and the eastern powers backed conservative claimants to each throne. In the east, the configuration was somewhat different: in two 'Mehemet Ali crises'—in 1833 and again in 1839–41—Britain and Russia cooperated in defending the Turkish Sultan against his vassal, Mehemet Ali, the Pasha of Egypt, who found backing from the French. By the late 1830s, Louis Philippe of France was actually moving away from Britain and closer to Metternich and Austria. In 1836, Louis Philippe even proposed a new European congress for revising the Vienna settlement—'an entente of the five Powers for the solution of all the great political questions ... for settling all those questions with a general and European interest ... for guaranteeing the *status quo* of the territorial delimitation of Europe'—but his call was swiftly rebuffed by the other powers.[198] (In 1863, a proposal for a new congress by Napoleon III would meet a similar fate.)

The battles for influence of the 1830s and early 1840s were suddenly overshadowed when almost all of Europe was struck by a tidal wave of revolution in 1848. Popular uprisings erupted in Paris, Copenhagen, Sicily, Milan, Florence, Turin, Rome, Venice, Berlin, Prague, Budapest, Frankfurt and even Vienna. Metternich, still in the Ballhausplatz after all these years, finally fell from power. With his resignation, the last of the founding fathers of the Congress System was gone. Although there was no longer any Congress System, the three eastern powers continued to collaborate in opposing popular revolution. General Joseph Radetzky, Schwarzenberg's chief-of-staff in the final campaign against Napoleon 30 years before, commanded Austrian forces against the revolutionaries.[199] Austria received the assistance of 300,000 Russian troops, who marched into Hungary, much as she had enjoyed the benefit of Russian troops in the background in 1821. The legacy of international cooperation against revolution still survived, at least in the east.

But eventually, all the seams sewn together by the statesmen at Vienna tore apart. The 'Eastern Question'—the anxious concern of the great powers over the survival of the Ottoman Empire and the fate of its territories if it dissolved—led to the Crimean War in 1854 with France, Britain and Turkey ranged on one side and Russia on the other; the failure of Austria and Prussia to come to the assistance of Russia against the constitutional states of Britain and France led to disillusionment in Russia and the collapse of the 'Neo-Holy Alliance'. Historians generally agree that this created the opening needed for the unification of Italy and Germany without Russian interference. The boundaries of Europe were thus being progressively redrawn on the basis of nationality. Only two further congresses were held for the rest of the century: the Congress of Paris in 1856 at the end of the Crimean War, and the Congress of Berlin in 1878 to rewrite the Treaty of San Stefano after yet another Russo-Turkish war. Both of these congresses were of an older, war-termination variety, and not true revivals of the Congress System. The unification of Germany in 1871 was followed by the creation of a system of separate, less flexible alliances. Bismarck tried to restore the old alliance of the three eastern courts, but Russia eventually gravitated towards France, much as Richelieu and Capodistrias had once aspired to do. By 1914, exactly one century after the Congress of Vienna, the stage was set for a 'total war' even more terrible than that of the *anni horribiles* of 1792 to 1815.

8

The Legacy of the Congress System: Success or Failure?

AS a result of the French Revolution, the limited *Kabinettskriege* of the eighteenth century were replaced by mass conscription and nearly two decades of total warfare (*guerre à l'outrance*). Not surprisingly, the statesmen of the post-war years, just as in the periods immediately following the First and Second World Wars, attempted to avoid further upheaval and bloodshed by creating new methods of international cooperation to regulate their disagreements. The Congress System that resulted constituted an audacious experiment. It was the first time in history that statesmen attempted to establish institutional mechanisms to superintend relations between sovereign states with the aim of maintaining world peace and stability. Although the system failed to endure, it marked a decisive step in the evolution of international institutions, serving as a direct precursor to the conference diplomacy of the later nineteenth century, the League of Nations and the United Nations, as well as of later great power summit diplomacy and the European Union.

If references to the Congresses of Vienna, Aix-la-Chapelle, Troppau, Laibach and Verona are no longer commonplace today, the memory of this great experiment in diplomacy hardly deserves to be forgotten. For this was the first occasion on which governments had to cope with reconciling the 'forces of movement'—the demand for popular sovereignty and greater socio-economic equality unleashed by the Atlantic Revolutions—with the 'forces of order', the need to preserve systems of law, property rights, and mechanisms of political authority. It was a pivotal moment in the history of much of Europe and even beyond it—France, Germany, Italy, Spain, Russia, Portugal, Greece, Romania, Ottoman Turkey and Latin America. Rulers and their landowning aristocratic elites no longer justified their rule on the basis of divine right, but now legitimized their power on new, post-revolutionary utilitarian grounds—their firm control at the helm was needed, so they argued, to prevent society from lapsing into the anarchy of revolution and popular upheaval. This was a time when ruling elites struggled to develop a new form of international cooperation and even a nascent world government in order to suppress revolution and to moderate armed conflict. Their efforts gave rise to new norms and procedures that would become enshrined as the recognized methods and traditions of diplomacy. At the same time, the elites who operated the system exhibited little sympathy for the lower classes or understanding of their problems.

The Congress System was essentially the brainchild of three men—Tsar Alexander, Viscount Castlereagh and Prince Metternich. Each statesman possessed slightly different motivations for wishing to extend their wartime collaboration into peacetime, and these variations led to subtle differences in nuance in how each of them thought the new system should work. For Alexander, the notion of a European alliance dated back at least to Czartoryski's memorial of 1803, and was literally meant to provide stability and peace in the form of a supra-European form of government. There were both liberal and Christian overtones to his vision. Each monarch would be guaranteed his throne and territory by the other members of the alliance, yet each would also be required to provide his subjects with liberal institutions. At the same time, the entire framework was to be permeated with a spirit of Christian solicitude. In one respect, Alexander's conception of the alliance can be viewed as an attempt by Russia, still a relatively new power, to integrate itself into the European state system and to achieve a greater degree of recognition from the other powers. At the same time, the Tsar—even in his 'liberal phase'—had never completely worked out the full implications of his vision of a confederation of enlightened despots informed by national assemblies. There was always the paradox that the most absolute ruler in Europe was also the sponsor of the most liberal programme of reform. It was a contradiction rooted deeply in Russian history itself, arising out of Peter the Great's legacy of Westernization 'from above'. For what if a people, after having been granted liberal institutions, criticized their monarch or even rejected the monarchical order itself? Indeed, this is what happened, to the Tsar's great annoyance, in Poland and within his own palace guard. This obvious weak point, combined with the fear of revolution, permitted Metternich to manipulate the Tsar from 1819 onwards. The Tsar abandoned the liberal aspects of his vision, and the Holy Alliance genuinely became an alliance of monarchs—just as Metternich had presciently rewritten the provisions of Alexander's original treaty of the Holy Alliance in September 1815.[1]

Next, there was Castlereagh, frequently credited by British historians as the principal architect of the Congress System. His earliest hopes for a system of European cooperation also dated back at least as far as the exchange between his mentor Pitt and Czartoryski. To defeat Napoleon, Castlereagh recognized the necessity of a European coalition in which all the allied great powers acted in unison. The experiences of 1812 to 1814 had proved with a vengeance that the Continental powers might collaborate with complete disregard for British interests. To prevent this danger, Castlereagh embarked for the Continent and, using his control of British subsidies, brought the allied powers together in the Treaty of Chaumont in 1814; he also encouraged them to renew their partnership in the Quadruple Alliance of 20 November 1815. The fruitful cooperation between the allied leaders that brought the contest with Bonaparte to a victorious conclusion thoroughly convinced Castlereagh of the absolute superiority of face-to-face negotiations over the usual channels of diplomatic discourse. His notion of a Congress System consisted primarily of an agreement to hold periodic conferences or summit meetings to discuss important issues and to attempt to resolve them peacefully through negotiation and compromise. In an age before the telegraph and telephone, this made perfect sense. It also gave full rein to his formidable bargaining talents. The other important part of his conception, often not emphasized enough, was that Britain would continue to act with the Continental powers instead of in splendid isolation. Castlereagh anticipated that he would continue to exploit his personal contacts with other European leaders to make certain that important issues were resolved in a manner conducive to British interests. The system would prevent the Continental powers from acting without Britain and defuse important problems before they led to war. To sell the idea to his own countrymen and to prevent a total detachment of Britain from Continental politics, Castlereagh had to emphasize those elements of his programme designed to prevent the resurgence of France. He therefore described the alliance as providing a bulwark against French aggression, and he opposed plans to turn the alliance, at least publicly, into an instrument of counter-revolution as a matter of general principle.

But Castlereagh had always understood that there was more to the alliance than this. Like the other allied leaders, he remained steadfast in his opposition to the spread of revolution in Europe. Indeed, he had more personal experience than any of them in confronting revolution, since he had witnessed unrest on his father's own estates and had played a prominent role in suppressing the Irish Rebellion of 1798. Castlereagh was extremely suspicious of public opinion, but he also felt that with proper skill and effort, it could be managed effectively. Therefore, his idea of the Congress System was to cooperate with the Continental states in repressing the revolutionary spirit still stalking Europe, but to manage this collaboration in such a manner that it could withstand parliamentary scrutiny, or even better, avoid it altogether.

The collaboration with the allied powers was to be achieved through secret, not open, diplomacy. In most cases, he opposed foreign intervention, not because he favoured the 'forces of movement', but because he believed local rulers could restore order on their own. Only when local counter-revolutionary resources proved deficient was Castlereagh willing to consider bringing the powerful machinery of the European alliance to bear on the problem and even then preferably in clandestine ways that would escape the notice of the British Parliament. Always conscious of the fact that the British system of government was itself the product of a revolutionary settlement, Castlereagh appreciated that he could only bring his countrymen so far; accordingly, he was willing to give secret support to the Continental powers in their efforts to suppress revolution, but not so openly that it would directly involve Britain. Between the Congresses of Aix-la-Chapelle and Troppau, it seemed that Castlereagh might just pull off this delicate balancing act. But he was soon overtaken by events: the Continental statesmen grew ever more alarmed at the spread of revolutionary activity; the Tsar continued to insist on moving the alliance in the direction of a guarantee of the status quo; the French wished to broaden the alliance to shift its focus away from themselves; and even Metternich insisted on showing respect for the absolute powers of monarchs such as Ferdinand I of Naples and Ferdinand VII of Spain as a matter of principle. Not only the Tsar, but Continental statesmen like Gentz, too, believed that the best means for defeating the revolutionary movement was in a public display of the great powers' unshakable determination to uphold the alliance against revolutionary change. Castlereagh understood that such policies would be quite indefensible in the British Parliament.

For Metternich, the Congress System afforded a unique opportunity to use diplomacy and negotiation to achieve Austrian objectives rather than to rely solely on exertions of military power. Metternich was not subject to parliamentary pressures, like Castlereagh, nor did he hold strong messianic religious beliefs, like the Tsar; with the staunch support and even admiration of the Emperor Francis, Metternich enjoyed great freedom of action in these years. From the standpoint of great-power politics, he sought to prevent the strengthening of Russia, France or Prussia. At the same time, he sought to resist revolutionary change, in part because such change might threaten the fragile unity of the multi-ethnic Austrian Empire. These were statesmen who spent their whole lives battling revolution: like both Alexander and Castlereagh, Metternich believed he was engaged in mortal combat against a well-organized, highly disciplined, monolithic secret society, which stood behind all the multifarious manifestations of revolution breaking out across the face of Europe. Because he viewed these demonstrations of popular unrest as the product of a vast international conspiracy, Metternich believed that international cooperation was essential: like Alexander and Castlereagh, Metternich regarded the European alliance as the most powerful weapon in his arsenal for defeating the revolutionaries, whom he viewed with much the same horror as that with which many look on political terrorists today. Historian Alan Sked has recently reminded us that 'Metternich's career was dedicated to waging war on terror and he did this without resorting to torture, or undermining the rule of law, although he negotiated what would today be seen as international anti-terrorist conventions, employed a mild, if efficient censorship and used a secret intelligence service (or police) ....'[2]

Nor were these various objectives all that distinct in Metternich's mind, since he believed that expressions of political liberalism in Russia, France and Prussia were not only associated with territorial expansion but also encouraged the revolutionaries. Metternich subscribed to Pitt's view that in the midst of a storm, a homeowner should not repair his roof. 'I spend my time', Metternich lamented in 1822, 'shoring up crumbling edifices'.[3] Because his objectives were essentially to preserve the status quo, the creation of a tightly knit diplomatic system among the great powers was well-suited to his purposes. This spider's web was the perfect means for ensnaring the statesmen of the other powers and for persuading them to collaborate in his policy. Although Metternich harboured suspicions of Russian expansionism, he was willing to cooperate with the Tsar to defeat the greater danger posed by revolution. Sked points out that Metternich was also careful to maintain Austria's independence of action as much as possible—ensuring that 'her armies alone suppressed the Italian revolts, kept German policy within the confines of the *Bund*, and opposed unilateral French or Russian action in Spain'. Nowhere is Metternich's use of the Congress System to restrain Russia more evident than in his handling of the Eastern Question, where he dangled the possibility of allied support before the Tsar to prevent a Russo-Turkish War.

Salient characteristics of the Congress System

Despite these differences in nuance, there have been several attempts to define the characteristics of the Congress System as a whole, as it actually operated in the years from 1815 to 1823. Sir Charles Webster, for example, in a series of lectures in Calcutta in 1929, characterized the alliance as consisting of six 'aspects': (1) it was first and foremost a coalition of the great powers against France; (2) the idea of protecting the frontiers of France's neighbours gave rise to the idea that all the frontiers of Europe might be specially protected by a guarantee, although this was never concluded; (3) the alliance was seen as affording protection against revolution; (4) the alliance introduced the new system of 'diplomacy by conference'; (5) the alliance further introduced the use of ambassadorial conferences; (6) and finally, the emotions provoked by the war led to the Holy Alliance, although this latter agreement contained no specific obligations. The historian Richard B. Elrod launched a more recent discussion on the nature of the system in 1976 by publishing an article in the influential journal *World Politics*: he argued that the Congress System had four 'essential precepts', that were later incorporated into the Concert of Europe: 'great-power tutelage over the rest of Europe'; 'territorial changes in Europe were subject to the sanction of the great powers'; 'essential members of the states system must protected and defended'; and 'great powers must not be humiliated'.

With the benefit of hindsight, it would seem that the Congress System can, in fact, be best characterized as consisting of the following set of conditions, characteristics and goals:

Conditions

(1) Europe was 'multipolar', consisting of several independent, sovereign states, none of which exercised hegemonic power.[4]
(2) Foreign policy remained in the hands of elite practitioners who were relatively free of constraints and immune to public pressures. In some cases these practitioners were monarchs; in others, their chief ministers. Most often, decisions were made collaboratively by monarchs and their chief advisors. European society remained aristocratic, and these elite decision-makers were generally quite cosmopolitan. However, new social forces were emerging as a result of the Enlightenment, economic progress, the French Revolution and the Napoleonic Wars.
(3) European elites perceived a common danger—the spread of revolution. This provided the main impetus for the formation of the Congress System.
(4) There was a temporary absence of direct conflict among the great powers, due to the defeat of France and the compromises on territorial allocations reached at the Congress of Vienna and incorporated into the Vienna Final Act.

Characteristics

(5) Membership in the Congress System was restricted to the great powers.
(6) During the heyday of the Congress System, the great powers consulted among themselves and attempted to reach a consensus on most issues. These consultations took place either through 'Congresses' in which sovereigns, chief ministers and foreign ministers were present, or through

ambassadorial conferences. Under Article VI of the Quadruple Alliance, the members agreed to hold periodic meetings, although the 'periods' were never specified and this provision was never enforced. At the Congress of Aix-la-Chapelle, France was invited to join the other members as a participant in the system. Later Congresses (Troppau, Laibach and Verona) were held in response to particular crises rather than based on fixed periods. These meetings fostered greater 'transparency' and a sense of social community among the statesmen.

(7) Britain participated in the system and acted with the Continent. (However, Britain and France only participated as observers at the Congresses of Troppau and Laibach, and Britain was virtually isolated at the Congress of Verona.)

(8) Collectively, the members of the system had an overwhelming preponderance of force at their disposal. (In their defeat of Napoleon in the campaign of 1815 and their excursions into Naples and Spain, these nineteenth-century powers were actually more successful in rapidly achieving their objectives than twenty-first century interventions in Iraq and Afghanistan.)

(9) There were no clear rules regarding voting, whether a majority or unanimity was required, or any other determinations for establishing procedures, except that decisions were generally recorded in conference protocols, parts of which were occasionally made public. It was hoped that the great powers would first agree among themselves and then impose their unanimous will on the rest of Europe, but such unanimity was not always achieved.

(10) There was little development of international public law, of precedent, or of permanent institutions by the Congress statesmen. The system remained primarily a cooperative method of ad hoc, secret diplomacy. Since efforts to establish a general territorial guarantee, a timetable of future meetings based on fixed periods, or even a permanent conference centre all failed, there was little institutional growth. Ironically, the British desire to avoid parliamentary scrutiny placed constraints on the system that sharply inhibited its institutional development.

Goals

(11) The new system was directed, above all, to combating any new revolution arising in France. Nevertheless, at their meetings, the members also discussed a wide array of other topics. There was some ambiguity as to whether the system should also apply to revolutions occurring outside of France. Russia felt that the new system was necessarily directed against

the forces of revolution wherever they might arise, and the French had never wanted the system to be directed solely at themselves; but the British felt a great need to restrict the operation of the system to actions against France, because any other actions would have been difficult to defend in a hostile Parliament. Austria vacillated between the British and Russian view (depending upon her strategic interests).

(12) Efforts to push the system further, in the direction of a guarantee of all territories or even of all existing internal political arrangements, failed to win the support of all its members. Efforts to extend the system beyond the perimeters of Europe, into Latin America or the Ottoman Empire, similarly failed. Yet it would seem wrong to say that there was an understanding *ab initio* that the European possessions of the Ottoman Empire or the Spanish American colonies lay outside the system; rather, the parties simply failed to come to an agreement about what should be done there.

The exercise of mutual self-restraint, lauded by many historians and political scientists, was more of an incidental by-product of these conditions than an essential characteristic of the system. Most often, this restraint was exercised by the Tsar, the staunchest advocate of the system, who was also acting in part out of religious conviction. The general fear of revolution, disdain for popular nationalism and the cosmopolitan nature of European aristocratic elites further contributed to the sense of moderation and self-control. But because the system never went beyond the methods of *ad hoc*, secret diplomacy, its members were always free to pursue their individual interests at any time.

A post-hegemonic international security regime?

Political scientists have also attempted to identify the main elements of the Congress System in order to compare it more meaningfully with other systems. In 1982, the American political scientist Robert Jervis identified the Congress System—which he saw as the 'strongest' phase of the 'Concert of Europe'—as a type of 'security regime'.[5]

In political science parlance, international 'regimes' are 'rules of the game' or common 'principles, norms, rules and decision-making procedures' shared by actors across national boundaries. Members of the same 'regime' agree, explicitly or tacitly, to follow the same norms and rules, even though they are not subject to a common sovereign or penalized for not doing so. A 'security regime', according to Jervis, is a 'regulated environment' consisting of 'those principles, rules, and norms that permit nations to be restrained in their behavior in the belief that others will reciprocate'.

The Legacy of the Congress System

The Congress System provides, in Jervis' view, the 'best example of a security regime'. Rather than acting to maximize their own power or take advantage of others, Jervis argues that the great powers made concessions and refused to exploit each other's weaknesses: 'In short, they moderated their demands and behavior as they took each other's interests into account in settling their own policies.'[6] He cites, for example, Castlereagh's instructions of 1816 to British diplomats to subordinate all 'petty intrigue' and 'secondary and separate interests' to the common cause of peace and good will. The new Congress System, he notes, 'did not banish conflict' but 'regulate[d]' it: the great powers cooperated and seldom resorted to war.[7]

A few years later, Jervis tackled the topic again by comparing the Concert of Europe, especially during the era of the congresses, with the operation of the balance of power.[8] Jervis noted that while there has never been a world government, the Congress System remains the closest that states have ever reached towards that goal.[9] He sees such systems as arising only after the experience of fighting a total war against a hegemon like Napoleon or Hitler: 'concert systems form after, and only after, a large war against a potential hegemon because such a conflict produces significant ties between the allies, undermines the acceptability of war as a tool of statecraft, and perhaps most important, increases the incentives to cooperate.'[10] Jervis argues—through an application of game theory—that concert systems arise because of shifts in the 'payoffs' from cooperation and non-cooperation: war is no longer perceived as a legitimate instrument of statecraft, defensive actions become preferable to offensive ones, fears of war and revolution increase the perceived risks of non-cooperation, personal ties broaden the benefits of cooperation, and states form alliances more easily.

Louise Richardson, another American political scientist, likewise regards the Congress System as the strongest phase of the Concert of Europe, itself a 'contemporary international security institution' that 'facilitated adaption to change in the international distribution of power.'[11] As a security institution, she finds the Concert of Europe consisted of a series of norms, rules and procedures: 'The Concert's norms were: self-restraint; consultation in time of crisis; willingness to act together (and its corollary), refusal to act unilaterally; and constant assurances of one another of their pacific intent and commitment to the maintenance of stability.' Alongside these norms, she identifies several explicit rules of behaviour: the use of conference diplomacy to deal with crises; approval by the great powers for all territorial changes; the essential members of the system were to be protected; and the interests and honour of great powers could not be challenged. Finally, borrowing from the work of historian Paul Gordon Lauren, Richardson identifies a series of procedures that she believes created 'an elaborate crisis prevention system'; these included 'mutual consultation and collective decision-making'; 'creation of buffer states'; 'delineation of interests and areas of involvement'; 'intervention by multilateral action'; 'pacific settlement of disputes': and 'communication and provision of advance notification'.[12]

Most other political scientists have taken a similar approach. For example, Charles Kupchan categorizes the Concert of Europe as a 'security community':

> The Concert operated as a directorate of Europe's major powers, providing a forum in which they forged a set of rules and norms for regulating their relations and peacefully resolving disputes. War among the members of the Concert did not become unthinkable; an undercurrent of strategic rivalry continued to animate their relations. But the Concert did constitute a security community inasmuch as strategic rivalry was significantly muted and armed force effectively eliminated as a legitimate tool of statecraft among its members.[13]

Ian Clark refers to their cooperation as a form of 'collective hegemony'—defined as 'great-power control over international society'.[14] Matthias Schulz (a German historian) sees the system as a form of 'security council' while Kevin McMillan evaluates it as a form of international governance.[15]

A number of political scientists have examined specific aspects of the system: one finds that it actually created its own 'social community', facilitating diplomatic transactions.[16] Another marvels at its 'transparency'—under the Congress System, statesmen could better see and understand the manoeuvres of other participating diplomats.[17] Like Castlereagh, this scholar—Dan Lindley—believes such transparency constituted the chief merit of the system.[18] This emphasis accords well with Robert Keohane's more general explanation of why international regimes often arise to begin with—'International regimes—clusters of principles, norms, rules and decision-making procedures—reduce transaction costs for states, alleviate problems of asymmetrical information, and limit the degree of uncertainty that members of the regime face in evaluating each others' policies'.[19] In other words, the Congress System helped to reduce both uncertainty and 'transaction costs'.

One group of political scientists—often depicting themselves as 'realists' in contrast to more pro-Congress 'institutionalists'—has questioned whether there was really much of a Congress System at all. In a detailed analysis of the Greek crisis of the 1820s, Korina Kagan found that each of the great powers essentially pursued its own interests, and therefore concluded that the Congress System was 'a weak and ineffective institution that was largely irrelevant to great power behavior'.[20] Branislav Slantchev has argued that the great powers essentially achieved what they wanted at Vienna, where they established spheres of influence; afterwards, according to Slantchev, the system became self-enforcing: 'The Vienna territorial settlement structured incentives in such a way as to make enforcement endogenous—it generated credible commitments to uphold it because it delineated spheres of influence such that any significant changes would impinge directly on the interests of enough powers to allow them to counter any such revisionism.' He contends it was this careful alignment of interests that accounted for the powers' subsequent behaviour 'rather than some illusory system of normative and legalistic checks and balances....'[21] Matthew Rendall has combined these various approaches to explain why the powers sometimes doggedly pursued their separate interests and why, at other times, they seemed to exercise a remarkable degree of self-restraint.[22]

What all of these political science analyses have in common is that they help us to appreciate the Congress System more abstractly as a type of international system that tends to arise under particular conditions and that displays a set of typical characteristics.

Why the system failed

Once we grasp the fundamental nature of the Congress System, the next question is: why did it eventually fail? A wide array of answers has been offered, and it was doubtless the combined effect of several factors that led to its downfall. The first explanation—and certainly the most obvious one—was the one offered at the time by both Canning and Gentz. The purpose of the Congress System was counter-revolutionary: as the memory of the great revolution faded, national rivalries revived and slowly tore the Congress System apart. Countries like England and France thought they could do better on their own. '[T]he so-called Congress System broke down under the pressure of divergent national interests', writes Alan Sked. Robert Jervis believes this explanation has more general application, transcending the experiences of 1815 to 1823:

> Concert systems decay ... [I]n general the passage of time alters the unusual postwar situation and reestablishes the balance-of-power assumptions. As the memories of war fade, the bonds erode that helped to hold the blocking coalition together. Friction tends to build as each state believes that it is sacrificing more for unity than are the others. Because of perceptual dynamics, each will remember the cases in which it has been restrained, and ignore or interpret differently cases in which others believe they acted for the common good. Fear of the state that had earlier sought

hegemony is also likely to decline over time … The painful memories of the enormous costs of war also become dimmer as time passes, and a new generation, with no first-hand experience, comes to power.[23]

One objection to this explanation is that in 1823 the cycle of European revolutions was far from complete. Although the memory of the French Revolution may have faded, new revolutions were constantly occurring to take its place. Why should European conservatives have been willing to abandon their system when they had just confronted the Revolutions of the 1820s and continued to face revolutionary turbulence across the face of Europe?

A second explanation, a variation in some ways of the first, is that the Congress System was riddled with ambiguity and misunderstanding from the outset. The Russians intended it as an embryonic world government; the British as a system of conference diplomacy; the Austrians as a way to contain the Russians and Prussians; and the French as a means for redirecting the focus of the allies away from themselves. It can be argued that these dissimilarities in interpretation reflected deeper ideological, political, social, strategic and economic differences among its members. Britain and France, with their constitutional systems and active middle classes, could not effectively be bound together with the more autocratic eastern powers.

Although there were these conflicting aims within the alliance from the outset, this explanation begs the question of why these differences widened instead of narrowed. Once the institutions of the Congress System were established at Paris and Aix-la-Chapelle, why was the new system unable to strengthen itself, or even to acquire new functions as time passed? Why, instead, did those tensions tear it apart less than five years after the Congress at Aix?

Both Wellington and Castlereagh's half-brother Lord Stewart blamed the collapse of the Congress System on the failure of the eastern powers to take Britain's special constitutional system sufficiently into account and for proceeding instead in a manner that the British ministers were unable to defend in Parliament. They therefore dated the rift in the alliance to Troppau and placed the blame for it largely on the Tsar and Metternich. After the death of Castlereagh and the Congress of Verona, Wellington—an adherent of the system—sent this frank assessment to the Austrian Chancellor:

> The first manifest disunion was at Troppau. There had been at Aix-la-Chapelle a good deal of discussion between the Russian Cabinet and us respecting the *Casus Foederis* of the Treaty of November 1815. But this dispute was brought before the public without the knowledge of our plenipotentiary by the *Protocole préliminaire*, and the Circular from Troppau;

to the last of which we were obliged in our own defence to reply. Then followed the Congress at Verona; and I beg leave to recall to your recollection the various occasions on which I ventured to foretell to your Highness the consequence to the Alliance in general of the state of *isolement* [isolation] in which I was left. Observe that I don't pretend that upon either occasion the Allies were bound to abandon their object to please the councils of this country; but I contended then as I do now, that as it was an object to the Allies upon both occasions to carry this government with them as far as it could go, it would have been wise to conduct these transactions in such a manner as that at least it might not be apparent to the world that we were separated from the Allies; and that the well-meaning people of this country might not have been accustomed to consider that separation as a benefit, instead of an evil ... Thus you will see that it is neither *les choses* [the things] themselves nor *les hommes* [the men] who have transacted them, that have occasioned the mischief; but the mode in which the transactions which have taken place have been carried on, the pains taken by some to disgust us with the Alliance, and the little pains taken by others to conciliate us towards it, and finally, the unmerited calumnies of which we have been the object, which have been circulated by the former, and have not been too liberally discouraged by the latter.[24]

At the end of the Cold War a prominent international relations theorist made the claim that 'avoiding military conflict in Europe after the Cold War [will depend] greatly on whether the next decade is characterized by a continuous pattern of institutionalized cooperation'.[25] It might be argued by analogy that the Congress System did not last because of the failure of its leading statesmen to establish just such 'institutionalized cooperation'.[26] The Congress statesmen were on the verge of establishing periodic summit conferences at fixed intervals, territorial guarantees and even the enunciation of a set of general principles to govern intervention, but then pulled back. Historians tend to dismiss these projects as chimerical, and often take the British view that the Continental powers hijacked the system beyond its original intent. If, in fact, the direction of the Congress System had not become exclusively counter-revolutionary, then Britain might have participated more fully in it. Ironically, it was Castlereagh who insisted that the workings of the system be kept shrouded in secrecy because he knew its largely counter-revolutionary aims could not be sustained in the British Parliament. This meant, however, that the Congress System had no chance to develop more permanent institutions or to evolve. In this sense, the system may have been stillborn. If more durable international institutions had been established between 1815 and 1823, perhaps it might have survived. We say 'perhaps' because, although the absence of institutions may have doomed the Congress System, their existence would not necessarily have guaranteed its success—as the later League of Nations would show.

A third explanation for the failure of the Congress System is that it was overly dependent on the handful of individuals who formed it. It was a partnership that never became a corporation. As a virtually secret society, the system could not outlast its founders. This is actually the reverse side of the same coin as the last explanation. The meetings of the Congress System, despite the provisions of the Quadruple Alliance, remained largely ad hoc. The alliance created no permanent body, formal rules or secretariat with an institutional memory. It was as if the operation of the United States Constitution had depended on the continuing personal participation of the framers. It was less an agreement by the powers than by a particular group of leaders, who had developed great personal familiarity during the final stage of the Napoleonic Wars. As the individuals who formed the Congress System passed away, the system itself evaporated. Their replacements did not share their experiences, views, or commitments. Canning did not possess the enthusiasms of Castlereagh, and Tsar Nicholas did not hold the strong internationalist beliefs of his older brother, Alexander.

A fourth explanation is that the system failed because of subsequent economic, social and political changes. Establishment of the Congress System, wedding the constitutional monarchy of Britain on the western edge of Europe with autocratic Russia to the east, was already difficult in 1815. 'The present difficulties', Stewart wrote from Vienna on the eve of Troppau,

> have undoubtedly brought forcibly into consideration the advantages and disadvantages of the present Great Alliance. Out of the five Powers that compose it three have pure Monarchical Institutions. The other two, England and France, have Constitutional Governments. The measures of the former in all points connected with their publick Administration and Safety should be vigorous, prompt and immediate. In the Constitutional Governments, they can be committed to nothing without previous deliberation and discussion ...[27]

As England continued to industrialize, the gulf between Western and Eastern Europe widened. After the July Revolution in France and the passage of the Reform Bill in England, so the argument goes, the bonds had stretched so far that they simply burst. The troubling problem with this argument is that it implies that international cooperation can only succeed between similar states (or at least between states that are not too dissimilar). Indeed, some political scientists have argued that peace is more likely to endure between societies with similar political systems—whether they are democracies or autocracies.[28] Perhaps the collapse of the Congress System provides additional support for this hypothesis.

A fifth explanation, closely related to the fourth, is that the system failed because its authors did not sufficiently take into account the twin forces of liberalism and nationalism. Among liberals and nationalists, the 'Holy Alliance' was viewed as an instrument of repression and became a term of abuse. As early as 1815, on the floor of the House of Commons, the Whig leader Henry Brougham challenged Castlereagh, asking why the three monarchs had drawn up a treaty, and why Britain had been excluded—'When the crowned heads met, the result of their united councils was not always favorable to the interests of humanity.'[29] In 1821, at the time of the Austrian expedition to Naples, the radical publicist William Hone wrote the pamphlet, *The Divine Right of Kings to Govern Wrong*, which he dedicated to the 'Members of the Holy Alliance', admonishing his readers:

> Kingcraft rears up its terrific mass, muffled in the mantle of Legitimacy; its head cowled and crowned, and dripping with the holy oil of Divine Right; its eyes glaring deadly hate to human happiness; its lips demanding worship for itself. Denouncing dreadful curses against the free, and yelling forth threatenings and slaughter, it stamps with its hoof, and coils together its frightful force to fall on young Liberty and squelch it. Its red right-arm is bared for the butchery of the brave who love Freedom and dare contend for it. It has prepared its chains and dug its dungeons, erected its scaffolds, and sharpened its axes for the wise and excellent of the earth; and its bloody banners are unfurled in insolent anticipation of unholy triumph!

Certainly this was the view held by many liberal scholars in the late nineteenth and early twentieth centuries. They saw the Congress statesmen as ogres fighting against the tide of history. The greater democratization of Britain and France in the early 1830s led to increasing public condemnation of the actions of the eastern autocracies, making international cooperation ever more difficult. The failure of the system, it is argued, was caused by its identification with the preservation of an autocratic and aristocratic way of life. The alliance was on the wrong side of history.

The strengthening of nationalist feelings, which the Congress statesmen had tried to suppress, it is further claimed, led to a resumption of armed conflicts later in the century. All of the fault lines that had appeared as cracks at Vienna, and which the Congress statesmen had tried to paper over, eventually reappeared and led to either revolution or war—the Austro-French dispute over Italy; Britain, the Netherlands and France on Belgium; the revolutions of 1848; Britain and Russia on the future of the Ottoman Empire; the 1863 revolution in Poland; Prussia and Austria for control of Germany; and Prussia and France contesting the eastern frontier of France. The Congress System consequently failed because it tried to suppress both liberalism and nationalism. Sensible as this argument may appear, it still leaves two unanswered questions—first, why did the system disintegrate as early as 1823–25, and second, why did it prove unable to accommodate these rising forces?

A sixth explanation for the failure of the Congress System, related to the third one above, looks to the international system. The member states failed to surrender any of their sovereignty; for this reason alone, it could be said, the system was doomed from the start. The Congress statesmen repeatedly discussed the idea of drafting a general guarantee, and even came close to concluding one at Vienna and Aix-la-Chapelle, but they never actually did so. No institutions emerged; no new body of public international law was created; and no new enforcement mechanisms were introduced. The Congress System was ephemeral because the international system remained in its natural Hobbesian state of anarchy.

The final explanation is, paradoxically, the very opposite of all the foregoing ones. It is the view that the system did not really fail or pass away at all but, rather, that it evolved. The British historian F.H. Hinsley epitomized this view:

> Castlereagh's principles survived when the Holy Alliance collapsed. It is one of the ironies of international history—and perhaps it is also one of the lessons—that the failure of the Congress system marked not the end but the beginning of an age of collaboration between the Great Powers because they then fell back on the Congress system as it had been interpreted by Castlereagh ... When the Congress system proved unworkable the notion of a coalition of leading states, founded on a public law for the defence of that law, was not abandoned. It was set free from its earlier association with the determination to govern the world—from the form the Congress idea first assumed when it at last replaced, at the beginning of the nineteenth century, the aspiration to universal monarchy. A looser association of the Great Powers continued in existence—an attenuated Congress system limited to dealing with problems as they arose, not seeking to anticipate them or to iron them out of existence ... [which] came to be called the Concert of Europe.[30]

Political scientists, as we have seen, often characterize the Congress System as an 'international security regime'. Like Hinsley, they point out that many of the norms, rules and procedures that the Congress statesmen first developed became standard diplomatic practices. Thus, the Congress System was transformed into the later 'Concert of Europe', in which the great powers collaborated, usually through ambassadorial conferences, in response to specific crises, such as the Belgian and Greek Revolutions and the Mehemet Ali crises. Because of the creation of these new practices, the 'long nineteenth century' from 1815 to 1914, it has been argued, was far more peaceful than the early twentieth.

This defence of the Congress System is also less than satisfactory. That is because the Congress System, and the later Concert of Europe, though related, were far from the same—the Congress System was an attempt to devise an 'institutionalized cooperation'—even a new world government—in order to break the cycle of revolutions that had disrupted the entire adult lives of the Congress statesmen. The later Concert of Europe had no such aspirations.

Imagine, for a moment, that the Congress System had succeeded. What if the foreign ministers of the great powers had been meeting in periodic summit conferences every two or three years throughout the 'long' nineteenth century? Imagine that the statesmen in 1914—a hundred years after the Treaty of Chaumont and the First Peace of Paris—were on the same familiar terms as Alexander, Castlereagh and Metternich. Would the crisis of July 1914 have ended in the same way? In 1914, Tsar Nicholas II of Russia actually made a personal appeal to Kaiser Wilhelm II of Germany to prevent the outbreak of war, but his entreaties were ignored. Suppose an appeal had been made between leading ministers on cordial terms? Suppose a new congress had been held to resolve the crisis. Would the history of Europe have been the same?

Or would the result, if the Congress System had actually survived, have been an unmitigated disaster? Would the leading powers of Europe have stifled all change, preventing the unifications of Italy and Germany and the collapse of the conservative autocratic eastern empires that followed the First World War? Either way, it is clear that the Congress System was not quite the same as the later Concert of Europe. Therefore, we need some explanation of why the one metamorphosed into the other.

The legacy of the Congress System

The Congress System provided an international 'learning experience' that repressed the revolutions of the 1820s, established many of the procedures followed by the later Concert of Europe, and served as a precursor to the League of Nations, the United Nations and even the European Union. We can laud these statesmen for their vision of international organization even as we condemn their specific policies for obstructing social change.

Although the creation of the League of Nations in 1919 was based on President Wilson's Fourteen Points, Wilson himself curiously failed to develop detailed plans for the League. These came mainly from the British: Lord Robert Cecil suggested to the Foreign Secretary that a working committee be established to look 'particularly from a juridical and historical point of view, into the various schemes for establishing by means of a League of Nations, or other device, as an alternative to war as a means of settling international disputes'.[31] One of the most important issues was the role that the great powers would have in the future League. In examining international organization from the 'historical point of view', the new committee, chaired by Sir Walter Phillimore, was well aware of the Congress System. It proposed a 'conference of Allied States' that might have been taken straight out of the Quadruple Alliance—holding its meetings as the occasion required.[32] The Phillimore Committee would have preferred to restrict the new League to those great powers whose efforts had won the war—in effect, a rebirth of the Congress System. This view was rejected on the grounds that all nations should be given some opportunity to participate in the League. But the idea of a special role for the great powers did not die—it was simply submerged into the organization of the League as a whole. In November 1918, Lord Cecil presented a new plan; his ideas were combined with the recommendations of the Phillimore Committee and became known as the 'Cecil Draft'; this new plan was then shared with the American delegation in January 1919 and effectively became the first draft of the later 'Covenant of the League of Nations'. It was the first step in fixing the organizational structure of the League, and proposed a permanent secretariat, an assembly of all member states that would meet every four years, and a 'Council' of the five great powers, to meet for 'regular conferences' on an annual basis—again a recognizable successor to the earlier Congress System. 'Universal war places the main responsibility for all major activities on the great powers', wrote Sir Charles Webster, 'a responsibility which is inevitably extended into the period of peace. From that fact came the European Alliance of the great powers in 1815, and in 1919 Lord Cecil at first suggested that the Council of the League should be solely composed of the great powers'.[33] The 'Cecil Draft' was modified to add rotating members to the League's 'Executive Council', chosen by the Assembly, but otherwise this largely became the structure of the new League.

And through this conduit, the Congress System in fact exercises a continuing, if largely unrecognized, influence even to this day: for during World War II, the allies decided to scrap the League of Nations in favour of a new organization, the 'United Nations'. The three leading allied powers—Britain, the Soviet Union and the United States—were convinced that the main problem with the League had been its weakness. What they felt was required was a strengthening of the role of the great powers—in a sense, a return to the original conception of the Congress System. 'Britain, Russia, China and the United States and their allies represent more than three-quarters of the total population of the earth', Roosevelt declared in 1943. 'As long as these four nations with great military power stick together in determination to keep the peace there will be no possibility of an aggressor nation arising to start another war.'[34] US Secretary of State Cordell Hull and his assistant Leo Pasvolsky drew up a plan for the new United Nations essentially based on the League of Nations. While Churchill favoured the creation of regional councils to strengthen Britain's role in Europe, the Foreign Office staff, including permanent undersecretary Alexander Cadogan and historian Charles K. Webster, favoured the American ideal of a strengthened League of Nations.[35] Even the Soviets, though distrustful of the West, wanted a continuation of some kind of the wartime alliance to protect their borders and to keep Germany in place. They favoured the creation of a small council of great powers exercising veto powers.[36]

Not only the name of the organization as a whole, but those of its principal parts were changed so that it might not be confused with its unfortunate predecessor; at talks at Dumbarton Oaks in Washington DC in the summer of 1944, the League's 'Executive Council' became the 'Security Council' (a name suggested by the Soviets), the 'Assembly' became the 'General Assembly' and the 'Covenant' itself was replaced by a 'Charter'. But the roots of today's Security Council can still be clearly traced through the 'Executive Council' of the League of Nations back to the Congress System itself.[37]

The uncanny resemblance between the five veto-wielding permanent members of the Security Council and the European pentarchy of old is therefore no accident. Its current members are the victors of the Second World War, just as the original members of the Quadruple Alliance were the victors of the Napoleonic Wars. Like the Congress System, the Security Council can be accurately described as a wartime coalition extended into peacetime. The leading allied powers decided on the structure of the United Nations and then invited the other nations to participate, just as the Congress of Vienna was announced by the allied powers, who invited the other states to attend. The members of the General Assembly could be compared to those plenipotentiaries who gathered in Vienna while the allied powers held their private negotiations. In 1818, the European alliance faced the problem of what to do with France. The permanent members of the Security Council have much the same issue with respect to the 'G4'—Brazil, Germany, India and Japan—countries whose population size or wealth would seemingly entitle them to become permanent members. But the current members have not been as willing to open their ranks—perhaps, the system works well enough as it is;

perhaps the veto prevents expansion from becoming a realistic possibility (China will always veto the admission of Japan); perhaps nine veto-wielding members would induce paralysis into the organization. In 1818, the alliance members faced a different problem: they were still concerned about the threat that France posed to their own security. However, they proved flexible enough to preserve the alliance and yet allow France into their congresses. NATO has proved similarly flexible. Could the structure of the United Nations demonstrate similar versatility—perhaps by creating a new category of permanent membership for the 'G4' nations without veto powers—affording representation to a nation such as India, which represents one-fifth of humanity, without reducing the effectiveness of the council?

The links from the Congress System to the European Union are somewhat more tenuous. The origins of the EU, like those of the Congress System, are to be found in mutual exhaustion after a great war. As early as 1946, Winston Churchill announced the need to 'build a kind of United States of Europe' and two years later he organized a landmark 'Congress of Europe' at The Hague, attended by Europe's leading statesmen and politicians. Churchill was accompanied by Count Richard von Coudenhove-Kalergi, an admirer of the Abbé de Sainte Pierre and Kant, the author of *Paneuropa* in 1923, and the organizer of the first Pan-European Congress, held appropriately enough at Vienna in 1926. But the principal progenitor of the future European Community was in fact Jean Monnet, a cognac merchant who had attended the Paris Peace Conference in 1919 and who then worked for three years at the League of Nations before becoming gravely disillusioned; Monnet subsequently dealt with issues of joint industrial production during the Second World War. Just as the Congress System had a very specific motive—to combat revolution—Monnet and the French foreign minister, Robert Schuman, had a specific need—France required German coal to produce steel. At the same time, French leaders feared the consequences of a German economic revival, while British and American leaders wanted German support in their new contest against the Soviet Union. In 1950, French foreign minister Schuman presented Monnet's plan for the creation of a supranational authority, the European Coal and Steel Community, to be given control over coal and steel production in France, Germany and the Benelux countries. While the Congress System of 1815 to 1823 had taken a 'top-down' approach to the federation of Europe, Monnet and Schuman favoured an incremental approach to European unity—'the way to proceed was not at the top, at national level,' writes one historian, 'but rather "functionally", where collaboration could be shown to benefit all concerned'.[38]

Other changes were also taking place in the post-war years—Europe's loss of colonies, the introduction and improvement of nuclear weapons and the long rivalry of the two superpowers during the Cold War. These circumstances caused Europeans to lose interest in conventional military forces and to focus on achieving economic growth and greater social equality rather than on military might. The result, American historian James Sheehan writes, has been the transformation of Europe into a collection of pacific 'civilian' states, bound together by economic interdependence and a common aversion to warfare as much as by the institutions of the European Union. The most elusive goal of all has been the one shared with the Congress System—that of a common foreign policy. European states recognized the need for a common foreign policy in the Treaty of Maastricht—which called for 'the implementation of a common foreign and security policy including the eventual framing of a common defence policy'—but they have yet to achieve it.[39]

There is still another legacy—this one in the direction of international law. The dream of attaining international stability through a general guarantee—first suggested by the speculative philosophers, then incorporated into the proposals of Czartoryski and Pitt, next initiated by Castlereagh at Vienna and finally re-introduced by Ancillon and the Tsar at the Congress of Aix-la-Chapelle—also has its sequel. The Covenant of the League of Nations (Article 10) attempted to prevent external aggression threatening the territorial integrity of its member states. After the Nazi atrocities in World War II, the international tribunal at Nuremberg established not only 'crimes against humanity' but also 'crimes against peace'—defined as the 'planning, initiation or waging of a war of aggression or a war in violation of international treaties, agreements or assurances'. In Article 2 of the United Nations Charter, all signatories pledged to 'refrain in their international relations from the threat or use of force against the territorial integrity or political independence of any state'. Although this provision theoretically froze all existing borders between states, there was no strict mechanism for its enforcement in the Charter. Instead, the power to determine acts of aggression was handed over to the Security Council (Article 39). However, in the wake of North Korea's attack on South Korea in 1950, a new UN commission was formed with the task of defining international aggression; it concluded that 'aggression' was 'the use of force by a State or Government against another State or Government, in any manner ... for any reason or any purpose other than individual or collective self-defence or in pursuance of a decision ... of the United Nations'. Two decades later, on 14 December 1974, the General Assembly passed Resolution 3314, defining aggression as any armed invasion, attack, bombardment or violation by one state of the territory of another, and proscribing all wars of aggression as 'crime[s] against international peace'—but this resolution had no binding effect under international law. However, in 1998 the Rome Statute for an International Criminal Court—a voluntary compact—was finally enacted with the approval of 120 member states and went into effect in 2002. As recently as May 2010, at a conference at Kampala, Uganda, members of the International Criminal Court refined their definition of the crime of aggression and determined that parties could be tried for aggression commencing in 2017. Participation remains voluntary and states can even join the International Criminal Court while opting out of the rules covering international aggression. The jurisdiction of the court thus remains limited and still a far cry from the guarantee of all existing borders and territories from attack sought by many of the Congress statesmen two centuries ago.[40]

Like the relationships of Czartoryski and Gentz with the earlier philosophers of perpetual peace, the connections between the Congress System and the institutions of our own day have often been palpable and direct. Here we have only to consider a few of the scholar-statesmen who devoted themselves to the study of the Congress System but who were also active in the events of their own times: Sir Charles Webster, C.M. Woodhouse, Henry Kissinger and Dominique Villepin.

Webster—whose name has appeared repeatedly across the pages of this book—was secretary to the military section of the British delegation at the Paris Peace Conference in 1919. He famously wrote a study of the Congress of Vienna as one of the handbooks for the delegation, which noted that the defeated power, France, had attended the Congress and stirred up trouble for the victorious allied powers. The allies were careful not to repeat that mistake, and Germany did not participate in the peace conference, with disastrous results. Webster later became a strong supporter of the League of Nations. In the interwar years, he concluded an exhaustive study of the foreign policy of Castlereagh. Webster was not surprised at German rearmament, which he compared to that of France in 1818, but he was shocked at the way in which German rearmament was conducted by the Nazis, and at their 'use of violence in domestic affairs'; later, he opposed appeasement, criticizing the sacrifice of lesser states to aggressive nations like Germany and Italy. In 1939, Webster took leave from his academic post to work again at the British Foreign Office, where he was assigned the important task of helping to frame British policy towards the new United Nations; he participated in both the Dumbarton Oaks and San Francisco Conferences and contributed to the language of the Charter of the United Nations. There can be no doubt that the lessons of the Congress System were firmly in his mind as he helped shape the institutions of international cooperation for the future.[41] Soviet historians once took a more sinister view: they argued that from his study of early nineteenth-century diplomacy, Webster became a Russophobe; the object of the Congress System had been to keep Russia in check, and the new United Nations was deliberately designed to fulfil an analogous function towards the Soviet Union.

Another Congress scholar, C.M. Woodhouse, author of a biography of Capodistrias as well as several histories of modern Greece, helped organize resistance against the Nazis behind enemy lines in Greece during World War II. Later, he opposed the military dictatorship in Greece. Woodhouse was also active in the Anglo-American decision to overthrow Mossadegh, the Prime Minister of Iran, in the 1950s.

The most famous of all the Congress scholars by far, however, has been Henry Kissinger, National Security Adviser to President Nixon and Secretary of State to Presidents Nixon and Ford. His doctoral dissertation at Harvard, later published as the book *A World Restored*, was a detailed study of the Congress System. Kissinger viewed the central problem of the period as the confrontation with a revolutionary power (France) that did not recognize the 'legitimacy' of the existing international order. According to Kissinger, Metternich, 'the Continental statesman', used diplomacy to achieve his objectives because he no longer trusted in Austria's own military strength; Castlereagh, 'the Insular statesman', established close ties with the Continent to maintain a balance of power that would promote British commercial interests.[42] Metternich, says Kissinger, succeeded because he patiently separated Austria from Napoleon without embracing a form of popular nationalism that would have been destructive to the polyglot Austrian empire; Castlereagh succeeded because he rejected the demands of his countrymen for a punitive peace in favour of establishing a Continental equilibrium. Both, according to this future American Secretary of State, exhibited qualities of 'great' statesmanship:

> The test of a statesman, then, is his ability to recognize the real relationship of forces and to make this knowledge serve his ends. That Austria should seek stability was inherent in its geographic position and domestic structure. But that it would succeed, if only temporarily and however unwisely, in identifying its domestic legitimizing principle with that of the international order was the work of its Foreign Minister. That Great Britain should attempt to find security in a balance of power was the consequence of twenty-three years of intermittent warfare. But that it should emerge as a part of the concert of Europe was due to the efforts of a solitary individual.[43]

These statesmen were heroes in Kissinger's eyes, in part, because they brazenly pursued what they deemed as necessary policies even in defiance of popular opinion. The study of this period thus led Kissinger to value order and hierarchy in the international system, secrecy in negotiations, a willingness (for better or worse) to pursue policies that might be unpopular or misunderstood, the use of trade-offs and a willingness to the cooperate with different types of states.[44] Kissinger largely overlooked domestic considerations in favour of the *Primat der Aussenpolitik*—the primacy of foreign policy. Perhaps it was his very familiarity with the diplomacy of Castlereagh, Metternich, Alexander and Talleyrand that caused Kissinger to push for conversion of the bipolar world of the early Cold War into a more flexible multipolar system. Is it too great a stretch to see Nixon and Kissinger's reaching out to China during the Vietnam War as an echo of the *rapprochement* of Castlereagh and Metternich with France during the Polish-Saxon crisis at the Congress of Vienna? Was American involvement in the overthrow of Salvador Allende in Chile in 1973 analogous to the Austrian overthrow of revolutionary government in Naples or the French in Spain during the 1820s? Was Kissinger's practice of diplomacy, especially the veil of secrecy that surrounded his talks with the North Vietnamese, inspired by Castlereagh, who, as the foreign minister of a parliamentary state, resorted to secrecy in pursuing unpopular policies in his dealings with Continental autocrats?

Dominique Villepin, a French diplomat, published a detailed study of the Hundred Days in 2001, which won the prestigious *Grand Prix d'Histoire* of the Napoleonic Foundation. Two years later, Villepin caused a stir as French foreign minister when he opposed Anglo-American intervention in Iraq. Was it his extensive knowledge of the French experience, as the object of allied intervention in 1815, that made him acutely sensitive to the problems that might arise during an allied occupation of Iraq and which therefore caused him to urge a more cautious approach on Britain and the United States?

* * *

After the Congress of Verona, the Congress System lay in shambles. The dream of a system of formal cooperation by the great powers to supervise the destinies of Europe was quickly fading. No more great peacetime congresses would be held. The resolution of international disagreements through diplomacy rather than through conflict, the notion of negotiation among the great powers who, having resolved questions to their own satisfaction, would then impose their will on the rest of the world, was no more.

Nevertheless, the story of the Congress System continues to inspire, even as we may condemn the direction that it took, as a bold attempt by men in power—not merely philosophers—to set in motion a system to redirect the world from 20 years of war to peace. On 4 January, in the magnificent setting of a ball at the *Redoutensaal* of the Hofburg Palace—surrounded by dancers and musicians, the shimmering lights of a thousand candles, white and gilded rococo walls, parquet floors, French chairs lined with red satin and liveried servants—a buoyant Lord Castlereagh optimistically whispered into the ear of the Tsar, believing that the interminable Polish-Saxon Question had finally been resolved: '*Il commence l'âge d'or*—Now, the golden age begins.'[45] Whether their inspiration was to avoid the slaughter of total warfare, or the more selfish desire of preserving their own wealth, power and privilege from the onslaught of revolution—whether the mechanism they devised preserved the peace of Europe or was chiefly a means of repression—it was a sincere effort to reduce violence through collective action. As we look towards our own future in an increasingly multipolar world, we must ask—can such diverse powers as the United States, China, India, Russia and the European Union be similarly bound?[46] Are the threats posed by cyberwar, terrorism, global financial collapse and environmental disaster sufficient to draw nation-states together, as the threats of revolution and war once drew together the powers of Europe in 1815? Is there, in fact, the possibility of an evolution of world politics as a whole, 'from an international system to an international society, or from an international society to a world society'?[47] And if so, does the example of the earlier Congress System furnish any kind of useful paradigm? Will the 'great powers' of today be able to forge a more durable structure than their predecessors did in the Congress System?

If political scientists tend to look at the Congress System in terms of regimes and institutions, the historian has a broader mandate. The historian must consider the general context and the impact of the alliance on European society as a whole. For there can be no doubt that the Congress System has become a byword for reaction. It was the Congress System that restored Louis XVIII to the throne a second time in 1815 and kept him there; that enabled the conservative elites of Europe to stifle the student associations, the press, and the movement to establish liberal constitutions in Germany; that issued the counter-revolutionary declaration from Troppau; that crushed the constitutional monarchies in Naples, Piedmont and Spain without compromise. If the Congress System was intended to diminish violence, it also added to it by sending troops where revolutions had been bloodless. It was the great European alliance that permitted the execution of Marshal Ney and the hanging of Riego. So here, at the end of our journey, we arrive at the very problem with which we started. With revolutions against oppressive governments just two decades ago in Eastern Europe and with fresh revolutions having just occurred in Tunisia, Egypt, Libya, Syria and Yemen during the recent 'Arab Spring', there is a clear sense of the continuing struggle between the forces of democratization and the desperate efforts of elites to hold onto their power at almost any cost. Were the Congress statesmen reactionaries merely propping up 'decaying edifices' to preserve their own privileges? Did the Congress System impede social progress? One leading historian has written that we should not hold diplomats and statesmen responsible for achieving greater social and economic justice in their societies. Why not?

Yet, in wresting power from elites, there is also the quite evident danger that popular movements can lead to violence, anarchy and demagoguery. The Congress statesmen saw themselves as the champions of order, without which liberty is meaningless. So we must further ask: were the peoples in many parts of Europe—largely agricultural and illiterate—ready for the popular sovereignty demanded by radical and nationalist leaders in the first decade after the Napoleonic Wars? Would the granting of their demands have led to chaos, as it did at moments during the French Revolution? Is it always necessary, as one political scientist has recently suggested, for closed, authoritarian societies to experience a period of painful instability as they make the transition into becoming more open, democratic states?[48] And does this further mean that the methods of repression of the Congress statesmen were in some degree justified?

Or was there a middle ground between these extremes? Perhaps the true failure of the Congress statesmen was not in their resistance to the threat of violent revolution, but in their failure, arising from their paranoia, to countenance a greater degree of moderate change.[49] Should limits have been placed on the discretion of the restored kings of Naples and Spain, or restraints have been placed sooner on the Sultan in his massacres of the Greeks? Europe may well have been at a 'tipping point'—not only in France, but in Prussia, Russia, Poland, Spain, Portugal, Naples and Piedmont. Might new constitutions have been successfully established throughout the Continent with representative elements? Would the vision of the 'liberal' Tsar of 1814–18, assisted by Czartoryski and Capodistrias, for a federation of liberal states with national assemblies based on limited franchises, have been more appropriate than abandoning the alliance altogether or restricting its scope to the support of absolutist kings? Was this a great opportunity lost? Would such steps have led to gradual and peaceful changes that might have averted two world wars? Or would such efforts, at this moment in history and built upon such frail socio-economic foundations, have necessarily failed? Must we simply reconcile ourselves to praising the Congress statesmen for their contribution to procedures of international cooperation, while condemning the use they made of those procedures? And here, perhaps, is the crux of the dilemma faced in the decade of the Congresses that we are still facing today: how is it possible to achieve transformative social and political change, often injurious to powerful vested interests, and yet to preserve the rule of law—especially when the existing legal order has largely been created to protect those very vested interests? If change is achieved by pushing the rule of law aside, chaos results; if the rule of law is preserved, substantial change may be impeded. And an equally stubborn conundrum persists at the international level, where nations strive to develop and maintain mechanisms of cooperation without sacrificing their sovereignty. *'Il commence l'âge d'or'*, whispered Castlereagh to the Tsar in the first week of 1815. Two hundred years later, humankind is still waiting expectantly for the promised golden age to begin.

CHRONOLOGY

1769	Births of Napoleon, Castlereagh and Wellington.
1772	First Partition of Poland.
1773	Birth of Metternich.
1777	Birth of Alexander.
1789	Meeting of the Estates General at Versailles; storming of the Bastille.
1790	Talleyrand officiates at the *Fête de la Fédération*.
1792	Fall of the French monarchy; beginning of French Revolutionary Wars.
1793	Execution of Louis XVI; beginning of the 'Reign of Terror'; Second Partition of Poland.
1794	Fall of Robespierre.
1795	Kant's essay 'On Perpetual Peace'; French Directory formed; Third Partition of Poland.
1796	Bonaparte begins his Italian campaign.
1799	French Consulate.
1801	Murder of Paul I of Russia; Alexander becomes Tsar.
1802	Peace of Amiens.
1803	Czartoryski's memorandum to the Tsar.
1804	Francis I declares himself Emperor of Austria; Czartoryski drafts instructions for Russian envoy to Pitt; execution of Duc d'Enghien; Napoleon makes himself Emperor of the French.
1805	Pitt's reply to Russian post-war plans; Third Coalition; Battle of Austerlitz; Naval battle at Trafalgar.
1806	Creation of Confederation of the Rhine; end of Holy Roman Empire; defeat of Prussia at Battle of Jena; creation of Continental System; Metternich made ambassador to France.
1807	Battles of Eylau and Friedland; Peace of Tilsit; creation of Duchy of Warsaw; Stein's reforms in Prussia; Hardenberg's 'Riga Memorial'.
1808	German princes at Erfurt; Joseph made King of Spain; Spanish uprising.
1809	Wellington advances into Spain; defeat of Austria at Battle of Wagram; duel between Castlereagh and Canning; Metternich becomes foreign minister.
1810	Marriage of Napoleon and Marie Louise; appointment of Hardenberg.
1812	Napoleon's invasion of Russia; *Junta* of Cadiz drafts Constitution of 1812; Battle of Borodino; burning of Moscow; Napoleon's retreat; General Yorck signs Convention of Taurrogen; Castlereagh appointed Foreign Secretary.

1813 Metternich's Dresden interview with Napoleon; Treaties of Kalisch and Reichenbach; Battle of Leipzig; Frankfurt Proposals; Battle of Vitoria; Castlereagh's mission to the continent.

1814 Castlereagh and Metternich at Basel; allied conferences at Langres; allied invasion of Switzerland and France; negotiations at Châtillon; Treaty of Chaumont; royalist declaration at Bordeaux; allied occupation of Paris; Alexander with Talleyrand; abdication of Napoleon and Treaty of Fontainebleau; restoration of the Bourbons; Louis XVIII grants *Charte*; Talleyrand Ministry; French keep stolen artworks; First Treaty of Paris; Belgian provinces united with Netherlands; Austria gains control of North Italy; Hardenberg's memorandum in Paris; visit of the allied sovereigns to London; Congress of Vienna assembles in September; procedural question; Polish-Saxon dispute; Castlereagh's audiences with the Tsar; Hardenberg cooperates with Austria and Britain; 'Conspiracy of 23 October'; King of Prussia repudiates Hardenberg; Metternich and Castlereagh retract offer of Saxony to Prussia; Rhineland proposal for the King of Saxony; Hardenberg's outburst; Treaty of Ghent concludes War of 1812.

1815 Secret Alliance of 3 January between Austria, France and Britain; meetings of the Statistical Committee; final negotiation of territorial settlement of Central Europe; negotiations of German Committee on future German Confederation; Austria agrees to oust Murat; discussion of possible 'General Guarantee'; Castlereagh leaves Vienna; continuing negotiations on Switzerland, Scandinavia, rights of German Jews, slave trade, European rivers, and diplomatic precedence; Napoleon lands near Antibes and marches to Paris; Allied Declaration against Napoleon; 'Hundred Days' (*les Cent Jours*); defeat of Murat; King of Prussia promises his subjects a constitution; Vienna Final Act; Battle of Waterloo; second restoration of Louis XVIII; Talleyrand-Fouché Ministry; Treaty of the Holy Alliance; Second Peace of Paris with return of stolen artworks, payment of reparations, losses of territory and occupation of France by allied armies; resignation of Talleyrand and appointment of Richelieu government in France; Quadruple Alliance; unrest in Britain against Corn Laws; trial and execution of Ney.

1817 *Burschenschaften* members celebrate at Wartburg (*Wartburgfest*); reduction of allied occupation forces in France.

1818 Spain seeks help of allied powers against rebellious colonies; Congress of Aix-la-Chapelle; France borrows from Baring to pay reparations; evacuation of France by allies; debate on future of the European Alliance; Quadruple Alliance preserved but France invited to allied reunions; Castlereagh rejects the Russian interpretation of the alliance; allies agree to British terms for mediation between Spain and her colonies; allies discuss Ancillon's proposed treaty to guarantee borders but not thrones; allies also discuss slave trade, piracy, status of German Jews, Treaty of Kiel and Baden-Bavarian dispute.

1819 Assassination of Kotzebue; Metternich meets Hardenberg and King of Prussia at Teplitz; Carlsbad Decrees; meeting of Diet of German Confederation;

	Peterloo; Six Acts; dismissal of liberals Humboldt and Boyen from Prussian cabinet and defeat of Prussian reform movement.
1820	Riego's *Pronunciamento* and rebellion in Spain; Cato Street conspiracy; assassination of Duc de Berri in France; Second Richelieu government in Paris; Ferdinand VII accepts Spanish Constitution of 1812; Tsar proposes allied intervention in Spain; Castlereagh's State Paper of 5 May 1820; conclusion of final terms for German Confederation; revolution in Naples; King of Naples accepts Spanish Constitution of 1812; revolution in Portugal; Tsar attends Polish *Sejm*; Congress of Troppau; rivalry of Metternich and Capodistrias; mutiny in the Semenovsky Regiment; drafting of counter-revolutionary documents: 'System of Conduct', *Protocole préliminaire*, 'Act of Guarantee', Troppau Circular; allied invitation to King of Naples.
1821	Congress of Laibach; arrival of King of Naples; Austrian military preparations; revolution in Piedmont; movement of Russian troops; Austrian victory against Neapolitan constitutionalists at Rieti; defeat of Piedmontese revolutionaries; Austrian occupation of Naples and Piedmont; Prince Ypsilantis' Orthodox Christian uprising in Moldavia; Alexander rejects Ypsilantis' request for Russian support; flight of Ypsilantis; spread of the Greek rebellion to the Peloponnese; Russia permits Ottoman force to enter Danubian Principalities; brutal murder of the Patriarch of Constantinople; Russian 'Four Points'; Stroganov's withdrawal from Constantinople; Capodistrias urges Russian intervention; death of Napoleon; Castlereagh meets Metternich in Hanover; fall of Richelieu government in Paris.
1822	Alexander avoids war against Sultan; Tatishchev mission in Vienna; continuing massacres of Christians and Muslims in Ottoman Empire; resignation of Capodistrias; Castlereagh's suicide; Canning becomes Foreign Secretary; Congress of Verona; Montmorency's 'Three Questions'; Parallel Instructions for Envoys in Madrid; resignation of Montmorency in Paris.
1823	Chateaubriand becomes foreign minister; Louis XVIII asks Chambers to intervene in Spain; French expedition under Duc d'Angoulême restores Ferdinand's authority; Ferdinand's reactionary rule; Byron goes to Greece; Polignac Memorandum; President Monroe issues 'Monroe Doctrine'; Ferdinand proposes conference in Paris on Spanish colonies, which Canning refuses.
1824	Tsar Alexander proposes new Congress for Greek question; Canning refuses; death of Louis XVIII; Ibrahim Pasha plans depopulation of the Peloponnese; Tsar plans campaign against Ottoman Empire.
1825	Death of Alexander I; Decembrist revolt; Nicholas I becomes Tsar.
1826	Wellington sent to St Petersburg; Mahmud II destroys Janissaries.
1827	Treaty of London; Battle of Navarino; Canning becomes Prime Minister but dies four months later.
1829	Catholic Emancipation in Great Britain.
1830	July Revolution overthrows Charles X in France; Metternich and Nesselrode conclude '*Chiffon de Carlsbad*'; revolutions in Belgium, Poland and Italy;

Belgian question handled by ambassadorial conference in London; Belgium made independent; Polish rebels crushed; fall of Wellington's government in Britain.
1832 Passage of Reform Bill in Great Britain.
1833 First Mehemet Ali crisis; Münchengrätz Alliance of Austria, Russia and Prussia.
1834 Palmerston's 'Quadruple Alliance' of Britain, France, Spain and Portugal.
1839 Beginning of Second Mehemet Ali Crisis.
1848 Revolutions of 1848.
1852 Death of Wellington.
1854 Start of Crimean War.
1856 Congress of Paris.
1859 Unification of Italy; death of Metternich.
1863 Revolution in Poland.
1871 Unification of Germany.
1878 Congress of Berlin.
1914 Outbreak of World War I.

DRAMATIS PERSONAE

The rulers of Europe

Alexander I, Tsar of Russia (1777–1825). All-powerful Emperor of Russia, who began his reign in 1801 after the murder of his father, Paul I.

Ali Pasha of Janina (1740–1822). Independent Governor of Epirus in the Ottoman Empire.

Charles XIV Jean, King of Sweden (1763–1844). Born as Jean Bernadotte, this French general was elected Crown Prince of Sweden in 1810 and became King of Sweden and Norway in 1818.

Ferdinand IV, King of Naples (1751–1825). Bourbon King who fled from Naples to Sicily during the Napoleonic Wars but was later restored in Naples after the fall of Murat.

Ferdinand VII, King of Spain (1784–1833). Bourbon King held captive in France by Napoleon from 1808 until his restoration in 1814.

Francis, Emperor of Austria (1768–1835). Habsburg prince who became Holy Roman Emperor in 1792, founded the Austrian Empire in 1804 and abandoned the title of Holy Roman Emperor in 1806.

Frederick Augustus I, King of Saxony (1750–1827). One of the last monarchs in Europe to abandon Napoleon.

Frederick William III, King of Prussia (1770–1840). Starting his reign in 1797, he at first pursued a policy of neutrality in the Napoleonic wars. Devoted to his beautiful wife, Queen Louise, who died in 1810, he vacillated in his relations with Napoleon, Stein, Hardenberg, the Tsar and Metternich.

George IV, King of the United Kingdom (1762–1830). Prince Regent from 1811 to 1820, his scorn for his wife, Queen Caroline, led to a national crisis when he ascended the throne.

Louis XVI, King of France (1754–93). By summoning the Estates General to Versailles in 1789, this ruler inadvertently precipitated the French Revolution.

Louis XVIII, King of France (1755–1824). A younger brother of Louis XVI, who emigrated to Russia and England before being restored to the French throne in 1814.

Mahmud II, Sultan of the Ottoman Empire (1785–1839). The all-powerful ruler of the Ottoman Empire, who took control after the fall of Selim III and faced threats from provincial governors, Christian subjects and European powers.

DRAMATIS PERSONAE

Joachim Murat, King of Naples (1767–1815). French cavalry commander who married Caroline Bonaparte and became ruler of Naples in 1808. After the Battle of Leipzig, he deserted Napoleon and concluded a treaty with Austria.
Napoleon Bonaparte (1769–1821). French General, First Consul, and 'Emperor of the French' from December 1804 until his abdication in May 1814, and briefly during the 'Hundred Days' (*Cent Jours*) from March to June 1815.
Nicholas I, Tsar of Russia (1796–1855). Youngest brother of Alexander I.

* * *

Statesmen, diplomats, generals and others

William A'Court (1779–1860). British ambassador to Sicily, Naples and Spain.
Johann Peter Friedrich von Ancillon (1767–1837). Conservative Prussian court councillor, tutor to the Crown Prince and senior official in the Prussian foreign ministry.
Duc d'Angoulême (1775–1844). Eldest son of Charles X, who fought along with the *émigrés* and commanded the French forces invading Spain in 1823. He married his cousin, the daughter of Louis XVI and Marie Antoinette.
Comte d'Artois (1757–1836). Younger brother of Louis XVIII and the leader of the ultra-royalist party. He reigned from 1824 to 1830 as Charles X.
Count von Bernstorff (1769–1835). Danish foreign minister who represented Denmark at the Congress of Vienna. He became Danish minister to Berlin, but in 1818 he changed his allegiance to become foreign minister of Prussia.
George Canning (1770–1827). British Foreign Secretary from 1807 to 1809, ambassador to Portugal from 1814 to 1816, Foreign Secretary a second time from 1822 to 1827, and Prime Minister for four months in 1827.
Stratford Canning (1786–1880). Cousin of George Canning, who served as British envoy to Switzerland, attended the Congress of Vienna and became British ambassador in Constantinople.
Count John Capodistrias (1776–1831). Cypriot Greek who rose in the Tsar's service and became co-foreign minister with Nesselrode until his resignation in 1822. Later he was the first President of Greece.
Marquis de Caraman (1762–1839). French ambassador to Austria, who attended the Congresses of Troppau, Laibach and Verona.
Lord Castlereagh (1769–1822). Politician and statesman from Ireland who became Chief Secretary of Ireland, steered the Act of Union through the Irish Parliament, became Secretary for War and Colonies, fought a duel with George Canning in 1809, and served as Foreign Secretary of Great Britain from 1812 to 1822.
Marquis de Caulaincourt (1773–1827). Appointed ambassador to Russia in 1807, he accompanied Napoleon on his retreat from Moscow in 1812, became Napoleon's foreign minister, represented France at the Congress of Châtillon, and negotiated the Treaty of Fontainebleau with Alexander.

François-René de Chateaubriand (1768–1848). French writer who first sympathized with Bonaparte, later advocated the return of the Bourbons, joined the ultra-royalists, became ambassador to England, represented France at the Congress of Verona and became French foreign minister.

Grand Duke Constantine of Russia (1779–1831). A younger brother of Alexander I, who served as the Governor of Poland.

Prince Adam Czartoryski (1770–1861). A prince from an aristocratic Polish family who was sent to St Petersburg as a young man, where he befriended Alexander, the future Tsar. Czartoryski served as Russian foreign minister from 1804 to 1806, advised Alexander on Polish matters at the Congress of Vienna, and helped organize the unsuccessful Polish Revolution of 1830.

Prince Esterhazy (1786–1866). Wealthy Hungarian noble who became Austrian ambassador to Great Britain.

Joseph Fouché, Duc d'Otrante (1759–1820). A former Jacobin who voted to execute Louis XVI, later helped bring down Robespierre, became Napoleon's chief of police and played an important role in securing the second restoration of Louis XVIII in 1815.

Friedrich von Gentz (1764–1832). A student of Immanuel Kant's, who translated Burke's *Reflections on the Revolution in France* into German, entered the Prussian diplomatic service and became an important writer and publicist. Later he entered Austrian service and became the chief assistant to Metternich and 'Secretary' to all of the European Congresses.

Prince Alexander Golitsyn (1773–1844). A boyhood friend of Alexander's, who later became the head of the Holy Synod.

Count Yuri Golovkin (1762–1846). Russian ambassador to Austria, 1818 to 1822.

Robert Gordon (1791–1847). Younger brother of the Earl of Aberdeen, who acted as an envoy to Austria, participated in the Congresses of Troppau and Laibach, and became British ambassador to Austria from 1841 to 1847.

Patriarch Gregorius V of Constantinople (1746–1821). Spiritual leader of the Orthodox Christians in the Ottoman Empire.

Prince Karl August von Hardenberg (1750–1822). Hanoverian who entered Prussian service, becoming chief minister in 1810 until his death in 1822.

Wilhelm von Humboldt (1767–1835). Prussian thinker, linguist, reformer and diplomat, who assisted Hardenberg at the Congress of Vienna.

Johann Heinrich Jung-Stilling (1740–1817). German Pietist whose works influenced Tsar Alexander I.

August von Kotzebue (1761–1819). German writer and dramatist, who held positions in Vienna and St Petersburg, but was assassinated in 1819.

Baroness Julie von Krüdener (1764–1824). Mystical widow who developed spiritual ties with Tsar Alexander I.

General von Krusemarck (1767–1822). Prussian General who attended the Congresses of Vienna and Troppau.

Marqués de Labrador (1755–1852). Spanish envoy to the Congress of Vienna.

Dramatis Personae

Comte de La Ferronnays (1777–1842). French ambassador to Russia, who attended the Congresses of Troppau, Laibach and Verona.

Frédéric César de La Harpe (1754–1838). Swiss liberal employed by Catherine the Great as a tutor to the Grand Dukes Alexander and Constantine.

Francisco Martinez de La Rosa (1787–1862). Spanish poet who headed a moderate constitutional government during the Spanish Revolution.

Count Lebzeltern (1774–1854). Austrian ambassador to Russia.

Count Lieven (1774–1839). Russian ambassador to Britain.

Countess Lieven (1785–1857). Wife of Count Lieven.

Prince de Ligne (1735–1814). Austrian Field Marshal and famous wit at the Congress of Vienna.

Earl of Liverpool (1770–1828). British Prime Minister from 1812 to 1827, who supported the policies of both Castlereagh and Canning.

Louis Philippe, Duc d'Orléans (1773–1850). Cousin of the Bourbons, who became 'King of the French' after the July Revolution in 1830.

Marie Louise (1791–1847). Daughter of Emperor Francis I of Austria, who married Napoleon in 1810; after Napoleon's fall, she became the Duchess of Parma.

Count von Merveldt (1764–1815). General in the Austrian army, who became Austrian ambassador to Great Britain from 1814 until his death in 1815.

Prince Clemens von Metternich (1773–1859). Wealthy Rhenish nobleman who followed his father's footsteps in entering the service of the Habsburgs. He married the granddaughter of Prince von Kaunitz and became Austrian ambassador in Dresden, Berlin and Paris. He then served as Austrian foreign minister from 1809 until 1848, also becoming Chancellor in 1821. Metternich presided over the allied proceedings at the Congresses of Vienna, Aix-la-Chapelle, Troppau, Laibach and Verona.

Duc de Montmorency (1767–1826). Liberal French nobleman who turned against the Revolution during the Reign of Terror and became a royalist conspirator. He was appointed foreign minister in 1821 and represented France at the Congress of Verona.

Count Münster (1766–1839). Hanoverian diplomat who attended the Congress of Vienna and reported to George IV as ruler of Hanover.

Count Karl Robert Nesslerode (1780–1862). Baltic German who entered the Russian navy, joined the Russian diplomatic service and became foreign minister of Russia. Nesselrode attended the Congresses of Vienna, Troppau, Laibach and Verona.

Marshal Ney (1769–1815). French cavalry commander, known as 'the bravest of the brave', who fought in the French Revolutionary Wars and under Napoleon at Jena, Eylau, Friedland, Borodino and Waterloo. Ney was tried and executed for treason in 1815.

Duc de Pasquier (1767–1862). Member of the liberal nobility who was arrested during the Reign of Terror and was released after Robespierre's death. Pasquier became an official under the Napoleonic Empire and foreign minister under Louis XVIII from November 1819 to December 1821.

General Pepe (1783–1855). Commander of the Neapolitan constitutional army during the Neapolitan Revolution.

William Pitt the Younger (1759–1806). Prime Minister of Great Britain from 1783 to 1801 and from 1804 to 1806; a mentor to both Castlereagh and Canning.

Prince Jules de Polignac (1780–1847). Ultra-royalist who became French ambassador to Britain, held important conferences with Canning on Spain's former colonies, and became head of the French government under Charles X.

Count Charles-André Pozzo di Borgo (1764–1842). Corsican rival to Napoleon, who entered the Russian service and became Russian ambassador to France from 1814 to 1835.

General Radetzky (1766–1858). Austrian Chief-of-Staff during the final stages of the Napoleonic Wars; he later commanded Austrian forces suppressing the Revolutions of 1848.

Count Razumovsky (1752–1836). Russian envoy to Austria, whose splendid palace burnt down during the Congress of Vienna.

Duc de Richelieu (1766–1822). Descendent of the famous cardinal, who became an *émigré* during the French Revolution, was made Governor of Novorossiya (or 'New Russia', an area including Odessa and the Crimea) by Alexander I, was appointed French foreign minister in 1815 and represented France at the Congress of Aix-la-Chapelle in 1818.

Major Riego (1784–1823). Army officer, whose *pronunciamento* triggered the Spanish Revolution of 1820.

Maximilien Robespierre (1758–1794). French revolutionary leader who sponsored the 'Reign of Terror'.

Jean-Jacques Rousseau (1712–1778). Genevan writer and philosopher whose ideas stirred the French revolutionaries as well as the later romantics.

Prince Ruffo. Representative of the King of Naples at the Congress of Laibach.

Duchess Dorothée von Sagan (1793–1862). Youngest daughter of the Duchess of Courland, who married Talleyrand's nephew and accompanied Talleyrand to the Congress of Vienna.

Duchess Wilhelmine von Sagan (1781–1839). Eldest daughter of the Duchess of Courland, who had an affair with Metternich, which she ended at the time of the Congress of Vienna.

Abbé de Saint-Pierre (1658–1743). Author of a plan for 'perpetual peace'.

Baron vom und zum Stein (1757–1831). Imperial knight from Nassau, who entered Prussian service and became chief minister after the Prussian defeat at Jena. He introduced the abolition of serfdom, municipal reform, free trade in land, and universal conscription. Napoleon forced his dismissal at the end of 1808. Stein later enlisted in the Tsar's service and attended the Congress of Vienna as the Tsar's chief advisor on German affairs.

Lord Charles Stewart (1778–1854). Younger half-brother of Lord Castlereagh, who fought in the Peninsula Wars, served as ambassador to Prussia from 1813 to 1814 and as ambassador to Austria from 1814 to 1823.

Dramatis Personae

Alexander Stourdza (1791–1854). Conservative Orthodox Christian intellectual of Greek and Romanian descent, brother of Roxanne Stourdza, diplomat at the service of the Tsar, assistant to Capodistrias and main draftsman of the Holy Alliance.

Roxanne Stourdza (1786–1844). Lady-in-waiting to the Empress Elizabeth, follower of Jung-Stilling and Madame de Krudener and 'spiritual wife' of Tsar Alexander I.

Lord Strangford (1780–1855). British ambassador to Constantinople.

Baron Stroganov (1769–1857). Russian ambassador to Constantinople.

Sir Charles Stuart (1779–1845). British ambassador to France from 1815 to 1824.

Duc de Sully (1560–1641). Author of an early plan for European confederation.

Prince Talleyrand (1754–1838). French nobleman and cleric who sided with the early French revolutionaries, fled to America during the Reign of Terror and served as foreign minister to the Directory, Napoleon and Louis XVIII. Talleyrand helped to bring Napoleon to power in 1799 and to restore the French King in 1814. He negotiated the First Peace of Paris and represented France at the Congress of Vienna, but resigned during the negotiation of the Second Peace of Paris.

Count Tatishchev (1767–1845). Russian diplomat, who served as ambassador to Spain.

Comte de Villèle (1773–1854). President of the French Council and head of the French government from 1822 to 1827.

Baron de Vitrolles (1774–1854). French nobleman who played a key role in the restoration of Louis XVIII in 1814.

Tudor Vladimirescu (1780–1821). Rebel leader of Romanian peasants in 1821.

Count Vorontsov (1744–1832). Russian diplomat in London.

Sir Henry Wellesley (1773–1847). Duke of Wellington's youngest brother and British ambassador to Spain, 1809 to 1821, and to Austria, 1823 to 1831.

Duke of Wellington (1769–1852). Anglo-Irish nobleman who attended military academy in France, became a leading British general after serving in Ireland, India and the Peninsular Wars, defeated the French in Spain in 1814, defeated Napoleon at Waterloo in 1815 and was placed in charge of the occupation army in France. Wellington attended the Congresses of Vienna, Aix-la-Chapelle and Verona, and later became Prime Minister of the United Kingdom.

Baron von Wessenberg (1773–1858). Austrian diplomat who assisted Metternich at the Congress of Vienna.

William Wilberforce (1759–1833). English Member of Parliament and friend of William Pitt the Younger, who led the movement against the slave trade.

Prince Wittgenstein (1770–1851). Conservative councillor to the King of Prussia.

Prince Alexander Ypsilantis (1792–1828). Greek Phanariot *aide-de-camp* to Tsar Alexander I, who crossed into the Principalities and proclaimed a rebellion against the Ottoman Sultan in 1821.

Count Zichy. Austrian ambassador to Prussia.

NOTES

1. The European State System and the Napoleonic Wars

1. In *The Age of Democratic Revolution*, R.R. Palmer applied this threefold classification scheme to describe the political institutions of *ancien régime* Europe. In particular, for the 'middle zone' he wrote: 'Between the eastern monarchies and France there was a broad middle zone, a world of miniscule states, princely, ecclesiastical, and republican, into which Germany, Italy, Switzerland, and the Netherlands were divided.' French historians Roland Mousnier and Ernest Labrousse in *Le XVIIIe Siècle: Révolution Intellectuelle, Technique et Politique, 1715–1815* (Paris: PUF, 1953) preferred to distribute the states of eighteenth-century Europe geographically into five groups: Western (Britain, Holland and France), Southern (Spain, Portugal and Italy), Eastern (Russia, Poland, Turkey), Central (Switzerland, the German and Danubian States, the Holy Roman Empire, the Imperial Princes, the Habsburgs, the Hohenzollerns) and Northern (Denmark and Sweden). Even earlier, the German historian A.H.L. Heeren simply bifurcated *ancien régime* Europe into a 'Southern' and 'Northern European States-System': Heeren, *A Manual of the History of the Political System of Europe and Its Colonies* (London: H.G. Bohn, 1846). In *Inventing Eastern Europe* (Stanford, 1994), cultural historian Larry Wolff argues that the division of Europe between East and West was in part an invention of the Enlightenment, and that French *philosophes* deliberately exaggerated the backwardness of the East. On the variety of *ancien régime* states, see also Philip Bobbitt, *The Shield of Achilles: War, Peace and the Course of History* (London: Allen Lane, 2002).
2. Sergei F. Platonov, *The Time of Troubles: A Historical Study of the Internal Study of the Internal Crisis and Social Struggle in Sixteenth and Seventeenth Century Muscovy* (Lawrence: University Press of Kansas, 1970).
3. Alexander Bitis, *Russia and the Eastern Question: Army, Government and Society, 1815–1833* (Oxford: Oxford University Press/British Academy, 2006), p. 44.
4. Bitis, *Russia and the Eastern Question*, pp. 19–21, 24.
5. Bitis, *Russia and the Eastern Question*, pp. 44–50. These included more reliance on skirmishers, the training of recruits under simulated battlefield conditions, a greater use of bayonet charges and the granting of greater freedom of action to the infantry. According to historian Janet Hartley, Russia possessed 104,654 infantry in 1763 and an army of 446,654 infantry by 1801. See Janet Hartley, *Russia, 1762–1825: Military Power, the State and the People* (London, 2008), pp. 8–9.

6. Michael Speransky, cited in Marc Raeff, *Michael Speransky, Statesman of Imperial Russia, 1772–1839* (The Hague: M. Nijhoff, 1957), pp. 121–22.
7. By 1801, Russia's population had reached 40 million, including 225,000 nobles, 215,000 clergy, 119,000 merchants and 15,000 officers and bureaucrats. Eighty-five per cent of the country were serfs, of whom 20 million were privately owned and 13 million were state peasants. See Marie-Pierre Rey, *Alexandre I* (Paris: Flammarion, Grandes Biographies, 2009), pp. 118–19.
8. The question of the 'decline' of the Ottoman Empire, once one of the great certitudes of nineteenth-century history, has now become controversial. See M.S. Anderson, *The Eastern Question, 1774–1923: A Study in International Relations* (London: St Martins' Press, 1966), p. xiv: 'The dangerous weakness of the Ottoman Empire which was made explicit by this war had been visible well before 1768'; D.G. Clayton, *Britain and the Eastern Question: Missolonghi to Gallipoli* (London: University of London Press, 1971); Stanford Shaw, *Between Old and New: The Ottoman Empire under Sultan Selim III, 1789–1807* (Cambridge, MA: Harvard University Press, 1971); Malcolm Yapp, *The Making of the Modern Middle East, 1798–1923* (London: Longman, 1987), argues that the Ottoman Empire was in fact making a recovery in this period; H. İnalcık and D. Quartaert, *An Economic and Social History of the Ottoman Empire, 1300–1914* (Cambridge: Cambridge University Press, 1994); A.L. Macfie, *The Eastern Question, 1774–1923* (London: Longman, 1996), pp. 5–7, dates the decline from as early as the sixteenth century: 'For a complex variety of reasons—including a weakening of the authority of the Sultanate; the collapse of the *devshirme* (Christian slave levy) and *timar* (land holding) systems; inadequate tax revenue; over-population; loss of trade (in the second half of the sixteenth century the India trade was increasingly transferred to the Atlantic route); and widespread corruption—the heavily centralised system of government created by the early sultans came under increasing strain'; Cemal Kafadar, 'The question of Ottoman decline', *Harvard Middle Eastern and Islamic Review* 4 (1997–98), pp. 30–75; Donald Quataert, *The Ottoman Empire, 1700–1922* (Cambridge: Cambridge University Press, 2000), p. 54: 'During the long nineteenth century, 1798–1922, the earlier Ottoman patterns of political and economic life remained generally recognizable in many ways. Territorial losses continued and frontiers shrank; statesmen at the center and in the provinces continued their contestations for power and access to taxable resources; and the international economy loomed ever more important. And yet, much was new. The forces triggering the losses now became increasingly complex, now involving domestic rebellions as well as the familiar imperial wars'; Caroline Finkel, *Osman's Dream: The Story of the Ottoman Empire, 1300–1923* (New York: Basic Books, 2005); Karen Barkey, *The Empire of Difference: the Ottomans in Comparative Perspective* (Cambridge: Cambridge University Press, 2008), emphasizes elements of resilience and longevity but argues that the attempt to reform the empire by turning it into a nation-state inevitably created strains and ended earlier policies of toleration; M. Şükrü Hanioğlu, *A Brief History of the Late Ottoman Empire* (Princeton, NJ: Princeton University Press, 2008), p. 203: 'The history of the

Ottoman Empire exhibits several major dynamics that overlap and, at times, contradict each other. First among these is the struggle between center and periphery. Perhaps the central theme of late Ottoman history is the attempt of the central government in the imperial capital to assert its control over a loosely held periphery which had gradually accumulated administrative, economic and even diplomatic independence of the center. The seepage of power to the periphery peaked in 1808 ... Defense of the empire in the age of modern warfare demanded a large and professional army and navy equipped with advanced weaponry; the maintenance of such military focus depended on effective taxation; and effective taxation was not commensurate with the rule of local notables. Instead it required an effective, centralized bureaucracy'; Baki Tezcan, *The Second Ottoman Empire: Political and Social Transformation in the Early Modern World* (Cambridge: Cambridge University Press, 2010), pp. 9–10, notes that 'the conventional narrative of Ottoman history—that in the late sixteenth century the Ottoman Empire entered a prolonged period of decline marked by steadily increasing military decay and institutional corruption has been discarded', and further argues, on pp. 191–244, that there was a transformation of the empire from 1580 to 1826, a 'relative democratization of political privileges', which led to the subjection of non-Muslims to second class status, attracting the intervention of the European Powers, and this in turn contributed to the collapse of 1826, rather than a straightforward decline.

9. H. Arnold Barton, *Scandinavia in the Revolutionary Era, 1760–1815* (Minneapolis, 1986), pp. 3–60; R.M. Hatton, 'Scandinavia and the Baltic', *The New Cambridge Modern History*, vol. vii (Cambridge, 1966), pp. 339–64; David G. Kirby, *Northern Europe in the Early Modern Period: The Baltic World, 1492–1772* (London, 1990) and *The Baltic World, 1772–1993: Europe's Northern Periphery in an Age of Change* (London, 1995), pp. 46–74.
10. Piotr S. Wandycz, *The Price of Freedom: A History of East Central Europe from the Middle Ages to the Present*, 2nd edn (London: Routledge, 2001), pp. 85–90: 'Like contemporary Spain, the Commonwealth had grown too big and lost its capability of translating potential power into actual strength' (p. 87).
11. W.H. Zawadzki, *A Man of Honour: Adam Czartoryski as a Statesman of Russia and Poland, 1795–1831* (Oxford: Oxford University Press, 1993), pp. 12–13.
12. Zawadzki, *A Man of Honour*, p. 12.
13. These powers deliberately stirred up further trouble by demanding toleration for Protestant and Orthodox Christian dissenters in Catholic Poland.
14. 'The first partition had occurred because of the Commonwealth's weakness; the second and third took place when it was reforming itself and gaining strength. This the partitioning powers would not tolerate ... Polish and foreign historians have endlessly debated whether the Commonwealth fell because of its internal decomposition or because its neighbors were determined to pull it down. There is no single answer, since various elements entered into the picture. The Commonwealth, having failed to resolve its internal problems in the seventeenth century ... gradually ceased to be a factor of power and stability in the region.

It had either to reform itself or fall victim to the partitioning principle then practiced.' Wandycz: *Price of Freedom*, pp. 133–34. See also, Herbert H. Kaplan, *The First Partition of Poland* (New York: Columbia University Press, 1962); Robert H. Lord, *The Second Partition of Poland: A Study in Diplomatic History* (Cambridge, MA: Harvard University Press, 1915); Adam Zamoyski, *The Last King of Poland* (London: Jonathan Cape, 1992); Jerzy T. Lukowski, *The Partitions of Poland, 1772, 1793, 1795* (Harlow: Addison Wesley Longman Higher Education, 1998); Larry Wolff, *The Vatican and Poland in the Age of the Partitions* (New York: distributed by Columbia University Press, 1988) and *The Idea of Galicia: History and Fantasy in Habsburg Political Culture* (Stanford: Stanford University Press, 2010), pp. 13–62; Norman Davies, *God's Playground: A History of Poland* (New York: Columbia University Press, 1982), vol. 1: *The Origins to 1795*, pp. 409–12, 511–46; Adam Zamoyski, *Poland: A History* (New York: Hippocrene, 2012), pp. 189–217; and Jerzy Lukowski and W. Hubert Zawadzki, *A Concise History of Poland* (Cambridge: Cambridge University Press, 2001), pp. 90–106.

15. For centuries, the Habsburgs had been the most distinguished ruling house of Europe. In the sixteenth century, Charles V had inherited the Netherlands, Spain, Austria, Naples, Sicily, Sardinia and the Franche-Comté. Charles later divided his empire between his son Philip, who became King of Spain, and his younger brother Ferdinand, who became the Holy Roman Emperor. Through his wife, Ferdinand also inherited the kingdoms of Bohemia and Hungary. After the War of the Spanish Succession, Spain was ruled by a branch of the Bourbon family, but the Austrian Habsburgs obtained the Austrian Netherlands (Belgium), Milan and Naples. This gave them an interest in Italy as well as Central Europe.

16. For a brief survey of developments in Austria under the *ancien régime*, see Charles W. Ingrao, *The Habsburg Monarchy, 1618–1815*, 2nd edn (Cambridge: Cambridge University Press, 2000).

17. Friedrich Meinecke, *The Age of German Liberation, 1795–1815*, ed. Peter Paret (Berkeley: University of California Press, 1977), p. 4.

18. For an account of Switzerland in the seventeenth and eighteenth centuries, see J. Murray Luck, *A History of Switzerland* (Palo Alto, CA: SPOSS, 1985), pp. 175–304. See pp. 305–16 for the French entry into Switzerland in 1798.

19. Christopher Duggan, *A Concise History of Italy* (Cambridge: Cambridge University Press, 1994), pp. 9–30, 60–86; John A. Davis, *Naples and Napoleon: Southern Italy and the European Revolutions* (Oxford: Oxford University Press, 2006), pp. 15–70; Franco Venturi, *Italy and the Enlightenment: Studies in a Cosmopolitan Century* (London: Longman, 1972), pp. 103–33, 154–64, 198–291; Michael Broers, *Napoleonic Imperialism and the Savoyard Monarchy, 1773–1821: State Building in Piedmont* (Lewiston: Edwin Mellen Press, 1997), pp. 51–163; Spencer M. DiScala, *Italy from Revolution to Republic: 1700 to the Present* (Boulder: Westview Press, 1995), pp. 3–19; Dino Carpanetto and Giuseppe Ricuperati, *Italy in the Age of Reason, 1685–1789* (London: Longman, 1987); Tim Blanning, *The Pursuit of Glory: Europe 1648–1815* (New York: Allen Lane, 2007), pp. 256–60; John Robertson, 'Enlightenment, Reform and Monarchy in Italy', in Gabriel

Paquette (ed.), *Enlightened Reform in Southern Europe and its Atlantic Colonies, c. 1750–1830* (Farnham: Ashgate, 2009); J.O. Lindsay, 'The Western Mediterranean and Italy', *The New Cambridge Modern History*, vol. vii (Cambridge: Cambridge University Press, 1966), pp. 280–85.

20. J.H. Elliott, *Imperial Spain, 1496–1716* (London: E Arnold, 1963), pp. 378–82; Richard Herr, *An Historical Essay on Modern Spain* (Berkeley, 1971), pp. 46–49.
21. Herr, *Historical Essay on Modern Spain*, pp. 50–64.
22. Jonathan Israel, *The Dutch Republic: Its Rise, Greatness, and Fall, 1477–1806* (Oxford: Clarendon Press, 1995), p. 1002.
23. Albert Sorel, *Europe and the French Revolution: the Political Traditions of the Old Regime* (London: Collins, 1969), p. 394.
24. For examples of this almost universal usage, see Talleyrand's references to 'Angleterre' in his letters to King Louis XVIII during the Congress of Vienna, Hardenberg's diaries, or Capodistrias' references to 'Angleterre' in his notes to Tsar Alexander I.
25. Mousnier and Labrousse, *Le XVIIIe Siècle*, p. 177.
26. In 1790, Britain's navy had 473 ships, compared to 324 in the French, 253 in the Spanish, 145 in the Russian and 123 in the Dutch navies. See Hartley, *Russia*, pp. 8–9. See also, more generally, John Brewer, *The Sinews of Power: War, Money and English State, 1688–1783* (London: Unwin Hyman, 1988); Paul Langford, *Modern British Foreign Policy* (London: Adams and Charles Black, 1976), vol. 3, *Eighteenth Century, 1688–1815*; Jeremy Black, *Eighteenth-Century Britain, 1688–1783* (Houndmills: Palgrave Macmillan, 2001), *Natural and Necessary Enemies: Anglo-American Relations in the Eighteenth Century* (London: Duckworth, 1986) and *Parliament and Foreign Policy in the Eighteenth Century* (Cambridge: Cambridge University Press, 2007); C.J. Bartlett, *Great Britain and Sea Power, 1815–1853* (Oxford: Clarendon Press, 1963); T.G. Otte, 'A Janus-like power: Great Britain and the European Concert, 1814–1853', in Wolfram Pyta (ed.), *Das europäische Mächtekonzert: Friedens- und Sicherheitspolitik vom Wiener Kongreß 1815 bis zum Krimkrieg 1853* (Cologne, Weimar and Vienna: Böhlau Verlag GMBH & CIE, 2009), pp. 125–53; J.R. Jones (ed.), *Britain and the World, 1649–1815* (Brighton: Harvester Press, 1980); and Kenneth Bourne, *The Foreign Policy of Victorian England, 1830–1902* (Oxford: Clarendon Press, 1970), pp. 1–25.
27. It is worth noting that up until 1782 there were still two Secretaries of State in Britain—one for the Northern and one for the Southern Department.
28. For a lucid summary of the debate on the origins and significance of the Revolution at the time of the bicentennial, see Jack R. Censer, 'Commencing the Third Century of Debate', *The American Historical Review* 94/5 (December 1989), pp. 1309–25; see also, William Doyle, *Origins of the French Revolution*, 3rd edn (Oxford: Oxford University Press, 1999); Bailey Stone, *Reinterpreting the French Revolution: A Global-Historical Perspective* (Cambridge: Cambridge University Press, 2002); Peter R. Campbell (ed.), *The Origins of the French Revolution* (London: Palgrave, 2006); Michael Sonenscher, *Before the Deluge: Public Debt,*

Inequality and the Intellectual Origins of the French Revolution (Princeton, NJ: Princeton University Press, 2007); and for a recent restatement of the traditional Marxist view, see Henry Heller, *The Bourgeois Revolution in France* (New York and Oxford: Berghahn Books, 2006). Some historians also emphasize that the prestige of the government had been weakened by its unsuccessful foreign policy, arguing that this contributed to the international instability that led to the crisis. See, e.g., Timothy Charles William Blanning, 'The European States-System at the Time of the French Revolution and Napoleonic Empire', in Pyta, *Das europäische Mächtekonzert*, pp. 79–102, especially pp. 80–81.

29. French legislators were further encouraged by popular animosity towards Austria.
30. For both the origins and the early years of the war, see Timothy C.W. Blanning, *The Origins of the French Revolutionary Wars* (London: Longman, 1986) and *The French Revolutionary Wars* (New York: Oxford University Press, 1996). Blanning traces the origins of the conflict back to the outbreak of war between Russia and the Ottoman Empire in 1787.
31. Censer, 'Commencing the Third Century of Debate', p. 1314, summarizing the arguments of François Furet: 'With politics reduced to a linguistic struggle, and Rousseauian thinking dominant, politicians could no longer exercise power in the traditional sense. Although some resisted, in the end they were forced to compete in the arena of discourse.'
32. Cited in R.R. Palmer, *Twelve Who Ruled* (Princeton, NJ: Princeton University Press, 1969), p. 67; see also Ruth Scurr, *Fatal Purity: Robespierre and the French Revolution* (New York: Metropolitan Books, 2006).
33. 'Whoever seeks to debase, divide or paralyze the Convention is an enemy of our country, whether he sits in this hall or is a foreigner. Whether he acts out of stupidity or from perversity, he is of the party of tyrants who make war upon us.' Robespierre before the Convention, 25 September 1793, cited in Palmer, *Twelve Who Ruled*, p. 71.
34. Robespierre before the Convention, 17 November 1793, cited in Palmer, *Twelve Who Ruled*, p. 125.
35. Robespierre before the Convention, 5 February 1794, cited in Palmer, *Twelve Who Ruled*, pp. 275–76.
36. Peter Paret, 'Napoleon and the Revolution in War', in Peter Paret (ed.), *Makers of Modern Strategy from Machiavelli to the Nuclear Age* (Princeton, NJ: Princeton University Press, 1986), pp. 123–42; Robert Bruce, Iain Dickie, Keven Kiley, Michael Pavkovic and Frederick Schneid, *Fighting Techniques of the Napoleonic Age, 1792–1815* (London: Amber Books, 2008).
37. Timothy C.W. Blanning, 'The European States System' in Pyta, *Das europäische Mächtekonzert*, p. 85.
38. See, for example, Jean-Clément Martin, *Violence et Révolution* (Paris: Éditions du Seuil, 2006).
39. David Andress, *The Terror: The Merciless War for Freedom in Revolutionary France* (New York: Farrar, Straus and Giroux, 2005), p. 2.

40. For the next sections, see generally: Thierry Lentz, *Nouvelle Histoire du Premier Empire* (Paris: Fayard, 2002–04); Thierry Lentz (ed.) *Napoleon et l'Europe* (Paris: Fayard 2004); David G. Chandler, *The Campaigns of Napoleon* (New York: Macmillan, 1966); Georges Lefebvre, *Napoleon* (New York: Columbia University Press, 1969); Owen Connelly, *Napoleon's Satellite Kingdoms* (New York: Free Press, 1965); Michael Broers, *Europe under Napoleon, 1799–1815* (New York: Edward Arnold, 1996); Charles Esdaile, *Napoleon's Wars: An International History, 1803–1815* (London: Penguin, 2007); Natalie Petiteau, *Napoléon, de la Mythologie à l'Histoire* (Paris: Seuil, 2004); and Paul Schroeder, *The Transformation of European Politics, 1763–1848* (Oxford: Oxford University Press, 1994), pp. 100–441.
41. Victor Monnier, *Bonaparte et la Suisse. Travaux préparatoires de l'Acte de Médiation* (Geneva and Basle: Helbing & Lichtenhahn, Slatkine, 2002).
42. Rey, *Alexandre I*, pp. 219–20; Alan Palmer, *Alexander I: Tsar of War and Peace* (London: Weidenfeld and Nicolson, 1974), p. 107; Janet Hartley, *Alexander I* (London: Longman), pp. 73–74. The Tsar's sarcastic comment to Kutuzov was immortalized in Tolstoy's *War and Peace* (Modern Library edition, p. 252).
43. Peter Paret, *The Cognitive Challenge of War: Prussia 1806* (Princeton, NJ: Princeton University Press, 2009).
44 Jean Tulard writes: 'The notion of the Grand Empire succeeded, starting from 1805, that of the Grand Nation' and Georges Lefbvre likewise explains that 'The war of 1805 inordinately extended the range of Napoleon's enterprises, and so made the French Empire merely the core of the "Grand Empire" which itself began to evolve through legislative acts'. See Jean Tulard, *Dictionnaire Napoléon* (Paris: Fayard, 1999), vol. I, p. 905; Georges Lefebvre, *Napoleon from 18 Brumaire to Tilsit, 1799–1807* (New York: Columbia University Press, 1969), p. 249.
45. Blanning argues that the revolutionaries had been shocked when the Germans and others did not welcome them with open arms—leading to a stern reaction in which 'liberated' peoples were exploited to meet the fiscal needs of the French army. See Timothy C.W. Blanning, *The French Revolution in Germany* (Oxford: Oxford University Press, 1983) and 'The European States-System at the Time of the French Revolution', in Pyta: *Das europäische Mächtekonzert*, pp. 79–102, especially pp. 86–87: 'It was a dismal experience for the revolutionaries. They had expected to be welcomed with open arms by a grateful humanity; so when they were rejected, they hardened their hearts and put France first. The rest of Europe, they concluded, had shown that they were still steeped in ignorance and prejudice, unworthy of liberation'.
46. The judgements of his contemporaries seem somewhat more balanced. Metternich described the French Emperor as a brilliant *parvenu*: 'Napoleon looked upon himself as being isolated from the rest of the world, made to govern it, and to direct everyone according to his own will' He took a very practical view of human nature and 'was persuaded that no man ... was guided or could be guided by any other motive than that of interest'. Metternich believed Napoleon's

natural talents were abetted by the unusual circumstances of his time: 'Surrounded by individuals who, in the midst of a world in ruins, walked at random without any fixed guidance, given up to all kinds of ambition and greed, he alone was able to form a plan, hold it fast, and conduct it to its conclusion ... As a war-chariot crushes everything which it meets on its way, Napoleon thought of nothing but advance.' Prince Richard Metternich (ed.), *The Memoirs of Prince Metternich* (New York Scribner's Sons, 1880), vol. i, 'Napoleon Bonaparte', pp. 273, 277, 281–83. And Talleyrand gave the following explanation for his failure: 'Napoleon had been raised to supreme power by the concourse of united wills against anarchy. The fame of his victories had caused him to be chosen; it was his sole claim; defeat revoked it as much as a glorious peace would have justified and affirmed it. But, dupe to his imagination that overruled his judgment, he said emphatically, that he must raise about France a rampart of thrones occupied by members of his family to replace that line of fortresses created previously by Louis XIV ... His success had so blinded him that he did not see that by pushing to extremes the political system he had foolishly embraced, as much at home as abroad, he would tire the French as well as other nations, and compel them all to seek, outside of himself, guarantees for a general peace, and, for the French, enjoyment of their civil rights.' Duc de Broglie, *Memoirs of the Prince de Talleyrand* (New York and London: G.P. Putnam's Sons, 1891), vol. ii, pp. 97–98. See also the discussion in Natalie Petiteau, *Napoléon, de la Mythologie à l'Histoire* (Paris: Editions du Seuil, 1999), pp. 260–68 ('Un souverain à l'ambition illimitée?'), reviewing several generations of historians on the issue of whether Napoleon aimed at a 'universal monarchy'. According to Petiteau, French historians Georges Lefebvres and Jacques Godechot both believed that Napoleon had an unbridled will to power, while Anglo-American historians Stuart Woolf and Alan Schom have argued that the empire developed in stages, not as a single idea. Finally, Jacques-Olivier Boudon has looked for an explanation in bureaucratic politics—based on the influence of Napoleon's army officers.

47. This was at least what Talleyrand professed in his later *Memoirs*. On the other hand, historian Alan Sked, citing Emile Dard, *Napoleon and Talleyrand* (London: Philip Allan and Co., 1937), argues that Talleyrand may in fact have been the true author of the Spanish usurpation and only abandoned Napoleon when he detected the change in the Emperor's fortunes. See Sked, 'Talleyrand and Metternich' (unpublished paper), pp. 17, 20–21 fn. 20. Sked believes that fear was the true motive behind Talleyrand's conduct.

48. Elizabeth York, *Leagues of Nations; Ancient, Mediaeval, and Modern* (London: The Swarthmore Press Ltd, 1919), pp. 100–03; David Ogg (ed.), *Sully's Grand Design of Henry IV* (Grotius Society Publications, No. 2) (London: Sweet and Maxwell, 1921); F.H. Hinsley, *Power and the Pursuit of Peace* (Cambridge: Cambridge University Press, 1967), pp. 23–29. In the 1745 edition of Sully's memoirs, these scattered references were finally consolidated into a single chapter. Sully said the Council was based on the Amphictyonic Council of ancient Greece, a league of city-states originally formed to protect the temple of Apollo at Delphi.

49. The Abbé de Saint-Pierre continually revised and modified his plan throughout his life. M.G. de Molinari, *L'Abbé de Saint-Pierre: Sa View et Ses Oeuvres* (Paris: Guillaumin, 1857), pp. 77–84, reprints the five articles that appeared in the original French version; for the English translation of the 12 articles printed in London in 1714, see York, *Leagues of Nations*, pp. 170–78; see also, Walter Alison Phillips, *The Confederation of Europe* (London: Longmans, Green and Co., 1920), pp. 26–27, for a restatement of Saint-Pierre's plan in six provisions.
50. Jean-Jacques Rousseau, *The Plan for Perpetual Peace, On the Government of Poland, and other Writings on History and Politics* (Hanover, NH: Dartmouth College Press, 2005), pp. 23–60; Grace G. Roosevelt, *Reading Rousseau in the Nuclear Age* (Philadelphia, PA: Temple University Press, 1990), pp. 90–119, 199–229; Hinsley, *Power and the Pursuit of Peace*, pp. 46–61.
51. Carl Friedrich (ed.), *The Philosophy of Kant: Immanuel Kant's Moral and Political Writings* (New York: Modern Library, 1949), pp. 441, 444; Hinsley, *Power and the Pursuit of Peace*, pp. 62–63, 68.
52. Eric Easley, *The War over Perpetual Peace: An Exploration into the History of a Foundational International Relations Text* (New York: Palgrave Macmillan, 2004); Paul Kennedy, *The Parliament of Man: the Past, Present and Future of the United Nations* (New York: Random House, 2006). According to Easley, these plans shared the notion of a 'restraint on state sovereignty through [the] establishment of a centralized authority, in the form of an international state or strong federation, above the collectivity of states' (pp. 2–3). And Kennedy similarly notes: 'It comes as no surprise that most of these texts were composed near the end of, or shortly after, a great and bloody war. They were efforts to find a way out of international anarchy, to escape the repeated struggles between cities, monarchies, and states, and to establish long-lasting peace. All of them sought to constrain selfish, sovereign power, usually by some form of league of nations that would take action against a country that broke the existing order. The mechanisms were therefore reactive, assuming humankind's propensity to conflict but trusting that such dangerous drives could be headed off ... To say that this was idealist would be gross understatement' (pp. 3–4).
53. For the flurry of contemporary peace movements in Britain in reaction to the war, see J.E. Cookson, *The Friends of Peace: Anti-War Liberalism in England, 1793–1815* (Cambridge: Cambridge University Press, 1982). Cookson mentions Kant's essay on perpetual peace, p. 30, but not Sully or Saint-Pierre.
54. Zawadzki, *A Man of Honour*, pp. 5–32; Marian Kukiel, *Czartoryski and European Unity, 1770–1861* (Princeton: Princeton University Press, 1955), pp. 3–16; Charles de Mazade (ed.), *Mémoires du Prince Adam Czartoryski et Correspondance ave l'Empereur Alexandre Ier* (Paris: E. Plon, Nourrit et Cie, 1887), vol. i, pp. 38–39; Patricia Kennedy Grimsted, *The Foreign Ministers of Alexander I: Political Attitudes and the Conduct of Russian Diplomacy, 1801–1825* (Berkeley: University of California Press, 1969), pp. 106–07.
55. Zawadzki, *A Man of Honour*, pp. 32–60.
56. Marian Kukiel, *Czartoryski and European Unity, 1770–1861* (Princeton, NJ: Princeton University Press, 1955), pp. 30–40; Zawadzki, *A Man of Honour*,

pp. 61–91, and 'Prince Adam Czartoryski and Napoleonic France, 1801–1805: A Study in Political Attitudes', *The Historical Journal* xviii/2 (1975), pp. 245–77; Hartley, *Alexander I*, pp. 66–67.

57. In fact, Saint-Pierre's project had appeared in Russian translation in 1771, while Rousseau's *Extrait du Projet de Paix Perpétuelle de Monsieur l'Abbé de Saint-Pierre* appeared in Polish in 1773, and Kant's essay on perpetual peace in Polish translations in both 1796 and 1797. See Zawadzki, *A Man of Honour*, pp. 88–89. Zawadzki argues that Czartoryski preferred Kant's moralism to Rousseau's pessimism.

58. Grimsted, *Foreign Ministers of Alexander I*, p. 118.

59. Mazade, *Mémoires du Prince Adam Czartoryski*, vol. ii, pp. 34–35. Adam Gielgud (ed.), *Memoirs of Prince Adam Czartoryski and his Correspondence with Alexander I* (London, 1888), vol. ii, pp. 41–51. See also, Kukiel, *Czartoryski*, pp. 41–51; Zawadzki, *A Man of Honour*, pp. 106–10; Adam Gielgud, *Memoirs of Prince Adam Czartoryski and his Correspondence with Alexander I* (London: Remington, 1888), vol. ii, pp. 47–48.

60. Gielgud, *Memoirs of Czartoryski*, p. 47; Mazade, *Mémoires du Czartoryski*, vol. ii, pp. 34–35.

61. Gentz published his article in the last issue of the *Historisches Journal*, an antirevolutionary periodical he published with Prussian support from 1799 to 1800. Although 'everlasting peace' was unrealizable, Gentz argued that mankind must strive towards it. See Paul Robinson Sweet, *Friedrich von Gentz: Defender of the Old Order* (Westport, CN: Greenwood Press, 1970), pp. 52–57.

62. Zawadzki, *A Man of Honour*, pp. 116–18; for other influences on Czartoryski, see pp. 87–90. For the earlier controversy over whether Piattoli was actually the author of this 'System', see Patricia Kennedy Grimsted, 'Czaroryski's System for Russian Foreign Policy, 1803: A Memorandum', in Nicholas Riasanovsky and Gleb Struve (eds.), *California Slavic Studies*, vol. v (Berkeley: University of California Press, 1970), pp. 22–24.

63. For Novosiltsov's report summarizing his discussions with Pitt in London, see Mazade, *Mémoires du Czartoryski*, vol. ii, pp. 45–56 ('Instructions secrètes à M. de Novosiltzow allant en Angleterre, le 11 Septembre 1804' and 'Papiers relatifs à la mission de M. de Novosiltzow à Londres'); Lord Harrowby to Count [Vorontsov], Downing Street, 26 June 1804, printed in John Holland Rose, *Select Despatches from the British Foreign Office Archives relating to the Formation of the Third Coalition against France, 1804–1805* (London: Royal Historical Society, 1904), pp. 14–19.

64. Pitt to Vorontsov, 19 January 1805, in N.A. (Kew), F.O. 65/57, attachment in Mulgrave to Leveson Gower (British Minister in St. Petersburg), 21 January 1805; printed in Webster, *British Diplomacy*, Appendix I; John Ehrman, *The Younger Pitt*, vol. iii (Stanford: Stanford University Press, 1996), pp. 695–701, 728–45.

65. Webster, *British Diplomacy*, Appendix i, p. 393.

66. Sweet, *Friedrich von Gentz*, p. 57.

67. John M. Sherwig, 'Lord Grenville's Plan for a Concert of Europe, 1797–1799', *The Journal of Modern History* 34/3 (September 1962), pp. 284–93. Pitt may have also been influenced by the advice he received from his new Foreign Secretary, Henry Phipps, Lord Mulgrave. See Edward Ingram, 'Lord Mulgrave's Proposals for the Reconstruction of Europe in 1804', *The Historical Journal* 19/2 (June 1976), pp. 511–20.
68. Sherwig, 'Lord Grenville's Plan', pp. 286–91. In 1805, the British ministers seem even to have considered transferring Holland to Prussia in a desperate effort to create a stronger maritime power on the borders of France. Ingram, 'Lord Mulgrave's Proposals', pp. 515, 519.

2. The Collapse of the Napoleonic Empire, 1812–14

1. Dominic Lieven, *Russia against Napoleon: the True Story of the Campaigns of War and Peace* (New York: Viking, 2010). See also, Rey, *Alexandre I*, pp. 302–30; Esdaile, *Napoleon's Wars*, pp. 460–80; Chandler, *Campaigns of Napoleon*, pp. 739–861, especially pp. 852–61 for Chandler's analysis of Napoleon's errors ('The problems of space, time and distance proved too great for even one of the greatest military minds that has ever existed'); Hartley, *Alexander I*, pp. 111–19; Palmer, *Alexander I*, pp. 216–56.
2. Peter Paret, *Yorck and the Era of Prussian Reform, 1807–1815* (Princeton, NJ: Princeton University Press, 1966), ch. 6 and *Clausewitz and the State* (Oxford: Oxford University Press, 1976), pp. 229–32; Enno Kraehe, *Metternich's German Policy, 1799–1814* (Princeton, NJ: Princeton University Press, 1963), pp. 153–56; Schroeder, *Transformation of European Politics*, pp. 450–59.
3. Agreement at Kalisch, 28 February 1813, in L.J. Chodzko, Comte d'Angeberg, *Le Congrès de Vienne et les Traités de 1815* (Paris: Amyot, 1864), vol. i, p. 1; see also Edward Vose Gulick, *Europe's Classical Balance of Power* (New York: W.W. Norton, 1955), pp. 108–09; Sir Charles Kingsley Webster, *The Foreign Policy of Lord Castlereagh, 1812–1815: Britain and the Reconstruction of Europe* (London: G. Bell and Sons, 1931), pp. 119–34; Kraehe, *Metternich's German Policy*, pp. 156–58; Hartley, *Alexander I*, pp. 120–22; Douglas Dakin, 'The Congress of Vienna, 1814–1815, and its Antecedents', in Alan Sked (ed.), *Europe's Balance of Power, 1815–1848* (London: Macmillan, 1979), pp. 15–18.
4. Treaty of Reichenbach, 14 June 1813, in d'Angeberg, *Congrès de Vienne*, vol. i, p. 9.
5. Agreement at Toeplitz, 9 September 1813, in d'Angeberg, *Congrès de Vienne*, vol. i, p. 50.
6. At Leipzig, 360,000 allied troops faced 200,000 French forces. Historian Alan Sked argues that Austrian entry into the allied coalition proved to be the decisive factor—not simply because of the increase in numbers but also in leadership: Schwarzenberg, assisted by the capable Radetzky, now assumed command of allied forces. Alan Sked, *Radetzky: Imperial Victor and Military Genius* (London: I.B.Tauris, 2011), pp. 36–51. See also, Esdaile, *Napoleon's Wars*, pp. 513–17;

Chandler: *Campaigns of Napoleon*, pp. 912–36.
7. Lord Aberdeen, 22 October 1813, Leipzig, in Lady Francis Balfour, *The Life of George, Fourth Earl of Aberdeen* (London, 1923), vol. i, p. 125.
8. Sked, *Radetzky*, pp. 54–55.
9. Webster, *Foreign Policy of Castlereagh, 1812–1815*, pp. 166–89; Kraehe, *Metternich's German Policy*, pp. 250–52, 283–85; Michael Leggiere, *The Fall of Napoleon: The Allied Invasion of France* (Cambridge: Cambridge University Press, 2007), pp. 49–56; Schroeder, *Transformation of European Politics*, pp. 490–91.
10. Alexander I to Lieven and Pozzo di Borgo, 6 December 1813, Frankfurt-am-Main, and Lieven and Pozzo di Borgo to Nesselrode, 22 December 1813, London, in USSR, Ministry of Foreign Affairs, *Vneshniaia Politika Rossii XIX i nachala XX veka: Dokumenty rossiskogo Ministerstva inostrannykh del*, 1st Series (1801–1815) vol. vii (January 1813–May 1814) (Moscow: Nauka, 1970), pp. 492–47, 514–18.
11. Memorandum of Cabinet, 26 December 1813, in Webster: *British Diplomacy*, pp. 123–28; Webster, *Foreign Policy of Castlereagh, 1812–1815*, pp. 193–98.
12. Mark Jarrett, 'Castlereagh, Ireland and the French Restorations of 1814–1815', PhD thesis (Stanford University, 2006), pp. 250–68.
13. Jarrett: 'Castlereagh, Ireland and the French Restorations', pp. 279–86; Franklin D. Scott, 'Bernadotte and the Throne of France, 1814', *Journal of Modern History* V (1933), pp. 465–78, and *Bernadotte and the Fall of Napoleon* (Cambridge, MA: Harvard University Press, 1935); Torvald Hojer, *Carl XIV Johan*, vol. ii (Stockholm: P.A. Nordstedt & Söners Förlag, 1939–60), pp. 236–44.
14. Castlereagh to Liverpool, Basel, 22 January 1814, in Webster, *British Diplomacy*, pp. 133–38; see also, Jarrett: 'Castlereagh, Ireland and the French Restorations', pp. 271–79; August Fournier, *Der Congress von Chatillon*; Webster, *Foreign Policy of Castlereagh, 1812–1815* (Vienna and Prague: Tempsky, 1900), pp. 200–03; Kraehe, *Metternich's German Policy, 1799–1814*, pp. 283–87; Leggiere, *The Fall of Napoleon*, pp. 542–44.
15. Wilhelm Oncken, 'Lord Castlereagh und die Ministerconferenz zu Langres am 29. January 1814', *Historisches Taschenbuch* 6te Folge, Jhrg. 4 (1885), pp. 9–36; Jarrett, 'Castlereagh, Ireland and the French Restorations', pp. 286–99; Fournier, *Der Congress von Chatillon*, pp. 56–79; Kraehe, *Metternich's German Policy, 1799–1814*, pp. 288–90; Webster, *Foreign Policy of Castlereagh, 1812–1815*, pp. 205–10.
16. Circular of Lord Castlereagh to Metternich, Nesselrode and Hardenberg, 1 March 1814, Chaumont, National Archives (Kew), F.O. 92/3, ff. 69–70.
17. Castlereagh to Liverpool, Chaumont, 10 March 1814, in Webster, *British Diplomacy*, p. 165.
18. For the Treaty of Chaumont, see especially, Jarrett, 'Castlereagh, Ireland and the French Restorations', pp. 304–07; Gulick, *Europe's Classical Balance of Power*, pp. 151–60, which includes the text of the treaty; Webster: *Foreign Policy of Castlereagh*, pp. 211–32; Kraehe: *Metternich's German Policy*, pp. 302–10; Fournier, *Der Congress von Chatillon*, pp. 178–83.

19. Jean Tulard, *Napoleon: The Myth of the Saviour*, trans. Teresa Waugh (London: Weidenfeld and Nicolson, 1984), pp. 242–45; D.M.G. Sutherland, *France 1789–1815: Revolution and Counter-Revolution* (Oxford: Oxford University Press, 1985), pp. 390–91. For this section generally, see also: Lentz: *Nouvelle Histoire du Premier Empire*, vol. ii: *L'effrondrement du système napoléonien, 1810–1814*; Felix Ponteil, *La Chute de Napoléon 1er* (Paris: Aubier, 1943); Henry Houssaye, *1814* (Paris: Perrin, 1907), ch. 1 ('La France au Commencement de 1814'), pp. 1–59; Guillaume de Bertier de Sauvigny, *The Bourbon Restoration* (Philadelphia: University of Pennsylvania Press, 1966), pp. 3–16; Louis Bergeron, *L'Épisode napoléonien: Aspects intérieurs, 1799–1815* (Paris: Éditions du Seuil, 1972), pp. 85–118 ('La fin de l'Empire, en 1814', Bergeron writes, 'est bien l'histoire d'une décomposition interne'); Georges Lefebvre, *Napoleon from Tilsit to Waterloo, 1807–1815* (New York: Columbia University Press, 1969), pp. 346–47, 351–52, 358–59; Philip Mansel, *Louis XVIII* (London: Bland & Briggs, 1981), pp. 157–276; J. Regnault, 'L'Empereur et l'opinion publique, 1813–1814', *Revue hist. de L'Armée* xiii (1957), pp. 29–50, Steven Englund, *Napoleon: A Political Life* (New York: Scribner, 2004), pp. 379–89, 395–96, 401–06; Emmanuel de Waresquiel and Benoît Yvert, *Histoire de la Restauration, 1814–1830: Naissance de la France moderne* (Paris: Perrin, 1996), pp. 13–20. For a recent overview of the historiography of the empire, see Natalie Petiteau, *Napoléon, de la Mythologie à l'Histoire* (Paris: Éditions du Seuil, 2004), chs 5, 6, 8, and 10.
20. Sutherland, *France, 1789–1815*, p. 385.
21. Tulard, *Napoleon*, p. 188.
22. Ponteil, *La Chute de Napoleon 1er*, pp. 15–22; Houssaye, *1814*, pp. 4–7; Tulard, *Napoleon: the Myth of the Saviour*, pp. 317–18.
23. Sutherland, *France, 1789–1815*, p. 421; Houssaye, *1814*, pp. 6–10.
24. Declaration of the Allies, 25 March 1814 in d'Angeberg, *Congrès de Vienne*, vol. i, pp. 143–46.
25. For the rest of this section, see Jarrett, 'Castlereagh, Ireland and the French Restorations', pp. 309, 314–50; Bathurst to Castlereagh, 22 March 1814 (No. 8), Castlereagh to Liverpool, 30 March (No. 45) and 4 April 1814 (No. 50), Dijon, and 13 April 1814 (No. 54), Paris, in Webster: *British Diplomacy*, pp. 171–77; Bertier de Sauvigny, *Bourbon Restoration*, pp. 24–47; Philip Mansell, *Louis XVIII* (London: John Murray, 2005), pp. 170–88; de Waresquiel and Yvert: *Histoire de la Restauration*, pp. 11–56; G. Lacour-Gayet, *Talleyrand* (Paris: Payot, 1930), vol. ii, pp. 343–402; Pierre Rain, *L'Europe et la Restauration des Bourbons, 1814–1818* (Paris: Perrin, 1908); David Hamilton-Williams, *The Fall of Napoleon: The Final Betrayal* (New York: Wiley, 1994), pp. 87–126; Michel Verpeaux, 'La vacance du pouvoir et le droit', in Yves-Marie Bercé (ed.), *La Fin de l'Europe Napoleonienne 1814: La Vacance du Pouvoir* (Paris: H. Veyrier, 1990), pp. 293–313; Jean Orieux, *Talleyrand ou Le Sphinx Incompris* (Paris: Flammarion, 1998), pp. 565–85; Emmanuel de Waresquiel, *Talleyrand: le prince immobile* (Paris: Fayard, 2003), pp. 431–56.
26. Treaty of Fontainebleau, 11 April 1814, in d'Angeberg, *Congrès de Vienne*, vol. i, pp. 149–56.

27. Webster, *Foreign Policy of Castlereagh, 1812–1815*, pp. 263–76; Castlereagh to Liverpool, 19 April and 5 (No. 58), 19 (No. 59) and 23 May 1814, Paris, in Webster, *British Diplomacy*, pp. 177–78, 180, 183–86; Bertier de Sauvigny, *Bourbon Restoration*, pp. 47–51; Charles Dupuis, *Le Ministère de Talleyrand* (Paris: Plon, 1920), vol. i, pp. 354–78; Lacour-Gayet, *Talleyrand*, vol. ii, pp. 403–19; Waresquiel and Yvert, *Restauration*, pp. 63–64; Waresquiel *Talleyrand*, pp. 463–69. For the armistice of 23 April 1814, see d'Angeberg, *Congrès de Vienne*, vol. i, pp. 156–60. For the Peace of Paris, 30 May 1814, including the secret articles and particular articles concluded between France and individual powers, see d'Angeberg, *Congrès de Vienne*, vol. i, pp. 161–78.
28. The term 'equilibré' was once routinely translated as 'a balance of power', but more recently, historian Paul Schroeder has argued that a system of equilibrium and a balance of power were not equivalent. For a critique of Schroeder's view, see Alan Sked, *Metternich and Austria: An Evaluation* (Houndsmill: Palgrave Macmillan, 2008), pp. 54–63. See also Paul Sonnino, 'What Kind of Idea is the Idea of the 'Balance of Power'?', in Peter Krüger and Paul Schroeder (eds), *'The Transformation of European Politics, 1763–1848': Episode or Model in Modern History?* (Münster: Lit Verlag, 2002), pp. 63–76.
29. Treaty of Paris, 30 May 1814, in d'Angeberg, *Congrès de Vienne*, vol. i, p. 170: 'Dans le délai de deux mois, toutes les puissances qui ont été engagées de part et d'autre dans la présente guerre enverront des plénipotentiaires à Vienne, pour régler, dans un congrès general, les arrangements qui doivent completer les dispositions du présent Traité'.

3. The Congress of Vienna, 1814–15

1. On the origins of the plan to hold a congress, see Karl Griewank, *Der Wiener Kongress und die Neuordnung Europas 1814/15* (Leipzig: Koehler & Amelang, 1942), p. 64; Thierry Lentz, *Le congrès de Vienne* (Paris: Perrin, 2013), pp. 17–18.
2. D'Angeberg, *Congrès de Vienne*, vol. i, pp. 362–64. This is one of the most frequently cited passages about the Congress: see Sir Ernest Satow, *A Guide to Diplomatic Practice* (London: Longmans, Green & Co., 1922), vol. ii, pp. 2–3 (Satow notes that Metternich published this description in a 'semi-official article'); Gordon A. Craig and Alexander L. George, *Force and Statecraft: Diplomatic Problems of Our Time* (New York: Oxford University Press, 1983), p. 29; and Richard Langhorne, 'Reflections on the Congress of Vienna', *Review of International Studies* xii/4 (October 1986), p. 318.
3. Peter Thielen, *Karl August von Hardenberg 1750–1822: Ein Biographie* (Cologne: Grote, 1967), pp. 300–02; Thomas Stamm-Kuhlmann (ed.), *Karl August von Hardenberg, 1750–1822: Tagebücher und autobiographische Aufzeichnungen* (Munich: Harald Boldt Verlag, 2000), 'Einleitung', pp. 65–66; Kraehe, *Metternich's German Policy*, vol. i, p. 316; Heinrich von Treitschke, *History of Germany in the Nineteenth Century*, trans. Eden and Cedar Paul (London: Jarrold & Sons, 1915), vol. i, pp. 661–63; Webster, *Foreign Policy of Lord Castlereagh, 1812–1815*,

pp. 280–81; Castlereagh to Liverpool, 5 May 1814 (No. 58), Paris, in Webster, *British Diplomacy*, p. 180 ('I now send you a report ... drawn up by the Chancellor Hardenberg after repeated discusions'); Griewank, *Wiener Kongress und Neuordnung Europas*, pp. 63–64; Karl Erich Born, 'Hardenbergs Pläne und Versuch zur Neuordnung Europas und Deutschlands 1813/1815', *Geschichte in Wissenschaft und Unterricht* viii (1957), pp. 550–65.

4. Janet M. Hartley, '"It is the Festival of the Crown and Sceptres": The Diplomatic, Commercial and Domestic Signficance of the Visit of Alexander I to England in 1814', *The Slavonic and East European Review* 73/2 (April 1995), pp. 246–68; Francis Ley, *Alexandre Ier et sa Sainte-Alliance* (Paris: Fischbacher, 1975), pp. 79–83; August Fournier, 'London Präludien zum Wiener Kongress', *Deutsche Revue* 43 (1918), I, pp. 125–36, 205–16; II, pp. 24–33.

5. They were assisted by several capable 'civil servants'—Gentz and Wessenberg for Austria; Earl Clancarty, Lord Cathcart, Edward Cooke and Joseph Planta for Britain, d'Alberg and La Besnardier for France; Hoffmann for Prussia; and Nesselrode, Czartoryski, Stein and Capodistrias for Russia.

6. For further background on Metternich, see Sked, *Metternich and Austria*; Alan Palmer, *Metternich* (London: Weidenfeld and Nicolson, 1972); Desmond Seward, *Metternich, the First European* (New York: Viking, 1991); Guillaume de Bertier de Sauvigny, *Metternich and His Times* (London: Darton, Longman & Todd, 1962) and *Metternich* (Paris: Fayard, 1986); Heinrich Ritter von Srbik, *Metternich, der Staatsmann und der Mensch* (Munich: F. Bruckmann, 1925, 1957); and Metternich, *Memoirs of Prince Metternich*.

7. For Talleyrand, see Waresquiel, *Talleyrand*; Orieux: *Talleyrand ou Le Sphinx Incompris*; Lacour-Gayet: *Talleyrand*; Duff Cooper, *Talleyrand* (New York, 1967); David Lawday, *Napoleon's Master: A Life of Prince Talleyrand* (New York: St Martin's Press, 2006); Philip G. Dwyer, *Talleyrand* (London: Longman, 2002); and Charles Maurice de Talleyrand-Perigord, *Memoirs of the Prince de Talleyrand* (New York: G.P. Putnam's Sons, 1891–92).

8. Waresquiel, *Talleyrand*, p. 69.

9. For Hardenberg, see Ingo Hermann, *Hardenberg: der Reformkanzler* (Berlin: Siedler, 2003); Thielen, *Hardenberg*; and Thomas Stamm-Kuhlmann (ed.), *'Freier Gebrauch der Kräfte': Eine Bestandsaufnahme der Hardenberg-Forschung* (Munich: R. Oldenbourg Verlag, 2001).

10. For the earlier career of Castlereagh, see Jarrett, 'Castlereagh, Ireland and the French Restorations', pp. 1–255; Giles Hunt, *The Duel: Castlereagh, Canning and Deadly Cabinet Rivalry* (London: I.B.Tauris, 2008); H. Montgomery Hyde, *The Rise of Castlereagh* (London: Macmillan, 1933); Patrick Geoghegan, *Lord Castlereagh* (Dundalk: Dundalgan Press, 2002); Wendy Hinde, *Castlereagh* (London: Collins, 1981); John Bew, *Castlereagh: Enlightenment, War, and Tyranny* (London: Quercus, 2011); John Derry, *Castlereagh* (London: Allen Lane, 1976); Sir Archibald Alison, *Lives of Lord Castlereagh and Sir Charles Stewart, the Second and Third Marquesses of Londonderry* (London: J.M. Dent & Sons, 1861); and Charles [Stewart] Vane, Third Marquess of Londonderry (ed.),

Memoirs and Correspondence of Viscount Castlereagh (London: H. Colburn, 1848–54).

11. For general background on Alexander, see Rey, *Alexandre Ier*; Palmer, *Alexander I*; Hartley, *Alexander I*; Ley, *Alexandre Ier et sa Sainte-Alliance*; Patricia Kennedy Grimsted, *The Foreign Ministers of Alexander I: Political Attitudes and the Conduct of Russian Diplomacy, 1801–1825* (Berkeley: University of California Press, 1969); and K. Waliszewski, *La Russie Il y a Cent Ans: Le Regne d'Alexandre Ier* (Paris: Plon, 1924). See also Grand Duke Nicholai Mikhaïlovich, *Imperator Aleksandr I* (St Petersburg: Manufacture of Government Papers, 1912) and Theodor Schiemann, *Die Geschichte Russlands unter Kaiser Nikolaus I*, vol. 1: *Kaiser Alexander I under die Ergebnisse seiner Lebensarbeit* (Berlin: G. Reimer, 1904), which contain a large number of original letters in French, and Gielgud, *Memoirs of Prince Adam Czartoryski*.
12. Rey, *Alexandre I*, pp. 131–70; Hartley, *Alexander I*, pp. 30–49; Marc Raeff, *Michael Speransky: Statesman of Imperial Russia, 1772–1839* (The Hague: Martinus Nijhoff, 1957), pp. 34–40. Raeff argues that the Tsar was not a hypocrite but had a different understanding of the term 'constitution' than we have today: 'What they called a constitution should perhaps be termed "fundamental principles of administrative organization". The term constitution conveyed to them the idea of an orderly system of government and administration, free from caprices and demoralizing tyranny of arbitrariness. To give Russia a constitution, therefore, implied bringing clarity and order to the administration and basing the relationship between the government and the individual subject on the rule of law.'
13. She had had broken off her relationship with the Tsar on his return to St Petersburg in June 1814, although he apparently kept visiting her at the Congress of Vienna, which she attended with her husband, until she finally insisted that he stay away. See Rey, *Alexandre I*, pp. 172–357, 358; Ley, *Alexandre Ier et sa Sainte-Alliance*, p. 97. Although some writers have accused the Tsar of having a voracious sexual appetite, his most recent biographer convincingly argues his promiscuity at the Congress was a reaction to his rejection by Naryshkina. See Rey, *Alexandre I*, p. 360.
14. Stanley Lane-Poole, *Life of the Right Honourable Stratford Canning: Viscount Stratford de Redcliffe* (London: Longmans, Green & Co., 1888), vol. i, p. 213. For Castlereagh's character, see also Hunt, *The Duel*, pp. 29–46.
15. Bertier de Sauvigny, *Metternich and His Times*, p. 23.
16. Bertier de Sauvigny, *Metternich and his Times*, p. 306.
17. Castlereagh to Lord Stewart, 5 January 1821, in Alison, *Lives of Lord Castlereagh and Sir Charles Stewart*, p. 217.
18. Hardenberg to Count Münster, 24 May 1812, in Wilhelm Oncken, *Oesterreich und Preussen in Befreiungskriege* (Berlin: G. Gratte, 1879), vol. ii, pp. 87–89; cited in Henry Kissinger, *A World Restored: Metternich, Castlereagh and the Problems of Peace 1812–1822* (New York: Houghton Mifflin, 1964), p. 11.
19. Kissinger, *A World Restored*, p. 21.

20. Lieven, *Russia against Napoleon*, p. 57.
21. Lane-Poole, *Life of the Right Honourable Stratford Canning*, vol. i, p. 236.
22. 'On the Necessity of a General Arming of the People on the Frontiers of France, by a Friend of Universal Peace' (1794), in Metternich, *Memoirs*.
23. Bertier de Sauvigny, *Metternich and his Times*, p. 52.
24. Heinrich von Srbik, 'Metternichs Plan der Neuordnung Europas 1814/1815', *Mitteilungen des Instituts für österreichische Geschichtsforschung*, vol. xl (1925), trans. and reprinted in Henry Schwarz (ed.) *Metternich, the 'Coachman of Europe'* (Boston: D.C. Heath, 1962), p. 8.
25. Castlereagh to William Wickham, 12 June 1798, Dublin Castle, in Stewart, *Memoirs and Correspondence of Viscount Castlereagh*, vol. i, pp. 219–20.
26. Castlereagh to Camden, 9 July 1797, Dublin Castle, in Centre for Kentish Studies (Maidstone), Pratt Mss., U840 C98/2.
27. Raeff, *Michael Speransky*, pp. 119–69; Nicholas Riasanovsky, *Russian Identities: A Historical Survey* (New York: Oxford University Press, 2005), pp. 117–20.
28. Cited in James Sheehan, *German History, 1770–1866* (Oxford: Clarendon Press, 1989), p. 305.
29. Meinecke, *The Age of German Liberation*, p. 54.
30. For background on Humboldt, see Paul Robinson Sweet, *Wilhelm von Humboldt: A Biography* (Columbus: Ohio State University Press, 1978–80).
31. On a generational approach to the Congress statesmen, see also, Sven Externbrink, 'Kulturtransfer, Internationale Beziehunge und die "Generation Metternich" zwischen Französischer Revolution, Restauration und Revolution von 1848', in Pyta, *Das europäische Mächtekonzert*, pp. 59–78.
32 Broers, *Napoleonic Imperialism and the Savoyard Monarchy*, p. 482.
33. Friedrich von Gentz, *Fragments upon the Present State of the Political Balance of Europe* (London: M. Peliter, 1806), ch. 1, pp. 56 and 61.
34. For one set of Russian plans prior to the Congress, see Nesselrode's short 'Basis of a General Arrangement', 31 July (12 August) 1814, in USSR, *Vneshniaia Politika Rossii, 1801–1815*, Series 1, vol. viii, pp. 87–88.
35. Castlereagh to Wellington, 1 October 1814, in Webster, *British Diplomacy*, pp. 195–97.
36. Instructions of Louis XVIII to his ambassador to the Congress of Vienna, September 1814, in d'Angeberg, *Congrès de Vienne*, vol. i, pp. 215–38. See also the 'general ideas' that Talleyrand conveyed to the Austrian envoy Baron Vincent before leaving Paris for Vienna, in Griewank, *Wiener Kongress*, p. 310.
37. Paul Kennedy, *The Rise and Fall of the Great Powers* (New York: Vintage Books, 1987), pp. 99, 154.
38. Castlereagh to Liverpool, 24 September 1814, in Webster, *British Diplomacy*, pp. 193–95.
39. Castlereagh, 'Memorandum upon the Measures to be adapted Preparatory to the Meeting of the Congress in Form for the Despatch of Business', Vienna, September 1814, in Webster, *The Congress of Vienna*, Appendix II, pp. 170–71, and Two 'Projets', Appendix III, pp. 172–74.

40. Humboldt, *Projet*, September 1814, in Webster, *The Congress of Vienna*, Appendix IV, pp. 175–83, 'Proposal to Publish a Declaration', Appendix V, pp. 183–85 and Appendix VI, p. 185. See also, Griewank, *Wiener Kongress*, pp. 104–08.
41. 'Niederschrift Binders über die erste Konferenz zwischen Castlereagh, Metternich und Nesselrode in Wien am 16. September 1814', in Griewank, *Wiener Kongress*, p. 311.
42. Stuart to Castlereagh, Paris, 18 August 1814, cited in Eugeniusz Wawrzkowicz, *Anglia a prawa polska 1813–1815* (Kraków and Warsaw: Druk W.L. Anczyca i spólki, 1919), pp. 370–71.
43. Castlereagh to Liverpool, 3 September 1814, in Webster, *British Diplomacy*, pp. 191–93. The Duc de Berri had also been sent to London that summer to concert with the British on matters expected to come before the Congress. See Alexandra von Ilsemann, *Die Politik Frankreichs auf dem Wiener Kongress: Talleyrands aussenpolitische Strategien zwischen Erster und Zweiter Restauration* (Hamburg: Krämer, 1996), pp. 144–53, 157–58. Ilsemann contends that Talleyrand's plan was to create special committees which would submit their work to a general committee, which in turn would submit its work to a plenary session of the Congress. Ilsemann notes, on the other hand, that there was nothing about the organization of the Congress in Talleyrand's instructions.
44. Talleyrand-Perigord, *Memoirs*, vol. ii, pp. 202–04; Talleyrand to Louis XVIII, 4 October 1814, in M.G. Pallain, *The Correspondence of Prince Talleyrand and King Louis XVIII during the Congress of Vienna* (New York: Charles Scribner's Sons, 1881), p. 117 and in Talleyrand-Perigord, *Memoirs*, vol. ii, pp. 229–34; see also the 'King's Ambassadors at the Congress to Minister of Foreign Affairs', 4 October 1814, Vienna, in Talleyrand Perigord, *Memoirs*, vol. ii, pp. 227–28.
45. Talleyrand to Louis XVIII, 4 October 1814, in Pallain, *The Correspondence of Talleyrand and Louis XVIII*. p. 117 and in Talleyrand-Perigord, *Memoirs*, vol. ii, pp. 229–34.
46. Castlereagh to Liverpool, 9 October 1814, in Webster, *British Diplomacy*, pp. 202–03; Griewank, *Wiener Kongress*, pp. 108–10; Lentz, *Congrès*, pp. 85–88.
47. Castlereagh to Liverpool, 9 October 1814, in Webster, *British Diplomacy*, pp. 202–03. See also Webster, *Foreign Policy of Lord Castlereagh, 1812–1815*, pp. 342–43; Webster, *Congress of Vienna*, pp. 86–87; Lentz, *Congrès*, pp. 89–90.
48. Castlereagh visited Talleyrand around 9 October, when he explained that he would lose all influence with the allies on Naples if he did not stop intriguing against them; he also reminded Talleyrand that it was the allied powers who had restored the French monarchy. Castlereagh to Liverpool, 9 October 1814, in Webster, *British Diplomacy*, pp. 203–05; Webster, *Congress of Vienna*, pp. 88–89.
49. Griewank, *Wiener Kongress*, pp. 110–11; Webster, *Congress of Vienna*, p. 90.
50. For the social life of the Congress, see especially Comte August de La Garde-Chambonas, *Souvenirs du Congrès de Vienne, 1814–1815* (Paris: Librarie Émile-Paul, 1904) (trans. as *Anecdotal Recollections of the Congress of Vienna* (London: Chapman and Hall, 1902); Dorothy McGuigan, *Metternich and the Duchess: The Public and Private Lives of the Congress of Vienna* (Garden City, NY: Double-

day, 1975); Hilde Spiel, *The Congress of Vienna: An Eyewitness Approach*, trans. Richard H. Weber (Philadelphia: Chilton Book Co., 1968); Gregor Dallas, *The Final Act: The Roads to Waterloo* (New York: Henry Holt & Co., 1997); Adam Zamoyski, *Rites of Peace: The Fall of Napoleon and the Congress of Vienna* (New York: HarperCollins, 2007); and David King, *Vienna, 1814: How the Conquerors of Napoleon Made Love, War, and Peace at the Congress of Vienna* (New York: Harmony Books, 2008); Lentz, *Congrès*, pp. 107–25; Brain Vick, *The Congress of Vienna: Power and Politics after Napoleon* (Cambridge, Mass: Harvard University Press, 2014).

51. August Fournier, *Die Geheimpolizei auf dem Wiener Kongress* (Vienna: Tempsky, 1913); Commandant Maurice Henri Weil, *Les Dessous du Congrés de Vienne* (Paris: Librairie Payot, 1917), vols 1 and 2.
52. Zawadzki, *A Man of Honour*, pp. 236–38.
53. ibid.
54. Max Lehmann, 'Tagebuch des Freiherrn vom Stein während des Wiener Kongresses', *Historische Zeitschrift*, New Series xxiv (1888), pp. 392–93 (Stein's entry for 19 October 1814); Zawadzki, *A Man of Honour*, pp. 235–37.
55. 'If we consider the power of Russia', wrote Castlereagh's half-brother, Charles Stewart, 'unassailable as she is in front and rear, with an immense front, mistress of the Caspian, the Euxine and the Baltic, with forty millions of brave, hardy, docile, enthusiastic, and submissive inhabitants, with immense armies highly disciplined, excellently appointed, with innumerable hordes of desolating cavalry, her adoption of French maxims in war, of making the countries where her armies march, feed and maintain them, what may we not fear from her?' Stewart, *Narrative of the War in Germany and France*, p. 185, also in Alison: *Lives of Castlereagh and Stewart*, vol. i, p. 341. See also, Knesebeck's memorandum of November 1814, discussed below, and Merveldt to Metternich, 9 July 1814, London, on the growth of Russian power, in Wawrzkowicz, *Anglia a prawa polska*, pp. 354–55.
56. Talleyrand to Louis XVIII, 9 October 1814, in Palain, *The Correspondence of Prince Talleyrand and King Louis XVIII*, p. 37. On the other hand, it is worth noting that just three years earlier Metternich had been actively promoting the exchange of landlocked Galicia with Napoleon in exchange for the Illyrian provinces and their access to the sea. See Larry Wolff, *The Idea of Galicia: History and Fantasy in Habsburg Political Culture* (Stanford, CA: Standford University Press, 2010), p. 64.
57. 'The unhappy Polish question has threatened the tranquillity of Europe for almost a year. It divides itself, in its turn, into two distinct propositions, which are equally alarming—1. The reunion of the Duchy of Warsaw with Russia, which would menace the frontiers of Austria and Prussia; 2. The re-establishment of the kingdom of Poland, the existence of which would compromise the tranquillity of the Polish provinces still possessed by Austria and Prussia.' Münster to the Prince Regent, Vienna, 27 November 1814, in George Herbert, Count Münster, *Political Sketches of the State of Europe from 1814–1867* (Edinburgh: Edmonston and Douglas, 1868), p. 189.

58. Throughout the summer of 1814, the Austrian ambassador in London, Count Merveldt, had been explaining the dangers of the Russian acquisition of Poland to Austria and Prussia. In particular, Merveldt had a verbal exchange with Czartoryski in order to impress Castlereagh with his arguments. Austria had originally opposed the first partition, he claimed, and would look with favour on the creation of an independent Poland, but not one under the Russian Tsar's sceptre, which would only serve to increase the number of Russian troops menacing the borders of Austria and Prussia. Merveldt felt that Castlereagh was aware of these dangers, but not the rest of the British cabinet. Merveldt to Metternich, 22 July 1814, London, in Wawrzkowicz, *Anglia a prawa polska*, pp. 355–61.
59. Nesselrode to Alexander I, Vienna 13 (25) September 1814, in USSR, *Vneshniaia Politika Rossii, 1801–1815*, Series 1, vol. viii, pp. 103–08; Münster: *Political Sketches of Europe*, p. 187; Zawadzki, *A Man of Honour*, p. 238. The Russians claimed this territory by right of conquest, since they had marched into Poland without the help of the alliance. Metternich insisted that Russia must refrain from taking Kraków and Zamość, since their acquisition would expose Vienna and Galicia, respectively, to invasion.
60. Kraehe, *Metternich's German Policy*, vol ii, *The Congress of Vienna* (Princeton, NJ: Princeton University Press, 1983), pp. 130–31.
61. Castlereagh to Liverpool, 2 October 1814, in Webster, *British Diplomacy*, pp. 197–99.
62. Castlereagh to Liverpool, 2 October 1814, in Webster, *British Diplomacy*, pp. 199–201.
63. The Tsar's dilemma is described most eloquently by Zawadki, *A Man of Honour*, pp. 238–39: 'There was another obstacle facing Alexander's Polish policy: the susceptibilities of Russian opinion, especially in St. Petersburg. As explained by Alexander's trusted aide-de-camp General A.I. Chernyshev, many Russians opposed the surrender of Catherine II's conquests; they doubted long-term Polish loyalty ... It was this ambiguity, resulting from Alexander's inability to translate his Polish dream into reality, that was the root cause of the Polish crisis; for to the ministers of the other powers, Alexander's proposals appeared as an excessive and dangerous extension of Russian influence in Europe rather than a clearcut act of justice on behalf of the Poles.' These problems are made quite apparent in the reports of Lebzeltern, the Austrian ambassador to the Russian court, in the aftermath of the Congress of Vienna; see, e.g, Lebzeltern to Metternich, 20 March 1817, in Grand-Duc Nicolas Mikhaïlowitch, *Les Rapports Diplomatiques de Lebzeltern, Ministre d'Autriche à la Cour de Russie, 1816–1826* (St Petersburg: Manufacture of Government Papers, 1913), p. 12; see also Kraehe, *Congress of Vienna*, pp. 132–33.
64. Griewank, *Wiener Kongress*, p. 147.
65. Kraehe, *Congress of Vienna*, pp. 100–01, 148, 153, 162–63, 166–72, 218–24.
66. Castlereagh to Liverpool, 9 October 1814 (No. 6), in Webster, *British Diplomacy*, pp. 201–02. For a direct Saxon appeal to Castlereagh opposing absorption into Prussia, see Ernest, Duc de Saxe Coburg to Castlereagh, 14 October 1814,

Vienna, in Rudolf Jenak, *Sachsen, der Rheinbund und die Exekution der Sachsen betreffenden Entscheidungen des Wiener Kongresses (1803–1816)* (Neustadt an der Aisch: Ph. C.W. Schmidt, 2005), pp. 203–05. Jenak includes correspondence between the King of Saxony and his plenipotentiary to the Congress, Count Schulenburg, which contains extensive analyses of British policy and detailed 'balance sheets' showing ways of redistributing territories to satisfy the Prussian demand for population while maintaining Saxony (pp. 206–30).

67. Hardenberg to Castlereagh and Metternich, 9 October 1814, in Haus-, Hof- und Staatsarchiv (Vienna), Staatskanzlei, Kongressakten, Karton 7, ff. 93–96; also in d'Angeberg, *Congrès de Vienne*, vol. iv, Appendice', pp. 1934–39; see also, Castlereagh to Liverpool, 9 October 1814 (No. 9), in Webster, *British Diplomacy*, p. 208; Kraehe, *Congress of Vienna*, pp. 158–59.
68. Webster, *British Diplomacy*, pp. 206–07.
69. Talleyrand to Louis XVIII, 4 October 1814 in Talleyrand, *Memoirs*, vol. ii, p. 236, Pallain, *Correspondence of Talleyrand and Louis XVIII*, p. 24; Waresquiel, *Talleyrand*, p. 475; Fournier, *Geheimpolizei*, p. 200.
70. 'Note de lord Castlereagh au prince de Hardenberg' and 'Note verbale de lord Castlereagh au prince de Hardenberg' 11 October 1814, in d'Angeberg, *Congrès de Vienne*, vol. ii, pp. 274–78; Webster, *Foreign Policy of Castlereagh, 1812–1815*, pp. 344–45; Kraehe, *Congress of Vienna*, pp. 171–73; also in Haus-, Hof- und Staatsarchiv (Vienna), Staatskanzlei, Kongressakten, Karton 7, ff. 101–03.
71. Castlereagh to Liverpool, 14 October 1814 (No. 9), in Webster, *British Diplomacy*, pp. 206–10.
72. Webster, *British Diplomacy*, pp. 208–10; Wawrzkowicz, *Anglia a prawa polska*, pp. 425–26; 'Memorandum de lord Castlereagh, au sujet des traités entre les allies relatifs au duché de Varsovie', 4 October 1814, in d'Angeberg, *Congrès de Vienne*, vol. ii, pp. 265–70. Some of these ideas may have been suggested to Castlereagh that summer by Count Merveldt, the Austrian ambassador in London. Merveldt did not try to hide his alarm at the growth of Russian power—specifically pointing to her acquisition of Finland at the expense of Sweden, of part of Galicia at the expense of Austria and of Białystok at the expense of Prussia—in a conversation with Czartoryski in London that July. See Jacob Kloest to King Frederick William III, 11 July 1814, London, in Wawrzkowicz, *Anglia a prawa polska*, p. 363. The same list of Russian aggrandizements also appears in Knesebeck's memorandum of early November (see below). Castlereagh later explained to the British cabinet that the memorandum he gave to the Tsar at the conclusion of this interview was a paper that was being prepared for the other allied ministers.
73. Zawadzki, *A Man of Honour*, p. 240.
74. Wawrzkowicz, *Anglia a prawa polska*, pp. 366–67.
75. Zawadzki, *A Man of Honour*, p. 240.
76. Hardenberg to Metternich, 21 October 1814, in Haus-, Hof- und Staatsarchiv (Vienna), Staatskanzlei, Kongressakten, Karton 7, f. 154. 'Le temps presse—Il me parait que nous devions enfin décider finalement les objets principaux qui nous occupent et avant le depart des Souverains pour Bude [Time is running out—it

appears to me we must at last finally decide the main objects that occupy us and before the departure of the Sovereigns for Buda]. Hardenberg ended his note affectionately: 'je vous embrasse de tout mon coeur [I embrace you with all my heart].'

77. For a copy of Metternich's note to Hardenberg see Haus-, Hof- und Staatsarchiv (Vienna), Staatskanzlei, Kongressakten, Karton 7, ff. 156–63, or in the French archives, see Archives des Affaires Étrangères (La Courneuve), Mémoires et Documents (France), vol. 684 ('Congrès de Vienne'), ff. 146–47. It contained the condition that Austria should be able to 'count on the reciprocal support and absolute uniformity in the steps taken by the two courts on the Polish Question' ('compte sur l'appui reciproque et sur une uniformité absolue de marche des deux Cours, dans la question poloniaise'). See also, Metternich to Castlereagh, 22 October 1814, Vienna, 'Confidentielle', in Haus-, Hof- und Staatsarchiv (Vienna), Staatskanzlei, Kongressakten, Karton 7, ff. 173–74.

78. Peter Burg, *Der Wiener Kongress* (Munich: Deutscher Taschenbuch Verlag, 1984), p. 9; Kraehe, *Congress of Vienna*, pp. 207–10; Zawadzki, *A Man of Honour*, pp. 240–44.

79. 'Mémoire of Lord Castlereagh on the Polish Question' submitted to Prince Metternich, 23 October 1814, in Haus-, Hof- und Staatsarchiv (Vienna), Staatskanzlei, Kongressakten, Karton 7, ff. 167–72: 'It is conceived of the utmost importance even before H[is] I[mperial] M[ajesty] [the Tsar] proceeds to Bude, that he should be apprised of the serious purpose upon which His Allies entertain of pressing upon H.I.M. what they consider themselves, as well as by their treaties, as by General Principles of Policy & Justice entitled to claim from H.I.M.'; also in Castlereagh to Liverpool, 24 October 1815, in Webster, *British Diplomacy*, pp. 212–15; Webster, *Castlereagh, 1812–1815*, pp. 346–47; see also, 'Points de proposition à faire à la Russie par l'Entretien du Cabinet Britannique' in Haus-, Hof- und Staatsarchiv (Vienna), Staatskanzlei, Kongressakten, Karton 7, ff. 287–88. In pencil: 'à Hardenberg le 2 Novembre'.

80. Talleyrand to Louis XVIII, 31 October 1814, in Pallain, *Correspondence of Talleyrand and Louis XVIII*, pp. 99–110.

81. Zawadzki, *A Man of Honour*, pp. 240–41; Arthur Wellesley, Duke of Wellington (ed.), *Supplementary Despatches, Correspondence and Memoranda of Field Marshal Arthur [Wellesley] Duke of Wellington*. (London: J. Murray, 1858–72), vol. ix, pp. 368, 388–92. Zawadzki contends that the memorandum was initially composed by Czartoryski and his assistant, Szaniawski and then personally edited by the Tsar and a seasoned diplomat, Jean Anstett. Zamoyski has more recently argued that Czartoryski was not its author based on comments in his diary that 'Castlereagh is angry with me over Anstett's reply. All fury is directed against me.' Zamoyski: *Rites of Peace*, p. 335. However, his comment would still seem *à propos* if Anstett performed the final redaction and Czartoryski provided the initial ideas, and Zawadzki provides his own evidence of Czartoryski's involvement based on the Czartoryski manuscripts in Kraków and documents published in Wawrzkowicz, *Anglia a prawa polska*, pp. 435–38.

82. Zawadzki, *A Man of Honour*, p. 242.
83. 'Mémoire de Lord Castlereagh on Poland', 4 November 1814, in Haus-, Hof- und Staatsarchiv (Vienna), Staatskanzlei, Kongressakten, Karton 7, ff. 7–28; 234–37, 251–67; also in Archives des Affaires Étrangères (La Courneuve), Mémoires et Documents (France), vol. 684 ('Congrès de Vienne'), ff. 100–1; enclosed in Castlereagh to Liverpool, 17 November 1814, in Wawrzkowicz, *Anglia a prawa polska*, p. 453; d'Angeberg, *Congrès de Vienne*, vol. ii, pp. 394–401; Wellington, *Supplementary Despatches*, vol. ix, pp. 410–16; Webster, *British Diplomacy*, pp. 226–27; Kraehe, *Congress of Vienna*, p. 234. Kraehe believes Castlereagh's response was drafted by Edward Cooke.
84. Castlereagh, Mémoire 'On Poland', 4 November 1814, Haus-, Hof-, und Staatsarchive (Vienna), Staatskanzlei, Kongressakten, Karton 7, ff. 8–10; also Wellington, *Supplementary Despatches*, vol. ix, p. 411; Webster, *British Diplomacy*, p. 226.
85. Castlereagh, Mémoire 'On Poland', 4 November 1814, Haus-, Hof-, und Staatsarchive (Vienna), Staatskanzlei, Kongressakten, Karton 7, ff. 1011; also Webster- *British Diplomacy*, p. 226.
86. Zawadzki, *A Man of Honour*, p. 239.
87. Zawadzki, *A Man of Honour*, p. 241.
88. Enclosed in Castlereagh to Liverpool, 11 November 1814, and printed in Wawrzkowicz, *Anglia a prawa polska*, pp. 439–42. Knesebeck explained that even a mere glance at the map showed that with her recent gains in Finland, Besserabia and on the Persian frontier, Russia had become practically invulnerable to attack. The security of a strong defence at three points, Knesebeck explained, did not in itself guarantee an offensive on the fourth. However, the first concern of a military commander in preparing an offensive was always how to cover one's flanks and retreat. The system of defence that Russia had established in the north and the east therefore inspired fears that Russia had offensive aims in the west. If Russia were to acquire Poland up to Kalisch, as the Tsar demanded, she could cover her right flank with Siearadz, Modlin, and Thorn and her left flank with Zamosc, the Vistula River, and Kraków. 'Is this a defensive position that she takes against Austria and Prussia? ... It is a strange enough system, and a new kind of defence, to advance a so-called point extending from Thorn to Cracow, a front sufficient for 800,000 combattants, and whose flanks are covered by the Vistula and numerous fortresses. To believe in such a defence, with the gains already made along her other borders and her army of 700,000 troops ready to march, one has to hide the map, close one's eyes, and see only the heart of Alexander, the sole guarantee for the security of other states.' Knesebeck then compared this to Prussia's situation—her territories were dispersed along the Rhine, the Elbe and the Vistula, leaving her no more than five million inhabitants in the centre and detached groups threatened by Russia to the east. 'None of her frontiers are secured: does her defence begin at the Oder or the Elbe? How different is this picture from that of Russia—a contiguous mass of territory with 43 million inhabitants, her borders on the north, south and east secure from attack by her neighbors. With this, an army of 5 to 700,000 men, always ready to march ... in cantonments along

her borders, where they are assembled in camps.' And even if the Russian army were lodged behind the borders of Poland, Knesebeck argued, this would change nothing, because 'Poland is a part of Russia, and the Polish troops are merely the advance guard of the Russian army'. The Russian view was that, because of the vast extent of their empire, they needed this large military force, which took so long to mobilize that it did not pose any threat to their neighbours; in addition, Russian conscripts served for life and could not be easily integrated back into the countryside, while ordinary serfs were not otherwise called up for service. See, e.g., Jacobi-Kloest to King Frederick William III, 11 July 1814, London, in Wawrzkowicz, *Anglia a prawa polska*, p. 363 ('ce qui avait cependant pu rassurer un peu l'Autriche, la Prusse et la Suède, était la trop grande étendue de territoire que couvrait cette population, ce qui par consequent faisait naître une certaine difficulté de rassembler assez vite ces moyens de guerre si prépondérants') and Lebzeltern to Metternich, 19 August 1816, St Petersburg, reporting the Tsar's claim that despite his large army, he has few troops at his disposal—they are separated into divisions on the borders of Chine, Persia, Khirgis: 'What remains for an expanse from the Baltic to the Black Sea? An immense line without depth! I cannot put 400,000 men into a campaign.' In contrast, he claimed the Prussians had 500,000 men on a war footing as well as their militia (*Landwehr*): 'They can assemble 300,000 men in 15 days and 500,000 men in six weeks. It would take me three and a quarter months to assemble an inferior force.' Mikhaïlowitch, *Les Rapports Diplomatiques de Lebzeltern*, pp. 2–3; see also, Geoffrey Hosking, *Russia: People and Empire* (Cambridge, MA: Harvard University Press, 1997), pp. 183–93.
89. Cooke to Liverpool, [7] December 1814, in Wellington, *Supplementary Despatches, Correspondence and Memoranda*, vol. ix, p. 473; see also, McGuigan, *Metternich and the Duchess*, pp. 391–92; Webster, *Foreign Policy of Castlereagh, 1812–1815*, p. 360; Zamoyski, *Rites of Peace*, pp. 330–31; King: *Vienna 1814*, pp. 134–35.
90. Maria Ulrichová (ed.), *Clemens Metternich-Wilhelmine von Sagan: Ein Briefwechsel* (Graz and Köln, 1966), p. 270. For suspicions of the Tsar's deliberate efforts to stir up trouble for the Duchess of Sagan to separate her from Metternich, see the Austrian police report of 1 November 1814 in Weil: *Les Dessous*, vol. i, pp. 443–44 (No. 635).
91. Max Lehmann, 'Tagebuch des Freiherrn vom Stein während des Wiener Kongresses', *Historische Zeitschrift*, New Series, vol. xxiv (1888) pp. 400–01 (entry for 5 November).
92. Hardenberg's diary entry on the explosive events of 5 October is somewhat laconic: 'Conference at the Emperor of Russia's on the affairs of the Congress, Saxony, Poland and Italy, then at the King's. The opinion of the Emperor to Humboldt is that I am refusing—dinner at home, Castlereagh came over.' See Stamm-Kuhlmann, *Hardenberg: Tagebücher*, p. 803.
93. Lehmann, 'Tagebuch', p. 399 (entry for 29 October–7 November: 'polnische Sache'). See also, Webster, *Foreign Policy of Castlereagh, 1812–1815*, pp. 347–48.

94. D'Angeberg, *Congrès de Vienne*, vol. ii, pp. 413–14; Webster, *Foreign Policy of Castlereagh, 1812–1815*, p. 354. For Repnin's administration of Saxony since 1813, see Jenak, *Sachsen, der Rheinbund und die Exekution der Sachsen*, pp. 191–98.
95. Hardenberg apologized for the debacle of 5 November: Hardenberg to Metternich, 7 November 1814, 'Confidential', Haus-, Hof- und Staatsarchiv (Vienna), Staatskanzlei, Kongressakten, Karton 7, ff. 296–303: 'The long conversation that I have had in the presence of the King with the Emperor of Russia can scarcely have produced more of an effect than that on Lord Castlereagh and Prince Metternich ... His Imperial Majesty persists in complaining of the obstacles placed before his plans despite the great services he had rendered to the common cause.' Nonetheless Hardenberg hoped to maintain their entente. See Hardenberg to Metternich, 9 November 1814, Vienna, at '3 in the afternoon', Kongressakten, Karton 7, ff. 295: 'I prefer to concert confidentially with you.'
96. The Nida River is a tributary of the Vistula; the Warta River is a tributary of the Oder. Although the two rivers come near to one another just north of Kraków, they never actually meet.
97. Hardenberg to Metternich, 24 November 1814, in Haus-, Hof- und Staatsarchiv (Vienna), Staatskanzlei, Kongressakten, Karton 7, f. 330: 'I have passed by you to tell you all that took place. I am content with the long conversation I had yesterday evening with Tsar Alexander. I hope that we will arrange things. His Majesty promised to let me know his counter-proposals in a day [au premier jour].'
98. Kraehe, *Congress of Vienna*, p. 260.
99. Kraehe, *Congress of Vienna*, pp. 261–63.
100. Castlereagh to Liverpool, 7 December 1814, in Webster, *British Diplomacy*, pp. 255–57; Wawrzkowicz, *Anglia a prawa polska*, pp. 366–67.
101. Metternich to Hardenberg, 10 December 1814, copy in Archives des Affaires Étrangères (La Courneuve), Mémoires et Documents (France), vol. 684 ('Congrès de Vienne'), f. 148.
102. Lehmann, 'Tagebuch', pp. 412–13.
103. Kraehe, *Congress of Vienna*, pp. 267–69; Webster, *Foreign Policy of Castlereagh, 1812–1815*, p. 362.
104. Stamm-Kuhlmann, *Hardenberg: Tagebücher*, p. 807. ('12 [December]': 'Metternich chez moi—embarassé—voulant montrer tous les papiers à l'Empereur'.)
105. Stamm-Kuhlmann, *Hardenberg: Tagebücher*, p. 807, fn. 447. ('Zugleich kam er selbst ... Früh zum St[aats] k[anzler], um ihm zu beweisen, dass das Schreiben nicht offiziell, sondern konfidentiell gewesen, dass man ja noch mehr von Sachsen oder Polen habe fordern können.') According to Stamm-Kuhlmann, the dates given by Stein in his diary are not always accurate, so the interview he recorded for 13 December would seem more likely to have occurred on 12 December.
106. Kraehe, *Congress of Vienna*, pp. 264–68; Castlereagh to Liverpool, 17 December 1814, in Webster, *British Diplomacy*, pp. 257–59.

107. Hermann Freiherrn v. Egloffstein (ed.), *Carl Bertuchs Tagebuch vom Wiener Kongress* (Berlin: Gebrüder Paetel, 1916), p. 69.
108. Ferdinand Troska, *Die Publizistik zur Sächsischen Frage auf dem Wiener Kongress* (Halle: M. Niemeyer, 1891), pp. 13–32.
109. Kraehe, *Congress of Vienna*, p. 272.
110. Webster, *Foreign Policy of Castlereagh, 1812–1815*, pp. 356–57, 551–57: 'I am firmly convinced ... that Europe will not know how to rest in peace if the Emperor of Russia wants, sword in hand, to decide his interests without listening to the other powers, who oppose him with the sanctity of treaties.'
111. Castlereagh to Liverpool, 5 December 1814, in Webster, *British Diplomacy*, pp. 251–52; also in Wellington, *Supplementary Despatches*, vol. ix, p. 462.
112. Castlereagh to Liverpool, 5 December 1814, Vienna, in Webster, *British Diplomacy*, p. 248; Webster, *Foreign Policy of Castlereagh, 1812–1815*, pp. 357–58.
113. Police report of 6 December 1814, in Fournier, *Geheimpolizei*, p. 295.
114. Zawadzki, *A Man of Honour*, p. 243; copy of Grand Duke Constantine's Proclamation, Warsaw, 11 December 1814, in Archives des Affaires Étrangères (La Courneuve), Mémoires et Documents (France), vol. 684 ('Congrès de Vienne'), f. 159.
115. J. Erich Bollmann to Frau Reinhard, 14 December 1814, in Fournier, *Geheimpolizei*, pp. 324–35.
116. Bartsch, report of 22 December 1814, in Fournier, *Geheimpolizei*, p. 309.
117. Police report of 29 December 1814, in Fournier, *Geheimpolizei*, pp. 324–25.
118. Summary of various reports for 16 December 1814, in Fournier, *Geheimpolizei*, p. 304.
119. According to Talleyrand, the Austrians had held talks with the Bavarians as early as September on their common defence: 'At the very time when M. de Schwartzenberg was representing war as inevitable sooner or later, the movements of a body of Austrian troops in Galicia seemed to indicate that it might be near at hand. The Cabinet of Vienna seems to be waking up from its lethargy. M. de Metternich talked to Prince de Wrede of an alliance, asking him whether Bavaria would not now add twenty-five thousand men to the Austrian forces ...' Talleyrand to Louis XVIII, 17 September 1814, *Correspondence of Talleyrand and Louis XVIII*, p. 147; then in late November, he writes again: 'Prince Schwartzenberg inclines to war, saying that it can be made now with more advantage than some years hence. A plan of campaign has been already drawn up at the Chancellery of War; and Prince de Wrede [of Bavaria] has also made one. Austria, Bavaria and the other German states would put three hundred and twenty thousand men in the field ... The campaign would not commence before the end of March.' Talleyrand to Louis XVIII, 25 November 1814, Vienna, *Correspondence of Talleyrand and Louis XVIII*, pp. 167–68.
120. Kraehe, *Congress of Vienna*, pp. 279–83. The plan called for a single chamber in which each state would be represented equally, and Austria would hold the permanent presidency.
121. Egloffstein, *Carl Bertuchs Tagebuch vom Wiener Kongress*, p. 71; Zamoyski, *Rites of Peace*, p. 365.

122. Castlereagh to Liverpool, 17 December 1814, in Webster, *British Diplomacy*, pp. 257–59.
123. Kraehe, *Congress of Vienna*, p. 271.
124. Kraehe, *Congress of Vienna*, pp. 271, 284–85. The dates in Hardenberg's diary differ slightly from this account. Hardenberg records that he met with Czartoryski, Stein, Capodistrias, Knesebeck and Humboldt on 14 December; met with King Frederick III to read the Austrian 'pieces' (the correspondence handed over by Metternich) and then had an audience with the Tsar on 15 December; had another meeting with Czartoryski, Stein, Capodistrias, and Humboldt on 16 December at which they drafted the note for Alexander; sent the note to Alexander on 17 December; met with Metternich on the 18th; and met with Castlereagh alone on 19 December and then again with Stein, Czartoryski and Humboldt. See Stamm-Kuhlmann, *Hardenberg: Tagebücher*, pp. 807–09, for diary entries for 14–21 December 1814. See also, Count Münster to the Prince Regent, 18 December 1814, in Münster, *Political Sketches of Europe*, pp. 207–08; Webster, *Foreign Policy of Castlereagh, 1812–1815*, pp. 366–67.
125. In a letter to Metternich on 21 December, Hardenberg explained that the memorandum, which he had previously described, would be officially conveyed to him by Castlereagh and to the Austrian Emperor by the Tsar. 'In the name of friendship', Hardenberg implores Metternich to consider most carefully the proposal for moving the King of Saxony to the left bank of the Rhine. This would not only take care of the needs of the King of Saxony and his family, Hardenberg points out, but it would also establish peace on a solid basis without creating resentment in Prussia. There seems little reason to doubt Hardenberg's sincerity. See Hardenberg to Metternich, 21 December 1814, 'Confidentielle', in Haus-, Hof- und Staatsarchiv (Vienna), Staatskanzlei, Kongressakten, Karton 7, f. 402. See also, Kraehe, *Congress of Vienna*, p. 285. The transfer was contemplated by the Russians before the Congress.
126. Castlereagh to Liverpool, Vienna, 5 January 1815, in Webster, *British Diplomacy*, pp. 282–83.
127. Münster to the Prince Regent, 24 December 1814, Vienna, in Münster, *Political Sketches of Europe*, pp. 216–17. The Austrians, in fact, accused the Prussians of distorting the numbers in a new form of 'statistical aggrandizement'. See Kraehe, *Congress of Vienna*, p. 284–86. For a copy of Castlereagh's *projet* for the formation of the Statistical Committee, see Sir Charles Kingsley Webster, *The Congress of Vienna* (London: H. Milford, 1919), Appendix VII, p. 186. Castlereagh gave his proposal to the Russian and Prussian ministers at the conference of 20 December: see Castlereagh to Liverpool, 24 December 1814, in Webster, *British Diplomacy*, pp. 268–71. See also Lentz, *Congrès*, pp. 101–03.
128. Archives des Affaires Étrangères (La Courneuve), Mémoires et Documents (France), vol. 684 ('Congrès de Vienne').
129. Czartoryski to Anstett, Vienna, 2 (14) January 1815, in USSR, *Vneshniaia Politika Rossii, 1801–1815*, Series 1, vol. viii, pp. 173–74.
130. Castlereagh to Liverpool, 24 December 1814, in Webster, *British Diplomacy*, pp. 268–71.

131. Kraehe, *Congress of Vienna*, p. 262.
132. Ilsemann, *Die Politik Frankreiches auf dem Wiener Kongress*, pp. 169–90.
133. Gulick, *Europe's Classical Balance of Power*.
134. Talleyrand to Metternich, 19 December 1814, Archives des Affaires Étrangères (La Courneuve), vol. 684, ff. 167–73; also in d'Angeberg, *Congrès de Vienne*, vol. ii, pp. 540–44. It has been suggested that his note was primarily an attempt to allay Austro-British concerns by tacitly conveying the message that France no longer had territorial ambitions in Belgium or the Rhineland. See Kraehe, *Congress of Vienna*, p. 284. In fact, Kraehe praises Talleyrand's response as 'his finest moment at the congress'.
135. Alexander I to Count Lieven, Vienna, 15 (27) December 1814, in USSR, *Vneshniaia Politika Rossii, 1801–1815*, pp. 139–40.
136. Instructions attached to Alexander I's letter to Count Lieven, Vienna, 15 (27) December 1814, in USSR, *Vneshniaia Politika Rossii, 1801–1815*, pp. 140–45.
137. Report of 29 December 1814, in Fournier, *Der Congress von Châtillon*, p. 321 ('On sait dans le public qu'Alexandre ne veut pas traiter avec lui et qu'il a destiné Razumowsky'); Webster, *Foreign Policy of Castlereagh, 1812–1815*, p. 369.
138. Capodistrias, 'Aperçu de ma carrière publique depuis 1798 jusqu'à 1822', in *Sbornik imperatorskogo russkogo istoricheskogo obshchestva* [Transactions of the Russian Imperial Historical Society], vol. iii (St Petersburg: Russian Imperial Historical Society, 1868), pp. 197–200; C.M. Woodhouse, *Capodistria: the Founder of Greek Independence* (London: Oxford University Press, 1973), pp. 121–22.
139. Metternich to Razumovsky, 26 December 1814, No. 1, Vienna; Razumovsky to Metternich, 27 December 1814, Vienna; Metternich to Razumovsky, 27 December 1814, No. 3, Vienna, in Haus-, Hof- und Staatsarchiv (Vienna), Staatskanzlei, Kongressakten, Karton 7, ff. 537–40; see also, Kraehe, *Congress of Vienna*, p. 287; Zamoyski, *Rites of Peace*, p. 389.
140. Note [by Czartoryski], 30 December 1814 (11 January 1815), in USSR, *Vneshniaia Politika Rossii, 1801–1815*, Series 1, vol. viii, pp. 157–62.
141. Zawadzki, *A Man of Honour*, p. 244.
142. Kraehe, *Congress of Vienna*, pp. 288–91. At the same time, Metternich further proposed that the Saxon king should be moved from Prussian custody to Vienna.
143. Webster, *Foreign Policy of Castlereagh, 1812–1815*, p. 370. Did Hardenberg even realize he had given such offence? His own diary makes no mention of it—only that the committee had discussed the admission of France. Stein's diary also makes no mention of the outburst, but he does refer to the discussion over the comprehensive memorandum on Poland. Lehmann, 'Tagebuch', p. 422 (entry for 31 December). In his diary, Gentz likewise fails to mention Hardenburg's eruption.
144. Russian Projet, 30 December 1814, in Archives des Affaires Étrangères (La Courneuve), Mémoires et Documents, vol. 684, ff. 174–89.
145. McGuigan, *Metternich and the Duchess*, pp. 424–28.

146. 'Note of Lord Castlereagh', 5 January 1815, in Alison, *Lives of Castlereagh and Stewart*, vol. ii, p. 556, unnumbered footnote.
147. Webster, *Foreign Policy of Castlereagh, 1812–1815*, p. 372.
148. Merveldt to Metternich, 22 July 1814, in Wawrzkowicz, *Anglia a prawa polska*, pp. 355–61: Merveldt told Czartoryski that the first step in French aggression had been to secure the Low Countries; Russia was now similarly securing Poland. 'On my side, I repeated my way of viewing this question, which is that it will be easier to stop Russia now than later, when she has organized all of her means, which have increased her power.'
149. Merveldt to Metternich, 22 July 1814, London, in Wawrzkowicz, *Anglia a prawa polska*, pp. 355–61; Jacobi-Kloest to King Frederick William III, 11 July 1814, London, in Wawrzkowicz, *Anglia a prawa polska*, pp. 362–68, reporting the same conversation.
150. Talleyrand to Louis XVIII, 17 September 1814, in Pallain, *The Correspondence of Prince Talleyrand and King Louis XVIII*, pp. 146–47.
151. Castlereagh to Liverpool, 21 November 1814, Vienna, in Webster, *British Diplomacy*, p. 240; also in Wellington, *Supplementary Despatches*, vol. ix, p. 447 and Zamoski, *Rites of Peace*, p. 368.
152. Zamoyski, *Rites of Peace*, p. 369.
153. Lehmann, 'Tagebuch', p. 421.
154. Zamoyski, *Rites of Peace*, p. 390, citing F.O. 92/10, f. 58; see also Andrew Roberts, *Napoleon and Wellington: The Battle of Waterloo* (New York: Simon and Schuster, 2001), p. 137.
155. 'Die Österreicher zogen unterdessen eine Armee in Böhmen zusammen ... eine Armee von Franzosen soll vom Rhein her auf die Elbe vorgehen. Es sollte also Deutschland von neuem einem bürgerlichen und französischen Krieg preisgegeben werden wegen des Interesses eines Anhängers von Napoleon und über die Frage, ob es besser sei, ihn auf das linke Rheinufer zu versetzen oder Sachsen zu zerreissen und ihm dort ein Fragment anzuweisen. Welche Verblendung!' Stamm-Kuhlmann, *Hardenberg: Tagebücher*, p. 810, fn. 470.
156. [? Schwarzenberg] to Emperor Francis, 5 January 1815, Vienna, in Haus-, Hof- und Staatsarchiv (Vienna), Kriegsakten 428 (alt 492), ff. 10–13. I wish to thank Professor Alan Sked of the London School of Economics for his help in translating this letter from the old German cursive script (*Fraktur Handschrift*).
157. Merveldt to Metternich, 22 July 1814, in Wawrzkowicz, *Anglia a prawa polska*, p. 359. Metternich wrote to the Emperor Francis that this demonstrated that the British had a low opinion of the state of preparedness of the Austrian army, and that they should strive to correct this view. Metternich, 6 August 1814, Baden, in Wawrzkowicz, *Anglia a prawa polska*, p. 362.
158. Jacobi-Kloest to King Frederick William III, 11 July 1814, London, in Wawrzkowicz, *Anglia a prawa polska*, p. 365.
159. Talleyrand to Louis XVIII, 12 November 1814, Vienna, in Pallain, *Correspondence of Talleyrand and Louis XVIII*, pp. 132–33.

160. Talleyrand to Louis XVIII, 17 October 1814, in Pallain, *Correspondence of Talleyrand and Louis XVIII*, p. 64.
161. Talleyrand to Louis XVIII, 8 February 1815, in Pallain, *Correspondence of Talleyrand and Louis XVIII*, p. 304.
162. Webster, *Foreign Policy of Castlereagh, 1812–1815*, pp. 358–60.
163. Castlereagh to Liverpool, Vienna, 2 January 1815, in Webster, *British Diplomacy*, p. 280: 'I hope you will not think my Treaty an improvident one. It pledges you absolutely to nothing beyond the value in money at which the force is calculated ....'
164. Nesselrode to Pozzo di Borgo, 15 (27) September 1814, in Charles-André Pozzo di Borgo, *Correspondance diplomatique du comte Pozzo di Borgo, ambassadeur de Russie en France et du comte de Nesselrode depuis la restauration des Bourbons jusqu'au congrès d'Aix-la-Chapelle, 1814–1818* (Paris: Calmann Lévy, 1890), vol. 1, p. 83; also cited in Matthew Rendall, 'Defensive Realism and the Concert of Europe', *Review of International Studies* 32/3 (2006), p. 530.
165. Hardenberg's diary entry for 21 December 1814, in Stamm-Kuhlmann, *Hardenberg: Tagebücher*, p. 809.
166. Kraehe, *Congress of Vienna*, p. 292. The Soviet historian Zak reached a similar conclusion: 'Although by [3 January 1815,] the hostilities between England and the United States had already ceased (which was actually an additional push for England to enter into an alliance with Austria and France) and the English government could freely dispose of its military forces, Castlereagh managed to negotiate for England the right to replace them with mercenaries or merely to provide money for supporting the necessary military contingents (£20 per each infantryman and £30 per each cavalryman). Notably, Castlereagh wrote to Liverpool that the treaty was the best way to ensure English interests on the Continent without imposing any serious obligations on the English government. In a hurry to conclude the treaty, Castlereagh signed it even before receiving official approval from his government. In England, his actions worried some members of the government, who insisted that Castlereagh should be given detailed instructions. It is likely that neither Austria nor (especially) France seriously considered supplying such a significant military contingent as was provided for under the treaty; neither could Castlereagh firmly count on the Parliament approving the subsidies provided for in the treaty. However, both Castlereagh and Metternich, who had long thought about the possibility of becoming closer with France, believed that the entry into the treaty would in and of itself be a strong means of influencing Russia as well as Prussia. It should be noted that both Austria and especially England, which had bet on the Prussian card, believed, as Castlereagh clearly wrote to Lord Liverpool on 2 January 1815, that the purpose of the secret treaty was not to damage the interest of Prussia so much as to pull her away from Russia.' L.A. Zak, *Monarkhi protiv narodov* [Monarchy against the People] (Moscow, 1966), pp. 197–98. I wish to thank my friend Elena Speed, an attorney at the San Francisco office of the international law firm of Baker & McKenzie, for her kind assistance in translating this passage. See also the

discussion by political scientist Rendall: 'Defensive Realism and the Concert of Europe', pp. 526–30.
167. These suggestions are made by Rory Muir in his *Britain and the Defeat of Napoleon, 1807–1815* (New Haven, CT: Yale University Press, 1996), p. 341. The sacrifice of Saxony had been criticized by the opposition in the House of Commons in November.
168. British Library Manuscripts Loan 72 ('Liverpool Mss. on Loan'), vol. 15, ff. 98–99, Lord Mulgrave to Lord Bathurst, 18 January 1815, 'Private'.
169. Hardenberg's entry for 16 December 1814 ('Es soll eine geheime Convention zwischen Oest[er]reich, England, Frankreich, Bayern geschlossen seyn wegen Pohlen und Sachsen') in Stamm-Kuhlmann, *Hardenberg: Tagebücher*, p. 808.
170. Hardenberg's diary entry for 4 January 1815 in Stamm-Kuhlmann, *Hardenberg: Tagebücher*, p. 811. Hardenberg subsequently dined with Castlereagh.
171. Castlereagh to Liverpool, 5 January 1814 (No. 49), in Webster, *British Diplomacy*, pp. 282–83.
172. Hardenberg's diary entries in Stamm-Kuhlmann, *Hardenberg: Tagebücher*, pp. 811–13. On 7 January, he recorded 'Castlereagh wanted to have the King of Saxony at Prague and showed me a memorandum he has written on the non-necessity of [the King's] consent'. The reference to Prague was presumably a reference to the Saxon King's captivity. On 13 January, Hardenberg recorded in his diary that he was unhappy with Castlereagh's way of explaining himself and how he seemed to favour the views of Prussia's adversaries. Stamm-Kuhlmann, *Hardenberg: Tagebücher*, p. 812.
173. Castlereagh to Liverpool, 8 January 1815, No. 50, in Webster, *British Diplomacy*, p. 284.
174. Webster, *Foreign Policy of Castlereagh, 1812–1815*, p. 373.
175. Jaucourt to Talleyrand, 27 March and 2 April 1815, and Reinhardt to Talleyrand, Brussels, 28 March 1815, in Pallain, *Correspondence of Talleyrand and Louis XVIII*, pp. 424–25 and 435–36.
176. Waliszewski, *Le Règne d'Alexandre Ier*, p. 312 (based on N.K. Schilder *Imperator Aleksandr Pervyi*, vol. iii (St Petersburg: A.S. Suvorin, 1897), p. 306); Lehmann, 'Tagebücher', pp. 447–48 (Stein's entry for 8 April 1815); Nesselrode to Pozzo di Borgo, 1 (13) May 1815, in Pozzo di Borgo, *Correspondence Diplomatique*, vol. i, p. 143; Alan Schom, *One Hundred Days: Napoleon's Road to Waterloo* (New York: Atheneum, 1992), p. 246.
177. Webster, *Foreign Policy of Castlereagh, 1812–1815*, p. 372.
178. Castlereagh to Liverpool, 5 January 1814 (No. 49), in Webster, *British Diplomacy*, pp. 282–83.
179. Historian Enno Kraehe observes: 'Despite its important role in the negotiations, Castlereagh seems not to have sent a copy home; it is not to be found in his correspondence in the PRO.' Kraehe, *Congress of Vienna*, p. 295, fn. 88.
180. Castlereagh, 'Note', 5 January 1815, in Haus-, Hof- und Staatsarchiv (Vienna), Staatskanzlei, Kongressakten, Karton 7, ff. 549–54, described in the archives index as 'Castlereagh's Plan for the Reconstruction of the Kingdom of Prussia':

'Les données suivantes suffiront pour faire voir que sans réunir la Saxe Royale entière á la Prusse et sans l'empêcher de former un corps d'état independant, on peut suffire aux moyens pour rétablir comme le veut le Traité de Kalisch, la force réelle de la Prusse au point vu elle se trouvait avant 1806, pour assurer au Hanovre les arrondissements voulus par le traité, pour accorder à Saxe Wiemar l'augmentation de 50,000 ames qu'on lui a fait esperer, et pour indemniser le Grande Duché de Darmstadt de la perte qui'il éprouverait en cedant le Duché de Westphalie à la Prusse.'

181. Alexandra von Ilsemann, for example, points out that after the conclusion of the secret treaty ('Geheimvertrag'), the Polish-Saxon Question was quickly resolved. See Ilsemann. *Die Politik Frankreichs auf dem Wiener Kongress*, pp. 209–10. Castlereagh himself claimed as much in a later letter to the British cabinet, although his assertion may have been influenced by a natural desire to justify his earlier conduct. See Castlereagh to Liverpool, 13 February 1815, No. 70, Vienna, in Webster, *British Diplomacy*, pp. 303–05: 'I consider that the Defensive Treaty signed on the third ultimo with Austria and France, and since acceded to by Holland, Bavaria, and Hanover, has been productive of all the good consequences, I may say more, than I had ventured to hope for, when I proposed that measure for the adoption of those Powers.'

182. Castlereagh to Liverpool, 25 December 1814, in Webster. *British Diplomacy*, p. 272. Talleyrand told Count Münster the same: 'Prince Talleyrand assures me that the Emperor of Russia, after having obtained his end in Poland, would desire to see Prussia give up Saxony.' Count Münster to Prince Regent, 29 December 1814, Vienna, in Münster, *Political Sketches of Europe*, p. 218.

183. Kraehe, *Congress of Vienna*, p. 291. Kraehe makes it seem that this was tantamount to a refusal, whereas it would seem more accurate to say the Tsar's support was lukewarm; in his diary for that day, Hardenberg jotted: '[a]mbiguous explanations on what would be done in the case of war, at least not very pronounced.'

184. Webster, *Foreign Policy of Castlereagh, 1812–1815*, p. 228, fn. 1 and p. 352.

185. Rey, *Alexandre I*, pp. 359–60; Zawadzki, *Man of Honour*, pp. 251–52; Zamoyski, *Rites of Peace*, pp. 353, 410–11, 483.

186. Ley, *Alexandre Ier et sa Sainte Alliance*, pp. 85–105 ('Un Pacte Trinitaire').

187. See Chapter 4, below.

188. 'Troisième Protocole de la séance du 12 janvier 1815', in d'Angeberg. *Le Congrès de Vienne*, vol. iv ('Appendice'), p. 1883; Castlereagh to Liverpool, 11 January 1815 (No. 51), 22 January 1815 (No. 57), and 29 January 1815 (No. 63) in Webster, *British Diplomacy*, pp. 285–86, 292–98; and Kraehe: *Congress of Vienna*, p. 299. Hardenberg's plan of 12 January stated that Prussia required 3,411,715 inhabitants to reach its 1805 population and was entitled to an additional 681,914 to match the gains of the other powers. Hardenberg proposed that she obtain 2,051,240 new residents by acquiring the Kingdom of Saxony, as well as 810,268 from the Duchy of Warsaw, 299,877 from the Duchy of Berg, 131,888 from Westphalia, and 729,228 from the Left Bank of the Rhine. Protocole de

la Conférence, le 12 janvier 1815, Annexe A, 'Plan pour la reconstruction de la Prusse' in Great Britain, Foreign Office, *British and Foreign State Papers*, vol. ii (London: James Ridgway and Sons, 1839) pp. 602–03; see also Gulick, *Europe's Classical Balance of Power*, pp. 249–51, Zamoyski, *Rites of Peace*, p. 396.
189. Webster, *Foreign Policy of Castlereagh, 1812–1815*, p. 380.
190. Castlereagh to Liverpool, 8 January 1815 (No. 50), in Webster, *British Diplomacy*, p. 285.
191. Castlereagh to Liverpool, 22 January 1815 (No. 57) and 29 January 1815 (No. 63), in Webster, *British Diplomacy*, pp. 292–98; Webster, *Foreign Policy of Castlereagh, 1812–1815*, pp. 380–82.
192. Hardenberg's diary entry for 23 January 1815, in Stamm-Kuhlmann, *Hardenberg: Tagebücher*, p. 813.
193. Under the Austrian proposal, Prussia needed 3,400,065—less than Hardenberg's claim of 3,411,715 but closer to this than to Castlereagh's 5 January estimate of 2,657,835. On the other hand, the Austrian proposal gave the Prussians only 782,249 Saxon residents—far closer to Castlereagh's award of 695,235 Saxons than to Hardenberg's most recent demand for 2,051,240 Saxons. The Austrian proposal was accompanied by a balance sheet showing Austrian gains and losses, alleging that Austria would gain only 166,376 additional inhabitants based on the treaties. See Protocole de la Conférence, le 28 janvier 1815, Annexe B, 'Mémoire Autrichien en Réponse au Plan Prussien' and Sous-Annexe, 'Contre-Projet Autrichien au Plan Prussien', in Great Britain, *British and Foreign State Papers*, vol. ii, pp. 606–12; see also Gulick, *Europe's Classical Balance of Power*, p. 251.
194. Castlereagh to Liverpool, 6 February 1815 (No. 66), in Webster, *British Diplomacy*, pp. 299–302; Webster, *Foreign Policy of Castlereagh, 1812–1815*, p. 382.
195. Webster, *Foreign Policy of Castlereagh, 1812–1815*, p. 382.
196. Webster, *Foreign Policy of Castlereagh, 1812–1815*, p. 383. Hardenberg submitted a new memorandum to the other powers on 8 February, again asserting that Prussia should be awarded Leipzig but submitting to the new arrangements. According to Hardenberg's new calculations, Prussia actually received 855,305 Saxons, 810,268 Poles from the Duchy of Warsaw, 1,100,000 inhabitants from the Left Bank of the Rhine, 299,877 inhabitants from the Duchy of Berg, 131,888 inhabitants from Westphalia, 127,000 inhabitants from the House of Orange, and 20,000 inhabitants from Thorn and its outskirts—giving her a surplus of 41,630 over her losses. 'Mémoire Prussien, en Réponse au Contre-Projet Autrichien', in Great Britain, *British and Foreign State Papers*, vol. ii, pp. 616–29.
197. Castlereagh, Note on Polish affairs, 12 January 1815, Archives des Affaires Étrangères (La Courneuve), Mémoires et Documents, vol. 684, f. 190; also in Webster, *British Diplomacy*, pp. 287–88.
198. See Kraehe, *Congress of Vienna*, pp. 327–44; Webster, *The Congress of Vienna*, pp. 147–53; Lentz, *Congrès*, pp. 147–50, pp. 153–58; and Enno Kraehe, 'Wellington and the Reconstruction of the Allied Armies during the Hundred Days', *International History Review* 11/1 (February 1989), pp. 84–97.

199. Michael Hundt, *Die Mindermächtigen deutschen Staaten auf dem Wiener Kogress* (Mainz: P. von Zabern, 1996), pp. 109–49, 352–53. The smaller German states held 56 meetings from 14 October 1814 to 9 June 1815. Nineteen delegates attended the first meeting, held by Freiherr von Gagern. See Hundt, *Die Mindermächtigen*, pp. 109–10.
200. For the treatment of Italy at the Congress of Vienna, see Webster, *Congress of Vienna*, pp. 142–47, and *Foreign Policy of Castlereagh, 1812–1815*, pp. 313–18, 397–412; Lentz, *Congrès*, pp. 173–96, pp. 219–23; Guglielmo Ferrero, *The Reconstruction of Europe: Talleyrand and the Congress of Vienna, 1814–1815*, trans. Theodore Jaeckel (New York, 1941), pp. 196–207, 255–57, 301–10; Hannah Alice Straus, *The Attitude of the Congress of Vienna toward Nationalism in Germany, Italy and Poland* (New York: Columbia University Press, 1949), pp. 85–122; Alan J. Reinerman, *Austrian and the Papacy in the Age of Metternich* (vol. i): *Between Conflict and Cooperation, 1809–1830* (Washington DC: Catholic University Press, 1979), pp. 7–19 (Reinerman argues that Metternich supported the Papacy's claims for a restoration of the Legations); 'Memoir by Friedrich von Gentz', 12 February 1815, in Metternich, *Memoirs of Prince Metternich*, vol. ii, pp. 579–84 ('Affairs of Italy'); and the correspondence between Wellington and Castlereagh and between Talleyrand to Louis XVIII. See, e.g., Talleyrand to Louis XVIII, 15 February 1815, in Talleyrand: *Correspondence of Talleyrand and Louis XVIII*, pp. 316–33 (on French proposals and Austrian counter-proposals on Italy). For the Restoration in Italy generally, see Marco Meriggi, 'State and Society in Post-Napoleonic Italy', in David Laven and Lucy Riall (eds), *Napoleon's Legacy: Problems of Government in Restoration Europe* (Oxford: Berg, 2000), pp. 49–63; David Laven, *Venice and Venetia under the Habsburgs* (New York: Oxford University Press, 2002) and 'Austria's Italian Policy Reconsidered: Revolution and Reform in Restoration Italy', *Modern Italy* 3 (1997), pp. 3–33; R. John Rath, *The Provisional Austrian Regime in Lombardy-Venetia* (Austin: University of Texas, 1969); Michael Broers, *Napoleonic Imperialism and the Savoyard Monarchy, 1773–1821: Statebuilding in Piedmont* (Lewiston, NY: Edwin Mellen Press, 1997) and *The Napoleonic Empire in Italy, 1796–1814: Cultural Imperialism in a European Context?* (London: Palgrave Macmillan, 2005); and John A. Davis, *Naples and Napoleon: Southern Italy and the European Revolutions, 1780–1860* (Oxford: Oxford University Press, 2006).
201. Napoleon to Joseph, 22 April 1806, in John Santore, *Modern Naples: A Documentary History, 1799–1999* (New York: Italica Press, 2001), p. 66.
202. Davis, *Naples and Napoleon*, pp. 260–61; Harold Acton, *The Bourbons of Naples (1734–1825)* (London: Methuen, 1956), pp. 622–23.
203. John Rosselli, *Lord William Bentinck: The Making of a Liberal Imperialist, 1774–1839* (Berkeley: University of California Press, 1974), pp. 147–80 and *Lord William Bentinck and the British Occupation of Sicily* (Cambridge: Cambridge University Press, 1956).
204. William A'Court, 'Minutes of a Conversation with Lord Castlereagh in Paris, 16 May 1814', British Library, Additional Manuscript ('Add. Mss.') 41515, ff. 62–66.

205. Note of Nesselrode to Alexander, 20 January (1 February) 1815, and Note on Status of Negotiations, 28 January (9 February) 1815, in USSR, *Vneshniaia Politika Rossii, 1801–1815*, Series 1, vol. viii, pp. 181–82, 188.
206. Castlereagh to Liverpool, 18 December 1814, in Webster, *British Diplomacy*, pp. 261–63, and Wellington, *Supplementary Despatches*, vol. ix, p. 485. See also, Liverpool to Castlereagh, 23 December 1814 and 20 February 1815, Wellington to Liverpool, 25 December 1814, and Liverpool to Wellington, 11 January 1815, and Castlereagh to Wellington, 12 March 1815, in Webster, *British Diplomacy*, pp. 264–65, 273–74, 288–90, 310–11.
207. Clancarty to Castlereagh, 3 April 1815, Vienna, 'Private', in Public Record Office of Northern Ireland (Belfast), D3030/4485, on the delay in the negotiation of a Franco-Austrian treaty for the removal of Murat: 'The Treaty between Austria and France respecting Murat has not yet made all the progress I could have wished, circumstances have rendered it less pressing.'
208. Acton, *Bourbons of Naples*, pp. 634–39, 645–47; Davis, *Naples and Napoleon*, pp. 263–64; Santore, *Modern Naples*, pp. 86–88; Rath, *Austrian Regime in Lombardy-Venetia*, pp. 316–61; Jean Vanel, 'Murat', in Jean Tulard (ed.), *Dictionnaire Napoléon* (Paris: Fayard, 1999), vol. ii, pp. 358–60; Jean Tulard, *Murat ou l' Éveil des Nations* (Paris: Hachette, 1983).
209. One recent historian of Restoration Italy aptly observes: 'The major victory of Metternich and Francis I at the Congress of Vienna was to establish Austrian hegemony in Italy. This was secured principally through the direct reacquisition of Lombardy and Venetia, two of the most populous and fertile regions in the peninsula. In addition, the thrones of a number of smaller states—Modena, Parma, and Tuscany—fell to members of the House of Habsburg. Metternich's plan to erect an Italian Confederation along the lines of that established in Germany came to nothing. The King of Sardinia– Piedmont and the Pope blocked the proposal, refusing to countenance Habsburg presidency. Marriage alliances and military conventions went a long way towards compensating for this setback.' Laven: *Venice and Venetia under the Habsburgs*, p. 78.
210. Lane-Poole, *Life of the Right Honourable Stratford Canning*, vol. i, p. 226; Capodistrias, 30 July (11 August) 1814, and 22 September (4 October) 1814 and 18 (30) January 1815 in USSR, *Vneshniaia Politika Rossii, 1801–1815*, Series 1, pp. 81–85, 111–12, 176–79. See also Ferrero, *Reconstruction of Europe*, pp. 208–16, 295–96; Webster, *Congress of Vienna*, pp. 153–54; Webster, *Foreign Policy of Castlereagh, 1812–1815*, pp. 395–96; Lentz, *Congrès*, pp. 167–71.
211. Woodhouse, *Capodistria*: pp. 82–105, 11–13; Webster, *The Congress of Vienna*, p. 153; Murray Luck, *History of Switzerland*, pp. 258–385, 305–42; Lane-Poole, *Life of the Right Honourable Stratford Canning*, vol. i, pp. 222–35. A year later, Switzerland's border with Piedmont was settled in the Treaty of Turin.
212. For this section generally, see H. Arnold Barton, *Scandinavia in the Revolutionary Era*, pp. 275–358; D. Kirby, *The Baltic World, 1772–1993*, pp. 30–45; Päiviö Tommila, *La Finlande dans la politique européene dans 1809–1815* (Helsinki: Finnish Historical Society, 1962).

213. The King's illegitimate son, Carl Löwenhelm, actually represented Sweden at the Congress of Vienna.
214. At his funeral, Count Axel von Ferson, suspected lover of Marie Antoinette, who had also helped Washington at Yorktown and who had arranged for Louis XVI's 'flight to Varennes', was falsely blamed and scandalously beaten to death by a street mob as troops impassively looked on.
215. Webster, *Foreign Policy of Castlereagh, 1812–1815*, pp. 306–09, 390–92. Bernadotte continued to successfully evade some of Sweden's obligations, and the question of the enforcement of the treaty would again arise three years later at the Congress of Aix-la-Chapelle.
216. H. Arnold Barton, *Scandinavia in the Revolutionary Era*, p. 354. Barton cites Tommali, *La Finlande dans la politique européene*, p. 417, who is in fact citing the Tsar's letter to Castlereagh in response to the latter's first memorandum on Poland, in d'Angeberg, *Congrès de Vienne*, vol. ii, p. 351 The quotation is taken slightly out of context since the Tsar was actually pointing out, in response to a point previously made by Castlereagh, that, although the acquisition of Norway gave Sweden important maritime advantages *vis-à-vis* Russia, this was offset by the fact that his capital had become impregnable, while, since Sweden was more concentrated, both sides had gained in security: 'Vous me faites entendre que l'Angleterre n'a consenti à l'acquisition de la Norwége, en faveur de le Suède, que pour me garantir l'acquisition antérieure de la Finlande ... Je ne pouvais perdre de vue les grands advantages maritimes que la Norwége donnait à la Suède contra moi. Cependant, tout compensé, ma capitale était devenue inattaquable, tandis que la Suède, mieux concentrée, n'avait plus rien à redouter. De cette façon on gagnait de part et d'autre en sûreté.'
217. Max James Kohler, *Jewish Rights at the Congresses of Vienna (1814–1815) and Aix-la-Chapelle* (New York: American Jewish Committee, 1918), pp. 1–49, and on Humboldt's views, pp. 63–83; Salo Baron, *Die Judenfrage auf dem Wiener Kongress* (Vienna and Berlin: R. Löwit, 1920); Michael Hundt, 'Die Vertretung der jüdischen Gemeinden Lübecks, Bremens, Hamburgs auf der Wiener Kongress', *Blätter für deutsche Landesgeschichte* 130 (1994), pp. 143–90; for further background, see Thomas Stamm-Kuhlmann, 'Der Staatskanzler von Hardenberg, die Bankiers und die Judenemanzipation in Preussen', *Vierteljahrschrift für Sozial- und Wirtschaftsgeschichte* 83/3 (1996), pp. 334–46; Niall Ferguson, *The House of Rothschild: Money's Prophets, 1798–1848* (New York: Viking Press, 1998), pp. 172–76; Ruth Gay, *The Jews of Germany: A Historical Portrait* (New Haven, CT and London: Yale University Press, 1992), pp. 98–138; Nachum T. Gidal, *Jews in Germany from Roman Times to the Weimar Republic* (Köln: Könemann Verlagsgesellschaft mbH, 1988), pp. 112–49.
218. In July 1815 Hardenberg also acted to ban the performance of an anti-Semitic play in Berlin on the grounds of Jewish sacrifices during the course of the war.
219. Kohler, *Jewish Rights*, pp. 27–28; Baron, *Judenfage*, pp. 100–16.
220. Baron, *Judenfrage*, pp. 178–206; Castlereagh to Clancarty, 8 July 1816, in Kohler, *Jewish Rights*, p. 47.

221. David Brion Davis, *The Problem of Slavery in the Age of Revolution, 1770–1823* (Ithaca, NY: Cornell University Press, 1975), pp. 27–31, 94–100, 107–12, 137–51, 557–58.
222. Conditions were so bad on these islands, where the death rate regularly exceeded the birth rate, that a continuous replenishment of the labour force was considered necessary.
223. Webster, *Foreign Policy of Castlereagh, 1812–1815*, pp. 269–72, 413–24.
224. Castlereagh to Talleyrand, 16 July 1814, in Wellington, *Supplementary Despatches*, vol. ix, p. 163.
225. Castlereagh, 'Memorandum as to the mode of conducting the negotiations in Congress for the final Abolition of the Slave Trade', 21 November 1814, in Webster, *British Diplomacy*, pp. 233–35, and Webster, *Foreign Policy of Castlereagh, 1812–1815*, pp. 419–20: 'I particularly recommend to your consideration', he wrote, 'the advantage of having a sort of permanent European Congress in existence as therein proposed upon this particular subject. I am of opinion that this may be made in itself a most powerful instrument to enforce with good faith the engagements of the several Powers.'
226. An ambassadorial conference consisted of the foreign minister of the host state together with the diplomatic corps in that capital.
227. The French decided to abandon their plans for the reconquest of Haiti, which reduced their anticipated demand for new slaves.
228. Stefan Krause, *Die Ächtung des Sklavenhandels auf dem Wiener Kongress: Ein Sieg der Humanität oder der Machtpolitik?* (Norderstedt, 2009), pp. 9–13.
229. Great Britain, Foreign Office, *British Foreign and State Papers*, vol. iii, 1815–1816 (1838), pp. 196–99, 945–75; Lentz, *Congrès*, pp. 233–39.
230. Webster, *Foreign Policy of Castlereagh, 1812–1815*, p. 427.
231. Webster, *Foreign Policy of Castlereagh, 1812–1815*, p. 427. In Pitt's case, as Webster points out, this may have been less a plan for perpetual peace than one to simply unite Europe against Napoleonic hegemony.
232. Webster, *Foreign Policy of Castlereagh, 1812–1815*, p. 428. Webster suggests that on the eve of his departure from Vienna, Castlereagh was aware of potential divisions in Europe, especially if France and Austria insisted on the removal of Murat by military force and Russia and Prussia opposed it. Agreement on a guarantee might have averted any such conflict.
233. Webster, *Foreign Policy of Castlereagh, 1812–1815*, p. 429.
234. Schroeder, *The Transformation of European Politics*, pp. 573–74.
235. Gentz to Prince Karadja, Hospodar of Walachia, 1 January 1816, in Anton von Prokesch-Osten (ed.), *Dépêches Inédites du Chevalier de Gentz aux Hospodars de Valachie* (Paris, 1876), vol. i, pp. 198–99.
236. Webster, *Foreign Policy of Castlereagh, 1812–1815*, pp. 431–32. Moreover, the Tsar later accused the British of abandoning the plan for a general guarantee. In 1816, Gentz also wrote that it was the British who had in fact refused to agree to the guarantee. Prokesch-Osten (ed.), *Dépêches Inédites du Chevalier de Gentz aux Hospodars de Valachie* (Paris: Plon, 1876–77), vol. i, pp. 198–99 ('the

ministers of England declared they were not authorized to sign it, and the article was abandoned').

237. See discussion of Gentz's 'projet' for the arrangement of the comprehensive treaty in Clancarty to Castlereagh, Vienna, 3 April 1815 (No. 3), in N.A. (Kew), F.O. 92/17. For excerpts from the Final Act, see Lentz, *Congrès*, pp. 328–51.
238. 'Au sixième protocole de la séance des cinqs Puissances, du 10 février 1815', in d'Angeberg, *Congrès de Vienne*, vol. iv ('Appendice'), pp. 1888–89.
239. Memoir by Friedrich von Gentz, 12 February 1815 in Metternich, *Memoirs of Prince Metternich*, vol. ii, p. 553.
240. Zamoyski, *Rites of Peace*, p. 558.
241. Schroeder, *The Transformation of European Politics*, p. 577.
242. In his letters to Louis XVIII, Talleyrand himself differentiated between these two concepts. See, e.g., Talleyrand to Louis XVIII, 10 January 1815, in Pallain, *Correspondence of Talleyrand and Louis XVIII*, pp. 258–59 ('Of the two principles involved in the question of Saxony, one, of legitimacy, will be absolutely respected, and this is the most important to us. The other, that of equilibrium, will be less completely safe.')
243. Since the Polish-Saxon Question constituted the major issue of the Congress, to say that the Congress statesmen had otherwise abandoned balance-of-power principles is like saying the dinner was delicious except for the main course.
244. Paul W. Schroeder, 'Did the Vienna Settlement Rest on a Balance of Power', *American Historical Review* 97 (1992), p. 705.
245. Andreas Ossiander, *The States System of Europe, 1640–1990: Peacemaking and the Conditions of International Stability* (Oxford: Oxford University Press, 1994), p. 232.
246. Ossiander, *The States System of Europe*, pp. 232–33.
247. In his *Memoirs*, Talleyrand takes a very different view of 'principle', accusing the great powers at the Congress of disregarding his own advice and ignoring principles: 'This deplorable disregard for all principle must be attributed to the disorganization and agitation that Europe has experienced during twenty-five years. So many sovereigns have been forced by the sway of irresistible circumstances to recognize usurpers, to treat and even to ally themselves with them. They have thus, little by little, been led to sacrifice their scruples for safety.' De Broglie, *Memoirs of the Prince de Talleyrand*, vol ii, p. 206. Talleyrand argued for adopting 'legitimacy' as the guiding principle in the reconstruction of Europe, but in a strange way the absence of principle he complains of—the arrogation of all decision-making by the leading powers—actually anticipates Osiander's 'great power' principle.
248. G. John Ikenberry, *After Victory: Institutions, Strategic Restraint and the Rebuilding of Order after Major Wars* (Princeton: Princeton University Press, 2001), p. 114.
249. John A. Vasquez, 'Conclusion: The Vienna System: Why It Worked and Why It Broke Down', in Peter Kruger and Paul W. Schroeder (eds), *The Transformation*

of European Politics, 1763–1848: Episode or Model in Modern History (Münster: LIT Verlag, 2002), pp. 235–241.
250. Sked, Metternich and Austria, pp. 57–58.
251. Kraehe, Congress of Vienna, p. 289.
252. Castlereagh to Liverpool, 21 November 1814, F.O. Congress 8, cited in Wawrzkowicz, Anglia a prawa polska, p. 450.
253. See, especially, Kenneth Waltz, *Man, the State and War* (New York: Columbia University Press, 1959). Waltz preferred to refer to these levels as 'images'.
254. While Frederick the Great had seized Silesia, Britain had taken France's colonies in Canada and India, and the eastern powers had begun their partitioning of Poland before 1789, the rapidity of territorial and dynastic change unleashed by the French Revolution and Napoleon constituted more than just a quantitative difference.
255. Much ink has now been spent by both historians and political scientists on the differences between territorial aggrandizement, balance-of-power and international equilibrium, but are these always contradictory? We can leave it to Gentz, the pupil of Kant, to challenge our thinking on these 'antimonies'.

4. The Birth of the Congress System, 1815–18

1. For this section see Jarrett, 'Castlereagh, Ireland and the French Restorations', chs 7–11, pp. 358–698.
2. Jarrett, 'Castlereagh, Ireland and the French Restorations', p. 478
3. Jarrett, 'Castlereagh, Ireland and the French Restorations', p. 516.
4. Jarrett, 'Castlereagh, Ireland and the French Restorations', pp. 589–91, citing Public Record Office of Northern Ireland, D3030/4543 and D3030/4544; also in Webster, *Foreign Policy of Castlereagh, 1812–15*, pp. 545–48.
5. For a short but perceptive description of the battle, see Andrew Roberts, *Waterloo June 18, 1815: The Battle for Modern Europe* (London: HarperCollins, 2005).
6. Capodistrias, 'Agenda—Résumé de tous les rapports reçu de nos missions', 11 April 1820, in USSR, *Vneshniaia Politika Rossii, 1815–1830*, vol. iii, p. 337.
7. Great Britain, National Archives (hereafter, 'N.A.') (Kew), F.O. 92/23 ff. 99–109, 'Austrian Memoir'.
8. N.A. (Kew), F.O. 92/23 ff. 171–77, Wellington to Castlereagh, 11 August 1815, Paris.
9. N.A. (Kew), F.O. 92/29, ff. 121–28, Russian 'Projet', enclosed in Castlereagh to Liverpool, 15 October 1815 (No. 80). A copy of the proposed treaty, in Russian, is found in USSR, *Vneshniaia Politika Rossii, 1801–1815*, vol. viii, pp. 694–95, fn. 271. On its authorship, see Woodhouse, *Capodistria*, p. 135, and Castlereagh's letter to Stewart of 6 November 1815, below.
10. 'Ces mesures ont pour principe inaltérable de procurer á la France le temps et les moyens nécessaires pour affirmer l'Autorité Royale sur base de la légitimité et sur les Salutaires Maximes consacrées par la Charte Constitutionelle.'
11. The second article thus stated: 'Si quelques tentatives criminelles suites du délire

des Passions Révolutionnaires pourroient être faites pour exclure la Dynastie régnante du Trone soit pour lui substituer un individu de la Famille de Bonaparte ou pour introduire en France un ordre de choses qui menaçeroit de nouveau la sureté de L'Europe, Les Hautes Parties contractantés pour preserver intact Le Principe établi dans l'Article précédent, promettent de vouer leurs efforts au maintien de la Royauté et de l'ordre Constitutionnel.' The proposed third article pledged the signatories to mobilize forces in support of the temporary army of occupation if required, while the fourth engaged them to renew, when the occupation expired, 'treaties of reciprocal guarantee of their respective possessions, as well as for the peace and general tranquillity [... de renouveller entr'Elles lors de l'expiration du terme des occupations temporaires en question, des Traités de Garantie reciproque pour le maintien de Leurs Possessions respectives, ainsi que pour celui de la Paix et de la tranquillité générale]'. The fifth reserved to the signatories their full rights of conquest and the power to take additional measures to protect Europe in the event that the war with France should ever be renewed.

12. Castlereagh to Liverpool, 15 October 1815, N.A. (Kew), F.O. 92/29, ff. 114–20, also printed in Webster, *British Diplomacy*, pp. 386–88.
13. Castlereagh, 'Projet de Traité entre les quatre Puissances', in N.A. (Kew), F.O. 92/29, ff. 132–39.
14. Note of Razumovsky and Capodistrias to Nesselrode, 'Observations on the Projet for a Treaty of Alliance, redrafted by Viscount Castlereagh', 5 (17) October 1815, Paris, in USSR, *Vneshniaia Politika Rossii, 1801–1815*, vol. viii, pp. 551 and 560–62.
15. Razumovsky and Capodistrias, transmitted to the Austrian, British and Prussian Plenipotentiaries, 'Observations on the Projet for a Treaty of Alliance', 9 (21) October 1815, Paris, in USSR, *Vneshniaia Politika Rossii, 1801–1815*, vol. viii, pp. 565–67.
16. Castlereagh, 'Projet de Traité entre les quatre Puissances', in N.A. (Kew), F.O. 92/29, ff. 132–39.
17. N.A. (Kew), F.O. 92/29, f. 132 verso (Bathurst's comment in pencil, signed 'B^t').
18. Castlereagh to Sir Charles Stewart, [6] November [1815], Paris, 'Private', in Public Record Office of Northern Ireland (Belfast), Castlereagh Papers, D3030/Q2/1, ff. 153–54.
19. E.E. Hertslet, *The Map of Europe by Treaty* (London: Butterworths, 1875), vol. i, pp. 372–75; d'Angeberg, *Le Congrès de Vienne*, vol. ii, pp. 1636–38; see also, Russian-Austrian treaty, 8 (20) November 1815, Paris, in USSR, *Vneshniaia Politika Rossii, 1801–1815*, vol. viii, pp. 609–12.
20. Same as above.
21. Confidential Note to Richelieu, 20 November 1815, Paris, in Haus-, Hof- und Staatsarchiv (Vienna), Staatskanzlei, Verträge betreffende Akten, Karton 6, 20 September–22 November 1815, Konferenzen den 4 Alliierten Ministerien, enclosed in Conference 33 (17 November), 'Note Confidentielle' dated for 20 November 1815, ff. 191–94.

22. N.A. (Kew), F.O. 92/29 ff. 177–79: Allied Instructions to Wellington as Commander of Occupation Force, in English translation. For these same instructions in French, see N.A. (Kew), F.O. 92/30 ff. 133–36; also in Wellington, *Supplementary Despatches*, vol. xi, pp. 240–42.
23. Rain, *L'Europe et la Restauration des Bourbons*, pp. 207–09, 270–84, and the appendices, pp. 479–90, with several of the protocols from their sessions; Reiner Marcowitz, *Grossmacht auf Bewährung: Die Interdependenz französischer Innen- und Aussenpolitik und ihre Auswirkungen auf Frankreichs Stellung im europäischen Konzert, 1814/15–1851/52* (Stuttgart: Thorbecke, 2001), p. 48.
24. N.A. (Kew), F.O. 92/30 ff. 138–40, Castlereagh to Sir Charles Stuart.
25. Webster, *Foreign Policy of Castlereagh, 1812–1815*, p. 462, note 1.
26. N.A. (Kew), F.O. 92/26, ff. 111–16, Castlereagh to Liverpool, 11 September 1815 (No. 50), enclosing Castlereagh's memorandum on the return of artworks from the Louvre (ff. 117–23), and Russian memorandum on the same (ff. 125–28); also, N.A. (Kew), F.O. 92/28, Castlereagh to Liverpool, 21 September 1815 (No. 61) and 25 September 1815 (No. 66) on the 'spoliation' of the Louvre.
27. N.A. (Kew), F.O. 92/23, ff. 96–98, Castlereagh to Liverpool, 12 August 1815. For Wellington's objections to Prussian demands, presented in a memorandum by Humboldt, see his letter to Castlereagh of 11 August 1815, in N.A. F.O. 92/23, ff. 171–77. He concludes: 'Revolutionary France is more likely to disturb the World, than France, however strong her Frontier, under a regular Government, and that is the situation in which we ought to endeavour to place her' (f. 175); see also Webster, *British Diplomacy*, pp. 339–41, 345–47, 353–76, 378–79.
28. Liverpool to Castlereagh, 28 August 1815, in Webster, *British Diplomacy*, pp. 372–73.
29. Castlereagh to Liverpool, 4 September 1815 in N.A. (Kew), F.O. 92/26, also reprinted in Webster, *British Diplomacy*, pp. 375–76; Webster, *Foreign Policy of Castlereagh, 1812–1815*, pp. 465–75; Albert Sorel, *Le Traité de Paris du 20 Novembre 1815* (Paris: G. Baillière, 1872), pp. 68–131.
30. Webster, *Foreign Policy of Castlereagh, 1812–1815*, pp. 481–83.
31. Alexander to Prince Regent, 2 July 1812, in Schilder, *Imperator Aleksandr Pervyi*, iii, p. 500, cited in H.G. Schenk, *The Aftermath of the Napoleonic Wars—An Experiment* (Oxford: Oxford University Press, 1947), p. 34.
32. '… que lorsque l'édifice de la pacification générale reposera sur les mêmes bases qui ont assuré le succès de leurs armes, savoir sur l'identité de leurs vues et maximes politiques, ainsi que l'association franche et loyale de leurs intérêts les plus chers. Pénétrés également des principes immutables de la religion chrétienne commune à tous, c'est sur cette base unique de l'ordre politique comme l'ordre social que les souverains fraternisant entr'eux épureront leurs maximes d'état et garantiront les rapports entre les peuples que la providence leur a confiés …'. Cited in Schenk, *Aftermath of the Napoleonic Wars*, p. 35; Ley, *Alexandre Ier and la Sainte Alliance*, pp. 98–99; Maurice Bourquin, *Histoire de la Sainte Alliance* (Geneva: George, 1954), p. 134.
33. Castlereagh to Liverpool, 28 September 1815, in Webster, *British Diplomacy*, p. 382.

34. Stella Ghervas, *Reinventer la Tradition: Alexandre Stourdza et l'Europe de la Saint-Alliance* (Paris: Honoré Champion, 2008), pp. 72–73.
35. Ghervas, *Reinventer la Tradition*, pp. 180–86.
36. Werner Näf, *Zur Geschichte der Heiligen Allianz* (Bern, 1928), 'Dokumentischer Anhang', pp. 34–37; Ley, *Alexandre Ier et sa Sainte-Alliance*, pp. 107–65, especially pp. 149–53, for Metternich's redactions; Schenk, *Aftermath of Napoleonic Wars*, pp. 31–43; E.J. Knapton, 'The Origins of the Holy Alliance', Historical Revision N. XCVIII, *History*, New Series 26/2 (September 1941), pp. 131–40; Guillaume de Bertier de Sauvigny, 'Sainte-Alliance et Alliance dans les conceptions de Metternich', *Revue historique* 223 (1960), pp. 249–74; Philipp Menger, 'Die Heilige Allianz—"La garantie religieuse du nouveau système Européen"?', in Pyta, *Das europäische Mächtekonzert*, pp. 209–36; Bourquin: *Histoire de la Sainte Alliance*, pp. 133–46.
37. The entire treaty in contemporary translation into English can be found in Hertslet, *Map of Europe by Treaty*, i, pp. 317–19. The final text of the Holy Alliance in French can also be found in *British Foreign and State Papers*, vol. iii, pp. 211–12.
38. Castlereagh to Liverpool, 28 September 1815, in Webster, *British Diplomacy*, p. 383. See also N.A. (Kew), F.O. 165/28, Castlereagh to A'Court, 26 January 1816: 'Previous to my leaving Vienna, I had prepared a project of Declaration to be promulgated by the Congress on the completion of their labours, in which the Sovereigns were made to pledge themselves in the face of Europe to preserve and uphold the Peace and Settlement they had thus concluded, engaging to turn their Arms against whatever Power might violate or disturb the same. The Emperor, who has been at all times strongly tinctured with Religious Impressions, increased this disposition very much at Paris, in the Society of a Lady of an advanced time of life, who is a celebrated exaltée of the name of Madame de [K]ruedener—His Imperial Majesty, referring to the declaration above mentioned, expressed to me a wish to give to it the more solemn character of a Treaty, and informed me he was employed upon such an Instrument, which I believe he drew entirely himself. Thus originated the Treaty in question, the engagements taken in which were perfectly laudable and innocent, but being cloathed in a language not suited to Diplomatic Transactions, his Imperial Majesty was induced to propose it to his Allies as an autobiographical engagement between them as Sovereigns, in which their Ministers were not by signature to intervene; and as such it was executed.'
39. Näf, *Geschichte der Heiligen Allianz*; W.P. Cresson, *The Holy Alliance: the European Background of the Monroe Doctrine* (New York: Oxford University Press, 1922).
40. Castlereagh to Liverpool, 28 September 1815, in Webster, *British Diplomacy*, p. 383. A copy of the Holy Alliance is in N.A. (Kew), F.O. 92/28, with a copy of the letter sent to the Prince Regent and a 'Projet de l'Acte d'Accession'.
41. Ghervas, *Reinventer la Tradition*, pp. 186–91.
42. N.A. (Kew), F.O. 92/23 ff. 161–68, Castlereagh's Memorandum on the Russian, Austrian, and Prussian Confidential Notes, August 1815, Paris.

43. Thomas Dwight Vere, *The Duke of Wellington and the British Army of Occupation in France, 1815–1818* (Westport, CT: Greenwood Press, 1992), pp. 1–31, 93–106.
44. Treitschke, *History of Germany*, vol. iii, pp. 82–84; Guillaume de Bertier de Sauvigny, *France and the European Alliance 1816–1821: The Private Correspondence of Metternich and Richelieu* (Notre Dame, IN: University of Notre Dame Press, 1958), pp. 22–35.
45. Castlereagh to Cathcart, 27 March 1818, in Wellington, *Supplementary Despatches*, vol. xii, pp. 445–46. Castlereagh specifically instructed that his message should be shown to the courts of Russia, Austria and Prussia, but not of France.
46. Treitschke, *History of Germany*, vol. iii, pp. 81–82.
47. Neumann to Metternich, 27 August 1818, No. 68 B, in Haus-, Hof- und Staatsarchiv (Vienna), 1818, Grossbritannien, Berichte, Karton 158, bundle 2, first series of folios.
48. Hardenberg's diary entry for 9 October 1818, in Stamm-Kuhlmann: *Hardenberg: Tagebücher*, p. 866 ('Clausewitz war Commmandant von Aachen'.) See also Paret, *Clausewitz and the State*, p. 271.
49. 'The evacuation of territory alone does not constitute the entire liberation of France. The alliance, based on the Treaty of Chaumont, renewed in the Treaty of 20 November, which continues to hold France under its yoke ... must also be broken'. Instructions to the Duc de Richelieu, in Bourquin: *Histoire de la Sainte Alliance*, p. 223.
50. Charles Kingsley Webster, *The Foreign Policy of Lord Castlereagh, 1815–1822: Britain and the European Alliance* (London: G. Bell & Sons, 1925), pp. 134–40, 152.
51. N.A. (Kew), F.O. 92/35, ff. 10–17, Castlereagh to Bathurst, 3 October 1818, No. 2, Aix-la-Chapelle.
52. Phillips, *The Confederation of Europe*, pp. 161–62. For Metternich's views on the internal situation in France, see Bertier de Sauvigny, *France and the European Alliance*, pp. 36–56.
53. Satow, *A Guide to Diplomatic Practice*, pp. 270–85: 'During a congress or a conference, no matter for what object or purpose, the minutes of the plenipotentiaries are styled either protocol or *procès-verbal*, indifferently. Perhaps the former word is more dignified. Obviously protocol in this sense does not mean an agreement; *procès-verbal* would be better, as it means nothing else' (p. 271); Sir Charles Kingsley Webster, *The European Alliance, 1815–1825* (Calcutta: University of Calcutta, 1929), p. 39: 'To a certain extent, the procedure of international conferences had been fixed at the Congress of Vienna and become largely a matter of routine. There was a council of ministers, the ministers of the Great Five Powers, who met every day. They kept a record (Protocol) of their proceedings, not a record as full as was made at the Paris Peace Conference of 1919, not recording the words of the ministers, but simply stating the decisions arrived at, and sometimes stating the reasons for them. Attached to the Protocol there would be Memoranda or Papers put in by the various Powers'. A list of the

protocols from the Congress of Aix-la-Chapelle can be found in Haus-, Hof- und Staatsarchiv (Vienna), Staatskanzlei, Friedensakten, Karton 103, ff. 37–47; the protocols themselves are in Kongressakten, Karton 17; finally, there is a summary of the conferences in Haus-, Hof- und Statsarchiv (Vienna), Gesandtschaftsarchiv Berlin, Karton 68; copies of the protocols may also be found in Archives des Affaires Étrangères (La Courneuve), Mémoires et Documents (France), vol. 712.

54. '[Trois]ème Conférence du 1 Oct. 1818 entre les 4 Cabinets', in Haus-, Hof- und Staatsarchiv (Vienna), Gesandtschaftsarchiv Berlin, Karton 68, and Staatskanzlei, Kongressakten, Karton 17, f. 5, Protocol No. 4, 2 October 1818, on the unanimity of the four allied courts on the evacuation of allied troops from France.

55. Austrian memorandum of 7 October 1818, in N.A. (Kew), F.O. 92/35, ff. 138–47, Castlereagh to Bathurst, 19 October 1818 (No. 13); also cited in Phillips, *Confederation of Europe*, pp. 159–60.

56. N.A. (Kew), F.O. 92/35, ff. 20–26, Castlereagh to Bathurst, 3 October 1818, No. 4, Aix-la-Chapelle; Webster, *Foreign Policy of Castlereagh, 1815–1822*, pp. 143–44.

57. N.A. (Kew), F.O. 92/35, ff. 20–26, Castlereagh to Bathurst, 3 October 1818, No. 4, Aix-la-Chapelle;

58. 'Conférence du 12 Oct, 4 Cabinets', Haus-, Hof- und Staatsarchiv (Vienna), Gesandtschaftsarchiv Berlin, Karton 68: 'They took into consideration issues relating to the treaty of alliance of 20 November 1815 and the measures to be adopted to determine future relations between the four powers and France in the manner most consistent with the common interest of Europe. [Ils ont pris encore en consideration les questions relative au traité d'Alliance du 20 Nov. 1815 et les mesures à adopter pour determiner de la manière le plus conforme a l'intérêt commun de l'Europe les relations futures entre les 4 puissances Alliées et la France]'; see also, Webster, *Foreign Policy of Castlereagh, 1815–1822*, p. 145.

59. N.A. (Kew), F.O. 92/35, ff. 138–47, Castlereagh to Bathurst, 19 October 1818 (No. 13), Aix-la-Chapelle.

60. Most historians accept that the memorandum, although dated 8 October, was not submitted for discussion until 14 October. See, e.g., Webster, *Foreign Policy of Castlereagh, 1815–1822*, p. 149, n. 2. A folder in the Austrian state archives, entitled 'Acts relative to the Quadruple Alliance and the establishment of its relations with France', lists the memorandum with the date of 14 October: Haus-, Hof- und Staatsarchiv (Vienna), Staatskanzlei, Kongressakten, Karton 17 (Alt 30), No. 5. 'Projet de Protocole par le cabinet russe', followed by No. 6. 'Remarques de Mr. Gentz sur le projet ci-devant'. Based on Castlereagh's reports to the British cabinet in London, it may have even been discussed after that date: see N.A. (Kew), F.O. 92/35, ff. 138–47, Castlereagh to Bathurst, 19 October 1818, Aix-la-Chapelle (No. 13), which encloses the Russian memorandum, found at ff. 159–88, with an addition at ff. 190–97, but which does not yet report any allied discussion of it. These enclosures bear the dates of 26 September/8 October. Nonetheless, one historian has found an earlier reference to the proposal in the Prussian archives, dated 10 October. See Lawrence J. Baack, *Christian Bernstorff and Prussia: Diplomacy and Reform Conservatism, 1818–1832* (New Brunswick,

NJ: Rutgers University Press, 1980), p. 44, fn. 12. Baack believes that the discussion on the Russian proposal was in fact launched on 8 October, although this would seem to contradict Castlereagh's reports to the British cabinet. See Castlereagh to Bathurst, 9 November 1818 (No. 29), found at F.O. 92/37, ff. 110–32.
61. Hartley, *Alexander I*, p. 144.
62. Bourquin, *Histoire de la Sainte Alliance*, p. 231. See also Philips: *Confederation of Europe*, p. 166: 'The language of this memorandum recalls that of the instructions to Novosiltsov in 1804. Both in principles and in its proposals for its practical application it is all but identical with the scheme submitted by Alexander to Pitt. The only difference is that for the Dual Alliance of Russia and Great Britain, which, under the original scheme, was to be maintained as a sort of directorate of the European Concert, had been substituted the Quadruple Alliance.'
63. Their discussion of this question seems to have ended on 19 October. See Haus-, Hof- und Statsarchiv (Vienna), Staatskanzlei, Kongressakten, Karton 17, ff. 57-67, Protocol Nos. 15 and 16; see also Haus-, Hof- und Statsarchiv (Vienna), Gesandtschaftsarchiv Berlin, Karton 68, 'Conférences du 18 & 19 Octobre' ('The Ministers of the four Courts have completed their consideration of the draft of a protocol which had occupied them for the last several days.... .[Messrs les Ministres du 4 Cours ont terminé l'examen du projet de protocolle dont ils s'etaient occupés pendant les derniers jours. Conserver dans toute la force la quadruple alliance ... Conserver également dans toute la pureté le principe moral de l'union entre les 4 Cabinets ... inviter la France à s'assoir aux 4 puissances a l'effet de presenter à l'Europe dans l'union et dans l'accord fraternel et chrétien qui caracterisent leur politique, le moyen le plus sur de maintenir l'inviolabilité des transactions sur les quelles repose la paix générale.]'
64. Metternich, *Memoirs*, vol. iii, pp. 182–83 ('The Act of Guarantee'). Although this document in Metternich's published memoirs probably applies to the treaty of guarantee, discussed below, Metternich no doubt applied the same reasoning to this earlier debate.
65. To the extent that the treaties created a 'moral guarantee', Castlereagh affirmed that a state might be justified in acting unilaterally against their breach if it were adversely affected: 'There is no doubt that a breach of the Covenant by any one State is an injury, which all the other States may, if they shall think fit, either separately or collectively resent, but the Treaties do not impose, by express stipulation, the doing so, as [a] matter of positive obligation. So solemn a Pact, on the faithful Execution and the Observance of which all Nations should feel the strongest Interest, may be considered as under the Protection of a Moral Guarantee of the Highest Nature, but as those who framed these Acts probably did not see how the whole Confederacy could, without the utmost inconvenience, be made collectively to enforce the observance of these Treaties, the Execution of this Duty seems to have been deliberately left to arise out of the Circumstances of the Time and of the case, and the offending state to be brought to reason by such of the injured states as might, at the moment, think fit to charge themselves with the Task of defending their own Rights thus invaded'. Castlereagh, 'Memorandum', in

Webster, *Congress of Vienna*, Appendix viii, p. 188; Haus-, Hof- und Staatsarchiv (Vienna), Staatskanzlei, Karton 17 (Alt. 30), ff. 78–79.

66. Webster, *The Congress of Vienna*, Appendix, viii; Webster, *Foreign Policy of Castlereagh, 1815–1822*, pp. 150–53; Phillips, *Confederation of Europe*, pp. 173–75. Webster thought that none of the other allied powers ever received a written copy of this important pronouncement, but Metternich clearly did: there is a copy in the Austrian state archives, entitled 'Memorandum on the English point of view on the *casus foederis*', on which is written in pencil: 'communicated only to the Austrian Cabinet. [Communiqué au seul Cabinet autrichien]'. Haus-, Hof- und Staatsarchiv (Vienna), Staatskanzlei, Karton 17 (Alt. 30), ff. 75–93.

67. Bathurst to Castlereagh, 20 October 1818, Downing Street, in Stewart, *Memoirs and Correspondence of Viscount Castlereagh*, xii, pp. 55–58. See also, Phillips, *Confederation of Europe*, p. 168.

68. Richelieu to Louis XVIII, 12 October 1818, in Raoul de Cisternes, *Le Duc de Richelieu, son Action aux Conférences d'Aix-la-Chapelle, sa retrait du pouvoir* (Paris: Calmann Lévy, 1898), p. 80.

69. Castlereagh to Bathurst, Aix-la-Chapelle, 20 October 1818 (No. 15), in N.A. (Kew), F.O. 92/36, ff. 62–70.

70. Castlereagh to Bathurst, Aix-la-Chapelle, 20 October 1818 (No. 15), in N.A. (Kew), F.O. 92/36, ff. 62–70.

71. Castlereagh to Bathurst, Aix-la-Chapelle, 20 October 1818 (No. 15), in N.A. (Kew), F.O. 92/36, ff. 62–70. See also the similar memorandum by Metternich, 'Abridged Summary of the Situation on November 1, 1818', in Metternich, *Memoirs*, vol. iii, pp. 185–88; see also, USSR, *Vneshniaia Politika Rossii, 1815–1830* (Moscow: Nauka, 1976), Series 2, vol. ii (October 1817–April 1819), pp. 514–15: 14 October, 1818, 'Analysis of the Treaty of Chaumont and the Quadruple Alliance', pp. 519–20: Protocol No. 16, 19 October 1818, Aix-la-Chapelle; and pp. 531–32: Capodistrias, 'Marche de la négociation', 1 November 1818.

72. Capodistrias, 'Premier projet le Cte de Capo d'Istria du Protocol', 22 October 1818, Haus-, Hof- und Staatsarchiv (Vienna), Staatskanzlei, Kongressakten, Karton 17, ff. 75–78.

73. N.A. (Kew), F.O. 92/36, ff. 88–94, Castlereagh to Bathurst, 29 October 1818 (No. 19), Aix-la-Chapelle, enclosing, ff. 96–104, 'Projét de Protocole reservé à la Connaissance des Puissances Signataires du Traité de Quadruple Alliance du 20 Novembre 1815'.

74. Richelieu to Louis XVIII, [October 1818], in Cisternes, *Duc de Richelieu*, p. 88.

75. Castlereagh to Bathurst, Aix-la-Chapelle, 2 November 1818, No. 23, 'Private and Confidential', in N.A. (Kew), FO 92/37, ff. 15–23. Selective parts of this dispatch can be found in Webster, *Foreign Policy of Castlereagh, 1815–1822*, pp. 156–59.

76. 'Que cette garantie solidaire ait été explicitement statuée ou non, que les actes diplomatiques l'annoncent comme une obligation positive ou seulement virtuelle, cette garantie n'en pas moins sacrée aux yeux de l'empereur. S. M. en retrouve le principe générateur dans la sens comme dans la teneur littérale de l'Acte fraternel

du 14 (26) septembre 1815, et surtout dans la nature des motifs qui ont dicté cet engagement et qui l'ont fait accueillir par tous les gouvernements européens avec l'unanimité la plus imposante.' Russian Memorandum to Austria, Great Britain, Prussia and France, Aix-la-Chapelle, 23 November 1818, in USSR, *Vneshniaia Politika Rossii, 1815–1830*, Series 2, vol. ii, pp. 589–91.

77. There is an interesting document comparing the views of Castlereagh and Richelieu in opposing columns. Richelieu's side begins: 'Although the Treaty of the Quadruple Alliance has not been formally annulled or dissolved, by the conditions that are established today, it can no longer be considered as applicable to the state of peace.' Castlereagh provides a contrary and ultimately prevailing view: 'The Treaty of the Quadruple Alliance of 20 November 1815 should not be regarded as annulled by the union or pacific concert that has been established with France for the maintenance of the peace and of the existing treaties, but rather as continuing to exist in full force and usefulness [mais comme encore subsistant en pleine Force et Valeur]'. Identical copies of this illuminating comparison can be found in both N.A. (Kew), F.O. 92/39, ff. 11–12 and F.O. 120/34 (unnumbered).

78. Haus-, Hof- und Staatsarchiv (Vienna), Staatskanzlei, Kongressakten, Karton 17, ff. 157–58, Protocol No. 33 (Four Courts), 15 November 1818; ff. 161, 164–65, signed protocol, 15 November 1818; ff. 162-163, printed version of the same; f. 159, Protocol No. 34 (Five Courts), 15 November 1818; ff. 167–171, secret protocol (Protocol reservé à la connaissances des Puissances signataires du traité de la Quadruple Alliance du 15 Novembre 1815). For Richelieu's suggested changes, see Archives des Affaires Étrangères (La Courneuve), Mémoires et Documents (France), vol. 713, ff. 275–80, 311–13.

79. See Baack, *Bernstorff*, p. 45; for the attribution of the proposal to Hardenberg; see Webster, *Foreign Policy of Castlereagh, 1815–1821*, p. 161; USSR, *Vneshniaia Politika Rossii, 1815–1830*, Series 2, vol. ii, pp. 589–91, 15 November 1818. However, Castlereagh himself wrote to the cabinet on 9 November that Metternich had informed him that the Prussians were about to raise the issue, and Castlereagh also wrote that he had received a confidential memorandum on a plan for a guarantee from Hardenberg.

80. 'People who knew France's internal conditions intimately see new revolutions as entirely possible, one might say probable ... As France's neighbour, and as a state in possession of provinces which she wants, Prussia is and will remain for a long time the sole object of her revenge, hate and plans for conquest'; cited in Gertrud Steckhan, *Preussen und die Neuorientierung der europäischen Staatengesellschaft auf dem Aachener Kongress, 1818* (Berlin: Bottrop, 1934), p. 91, and in Baack, *Bernstorff*, p. 46.

81. Webster, *Foreign Policy of Castlereagh, 1815–1822*, pp. 161–62.

82. Steckhan, *Preussen und die Neuorientierung der europäischen Staatengesellschaft*, p. 81.

83. Haus-, Hof- und Staatsarchiv (Vienna), Staatskanzlei, Kongressakten, Karton 18 (Alt 32), f. 56, untitled document, 10/22 November 1818, Aix-la-Chapelle: 'This

major question [of a guarantee] has been frequently discussed in the negotiations at Aix-la-Chapelle. In 1816, the Cabinet of Berlin had posed it in very specific terms. A copy of this communication can be found attached here. The Russian minister, appreciating the views expressed by the Cabinet of Berlin, reproduced them in his confidential memorandum of 5 October'. For the excerpt from Ancillon's proposal, see ff. 57–60. Although the cover memorandum is incomplete and bears a different date, it appears to be the same as that published in USSR, *Vneshniaia Politika Rossii, 1815–1830*, Series 2, vol. ii, pp. 589–91. The copy of Ancillon's paper in Vienna seems to propose preserving thrones as well as borders, at least for the five great powers. He argues that the five powers should guarantee both the current state of their possessions and their 'situations': 'les cinq grandes puissances déclarent qu'elles maintiendraient par tous en Europe et reciproquement les unes envers les autres la Souverainté légitime; qu'elles ne permettent pas qu'il y soit atteinte par des moyens violens, pas des changements fait de bas en haut et par des revolutions quelconques'.

84. Cresson, *The Holy Alliance*, pp. 133–34.
85. N.A. (Kew), F.O. 92/37, ff. 110–32, Castlereagh to Bathurst, 9 November 1818 (No. 29) Aix-la-Chapelle.
86. N.A. (Kew), F.O. 92/37, ff. 110–32, Castlereagh to Bathurst, 9 November 1818 (No. 29) Aix-la-Chapelle.
87. N.A. (Kew), F.O. 92/37, ff. 110–32, Castlereagh to Bathurst, 9 November 1818 (No. 29) Aix-la-Chapelle. Castlereagh's ambivalence was so great that in his next report to London he explained that his previous dispatch may have appeared more favourable than he really felt; he saw both advantages and disadvantages to the proposal. See N.A. (Kew), F.O. 92/37, Castlereagh to Bathurst, 9 November 1818, Aix-la-Chapelle.
88. N.A. (Kew), F.O. 92/37, ff. 163–67, Castlereagh to Bathurst, 12 November 1818 (No. 31), Aix-la-Chapelle.
89. N.A. (Kew), F.O. 92/39, ff. 82–86, Castlereagh to Bathurst, 19 November 1818 (No. 37), Aix-la-Chapelle.
90. Nesselrode, 'Résumé des discussions sur la médiation entre l'Espagne et ses colonies', 25 October 1818, in USSR, *Vneshniaia Politika Rossii, 1815–1830*, Series 2, vol. ii, pp. 522–24. According to the records in the Austrian state archives, the discussions on the Spanish colonies began on 23 October.
91. Castlereagh to Sir Hew Dalrymple, 23 May 1808, 'Private and Secret' and Castlereagh to Duke of Manchester, 4 June 1808, No. 2, in N.A. (Kew), CO 324/68; see also, Castlereagh, Memorandum of 21 December 1807, St James Square, in Public Record Office of Northern Ireland (Belfast), D3030/2544: 'If we are again to look to any operation against the possessions of Spain in South America, particularly in Rio de la Plata, the present moment seems to be particularly favorable to such an attempt.'
92. Cabinet Memorandum of 28 August 1817, discussed in Webster, *Foreign Policy of Castlereagh, 1815–1822*, pp. 413–14. Webster argues that Castlereagh had held to these principles since first becoming Foreign Secretary in 1812 (p. 408).

See also Sir Charles Kingsley Webster (ed.), *Britain and the Independence of Latin America* (Oxford: Oxford University Press, 1938), vol. ii. Wellington complained to Castlereagh that the Spanish, after being rebuffed in London, tried to bring the matter before the ambassadorial conference in Paris. See Wellington to Castlereagh, 21 July 1817, Paris, in N.A. (Kew), F.O. 92/32, ff. 70–73: 'It was clear that the object of the Spaniards was by applying to the Conference to force Great Britain with measures to which the Govt. had refused to listen ... I never saw the Duke [de Richelieu] more fair or cordial than he was in his answer. He agreed entirely with me that these applications ought to be discouraged. He urged however strongly the expediency & even necessity of our making some exertion to put an end to the existing troubles in S. America which he says are becoming daily more an object of attention and of hope to the disaffected in France & to the Jacobins throughout the World, and that he conceives that the other Powers of Europe ought to place themselves at the back of England to support her in her measures to put an end to the Slave Trade and to tranquillize S. America.'

93. Neumann to Metternich, 1 September 1818, No. 68 A, in Haus-, Hof- und Staatsarchiv (Vienna), 1818, Grossbritannien, Berichte, Karton 158, bundle 2, second series of folio nos., ff. 1–18. On the other hand, a year later, when Spain failed to follow his recommendations, Castlereagh explained to his half-brother that it was not true that Britain was only pursuing her commercial interests in this matter: 'In a commercial sense, this Govt. feels less solicitude upon this question than is generally supposed; in some way or other the wants of South America will be supplied, this supply must come from Europe, and this Country will in some mode or other furnish its full share of this supply; but they look with regret and alarm to the decision and especially for the best interests of Spain Herself, not merely from forcing commerce into the pernicious channels of a contraband intercourse, to the great prejudice of her true financial policy, but as laying the seeds of future discontent and successive insurrections throughout South America.' Castlereagh to Stewart, 24 September 1819, in N.A. (Kew), F.O. 7/142.
94. William S. Robertson, *France and Latin American Independence* (Baltimore, MD: Johns Hopkins Press, 1939), pp. 136–37.
95. Robertson, *France and Latin American Independence*, pp. 147–55.
96. Capodistrias, 'Pacification des colonies espagnoles', Aix-la-Chapelle, 1 November 1818, in USSR, *Vneshniaia Politika Rossii, 1815–1830*, Series 2, vol. ii, pp. 525–28.
97. Nesselrode, 'Résumé des discussions sur la médiation entre l'Espagne et ses colonies', Aix-la-Chapelle, 25 October 1818, in USSR, *Vneshniaia Politika Rossii, 1815–1830*, Series 2, vol. ii, pp. 522–24.
98. N.A. (Kew), F.O. 92/36, ff. 176–79, Castlereagh to Bathurst, 2 November 1818 (No. 22), and ff. 181–201, for Castlereagh's 'Queries' on the question of mediation between Spain and her colonies.
99. For his post-1820 preference for monarchies in the Americas, see Webster, *Britain and the Independence of Latin America*, vol. ii, Nos 531–34; Castlereagh, 'Memorandum on South America', 1 May 1807, in Stewart, *Memoirs and*

Correspondence of Viscount Castlereagh, vii, p. 314. The viability of such a solution was demonstrated four years later by Brazil.

100. Castlereagh to Metternich, 7 November 1818, Aix-la-Chapelle, in Haus-, Hof- und Staatsarchiv (Vienna), Staatskanzlei, Kongressakten, Karton 17 (Alt. 31), ff. 7–26. The allied ministers were agreed, Castlereagh noted, that they could not intervene militarily, so the only issue was whether this should be avowed or kept to themselves. Could they proceed without telling the insurgents? Would such uncertainty induce the colonists to agree to whatever terms were offered to them? 'Can the Powers thus forcibly compel submission without making themselves morally responsible for the fate of these people hereafter under the Government of Spain? ... Can they thus awe them into submission and with justice refuse to guarantee the settlement they impose on them?' Would the powers agree to arbitrate all future disputes between Spain and her colonies? Would Spain let her agents in South America know? If not, would these agents misinform the insurgents that the allies intended to intervene with force? If the agents knew the truth, would not the rebels also soon find out? Another issue he raised was how the British could justify such conduct in Parliament. And finally, would not the agents themselves disagree? 'What are the risks of disunion between so many commissioners of equal authority, acting at such a distance from their Courts, upon political questions of such magnitude and delicacy? What are the chances of delay from indecision, from a reluctance to incur responsibility, and from endless references to Europe?' And what if the agents on the spot act on different principles with respect to the use of armed force? 'Can these difficulties occur in South America without recoiling here and becoming in Europe a serious embarrassment? What is the danger of embarrassing the harmony of the European System by the complications that may grow out of such a course of proceeding ...' In other words, he argues that withholding the truth from the insurgents in South America might actually imperil the harmony of the alliance in Europe!
101. Cresson, *The Holy Alliance*, p. 76.
102. Webster, *Foreign Policy of Castlereagh, 1815–1822*, pp. 419–20; Cisternes, *Duc de Richelieu*, pp. 98–99, 142, 148; Wellington, *Supplementary Despatches*, xii, p. 805; Cresson, *The Holy Alliance*, pp. 79–80.
103. N.A. (Kew), F.O. 92/41, ff. 22–35, Castlereagh to Bathurst, 24 November 1818 (No. 48); ff. 78–87, Castlereagh to Bathurst, 24 November 1818 (No. 49), 'Most Secret and Confidential'.
104. Robertson, *France and Latin American Independence*, pp. 154–55.
105. Schroeder, *Transformation*, pp. 573–575. Capodistrias was sent to Paris and London in the summer of 1819 to concert with the allies on the stability of France after the fall of the Richelieu government, as well as to attempt to resolve the issues surrounding the Spanish colonies, piracy and the slave trade. See Nesselrode to Capodistrias, 20 May 1819; Capodistrias to Alexander I, 15 (27) July 1819, Paris; Memorandum of Capodistrias, 12 (24) August 1819, London; Nesselrode to Lieven, 22 November (4 December) 1819; Nesselrode to Seroskern (in Rio de Janeiro); and 'Aperçu des relations politiques entre les cours alliées depuis

les conferences d'Aix-la-Chapelle jusqu'à ce jour', 23 December 1819 (4 January 1820), all in USSR, *Vneshniaia Politika Rossii, 1815–1830*, Series 2, vol. iii (May 1819–February 1821), pp. 23–25, 55–66, 94–100, 173–75, 177 and 207.

106. Satow, *A Guide to Diplomatic Practice*, vol. ii, pp. 84–85; Webster, *Foreign Policy of Castlereagh, 1815–1822*, pp. 167–85, 463–64; Bourquin, *Histoire de la Sainte Alliance*, pp. 237–46; Steckhan, *Preussen und die Neuorientierung der europäischen Staatengesellschaft*, pp. 94–99.

107. See Haus-, Hof- und Staatsarchiv (Vienna), Staatskanzlei, Kongressakten, Karton 17 (Alt. 30), ff. 38–40, for the Austrian memorandum on the slave trade; f. 42 for the Prussian; ff. 44–54 for the French; ff. 111–34 for the British; and ff. 140–44 for the Russian. Also see Protocol No. 25, 7 November 1818, and No. 37, 11 November 1818; see also Protocol No. 38, 19 November 1818, and ff. 196–211 for an additional British memorandum on this topic.

108. See Gentz to Prince Karadja, 24 March 1818, Vienna, in Prokesch-Osten, *Dépêches Inédites*, vol. i, pp. 343–53.

109. See Protocol No. 31, 13 November 1818, and Haus-, Hof- und Staatsarchiv (Vienna), Staatskanzlei, Kongressakten, Karton 17, ff. 146–54 for the Russian memorandum of 7 November 1818 on the Barbary pirates. See Capodistrias to Tatishchev, 13 (25) December 1818, in USSR, *Vneshniaia Politika Rossii, 1815–1830*, Series 2, vol. ii, pp. 602–07, for subsequent discussions.

110. Egon Corti, *The Rise of the House of Rothschild* (London: Europa-Verlag, 1928); Ferguson, *House of Rothschild*, pp. 122–27, 153–55.

111. See Protocol No. 44, 21 November 1818, in Haus-, Hof- und Staatsarchiv (Vienna), Staatskanzlei, Kongressakten, Karton 17, f. 253; Kohler, *Jewish Rights*, pp. 50–62; Metternich, 'On the Question of the Jews' (1818), in Metternich, *Memoirs*, vol. iii, pp. 209–10.

112. Ferguson, *House of Rothschild*, pp. 177–78.

113. Conference of 29 October 1818, in Haus-, Hof- und Staatsarchiv (Vienna), Gesandtschaftsarchiv Berlin, Karton 68.

114. Bourquin: *Histoire de la Sainte Alliance*, p. 245; Metternich, *Memoirs*, vol. iii, p. 127. On 21 November 1818, he wrote her again (pp. 149–50): 'I have never seen more perfect agreement between the Cabinets.'

115. 'Memoir' by Friedrich von Gentz, Aix-la-Chapelle, November 1818, in Metternich, *Memoirs*, vol. iii, pp. 189–96.

116. Castlereagh to Liverpool, 20 October 1818, in Schenk, *Aftermath of the Napoleonic Wars*, p. 126. After the Congress of Aix-la-Chapelle, Castlereagh explained to the Austrian ambassador that he saw only three legitimate *casus foederis* under the present alliance: '(1) In an attack by France on another power; (2) The return of Bonaparte; and (3) An imminent danger menacing Europe, on which it would be necessary to understand one another.' Esterhazy to Metternich, 16 May 1819, London, No. 104, Litt. A, in Haus-, Hof-, und Staatsarchiv (Vienna), Grossbritannien, Karton 160, Berichte (1819).

117. Earl of Ripon to Marquess of Londonderry, 6 July 1839, in *Castlereagh Correspondence*, vol. i, p. 128; also cited in Webster, *Foreign Policy of Castlereagh,*

1815–1822, p. 56; Jacques-Alain de Sédouy, *Le Concert Européen: Aux origins de l'Europe, 1814–1914* (Paris: Fayard, 2009), p. 23. Sédouy, a former diplomat, shows immediate appreciation for the significance of Castlereagh's parliamentary experience, which set him apart from the continental statesmen as a negotiator. Ripon was referring to Castlereagh's mission to the Continent in December 1813.

5. The Alliance in Operation, 1819–20

1. Metternich to Emperor Francis, 27 October 1817, in Metternich, *Memoirs*, vol. iii, pp. 74–87; Sheehan, *German History*, pp. 418–19; 429–30; Sked, *Metternich and Austria*, pp. 107–22. German historian Gunther Heydemann views the inability of Austria to achieve genuine constitutional reform as one of the keys to Metternich's entire policy: 'Granting even one nation or portion of this empire a constitution which enabled it to share in the general government of the realm would not only mean the end of absolute rule to which Francis (1792–1835) and his successor Ferdinand I (1835–48) clung, but could and in the long run probably would mean the breakup and dissolution of an empire held together mainly by the monarch. Thus, Metternich's unconditional rejection of all attempts to meet the threat of revolution through modern representative institutions, such as Great Britain proposed for Germany and Italy, must be seen in the context of this fundamental threat to Austria's existence.' Heydemann, 'The Vienna System between 1815 and 1848 and the Disputed Antirevolutionary Strategy: Repression, Reforms or Constitutions?' in Krüger and Schroeder, *'The Transformation of European Politics, 1763–1848'*, pp. 195–96.
2. Sheehan, *German History*, p. 403.
3. Hundt, *Die mindermächtigen deutschen Staaten*, pp. 268–341; Sheehan, *German History*, pp. 403–05. For Austrian interests as both a German and European power, see Wolf D. Gruner, 'Der Beitrag der Grossmächte in der Bewährungs- und Ausbauphase des europäischen Mächtekonzerts: Österreich 1800–1853/56', in Pyta, *Das europäische Mächtekonzert*, pp. 175–208.
4. Heinrich von Gagern to his father, 17 June 1818, Jena, in Mack Walter (ed.), *Metternich's Europe* (New York: Harper & Row, 1968), pp. 44–63.
5. Sheehan, *German History*, p. 4056; Treitschke, *History of Germany*, vol. iii, pp. 3–44, for student associations, pp. 50–53 for the origins of the *Burschenschaft* in particular and pp. 44–50, on anti-Semitism among the *Burschenschaften* (which Treitschke lamentably tried to justify); for anti-Semitism in the *Burschenschaften*, see also Lars Fischer, 'Hegel in Support of Jewish Emancipation: A Deliberate Political Act?', *The Owl of Minerva*, 37:2 (Spring/Summer 2006), pp. 127–57.
6. George Rose to Castlereagh, 29 October 1817, No. 69, Berlin, N.A. (Kew), F.O. 64/108, and cited in Sabine Freitag and Peter Wende, *British Envoys to Germany, 1816–1866*, vol. i, *1816–1829* (Cambridge: Cambridge University Press, 2000), pp. 76–77. For further reactions, see Rose's reports of 11 and 18 November and 23 December 1817. Also see the description of the Wartburg Festival by Lorenz

Oken, a professor at Jena, in G.A. Kertesz (ed.), *Documents in the Political History of the European Continent* (Oxford: Clarendon Press, 1968), pp. 64–67.
7. Sheehan sees important geographic variations in these constitutions. In the new Napoleonic states of the southwest, constitutions created assemblies—rulers may have seen these constitutional changes as weapons against attempts by former imperial knights to revive their privileges. Thus Baden, a new state, established the most representative system. In the north, the new constitutions were based on traditional estates. See Sheehan, *German History*, pp. 411–17, 426–27.
8. Walter Simon, *The Failure of the Prussian Reform Movement, 1807–1819* (Ithaca, NY: Cornell University Press, 1955), p. 109. See also, Brendan Simms, *The Struggle for the Mastery of Germany, 1779–1850* (New York: St Martin's Press, 1998), pp. 75–90, 120–22; Hagen Schulze, 'The Prussian Reformers and their Impact on German History', in T.C.W. Blanning and Peter Wende (eds), *Reform in Great Britain and Germany, 1750–1850* (Oxford: Oxford University Press, 1999).
9. Thomas Stamm-Kuhlmann, 'Restoration Prussia', in Philip G. Dwyer (ed.), *Modern Prussian History, 1830–1947* (Harlow: Longman, 2001), p. 63.
10. Thomas Stamm-Kuhlmann, *König in Preussens grosser Zeit: Friedrich Wilhelm III, der Melancholiker auf dem Thron* (Berlin: Siedler, 1992), pp. 419–22.
11. Stamm-Kuhlmann, *Friedrich Wilhelm III*, pp. 417–18, 424–26; Simon, *Prussian Reform Movement*, pp. 181–93; Baack, *Bernstorff*, pp. 70–71.
12. Simon, *Prussian Reform Movement*, p. 133.
13. Ghervas, *Reinventer la Tradition*, pp. 78–80; Treitschke, *History of Germany*, vol. iii, pp. 127–28.
14. Stamm-Kuhlmann, *Friedrich Wilhelm III*, pp. 424–25; Treitschke, *History of Germany*, vol. iii, pp. 418–19, 438.
15. Simon, *Prussian Reform Movement*, p. 206.
16. Stamm-Kuhlmann, *Friedrich Wilhelm III*, pp. 432–33; George S. Williamson, 'What Killed August von Kotzebue? The Temptations of Virtue and the Political Theology of German Nationalism, 1789–1819', *Journal of Modern History* 72/4 (December 2000), pp. 890–943; Günther Heydemann, *Carl Ludwig Sand. Die Tat als Attentat* (Hof: Oberfrankische Verlagsanstalt, 1985); Varnhagen von Ense to Tetternborn, Karlsruhe, 24 March 1819 in Metternich, *Memoirs*, vol. iii, pp. 258–60.
17. Gentz to Metternich, 1 April 1819 and Metternich to Gentz, 9 April 1819, and 17 June 1819, in Metternich, *Memoirs*, vol. iii, pp. 253–57, 260–64, 286–92.
18. Simon, *Prussian Reform Movement*, pp. 207–11; Sheehan, *German History*, p. 423; Hardenberg's diary entries for 27 July–11 August 1819 in Stamm-Kuhlmann, *Hardenberg: Tagebücher*, pp. 872–74; Metternich to Emperor Francis, 30 July and 1 August 1819, in Metternich, *Memoirs*, vol. iii, pp. 295–99 and 299–308; Peter Thielen, *Karl August von Hardenberg*, pp. 352–53; Stamm-Kuhlmann, *Friedrich Wilhelm III*, pp. 433–36; Treitschke, *History of Germany*, vol. iii, pp. 206–13. For a copy of the Teplitz Convention, see Walter: *Metternich's Europe*, pp. 90–93.
19. Treitschke, *History of Germany*, vol. iii, pp. 254–55.
20. Treitschke, *History of Germany*, vol. iii, pp. 206–29. For Metternich's proposal to the German Confederation, based on the Carlsbad Decrees, see Metternich

to Count Buol and its enclosure, 1 September 1819 in Metternich, *Memoirs*, vol. iii, pp. 309–23. For the decrees themselves, see Kertesz: *Documents in Political History*, pp. 67–69.
21. Simon, *Prussian Reform Movement*, pp. 212–15.
22. One historian has remarked how the states of Germany could not agree to allow the free passage of grain despite conditions of famine, which they saw as an affront to their sovereignty, but readily agreed to the creation of a central bureau at Mainz to coordinate their counter-revolutionary activities. See Schenk, *Aftermath of the Napoleonic Wars*, pp. 97–99.
23. Simon, *Prussian Reform Movement*, pp. 215–28; Treitschke, *History of Germany*, vol. iii, pp. 260–76.
24. William had married the Tsar's favourite sister, Catherine, in 1816, but she died in January 1819. The Tsar's grandfather on his father's side was also the Duke of Württemberg, while his wife, the Empress Elizabeth, was the daughter of Charles Louis, Hereditary Prince of Baden (1755–1801).
25. Ghervas, *Reinventer la Tradition*, pp. 12, 78–80, 216.
26. Webster, *Foreign Policy of Castlereagh, 1812–1815*, pp. 190–93; Günther Heydemann, *Konstitution gegen Revolution: Die britische Deutschland- und Italienpolitik, 1815–1848* (Göttingen: Göttingen, 1995), pp. 46–48. Castlereagh later congratulated Neumann, the Austrian envoy in London, on Metternich's success in Germany, pointing to this practical success to make the point that in this instance the Austrians had followed 'the better line'—'the positive facts always speak louder than all the beautiful reasoning and speculative combinations', so that 'a policy based on principle will always triumph over one based on systems and abstract ideas': Neumann to Metternich, 14 January 1820, London, No. 131 A, in Haus-, Hof-, und Staatsarchiv (Vienna), Grossbritannien, Karton 162, Berichte (1820), first bundle, first series of folio numbers, ff. 19–21.
27. 'Aperçu des idées de l'empereur sur les affaires de l'Allemagne', 21 November (3 December) 1819, in USSR, *Vneshniaia Politika Rossii, 1815–1830*, Series 2, vol. iii, pp. 153–58. This Russian memorandum asserted that the 'intimate union' of the powers of the German Confederation offered the 'sole means' of overcoming the present danger: 'What is the role of the non-German powers: It is definite. The treaties prescribe it. Far from aggravating the evil ... the non-German powers should strive to bring to the rulers of Europe a more intimate union, and to reaffirm the ties of inalterable respect between governments and their governed.' The final phrase was a reference to constitutional reform.
28. Webster, *Foreign Policy of Castlereagh, 1815–1822*, pp. 193–98; Heydemann, *Konstitution gegen Revolution*, pp. 48–52.
29. Brian Fagan, *The Little Ice Age: How Climate Made History, 1300–1850* (New York: Basic Books, 2000), pp. 167–80. Scientists generally agree that this was the worst volcanic explosion in over a thousand years.
30. See, generally, Malcolm I. Thomis and Peter Holt, *Threats of Revolution in Britain, 1789–1848* (London: Archon Books, 1977); Charles Tilly, *Popular Contention in Great Britain, 1758–1834* (Cambridge MA: Harvard University Press, 1995);

E.P. Thompson, *The Making of the English Working Class* (London: Victor Gollancz, 1963).
31. Joyce Marlow, *The Peterloo Massacre* (London: Panther Books, 1971); Thompson, *Making of the English Working Class*, pp. 669–700, 709–10; J.E. Cookson, *Lord Liverpool's Administration, 1815–1822* (Edinburgh & London: Scottish Academic Press, 1975), pp. 178–99; Norman Gash, *Aristocracy and People: Britain 1815–1832* (London: Edward Arnold, 1979), pp. 96–99; John Bew, *Castlereagh: Enlightenment, War and Tyranny* (London: Quercus, 2011), pp. 462–68; Boyd Hilton, *A Mad, Bad and Dangerous People: England 1783–1846* (Oxford: Oxford University Press, 2006) pp. 252–53; Elie Halévy, *The Liberal Awakening*, trans. E.I. Watkin and D.A. Barber (London, 1949). Hilton points out that the ministers resisted the demands of the Duke of York for an increase in the standing army, while Bew notes that Castlereagh conceded in debate that the corrupt borough of Grampound should be disenfranchised in favour of Leeds.
32. Debate on the Seditious Meetings Bill, 29 November 1819, in T.C. Hansard, *The Parliamentary Debates from the Year 1803 to the Present Time*, vol. xli (23 November 1819–28 February 1820) (London), col. 412.
33. Hansard, *Parliamentary Debates*, vol. xli, col. 401 (debate of 29 November 1819).
34. Hansard, *Parliamentary Debates*, vol. xli, col. 381. Castlereagh was so impassioned in this debate that when the bill was again considered on 3 December 1819, opposition leader George Tierney accused him of 'wrath against the people'. Castlereagh replied: 'I feel no wrath against the people. I am only doing my duty.' Hansard, *Parliamentary Debates*, vol. xli, col. 702.
35. Hansard, *Parliamentary Debates*, vol. xli , cols. 383, 387–88 (debate of 29 November 1819).
36. That Castlereagh sincerely held the beliefs he espoused in Parliament is scarcely to be doubted. He sent a similar description to his envoys abroad: '[A] number of itinerate orators of very low condition in life ... have gone about exciting the passions of these people, and persuading them that nothing but an entire change of the constitution, the destruction of the National Debt, and the extinction of the great mass of the taxes could relieve their distress, and some of them have even inspired them with a due disposition to seize upon and divide the property of their neighbours. The lowest orders of the manufacturing population had been thus worked upon, previous to the first Manchester Meeting ... The disturbances in question are confined to the very lowest orders of the people. The extent of the mischief is locally very limited, and the rest of the Kingdom is both quiet, contented and prosperous, notwithstanding the licentiousness of the Press.' Castlereagh to Sir Charles Stuart (British ambassador to France), 14 September 1819, 'Private', in N.A. (Kew) F.O. 27/200.
37. Thompson, *Making of the English Working Class*, pp. 700–10.
38. Ignacio Fernández Sarasola, 'La portée des droits individuals dans la Constitution espagnole de 1812' and Jean-Baptiste Busaall, 'Constitution et "Gouvernement des Moderns dans l'Espagne du *Trenio Liberal* (1820–1823)', in Jean-Philippe

Luis (ed.), *La Guerre d'Independence Espagnole et le Libéralisme au XIXe Siècle* (Madrid: Casa de Velázquez, 2011), pp. 91–109, 111–24; Heydemann, *Konstitution gegen Revolution*, pp. 82–86.

39. Charles Esdaile, *Spain in the Liberal Age* (Oxford: Blackwell, 2000), pp. 31–35; Raymond Carr, *Spain 1808–1975*, 2nd edn (Oxford: Oxford University Press, 1982), pp. 86–115; Charles Esdaile, 'War and Politics in Spain, 1808–1814', *Historical Journal* 31 (1988), pp. 297–317; Marqués de Wenceslao Ramírez de Villa-Urritia, *Fernando VII Rey Consitucional: Historia Diplomática de España de 1820 a 1823* (Madrid: F. Beltrán 1922), pp. 7–141.

40. Esdaile, *Spain in the Liberal Age*, pp. 42–45; Carr, *Spain*, pp. 120–29; Villa-Urritia, *Fernando VII*, pp. 143–74; Josep Fontana, *La Crisis del Antiguo Régimen, 1808–1833* (Barcelona: Ariel, 1979), pp. 22–30; Jean-Philippe Luis, *L'Utopie réactionnaire* (Madrid: Casa de Velazquez, 2002), pp. 36–40.

41. Esdaile, *Spain in the Liberal Age*, p. 43.

42. Timothy E. Anna, 'Institutional and Political Impediments to Spain's Settlement of the American Rebellions', *The Americas* 34/4 (April 1982), p. 487.

43. Charles Wentz Fehrenbach, 'Moderados and Exaltados: The Liberal Opposition to Ferdinand VII, 1814–1823', *Hispanic American Historical Review* 50/1 (February 1970), p. 59.

44. Esdaile, *Spain in the Liberal Age*, pp. 45–49.

45. Fehrenbach, 'Moderados and Exaltados', pp. 59–60.

46. N.A. (Kew), F.O. 72/234 ff. 42–46, Sir Henry Wellesley to Castlereagh, Madrid, 7 January 1820, No. 10: 'It is believed that this Insurrection is more the work of Non-Commissioned Officers and Troops than of Officers: that very few of these have joined in it and that (although the Constitution has been proclaimed,) it arises principally from a Dislike to embark upon the Expedition.' See also: Richard Stites, *The Four Horsemen* (Oxford: Oxford University Press, 2014), pp. 28–31, 65–72; Esdaile, *Spain in the Liberal Age*, pp. 48–49; Carr, *Spain*, 124–29; Schroeder, *Metternich's Diplomacy Diplomacy at its Zenith, 1820–1823* (Austin: University of Texas Press, 1962), pp. 25–26; Villa-Urritia, *Fernando VII*, pp. 174–81; Alberto Gil Novales, *Rafael del Riego: La Revolución de 1820, día a día* (Madrid: Siglo Veintiuno, 1976), pp. 23–24 (introductory biographical note), pp. 34–67 (January and February 1820).

47. N.A. (Kew), F.O. 72/234 ff. 61–62, Wellesley to Castlereagh, Madrid, 17 January 1820 (No. 14) in cipher.

48. N.A. (Kew), F.O. 72/234 ff. 235–38, Wellesley to Castlereagh, Madrid, 23 February 1820 (No. 42).

49. Wellesley to Castlereagh, 24 January 1820 (No. 18), in N.A. (Kew), F.O. 72/234 ff. 101–05: 'Although the Court affects to make light of the revolt of the troops in Andalusia, it would appear by the letters enclosed in my letter of the 19th & by other private accounts that the insurgents are gaining strength.'

50. Wellesley to Castlereagh, 3 February 1820 (No. 25), in N.A. (Kew), F.O. 72/234, ff. 163–64: 'I have learned from authority that the Insurgents Army amounts to 10,000 Men including 500 Cavalry'; 7 February 1820 (Nos 29, 30, 31, 33, 34) in F.O. 72/234, ff. 182–207; 14 February 1820 (No. 37) in F.O. 72/234, ff. 217–18; and

21 February 1820 (No. 40) in F.O. 72/234, ff. 226–27: 'The Affair in Andalusia still continues without any considerable advantage having been gained either by the King's Troops or by those of the Insurgents ... There has been a slight disturbance at Saragossa [Zaragoza] where the People cried "[Vive] the Constitution" They however dispersed upon a promise from the authorities that their complaints should be submitted to the King. The Military did not interfere.'
51. Wellesley to Castlereagh, Madrid, 23 January 1820 (No. 42) in N.A. (Kew), F.O. 72/234 ff. 235–38. Wellesley continued: 'The state of the Government is certainly the most deplorable, and it ought to be a bitter reflection to the King's advisers that this state of things is solely attributable to their own obstinacy and inconsistency.'
52. Wellesley to Castlereagh, Madrid, 23 February 1820 (No. 42) in N.A. (Kew), F.O. 72/234, ff. 61–62; 24 February 1820 (No. 43), 28 February 1820 (Nos. 44 and 45) in F.O. 72/234; Wellesley to Castlereagh, 2 March 1820 (No. 46) in F.O. 72/234, ff. 255–57: 'The insurrection in Galicia is much more to be dreaded than that in Andalusia, since it appears that in Galicia the People have taken the part of the troops. It remains to be seen whether other Northern Provinces will declare against the King. It is in general believed they are ripe for insurrection. The edicts of the insurgents in Galicia are very severe. The punishment of death is awarded to anyone who speaks against the Constitution or obeys the King's orders until he has sworn to it ....'
53. Wellesley to Castlereagh, Madrid, 7 March 1820 (Nos 53 and 54) in N.A. (Kew), F.O. 72/234; Wellesley to Castlereagh, 7 March 1820, Madrid, 'Private and Confidential' in F.O. 72/234, ff. 300–02: 'I am afraid that this insurrection is taking a very bad turn for the King, and the want of decision of his ministers encreased the difficulties of his situation ... There is a very bad spirit among the lower classes in Madrid.' For Russian reports, see the three letters from Count Bulgari to Nesselrode of 24 February (7 March) 1820, Madrid, in USSR, *Vneshniaia Politika Rossii, 1815–1830*, Series 2, vol. iii, pp. 300–03, 306–09, and 312–13. See also, Fontana: *La Crisis*, pp. 31–41, for his view of the four stages of what Spanish historians refer to as the 'Trienio Liberal', or the three years of liberal rule; see Luis, *L'Utopie Réactionnaire*, pp. 41–47, for changes in administration in this period.
54. Wellesley to Castlereagh, Madrid, 20 January 1820 (No. 64) in N.A. (Kew), ff. 372–73; Wellesley to Castlereagh, 25 March 1820 (No. 66), in F.O. 72/234, ff. 394–95: 'It would seem that the mischievous publications issuing daily from the press have kept the public mind in a continued state of ferment. These publications are read and commented upon in clubs which have been established in different quarters of the town, and which are numerously attended'); see also Esdaile, *Spain in the Liberal Age*, pp. 49–55.
55. Nesselrode to Lieven, 3 (15) March 1820, in USSR, *Vneshniaia Politika Rossii, 1815–1830*, Series 2, vol. iii, p. 315–16; Guillaume de Bertier de Sauvigny, *Metternich et la France après le Congrès de Vienne*, vol. ii, *Les grands Congrès—1820/1824* (Paris: Hachette, 1970), pp. 305–10; Webster, *Foreign Policy of Castlereagh, 1815–1822*, pp. 228–32; Schroeder, *Metternich's Diplomacy*, pp. 26–27; Bourquin, *Histoire de la Sainte Alliance*, pp. 254–56.

56. Bertier de Sauvigny, *The Bourbon Restoration*, pp. 165–68. On the assassination of the Duc de Berri, see Gilles Malandain, *L'introuvable complot: Attentat, enquête et rumeur dans la France de la Restauration* (Paris: Éditions de l'EHESS, 2011).
57. Webster, *Foreign Policy of Castlereagh, 1812–1815*, pp. 230–34; Irby C. Nichols, Jr, *The European Pentarchy and the Congress of Verona, 1822* (The Hague: Martinus Nijhoff, 1971), p. 28.
58. Webster, *Foreign Policy of Castlereagh, 1815–1822*, pp. 228–29; Bertier de Sauvigny, *Metternich et la France*, vol. ii, pp. 309–11; Schroeder, *Metternich's Diplomacy*, pp. 27–28; Nesselrode to Golovkin, Lieven and Aleopus, 19 April (1 May) 1820, in USSR, *Vneshniaia Politika Rossii, 1815–1830*, Series 2, vol. iii, p. 351: 'What has saved Europe? The union of the allies—but is it strong enough to resist the revolutionary torrent? The Emperor wishes to invite his allies to reunite.' Capodistrias had submitted a strongly worded memorandum to the Tsar only a fortnight earlier: 'Résumé de tous les rapports reçu de nos missions', 30 March (11 April 1820) in USSR, *Vneshniaia Politika Rossii, 1815–1830*, Series 2, vol. iii, pp. 337–40—the revolution, having chosen its ground in Spain 'to exercise its ravages and threaten Europe with fresh catastrophes ... will it not be urgent for the powers to assemble to deliberate on the means to halt the progress of this evil?'
59. Bertier de Sauvigny, *Metternich et la France*, vol. ii, pp. 307–12; Schroeder, *Metternich's Diplomacy*, p. 29, fn. 14.
60. Wellington, 'Memorandum to Viscount Castlereagh regarding the propriety of interfering in Spanish Affairs', 16 April 1820, in Wellington, Arthur Wellesley, *Despatches, Correspondence and Memoranda of Field Marshal Arthur Duke of Wellington, K.G. Edited by his Son* (London: J. Murray, 1867), vol. i, p. 116–21; Webster, *Foreign Policy of Castlereagh, 1815–1822*, pp. 234–35.
61. Harold Temperley, *The Foreign Policy of Canning, 1822–1827*, 2nd edn (London: Archon, 1966), p. 14.
62. Castlereagh, 'Cabinet Minute', 30 April 1820, in Stewart, *Castlereagh Correspondence*, vol. xii, pp. 253–57; also in Alison, *Lives of Castlereagh and Stewart*, vol. iii, pp. 135–36.
63. State Paper of 5 May 1820, in Bourne, *Foreign Policy of Victorian England*, pp. 198–207, citing F.O. 120/39; also see Webster, *Foreign Policy of Castlereagh, 1815–1822*, pp. 235–46. Castlereagh read his paper aloud to the Russian ambassador, Count Lieven. See Lieven to Nesselrode, 4 (16) May 1820, London, No. 72, in USSR, *Vneshniaia Politika Rossii, 1815–1830*, Series 2, vol. iii, pp. 374–78. According to the Austrian ambassador, Prince Paul Esterhazy, Castlereagh also met with him, speaking not only as an individual but 'as the organ of the British Cabinet, which has examined this question with the most assiduous care, and the sentiments expressed [therein] are unanimously held by his colleagues and His Majesty the King'. Castlereagh then read a series of documents, including the State Paper itself; a letter from Ferdinand VII to George IV of England, announcing his acceptance of the new Spanish Constitution; George IV's response;

a report from the British ambassador in Madrid; and the instructions sent to Madrid and Rio de Janiero. See Esterhazy to Metternich, 5 May 1820 and 14 May 1820, No. 148 Litt. A, in Haus-, Hof-, und Staatsarchiv (Vienna), Grossbritannien, Karton 162, Berichte (1820), second bundle, first series of folio numbers, ff. 5–8, 15–20. Castlereagh further sent copies to the British ambassadors accredited to the Continental courts to read the State Paper to the foreign ministers of the allied powers.

64. Castlereagh to Stewart, 24 February 1820, in Alison, *Lives of Castlereagh and Stewart*, vol. iii, pp. 215–16.

65. Webster, *Foreign Policy of Castlereagh, 1812–1815*, pp. 243–45; Schroeder, *Metternich's Diplomacy*, pp. 27–30; Bertier de Sauvigny, *Metternich et la France*, vol. ii, pp. 305–11. The Spanish Revolution occurred while the allies were also in heated debate over a Russian proposal, made after the fall of the pro-Russian Richelieu government, for the allies to agree to a set of secret instructions specifying the precautions they would take in the event of the death of Louis XVIII of France; see Bertier de Sauvigny, *Metternich et la France*, vol. ii, pp. 284–305; Webster, *Foreign Policy of Castlereagh, 1815–1822*, pp. 200–14. Castlereagh's rejection of the Tsar's proposal for such 'eventual instructions', in his 'Memorandum on France' of 24 September 1819, was really a precursor to his State Paper of 5 May 1820. See Webster, *Foreign Policy of Castlereagh, 1815–1822*, pp. 207–09.

66. Davis, *Naples and Napoleon*, pp. 160–08, 276–94; George T. Romani, *The Neapolitan Revolution of 1820–1821* (Evanston, IL: Northwestern University Press, 1950), pp. 3–36; Stites, *Four Horsemen*, pp. 129–141; Di Scala, *Italy: From Revolution to Republic*, pp. 20–54; Mario Themelly, 'Introduction', in Luigi Minichini, *Luglio 1820: Cronaca di una Rivoluzione* (Rome: Bulzoni Editore, 1979), pp. vii-xxix; Heydemann, *Konstitution gegen Revolution*, pp. 69–80; Raffaele Scalamandrè, *Michele Morelli e la Rivoluzione Napoletana del 1820–1821* (Rome: Gangemi Editore, 1993), pp. 41–45, 53–60; Annibale Alberti (ed.), *Atti del Parlamento delle Due Sicile 1820–1821* (Bologna, 1926–34), vols 4 and 5; Joseph Brady, *Rome and the Neapolitan Revolution of 1820–1821: A Study in Papal Neutrality* (New York: Columbia University Press, 1937); Etienne-Denis Pasquier, *Mémoires du Chancelier Pasquier*, vol. iv, 1818–1820 (Paris: Plon, 1894), pp. 514–17.

67. Davis, *Naples and Napoleon*, pp. 297–99; Gugliemo Pepe, *Memoirs of General Pepé* (London: Richard Bentley, 1846), vol. ii, pp. 161–78; Stites, *Four Horsemen*, pp. 141–151.

68. Pepe, *Memoirs*, vol. ii, pp. 182–85: 'I decided upon arresting the King, the Emperor, the Empress, Metternich, Medici, and Nugent. Their guard would be confided to a hundred officers and subalterns of the militia, who were Grand-Masters of the Carbonari. It was my intention to send them, thus escorted, to the city of Melfi in Basilicata.'

69. A'Court to Stewart, 26 April 1820, in British Library, Add. Mss. 41,532 (Heytesbury Papers), f. 53: 'The Spanish news has given great spirit to the disaffected all over Italy....'

70. Pietro Colletta, *History of the Kingdom of Naples, 1734–1825* (Edinburgh: T. Constable, 1858), vol. i, p. 327.

71. Davis, *Naples and Napoleon*, p. 303; Colletta, *History of the Kingdom of Naples*, vol. i, pp. 327–35; Scalamandrè, *Morelli*, pp. 81–133.
72. Pepe, *Memoirs*, vol. ii, pp. 218–34.
73. Webster, *Foreign Policy of Castlereagh, 1815–1822*, pp. 260–61.
74. A'Court to Castlereagh, 9 July 1820 ('Private'), in N.A. (Kew), F.O. 70/90.
75. '[T]he solemn public oaths to uphold the constitution taken by the prince regent had conferred full legitimacy on the constitutional regime established almost without a revolution. Even an official like the Intendent of Capitanata who was "perplexed as to his fate" now had no alternative but to support the constitutional municipalities that apparently had the full approval of the monarchy.' Davis, *Naples and Napoleon*, p. 304. According to Colletta, the King was threatened by five men who came to the palace on the night of 6 July claiming to be representatives of the *Carbonari*. Colletta, *History of the Kingdom of Naples*, vol. i, pp. 335–37.
76. Richard Keppel Craven, *A Tour through the Southern Provinces of the Kingdom of Naples* (London: Rodwell and Martin, 1821), Appendix, pp. 443–45; Scalamandrè, *Morelli*, pp. 137–40.
77. See also, Romani, *Neapolitan Revolution*, pp. 37–66; Minichini: *Luglio 1820*.
78. Back in 1815, both A'Court and Castlereagh had been annoyed by Ferdinand's disregard of the constitution in Sicily, even though they wished to see a strengthening of royal authority. At that time, they urged Ferdinand to follow the example of Louis XVIII and the French *Charte*. British Library, Add. Mss. 41,532 (Heytesbury Papers), f. 53. But in 1820 they believed the kingdom was peaceful. 'The quiet and prosperous state of these Kingdoms', A'Court had reported as recently as early March, 'affords but few subjects worthy of being brought under Your Lordship's notice'. A'Court to Castleareagh, 13 March 1820, Naples in N.A. (Kew), F.O. 165/31.
79. A'Court to Castleareagh, 2 August 1820 (No. 60) in N.A. (Kew), F.O. 165/31.
80. A'Court to Castlereagh, 9 July 1820, in N.A. (Kew), F.O. 70/90: 'The Chiefs are well persuaded that the non-interference of foreigners in their concerns must depend very much upon their abstaining from acts of violence, and they endeavour to inculcate this by every means in their power. This consideration may save us from personal violence, but we cannot be certain that it will.'
81. Romani, *Neapolitan Revolution*, pp. 67–104; Schroeder, *Metternich's Diplomacy*, pp. 30–35.
82. Romani, *Neapolitan Revolution*, pp. 128–37. In 1815, A'Court had urged that if Ferdinand were restored in Naples, the Hereditary Prince should rule in Sicily. See Castlereagh to A'Court, Vienna, 29 September 1814 (No. 7), British Library, Add. Mss. 41,515, ff. 141–44: 'It is with sentiments of deep regret that His Royal Highness has viewed the tenor of your despatches that, since His Majesty's return to the Administration of the Royal functions, his Government has been marked by such repeated violations of the Constitution which he promised to uphold ...'. The French foreign minister, Pasquier, thought that the outbreak of the Sicilian revolution would increase British concern in Naples: see Pasquier, *Mèmoirés*, vol. iv, p. 503.

83. A'Court to Castlereagh, 20 August 1820 (No. 68), in N.A. (Kew), F.O. 70/90.
84. A'Court to Castlereagh, 20 August 1820 (No. 68), in N.A. (Kew), F.O. 70/90. 'General Pepe, who is entirely lost in the opinion of the regular troops, is endeavouring to reconcile himself with Carbonari, hoping thro' their means to intimidate the Govt.'
85. A'Court to Castlereagh, 25 August 1820 (No. 72), in N.A. (Kew), F.O. 70/90.
86. A'Court to Castlereagh, 24 August 1820 (No. 71), in N.A. (Kew), F.O. 165/31.
87. A'Court to Castlereagh, 30 August 1820 (No. 73), in N.A. (Kew), F.O. 70/90.
88. A'Court to Castlereagh, 24 August 1820 (No. 71), in N.A. (Kew), F.O. 165/31. According to A'Court, the 'higher classes' would have preferred a constitution based on the French *Charte*, but the 'middling classes in the Provinces [were] satisfied with the present constitution'; and only the 'lowest classes' were indifferent or hostile.
89. Romani, *Neapolitan Revolution*, pp. 107–08; Schroeder, *Metternich's Diplomacy*, pp. 42–43.
90. Stewart had already conveyed to Castlereagh half a year earlier his opinion that the Austrian army was weak. N.A. (Kew), F.O. 7/144, Stewart to Castlereagh, 1 November 1819 (No. 23).
91. Metternich predicted that 'blood will flow in torrents'. Romani, *Neapolitan Revolution*, p. 107; Schroeder, *Metternich's Diplomacy*, p. 33; British Library, Add. Mss. 41532, ff. 56–58, Stewart to A'Court, 16 June and 4 August 1820.
92. Webster, *Foreign Policy of Castlereagh, 1815–1822*, pp. 264–65.
93. Castlereagh to Stewart, 29 July 1820, 'Most Secret and Confidential', in N.A. (Kew), F.O. 7/148 and British Library, Add. Mss. 41,532, ff. 65–73.
94. Webster, *Foreign Policy of Castlereagh, 1815–1822*, p. 263.
95. 'La chose doit être traitée comme une affaire *spéciale*, plutôt que générale; comme question *italienne*, plutôt qu'européenne, et, par conséquent, plus comme du domaine, de *l'Autriche* que celui de *l'Alliance*', Esterhazy to Metternich, 16 September 1820, London, cited in Heydemann, *Konstitution gegen Revolution*, p. 92. Heydemann adds that in his discussions with Esterhazy and Lieven in London, Castlereagh contemplated the survival of the constitutional regime in Naples if adequate modifications could be made to their adoption of the Spanish Constitution; perhaps this was an alternative strategy in the event that Austrian suppression of the regime failed.
96. Castlereagh to Stewart, 5 August 1820, Cray Farm, in N.A. (Kew), F.O. 7/160. Castlereagh presciently saw that the Continental powers would look upon the Neapolitan crisis as an occasion in which to introduce general principles: 'The remark of the French Minister originated in that disposition which the French as well as the Russian Government always feel to generalize every question & to try to bring it within the strict pale of the Alliance—Russia will always regard Her controul as complete, in proportion as the Governments of Europe can be made to form a single Machine, of which the Russian Military Power must ever constitute one of the very principal wheels. The French Govt., on the other hand, invariably wish to give to the Alliance some other and broader Character than that which

originally and really belonged to it—namely an alliance for the preservation of the Peace of Europe against French Revolutionary Danger—but neither Government will, I think, at this moment look with any favor on what is passing at Naples.'
97. Castlereagh to A'Court, 16 September 1820 (No. 7), 'Most Secret and Confidential' in N.A. (Kew), F.O. 70/89; Croker to Planta, 14 September 1820, Admiralty Office, in F.O. 165/31, stating that the *Leffy* (50 guns), *Active* (46 guns) and *Vengeur* (74 guns) had been ordered to the Bay of Naples; see also Schroeder, *Metternich's Diplomacy*, p. 47.
98. Hilton, *A Mad, Bad and Dangerous People?*, p. 269, citing Craig Calhoun, *The Question of Class Struggle: Social Foundations of Popular Radicalism during the Industrial Revolution* (Chicago: University of Chicago Press, 1982); Jane Robins, *The Trial of Queen Caroline: The Scandalous Affair that Nearly Ended a Monarchy* (New York: Free Press, 2006); Webster, *Foreign Policy of Castlereagh, 1815–1822*, pp. 217–25: 'The diplomatic history of the next twelve months cannot be understood unless the special difficulties and weaknesses of the British Government be taken into account.'
99. Alison, *Lives of Castlereagh and Stewart*, vol. iii, pp. 218–23.
100. Norman Gash, *Mr Secretary Peel* (London: Longmans, 1961), pp. 285–86.
101. *Morning Chronicle*, 21 July 1820.
102. Bertier de Sauvigny, *Metternich et la France*, vol. ii, p. 332; Woodhouse, *Capodistria*, pp. 239–40; Schroeder, *Metternich's Diplomacy*, p. 48, citing Vincent to Metternich, 21 August 1820.
103. In 1816, the eldest daughter of the Duke of Calabria, heir to the Neapolitan throne, had married the Duc de Berri, a younger son of the Comte d'Artois and nephew to Louis XVIII, further cementing their countries' ties.
104. Bertier de Sauvigny, *Metternich et la France*, vol. ii, pp. 331–32; Webster, *Foreign Policy of Castlereagh, 1815–1822*, pp. 265–66; Schroeder, *Metternich's Diplomacy*, pp. 49–51; Pasquier, *Mèmoires*, vol. iv, pp. 520–22. Prince Paul Esterhazy, the Austrian ambassador in London, mainly attributed the request to Pozzo di Borgo. See Esterhazy to Metternich, 14 November 1820, London, No. 173, Litt. B and B, in Haus-, Hof- und Staatsarchiv (Vienna), Grossbritannien, Karton 162, Berichte (1820), third bundle, third series of folios, ff. 23–24.
105. Bertier de Sauvigny, *Metternich et la France*, pp. 332–41; Webster, *Foreign Policy of Castlereagh, 1815–1822*, pp. 266–70; Schroeder, *Metternich's Diplomacy*, pp. 52–54.
106. Castlereagh to Stewart, 16 September 1820, Foreign Office, 'Most Private, Secret and Confidential' in N.A. (Kew), F.O. 7/160, and also printed in Stewart, *Castlereagh Correspondence*, vol. xii, pp. 311–18; Alison, *Lives of Castlereagh and Stewart*, vol. iii, pp. 136–40.
107. Same as above.
108. Webster, *Foreign Policy of Castlereagh, 1815–1822*, p. 266, 271–72; Bertier de Sauvigny, *Metternich et la France*: vol. ii, pp. 341–44; Schroeder, *Metternich's Diplomacy*, p. 53. On the importance that the Tsar attached to British participation, see Capodistrias to Lieven, 6 (18) September 1820, Warsaw, in USSR, *Vneshniaia Politika Rossii, 1815–1830*, Series 2, vol. iii, p. 504.

109. Webster, *Foreign Policy of Castlereagh, 1815–1822*, p. 274.
110. Romani, *Neapolitan Revolution*, p. 111, fn. 21, notes that the Italian *Carbonari* regarded Alexander 'somewhat as a patron'.
111. Bertier de Sauvigny, *Metternich et la France*, vol. ii, pp. 341–47; Webster, *Foreign Policy of Castlereagh, 1815–1822*, pp. 271–76; Schroeder, *Metternich's Diplomacy*, pp. 53–56; Stewart to Castlereagh, 2 October 1820 in N.A. (Kew), F.O. 7/160, also cited in Webster, *Foreign Policy of Castlereagh, 1815–1822*, pp. 521–24: 'Prince Metternich finds himself now obliged to decide ... either to forego having Russia (who if not for would be against) and France and to stand singly with England, or to sign and seal with the two former and trust to the known dispositions of the Great Britain.'
112. Castlereagh to Stewart, 21 September 1820, 'Most Private, Secret & Confidential' in N.A. (Kew), F.O. 7/160.
113. Bertier de Sauvigny, *Metternich et la France*, vol. ii, pp. 347–57.
114. Bertier de Sauvigny, *Metternich et la France*, vol. ii. pp. 374–79, 382–84; Pasquier, *Mémoires*, vol. iv, pp. 530–38. According to Pasquier, the French envoy M. de La Sensée met with Capodistrias on 22 September.
115. Thomas E. Skidmore, *Brazil: Five Centuries of Change*, 2nd edn (Oxford: Oxford University Press, 2010), pp. 41–46; Thomas Gallagher, *Portugal: A Twentieth-Century Interpretation* (Manchester: Manchester University Press, 1983), pp. 12–13; Angel Rivero, 'The Revolution of 1820 and the Advent of Liberalism in Portugal', unpublished paper presented at the Institute for the Study of the Americas, University of London, May 2010.
116. Webster, *Foreign Policy of Castlereagh, 1815–1822*, pp. 248–56. Castlereagh cautioned the British envoy in Lisbon not to perform any act that might be construed as 'formal recognition of the new order of things' but otherwise to protect British persons and interests and to pursue a conciliatory line of conduct. See Castlereagh to E.M. Ward, 18 October 1820 (No. 6) and 8 November (No. 7), in N.A. (Kew), F.O. 63/231, ff. 15–22.
117. Castlereagh to Stewart, 21 September 1820, 'Most Private, Secret & Confidential', in N.A. (Kew), F.O. 7/160.
118. Castlereagh sent this explanation to his half-brother for communication to the allies: 'I presume our refusal to send a Member of the Government to Troppau will be complained of, but if we had, we could have given him no other Instruction, nor in Truth any greater Latitude, than you have, whilst a Mission at the present Moment would have been productive of the greatest Misconception and Inconvenience ... I trust the Reasons which have been assigned to Lieven and Esterhazy for thus declining the Joint Request of their Courts will prove satisfactory ... I cannot disguise from you, however, that the Mode in which it was Claimed, and more especially in the Russian Communication, namely, as an obligation Imposed upon us by our Treaties, render'd it still more Impossible to alter the Line previously adopted, and declared, but had it even been urged upon the very grounds of my Dispatch of this date, that is upon our own terms,

still it would have been declined, so strongly do we feel the Inconvenience of at present rousing an alarm in this Country upon such questions ... [A]nd with the further Evil, that it would be hardly possible in such Case for us to render our Line Clear and Intelligible in Parliament, without bringing before both Houses more of the Allied Proceedings ....' Castlereagh to Lord Stewart, 15 October 1820, Cray Farm, 'Private', in N.A. (Kew), F.O. 7/160.
119. Webster, *Foreign Policy of Castlereagh, 1815–1822*, p. 283.
120. Webster, *Foreign Policy of Castlereagh, 1815–1822*, p. 284, citing Esterhazy to Metternich, 25 October 1820, London, No. 169, Litt. B, in Haus-, Hof- und Staatsarchiv (Vienna), Grossbritannien, Karton 162, Berichte (1820), third bundle, third series of folios, ff. 54–56. See also Esterhazy to Metternich, 15 October 1820, Litt. A and B, and 25 October 1820, Litt C (on views of George IV) in ibid.
121. Castlereagh to Stewart, 16 September, 1820, Foreign Office, 'Most Private, Secret and Confidential', N.A. (Kew), F.O. 7/160, and also in Stewart, *Castlereagh Correspondence*, vol. xii, pp. 311–18; Alison, *Lives of Castlereagh and Stewart*, vol. iii, pp. 136–40.
122. Note (*Zapiska*) of Secretary of State Capodistrias to Alexander I, 17 October 1820, Warsaw, in USSR, *Vneshniaia Politika Rossii, 1815–1830*, Series 2, vol. iii, pp. 540–44: 'Selon ce système, quel que soit le pays où la révolution détruise l'ordre de choses établi par l'alliance générale, les cours alliées doivent s'armer contre la révolution et chercher à la vaincre.'
123. USSR, *Vneshniaia Politika Rossii, 1815–1830, Series 2*, vol. iii, p. 542: 'Convenons de définir de la manière la plus positive les obligations nouvelles que nous allons contracter, pour nous liguer contre la révolution et pour détruire sa désastreuse influence. Signons par conséquent un traité qui nous soumettra à ces obligations précises.'
124. USSR, *Vneshniaia Politika Rossii, 1815–1830*, Series 2, vol. iii, p. 542.
125. On the abolition of serfdom in Livonia, see Nicholas V. Riasanovsky, *Russian Identities: A Historical Survey* (Oxford: Oxford University Press, 2005), p. 121. Riasanovsky notes that rural conditions were made worse because the peasants were emancipated without land.
126. Lebzeltern analyses the prospects for a constitution in his report to Metternich of 17 February 1820, printed in Mikhaïlovich: *Les Rapports Diplomatiques de Lebzeltern*, pp. 67–68: 'The Emperor thinks that there are already institutions in the Empire ready to receive a constitution—that is, the state assemblies of the nobles.' Article 13 of Novosiltsev's final draft provided that the 'legislative power shall be exercised by the Sovereign concurrently with the Diet of the Empire'. Decades earlier, Novosiltsev had been one of the members of the Tsar's liberal 'Unofficial Committee'. See Zawadzki: *A Man of Honour*, pp. 278–79; Marc Raeff, *Plans for Political Reform in Imperial Russia, 1730–1905* (Englewood Cliffs, NJ: Prentice Hall, 1966), pp. 110–20; Riasanovsky: *Russian Identities*, pp. 120–21; Rey: *Alexandre I*, pp. 405–08; Georges Vernadsky, *La Charte Constitutionnelle de l'Empire Russe de l'an 1820* (Paris: Librairie du Recueil Sirey,

1933); Theodor Schiemann, *La Charte Constitutionnelle de l'Empire de Russie* (Berlin: F. Gottheiner, 1903). Gentz noted that the Tsar intended the Polish Constitution to serve as a model for Russia itself. Gentz to Prince Karadja, 4 April 1818, Vienna, in Prokesch-Osten, *Dépêches Inédites*, vol. i, pp. 380–84. Novosiltsev's draft constitution, for reasons explained in the next chapter, was never published or promulgated and remained a secret until discovered during the Polish Revolution of 1830. See Rey, *Alexandre I*, fn. 72, p. 550.

127. Lebzeltern to Metternich, 10 October 1819, Warsaw, in Mikhaïlovich, *Les Rapports Diplomatiques de Lebzeltern*, p. 60; Thackeray, *Antecedents*, pp. 16–39, 73–81.

128. Zawadzki, *A Man of Honour*, pp. 279–85. The Grand Duke had issued the decree when one of his friends, an actress, was heckled at the National Theatre.

129. Ley, *Alexandre Ier et sa Sainte-Alliance*, p. 247; Thackeray, pp. 76–77.

6. Rift and Reunion, 1820–22

1. Archives des Affaires Étrangères (La Courneuve), Mémoires et Documents (France), No. 720, f. 24 ('Recit historique de Boislecomte'); Hardenberg's diary entry for 1 November 1820 in Stamm-Kuhlmann, *Hardenberg: Tagebücher*, pp. 900–1.

2. Grimsted, *The Foreign Ministers of Alexander I*, pp. 226–68; Woodhouse, *Capodistria*; Ghervas: *Reinventer la Tradition*, pp. 349–74; Capodistrias, 'Aperçu de ma carrière publique depuis 1798 jusqu'à 1822', in *Sbornik imperatorskogo russkogo istoricheskogo obshchestva*, vol. iii.

3. Stewart to Castlereagh, 3 February 1820, Vienna, 'Most Private and Confidential', in N.A. (Kew), F.O. 7/160.

4. Bertier de Sauvigny, *Metternich et la France*, vol. ii, pp. 366–67; Metternich, *Memoirs*, vol. iii, p. 374, Metternich to Comtesse de Lieven, 21 October 1820; Ley: *Alexandre Ier et sa Sainte-Alliance*, p. 244; Hans W. Schmalz, *Versuche einer gesamteuropäischen Organisation, 1815–1820, mit besonderer Berücksichtigung der Troppauer Interventionspolitik* (Aarau: H.R. Sauerländer, 1940), pp. 69–70.

5. Webster, *Foreign Policy of Castlereagh, 1815–1822*, p. 289; Woodhouse, *Capodistria*, p. 245.

6. Bertier de Sauvigny, *Metternich et la France*, vol. ii, p. 361.

7. Bertier de Sauvigny, *Metternich et la France*, vol. ii, pp. 367–70; Webster, *Foreign Policy of Castlereagh, 1815–1822*, pp. 289–90; Schroeder, *Metternich's Diplomacy*, pp. 63–64; Schmalz, *Versuche einer gesamteuropäischen Organisation*, pp. 70–1; N.A. (Kew), F.O. 7/160, Stewart to Castlereagh, 4 November 1820, Troppau, 'Secret and Confidential'.

8. Bertier de Sauvigny, *Metternich et la France*, vol. ii, p. 373. Bernstorff privately dissented; he felt that poor governance in Naples had caused the insurrection, and he opposed Austrian plans to intervene. See Baack: *Christian Bernstorff*, pp. 82–83. According to Schmalz, *Versuche einer gesamteuropäischen Organisation*, p. 71, the Prussians told the Austrians and Russians they would defer to them, and Treitschke argues they were completely distracted by issues of domestic reform in Berlin.

9. Capodistrias and Nesselrode, 'Premier entretien confidential avec M. le prince de Metternich', 26 October 1820, and 'Second entretien confidential avec M. le prince de Metternich', 27 October 1820, in USSR, *Vneshniaia Politika Rossii, 1815–1830*, Series 2, vol. iii, pp. 555–64.
10. USSR, *Vneshniaia Politika Rossii, 1815–1830*, Series 2, vol. iii, pp. 555–64. The anxiety with which the allies regarded the survival of Lord Liverpool's government was discerned by Stewart, who reported to his half-brother a few weeks later: 'Your Lordship must feel the particularly nervous position which the British Government is now looked at, and the great dread that a change of men would be followed by a change of measures (which I have already reported as operating on the Sovereign's [sic] and Minister's [sic] minds here) tends in no small degree to throw together the three cabinets into a common consultation as to their conduct and proceedings in such an event.' Stewart to Castlereagh, 15 November 1820, Troppau, 'Most Secret and Confidential-A' and 'Separate', in N.A. (Kew), F.O. 7/160. The three eastern powers were especially concerned that if the opposition came to power in London, they would release Napoleon.
11. Hardenberg's diary entry for 29 October 1820 in Stamm-Kuhlmann, *Hardenberg: Tagebücher*, pp. 899–900.
12. Webster, *Foreign Policy of Castlereagh, 1815–1822*, pp. 290–91. See also, Schroeder, *Metternich's Diplomacy*, pp. 65–66; Bertier de Sauvigny, *Metternich et la France*, pp. 379–81; Schmalz, *Versuche einer gesamteuropäischen Organisation*, pp. 71–75. Stewart thought the Russian memorandum 'mixes up too much the two Revolutions of Spain and Naples in one general conclusion, whereas, there is a vast and decided difference, which has been forcibly dwelt upon in my instructions', N.A. (Kew), F.O. 7/160, Stewart to Metternich, 3 November 1820, Troppau. Back in late October, Castlereagh had already sent Stewart this warning in anticipation: 'It is not possible for the British Government, as I very early apprized you, to take to the field fruitlessly denouncing by a sweeping & joint declaration, the Revolutionary dangers of the present day, to the existence of which, they are sufficiently alive: nor can they venture to embody themselves, en corps, with the non-representative gov[ernmen]ts in what would seem to constitute a scheme of systematic [interference] in the internal affairs of other states; besides, they do not regard mere declarations as of any real or solid value independent of some practical measure actually resolved on; and what that measure is, which can be generally and universally adopted against bad principles overturning feeble and ill administered governments they have never as yet been able to divine. We shall however wait with patience and deference for the views which may be disclosed at Troppau ….' Castlereagh to Stewart, 28 October 1820, Foreign Office, 'Private and Confidential', in N.A. (Kew), F.O. 7/160.
13. Schroeder, *Metternich's Diplomacy*, pp. 65–66; Bertier de Sauvigny, *Metternich et la France*, vol. ii, pp. 379–81; for Gentz's scathing critique, see Schmalz, *Versuche einer gesamteuropäischen Organisation*, pp. 74–75 and Schroeder, *Metternich's Diplomacy*, pp. 67–69.
14. Hardenberg's diary entry for 3 November 1820 in Stamm-Kuhlmann, *Hardenberg: Tagebücher*, p. 902.

15. Nesselrode and Capodistrias to Alexander I, 'Premier Agenda' and 'Second Agenda', 5 November 1820, in USSR, *Vneshniaia Politika Rossii, 1815–1830*, Series 2, vol. iii, pp. 567–69 and 572–74.
16. Of course, these diplomats might have been accused of the grossest hypocrisy, since Russia still lacked her own constitution; but their view seems to have been, and not without justification, that these Western countries were more ready for reform. 'Thus it was not entirely inconsistent', argues British historian Janet Hartley, 'for Alexander to encourage the introduction of constitutions elsewhere in Europe, and even in the non-Russian parts of his own Empire, while not introducing one into Russia itself'. Hartley, *Alexander I*, p. 34.
17. Bertier de Sauvigny, *Metternich et la France*, vol. ii, pp. 348, 374–79.
18. Bertier de Sauvigny, *Metternich et la France*, vol. ii, p. 383; Schroeder, *Metternich's Diplomacy*, p. 93; Romani, *Neapolitan Revolution*, pp. 113–17.
19. Schroeder, *Metternich's Diplomacy*, p. 69–71.
20. Hardenberg's diary entry for 10 November 1820 in Stamm-Kuhlmann, *Hardenberg: Tagebücher*, pp. 905–06; Bertier de Sauvigny, *Metternich et la France*, pp. 384–85; Romani, *Neapolitan Revolution*, pp. 143–44; Schroeder, *Metternich's Diplomacy*, pp. 73–74.
21. [Capodistrias], 'Bases d'un transaction', 14 November 1820, in USSR, *Vneshniaia Politika Rossii, 1815–1830*, Series 2, vol. iii, pp. 585–86; Schmalz, *Versuche einer gesamteuropäischen Organisation*, p. 78; Schroeder, *Metternich's Diplomacy*, pp. 74–75.
22. N.A. (Kew), F.O. 7/160, Stewart to Castlereagh, 15 November 1820, Troppau; Nesselrode to Maxim Alopeus and Anstett, 17 November 1820, Troppau, enclosing note of 19 October, St Petersburg, in USSR, *Vneshniaia Politika Rossii, 1815–1830*, vol. iii, pp. 587–88.
23. On the importance of the regiment, see Bitis, *Russia and the Eastern Question*, pp. 39, 47–48, 66–67; 'Au Service des Tsars: La Garde Impériale Russe, de Pierre le Grand à la Révolution d'Octobre' (Exhibition at the Musée de l'Armée in the Hôtel des Invalides, Paris, from 9 October 2010 to 23 January 2011); J.L. Wieczynski, 'The Mutiny of the Semenovsky Regiment in 1820', *Russian Review* XXIX (1970), pp. 167–68.
24. Comte de Gabriac to La Ferronnays, 2, 8, 11, 17, 30 November 1820, and 23 January, 30 May 1821, St Petersburg, in Mikhaïlovich, *Imperator Aleksandr I*, vol ii, pp. 345–53 and pp. 539–44 ('History of the Semenovsky Regiment, 1820'). On 2 November 1820, Gabriac reported that no officer was directly involved, but he believed they nonetheless must have been implicated, and even the Masonic organizations may have played a role ('Aucun officier n'a été ostensiblement impliqué dans cette désobéissance. Cependant beaucoup de gens les croient complices. Ils supposent en outré qu'il existe parmi eux des associations maçonniques redoutables'), Mikhaïlovich, *Imperator Aleksandr I*, vol ii, p. 346. See also, Rey, *Alexandre I*, p. 411 and fn. 79 on p. 551, citing the report of Kochubei, who wrote that the mutiny had been caused by Schwartz's brutality alone; see also Wieczynski, 'Mutiny of the Semenovksy Regiment', pp. 168–72. Russian police subse-

quently discovered notices in the barracks attacking not only Schwartz but the Tsar himself and calling for the formation of a representative government. See Wieczynski, 'Mutiny of the Semenovksy Regiment', pp. 172–74; Rey, *Alexandre I*, pp. 411–12.

25. N.A. (Kew), F.O. 7/160, Stewart to Castlereagh, 15 November 1820, Troppau; see also Webster, *Foreign Policy of Castlereagh, 1812–1815*, p. 294.
26. Alexander to Arakcheev, 17 November 1820, in Palmer, *Alexander I*, pp. 373–74, citing Schilder: *Imperator Aleksandr Pervyi*, vol. iv, p. 185. See also Wieczynski, 'Mutiny of the Semenovksy Regiment', pp. 176–77. Hartley, *Alexander I*, pp. 150–51, suggests that Alexander felt that he was being confronted by the work of the devil himself. Later, a military tribunal found Schwartz guilty of multiple infractions and several hundred members of the regiment guilty of treason. The presiding officer recommended 50 lashes each but the Tsar followed Arakcheev's recommendation that the men run a gauntlet through the battalion six times, resulting in thousands of lashes each. Schwartz was dismissed from service but re-appointed two years later. All the remaining men were dispersed to other regiments outside of St Petersburg, and the Semenovksy Regiment was reconstituted the following year with entirely different men. See Wiecynski, 'Mutiny of the Semenovksy Regiment', pp. 175–76. The survivors of the Semenovsky later played a key role in the Decembrist revolt of 1825.
27. See, for example, Lebzeltern to Metternich, 17 February 1820, in Mikhaïlovich, *Les Rapports Diplomatiques de Lebzeltern*, pp. 67–68, in which the nobles claim that the Tsar should grant them individual freedom before asking them to free their serfs: 'Et lorsque l'Empereur a conçu l'idée d'accorder la liberté aux paysans dans les provinces russes, les nobles propriétaires ont observe qu'avant de libérer leurs serfs, il fallait qui'ils le fussent eux-mêmes, non en doctrine nominale, mais en practique. Dès que l'Empereur garantirait leur liberté individuelle, il la guarantiraient à leurs paysans.' For the influence of Golitsyn and Karamzin, see Rey, *Alexandre I*, pp. 408–11; Iver B. Neumann, *Russia and the Idea of Europe* (London: Routledge, 1996), pp. 13–27 and Richard Pipes (ed.), *Karamzin's Memoir on Ancient and Modern Russia* (Ann Arbor: University of Michigan Press, 2005). Marc Raeff, however, points out that the Tsar continued to flirt with constitutional projects even after 1820.
28. Bertier de Sauvigny, *Metternich et la France*, vol. ii, pp. 386–88, 393–400; Haus-, Hof- und Staatsarchiv (Vienna), Staatskanzlei, Kongressakten, Karton 21, ff. 246–47, Note Verbale, November 1820.
29. Bertier de Sauvigny, *Metternich et la France*, vol. ii, p. 380, sees this as a triumph for Metternich, but Webster, *Foreign Policy of Castlereagh, 1815–1822*, believes Metternich was truckling to Russia because he could no longer count on Britain for support.
30. 'Protocole préliminaire', 19 November 1820, Troppau, in USSR, *Vneshniaia Politika Rossii, 1815–1830*, Series 2, vol. iii, pp. 589–91; Bertier de Sauvigny, *Metternich et la France*, pp. 388–90 and for a copy of the text, see pp. 413–15; Webster, *Foreign Policy of Castlereagh, 1815–1822*, p. 295; Schmalz, *Versuche*

einer gesamteuropäischen Organisation, pp. 78–79; Schroeder, *Metternich's Diplomacy*, pp. 80–82.

31. As late as 28 October, Castlereagh was hopeful that the Continental allies would avoid public declarations of principle that would separate them from Britain. Thus, while the eastern powers were drafting the *Protocole préliminaire*, Castlereagh wrote the following message to his half-brother: 'If I may judge from the tone in which those papers are written, the Russian language is moderated and I should hope no difficulty will occur in the opening of the business at Troppau; but I do not see my way to any result of a different character to that which I have before hinted at. It is not possible for the British Government[,] as I very early apprized you, to take the field fruitlessly denouncing by a sweeping & joint Declaration, the Revolutionary dangers of the present day, to the existence of which, they are nevertheless sufficiently alive: nor can they venture to embody themselves, en corps, with the Non-Representative Govts. In what would seem to constitute a scheme of Systematic [interference] in the Internal Affairs of other States; besides, they do not regard mere Declarations as on any real or solid value independent of some practical measure actually resolved on; and what that measure is, which can be generally and universally adopted against bad Principles overturning feeble and ill administered Governments, they have never as yet been able to divine. We shall however wait with patience & deference for the views which may be disclosed at Troppau, and be prepared frankly to explain ourselves, whenever the plans to be there developed are sufficiently matured to admit of their being taken into consideration by this Govt.' Castlereagh to Lord Stewart, 28 October 1820, Foreign Office [London], 'Private & Conf[idential]', in N.A. (Kew), F.O. 7/160.
32. For a copy of Metternich's secret instructions to Prince Ruffo, on how the King should react to the allied invitation, which were furnished to Stewart, see British Library, Add. Mss. 41532, f. 95. Stewart had been under the impression that Metternich was keeping him well informed about developments at Troppau, but such had not been the case: see, Stewart to Castlereagh, 15 November 1820, 'Private & Confidential-A, Separate' in N.A. (Kew), F.O. 7/160.
33. N.A. (Kew), F.O. 7/160, Stewart to Castlereagh, 20 November 1820, Troppau, 'Most Secret & Confidential', also in Webster, *Foreign Policy of Castlereagh, 1815–1822*, pp. 527–33. See also, USSR, *Vneshniaia Politika Rossii*, Series 2, vol. iii, pp. 610–12, 614–19, Nesselrode to Lieven 23 and 24 November 1820, Troppau; Bertier de Sauvigny, *Metternich et la France*, vol. ii, pp. 389, 393; Webster, *Foreign Policy of Castlereagh, 1815–1822*, pp. 295–97; Schroeder, *Metternich's Diplomacy*, pp. 81–84; Woodhouse, *Capodistria*, pp. 246–48.
34. N.A. (Kew), F.O. 7/148, Castlereagh to Stewart, 4 December 1820, 'Most Secret', 'Draft'; also referred to in Webster, *Foreign Policy of Castlereagh, 1815–1822*, pp. 298–99.
35. Webster, *Foreign Policy of Castlereagh, 1815–1822*, pp. 298–99.
36. Esterhazy to Metternich, 29 November 1820, London, No. 174, Litt. A and B, in Haus-, Hof- und Staatsarchiv (Vienna), Grossbritannien, Karton 162, Berichte

(1820), third bundle, second series of folios, ff. 33–34, 41–43; also in Webster, *Foreign Policy of Castlereagh, 1815–1822*, p. 299. See also Esterhazy to Metternich, 4 December and 10 December 1820, London, No. 175, Litt. C, No. 176, Litt. A & B, in Haus-, Hof- und Staatsarchiv, Grossbritannien, Karton 162, 1820, Berichte (1820), third bundle, fourth series, ff. 15–19, 21–23; also cited in Schroeder, *Metternich's Diplomacy*, pp. 85–86.
37. Lieven to Nesselrode, 21 December 1820, in Webster, *Foreign Policy of Castlereagh, 1815–1822*, pp. 305, 573–75.
38. Webster, *Foreign Policy of Castlereagh, 1815–1822*, pp. 298–305.
39. Webster, *Foreign Policy of Castlereagh, 1815–1822*, p. 305; Lieven to Nesselrode, 8 December 1820, in USSR, *Vneshniaia Politika Rossii*, Series 2, vol. iii, pp. 628–32.
40. N.A. (Kew), F.O. 7/160, Stewart to Castlereagh, 15 November 1820, 'Most Secret & Confidential'; Webster, *Foreign Policy of Castlereagh, 1815–1822*, p. 293.
41. Schmalz, *Versuche einer gesamteuropäischen Organisation*, pp. 84–85.
42. Schmalz, *Versuche einer gesamteuropäischen Organisation*, pp. 84–92, with the text of the proposed guarantee on pp. 87–88, fn. 71; Schroeder, *Metternich's Diplomacy*, p. 87.
43. The opening three tenets of the 'Act of Guarantee' were followed by a series of 'Moral Guarantees', which spelt out the steps to be taken when a change occurred; see Schroeder, *Metternich's Diplomacy*, pp. 86–90.
44. Schroeder, *Metternich's Diplomacy*, pp. 91–92; 'Questions que présente le développement ultérior de la première partie du protocole du 7 (19) Novembre', 17 December 1820, Troppau, in USSR, *Vneshniaia Politika Rossii, 1815–1830*, Series 2, vol. iii, pp. 648–52.
45. For the text of the circular, see Metternich, *Memoirs*, vol. iii, pp. 444–47; d'Angeberg, *Congrès de Vienne*, vol. iv, pp. 1801–04. See also Bertier de Sauvigny, *Metternich et la France*, vol. ii, pp. 400–01; Woodhouse, *Capodistria*, p. 248.
46. Bertier de Sauvigny, *Metternich et la France*, vol. ii, pp. 403–10; Schroeder, *Metternich's Diplomacy*, pp. 109–10, 130–39. One ticklish issue was whether A'Court, the British minister in Naples, would participate in the ambassadorial conference guiding the restored King, since Britain was not participating in the allied intervention. See Gordon to Castlereagh, 5 March 1821, Laibach, No. 12, in N.A. (Kew), F.O. 165/35 ('It is evident that in many respects these duties can only be considered as proceeding with a system of measures in which Gt. Britain has taken no part, and yet it is felt that the absence of the British Envoy at Naples might be directly prejudicial to the interests of the three powers, unless it be expressly grounded upon the strict neutrality of his Government upon the whole Neapolitan Question').
47. Bertier de Sauvigny, *Metternich et la France*, vol. ii, pp. 393–410.
48. Bertier de Sauvigny, *Metternich et la France*, vol. ii, pp. 400–03; Schroeder, *Metternich's Diplomacy*, pp. 92–93; Haus-, Hof- und Staatsarchiv (Vienna), Staatskanzlei, Kongressakten, Karton 21, ff. 115–20, draft of Note from the three Cabinets to the Holy See; ff. 299–302, Note to the Pope, 12 December 1820; ff. 347–49, Démarche à Rome.

49. Haus-, Hof- und Staatsarchiv (Vienna), Staatskanzlei, Kongressakten, Karton 21, ff. 353–68, Metternich, 'Profession de foi du Prince de Metternich à Sa Majesté Impériale de Toutes les Russies'; also in Metternich, *Memoirs*, vol. iii, pp. 453–76, Metternich to the Emperor Alexander, 15 December 1820.
50. Romani, *Neapolitan Revolution*, pp. 120–25.
51. A'Court to Castlereagh, 8 February 1821, Naples, 'Private and Secret', British Library, Add. Mss. 41523, ff. 71–74.
52. Romani, *Neapolitan Revolution*, pp. 144–51; Schroeder, *Metternich's Diplomacy*, pp. 100–03; Bertier de Sauvigny, *Metternich et la France*, vol. ii, p. 418.
53. 'The Foreign Ministers were not consulted in subsequent messages to Parliament, by which the King bound Himself still more closely to the Constitution of the Cortes. That he did so under the immediate operation of fear, I have not the slightest doubt, but whether this be sufficient to justify, in the eyes of Europe, the violation of so many solemn oaths and promises, it is not for me to determine'. A'Court to Castlereagh, 8 February 1821, Naples, 'Private and Secret', British Library, Add. Mss. 41523, f. 74.
54. According to Romani, *Neapolitan Revolution*, pp. 149–50, this was simply a way of dismissing the ministry under the existing constitution.
55. Bertier de Sauvigny, *Metternich et la France*, vol. ii, p. 422; Romani, *Neapolitan Revolution*, pp. 150–53.
56. Bertier de Sauvigny, *Metternich et la France*, vol. ii, p. 417; Schroeder, *Metternich's Diplomacy*, p. 104.
57. Stewart to Castlereagh, 27 January 1821, Laibach, N.A. (Kew), F.O. 7/160; also in Webster, *Foreign Policy of Castlereagh, 1815–1822*, pp. 535–36.
58. Bertier de Sauvigny, *Metternich et la France*, vol. ii, pp. 427, 433.
59. Bertier de Sauvigny, *Metternich et la France*, vol. ii, pp. 434–36.
60. Bertier de Sauvigny, *Metternich et la France*, vol. ii, p. 471.
61. Metternich, 10 January 1821, in Metternich, *Memoirs*, vol. iii, p. 480; from Gordon, 21 January 1821, encl.in Stewart to Castlereagh, 27 Jan. 1821, Laibach, "Most Secret & Confidential" N.A. (Kew), F.O. 7/160.
62. Bertier de Sauvigny, *Metternich et la France*, vol. ii, p. 441.
63. Bertier de Sauvigny, *Metternich et la France*, vol. ii, p. 442.
64. Bertier de Sauvigny, *Metternich et la France*, vol. ii, p. 443.
65. N.A. (Kew), F.O. 7/160, Stewart to Castlereagh, 21 January 1821, Laybach, 'Most Secret & Confidential'.
66. Bertier de Sauvigny, *Metternich et la France*, vol. ii, pp. 444–45.
67. Bertier de Sauvigny, *Metternich et la France*, vol. ii, pp. 444–45.
68. Bertier de Sauvigny, *Metternich et la France*, vol. ii, pp. 446–48; Schroeder, *Metternich's Diplomacy*, pp. 106–07; Stewart to Castlereagh, 31 January 1821, Laibach, in N.A. (Kew), F.O. 7/160.
69. Schroeder, *Metternich's Diplomacy*, pp. 106–07; Webster, *Foreign Policy of Castlereagh, 1815–1822*, p. 315; Bertier de Sauvigny, *Metternich et la France*, vol. ii, p. 450.
70. Bertier de Sauvigny, *Metternich et la France*, vol. ii, pp. 446–47; Webster, *Foreign Policy of Castlereagh, 1815–1822*, pp. 315–17.

71. Stewart to A'Court, 28 January 1821, Laibach, 'Private', N.A. (Kew), F.O. 7/160.
72. Bertier de Sauvigny, *Metternich et la France*, vol. ii, p. 447.
73. Alan J. Reinermann, *Austria and the Papacy in the Age of Metternich. Between Conflict and Cooperation* (Washington DC: Catholic University of America Press, 1979), pp. 83–85; Bertier de Sauvigny, *Metternich et la France*, vol. ii, pp. 448–50; Schroeder, *Metternich's Diplomacy*, pp. 107–08; Webster, *Foreign Policy of Castlereagh, 1815–1822*, p. 318.
74. Bertier de Sauvigny, *Metternich et la France*, vol. ii, p. 449; Schroeder, *Metternich's Diplomacy*, pp. 108–09.
75. Bertier de Sauvigny, *Metternich et la France*, pp. 453, 459–62; Schroeder, *Metternich's Diplomacy*, p. 114. Bertier de Sauvigny points out that the Austrians signed a military convention with Tuscany for the permanent passage of their troops. See Bertier de Sauvigny, *Metternich et la France*, p. 465.
76. Gentz to Soutzo, 22 January 1820, in Prokesch-Osten, *Depeches inédites*, vol. ii, pp. 121–23, cited in Schroeder, *Metternich's Diplomacy*, p. 105, fn. 6.
77. Stewart to Castlereagh, 31 January 1821, Laibach, in N.A. (Kew), F.O. 7/160.
78. A'Court to Stewart, 6 June 1821, Naples, 'Private', B.L. Add. Mss. 41,532, f. 143.
79. N.A. (Kew), F.O. 120/45, Gordon to Castlereagh, 16 February 1821, Laibach, No. 4; see also N.A. (Kew), F.O. 120/45, Gordon to Castlereagh, 25 February 1821, Laibach, No. 9, enclosing Ruffo's plan; cf. N.A. (Kew) F.O. 7/160 Stewart to Castlereagh, 3 February 1821, Laibach: 'It would however seem that the King will have a Constitution given to him ready cut and dry by Metternich and Capodistrias.'
80. Schroeder, *Metternich's Diplomacy*, pp. 109–10; Webster, *Foreign Policy of Castlereagh, 1815–1822*, p. 327. Meanwhile, the Austrian expedition had crossed the Papal States, leaving behind Austrian troops as they went and embittering relations between Austria and the Papacy. See Reinermann, *Austria and the Papacy*, pp. 85–90.
81. Gordon to Castlereagh, 24 February 1821, No. 7, Laibach, in N.A. (Kew), F.O. 120/45: the allies would prefer to destroy 'what was constructed without a proper license' and then 'rebuild another ... fabric' rather than to 'correct or modify' the existing constitutional government introduced by a revolutionary action.
82. Bertier de Sauvigny, *Metternich et la France*, pp. 451, 457–58.
83. Bertier de Sauvigny, *Metternich et la France*, p. 452.
84. Bertier de Sauvigny, *Metternich et la France*, p. 461; see also Webster, *Foreign Policy of Castlereagh, 1815–1822*, p. 327.
85. Esterhazy enclosed a copy of this issue of the *Morning Chronicle* in his report to Metternich of 19 January 1821, No. 179, Litt. B, in Haus-, Hof- und Staatsarchiv, Grossbritannien, Karton 163, Berichte (1821), first bundle, first series of folio numbers, f. 55.
86. N.A. (Kew), F.O. 83/81, Circular, 19 January 1821: '[N]o Government can be more prepared than the British Government is, to uphold the right of any State or States to interfere, where their own security, or essential interests, are seriously endangered by the internal transactions of another State. But ... they cannot

admit that this right can receive a general and indiscriminate application to all revolutionary movements ... or be made prospectively the basis of an Alliance.' See also Webster, *Foreign Policy of Castlereagh, 1815–1822*, pp. 320–25. Castlereagh's protest was communicated not only to the eastern powers, but also to the Italian courts, the German Confederation, Spain, and the British press.
87. T.C. Hansard, *Parliamentary Debates*, New Series, vol. iv (23 January–2 April 1821), cols 837, 844–46, 871–82, for 21 February 1821.
88. Schroeder, *Metternich's Diplomacy*, p. 113.
89. Castlereagh to Stewart, 13 March 1821, London ('Private') in Alison, *Lives of Castlereagh and Stewart*, vol. iii, pp. 218–23.
90. Gordon to Castlereagh, 24 February 1821, No. 8, Laibach, in N.A. (Kew), F.O. 120/45.
91. Gordon to Castlereagh, 25 February 1821, No. 10, Laibach, in N.A. (Kew), F.O. 120/45.
92. Bertier de Sauvigny, *Metternich et la France*, vol. ii, pp. 462, 475–77; Schroeder, *Metternich's Diplomacy*, pp. 114–15; Webster, *Foreign Policy of Castlereagh, 1815–1822*, p. 328.
93. Emperor Alexander I to Prince Alexander Golitsyn, 15 February 1821, in Mikhaïlovich, *Imperator Aleksandr I*, vol i, pp. 543–51.
94. Only five days after the Tsar's letter to Golitsyn, the French ambassador to Russia sent off the following remarkable report to Paris: 'Your Excellency ... seeks to know ... the source of the concerns that [the Tsar] still seems to harbour on the present state of France. I am certain today that these concerns are motivated neither by the steps taken by the royal government, nor by the personal dispositions of the ministers who compose the council of His Majesty. They come from the character of the Emperor, from the reports provided to him and from the fear that is caused to him by the attempts and audacity of a sect which, existing under different names in all the states of Europe, has, according to him, its principle and its leaders in France. All the private correspondence of the Emperor represents this sect as equally formidable in the number of its adepts and in the boldness of their projects, and as aiming at nothing less than the destruction of all religions and the overthrow of all legitimate thrones in Europe ... [T]he Emperor ... finds in France the cause of the events that we are witnessing' ('... Elles tiennent au caractère de l'Empereur, aux rappports qu'on lui fait et à l'effroi qui ont du lui causer les tentatives et l'audace d'une secte qui, répandue sous differens noms dans tous les Etats de l'Europe, doit, selon lui, avoir son principe et ses chefs en France. Toutes les correspondances particulières de l'Empereur s'attachent à lui représenter cette secte comme aussi formidable par le nombre de ses adepts que par la hardiesse de leurs projets, et ne tendant à rien moins qu'à détruire toute espéce de religion et a renverser tous les trônes légitimes de l'Europe. Nos ennemis ont un grand intérêt à entretenir cette prévention l'Empereur, qui lui fait toujours chercher en France la cause des évènenmens dont nous sommes témoins'), La Ferronnays to Pasquier, 20 February 1821, 'Confidentielle', Laybach, in Archives des Affaires Étrangères (La Courneuve), Mémoires et Documents, vol. 719, ff. 48–52.

95. Broers, *Savoyard Monarchy*, pp. 480–524; Michael Broers, 'The Restoration in Piedmont-Sardinia, 1814–1848: Variations on Reaction' in David Laven and Lucy Riall (eds), *Napoleon's Legacy: Problems of Government in Restoration Europe* (Oxford: Berg, 2000), pp. 151–64.
96. Schroeder, *Metternich's Diplomacy*, pp. 116–17.
97. Bertier de Sauvigny, *Metternich et la France*, vol. ii, p. 478; Schroeder, *Metternich's Diplomacy*, pp. 117–18; Di Scala, *Italy from Revolution to Republic*, p. 57; Duggan, *Concise History of Italy*, p. 104. For British diplomatic correspondence from Turin, see Frederico Curato, *La Relazioni diplomatiche fra la Gran Bretagna e il Regno di Sardegna* (Roma: Instituto Storico Italiano per l'Eta moderna e contemporanea, 1972), Part 2, Series 1 (1814–1830), vol. 1 (25 May 1814–25 April 1821); see also Giulio Ambroggio, *Santorre di Santarosa nella Restaurazione piemonetse* (Turin: Pintore, 2007); Rosario Romeo, *Dal Piemonte sabaudo all'Italia liberal* (Bari: Laterza, 1974).
98. Bertier de Sauvigny, *Metternich et la France*, vol. ii, p. 481.
99. N.A. (Kew), F.O. 165/35, Castlereagh to Gordon, 5 April 1821, Foreign Office, 'Secret & Confidential'; also in British Library, Add. Mss. 41523, ff. 134–38, enclosed in Castlereagh to A'Court, 5 April 1821 (No. 5). In *The Foreign Policy of Castlereagh, 1815–1822*, Webster refers briefly this dispatch on page 330 but without emphasizing its significance: 'He was only less opposed to the use of Russian troops, which, however, he preferred to both French and Austrian, if force must be used.'
100. Broers, *Savoyard Monarchy*, p. 524.
101. Barbara Jelavich, *History of the Balkans: Eighteenth and Nineteenth Centuries* (Cambridge: Cambridge University Press, 1983), pp. 1–36; Peter F. Sugar, *Southeastern Europe under Ottoman Rule, 1354–1804* (Seattle: University of Washington Press, 1977).
102. Moldova, east of the Pruth River, became Russian Bessarabia in 1812.
103. Christine M. Philliou, *Biography of an Empire: Governing Ottomans in an Age of Revolution* (Berkeley: University of California Press, 2011), pp. xx–xxi, 5–37; Richard Clogg, *A Concise History of Greece*, 2nd edn (Cambridge: Cambridge University Press, 2002), pp. 20–25; Bitis, *Russia and the Eastern Question*, p. 99, fn. 5: 'The Phanariots were a Greek or Hellenized Christian aristocracy, loyal to the Sultan and entrusted with the highest posts in the Ottoman administration.' Clogg considers the Phanariots the 'nearest approximation to a Greek *noblesse de robe*' or office-holding nobility. Richard Clogg (ed), *The Movement for Greek Independence, 1770–1821: A Collection of Documents* (London: Macmillan, 1976), pp. xiv–xv.
104. On the *millets*, see Jelavich, *History of the Balkans*, pp. 39–45, 48–53 ('Since the church hierarchy usually remained, the custom of using the leaders of the religious communities for government functions was established early ... The members of the accepted faiths were organized into communities, known as millets'); Clogg, *Concise History of Greece*, pp. 10–11 ('The *millets* enjoyed a wide degree of administrative autonomy and were ruled over by their respective

religious authorities'); Clogg, *Movement for Greek Independence*, xii–xiii ('In addition to spiritual jurisdiction over the Orthodox flock the Patriarch and the Holy Synod also enjoyed a wide jurisdiction in civil affairs, particularly in marital and testamentary matters. Not surprisingly the *millet* system played an important role in preserving a sense of corporate identity among the non-Muslim populations of the Empire. In return for the granting of these substantial privileges, the Ottoman Porte expected the Patriarch and the Orthodox hierarchy to act as guarantors of the loyalty of the Orthodox populations to the Ottoman state'); Sugar, *Southeastern Europe under Ottoman Rule*, p. 5 ('It involved a sort of self-government that under the Ottomans became institutionalized and known as the *millet* system, which was basically a minority home-rule policy based on religious affiliation'). Johann Strauss, however, points out that 'Ottomanists have paid little attention to certain aspects of the internal life of the various ethnic communities, subsumed under the convenient, but excessively vague term *millet*'. See Johann Strauss, 'Ottoman Rule Experienced and Remembered: Remarks on Some Local Greek Chronicles of the Tourkokratia', in Fikret Adanir and Suraiya Faroqhi (eds), *The Ottomans and the Balkans: A Discussion of Historiography* (Leiden and Boston: Brill, 2002), p. 193. In *Biography of an Empire*, pp. 6–7, Philliou argues that the millets were not 'fully institutionalized' before 1839, but provided a 'more fluid administrative apparatus'.

105. Avigdor Levy, 'Ottoman Attitudes to the Rise of Balkan Nationalism', in Belá K. Király and Gunther E. Rothenberg (eds), *War and Society in East Central Europe*, vol. 1 (New York: Columbia University Press, 1979), pp. 325–45; Jelavich, *History of the Balkans*, pp. 123–26; Hanioğlu, *A Brief History of the Late Ottoman Empire*, pp. 54–58. For European views of the Ottomans as an alien power, see Oliver Schulz, '"This clumsy fabric of barbarous power": Die europäische Aussenpolitik und der aussereuropäische Raum am Beispiel des Osmanischen Reiches', in Pyta, *Das europäische Mächtekonzert*, pp. 273–98.

106. Anderson, *The Eastern Question, 1774–1923*, pp. xi–xvi, 1–8; Bitis, *Russia and the Eastern Question*, pp. 19–20; Jelavich, *History of the Balkans*, pp. 68–72.

107. Jelavich, *History of the Balkans*, pp. 113–26; Finkel, *Osman's Dream*, pp. 384–418; Hanioğlu, *Late Ottoman Empire*, pp. 42–58; Anderson, *Eastern Question*, pp. 22–47; Bitis, *Russia and the Eastern Question*, pp. 30–31.

108. Stanford and Ezal Kural Shaw, *History of the Ottoman Empire and Modern Turkey*, vol. ii (*Reform, Revolution and Republic*) (Cambridge: Cambridge University Press, 1977), pp. 1–3.

109. The Sultan took measures against Molla Idris of Vidin (1812), Yillikoğlu Suleyman, *ayan* of Silistra (1813), and the *ayans* of Hezargrad and Didymoteichon in 1816, and of Thrace and Thessaly in 1818. See Levy, 'Ottoman Attitudes', pp. 332–36.

110. Katherine E. Fleming, *The Muslim Bonaparte* (Princeton, NJ: Princeton University Press, 1999); Gabriel Remeránd, *Ali de Tébélen: Pacha de Janina (1744–1822)* (Paris: Geuthner, 1928); Levy, 'Ottoman Attitudes', pp. 336–41; Douglas

Dakin, *The Unification of Greeece, 1770–1923* (London: Ernest Benn, 1972), pp. 24–27; David Brewer, *The Greek War of Independence: The Struggle for Freedom from Ottoman Oppression and the Birth of the Modern Greek Nation* (Woodstock and New York: Overlook Press, 2001), pp. 36–48.

111. Strauss, 'Ottoman Rule Experienced and Remembered', pp. 193–214; Clogg, *Movement for Greek Independence*, pp. 3–15. The Ottomans relied on village leaders to collect the taxes for which each village was responsible—see Allan Cunningham, *Anglo-Ottoman Encounters in the Age of Revolution* (London: F. Cass, 1993), vol. i, p. 197.
112. D.A. Zakythinos, *The Making of Modern Greece: From Byzantium to Independence*, trans. K.R. Johnstone (Oxford: Blackwell, 1976); S.K. Batalden, 'John Kapodistrias and the Structure of Greek Society on the Eve of the War of Independence: An Historiographical Essay', *East European Quarterly* XIII (1979), pp. 297–314.
113. Clogg, *Movement for Greek Independence*, pp. xvii–xviii, 70–76; J.A. Petropoulos (ed.), *Hellenism and the First Greek War of Liberation, (1821–1830)* (Thessaloniki: Institute for Balkan Studies, 1976); J.S. Koliopoulos, *Brigands with a Cause: Brigandage and Irredentism in Modern Greece* (Oxford: Clarendon Press, 1987).
114. Zakythinos, *Making of Modern Greece*, pp. 115–39.
115. Brewer, *Greek War of Independence*, pp. 17–25; Clogg, *Movement for Greek Independence*, pp. 119–46.
116. C.M. Woodhouse, *The Philhellenes* (London: Hodder and Stoughton, 1969), pp. 9–65; Theophilus C. Prousis, *Russian Society and the Greek Revolution* (DeKalb: Northern Illinois University Press, 1994), pp. 12–20, 84–104.
117. Zakythinos, *Making of Modern Greece*, pp. 140–79.
118. Zakythinos, *Making of Modern Greece*, pp. 157–67; Clogg, *Concise History of Greece*, pp. 28–31; Brewer, *Greek War of Independence*, pp. 17–21.
119. See the account of Emmanouil Xanthos, a founding member of the *Philiki Hetairia*, in Clogg, *Movement for Greek Independence*, pp. 182–200; Woodhouse, *Capodistria*, pp. 218–37, 250, 252–55; Clogg, *Concise History of Greece*, pp. 31–33; Jelavich, *History of the Balkans*, pp. 204–08; Brewer, *Greek War of Independence*, pp. 26–35.
120. Bitis, *Russia and the Eastern Question*, p. 99.
121. Zakythinos, *Making of Modern Greece*, p. 158.
122. Prousis, *Russian Society and the Greek Revolution*, p. 8.
123. Bitis, *Russia and the Eastern Question*, pp. 99–100.
124. Ypsilantis' proclamation is in Clogg, *Movement for Greek Independence*, pp. 201–03; a copy of Ypsilantis' proclamation can also be found in N.A. (Kew), F.O. 120/45. Alexandre Ypsilanti to the Tsar, Jassy, 24 February 1821 (Old Style), in Vasile Arimia et al. (eds), *Revoluția din 1821 Condusă de Tudor Vladimirescu: Documente Externe* (Bucharest: Editura Academiei Republicii Socialiste România, 1980), pp. 102–03; also in Anton von Prokesch-Osten, *Geschichte des Abfalls der Griechen vom Türkischen Reiche im Jahre 1821* (Vienna: C. Gerold's

Sohn 1867), vol. iii, pp. 61–62; see also Prince Sutzo to the Tsar, 24 February 1821 (Old Style), in Prokesch-Osten, *Geschichte des Abfalls der Griechen*, vol. iii, pp. 62–63; Hartley, *Alexander I*, p. 153; Kissinger, *A World Restored*, p. 287.

125. Bitis, *Russia and the Eastern Question*, pp. 98–104; Woodhouse, *Capodistria*, pp. 250–57.
126. Tsar to Golitsyn, 10 March 1821, Laibach, in Mikhaïlovich, *Imperator Aleksandr I*, vol. i, pp. 535–37; also in Ley, *Alexandre Ier et sa Sainte Alliance*, p. 260–63; Hartley, *Alexander I*, p. 153.
127. Metternich to Rechberg, 25 March 1821, Laibach, in Metternich, *Mémoires*, vol. iii, pp. 489–93: 'Dans un conseil qui a été tenu en presence de Leur Majestés, il a été décidé "que l'événement serait abandonné à lui-même". L'Empereur Alexandre casse et fait rayer des tableaux de son armée tous les militaires grecs qui prennent part à l'insurrection. Sa Majesté refuse tout appui et secours aux Grecs insurgés.'
128. Capodistrias to Ypsilantis, 14 (26) March 1821, Laibach in USSR, *Vneshniaia Politika Rossii, 1815–1830*, Series 2, vol. iv, p. 68; also in Prokesch-Osten, *Geschichte des Abfalls der Griechen*, vol. iii, pp. 65–67; see also Bitis, *Russia and the Eastern Question*, p. 104; Anderson, *Eastern Question*, p. 61.
129. Stroganov was a cousin to Paul Stroganov, who had been a member of the Tsar's 'Unofficial Committee'. Capodistrias to Stroganov, 14 (26) March 1821, Laibach, in Arimia et al.: *Revoluția din 1821 Condusă de Vladimirescu*, pp. 166–68; also in Prokesch-Osten, *Geschichte des Abfalls der Griechen*, vol. iii, pp. 68–70. See also, Capodistrias to Andrei Pisani, Russian Consul in Moldavia, 13 (25) March 1821, Laibach, in Arimia et al., *Revoluția din 1821 Condusă de Vladimirescu*, pp. 161–62, condemning Pisani's use of a consular official as an emissary to communicate with Ypsilanitis' forces: 'The Emperor is at peace with the Porte', Pisani was instructed, and since the security of the Principalities was already guaranteed by treaty, no act disturbing their tranquillity could ever 'obtain the support or sanction of the Emperor. Far from that, His Majesty wishes that the Ottoman government should adopt, without delay, the measures necessary to restore order and tranquillity.' See also Stroganov to Ypsilantis, 6 (18) March 1821, in Prokesch-Osten, *Geschichte des Abfalls der Griechen*, vol. iii, p. 70, telling him that his revolt was contrary to the principles of their Emperor but that perhaps he could still avert bloodshed.
130. Anderson, *The Eastern Question*, pp. 53–54.
131. Arimia et al., *Revoluția din 1821 Condusă de Vladimirescu*.
132. His internment in fact met with the approval of the Russian government; see Nesselrode to Golovkin, 17 (29) July 1821, USSR, *Vneshniaia Politika Rossii, 1815–1830*, Series 2, vol. iv, pp. 228–29.
133. Nesselrode to Stroganov, 13 May 1821, Laibach, in USSR, *Vneshniaia Politika Rossii, 1815–1830*, Series 2, vol. iv, pp. 149–51, explaining that they would not return the refugees, whether innocent or guilty, for humanitarian reasons since the Turks were sacrificing too many victims to the popular vengeance; the

Ottoman government was confounding 'crime and innocence' and exhibiting 'cruelty' to Christians, forcing the Greeks to resist out of sheer desperation. See the letter of General Major Kiselev to Prince Volkonsky, Toultzin, 9 March 1821, containing the report of Lieutenant Colonel Pestel, in Arimia et al., *Revoluţia din 1821 Condusă de Vladimirescu*, pp. 138–44; Schroeder, *Metternich's Diplomacy*, pp. 169–70; Woodhouse, *Capodistria*, p. 262; Bitis, *Russia and the Eastern Question*, pp. 105–07.

134. Jean Vlassopulo to Stroganov, 2 May 1821: 'Toute la Morée est aux armes', in USSR, *Vneshniaia Politika Rossii, 1815–1830*, Series 2, vol. iv, pp. 126–27; Douglas Dakin, *The Greek Struggle for Independence, 1821–1833* (Berkeley: University of California Press, 1973), p. 59; Gary J. Bass, *Freedom's Battle: The Origins of Humanitarian Intervention* (New York: Random House, 2008), p. 56.
135. Antoine Sandrini to Nesselrode, 30 April 1821, in USSR, *Vneshniaia Politika Rossii, 1815–1830*, Series 2, vol. iv, pp. 121–23.
136. Alan Palmer, *The Decline and Fall of the Ottoman Empire* (New York: M. Evans & Co., 1992), pp. 84–85; Charles A. Frazee, *The Orthodox Church and Independent Greece, 1821–1852* (Cambridge: Cambridge University Press, 1969), pp. 26–27.
137. Clogg, *Movement for Greek Independence*, pp. 203–06.
138. See the account of Robert Walsh, in Clogg, *Movement for Greek Independence*, pp. 206–08; Frazee, *Orthodox Church*, pp. 22–32; Palmer, *Ottoman Empire*, pp. 85–87. Ottoman sources describe a more orderly deposition and execution of Grigorios. Philliou, *Biography of an Empire*, pp. 72–73. The Patriarch's body was later sighted floating on the surface by refugees on a Russian grain ship and carried to Odessa.
139. Woodhouse, *Capodistria*, pp. 260–61; the British envoy Robert Gordon was still at Laibach: 'It is reported here to-day that the Patriarch of Constantinople has been murdered', Gordon to Castlereagh, 13 May 1821, Laibach, in Stewart, *Castlereagh Correspondence*, xii, p. 396.
140. Stourdza to Capodistrias, 2 (14) April 1821, Istria, in USSR, *Vneshniaia Politika Rossii, 1815–1830*, Series 2, vol. iv, pp. 94–95: 'I learn with a surprise mixed with emotions of joy and inquietude that Prince Alexander Ypsilanti has raised the standard for the deliverance of Greece … [I]t is important to speak clearly (*hautement*) to the consciences of the monarchs of Europe. It is a matter of telling them that the cause of Christians in the Orient should not be confused with that of the revolutionaries in France, Italy and Spain.' Capodistrias had written to Stourdza when the news had first been received that at a moment when Europe was being shaken by revolutionary convulsions, the same subversive principles had now appeared in Greece: 'If God, who is the sole arbiter of the destinies of peoples and nations, has decided in his impenetrable decrees that Europe should be saved in this moment of universal crisis by either the sacrifice of our unhappy country, or by its resurrection, the will of the Lord shall be accomplished.' Capodistrias to Stourdza, 18 (30) March 1821, USSR, *Vneshniaia Politika Rossii, 1815–1830*, Series 2, vol. iv, pp. 72–73.

141. Capodistrias to Nicolai, 4 July 1821, USSR, *Vneshniaia Politika Rossii, 1815–1830*, Series 2, vol. iv, pp. 192–94. However, Castlereagh denied that Strangford failed to give Stroganov support and even reviewed his reports with the Russian envoy in London to make this point; see Cunningham, *Anglo-Ottoman Encounters*, pp. 203–04. According to Cunningham, Stroganov actually engaged in deliberately provocative behaviour, such as ordering a Russian packet-boat into the Bosphorous without first obtaining Turkish permission, virtually forcing Strangford to advise the Ottomans to ignore Stroganov in favour of corresponding directly with Nesselrode.
142. Webster, *Foreign Policy of Castlereagh, 1815–1822*, pp. 354–55; notes of Stroganov to the Sublime Porte, 25 April, 22 May (3 June), 24 May (5 June) and undated, in Prokesch-Osten, *Geschichte des Abfalls der Griechen*, vol. iii, pp. 72–75, 81–84, 84–85, 95–101. The move to Buyukderi had been planned earlier. See Stroganov to Nesselrode, 9 June 1821, USSR, *Vneshniaia Politika Rossii, 1815–1830*, Series 2, vol. iv, pp. 162–65.
143. Dispatch to Stroganov, (4) 16 June 1821, St. Petersburg, in Prokesch-Osten, *Geschichte des Abfalls der Griechen*, vol. iii, pp. 89–92, and in Arimia et al., *Revoluția din 1821 Condusă de Vladimirescu*, pp. 322–25.
144. Cunningham, *Anglo-Ottoman Encounters*, p. 204.
145. Grand Vizier to Nesselrode, 27 June 1821, Constantinople, and communicated to France on 7 July, in Arimia et al., *Revoluția din 1821 Condusă de Vladimirescu*, pp. 339–43, based on the copy in the French archives, and in Prokesch-Osten, *Geschichte des Abfalls der Griechen*, vol. iii, pp. 131–40, in a different translation; see also Webster, *Foreign Policy of Castlereagh, 1815–1822*, p. 339; Schroeder, *Metternich's Diplomacy*, pp. 171–72.
146. Note presented by Stroganov to the Porte, 6 (18) July 1821 in Arimia et al., *Revoluția din 1821 Condusă de Vladimirescu*, pp. 363–66: 'Ce que l'empereur craignait le plus pour la Sublime Porte c'est que les mesures décretées par les ministère ottoman n'imprimassent à l'enterprise des auteurs de la révolution le caractère d'une défense légitime contre une destruction totale de la nation grecque et du culte qu'elle professe. Ces craintes, il faut bien en convenir, ces craintes ne semblent s'être que trop réalisées.' See also, Barbara Jelavich, *Russia's Balkan Entanglements, 1806–1914* (Cambridge: Cambridge University Press, 1991), pp. 58–59.
147. Note presented by Stroganov to the Porte, 18 July 1821 in USSR, *Vneshniaia Politika Rossii, 1815–1830*, Series 2, vol. iv, pp. 203–07; Prokesch-Osten, *Geschichte des Abfalls der Griechen*, vol. iii, pp. 95–101; Arimia et al., *Revoluția din 1821 Condusă de Vladimirescu*, pp. 363–66.
148. Cunningham, *Anglo-Ottoman Encounters*, pp. 204–05. However, Jelavich indicates that Ottoman officials said their reply would be three days late. Jelavich, *Balkan Entanglements*, p. 60.
149. Prokesch-Osten, *Geschichte des Abfalls der Griechen*, vol. iii, p. 95; Webster, *Foreign Policy of Castlereagh, 1815–1822*, pp. 355–57; Schroeder, *Metternich's Diplomacy*, pp. 172–73; Woodhouse, *Capodistria*, pp. 263–65; and Bitis, *Russia*

and the Eastern Question, pp. 108–09. For the response of the Sublime Porte to the note presented by Stroganov, see 30 July 1821, Constantinople, in Arimia et al., *Revoluția din 1821 Condusă de Vladimirescu*, pp. 374–76.

150. For the letters sent to the allied courts, see Bertier de Sauvigny, *Metternich et la France*, vol. ii, p. 518; see also Nesselrode to Golovkin, 22 June (4 July) 1821, in Prokesch-Osten, *Geschichte des Abfalls der Griechen*, vol. iii, pp. 86–88 and 101–04, explaining that the Russian army is ready to march, not to expand her frontiers, but to cooperate in the realization of a plan to bring peace and affirm equilibrium; Eberhard Schütz, *Die Europäische Allianzpolitik Alexanders I. unter der Griechische Unabhängigkeitskampf, 1820–1830* (Wiesbaden: Harrassowitz, 1975), pp. 47–50. It was actually Metternich who reduced the Russian propositions into four succinct points in a letter to the Austrian envoy, Lützow, on 17 July 1821.

151. Alexander to Francis, 'Copie d'une letter de Cabinet à S. M. l'Empereur d'Autriche', 11 July 1821, in Prokesch-Osten, *Geschichte des Abfalls der Griechen*, vol. iii, pp. 124–27 ('Excité et entretenu par les actes du Gouvernement Turc, le fanatisme des Musulmans demande obtient chaque jour de nouvelles victimes …'); also summarized in USSR, *Vneshniaia Politika Rossii, 1815–1830*, Series 2, vol. iv, p. 215; see also Bitis, *Russia and the Eastern Question*, p. 113; Nesselrode to Golovkin, 17 July 1821, in Prokesch-Osten, *Geschichte des Abfalls der Griechen*, vol. iii, pp. 127–28.

152. Bertier de Sauvigny, *Metternich et la France*, vol. ii, p. 518; on other approaches to France, see Hartley, *Alexander I*, p. 155; Schütz, *Europäische Allianzpolitik*, pp. 69–70, 76–77. At Vienna, the French ambassador even raised the possibility of a new Congress for possible allied intervention to protect the Christians in the Ottoman Empire; see Bertier de Sauvigny, *Metternich et la France*, pp. 517–18.

153. Pasquier to La Ferronnays, 18 June 1821, cited in Bertier de Sauvigny, *Metternich et la France*, vol. ii, p. 515.

154. Metternich, *Mémoires*, vol. iii, p. 465.

155. For example, Joseph Planta (former private secretary to Castlereagh and Under-Secretary of State after 1817) wrote to Stratford Canning that Stroganov's departure made it difficult to persuade the Sultan to evacuate the Principalities, therefore making war much more likely. Planta to Stratford Canning, 8 August 1821, in Webster, *Foreign Policy of Castlereagh, 1815–1822*, pp. 582–83; Cunningham, *Anglo-Ottoman Encounters*, p. 205.

156. Metternich to Lebzeltern, 1 August 1816, in Bertier de Sauvigny, *Metternich and His Times*, pp. 242–43.

157. Bertier de Sauvigny, *Metternich et la France*, vol. ii, pp. 512–13; Schroeder, *Metternich's Diplomacy*, pp. 123–24, 173–74.

158. Schroeder, *Metternich's Diplomacy*, pp. 178–79, especially fn. 46.

159. Castlereagh to the Tsar, 16 July 1821, Foreign Office, London, in Stewart, *Castlereagh Correspondence*, xii, pp. 403–08; see also Webster, *Foreign Policy of Castlereagh, 1815–1822*, pp. 360–61; Schroeder, *Metternich's Diplomacy*, p. 174.

160. Londonderry to Sir Charles Bagot, 5 August 1821, Foreign Office, No. 12, 'Draft', in N.A. (Kew), F.O. 65/126.
161. Schütz, *Europäische Allianzpolitik*, pp. 51–53.
162. Capodistrias to Bishop Ignatios, 28 July 1821, discussed in Woodhouse, *Capodistria*, p. 265.
163. La Ferronnays, 18 July 1821, St Petersburg, in Mikhaïlovich, *Aleksandr I*, vol. ii, p. 369; also in Ley, *Alexandre 1er et sa Sainte Alliance*, pp. 267–68; see also Albert Sorel, 'L'Alliance russe et la Restauration', in *Essais d'histoire et de critique*, 2nd edn (Paris: Plon, 1883), pp. 99–112.
164. Pozzo di Borgo to Nesselrode, 24 July 1821, in USSR, *Vneshniaia Politika Rossii, 1815–1830*, Series 2, vol. iv, p. 653, n. 104; also cited in Bitis, *Russia and the Eastern Question*, p. 110.
165. Ancillon's memorandum in Prokesch-Osten, *Geschichte des Abfalls der Griechen*, vol. iii, pp. 336–46; see also Bernstorff to Alopeus, 27 July 1821, Prokesch-Osten, *Geschichte des Abfalls der Griechen*, vol. iii, pp. 347–51, calling for a consensus on two points: support of the Greeks and a collective demand on the Porte; see also, Webster, *Foreign Policy of Castlereagh, 1815–1822*, p. 363; Schroeder, *Metternich's Diplomacy*, p. 178; Schütz, *Europäische Allianzpolitik*, pp. 49–51.
166. Ley, *Alexandre 1er et sa Sainte Alliance*, pp. 265–67 (letter of Comte de Gabriac, 13 June 1821, on Madame de Krüdener's views), pp. 267–68 (letter of La Ferronnays, 18 July 1821, on the same) and pp. 269–70 (on the Tsar's secret meeting of 7 September with Madame de Krüdener); see also, Palmer, *Alexander I*, p. 379.
167. See especially, La Ferronnays, 18 July 1821, in Mikhaïlovich, *Aleksandr I*, vol. ii, p. 369; Prousis, *Russian Society and the Greek Revolution*, pp. 26–54.
168. Capodistrias, 'Aperçu de ma carrière publique depuis 1798 jusqu'à 1822', in *Sbornik Imperatorskogo Russkogo Istoricheskogo Obshchestva*, vol. iii, p. 269; Ley, *Alexandre 1er et sa Sainte Alliance*, p. 269; Anderson, *Eastern Question*, p. 61; Kissinger, *A World Restored*, p. 296; Schütz, *Europäische Allianzpolitik*, pp. 77–81; Sked, *Metternich and Austria*, p. 70; Anderson, 'Russia and the Eastern Question', in Sked, *Europe's Balance of Power, 1815–1848*, p. 81.
169. Woodhouse, *Capodistria*, pp. 267–69.
170. Woodhouse, *Capodistria*, pp. 269–72; Capodistrias to Alexander, 10 August and 21 August 1821, in USSR, *Vneshniaia Politika Rossii, 1815–1830*, Series 2, vol. iv, pp. 242–46, 256–61.
171. Capodistrias to Alexander, 21 August 1821, in USSR, *Vneshniaia Politika Rossii, 1815–1830*, Series 2, vol. iv, pp. 256–61.
172. Schroeder, *Metternich's Diplomacy*, p. 174, citing Metternich to Lebzeltern, 24 August 1821; Webster, *Foreign Policy of Castlereagh, 1815–1822*, p. 364; Bertier de Sauvigny, *Metternich et la France*, vol. ii, p. 519; Emperor Francis to the Tsar, 22 August 1821, in Prokesch-Osten, *Geschichte des Abfalls der Griechen*, vol. iii, pp. 156–61.
173. Lettre de Cabinet à Lord Londonderry, St Petersburg, 29 August (10 September) 1821, in Prokesch-Osten, *Geschichte des Abfalls der Griechen*, vol. iii,

pp. 191–96; Circular from Nesselrode to Alopeus, Golovkin, Nikolai and Pozzo di Borgo, 29 August (10 September) 1821, in USSR, *Vneshniaia Politika Rossii, 1815–1830*, Series 2, vol. iv, pp. 279–80; Webster, *Foreign Policy of Castlereagh, 1815–1822*, p. 363. Nesselrode instructed the Russian diplomats to decline in advance all offers of mediation between Russia and the Porte received from the other allied powers; Russia aimed only at exercising her existing treaty rights, and only asked the allied courts for their opinions on the best mode of negotiation for establishing a concert of views and principles between Russia and her allies in the unfortunate event that no representation could secure an acceptable outcome with the Porte.

174. Conference of Austrian Internuncio and the Ottoman ministers, 22 November 1821, in Prokesch-Osten, *Geschichte des Abfalls der Griechen*, vol. iii, pp. 222–30. As noted above, Metternich reduced the Russian ultimatum to four succinct points, which were presented to the Porte again by Strangford and Lützow in November 1821; see Woodhouse, *Capodistria*, pp. 275–76.

175. Schroeder, *Metternich's Diplomacy*, p. 175. A conference was held between the Internuncio (the Austrian envoy to the Sultan, just below the rank of ambassador) and the Ottoman ministers on 22 November 1821; see Prokesch-Osten, *Geschichte des Abfalls der Griechen*, vol. iii, pp. 222–30.

176. Castlereagh to Robert Gordon, Aix-la-Chapelle, 1 October 1821, No. 17, in N.A. (Kew) F.O./161: 'If we look for a cure, the present menacing position of Russia may, in the hands of the allied ministers at Constantinople, be turned to good account, and the active excitement which may be produced by their uniform, but individual, exertions daily directed to rouse the Porte to new efforts for the pacification of the interior will probably have the best effects; let us, however, be cautious how we get into formal, still more into collective negotiation with the Ottoman Gov[ernmen]t, till the main danger has passed away and the irritation connected with it has subsided ... [S]ome temporary exercise of Turkish Authority ... might furnish a set-off against their acquiescing in the asylum afforded by Russia to the Greek fugitives.' Indeed, at this juncture Castlereagh sent scarcely any instructions at all to Strangford in Constantinople. See Cunningham, *Anglo-Ottoman Encounters*, pp. 216–17.

177. Webster, *Foreign Policy of Castlereagh, 1815–1822*, pp. 367–82; Schroeder, *Metternich's Diplomacy*, pp. 176–77; Bertier de Sauvigny, *Metternich et la France*, vol. ii, pp. 523–26; Bitis, *Russia and the Eastern Question*, pp. 112–13; Lieven to Nesselrode, 21 October 1821 (Old Style), USSR, *Vneshniaia Politika Rossii, 1815–1830*, Series 2, vol. iv, p. 435; John Charmley, *The Princess and the Politicians: Sex, Intrigue and Diplomacy, 1812–1840* (London: Viking, 2005), pp. 69–72; Schütz, *Europäische Allianzpolitik*, pp. 83–85.

178. Webster, *Foreign Policy of Castlereagh, 1815–1822*, pp. 374–75; Woodhouse, *Capodistria*, pp. 271–72.

179. Nichols, *The European Pentarchy and the Congress of Verona*, p. 11; Montgomery Hyde, *Princess Lieven* (London: George G. Harrap & Co., 1938), p. 131; Metternich to Francis I, 29 October 1821, Hanover, in Metternich, *Mémoires*,

vol. iii, pp. 558–59; Metternich to Lebzeltern, 31 October 1821, Hanover, in Mikhaïlovich. *Les Rapports Diplomatiques*, pp. 237–38.

180. Castlereagh to Bagot, 28 October 1821, Webster, *Foreign Policy of Castlereagh, 1815–1822*, pp. 375–79, citing F.O. 92/47; Woodhouse, *Capodistria*, pp. 273–74; Cunningham, *Anglo-Ottoman Encounters*, pp. 209–11.
181. Schroeder, *Metternich's Diplomacy*, pp. 178–79.
182. Nesselrode to Lieven, St Petersburg, 7 October 1821, in Prokesch-Osten, *Geschichte des Abfalls der Griechen*, vol. iii, pp. 196–202. The Porte agreed to evacuate the Principalities if Austria and England guaranteed that the retreat of Turkish forces would not be followed by the entry of Russian troops.
183. Anderson, *Eastern Question*, pp. 54–55.
184. Brewer, *Greek War*, pp. 111–23; Bass, *Freedom's Battle*, pp. 64–66; Cunningham, *Anglo-Ottoman Encounters*, p. 218.
185. Bitis, *Russia and the Eastern Question*, p. 113.
186. Woodhouse, *Capodistria*, p. 274.
187. Prokesch-Osten, *Geschichte des Abfalls der Griechen*, vol. iii, pp. 248–60; Anderson, *Eastern Question*, pp. 55; Brewer, *Greek War*, pp. 70–110; 124–34; 168–93.
188. Schroeder, *Metternich's Diplomacy*, p. 181, citing Lützow, the Austrian Internuncio (or envoy) at Constantinople, to Metternich, 8 December 1821.
189. Schroeder, *Metternich's Diplomacy*, pp. 182–83, citing Lebzeltern to Metternich, 9 and 10 January 1822, St Petersburg.
190. Webster, *Foreign Policy of Castlereagh, 1815–1822*, p. 385.
191. Schroeder, *Metternich's Diplomacy*, p. 183, citing Lebzeltern to Metternich, 6 February 1822. The report of this date, printed in Mikhaïlovich, *Rapports de Lebzeltern*, pp. 86–88, conveys Russian disappointment at Austrian hesitations respecting the Tsar's genuine devotion to peace and the alliance.
192. Castlereagh sent Bagot a chilling account of the recent progress of the revolutionary movement in order to discredit the Greeks: 'The first point that deserves the Emperor's attentive consideration is the wide and increasing spread of the revolutionary movement throughout the American as well as the European Continent. The events of the last few months in Mexico, Peru, the Caracas, and the Brazils, have nearly decided that both the Americas shall swell the preponderating catalogue of States administered under a system of government, founded upon a Republican or Democratic basis. The like spirit has been advancing in Europe with rapid strides; Spain and Portugal are in the very vortex of a similar convulsion. France fluctuates in her policy between extreme views and interests, both, in their very nature, seriously and perhaps equally menacing to her internal tranquility; and Italy, including the King of Sardinia's dominions, though, for the time, recovered from the grasp of the Revolutionists, is held only by the presence of the Austrian Army of Occupation ... In short, it is impossible that the Emperor should not see that the head of this revolutionary torrent is in Greece, that the tide is flowing in upon his southern provinces in almost an uninterrupted and continuous stream from the other side of the Atlantic; and it is

upon this principle, and not upon local views of policy, that his Imperial Majesty will, I doubt not, as a statesman, regulate his conduct.' Castlereagh to Sir Charles Bagot, 14 December 1821, in Stewart, *Castlereagh Correspondence*, vol. xii, pp. 443–46.

193. Webster, *Foreign Policy of Castlereagh, 1815–1822*, p. 387.
194. Webster, *Foreign Policy of Castlereagh, 1815–1822*, p. 388, citing Bagot to Castlereagh, 10 January and 22 February 1822.
195. Palmer, *Alexander I*, p. 380; Woodhouse, *Capodistria*, p. 283; Schroeder, *Metternich's Diplomacy*, pp. 177–79, 185–86. Palmer, a reputable scholar, seems to cite an incorrect source, but from everything we know of the Tsar, especially based on his letters to Golitsyn, this description of his conduct seems apt.
196. Woodhouse, *Capodistria*, pp. 283–84; Grimsted, *The Foreign Ministers of Alexander I*, pp. 266–67; for Tatishchev's instructions, see Alexander to Tatishchev, 5 (17) February 1822, in USSR, *Vneshniaia Politika Rossii, 1815–1830*, Series 2, vol. iv, pp. 426–28.
197. Bertier de Sauvigny suggests the Tatishchev mission was a means for the Tsar to retreat without 'loss of face'; Bertier de Sauvigny, *Metternich et la France*, vol. ii, p. 567.
198. Tatishchev to Nesselrode, 12 March, 22 March and 15 April 1822, Vienna, in USSR, *Vneshniaia Politika Rossii, 1815–1830*, Series 2, vol. iv, pp. 447–51, 454–56, 471–73; Tatishchev to Alexander, 28 March 1822, USSR, *Vneshniaia Politika Rossii, 1815–1830*, Series 2, vol. iv, p. 470; Metternich to Lebzeltern, 22 April 1822, in Prokesch-Osten, *Geschichte des Abfalls der Griechen*, vol. iii, pp. 364–66; Kissinger, *A World Restored*, pp. 302–03.
199. The Prussians had transmitted a protocol signed by Alopeus and Bernstorff, promising to break off relations with the Porte if Russia went to war (see Russian Circular of 15 April 1822, in USSR, *Vneshniaia Politika Rossii, 1815–1830*, Series 2, vol. iv, pp. 474–75, enclosing the signed Prussian protocol); Metternich recommended a mere oral declaration instead, and the French followed his example. He later explained frankly that his offer to withdraw was 'merely one of courtesy and would remain without effect, because he neither believed nor desired that His Britannic Majesty could be prevailed upon to withdraw his Ambassador from Constantinople, and he was from the first of opinion that such a measure should not be put in force unless it were unanimously adopted by the Allied Powers'. See Webster, *Foreign Policy of Castlereagh, 1815–1822*, pp. 395–96, citing Gordon to Castlereagh, 16 May 1822.
200. Schroeder, *Metternich's Diplomacy*, pp. 189–90; Metternich's Memorandum for the Emperor Alexander, 19 April 1822, Vienna, in Prince Richard Metternich-Winneburg (ed.), *Aus Metternich's Nachgelassene Papieren* (Vienna, 1881), vol. iii, pp. 539–45.
201. Capodistrias to the Tsar, 13 March 1822, USSR, *Vneshniaia Politika Rossii, 1815–1830*, Series 2, vol. iv, pp. 500–03.
202. Webster, *Foreign Policy of Castlereagh, 1815–1822*, pp. 393–94, citing Castlereagh to Bagot, 29 April 1822.

203. Bertier de Sauvigny, *Metternich et la France*, vol. ii, p. 569; Memoranda of Conferences in Vienna with Metternich, Tatishchev, Caraman and Robert Gordon, on 28 June, 17 July and 27 July 1821, in Prokesch-Osten, *Geschichte des Abfalls der Griechen*, vol. iii, pp. 393–98.
204. Webster, *Foreign Policy of Castlereagh, 1815–1822*, p. 397; Kissinger, *A World Restored*, p. 309; Grimsted, *Foreign Ministers of Alexander I*, p. 279; Bitis, *Russia and the Eastern Question*, p. 115, fn. 91.
205. Ley, *Alexander Ier et sa Sainte-Alliance*, p. 270. Stourdza had been suspended in October after submitting a memorandum to the Tsar urging intervention in favour of the Greeks.
206. Brewer, *Greek War*, pp. 154–67; Bass, *Freedom's Battle*, pp. 67–73.
207. John Howes Gleason, *The Genesis of Russophobia in Great Britain: A Study of Interaction of Policy and Opinion* (Cambridge, MA: Harvard University Press, 1950), pp. 42–71.
208. Bass, *Freedom's Battle*, pp. 68–71; Cunningham, *Anglo-Ottoman Encounters*, p. 218.
209. Webster, *Foreign Policy of Castlereagh, 1815–1822*, p. 399.
210. Matthew S. Anderson, 'Russia and the Eastern Question', in Sked, *Europe's Balance of Power*, p. 82.
211. Schroeder, *Transformation of European Politics*, p. 621.
212. Matthew Rendall, 'Russia, the Concert of Europe and Greece, 1821–29', *Security Studies* 9/4 (Summer 2000) and 'Defensive Realism and the Concert of Europe', pp. 523–40. Alexander Bitis lists several possible motives, from the influence of Metternich to the poor state of the Russian army, but concludes that the 'most convincing analysis' is that 'Alexander drew back from war in a genuine desire to preserve the unity of the alliance'. Bitis, *Russia and the Eastern Question*, p. 114.
213. Rendall, 'Russia, the Concert of Europe and Greece', pp. 64–71; Rendall, 'Defensive Realism', fn. 51.
214. Edward Ingram, 'Bellicism as Boomerang: The Eastern Question during the Vienna System', in Krüger and Schroeder, *Episode or Model*, pp. 205–25.
215. Schütz, *Europäische Allianzpolitik*.

7. The Twilight of the Congress System, 1822–23

1. Raymond Carr sees the *doceañistas* and *exaltados* as members of different social classes, but Charles Esdaile argues persuasively that their differences were primarily generational. See Carr, *Spain 1808–1975*, pp. 130–31 ('This division, essentially between liberals and democrats, between men of property and position and urban radicals, was common to European liberalism ...'); Esdaile, *Spain in the Liberal Age*, pp. 52–53 ('In so far as there was any difference at all, it was really one of age, reputation and success. Thus the *moderados* were drawn almost exclusively from men who were already well-established on the social scale thanks to a combination of a prosperous family background and successful ca-

reers in the army, the administration, the professions or big business. Whilst often sharing the same background, the *exaltados* were by contrast men who had yet to establish themselves ...'); see also Fehrenbach, 'Moderados and Exaltados, pp. 54–55: 'Most contemporaries, however, believed that the division among liberals was more a result of personal rivalries than of differences in ideological or parliamentary principles ... A careful examination of the evidence indicates that, for the most part, contemporaries were accurate in their assumptions.' Fehrenbach contrasts the men of 1812 and of 1820. See also, Gil Novales, *El Trienio Liberal*, pp. 15–16, 20–22; Timothy E. Anna, *Spain and the Loss of America* (Lincoln: University of Nebraska Press, 1983), p. 232; Christiana Brennecke, *Cádiz nach London: spanische Liberalismus im Spannungsfeld von nationaler Selbstbestimmung, Internationalität und Exil (1820–1833)* (Göttingen: Vandenhoeck & Ruprecht, 2010), pp. 60–80; Stites, *Four Horsemen*, pp. 76–79, 89–91.
2. For example, in September 1820, the Cortes debated placing curbs on the political clubs, abolished the law of entail, restored the properties of the *afrancesados*, and passed a press law. See Sir H. Wellesley to Castlereagh, 21 September 1820, Nos. 190, 191, and 192, in N.A. (Kew), F.O. 72/236, and Wellesley to Castlereagh, 4 January 1821, No. 3, in N.A. (Kew), F.O. 72/244; see also Esdaile, *Spain in the Liberal Age*, pp. 52–53; Stites, *Four Horsemen*, pp. 73–75, 81–82.
3. In September 1820, the Cortes also passed a law confiscating monastic lands in order to pay off the national debt, and a law restricting the press. Sir Henry Wellesley to Castlereagh, 28 September 1820, No. 195, in N.A. (Kew), F.O. 72/236. After the change in ministry in March, the Cortes voted to speed up the sale of church lands. Wellesley to Castlereagh, 22 March 1821, No. 49, in N.A. (Kew), F.O. 72/244; Gil Novales, *Trienio Liberal*, pp. 15–16; Carr, *Spain*, pp. 142–43.
4. Anna, *Spain and Loss of America*, p. 221; Wellesley to Castlereagh, 5 February 1821, Madrid, No. 19, in N.A. (Kew), F.O. 72/244, reporting receipt of news in Madrid of Morillo's November armistice with Bolivar.
5. Wellesley to Castlereagh, 2 January 1821, Madrid, No. 1, in N.A. (Kew), F.O. 72/244, f. 46.
6. Wellesley to Castlereagh, 2 January 1821, Madrid, No. 2, in N.A. (Kew), F.O. 72/244, f. 54.
7. Wellesley to Castlereagh, 18 January 1821, Madrid, No. 8, in N.A. (Kew), F.O. 72/244. He expressed the same views again on 27 January, No. 13: 'I am still of opinion that the best line of policy which the Allies could pursue with respect to this Country, even for the attainment of their own objects, would be to abstain from all interference with its affairs.'
8. Wellesley to Castlereagh, 27 January 1821, Madrid, 'Private and Confidential', in N.A. (Kew), F.O. 72/244, ff. 93–96.
9. Wellesley to Castlereagh, 19 and 27 February 1821, Madrid, Nos 27 and 30, 'Private and Confidential', in N.A. (Kew), F.O. 72/244.
10. Wellesley to Castlereagh, 7, 8 and 19 February 1821, Madrid, Nos 24, 25 and 29, in N.A. (Kew), F.O. 72/244; Esdaile, *Spain in the Liberal Age*, pp. 54–55; Carr, *Spain*, p. 134; Gil Novales, *Trienio Liberal*, p. 27.

11. Wellesley to Castlereagh, 25 February 1821, Madrid, 'Private and Confidential', in N.A. (Kew), F.O. 72/244, ff. 193–203.
12. Esdaile, *Spain in the Liberal Age*, p. 55.
13. Wellesley to Castlereagh, 7 March 1821, Madrid, 'Private and Confidential', in N.A. (Kew), F.O. 72/244.
14. Wellesley to Castlereagh, 7, 19 and 26 March 1821, Madrid, Nos. 40, 48 and 51, in N.A. (Kew), F.O. 72/244: 'Assurances have … been given to the Spanish Govt. by the ministers of the five powers … that these powers will abstain from interference in the affairs of Spain' (26 March 1821). Based on instructions from the Cortes, the Spanish government sent special couriers to all the allied courts asking each its intentions towards Spain. Wellesley to Castlereagh, 29 March and 2 April 1821, Madrid, Nos. 54 and 55, in N.A. (Kew), F.O. 72/244.
15. Esdaile, *Spain in the Liberal Age*, p. 55; Gil Novales, *Trienio Liberal*, pp. 27–28.
16. E. Christiansen, *The Origins of Military Power in Spain, 1800–1854* (Oxford: Oxford University Press, 1967), pp. 22–23.
17. Fehrenbach, 'Moderados and Exaltados', p. 63.
18. Esdaile, *Spain in the Liberal Age*, pp. 57–58; Carr, *Spain*, pp. 132–34; Fehrenbach, 'Moderados and Exaltados', p. 66.
19. Esdaile, *Spain in the Liberal Age*, pp. 56–57. According to Esdaile, these radical revolts deepened their differences with the *moderados* and even pushed some of the latter into the camp of counter-revolution. See also Gil Novales, *Trienio Liberal*, pp. 43–46.
20. Nichols, *Congress of Verona*, p. 29.
21. Gil Novales, *Trienio Liberal*, pp. 39–40. Gil Novales emphasizes that the outbreak was significant: 80,000 died in Barcelona alone.
22. Fehrenbach, 'Moderados and Exaltados', p. 66.
23. Nichols, *Congress of Verona*, p. 30; Gil Novales, *Trienio Liberal*, pp. 46–47.
24. Ferdinand made fresh approaches to the Tsar and Louis XVIII in late June and early July. Fehrenbach, 'Moderados and Exaltados', pp. 67–69. See below.
25. Gil Novales, *Trienio Liberal*, pp. 50–55; Carr, *Spain*, pp. 135–38 ('With the lamentable failure of Ferdinand in the Guards' rebellion, palace royalism was bankrupt'); Nichols, *Congress of Verona*, p. 31; Schroeder, *Metternich's Diplomacy*, pp. 195–96; Michael J. Quin, *A Visit to Spain* (London: Hurst, Robinson, 1823), pp. 61–67; Stites, *Four Horsemen*, pp. 94–95.
26. Carr, *Spain*, pp. 137–38; Fehrenbach, 'Moderados and Exaltados', p. 68; Nichols, *Congress of Verona*, p. 31; Stites, *Four Horsemen*, p. 95.
27. Chateaubriand, *Congress of Verona*, vol. i, p. 36.
28. Bertier de Sauvigny, *Metternich et la France*, vol. ii, p. 604; Schroeder, *Metternich's Diplomacy*, p. 196; Christiansen, *The Origins of Military Power*, p. 25; Nichols, *Congress of Verona*, pp. 29–30; Bertier de Sauvigny, *Bourbon Restoration*, p. 186; Quin, *Visit to Spain*, p. 82; Stites, *Four Horsemen*, pp. 96–97.
29. Schroeder, *Metternich's Diplomacy*, p. 197.
30. Nichols, *Congress of Verona*, pp. 29–30, 33. In August 1822, the French also sent the Comte de La Garde as their new ambassador to Madrid, furnished with

instructions for King Ferdinand to strengthen his power. Nichols, *Congress of Verona*, p. 30.
31. Bertier de Sauvigny, *Metternich et la France*, vol. ii, pp. 544–47.
32. Bertier de Sauvigny, *Metternich et la France*, vol. ii, pp. 551–54, 617–18; Schroeder, *Metternich's Diplomacy*, p. 199; Nichols, *Congress of Verona*, pp. 25–27; Bertier de Sauvigny, *Bourbon Restoration*, p. 179.
33. Bertier de Sauvigny, *Metternich et la France*, vol. ii, pp. 594–96; Schroeder, *Metternich's Diplomacy*, pp. 198–200.
34. Metternich himself made this observation: see Bertier de Sauvigny, *Metternich et la France*, vol. ii, p. 606.
35. Bertier de Sauvigny, *Metternich et la France*, vol. ii, pp. 604, 606 and 599, fn. 151; Schroeder, *Metternich's Diplomacy*, pp. 199–200.
36. Londonderry, 'Memorandum No. 3', 3 November 1822, Verona, in Wellington, *Despatches*, vol. i, pp. 486–87; Lebzeltern to Metternich, 7 (19) May 1822, St Petersburg, in Mikhaïlovich, *Rapports Diplomatiques de Lebzeltern*, p. 93: 'The Emperor thinks seriously ... of having 40,000 men march across the Austrian monarchy, Lombardy and the South of France into Spain to destroy the revolution' ('l'Empereur pense sérieusement, avec chaleur qu'il met à de hautes conceptions bien dignes de son grand coeur, à la possibilité et à la intérêt de faire marcher à travers toute la Monarchie Autrichienne, la Lombardie et le midi de la France quarante mille hommes en Espagne pour y combattre et tuer la révolution').
37. Bertier de Sauvigny, *Metternich et la France*, vol. ii, pp. 596–97.
38. Schroeder, *Metternich's Diplomacy*, pp. 200–04.
39. Bertier de Sauvigny, *Metternich et la France*, vol. ii, pp. 596–97; Schroeder, *Metternich's Diplomacy*, p. 286.
40. Schroeder, *Metternich's Diplomacy*, pp. 202–04, citing Lebzeltern's reports to Metternich from St Petersburg in April and May 1822.
41. Bertier de Sauvigny, *Metternich et la France*, vol. ii, p. 610; Schroeder, *Metternich's Diplomacy*, pp. 204–06.
42. Wellington, *Despatches*, vol. i, pp. 284–88; Nichols, *Congress of Verona*, pp. 19–23, 71–72; Temperley, *Foreign Policy of Canning*, pp. 53–55; J.E.S. Green, 'Castlereagh's Instructions for the Conferences at Vienna, 1822', *Transactions of the Royal Historical Society*, Third Series, 7 (1913), pp. 103–28.
43. Countess Dorothy Lieven to Metternich, 14 August 1822, in Peter Quennell, *The Private Letters of Princess Lieven to Prince Metternich* (London: J. Murray, 1937), pp. 157–58. On Castlereagh's suicide, see Harford Montgomery Hyde, *The Strange Death of Lord Castlereagh* (London: William Heinemann, 1959); Webster, *Foreign Policy of Castlereagh, 1815–1822*, pp. 482–89; Wendy Hinde, *Castlereagh* (London: Collins, 1981), pp. 277–81; Hunt, *The Duel*, pp. 175–86; and John Bew, *Castlereagh: Enlightenment, War and Tyranny* (London: Quercus, 2011), pp. 538–57. Giles Hunt argues persuasively that Castlereagh was suffering from the tertiary stages of syphilis, based upon a letter he has found among the Pratt papers in Kent.
44. Temperley, *Foreign Policy of Canning*, p. 27–34; Hunt, *The Duel*, pp. 161–67; Captain Josceline Bagot (ed.), *George Canning and His Friends* (New York: St Martin's

Press, 1909), vol. ii, pp. 1–132; Nichols, *Congress of Verona*, pp. 13–14; Hilton, *A Mad, Bad & Dangerous People*, pp. 280–88.

45. Temperley, *Foreign Policy of Canning*, pp. 43–44.
46. Bathurst to Castlereagh, 20 October 1818, in Stewart, *Castlereagh Correspondence*, vol. xii, pp. 56–57; Temperley, *Foreign Policy of Canning*, p. 45; Lane-Poole, *Stratford Canning*, vol. i, p. 291.
47. One scholar, Norihito Yamada, has recently challenged the older thesis of Harold Temperley that Canning deliberately set about destroying the Congress System. Yamada points, for example, to Canning's instructions to Wellington of 27 September 1822, in which he enjoined Wellington to discourage intervention in Spain in order to avoid allied disunion. Yamada concludes that, 'Canning expressed his desire to prevent Anglo-Continental disagreements over Spain from weakening the system of great-power concert'. Norihito Yamada, 'George Canning and the Spanish Question, September 1822 to March 1823', *The Historical Journal* 52/ 2 (June 2009), pp. 361–62. What this new evidence largely seems to reveal is that Canning was a confirmed pragmatist, willing to use all means at his disposal, including cooperation with the allied powers, for the promotion of British strategic and commercial interests.
48. Nichols, *Congress of Verona*, pp. 23–24.
49. Nichols, *Congress of Verona*, p. 35; Yamada, 'George Canning', pp. 349–51.
50. Wellington to Canning, 21 September 1822, in Wellington, *Despatches*, vol. i, pp. 288–94; Bertier de Sauvigny, *Metternich et la France*, vol. ii, pp. 626–28; Schroeder, *Metternich's Diplomacy*, p. 210; Nichols, *Congress of Verona*, pp. 25–27, 34–37; Bertier de Sauvigny, *Bourbon Restoration*, pp. 180–81, 187–88; Yamada, 'George Canning', pp. 354–55. Villèle, fearing that the British were obtaining important concessions from the emerging independent states of Latin America, also entertained a proposal to act as mediator between Spain and her colonies. If Spain refused this offer, he thought this might justify a rupture of diplomatic relations. Schroeder emphasizes that Wellington thought Villèle was committed to peace, whereas all he was really committed to was his own country's independence of action.
51. Canning to Wellington, 27 September 1823, in Wellington, *Despatches*, vol. i, p. 301–05. Canning instructed Wellington that 'discordance' between the allies 'may probably afford to your Grace an opportunity of evading the proposal of a joint declaration'; Temperley, *Foreign Policy of Canning*, pp. 63–65; Nichols, *Congress of Verona*, p. 37. Yamada points out that Canning still believed that allied action was unlikely and that this celebrated phrase was only added by Canning after Liverpool had criticized his original instructions. See Yamada, 'George Canning', pp. 349–50. See also, Green, 'Castlereagh's Instructions', and 'Wellington and the Congress of Verona', *English Historical Review* 35/138 (April 1920), pp. 200–11.
52. Bertier de Sauvigny, *Metternich et la France*, vol. ii, pp. 619–26; Nichols, *Congress of Verona*, pp. 44–45; Schroeder, *Metternich's Diplomacy*, p. 207. There was, moreover, some element of truth to both of these claims.

53. Yamada, 'George Canning', pp. 348–49, citing Londonderry (Stewart) to Bathurst, 12 and 15 September 1822, in N.A. (Kew), F.O. 7/172.
54. Bertier de Sauvigny, *Metternich et la France*, vol. ii, pp. 631–32, citing Gentz, 'Memorandum on the Affairs of Spain and Portugal'; Schroeder, *Metternich's Diplomacy*, pp. 207, 211–13; Treitschke, *History of Germany*, vol. iv, pp. 25–26.
55. Schroeder, *Metternich's Diplomacy*, p. 208, citing Vincent to Metternich, 27 October 1822, Paris, from the Austrian state archives (Haus-, Hof- und Staatsarchiv).
56. Montmorency had declined written instructions before leaving Paris, but after his appointment as President of the Council, Villèle completed these instructions and sent them along with Chateaubriand. In essence, the French delegation was told to preserve a free hand for France in Spain and to focus the energies of the Congress on Italy. However, as Villèle told Wellington, he also 'wished the Congress would take into consideration their actual position with respect to Spain, and the hypotheses under which they might be forced into a war and that the four other Powers should declare what line they would each take in case of the occurrence of any of the events which they conceived would force them to war'. Wellington to Canning, 21 September 1822, Paris, in Wellington, *Despatches*, vol. i, p. 292. For parts of the instructions, see Chateaubriand, *The Congress of Verona*, vol. i, pp. 111–13, and Alfred Nettement, *Histoire de la Restauration* (Paris & Lyon: Michel Lévy frères, 1868), vol. vi, pp. 231–34. See also, Jean Baptiste Villèle, *Mémoires et correspondance*, vols 1–5 (Paris: Hachette, 1887–90), vol. iii, pp. 33–34; Bertier de Sauvigny, *Metternich et la France*, vol. ii, pp. 615–17, 630; Schroeder, *Metternich's Diplomacy*, p. 210; Nichols, *Congress of Verona*, pp. 72–74.
57. Villèle to Montmorency, 15 October 1822, Villèle, *Mémoires*, vol. iii, p. 119.
58. Bertier de Sauvigny, *Metternich et la France*, vol. ii, pp. 596; Schroeder, *Metternich's Diplomacy*, p. 206.
59. Boislecomte, 'Résumé historique', Archives des Affaires Étrangères (La Courneuve), hereafter A.A.E., Mémoires et Documents, vol. 722, ff. 3, 55–57.
60. Nichols, *Congress of Verona*, pp. 42, 66–67; Schroeder, *Metternich's Diplomacy*, p. 208.
61. 'Le congrès de Vérone est le plus grand de tous ceux qui ayant en lieu depuis 1814', Metternich to Countess Lieven, 22 October 1822, in Bertier de Sauvigny, *Metternich et la France*, vol. ii, p. 632. See also, Boislecomte, 'Résumé historique', A.A.E., Mémoires et Documents, vol. 722, ff. 146–49; Schroeder, *Metternich's Diplomacy*, pp. 211–12; Nichols, *Congress of Verona*, pp. 75–80.
62. Boislecomte kept careful track of the sizes of the delegations, listing 15 delegates for Russia, 21 for Austria, and 29 for Prussia. See Boislecomte, 'Résumé historique', A.A.E., Mémoires et Documents, vol. 722, ff. 45–48. Bertier de Sauvigny calculates that France had one government minister, six ambassadors or ministers, and 26 secretaries or staff members: see Bertier de Sauvigny, *Metternich et la France*, vol. ii, p. 631.
63. Memorandum by Lord Londonderry, No. 1 (Lord Stewart), 29 October 1822, enclosed in Londonderry to Wellington, 31 October 1822, Verona, in Wellington,

Despatches, vol. i , pp. 475–77; Chateaubriand, *Congress of Verona*, vol. i, p. 123 ('We were indebted ... to M. de Villèle, who wished to have a friend at Verona'). It seems that Villèle had originally intended for Montmorency to attend just the conference in Vienna, as Castlereagh was planning to do, and for Chateaubriand to represent France at the later sessions in Verona on Italian matters. See Bertier de Sauvigny, *Bourbon Restoration*, pp. 187–88. Montmorency was sent to Vienna not Verona, so Chateaubriand actually reached Verona on 14 October, two days before him.

64. Chateaubriand, *Congress of Verona*, vol. i, pp. 107–10.
65. Egon Corti, *The Rise of the House of Rothschild* (London: Victor Gollancz, 1928) pp. 278–85; Nichols, *Congress of Verona*, p. 130; Ferguson, *House of Rothschild*, pp. 130, 158; Gentz, *Tagebücher*, vol. iii, pp. 114–15 (entries for 26, 28 and 30 November 1822).
66. Otto Wolff, *Ouvrard: Speculator of Genius*, trans. Stewart Thompson (London: Barrie and Rockliff, 1962), pp. 153–54.
67. For the Greek plenipotentiaries, see Prokesch-Osten, *Geschichte des Abfalls der Griechen*, vol. iii, pp. 447–50.
68. Chateaubriand, *Congress of Verona*, vol. i, p. 73.
69. Boislecomte, 'Résumé historique du Congrès' in A.A.E., Mémoires et Documents, vol. 722, ff. 2. For the significance of Boislecomte's *résumé*, see Bertier de Sauvigny, *Metternich et la France*, vol. ii, p. 614, n. 19, 'the great interest of this document is the fact that Boislecomte wrote each day, sometimes under the dictation of his patron La Ferrronnays'; see also, Nichols, *Congress of Verona*, p. 279. Other important sources are Wellington's letters to Canning, Montmorency's reports to Villèle, Chateaubriand's *Congress of Verona*, Gentz's diary, and the reports in the Austrian archives used by Schroeder, Nichols and Bertier de Sauvigny. The Prussian perspective is provided by Treitschke and by Ulrike Schmieder, *Preussen und der Kogress von Verona—eine Studie zur Politik der Heiligen Allianz in der spanische Frage* (Frankfurt: Egelsbach, 1992), translated into Spanish as *Prusia y el Congreso de Verona* (Madrid: Ediciones del Orto, 1998).
70. Boislecomte, 'Résumé historique', A.A.E., Mémoires et Documents, vol. 722, f. 70.
71. Chateaubriand, *Congress of Verona*, vol. i, p. 83.
72. Boislecomte, 'Résumé historique', A.A.E., Mémoires et Documents, vol. 722, ff. 70–71.
73. Boislecomte, 'Résumé historique', A.A.E., Mémoires et Documents, vol. 722, ff. 71–72. The victor of Waterloo assured the French delegates that their government had acted sagaciously in establishing a *cordon sanitaire* between Spain and France but otherwise warned them against taking further military action.
74. Through this means, Metternich was temporarily able to exclude Pozzo di Borgo, Chateaubriand and La Ferronnays from the discussions.
75. Boislecomte, 'Résumé historique', A.A.E., Mémoires et Documents, vol. 722, ff. 72–73; see also, Chateaubriand, *Congress of Verona*, vol. i, pp. 114–19; Nichols, *Congress of Verona*, pp. 43, 46–47, 85–86.

76. Bertier de Sauvigny, *Metternich et la France*, vol. ii, p. 633.
77. Boislecomte, 'Résumé historique', A.A.E., Mémoires et Documents, vol. 722, ff. 72–73.
78. For the famous three questions, see Boislecomte, 'Résumé historique', A.A.E., Mémoires et Documents, vol. 722, ff. 73; 'Precis des Communications verbales faites par M. le Vicomte de Montmorency ... à Vérone, le 20me Octobre 1822', in Wellington, *Despatches*, vol. i, pp. 403–04; Chateaubriand, *Congress of Verona*, vol. i, pp. 118–19; Bertier de Sauvigny, *Metternich et la France*, vol. ii, p. 633; Nichols, *Congress of Verona*, pp. 84–88; Temperley, *Foreign Policy of Canning*, pp. 65–67; Trietschke, *History of Germany*, vol. iv, pp. 26. Schroeder dismisses the three questions as a case of inept diplomacy: see *Metternich's Diplomacy*, pp. 212–13.
79. Boislecomte, 'Résumé historique', A.A.E., Mémoires et Documents, vol. 722, f. 74. Montmorency emphasized that the French did not desire war but were not afraid of it. According to Boislecomte, the three questions were not intended as a 'demand' but rather as a 'request' for assistance. See also, Nichols, *Congress of Verona*, p. 86.
80. Montmorency to Villèle, 11 November 1822, Verona, in Villèle, *Mémoires*, vol. iii, p. 199. Metternich later explained to Londonderry (formerly Lord Stewart) that his purpose was simply to have France commit herself, whether for or against intervention.
81. Boislecomte, 'Résumé historique', A.A.E., Mémoires et Documents, vol. 722, ff. 74–75. A copy of the appeal from Urgel can be found in Wellington, *Despatches*, vol. i, pp. 507–08.
82. Wellington to Canning, 29 October 1822, Verona, in Wellington, *Despatches*, vol. i, pp. 457–60: 'The Emperor of Russia, immediately upon the receipt of the French paper, declared himself ready to consent to all the demands of the French ministers, and to conclude a treaty with them, stipulating for the succours which he should give; and he declared his intention of marching an army of 150,000 men through Germany, which he should post in Piedmont, in readiness to fall either upon France, if the Jacobin party in France should take advantage of the absence of the army, or of its possible disaster in Spain, if the French government should require its assistance'. See also, Boislecomte, 'Résumé historique', A.A.E., Mémoires et Documents, vol. 722, f. 75–76; Bertier de Sauvigny, *Metternich et la France*, vol. ii, pp. 634–35; Nichols, *Congress of Verona*, p. 94. Presumably, the Russian troops would still have crossed France to reach Spain, although from Piedmont-Sardinia they could also have been transported by water.
83. Boislecomte, 'Résumé historique', A.A.E., Mémoires et Documents, vol. 722, ff. 75–76. Schroeder, *Metternich's Diplomacy*, p. 213, argues that Montmorency's three questions revived the Russian proposal, but they seem rather to have limited its scope.
84. Boislecomte, 'Résumé historique', A.A.E., Mémoires et Documents, vol. 722, f. 77: 'Ce n'est que par un frottement continu que les aspirités et les resistances [?s'usent] et s'adoucissent et il faut laisser les temps de limiter la volonté de la

Russe qui veut tout precipiter, et celles de l'Angleterre que ne veut rien faire.' See also Montmorency to Villèle, 28 October 1822, in Villèle, *Mémoires*, vol. iii, p. 159, on the need to 'concilier les ardeurs guerrières' of the Tsar with 'le système restrictif d'immobilité' of the English; Bertier de Sauvigny, *Metternich et la France*, vol. ii, pp. 634; Nichols, *Congress of Verona*, p. 89.

85. Boislecomte, 'Résumé historique', A.A.E., Mémoires et Documents, vol. 722, ff. 75–77. Boislecomte placed this section of his summary below this revealing rubric: 'It is established that France should act in the second line and as agent of the Alliance.'
86. Boislecomte, 'Résumé historique', A.A.E., Mémoires et Documents, vol. 722, ff. 79–80. Bertier de Sauvigny believes this dispatch, from Brunetti, arrived on the 21 or 22 October. See Bertier de Sauvigny, *Metternich et la France*, vol. ii, pp. 635–36; see also Nichols, *Congress of Verona*, p. 90.
87. Boislecomte, 'Résumé historique', A.A.E., Mémoires et Documents, vol. 722, ff. 81–82. Believing that he might have overstepped his authority, Wellington later claimed he had not actually offered Britain's good offices, but had merely invited the French to request them. Boislecomte, however, interpreted his offer the other way. Canning would later instruct Wellington to offer Britain's 'good offices' while in Paris on his way home.
88. Londonderry, Memorandum No. 1, 29 October 1822, Verona, in Wellington, *Despatches*, vol. i, pp. 475–77. According to Metternich, the Tsar assumed that the French intended to seize the initiative by attacking the Spanish revolutionaries with allied help, and only later realized that the cautious French government was merely willing to wage a war of defence.
89. Boislecomte, 'Résumé historique', A.A.E., Mémoires et Documents, vol. 722, ff. 78–79. The quotations in this section are attributed to the Tsar by Boislecomte, based upon his discussions with Montmorency. See also Nichols, *Congress of Verona*, p. 91.
90. Boislecomte, 'Résumé historique', A.A.E., Mémoires et Documents, vol. 722, ff. 78–79; Nichols, *Congress of Verona*, p. 91.
91. Montmorency, 'Conversation avec l'Empereur Alexandre, du 24 October' in Villèle, *Mémoires*, vol. iii, pp. 147–53; Boislecomte, 'Résumé historique', A.A.E., Mémoires et Documents, vol. 722, f. 78; Nichols, *Congress of Verona*, p. 91; Wellington to Canning, 29 October 1822, in Wellington, *Despatches*, vol. i, p. 457; Bertier de Sauvigny, *Metternich et la France*, vol. ii, pp. 634–35. The Tsar's pledge raised a further issue: was it restricted to the sending of troops into Spain or did it also extend to the movement of Russian troops in the direction of Spain (and therefore towards France)? Two days later, Montmorency requested clarification from Nesselrode on this vital point. See Montmorency to Villèle, 'commenced 28 October', Verona, in Villèle, *Mémoires*, vol. iii, pp. 158–68. When Pozzo di Borgo visited the French delegation on 29 October, he apparently brought Russian reassurances on this question.
92. Boislecomte, 'Résumé historique', A.A.E., Mémoires et Documents, vol. 722, ff. 83–84; Nichols, *Congress of Verona*, p. 91.

93. Boislecomte, 'Résumé historique', A.A.E., Mémoires et Documents, vol. 722, f. 83: 'il n'entera pas en France un seul soldat étranger sans la demande de votre gouvernement'.
94. Montmorency to Villèle, 29 October 1822, in Villèle, *Mémoires*, vol. iii, pp. 162 (Pozzo came to him on behalf of the Emperor 'pour commencer l'explication que m'était annoncée'); Wellington to Canning, 29 October 1822, in Wellington, *Despatches*, vol. i, p. 460 ('I have learnt that the Emperor of Russia had this morning sent General Pozzo di Borgo to Monsieur de Montmorency to talk to him on his plan for moving a body of troops into Piedmont; and that Monsieur de Montmorency had declared in positive terms that it would be highly injurious to France, not only that any troops should be moved in consequence of what should pass here, but that any orders should be given for the formation of an army with a view to its being moved forward hereafter'); Londonderry, Memorandum No. 3, 3 November 1822, Verona, in Wellington, *Despatches*, vol. i, pp. 486–89: 'The Emperor of Russia, by Prince Metternich's management, was evidently reduced from the idea of an immediate march of troops, to the consideration of an "*appui moral et matériel*" if it became necessary. With this point gained, Prince Metternich goes into conference, having exacted a promise from the French to decline all Russian force, except on their own requisition, and this declaration, Pozzo di Borgo was the messenger of, from M. de Montmorency to the Emperor Alexander'; Bertier de Sauvigny, *Metternich et la France*, vol. ii, pp. 634–35.
95. Alexander personally confirmed the pledge previously brought by Pozzo di Borgo. See Bertier de Sauvigny, *Metternich et la France*, vol. ii, p. 637.
96. Montmorency to Villèle, 9 November 1822, Verona, in Villèle, *Mémoires*, vol. iii, pp. 196: 'qu'il ne songerait jamais à passer par la France, que d'après notre désir et notre requisition formelle'.
97. Villèle to Montmorency, 6 November 1822, Paris, in Villèle, *Mémoires*, vol. iii, p. 182.
98. Schroeder, *Metternich's Diplomacy*, pp. 214–15, especially fn. 64.
99. Boislecomte, 'Résumé historique', A.A.E., Mémoires et Documents, vol. 722, ff. 119–20.
100. For example, even at Verona Metternich was still claiming to Wellington that the source of the unrest in Italy was actually to be found in Paris: 'Une conspiration s'est formée en 1821 pour le renversement des droits de souveraineté de l'Empereur sur ses païs en deça des Alpes ... l'une et l'autre ont reçu leur impulsion et leur direction du foyer révolutionnaire à Paris'. Metternich to Wellington, November 1822, Verona, in Wellington, *Despatches*, vol. i, p. 478. Back in February of 1821, the Tsar had expressed similar concerns to La Ferronnays: see La Ferronnays to Pasquier, 20 February 1821, 'Confidentielle', Laybach, in A.A.E., Mémoires et Documents, vol. 719: 'L'inquiétude que le Gouvernement a paru concevoir des dispositions de l'Espagne a été représentée à l'Empereur comme une preuve de notre faibless, ou même comme un secrete disposition a soutenir plutôt qu'à combattre l'ordre de choses qui s'y trouve établi.'

101. Bertier de Sauvigny, *Metternich et la France*, vol. ii, p. 637.
102. Boislecomte, 'Résumé historique', A.A.E., Mémoires et Documents, vol. 722, f. 89.
103. 'Memorandum by Lord Londonderry', No. 1, 29 October 1822, in Wellington, *Despatches*, vol. i, p. 476.
104. Wellington to Canning, 5 November 1822, Verona, in Wellington, *Despatches*, vol. i, p. 494.
105. Wellington to Canning, 19 November 1822, in Wellington, *Despatches*, vol. i, pp. 555–56: 'His Majesty went away as much impressed as ever with the necessity of interference in Spain, and the determination to press the interference upon France. When I pressed upon him the probable result of a successful operation against the Spanish revolution—viz., an occupation of Spain by French troops—he answered that it ought not to be done by French troops; and that, if such an occupation were necessary at all, it ought to be by an army composed of troops belonging to all the Allies.'
106. Wellington to Canning, 27 November 1822, in Wellington, *Despatches*, vol. i, pp. 613–14; Nichols, *Congress of Verona*, p. 124.
107. Villèle to Montmorency, 12 October 1822, Paris, in Villèle, *Mémoires*, vol. iii, pp. 113–16.
108. Schroeder, *Metternich's Diplomacy*, p. 218.
109. Canning to A'Court, 29 December 1822, in Augustus Granville Stapleton, *George Canning and his Times* (London: J.W. Parker, 1859), p. 389; Yamada, 'George Canning', p. 352.
110. Montmorency to Villèle, 'commencé le 28 Octobre' [1822], Verona, in Villèle, *Mémoires*, vol. iii, pp. 158–66; Bertier de Sauvigny, *Metternich et la France*, vol. ii, p. 638. Villèle had explicitly instructed Montmorency to avoid specifying in writing which conditions would lead France to withdraw her ambassador or to send in troops: see Villèle to Montmorency, 15 October 1822, Paris, in Villèle, *Mémoires*, vol. iii, p. 121. Thus far, Montmorency had obeyed Villèle's command by steering clear of precise commitments.
111. Londonderry, 'Memorandum No. 1', 29 October 1822, Verona, in Wellington, *Despatches*, vol. i, pp. 475–77 (Metternich 'now saw daylight in his operations').
112. Boislecomte, 'Résumé historique', A.A.E., Mémoires et Documents, vol. 722, f. 85; Villèle to Montmorency, 'commencé le 28 Octobre', in Villèle, *Mémoires*, vol. iii, pp. 158, 164–66; Bertier de Sauvigny, *Metternich et la France*, vol. ii, p. 638; Nichols, *Congress of Verona*, pp. 92–93.
113. Boislecomte, 'Résumé historique', A.A.E., Mémoires et Documents, vol. 722, ff. 84–88. Boislecomte wrote that France was 'drawn outside of her position' by agreeing to discuss the proposal, and Nichols viewed this as 'another piece of diplomatic strategy' and as a Metternichian 'maneuver'. The historian Bertier de Sauvigny, however, saw the proposal as having some worth: before providing France with a pledge of support, the other powers needed to know under what conditions she would go to war, and what steps might be taken to prevent it.

114. Boislecomte suspected that Metternich had manufactured this new task because he feared Montmorency intended to leave for Paris as soon as the answers to his three questions were received. Instead, Montmorency was now drawn into a more protracted discussion. See Boislecomte, 'Résumé historique', A.A.E., Mémoires et Documents, vol. 722, ff. 83–84.
115. Prussian aid was contingent on what her own internal situation would allow at the time and Austria would require further agreement among all the allies to furnish assistance, an impossibility. See Wellington, 'Minute of Conference of 30th October', in Wellington, *Despatches*, pp. 503–05, and for the allied responses, Wellington, *Despatches*, pp. 496–99. See also, Boislecomte, 'Résumé historique', A.A.E., Mémoires et Documents, vol. 722 ff. 90–96, summarizing the four allied responses officially submitted at the session of 31 October; Bertier de Sauvigny, *Metternich et la France*, vol. ii, pp. 639–40; Nichols, *Congress of Verona*, p. 94; Schroeder, *Metternich's Diplomacy*, p. 218.
116. Bertier de Sauvigny, *Metternich et la France*, vol. ii, pp. 639–40.
117. Wellington, 'Memoir on the Observation of the French Minister respecting Spain', 30 October 1822, Verona, in Wellington, *Despatches*, vol. i, pp. 499–501; Boislecomte, 'Résumé historique', A.A.E., Mémoires et Documents, vol. 722, ff. 92–95. Gentz had translated this phrase into French as 'prématurée, injuste et probablement inutile'. Boislecomte was delighted to hear Wellington mention the obligations incurred at Aix-la-Chapelle, which he believed the British had never recognized. See also, Bertier de Sauvigny, *Metternich et la France*, vol. ii, pp. 638–60; Nichols, *Congress of Verona*, pp. 94–97; Green, 'Wellington and the Congress of Verona, 1822'.
118. The English historian Temperley famously called this 'Wellington's bombshell'. See Temperley, *Foreign Policy of Canning*, pp. 67–68. Metternich had tried to soften the blow in private conversations with Wellington before the official disclosure of the allied responses.
119. Gentz, *Tagebücher*, vol. iii, p. 103, entry for 31 October 1822: 'Zweistündiges Gespräch, worin er mir sein ganzes, höchst unerbauliches System über die spanische Sache mittheilt'.
120. Treitschke makes this point in his *History of Germany*, vol. iv, p. 26–27. The Russian memorandum began: 'Dès le mois d'Avril de l'année 1820, la Russie avait signalé les consequences du triomphe de la révolution en Espagne' ['Since the month of April 1820, Russia has pointed out the consequences of the triumph of the Spanish revolution'], and Wellington similarly opened his response: 'Since the month of April 1820, the British government have availed themselves of every opportunity of recommending to his Majesty's Allies to abstain from all interference in the internal affairs of Spain.' See Wellington, *Despatches*, vol. i, pp. 496–97, 499.
121. Bertier de Sauvigny, *Metternich et la France*, vol. ii, p. 640.
122. Wellington to Canning, 5 November 1822, Verona, in Wellington, *Despatches*, vol. i, pp. 492–96; Boislecomte, 'Résumé historique', A.A.E., Mémoires et Documents, vol. 722, f. 97; Montmorency to Villèle, 5 November 1822, Paris, in Villèle,

Mémoires, vol. iii, p. 178–81; Bertier de Sauvigny, *Metternich et la France*, vol. ii, 639–40; Nichols, *Congress of Verona*, pp. 99–100.

123. Boislecomte, 'Résumé historique', A.A.E., Mémoires et Documents, vol. 722, f. 99.
124. The participants were Wellington, Metternich, Lebzeltern, Nesselrode, Pozzo di Borgo, Tatishchev, Lieven, Montmorency, Chateaubriand, La Ferronnays, Caraman, Bernstorff and Hatzfeldt. Gentz was also there. See Boislecomte, 'Résumé historique', A.A.E., Mémoires et Documents, vol. 722, f. 90; Schroeder, *Metternich's Diplomacy*, p. 216; Gentz, *Tagebücher*, vol. iii p. 103, entry for 31 October 1822 ('Um 8 Uhr Konferenz, die erste förmliche, bestehend, inclusive meiner, aus 13 Personen. Um 10 Uhr nach Hause'); Bertier de Sauvigny, *Metternich et la France*, vol. ii, p. 640; Nichols, *Congress of Verona*, p. 97.
125. 'Propositions du Cabinet Autrichien, 31 Octobre 1822', in Wellington, *Despatches*, vol. i, pp. 501–03.
126. Boislecomte, 'Résumé historique', A.A.E., Mémoires et Documents, vol. 722, f. 96; Wellington, Enclosure VII, 31 October 1822, Verona, attached to Wellington to Canning, 5 November 1822, in Wellington, *Despatches*, vol. i, p. 505; Bertier de Sauvigny, *Metternich et la France*, vol. ii, pp. 640–41; Nichols, *Congress of Verona*, pp. 97–98.
127. Boislecomte, 'Résumé historique', A.A.E., Mémoires et Documents, vol. 722, f. 96: Metternich proposed 'trois modes differens: Une déclaration collective ou spéciale. Une déclaration des quatres Puissances parlant au nom de la France. Une declaration que l'Angleterre addresserait au nom de tous les alliés'; Wellington to Canning, 5 November 1822, Verona, and 'Propositions du Cabinet Autrichien, 31 Octobre 1822', in Wellington, *Despatches*, vol. i, pp. 492–93; 501–03; Montmorency to Villèle, 5 November 1822, Verona, in Villèle, *Mémoires*, vol. iii, p. 178–81; Bertier de Sauvigny, *Metternich et la France*, vol. ii, pp. 640–41; Nichols, *Congress of Verona*, pp. 97–98; Schroeder, *Metternich's Diplomacy*, p. 216.
128. Boislecomte, 'Résumé historique', A.A.E., Mémoires et Documents, vol. 722, f. 96; Nichols, *Congress of Verona*, pp. 92–93, 98–99.
129. Wellington, Enclosure VII, 31 October 1822', in Wellington, *Despatches*, vol. i, p. 505; Bertier de Sauvigny, *Metternich et la France*, vol. ii, p. 637.
130. Wellington, 'Minute of Conference of the 1st Instant', 2 November 1822, Verona, in Wellington, *Despatches*, vol. i, pp. 505–07; Montmorency to Villèle, 5 November 1822, in Villèle, *Mémoires*, vol. iii, pp. 178–79; Nichols, *Congress of Verona*, pp. 101–02, Gentz, *Tagebücher*, vol. iii, pp. 103–04 (entry for 1 November): Gentz was not at the meeting, but Nesselrode and Bernstorff came afterwards to see him at midnight.
131. Boislecomte, 'Résumé historique', A.A.E., Mémoires et Documents, vol. 722, ff. 97–98; Nichols, *Congress of Verona*, p. 99–100.
132. Boislecomte, 'Résumé historique', A.A.E., Mémoires et Documents, vol. 722, ff. 97–98.
133. Boislecomte, 'Résumé historique', A.A.E., Mémoires et Documents, vol. 722, f. 98.

134. Boislecomte, 'Résumé historique', A.A.E., Mémoires et Documents, vol. 722, f. 98.
135. Boislecomte, 'Résumé historique', A.A.E., Mémoires et Documents, vol. 722, ff. 99–100, 102; Nichols, *Congress of Verona*, pp. 103–04; Green, 'Wellington and the Congress of Verona, 1822', p. 202. According to Boislecomte, the Russian ministers maintained that since the responses of the four courts had been officially presented and mentioned in the protocol, they should be kept there ('Les ministres Russes disaient au contraire que puis que les réponses du 4 Cours avaient été présentées officiellement et mentionnées au protocole, il fallait qu'elles fussent conservées'); Boislecomte, 'Résumé historique', A.A.E., Mémoires et Documents, vol. 722, f. 100.
136. Londonderry, Memorandum No. 2, 2 November 1822, Verona, in Wellington, *Despatches*, vol. i, p. 485.
137. Boislecomte, 'Résumé historique', A.A.E., Mémoires et Documents, vol. 722, f. 102; Bertier de Sauvigny, *Metternich et la France*, vol. ii, pp. 642–45; Schroeder, *Metternich's Diplomacy*, pp. 217–18; Nichols, *Congress of Verona*, pp. 103–06; Montmorency to Villèle, 5 November 1822, Verona, in Villèle, *Mémoires*, vol. iii, p. 180: Montmorency reported to Villèle that the diplomats were working and exchanging ideas each day.
138. Wellington to Stuart, 12 November 1822, in Wellington, *Despatches*, vol. i, p. 519; Boislecomte, 'Résumé historique', A.A.E., Mémoires et Documents, vol. 722, f. 101; Bertier de Sauvigny, *Metternich et la France*, vol. ii, p. 641; Nichols, *Congress of Verona*, p. 104.
139. Boislecomte, 'Résumé historique', A.A.E., Mémoires et Documents, vol. 722, ff. 101–02.
140. Boislecomte, 'Résumé historique', A.A.E., Mémoires et Documents, vol. 722, f. 102. Almost a century ago, the historian J.E.S. Green contended that Wellington carried a secret instruction to Verona that Britain would stay neutral in the event of a war. Green cited Wellington's speech in Parliament on 24 April 1823, in support of this proposition: see Green, 'Wellington and the Congress of Verona', pp. 203–04. Nichols was of the opinion that Wellington may have conveyed this message, but simply because he seemed to act without discretion; see, Nichols, *Congress of Verona*, pp. 280–81.
141. Londonderry to Canning, in Wellington, *Despatches*, vol. i, pp. 510 and 531; Nichols, *Congress of Verona*, pp. 105–06.
142. Boislecomte, 'Résumé historique', A.A.E., Mémoires et Documents, vol. 722, ff. 107–14.
143. Boislecomte, 'Résumé historique', A.A.E., Mémoires et Documents, vol. 722, ff. 106–07.
144. Boislecomte, 'Résumé historique', A.A.E., Mémoires et Documents, vol. 722, f. 101; Montmorency to Villèle, 'beginning 9 November [1822]', in Villèle, *Mémoires*, vol. iii, pp. 194–98.
145. 'The most convenient means for entering into the cases that cannot be foreseen or defined would be found in a conference established in Paris by the ministers

of the allied courts. This conference would offer the double advantage of facilitating with the cabinets and concerting on measures; even in a case foreseen in advance, the cabinets reserve for themselves the right to adopt a common accord and to give effect to their contingent engagements'. Metternich to Montmorency, 8 November 1822, in Bertier de Sauvigny, *Metternich et la France*, vol. ii, p. 644 (citing Haus-, Hof- und Staatsarchiv, Kongressakten 43); Schroeder, *Metternich's Diplomacy*, pp. 217–18.
146. Boislecomte, 'Résumé historique', A.A.E., Mémoires et Documents, vol. 722, ff. 103–06.
147. Wellington to Canning, 12 November 1822, Verona, in Wellington, *Despatches*, vol. i, pp. 523–29; Boislecomte, 'Résumé historique', A.A.E., Mémoires et Documents, vol. 722, ff. 114–17 for the conference on the 'Eastern Question' and ff. 117–19 for the discussions on Italian affairs.
148. Montmorency to Villèle, 11 and 12 November 1822, in Villèle, *Mémoires*, vol. iii, pp. 198–207; Londonderry to Canning, 8 November 1822, Wellington to Canning, 12 November 1822, and Wellington to Stuart, 12 November 1822, in Wellington, *Despatches*, vol. i, pp. 510–11, 518–23, 531–33; Bertier de Sauvigny, *Metternich et la France*, vol. ii, pp. 642–43; Nichols, *Congress of Verona*, pp. 104–05.
149. Bertier de Sauvigny, *Metternich et la France*, vol. ii, pp. 644–45; Schroeder, *Metternich's Diplomacy*, p. 218. For example, Montmorency wished to include attempts to deny the reigning family their rights to the throne, while Metternich believed this did not need to be listed as a separate *casus foederis* since it would only happen in conjunction with an attack on the King.
150. Boislecomte, 'Résumé historique', A.A.E., Mémoires et Documents, vol. 722, ff. 122, 130–33; Bertier de Sauvigny, *Metternich et la France*, vol. ii, pp. 644–46; Nichols, *Congress of Verona*, pp. 113–14; Schroeder, *Metternich's Diplomacy*, p. 218.
151. Wellington to Canning, 19 November 1822, Verona, in Wellington, *Despatches*, vol. i, pp. 555–59; Gentz, *Tagebücher*, vol. iii, pp. 105–01 (daily entries from 4 to 17 November 1822); Bertier de Sauvigny, *Metternich et la France*, vol. ii, pp. 646; Schroeder, *Metternich's Diplomacy*, p. 219, citing Gentz, 'Précis des Conférences du 18, 19 et 20 Novembre' and 'Spanische Frage', in the Austrian state archives (Haus-, Hof- und Staatsarchiv). Boislecomte noted that Gentz's 'Précis' was written for possible public use and may therefore not have been totally reliable. For the instructions themselves, see Chateaubriand, *Congress of Verona*, vol. i, pp. 139–49; Wellington, *Despatches*, vol. i, pp. 562–71; Boislecomte, 'Résumé historique', A.A.E., Mémoires et Documents, vol. 722, ff. 123–31; Nettement, *Restauration*, vol. vi, pp. 292–95.
152. Boislecomte, 'Résumé historique', A.A.E., Mémoires et Documents, vol. 722, ff. 131–37; Gentz, *Tagebücher*, vol. iii, p. 111 (entries for 19 and 20 November); Nichols, *Congress of Verona*, pp. 114–19; Bertier de Sauvigny, *Metternich et la France*, vol. ii, pp. 646–48, and 661 for a copy of the *procès-verbal* of 19 November 1822; Schroeder, *Metternich's Diplomacy*, pp. 218–20; Nettement, *Restauration*, vol. vi, pp. 295–97.

153. Wellington to Canning, 22 November 1822, Verona, in Wellington, *Despatches*, vol. i, pp. 562–69, especially p. 565; Schroeder, *Metternich's Diplomacy*, p. 219.
154. Boislecomte, 'Résumé historique', A.A.E., Mémoires et Documents, vol. 722, ff. 131–34; Nettement, *Restauration*, vol. vi, pp. 295–97. For a copy of the *procès-verbal*, see Metternich: *Memoirs of Prince Metternich*, vol. iii, pp. 651–53, and Bertier de Sauvigny, *Metternich et la France*, vol. ii, p. 661.
155. Nichols, *Congress of Verona*, pp. 115–17. According to Chateaubriand, the English plenipotentiary acted as though he were still commanding at Waterloo.
156. Schroeder, *Metternich's Diplomacy*, pp. 220–21.
157. Prokesch-Osten, *Geschichte des Abfalls der Griechen*, vol. iii, pp. 427–47; Boislecomte, 'Résumé historique', A.A.E., Mémoires et Documents, vol. 722, ff. 57–64, 114–17; Nichols, *Congress of Verona*, pp. 48–54, 24–58; Schroeder, *Metternich's Diplomacy*, pp. 223–24; Cunningham, *Anglo-American Encounters*, pp. 220–22.
158. Nichols, *Congress of Verona*, pp. 54–59, 191–217; Bertier de Sauvigny, *Metternich et la France*, vol. ii, pp. 653–60; Schroeder, *Metternich's Diplomacy*, pp. 225–28; Reinerman, *Austria and the Papacy*, vol. i, pp. 100–08.
159. Nichols, *Congress of Verona*, pp. 161–90.
160. Nichols, *Congress of Verona*, pp. 137–60; Chateaubriand, *Congress of Verona*, vol. i, pp. 100–02.
161. For a copy of the circular, see Metternich, *Memoirs of Prince Metternich*, vol. iii, pp. 655–62; see also, Nichols, *Congress of Verona*, p. 265.
162. Villèle to Chateaubriand, 28 November 1822, Paris, in Chateaubriand, *Congress of Verona*, vol. i, pp. 164–65.
163. Yamada, 'George Canning', pp. 353–54; Temperley, *Foreign Policy of Canning*, pp. 68–69; Bertier de Sauvigny, *Metternich et la France*, vol. ii, pp. 682–84.
164. Temperley, *Foreign Policy of Canning*, pp. 69–71; Bertier de Sauvigny, *The Bourbon Restoration*, pp. 189–90, and *Metternich et la France*, vol. ii, pp. 669–76, 681–82, 684–95; Waresquiel and Yvert, *Histoire de la Restauration, 1814–1830*, pp. 350–51; Nichols, *Congress of Verona*, pp. 302–07; Yamada, 'Canning', pp. 355–56. Villèle enjoyed the support of Louis' favourite, Madame de Cayla.
165. Chateaubriand, *Congress of Verona*, vol. i, p. 108: 'The idea of liberty in the minds of French people, who do not very well understand what liberty means, will never be equivalent to the idea of glory, which is their natural idea.'
166. Chateaubriand to Villèle, 31 October 1822, Verona, in Chateaubriand, *Congress of Verona*, vol. i, pp. 154–55; Guillaume de Bertier de Sauvigny, *Congrès de Verone* (Paris and Geneva: H. Champion, 1979), p. 73.
167. Bertier de Sauvigny, *The Bourbon Restoration*, pp. 189–90; Waresquiel and Yvert, *Histoire de la Restauration, 1814–1830*, pp. 351–55; Nichols, *Congress of Verona*, pp. 310–12; Speech of Louis XVIII in Great Britain, Foreign Office, *British and Foreign State Papers*, vol. x, 1822–1823 (1828), pp. 758–59.
168. Temperley, *Foreign Policy of Canning*, pp. 77–81.

169. Yamada, 'Canning', pp. 356, 358–59.
170. Temperley, *Foreign Policy of Canning*, pp. 83–86.
171. Temperley, *Foreign Policy of Canning*, pp. 86–88, 309; Cunningham, *Anglo-Ottoman Encounters*, pp. 257–58, 263–64.
172. Carr, *Spain*, pp. 141–43, 146–48; Esdaile, *Spain in the Liberal Age*, pp. 60–61; William Walton, *The Revolutions in Spain, from 1808 to the End of 1836*, vol. i (London: Richard Bentley, 1837), pp. 286–329; Josep Fontana, *De en Medio del Tiempo: La Segunda Restauración Española, 1823–1834* (Barcelona: Crítica, 2006), pp. 37–65; Jean-Philippe Luis, *L'utopie réactionnaire*, pp. 53–59; Gil Novales, *Trienio Liberal*, pp. 57–59; Wolff, *Ouvrard*, pp. 151–82; Temperley, *Foreign Policy of Canning*, pp. 86, 93, 96–97; Bertier de Sauvigny, *Metternich et la France*, vol. ii, pp. 743–46, 776–80; Stites, *Four Horsemen*, pp. 102–110.
173. Temperley, *Foreign Policy of Canning*, pp. 86, 93–98; Fontana, *De en Medio del Tiempo*, pp. 67–99, 125–40.
174. 'Protocols of Conferences of Representatives of the Allied Powers respecting Spanish America, 1824–1825', *American Historical Review* 22/3 (April 1917), p. 595; Temperley, *Foreign Policy of Canning*, p. 133.
175. Temperley, *Foreign Policy of Canning*, pp. 131–56; Cresson, *Holy Alliance*, pp. 113–26.
176. 'Protocols of Conferences on Spanish America, 1824–1825', pp. 595–616.
177. Temperley, *Foreign Policy of Canning*, pp. 133–54, 379–81; Cresson, *Holy Alliance*, pp. 113–26.
178. 'Over the Spanish question England had broken away altogether; France, though reluctantly concurring at the congress, revoked her assent immediately afterwards. To Metternich, this breach was very fatal to the Congress system; Its essence was that Europe should present an entirely united front to cow the revolutionaries in all parts of Europe, and the scene had been carefully staged at Verona for that purpose ... It was truly the last muster, the last splendid pageant of those forces which had ruled the world since 1815.' Temperley, *Foreign Policy of Canning*, p. 73.
179. Canning to Sir Charles Bagot, 3 January 1823, Foreign Office, in Bagot, *Canning and His Friends*, vol. ii, pp. 152–53.
180. Nichols, *Congress of Verona*, p. 320.
181. Nichols, *Congress of Verona*, p. 320.
182. 'It is impossible to tell the precise moment', wrote historian Maurice Bourquin, 'when the Holy Alliance reached its end.' Bourquin, *Histoire de la Sainte Alliance*, p. 457.
183. Soldiers were instructed to help in farming to make the army self-supporting; peasants were given property and provided with health care and schools, but they were also ordered to wear uniforms as they worked in the fields, conduct military exercises, and saw their lives increasingly regulated. See generally, Hartley, *Russia, 1762–1825*, pp. 190–208; Michael Jennings, *Arakcheev: Grand Vizier of the Russian Empire, 1769–1834* (New York: Dial Press, 1969), pp. 141–47, 183–98); Rey, *Alexandre I*, pp. 414–18; see also the reports of the Comte

de Wallmoden, Vienna, 28 October 1816, and Major Clam-Martiniz, July 1818, St Petersburg, in Mikhaïlovich, *Les Rapports Diplomatiques de Lebzeltern*, pp. 6–7, 54–56 An uprising of 28,000 peasants in one of the military colonies in June 1819 was put down with great brutality—275 men were forced to face 12,000 blows by running the gauntlet; 160 of them died; see Jennings, *Arakcheev*, pp. 194–95; Hartley, *Russia*, p. 207; Rey, *Alexandre I*, p. 418.

184. Temperley, *Foreign Policy of Canning*, pp. 326–27; Cunningham, *Anglo-Ottoman Encounters*, pp. 257–62.
185. Cunningham, *Anglo-Ottoman Encounters*, pp. 245–56; Temperley, *Foreign Policy of Canning*, 327–29.
186. Temperley, *Foreign Policy of Canning*, pp. 329–31; Bitis, *Russia and the Eastern Question*, p. 163.
187. Temperley, *Foreign Policy of Canning*, pp. 329–34.
188. Temperley, *Foreign Policy of Canning*, p. 335.
189. Temperley, *Foreign Policy of Canning*, p. 332.
190. Anderson, *Eastern Question*, p. 64; Temperley, *Foreign Policy of Canning*, pp. 338–39.
191. Anderson, *Eastern Question*, pp. 62–63; Temperley, *Foreign Policy of Canning*, pp. 336–51; Cunningham, *Anglo-American Encounters*, pp. 265–70; Woodhouse, *Capodistria*, pp. 318–29; Charmley, *The Princess and the Politicians*, pp. 108–31.
192. Anderson, *Eastern Question*, pp. 64–77; Temperley, *Foreign Policy of Canning*, pp. 390–409; Cunningham, *Anglo-American Encounters*, pp. 265–70; Charmley, *Princess and Politicians*, pp. 131–54; Prousis, *Russian Society and the Greek Revolution*, 52–54; Woodhouse, *Capodistria*, pp. 330–50, and for his assassination in 1831, pp. 488–507.
193. Sir Charles Webster, *The Foreign Policy of Palmerston, 1830–1841* (London: G. Bell, 1951), vol. i, p. 93.
194. Wellington, 'Memorandum upon the existing state of our relations with France, founded upon the Treaties of 1815–18', 14 August 1830, in Wellington, *Dispatches*, vol. vii, p. 162; Sir Charles Webster, 'Palmerston, Metternich and the European System 1830–41', in *The Art and Practice of Diplomacy* (New York: Barnes and Noble, 1962), pp. 155–56.
195. Emperor Francis to Metternich, Baden, 9 August 1830 in Metternich, *Memoirs of Prince Metternich*, p. 20.
196. Metternich, 6 August 1830, in Metternich, *Memoirs of Prince Metternich*, p. 19, fn. (unnumbered).
197. Although the apostle of legitimacy in 1814, Talleyrand wrote to Sebastiani, the French foreign minister, in 1831 that 'The King [Louis Philippe] knows that I am the partisan of no dynasty. Since the days of Louis XVI, I have served all governments out of my attachment to my country. I have abandoned them the moment they sacrificed the interests of France to personal interests'.
198. Hinsley, *Power and the Pursuit of Peace*, p. 215.
199. Sked, *Radetzky*, pp. 133–58.

8. The Legacy of the Congress System: Success or Failure?

1. The Tsar's view of the Congress System is greatly complicated by the fact that, having grown up under the contradictory directives of his father and grandmother, there appear to have been at least six 'Alexanders': (1) the Enlightened, reforming Tsar; (2) the son of Paul I, who loved military discipline and parades and who aspired to be a great general; (3) the religious and mystical Tsar, who admired Madame de Krüdener and sent long confessions to Golitsyn; (4) the internationalist Tsar, who employed Czartoryski and later Capodistrias and Stourdza; (5) the counter-revolutionary Tsar, who seems to have succumbed to Metternich and who sought international cooperation to defeat the 'Revolution' and the 'directing committee' in Paris; and (6) the Tsar who was the lifetime friend of Arakcheev, who ultimately rejected all attempts to curtail his own autocratic power and who planned the military colonies. Metternich perceived that these different faces of the Tsar were not simultaneous but a progression, and gave this characterization of the Tsar's swings in attitude in 1829: 'His judgment was always influenced by fanciful ideas ... Prolonged study of the Tsar's moral qualities and his political conduct led me to the discovery of what I have described ... as the periodicity of his mind. Each cycle covered a period of about five years ... The Emperor seized an idea and followed it out quickly. It took about two years to germinate in his mind so that it gradually acquired for him the value of a system. During the third year, he remained faithful to the system he had adopted, grew fond of it, listened with real fervour to its promoters. He was incapable of assessing its value or the dire consequences that might ensue from it. Some time in the fourth year, the sight of those consequences began to calm down his fervour; the fifth year showed an unseemly mixture of the old and nearly extinct system with the new idea. This new idea was often diametrically opposed to the one he just left.' Metternich, *Memoirs of Prince Metternich*, vol. i, pp. 315, 318–19; Bertier de Sauvigny, *Metternich and His Times*, pp. 237–39.
2. Sked, *Metternich and Austria*, p. 3.
3. Bertier de Sauvigny, *Metternich and His Times*, p. 24.
4. In his *The Tragedy of Great Power Politics* (New York: W.W. Norton, 2001), pp. 334–59, John Mearsheimer sees Europe in a period of 'balanced multipolarity' (absence of a clear hegemon with both the 'strongest army' and the 'greatest amount of wealth').
5. Robert Jervis, 'Security Regimes', *International Organization* 36/2 (Spring 1982), pp. 360–68, reprinted in Stephen Krasner (ed.), *International Regimes* (Ithaca, NY: Cornell University Press, 1983), pp. 173–94.
6. Jervis, 'Security Regimes', p. 179.
7. Jervis, 'Security Regimes', p. 179. See also, Regina Akopian, 'The Great Powers and the Establishment of Security Regimes. The Formation of the Concert of Europe, 1792–1815' (PhD dissertation, Rutgers University, 2008).
8. Robert Jervis, 'From Balance to Concert: A Study of International Security Cooperation', *World Politics* 38/1 (October 1985), pp. 61–62; and 'A Political

Science Perspective on the Balance of Power and the Concert', *American Historical Review* 97/3 (June 1992), pp. 716–24.
9. Jervis, 'From Balance to Concert', pp. 58–59.
10. Jervis, 'From Balance to Concert', p. 60.
11. Louise Richardson, 'The Concert of Europe and Security Management in the Nineteenth Century', in Helga Haftendorn, Robert O. Keohane and Celeste A. Wallander (eds), *Imperfect Unions: Security Institutions over Time and Space*) (Oxford: Oxford University Press, 1999), pp. 48–79.
12. Richardson, 'The Concert of Europe', pp. 48–77; Paul Gordon Lauren, 'Crisis Prevention in Nineteenth Century Diplomacy', in Alexander L. George (ed.), *Managing US-Soviet Rivalry: Problems of Crisis Prevention* (Boulder and London: Westview Press, 1983), pp. 31–64. See also, Charles Lipson, 'Is the Future of Collective Security Like the Past?', in George Downs (ed.), *Collective Security beyond the Cold War* (Ann Arbor: University of Michigan Press, 1994), pp. 105–32.
13. Charles A. Kupchan, *How Enemies Become Friends: the Sources of Stable Peace* (Princeton, NJ: Princeton University Press, 2010), pp. 188–89. Kupchan identifies a sequence of stages, starting with the 1805 exchange between Pitt and the Tsar and the self-restraint exercised by both Britain and Russia. Then he points out that Britain and Russia 'refrained from constructing a bipolar order, instead elevating the status of Prussia, Austria and France in order to put all of Europe's major states on a more level playing field' (p. 191). The next step was the creation of 'Concert diplomacy' followed by the creation of 'institutionalized restraint' (p. 192). The 'core strategic concept', according to Kupchan, 'was that the five powers would bind themselves to one another sublimating their individual interests to the preservation of group cohesion' (p. 192).
14. Ian Clark, *Hegemony in International Society* (Oxford: Oxford University Press, 2011), pp. 73–97 ('Collective Hegemony: The Concert of Europe, 1815–1914'). On page 74, Clark lists a number of issues that continue to divide international-relations theorists in dealing with the 'concert': whether it existed at all, what were its guiding rules, and whether it contributed to the relative peace of the nineteenth century.
15. Matthias Schulz, 'Das Europäische Konzert der Grossmächte als Sicherheitsrat: Normen und Praxis plurilateraler Friedenssicherung, 1815–1852' (Habilitationsschrift, University of Rostock, 2001), *Normen und Praxis: Das Europäische Konzert der Großmächte als Sicherheitsrat, 1815–1860* (München: R. Oldenbourg, 2009), pp. 537–77, and 'Internationale Politik und Friedenskultur. Das Europäische Konzert in politikwissenschaftlicher Theorie und historische Empirie' in Pyta, *Das europäische Mächtekonzert*, pp. 41–57; Kevin McMillan, 'The Emergence of International Governance: Practices of European Politics, 1700–1848' (PhD dissertation, Columbia University, 2008).
16. Bruce Cronin, *Community under Anarchy: Transnational Identity and the Evolution of Cooperation* (New York: Columbia University Press, 1999), pp. 3–4: 'political elites construct transnational communities by developing common social identities ... My claim is the following: transnational political communities form

when a set of political actors sharing a common social characteristic, a common relationship, a common experience, and a positive interdependence develop a political consciousness that defines them as a unique group'.
17. Dan Lindley, *Promoting Peace with Information: Transparency as a Tool of Security Regimes* (Princeton, NJ: Princeton University Press, 2007): 'Chapter 3. The Concert of Europe: Forum Diplomacy and Crisis Management'—'The Concert of Europe was the first peacetime multilateral crisis management forum. States before the Concert were limited to bilateral diplomacy, and never met together to manage crises. Compared to prior forum diplomatic practice, the chief benefit of meeting together should be the quicker flow of information. A greater flow of information should mean increased transparency—what states know about each other's intentions and capabilities' (p. 54). Compared to the 'opacity' of the eighteenth century, which had 'exacerbated misperceptions' and 'caused miscalculations', Lindley finds that the 'Concert' increased transparency in handling the Polish Question at the Congress of Vienna and the Belgian Question in 1830, and helped clarify deadlock during the revolutions in Spain and Naples in the 1820s.
18. Lindley, *Promoting Peace with Information*, see, for example, p. 84: 'I argue that the Concert was neither a normative transformation of politics nor a phenomenon devoid of institutional benefits. Rather, there was an institutional benefit provided by the Concert: that of transparency'.
19. Robert Keohane, *After Hegemony: Cooperation and Discord in the World Political Economy* (Princeton, NJ: Princeton University Press, 2005), p. xi.
20. Korina Kagan, 'The Myth of the European Concert', *Security Studies* 7/2 (Winter 1997–98), pp. 1–57 (p. 3).
21. Branislav L. Slantchev, 'Territory and Commitment: The Concert of Europe as Self-Enforcing Equilibrium', *Security Studies* 14/4 (October 2005), pp. 565–606. Slantchev correctly notes that 'The Concert worked without an overarching principle, a formal organization to resolve disputes, or a system of collective security to enforce its rules' (p. 566). In this, he sees evidence for his argument that the Congress System was essentially 'self-enforcing' and arose out of the territorial settlement at Vienna. However, it could be argued that the Congress System was equally a reaction to the Hundred Days and that the common fear of revolution led to an unparalleled decree of collaboration, although not to the formation of more permanent institutions. Slantchev also agrees with Jervis that concert systems tend to arise after a war against a hegemon, and in conditions in which short-term alliances are not profitable (p. 576).
22. Rendall, 'Defensive Realism and the Concert of Europe', pp. 523–40.
23. Jervis, 'From Balance to Concert', pp. 61–62.
24. Wellington to Metternich, 24 February 1824, in Wellington, *Despatches*, vol. ii, pp. 221–26.
25. Robert O. Keohane, 'The Diplomacy of Structural Change: Multilateral Institutions and State Strategies', in Helga Haftendorn and Christian Tuschhoff (eds), *America and Europe in an Era of Change* (Boulder, CO: Westview Press 1993), p. 53.

26. Among international relations theorists, Ian Clark thus poses the question, why did the Concert of Europe not 'tip' into a more institutionalized form? See Clark, *Hegemony in International Society*, p. 96.
27. N.A. (Kew), F.O. 7/160, Stewart to Castlereagh, 2 October 1820.
28. For example, Suzanne Werner finds that states that have dissimilar political systems are more likely to engage in war. See Suzanne Werner, 'The Effect of Political Similarity on the Onset of Militarized Disputes, 1816–1985', *Political Science Quarterly* 53/2 (June 2000), pp. 343–74. The 'democratic peace thesis', which argues that democracies do not wage war against one another, is based upon the same assumption. See Michael Doyle, 'Kant, Liberal Legacies, and Foreign Affairs', *Philosophy and Public Affairs* 12/3–4 (Summer–Autumn 1983), pp. 205–35, 323–53: 'Even though liberal states have become involved in numerous wars with nonliberal states, constitutionally secure liberal states have yet to engage in war with one another' (p. 213); Oneal and Russett take a more multivariate approach, arguing that either political similitude or participation in international organizations can make peace more likely: see John R. Oneal and Bruce Russett, 'The Kantian Peace: The Pacific Benefits of Democracy, Interdependence and International Organiziations, 1885–1992', *World Politics* 52/1 (1999), pp. 1–37 and *Triangulating Peace: Democracy, Interdependence and International Organizations* (New York: W.W. Norton, 2001). For example, Oneal and Russett write, in 'Kantian Peace', p. 4: 'Kant was convinced that a genuine, positive peace could be developed within a "federation" of liberal republics that rested more on the three Kantian supports—democracy, interdependence, and international law and organizations—than on power politics.'
29. T.C. Hansard, *Parliamentary Debates*, 11, col. 359.
30. Hinsley, *Power and the Pursuit of Peace*.
31. Cecil, cited in F.S. Northedge, *The League of Nations: Its Life and Times, 1920–1946* (New York: Holmes and Meier, 1986), p. 27.
32. Northedge, *The League of Nations*, p. 29; Charles Howard Ellis, *The Origin, Structure and Working of the League of Nations* (Boston: Houghton Mifflin, 1929), Chapter 5 ('Constitution and Membership of the League').
33. Sir Charles Webster, 'The Making of the Charter', in *The Art and Practice of Diplomacy* (New York: Barnes and Noble, 1962), p. 73.
34. David L. Bosco, *Five to Rule Them All: the UN Security Council and the Making of the Modern World* (Oxford: Oxford University Press, 2009), pp. 14–15.
35. Cadogan, for example, read history at Baillol College, Oxford, before the First World War, at a time when the events of the Napoleonic Wars and subsequent Congresses were intensively studied.
36. Bosco, *Five to Rule Them All*, pp. 14–19; Robert C. Hilderbrand, *Dumbarton Oaks: The Origins of the United Nations and the Search for Postwar Security* (Chapel Hill, NC: University of North Carolina Press, 1990), pp. 5–66. Under the American plan, completed by 14 August 1944, 'Peacekeeping authority was vested in a council composed of the five Great Powers (the United States, Great Britain, the Soviet Union, China and France) and three other nations to be elected for

annual terms; decisions were to be made by two-thirds majority vote including three-fourths of the permanent members'. Hilderbrand, *Dumbarton Oaks*, p. 25.
37. In summarizing the discussions at Dumbarton Oaks, political scientist David Bosco writes the following: 'After the obligatory welcoming festivities and speeches, the delegates sat down to work, and they quickly agreed on the basic architecture of the organization. A council of the leading powers would have sole responsibility for maintaining peace and security. The delegates agreed that they "were entitled to special position[s] on the Council by virtue of their exceptional responsibility for world security." At the suggestion of the Soviets, this council was dubbed the Security Council, and there was no doubt that it was where the power would lie. The draft produced during the conference stated, "Members of the Organization should by the Charter confer on the Security Council primary responsibility for the maintenance of international peace and security." They envisioned two separate roles for the council. When a dispute broke out between states, the council would act to facilitate negotiations and encourage mediation between the feuding parties. The council's advice in this capacity would be nonbinding but, it was hoped, influential. If the council determined that there was a threat to the peace or that an act of aggression had occurred, however, it could quickly assume the role of enforcer of the peace. And, as peace enforcer, the council's powers would be vast ...'. Bosco, *Five to Rule Them All*, pp. 20–21. See also, Hilderbrand, *Dumbarton Oaks*, pp. 122–58; Townsend Hoopes and Douglas Brinkley, *FDR and the Creation of the U.N.* (New Haven: Yale University Press, 2000), pp. 47–51.
38. J.A.S. Grenville, *A History of the World in the Twentieth Century* (Cambridge, MA: Harvard University Press, 1994), p. 554.
39. James J. Sheehan, *Where Have All the Soldiers Gone: The Transformation of Modern Europe* (Boston: Houghton Mifflin, 2008), pp. 161–62, and 172–227.
40. Bruce Broomhall, *International Justice and the International Criminal Court: Between Sovereignty and the Rule of Law* (Oxford: Oxford University, 2004); Benjamin B. Ferencz, 'What of Military Aggression in the 21st Century', *Global Brief* (Fall 2010), pp. 14–16. There remains, as Broomhall observes, a 'gulf' between the existing Westphalian system of state sovereignty and the 'sovereignty-limiting rationale' of the court (p. 2).
41. P.A. Reynolds and E.J. Hughes, *The Historian as Diplomat: Charles Kingsley Webster and the United Nations, 1939–1946* (London: Martin Robinson, 1976); Webster, 'The Making of the Charter of the United Nations', in *The Art and Practice of Diplomacy*.
42. Kissinger, *A World Restored*, p. 31.
43. Kissinger, *A World Restored*, p. 325.
44. In *Kissinger, A Biography* (New York: Simon and Schuster, 1992), Walter Isaacson writes: 'It is the mark of a true European-style conservative that he seeks stability even when it protects a system that is oppressive. Kissinger falls into that category' (p. 60). See also Robert D. Kaplan, 'Kisssinger, Metternich and Realism: Henry Kissinger's First Book (A World Restored)', *The Atlantic Monthly* 283/6 (June 1999), pp. 72–82; Jeremy Suri, *Henry Kissinger and the American Century* (Cambridge, MA: Harvard University Press, 2009), pp.127–28.

45. Webster, *Foreign Policy of Castlereagh, 1812–1815*, p. 372.
46. In *Great Power Coalition: Toward a World Concert of Nations* (New York: Rowman and Littlefield, 2002), political scientist Richard Rosecrance looks back nostalgically on the great power coalition of the nineteenth century, 'which succeeded in keeping the peace', and wonders if that might serve as the model for a future great power coalition of the United States, Japan, the European Union, China and Russia. It would certainly be easy enough for a historian to draw facile comparisons. Is China, with vast resources dwarfing other states but only just emerging as a fully fledged member of the world community, today's equivalent of early nineteenth-century Russia? Is the EU a modern analogue to the Germanic Confederation? Is the United States, as it recedes from a century of cultural, economic and military predominance, comparable to eighteenth-century France or nineteenth-century Britain?
47. Alex Bellamy (ed.), *International Society and Its Critics* (Oxford: Oxford University Press, 2005), p. 32.
48. Ian Bremmer, *The J Curve: A New Way to Understand Why Nations Rise and Fall* (New York: Simon and Schuster, 2006), pp. 5–6. Bremmer asserts that 'for a country that is "stable because it's closed" to become a country that is "stable because it's open," it must go through a transitional period of dangerous instability ... Movement from left to right along the J curve demonstrates that a country that is stable because it is closed must go through a period of dangerous instability as it opens to the outside world ... There are no shortcuts, because authoritarian elites cannot be quickly replaced with institutions whose legitimacy is widely accepted.' In the 1990s, leading development economists created the Human Development Index as a way to rank nations, based not simply on their economic production, but also on the standards of living, health and education care, personal freedom, and equality of opportunity that they provide to their citizens. Bremmer's 'J curve' concept and the Human Development Index together suggest an interesting possibility that goes beyond the scope of the present work. Might there be a way to quantify the degree of security, economic opportunity and well-being, participation in government and personal freedom in nations, both past and present, to draw more meaningful comparisons? Is it too fanciful to imagine constructing a composite index, like the Human Development Index, to permit historians to compare *ancien régime* states, those of the revolutionary and Napoleonic epoch, the restoration states of 1815–30 and those of more recent times? Would it then be easier to evaluate the claims of those historians who contend that Europeans were 'better off' under the *ancien régime* than in revolutionary and Napoleonic times, or under the stable if mildly repressive *régimes* of Metternichian Europe than under Napoleon, or under the *trienio liberal* than under the subsequent repression in Spain under Ferdinand VII ('la ominosa década'), and so on? Could we then better calculate the costs of movement along Bremmer's J curve?
49. Their outlook might be contrasted with that of subsequent reformers, especially those of the 1830s, discussed in T.C.W. Blanning and Peter Wende (eds), *Reform in Great Britain and Germany, 1750–1850* (Oxford: Oxford University Press, 1999) and in the later chapters of Heydemann, *Konstitution gegen Revolution*.

SELECT BIBLIOGRAPHY

Alberti, Annibale (ed.), *Atti del Parlemento delle Due Sicile 1820–1821* (Bologna, 1926–34).
Albrecht-Carrié, René, *The Concert of Europe* (New York: Walker, 1968).
Alison, Archibald, *Lives of Lord Castlereagh and Sir Charles Stewart* (London: J.M. Dent & Sons, 1861).
American Historical Association, 'Protocols of Conferences of Representatives of the Allied Powers respecting Spanish America, 1824–1825', *The American Historical Review* 22/3 (April 1917), pp. 595–616.
Anderson, Matthew, *The Eastern Question, 1774–1923: A Study in International Relations* (London: St Martins' Press, 1966).
Andress, David, *The Terror: The Merciless War for Freedom in Revolutionary France* (New York: Farrar, Straus and Giroux, 2005).
Angeberg, Comte d', see Chodzko.
Anna, Timothy E., 'Institutional and Political Impediments to Spain's Settlement of the American Rebellions', *The Americas* 34/4 (April 1982).
——, *Spain and the Loss of America* (Lincoln: University of Nebraska Press, 1983).
Antioche, Comte d', *Chateaubriand: Ambassadeur à Londres* (Paris: Perrin, 1912).
Argenti, Philip, *The Massacre of Chios Described in Contemporary Diplomatic Reports* (London: John Lane/The Bodley Head, 1932).
Arimia, Vasile, Gmulescu, Ielița, Moisuc, Elena, Moraru, Cornelia, Penelea, Georgeta, Poștăriță, Emilia, Veliman, Valeriu and Zaharia, Dumitru (eds), *Revoluția din 1821 Condusă de Vladimirescu: Documente Externe* (Bucharest: Editura Academiei Republicii Socialiste România, 1980).
Arjuzon, Antoine d', *Castlereagh, ou le defi à l'Europe de Napoleon* (Paris: Tallandier, 1995).
Arneth, Alfred Ritter von, *Johann Freiherr von Wessenberg: österreichischer Staatsmann des neunzehnten Jahrhunderts* (Vienna and Leipzig: W. Braumüller, 1898).
Baack, Lawrence J., *Christian Bernstorff and Prussia: Diplomacy and Reform Conservatism, 1818–1832* (New Brunswick, NJ: Rutgers University Press, 1980).
Baron, Salo, *Die Judenfrage auf dem Wiener Kongress* (Vienna and Berlin: R. Löwit, 1920).
Bartlett, Christopher John, *Castlereagh* (New York: Charles Scribner's Sons, 1966).

———, *Peace, War and the European Powers, 1814–1914* (Houndmills: Macmillan, 1996).
Bass, Gary J., *Freedom's Battle: The Origins of Humanitarian Intervention* (New York: Random House, 2008).
Bell, David, *The First Total War: Napoleon's Europe and the Birth of Warfare as We Know It* (New York: Houghton Mifflin, 2007).
Bercé, Yves-Marie (ed.), *La Fin de l'Europe Napoleonnienne, 1814: La Vacance du Pouvoir* (Paris: H. Veyrier, 1990).
Bertier de Sauvigny, Guillaume de, *France and the European Alliance 1816–1821: The Private Correspondence of Metternich and Richelieu* (Notre Dame, IN: University of Notre Dame Press, 1958).
———, 'Sainte-Alliance et Alliance dans les conceptions de Metternich', *Revue historique* 223 (1960), pp. 249–74.
———, *Metternich and His Times* (London: Darton, Longman & Todd, 1962).
———, *The Bourbon Restoration*, trans. Lynn Case (Philadelphia: University of Pennsylvania Press, 1966).
———, *Metternich et la France après le Congrès de Vienne, vol. i: De Napoléon à Decazes 1815/1820; vol. ii: Les grands Congrès—1820/1824* (Paris: Hachette, 1968, 1970).
———, *Metternich* (Paris: Fayard, 1986).
Bew, John, *Castlereagh: Enlightenment, War, Tyranny* (London: Quercus, 2011).
———, '"From an umpire to a competitor": Castlereagh, Canning and the issue of international intervention in the wake of the Napoleonic Wars', in Brendan Simms and D.B.J. Trim (eds), *Humanitarian Intervention: A History* (Cambridge: Cambridge University Press, 2011).
Bitis, Alexander, *Russia and the Eastern Question: Army, Government and Society, 1815–1833* (Oxford: Oxford University Press/British Academy, 2006).
Blanning, Timothy C.W., *The Origins of the French Revolutionary Wars* (London: Longman, 1986).
———, 'Paul Schroeder's Concert of Europe', *The International History Review* 16/4 (November 1994), pp. 701–14.
———, *The Pursuit of Glory: The Five Revolutions that Made Modern Europe* (London: Allen Lane, 2007).
Bosco, David L., *Five to Rule Them All: The UN Security Council and the Making of the Modern World* (Oxford: Oxford University Press, 2009).
Bourne, Kenneth, *The Foreign Policy of Victorian England, 1830–1902* (Oxford: Clarendon Press, 1970).
Bourquin, Maurice, *Histoire de la Sainte Alliance* (Geneva: George, 1954).
Brennecke, Christiana, *Cádiz nach London: spanische Liberalismus im Spannungsfeld von nationaler Selbstbestimmung, Internationalität und Exil (1820–1833)* (Göttingen: Vandenhoeck & Ruprecht, 2010).
Brewer, David, *The Greek War of Independence: The Struggle for Freedom from Ottoman Oppression and the Birth of the Modern Greek Nation* (Woodstock and New York: Overlook Press, 2001).

Bridge, F. Roy and Bullen, Roger, *The Great Powers and the European States System, 1814–1914*, 2nd edn (Harlow: Pearson, 2005).
Broers, Michael, *Napoleonic Imperialism and the Savoyard Monarchy, 1773–1821: State Building in Piedmont* (Lewiston: Edwin Mellen Press, 1997).
———, *Europe after Napoleon: Revolution, Reaction and Romanticism, 1814–1848* (Manchester: Manchester University Press, 1996).
———, Guimerá, Agustin and Hicks, Peter (eds), *The Napoleonic Empire and the New European Political Culture: War, Culture and Society, 1750–1850* (Houndmills: Palgrave Macmillan, 2012).
Broglie, Duc de (ed.), *Memoirs of the Prince de Talleyrand* (New York and London: G.P. Putnam's Sons, 1891).
Burg, Peter, *Der Wiener Kongress* (Munich: Deutscher Taschenbuch Verlag, 1984).
Büssem, Eberhard, *Die Karlsbader Beschlüsse von 1819. Die endgültige Stabilisierung der restaurativen Polilik im Deutschen Bund nach den Wiener Kongress von 1814/15* (Hildesheim: Verlag Dr. H. A. Gerstenberg, 1974).
Campbell, Peter R. (ed.), *The Origins of the French Revolution* (London: Palgrave, 2006).
Capefigue, J.B.H.R., *La Baronne de Krudner, l'Empereur Alexandre Ier au Congrès de Vienne et les Traités de 1815* (Paris, 1868).
Carr, Raymond, *Spain, 1808–1975*, 2nd edn (Oxford: Oxford University Press, 1982).
Censer, Jack R., 'Commencing the Third Century of Debate', *The American Historical Review* 94/5 (December 1989), pp. 1309–25.
Chandler, David G., *The Campaigns of Napoleon* (New York: Macmillan 1966).
Chateaubriand, François René de, *The Congress of Verona: Comprising a Portion of Memoirs of his Own Time* (London: Richard Bentley, 1838).
———, *Memoires d'Outre-Tombe* (Paris: Flammarion, 1898–1901).
Chodzko, L.J., Comte d'Angeberg, *Le Congrès de Vienne et les Traités de 1815* (Paris: Amyot, 1864).
Christiansen, E., *The Origins of Military Power in Spain, 1800–1854* (Oxford: Oxford University Press, 1967).
Cisternes, Raoul de, *Le Duc de Richelieu, son Action aux Conférences d'Aix-la-Chapelle, sa retrait du pouvoir* (Paris: Calmann Lévy, 1898).
Clark, Ian, *Hegemony in International Society* (Oxford: Oxford University Press, 2011).
Clayton, Gerald David, *Britain and the Eastern Question: Missolonghi to Gallipoli* (London: University of London Press, 1971).
Clogg, Richard (ed.), *The Movement for Greek Independence, 1770–1821: A Collection of Documents* (London: Macmillan, 1976).
———, *A Concise History of Greece*, 2nd edn (Cambridge: Cambridge University Press, 2002).
Colleta, Pietro, *History of the Kingdom of Naples, 1734–1825* (Edinburgh: T. Constable, 1858).
Cookson, J.E., *The Friends of Peace: Anti-War Liberalism in England, 1793–1815* (Cambridge: Cambridge University Press, 1982).

Cooper, Duff, *Talleyrand* (Stanford, CA: Stanford University Press, 1967).
Corti, Egon, *Metternich und die Frauen* (Zurich and Vienna: Europa-Verlag, 1948).
Cowles, Loyal, 'The Failure to Restrain Russia: Canning, Nesselrode, and the Greek Question', *The International History Review* 12/4 (November 1990), pp. 688–720.
Craig, Gordon A. and George, Alexander L., *Force and Statecraft: Diplomatic Problems of Our Time* (New York: Oxford University Press, 1983).
Craven, Richard Keppel, *A Tour through the Southern Provinces of the Kingdom of Naples* (London: Rodwell and Martin, 1821).
Cresson, W.P., *The Holy Alliance: the European Background of the Monroe Doctrine* (New York: Oxford University Press, 1922).
Cronin, Bruce, *Community under Anarchy: Transnational Identity and the Evolution of Cooperation* (New York: Columbia University Press, 1999).
Cunningham, Allan, *Anglo-Ottoman Encounters in the Age of Revolution* (London: F. Cass, 1993).
Dallas, Gregor, *The Final Act: The Roads to Waterloo* (New York: Henry Holt & Co., 1997).
Dard, Emile, *Napoleon and Talleyrand* (London: Philip Allan and Co., 1937).
Davis, David Brion, *The Problem of Slavery in the Age of Revolution, 1770–1823* (Ithaca, NY: Cornell University Press, 1975).
Davis, John A., *Naples and Napoleon: Southern Italy and the European Revolutions* (Oxford: Oxford University Press, 2006).
Delfiner, Henry A., 'Alexander I, the Holy Alliance and Clemens Metternich: A Reappraisal', *East European Quarterly* 37/2 (2003), pp. 127–50.
Di Scala, Spencer M., *Italy: From Revolution to Republic* (Boulder, CO: Westview Press, 1995).
Doyle, William, *Origins of the French Revolution*, 3rd edn (Oxford: Oxford University Press, 1999).
Dupuis, Charles, *Le Principe d'Equilibre et le Concert Européen* (Paris: Perrin, 1909).
——, *Le ministère de Talleyrand en 1814* (Paris: Plon, 1919).
Durchhardt, Heinz, *Der Wiener Kongress* (Munich: C.H. Beck, 2013).
Easley, Eric, *The War over Perpetual Peace: An Exploration into the History of a Foundational International Relations Text* (New York: Palgrave Macmillan, 2004).
Egloffstein, Hermann Freiherrn v. (ed.), *Carl Bertuchs Tagebuch vom Wiener Kongress* (Berlin: Gebrüder Paetel, 1916).
Ehrman, John, *The Younger Pitt: The Consuming Struggle* (Stanford, CA: Stanford University Press, 1996).
Esdaile, Charles, *Spain in the Liberal Age from Constitution to Civil War, 1808–1939* (Oxford: Blackwell, 2000).
——, *Napoleon's Wars: An International History, 1803–1815* (London: Penguin, 2007).
Eynard, Jean Gabriel, *Journal* (Paris: Plon, 1914).
Fehrenbach, Charles Wentz, 'Moderados and Exaltados: The Liberal Opposition to Ferdinand VII, 1814–1823', *Hispanic American Historical Review* 50/1 (February 1970), pp. 52–69.

Ferguson, Niall, *The House of Rothschild: Money's Prophets, 1798–1848* (New York: Viking Press, 1998).

Ferrero, Guglielmo, *The Reconstruction of Europe, Talleyrand and the Congress of Vienna, 1814–1815*, trans. T. Jaeckel (New York: W.W. Norton & Co., 1963).

Finkel, Caroline, *Osman's Dream: The Story of the Ottoman Empire, 1300–1923* (New York: Basic Books, 2005).

Fleming, David C., *John Capodistrias and the Conference of London* (Thessaloniki: Institute for Balkan Studies, 1971).

Flockerzie, Lawrence J., 'Saxony, Austria and the German Question after the Congress of Vienna, 1815–1816', *The International History Review* 12/4 (1990), pp. 661–87.

Fontana, Josep, *La crisis del Antiquo regimen, 1808–1833* (Barcelona: Ariel, 1979).

——, *De en Medio del Tiempo: La Segunda Restauración Española, 1823–1834* (Barcelona: Crítica, 2006).

Fournier, August, *Der Congress von Châtillon: Die Politik im Kriege von 1814* (Vienna and Prague: Tempsky, 1900).

——, *Die Geheimpolizei auf dem Wiener Kongress* (Vienna: Tempsky, 1913).

——, 'London Präludien zum Wiener Kongress', *Deutsche Revue* 43 (1918), I, pp. 125–36, 205–16; II, pp. 24–33.

Freitag, Sabine and Wende, Peter, *British Envoys to Germany, 1816–1866*, vol. i, *1816–1829* (Cambridge: Cambridge University Press, 2000).

Freksa, Frederick, *A Peace Congress of Intrigue: A Vivid, Intimate Account of the Congress of Vienna composed of the Personal Memoirs of its Most Important Inhabitants*, trans. Harry Hansen (New York: The Century Co., 1919).

Gentz, Friedrich von, *Fragments upon the Present State of the Political Balance of Europe* (London: M. Peliter, 1806).

Ghervas, Stella, *Reinventer la Tradition: Alexandre Stourdza et l'Europe de la Saint-Alliance* (Paris: Honoré Champion, 2008).

Gielgud, Adam, *Memoirs of Prince Adam Czartoryski and his Correspondence with Alexander I* (London: Remington, 1888).

Gil Novales, Alberto, *El Trienio Liberal* (Madrid: Siglo Veintiuno, 1980).

Grab, Alexander, *Napolean and the Transformation of Europe* (London: Palgrave Macmillan 2003).

Grabaud, Stephen, 'Castlereagh and the Peace of Europe', *Journal of British Studies* 3/1 (November 1963), pp. 79–87.

Green, J.E.S., 'Castlereagh's Instructions for the Conferences at Vienna, 1822', *Transactions of the Royal Historical Society*, Third Series, 7 (1913), pp. 103–28.

——, 'Wellington and the Congress of Verona', *English Historical Review* 35/138 (April 1920), pp. 200–11.

Griewank, Karl, *Der Wiener Kongress und die Neuordnung Europas 1814/15* (Leipzig: Koehler & Amelang, 1942).

Grimm, Dieter, *Deutsche Verfassungsgeschichte 1776–1866* (Frankfurt am Main: Suhrkamp, 1988).

Grimsted, Patricia Kennedy, *The Foreign Ministers of Alexander I: Political Attitudes and the Conduct of Russian Diplomacy, 1801–1825* (Berkeley: University of California Press, 1969).

Gruner, Wolf Dieter, *Grossbritannien, der Deutsche Bund und die Struktur des europäische Friedens im frühen 19. Jahrhundert. Studien zu den britisch-deutschen Beziehungen in einer Periode des Umbruchs 1812–1820* (Munich: Oldenbourg, 1979).

——— (ed.), *Gleichgewicht in Geschichte und Gegenwart* (Hamburg: R. Krämer, 1989).

Gulick, Edward Vose, *Europe's Classical Balance of Power* (New York: W.W. Norton, 1955).

Gurwood, Colonel John, *The Dispatches of Field Marshal the Duke of Wellington, during his Various Campaigns in India, Denmark, Portugal, Spain, the Low Countries and France, from 1799 to 1818* (London: John Murray, 1844).

Haas, Mark, *The Ideological Origins of Great Power Politics, 1789–1989* (Ithaca, NY: Cornell University Press, 2005).

Hammer, Karl, *Die Französische Diplomatie der Restauration und Deutschland 1814–1830* (Stuttgart: A. Hiersemann, 1963).

Hanioğlu, M. Şükrü, *A Brief History of the Late Ottoman Empire* (Princeton, NJ: Princeton University Press, 2008).

Hansard, T.C., *The Parliamentary Debates from the Year 1803 to the Present Time*, vol. xli *(23 November 1819–28 February 1820)*; New Series, vol. iv (23 January–2 April 1821) (London).

Hartley, Janet M., *Alexander I* (London: Longman, 1994).

———, '"It is the Festival of the Crown and Sceptres": The Diplomatic, Commercial and Domestic Significance of the Visit of Alexander I to England in 1814', *The Slavonic and East European Review* 73/2 (April 1995), pp. 246–68.

———, *Russia, 1762–1825: Military Power, the State and the People* (Westport, CN: Praeger, 2008).

Heller, Henry, *The Bourgeois Revolution in France* (New York and Oxford: Berghahn Books, 2006).

Herbert, George, Count Münster, *Political Sketches of the State of Europe from 1814–1867* (Edinburgh: Edmonston and Douglas, 1868).

Herr, Richard, *An Historical Essay on Modern Spain* (Berkeley: University of California Press, 1971).

Hertslet, E.E. *The Map of Europe by Treaty* (London: Butterworths, 1875).

Heydemann, Günther, *Carl Ludwig Sand. Die Tat als Attentat* (Hof: Oberfrankische Verlagsanstalt, 1985).

———, *Konstitution gegen Revolution: Die britische Deutschland- und Italienpolitik 1815–1848* (Göttingen and Zürich: Göttingen, 1995).

———, 'Das folgenschwere Zerwürfnis: Grossbritannien, Österreich und das europäische Staatensystem nach 1815', in Petronilla Gietl (ed.), *Vom Wiener Kongress bis zur Wiedervereininung Deutschlands* (Munich: Ernst Vögel, 1997).

Hilderbrand, Robert C., *Dumbarton Oaks: The Origins of the United Nations and the Search for Postwar Security* (Chapel Hill, NC: University of North Carolina Press, 1990).

Hilton, Boyd, *A Mad, Bad and Dangerous People? England, 1783–1846* (Oxford: Oxford University Press, 2006).
Hinsley, F.H., *Power and the Pursuit of Peace: Theory and Practice in the History of Relations between States* (Cambridge: Cambridge University Press, 1967).
Holbraad, Carsten, *The Concert of Europe: A Study in German and British International Theory* (London: Longmans, 1970).
Hotchkiss, Alice, 'The Concert of Europe: Its Evolution and Development', PhD thesis (University of California at Berkeley, 1940).
Houssaye, Henry, *1814* (Paris: Perrin, 1908).
Hundt, Michael, *Die mindermächtigen deutschen Staaten auf dem Wiener Kongreß* (Mainz: P. von Zabern, 1996).
Hunt, Giles, *The Duel: Castlereagh, Canning and Deadly Cabinet Rivalry* (London: I.B.Tauris, 2008).
Ikenberry, G. John, *After Victory: Institutions, Strategic Restraint and the Rebuilding of Order after Major Wars* (Princeton, NJ: Princeton University Press, 2001).
Ingram, Charles, *The Habsburg Monarchy, 1618–1815*, 2nd edn (Cambridge: Cambridge University Press, 2000).
Ingram, Edward, 'Lord Mulgrave's Proposals for the Reconstruction of Europe in 1804', *The Historical Journal* 19/2 (June 1976), pp. 511–20.
Ilsemann, Alexandra von, *Die Politik Frankreichs auf dem Wiener Kongress: Talleyrands aussenpolitische Strategien zwischen Erster und Zweiter Restauration* (Hamburg: Krämer, 1996).
Israel, Jonathan, *Revolutionary Ideas: An Intellectual History of the French Revolution from The Rights of Man to Robespierre* (Princeton: Princeton University Press, 2014).
Jarrett, Mark Jeffrey, 'Castlereagh, Ireland and the French Restorations of 1814–1815', PhD thesis (Stanford University, 2006).
Jaucourt, A.F. Comte de, *Correspondance du comte de Jaucourt, ministre intérimaire des Affaires étrangères avec le prince de Talleyrand, pendant le Congrès de Vienne* (Paris: Hachette, 1905).
Jelavich, Barbara, *History of the Balkans: Eighteenth and Nineteenth Centuries* (Cambridge: Cambridge University Press, 1983).
——, *Russia's Balkan Entanglements, 1806–1914* (Cambridge: Cambridge University Press, 1991).
Jenak, Rudolf, *Sachsen, der Rheinbund und die Exekution der Sachsen betreffenden Entscheidungen des Wiener Kongresses (1803–1816)* (Neustadt an der Aisch: Ph. C.W. Schmidt, 2005).
Jervis, Robert, 'Security Regimes', *International Organization* 36/2 (Spring 1982), pp. 360–68, reprinted in Stephen Krasner (ed.), *International Regimes* (Ithaca, NY: Cornell University Press, 1983), pp. 173–94.
——, 'From Balance to Concert: A Study of International Security Cooperation', *World Politics* 38/1 (October 1985), pp. 61–62.
——, 'A Political Science Perspective on the Balance of Power and the Concert', *American Historical Review* 97/3 (June 1992), pp. 716–24.

Johnson, Paul, *The Birth of the Modern: World Society, 1815–1830* (New York: HarperCollins, 1991).
Kafadar, Cemal, 'The Question of Ottoman Decline', *Harvard Middle Eastern and Islamic Review* 4 (1997–98), pp. 30–75.
Kagan, Korina, 'The Myth of the European Concert', *Security Studies* 7/2 (Winter 1997–98), pp. 1–57.
Kaplan, Robert D., 'Kisssinger, Metternich and Realism: Henry Kissinger's First Book (A World Restored)', *The Atlantic Monthly* 283/6 (June 1999), pp. 72–82.
Kennedy, Paul, *The Rise and Fall of the Great Powers* (New York: Vintage Books, 1987).
——, *The Parliament of Man: the Past, Present and Future of the United Nations* (New York: Random House, 2006).
Keohane, Robert O., 'The Diplomacy of Structural Change: Multilateral Institutions and State Strategies', in Helga Haftendorn and Christian Tuschhoff (eds), *America and Europe in an Era of Change* (Boulder, CO: Westview Press, 1993).
Kertesz, G.A. (ed.), *Documents in the Political History of the European Continent* (Oxford: Clarendon Press, 1968).
King, David, *Vienna, 1814: How the Conquerors of Napoleon Made Love, War, and Peace at the Congress of Vienna* (New York: Harmony Books, 2008).
Kissinger, Henry, *A World Restored: Metternich, Castlereagh and the Problems of Peace 1812–1822* (London: Houghton Mifflin, 1957).
——, *Diplomacy* (New York: Simon and Schuster, 1994).
Knapton, E.J., 'The Origins of the Holy Alliance', Historical Revision N. XCVIII, *History*, New Series 26/2 (September 1941), pp. 131–40.
Kohler, Max James, *Jewish Rights at the Congresses of Vienna (1814–1815) and Aix-la-Chapelle* (New York: American Jewish Committee, 1918).
Kraehe, Enno, *Metternich's German Policy, 1799–1814* (Princeton, NJ: Princeton University Press, 1963).
——, *Metternich's German Policy*, vol ii, *The Congress of Vienna* (Princeton, NJ: Princeton University Press, 1983).
——, 'Wellington and the Reconstruction of the Allied Armies during the Hundred Days', *The International History Review* 11/1 (February 1989), pp. 84–97.
Krüger, Peter and Schroeder, Paul, *'The Transformation of European Politics, 1763–1848': Episode or Model in Modern History?* (Münster: Lit Verlag, 2002).
Kukiel, Marian, *Czartoryski and European Unity, 1770–1861* (Princeton, NJ: Princeton University Press, 1955).
Kupchan, Charles A., *How Enemies Become Friends: the Sources of Stable Peace* (Princeton, NJ: Princeton University Press, 2010).
Lacour-Gayet, G., *Talleyrand* (Paris: Payot, 1930).
La Garde-Chambonas, Auguste, Comte de, *Souvenirs du Congrès de Vienne, 1814–1815* (Paris: Librarie Émile-Paul, 1904) (trans. as *Anecdotal Recollections of the Congress of Vienna* (London: Chapman and Hall, 1902)).
Lane-Poole, Stanley, *Life of the Right Honourable Stratford Canning: Viscount Stratford de Redcliffe* (London: Longmans, Green & Co., 1888).

Langhorne, Richard, 'Reflections on the Congress of Vienna', *Review of International Studies* xii/4 (October 1986).
Lauren, Paul Gordon, 'Crisis Prevention in Nineteenth Century Diplomacy', in Alexander L. George (ed.), *Managing US-Soviet Rivalry: Problems of Crisis Prevention* (Boulder, CO and London: Westview Press, 1983), pp. 31–64.
Laven, David and Riall, Lucy (eds), *Napoleon's Legacy: Problems of Government in Restoration Europe* (Oxford: Berg, 2000).
Lehmann, Max, 'Tagebuch des Freiherrn vom Stein während des Wiener Kongresses', *Historische Zeitschrift*, New Series xxiv (1888), pp. 385–467.
Lentz, Thierry, *Nouvelle Histoire du Premier Empire* (Paris: Fayard, 2002–04).
——, *Le congrès de Vienne: une refondation de l'Europe, 1814–1815* (Paris: Perrin, 2013).
—— *Les Vingts jours de Fontainebleau: La première abdication de Napoléon* (Paris: Perrin, 2014).
Levinger, Matthew, 'Hardenberg, Wittgenstein and the Constitutional Crisis in Prussia, 1815–1822', *German History* 8 (1990), pp. 257–77.
Levy, Avigdor, 'Ottoman Attitudes to the Rise of Balkan Nationalism', in Belá K. Király and Gunther E. Rothenberg (eds), *War and Society in East Central Europe*, vol. 1 (New York: Columbia University Press, 1979), pp. 325–45.
Ley, Francis, *Alexandre Ier et sa Sainte-Alliance* (Paris: Fischbacher, 1975).
Lieven, Dominic, *Russia against Napoleon: the True Story of the Campaigns of War and Peace* (New York: Viking, 2009).
Lindley, Dan, *Promoting Peace with Information: Transparency as a Tool of Security Regimes* (Princeton, NJ: Princeton University Press, 2007).
Longford, Elizabeth, *Wellington: The Years of the Sword* (London: Harper and Row, 1969).
——, *Wellington, Pillar of State* (London: Weidenfeld and Nicolson, 1972).
Lovie, Jacques and Palluel-Guillard, André, *L'épisode napoléonien: Aspects extérieurs, 1799–1815* (Paris: Éditions du Seuil, 1972).
Luck, J. Murray, *A History of Switzerland* (Palo Alto, CA: SPOSS, 1985).
Luis, Jean-Philippe, *L'Utopie Réactionnaire* (Madrid: Casa de Velazquez, 2002).
Mansel, Philip, *Louis XVIII* (Colchester: Frederick Muller Ltd, 1981).
Marcowitz, Reiner, *Grossmacht auf Bewährung: Die Interdependenz französischer Innen- und Aussenpolitik und ihre Auswirkungen auf Frankreichs Stellung im europäischen Konzert, 1814/15–1851/52* (Stuttgart: Thorbecke, 2001).
Mazade, Charles de (ed.), *Mémoires du Prince Adam Czartoryski et Correspondance avec l'Empereur Alexandre Ier* (Paris: E. Plon, Nourrit et Cie, 1887).
Mazower, Mark, *Governing the World: The History of an Idea* (New York: Penguin, 2012).
McGuigan, Dorothy, *Metternich and the Duchess: The Public and Private Lives of the Congress of Vienna* (Garden City, NY: Doubleday, 1975).
Mearsheimer, John, 'The False Promise of International Institutions', *International Security* 19/3 (Winter 1994–95), pp. 5–49.
——, *The Tragedy of Great Power Politics* (New York: W.W. Norton, 2001).

Meinecke, Friedrich, *The Age of German Liberation, 1795–1815*, ed. Peter Paret (Berkeley: University of California Press, 1977).
Metternich, Prince Richard (ed.), *Memoirs of Prince Metternich, 1773–1835* (New York: Scribner's Sons, 1880–82).
Minichini, Luigi, *Luglio 1820: Cronaca di una Rivoluzione* (Rome: Bulzoni Editore, 1979).
Mitzen, Jennifer, *Power in Concert: The Nineteenth Century Origins of Global Governance* (Chicago: University of Chicago Press, 2013).
Molinari, M.G. de, *L'Abbé de Saint-Pierre: Sa Vie et Ses Oeuvres* (Paris: Guillaumin, 1857).
Monnier, Victor, *Bonaparte et la Suisse. Travaux préparatoires de l'Acte de Médiation* (Geneva and Basle: Helbing & Lichtenhahn, Slatkine, 2002).
Montgomery Hyde, Harford, *Princess Lieven* (London: George G. Harrap & Co., 1938).
——, *The Strange Death of Lord Castlereagh* (London: William Heinemann, 1959).
Mousnier, Roland and Labrousse, Ernest, *Le XVIIIe Siècle: Révolution Intellectuelle, Technique et Politique, 1715–1815* (Paris: PUF, 1953).
Muir, Rory, *Britain and the Defeat of Napoleon, 1807–1815* (New Haven, CT: Yale University Press, 1996).
Näf, Werner, *Zur Geschichte der Heiligen Allianz* (Bern: Paul Haupt, 1928).
Nesselrode, A. de (ed.), *Lettres et Papiers du comte de Nesselrode, 1760–1850* (Paris: A. Lahure, 1908–12).
Nettement, Alfred, *Histoire de la Restauration* (Paris & Lyon: Michel Lévy frères, 1868).
Nicholai Mikhaïlovich, Grand Duke, *Imperator Aleksandr I* (St Petersburg: Manufacture of Government Papers, 1912).
——, *Les Rapports Diplomatiques de Lebzeltern, Ministre d'Autriche à la Cour de Russie, 1816–1826* (St Petersburg: Manufacture of Government Papers, 1913).
Nichols Jr, Irby C., *The European Pentarchy and the Congress of Verona, 1822* (The Hague: Martinus Nijhoff, 1971).
Nicholson, Sir Harold, *The Congress of Vienna: A Study in Allied Unity, 1812–1822* (New York: Harcourt Brace and Co., 1946).
Northedge, F.S., *The League of Nations: Its Life and Times, 1920–1946* (New York: Holmes and Meier, 1986).
Ogg, David (ed.), *Sully's Grand Design of Henry IV* (Grotius Society Publications, No. 2) (London: Sweet and Maxwell, 1921).
Olshausen, Klothilde von, *Die Stellung der Grossmächte zur sächsischen Frage auf dem Wiener Kongress und deren Rückwirkung auf die Gestaltung der preussischen Ostgrenze* (Quakenbrück: C. Trute, 1933).
Oncken, Wilhelm, *Oesterreich und Preussen in Befreiungskriege* (Berlin: G. Gratte, 1879).
Orieux, Jean, *Talleyrand ou le Sphinx Incompris* (Paris: Flammarion, 1998).
Osiander, Andreas, *The States System of Europe, 1640–1990: Peacemaking and the Conditions of International Stability* (Oxford: Clarendon Press, 1994).
Palewski, Gaston. *Le Miroir de Talleyrand: Lettres inedites a la duchesse de Courlande pendant le Congrès de Vienne* (Paris: Perrin, 1976).

Pallain, M.G., *The Correspondence of Prince Talleyrand and King Louis XVIII* (New York: Charles Scribner's Sons, 1881).

Palmer, Alan, *Metternich* (London: Weidenfeld and Nicolson, 1972).

——, *Alexander I: Tsar of War and Peace* (London: Weidenfeld and Nicolson, 1974).

Palmer, R.R., *The Age of Democratic Revolution* (Princeton, NJ: Princeton University Press, 1959–64).

——, *Twelve Who Ruled* (Princeton, NJ: Princeton University Press, 1969).

Paret, Peter, *Yorck and the Era of Prussian Reform, 1807–1815* (Princeton, NJ: Princeton University Press, 1966).

——, *Clausewitz and the State* (Oxford: Oxford University Press, 1976).

——, *The Cognitive Challenge of War: Prussia 1806* (Princeton, NJ: Princeton University Press, 2009).

Pasquier, Etienne-Denis, *Mémoires du Chancelier Pasquier* (Paris: Plon, 1894).

Peterson, Genevieve, 'Political Inequality at the Congress of Vienna', *Political Science Quarterly* 60/4 (December 1945), pp. 532–54.

Philliou, Christine M. *Biography of an Empire: Governing Ottomans in an Age of Revolution* (Berkeley: University of California Press, 2011).

Phillips, Walter Alison, *The Confederation of Europe*, 2nd edn (London: Longmans, Green and Co., 1920).

Pilbeam, Pamela (ed.), *Themes in European History 1780–1830* (London: Routledge, 1995).

Pirenne, Jacques-Henri, *La Sainte Alliance: Organisation européenne de la paix Mondiale* (Neuchatel: Éditions de la Baconnière, 1946).

Polovtsoff, A., *Correspondance Diplomatique des Ambassadeurs et Ministres de Russie en France et de France en Russie avec leurs Gouvernements de 1814 à 1830* (St Petersburg: Imperial Society of Russian History, 1907).

Ponteil, Felix, *La Chute de Napoleon 1er* (Paris: Aubier, 1943).

Pozzo di Borgo, Charles (ed.), *Correspondance diplomatique du comte Pozzo di Borgo, ambassadeur de Russie en France, et du comte de Nesselrode depuis la restauration des Bourbons jusqu'au congrès d'Aix-la-Chapelle, 1814–1818* (Paris: Calmann Lévy, 1890–97).

Prokesch-Osten, Anton von, *Geschichte des Abfalls der Griechen vom Türkischen Reiche im Jahre 1821* (Vienna: C. Gerold's Sohn 1867).

—— (ed.), *Dépêches Inédites du Chevalier de Gentz aux Hospodars de Valachie* (Paris: Plon, 1876–77).

Prousis, Theophilus C., *Russian Society and the Greek Revolution* (DeKalb: Northern Illinois University Press, 1994).

Pyta, Wolfram, 'Konzert der Mächte und kollecktives Sicherheitssystem: Neue Wege zwischenstaatlicher Friedenswahrung in Europa nach dem Wiener Kongress 1815', *Jahrbuch des Historischen Kollegs* 117 (1996), pp. 133–76.

—— (ed.), *Das europäische Mächtekonzert: Friedens- und Sicherheitspolitik vom Wiener Kongreß 1815 bis zum Krimkrieg 1853* (Cologne, Weimar and Vienna: Böhlau Verlag GMBH & Cie, 2009).

Quataert, Donald, *The Ottoman Empire, 1700–1922* (Cambridge: Cambridge University Press, 2000).
Quin, Michael J., *A Visit to Spain* (London: Hurst, Robinson, 1823).
Raeff, Marc, *Michael Speransky: Statesman of Imperial Russia, 1772–1839* (The Hague: Martinus Nijhoff, 1957)
——, *Plans for Political Reform in Imperial Russia, 1730–1905* (Englewood Cliffs, NJ: Prentice Hall, 1966).
Rain, Pierre, *L'Europe et la Restauration des Bourbons (1814–1818)* (Paris: Perrin, 1908).
Reinerman, Alan J., *Austria and the Papacy in the Age of Metternich. Between Conflict and Cooperation* (Washington DC: Catholic University of America Press, 1979).
Rendall, Matthew, 'Russia, the Concert of Europe, and Greece, 1821–29: A Test of Hypotheses about the Vienna System', *Security Studies* 9/4 (Summer 2000).
——, 'Defensive Realism and the Concert of Europe', *Review of International Studies* 32/3 (2006), pp. 523–40.
Rey, Marie-Pierre, *Alexandre I* (Paris: Flammarion, Grandes Biographies, 2009).
——, *1814– Un Tsar à Paris* (Paris: Flammarion, 2014).
Reynolds, P.A. and Hughes, E.J., *The Historian as Diplomat: Charles Kingsley Webster and the United Nations, 1939–1946* (London: Martin Robinson, 1976).
Riasanovsky, Nicholas V., *Russian Identities: A Historical Survey* (Oxford: Oxford University Press, 2005).
Richardson, Louise, 'The Concert of Europe and Security Management in the Nineteenth Century', in Helga Haftendorn, Robert O. Keohane and Celeste A. Wallander (eds), *Imperfect Unions: Security Institutions over Time and Space* (Oxford: Oxford University Press, 1999).
Roberts, Andrew, *Waterloo: June 18, 1815: The Battle for Modern Europe* (New York: HarperCollins, 2005).
——, *Napoleon: A Life* (New York: Penguin, 2014).
Roberts, John Morris, *The Mythology of the Secret Societies* (London: Secker and Warburg, 1972).
Robertson, William S., *France and Latin American Independence* (Baltimore, MD: Johns Hopkins Press, 1939).
Robins, Jane, *The Trial of Queen Caroline: The Scandalous Affair that Nearly Ended a Monarchy* (New York: Free Press, 2006).
Romani, George T., *The Neapolitan Revolution of 1820–1821* (Evanston, IL: Northwestern University Press, 1950).
Rose, John Holland, *Select Despatches from the British Foreign Office Archives relating to the Formation of the Third Coalition against France, 1804–1805* (London: Royal Historical Society, 1904).
Rosecrance, Richard (ed.), *Great Power Coalition: Toward a World Concert of Nations* (New York: Rowman and Littlefield, 2002).
Rosenkrantz, Neils, *Journal du Congrès de Vienne, 1814–1815* (Copenhagen: Georg Nørregård, 1953).

Rousseau, Jean-Jacques, *The Plan for Perpetual Peace, On the Government of Poland, and other Writings on History and Politics* (Hanover, NH: Dartmouth College Press, 2005).
Satow, Sir Ernest, *A Guide to Diplomatic Practice*, vol. ii (London: Longmans, Green & Co., 1922).
Sbornik imperatorskogo russkogo istoricheskogo obshchestva [Transactions of the Russian Imperial Historical Society], vol. iii (St Petersburg: Russian Imperial Historical Society, 1868).
Schenk, H.G., *The Aftermath of the Napoleonic Wars—An Experiment* (Oxford: Oxford University Press, 1947).
Schilder, N.K., *Imperator Aleksandr Pervyi*, vol. iii (St Petersburg: A.S. Suvorin, 1897).
Schmalz, Hans W., *Versuche einer gesamteuropäischen Organisation, 1815–1820, mit besonderer Berücksichtigung der Troppauer Interventionspolitik* (Aarau: H.R. Sauerländer, 1940).
Schroeder, Paul, *Metternich's Diplomacy at its Zenith, 1820–1823* (Austin: University of Texas Press, 1962).
——, 'The Transformation of Political Thinking, 1787–1848', in Jack Snyder and Robert Jervis (eds), *Coping with Complexity in the International System* (Boulder, CO: Westview Press, 1993), pp. 47–70.
——, *The Transformation of European Politics, 1763–1848* (Oxford: Oxford University Press, 1994).
——, *Systems, Stability and Statecraft* (New York: Palgrave Macmillan, 2004).
Schulz, Matthias, *Normen und Praxis: Das Europäische Konzert der Großmächte als Sicherheitsrat, 1815–1860* (München: R. Oldenbourg, 2009).
Schütz, Eberhard, *Die Europäische Allianzpolitik Alexanders I. und der Griechische Unabhängigkeitskampf, 1820–1830* (Wiesbaden: Harrassowitz, 1975).
Schwarz, Henry Frederick (ed.), *Metternich: the 'Coachman of Europe'* (Boston: D.C. Heath, 1962).
Scott, Ivan, 'Counter-Revolutionary Diplomacy and the Demise of Anglo-Austrian Cooperation, 1820–1823', *The Historian: A Journal of History* 34/3 (May 1972), pp. 465–84.
Scurr, Ruth, *Fatal Purity: Robespierre and the French Revolution* (New York: Metropolitan Books, 2006).
Šedivý, Miroslav, *Metternich, the Great Powers and the Eastern Question* (Pilsen: University of West Bohemia, 2013).
Sédouy, Jacques-Alain de, *Le Concert Européen: Aux origins de l'Europe, 1814–1914* (Paris: Fayard, 2009).
Sewart, Desmond, *Metternich: The First European* (New York: Viking, 1991).
Shaw, Stanford, *Between Old and New: The Ottoman Empire under Sultan Selim III, 1789–1807* (Cambridge, MA: Harvard University Press, 1971).
Sheehan, James J., *German History, 1770–1866* (Oxford: Clarendon Press, 1989).

──, *Where Have All the Soldiers Gone: The Transformation of Modern Europe* (Boston: Houghton Mifflin, 2008).
Sherwig, John M., *Guineas and Gunpowder: British Foreign Aid in the Wars with France 1793–1815* (Cambridge, MA: Harvard University Press, 1969).
Siemann, Wolfram, *Metternich* (Munich: C.H. Beck, 2010).
Simon, Walter, *The Failure of the Prussian Reform Movement, 1807–1819* (Ithaca, NY: Cornell University Press, 1955).
Singer, J. David, 'The Level-of-Analysis Problem in International Relations', in Klaus Knorr and Sidney Verba (eds), *The International System* (Princeton, NJ: Princeton University Press, 1961).
Sked, Alan (ed.), *Europe's Balance of Power, 1815–1848* (London: Macmillan, 1979).
──, 'Talleyrand and Metternich' (unpublished paper, nd).
──, *Metternich and Austria: An Evaluation* (Houndsmill: Palgrave Macmillan, 2008).
──, *Radetzky: Imperial Victor and Military Genius* (London: I.B.Tauris, 2011).
Slantchev, Branislav L., 'Territory and Commitment: The Concert of Europe as Self-Enforcing Equilibrium', *Security Studies* 14/4 (October 2005), pp. 565–606.
Sofka, James R., 'Metternich's Theory of European Order: A Political Agenda for Perpetual Peace', *The Review of Politics* 60/1 (1998), pp. 115–49.
Sonenscher, Michael, *Before the Deluge: Public Debt, Inequality and the Intellectual Origins of the French Revolution* (Cambridge, MA: Harvard University Press, 2007).
Sorel, Albert, *Europe and the French Revolution: the Political Traditions of the Old Regime* (London: Collins, 1969).
──, *Le Traité de Paris du 20 Novembre 1815* (Paris: G. Baillière, 1872).
Spiel, Hilde, *The Congress of Vienna: An Eyewitness Approach*, trans. Richard H. Weber (Philadelphia: Chilton Book Co., 1968).
Srbik, Heinrich Ritter von, *Metternich: der Staatsmann und der Mensch* (Munich: F. Bruckmann, 1925, 1957).
──, 'Metternichs Plan der Neuordnung Europas 1814/1815', *Mitteilungen des Instituts für österreichische Geshichtsforschung*, vol. xl (1925), trans. and reprinted in Henry F. Schwarz (ed.) *Metternich: the 'Coachman of Europe'.* (Boston: D.C. Heath 1962).
Stamm-Kuhlmann, Thomas, *König in Preussens grosser Zeit: Friedrich Wilhelm III, der Melancholiker auf dem Thron* (Berlin: Siedler, 1992).
──, (ed.), *Karl August von Hardenberg, 1750–1822: Tagebücher und autobiographische Aufzeichnungen* (Munich: Harald Boldt Verlag, 2000).
──, 'Der Staatskanzler von Hardenberg, die Bankiers und die Judenemanzipation in Preussen', *Vierteljahrschrift für Sozial- und Wirtschaftsgeschichte* 83/3 (1996), pp. 334–46.
──, 'Restoration Prussia', in Philip G. Dwyer (ed.), *Modern Prussian History, 1830–1947* (Harlow: Longman, 2001).
Steckhan, Gertrud, *Preussen und die Neuorientierung der europäischen Staatengesellschaft auf dem Aachener Kongress, 1818* (Berlin: Bottrop, 1934).

Stewart, Charles William Vane (ed.), *Memoirs and Correspondence of Viscount Castlereagh, Second Marquess of Londonderry* (London: H. Colburn, 1848–53).
Stites, Richard, *The Four Horsemen: Riding to Liberty in Post-Napoleonic Europe* (Oxford: Oxford University Press, 2014).
Stone, Bailey, *Reinterpreting the French Revolution: A Global-Historical Perspective* (Cambridge: Cambridge University Press, 2002).
Straus, Hannah Alice, *The Attitude of the Congress of Vienna toward Nationalism in Germany, Italy and Poland* (New York: Columbia University Press, 1949).
Strauss, Johann, 'Ottoman Rule Experienced and Remembered: Remarks on Some Local Greek Chronicles of the Tourkokratia', in Fikret Adanir and Suraiya Faroqhi (eds), *The Ottomans and the Balkans: A Discussion of Historiography* (Leiden and Boston: Brill, 2002).
Sweet, Paul Robinson, *Friedrich von Gentz: Defender of the Old Order* (Westport, CN: Greenwood Press, 1941).
——, *Wilhelm von Humboldt: A Biography* (Columbus: Ohio State University Press, 1978–80).
Talleyrand-Perigord, Charles Maurice de, *Memoirs of the Prince de Talleyrand* (New York: G.P. Putnam's Sons, 1891–92).
Temperley, Harold W.V., *The Foreign Policy of Canning, 1822–1827* (London: George Bell & Sons, 1925).
—— and Webster, Sir Charles Kingsley, 'British Policy in the Publication of Diplomatic Documents under Castlereagh and Canning', *Cambridge Historical Journal* 1/2 (1924), pp. 158–69.
Tezcan, Baki, *The Second Ottoman Empire: Political and Social Transformation in the Early Modern World* (Cambridge: Cambridge University Press, 2010).
Thackeray, Frank W., *Antecedents of Revolution: Alexander I and the Polish Kingdom* (Boulder: East European Monographs, 1980).
Thielen, Peter, *Karl August von Hardenberg, 1750–1822* (Cologne and Berlin: Grote, 1967).
Thompson, E.P., *The Making of the English Working Class* (London: Victor Gollancz, 1963).
Treitschke, Heinrich von, *History of Germany in the Nineteenth Century*, trans. Eden and Cedar Paul (London: Jarrold & Sons, 1915).
Troska, Ferdinand, *Die Publizistik zur Sächsichen Frage auf dem Wiener Kongress* (Halle: M. Niemeyer, 1891).
Tulard, Jean, *Napoleon: The Myth of the Saviour*, trans. Teresa Waugh (London: Weidenfeld and Nicolson, 1984).
USSR, Ministry of Foreign Affairs, *Vneshniaia Politika Rossii XIX i nachala XX veka: Dokumenty rossiskogo Ministerstva inostrannykh del*, 1st Series (1801–1815) vol. viii (May 1814–November 1815) (Moscow: Nauka, 1972).
——, *Vneshniaia Politika Rossii, 1815–1830* (Moscow: Nauka, 1976), Series 2, vol. ii (October 1817–April 1819); vol. iii (May 1819–February 1821); vol. iv (March 1821–December 1822).
Vere, Thomas Dwight, *The Duke of Wellington and the British Army of Occupation in France, 1815–1818* (Westport, CT: Greenwood Press, 1992).

Select Bibliography

Vick, Brian, *The Congress of Vienna: Power and Politics after Napoleon* (Cambridge, Mass: Harvard University Press, 2014).

Villa-Urritia, Wenceslao Ramírez de, Marqués de, *Fernando VII Rey Consitucional: Historia Diplomática de España de 1820 a 1823* (Madrid: F. Beltrán 1922).

Villèle, Jean Baptiste, *Mémoires et correspondance*, vols 1–5 (Paris: Hachette, 1887–90).

Waliszewski, K., *La Russie Il y a Cent Ans: Le Regne d'Alexandre Ier* (Paris: Plon, 1924).

Walter, Mack, *Metternich's Europe* (New York: Harper & Row, 1968).

Waltz, Kenneth, *Man, the State and War* (New York: Columbia University Press, 1959).

Wandycz, Piotr S., *The Price of Freedom: A History of East Central Europe from the Middle Ages to the Present*, 2nd edn (London: Routledge, 2001).

Waresquiel, Emmanuel de, *Talleyrand: le prince immobile* (Paris: Fayard, 2003).

———, *Cent Jours: la tentation de l'impossible, mars-juillet 1815* (Paris: Fayard, 2008).

——— and Yvert, Venoît, *Histoire de la Restauration, 1814–1830* (Paris: Perrin, 1996).

Wawrzkowicz, Eugeniusz, *Anglia a prawa polska 1813–1815* (Kraków and Warsaw: Druk W.L. Anczyca i spólki, 1919).

Webster, Sir Charles Kingsley, *The Congress of Vienna* (London: H. Milford, 1919).

———, *British Diplomacy, 1813–1815* (London: G. Bell and Sons, 1921).

———, *The Foreign Policy of Lord Castlereagh, 1815–1822: Britain and the European Alliance* (London: G. Bell and Sons, 1925).

———, *The European Alliance, 1815–1825* (Calcutta: University of Calcutta, 1929).

———, *The Foreign Policy of Lord Castlereagh, 1812–1815: Britain and the Reconstruction of Europe* (London: G. Bell and Sons, 1931).

——— (ed.), *Britain and the Independence of Latin America*, vols i and ii (Oxford: Oxford University Press, 1938).

——— (ed.), *The Art and Practice of Diplomacy* (New York: Barnes and Noble, 1962).

Weil, Maurice Henri, Commandant, *Les Dessous du Congrés de Vienne* (Paris: Librairie Payot, 1917).

Weiner, Margery, *The Sovereign Remedy: Europe after Waterloo* (London: Constable, 1971).

Wellesley, Arthur, Second Duke of Wellington (ed.), *Supplementary Despatches, Correspondence and Memoranda of Field Marshal Arthur [Wellesley] Duke of Wellington* (London: J. Murray, 1858–72).

——— (ed.), *Despatches, Correspondence and Memoranda of Field Marshal Arthur Duke of Wellington, K.G. Edited by his Son* (London: J. Murrary, 1867).

Wieczynski, J.L., 'The Mutiny of the Semenovsky Regiment in 1820', *Russian Review* XXIX (1970), pp. 167–68.

Williamson, George S., 'What Killed August von Kotzebue? The Temptations of Virtue and the Political Theology of German Nationalism, 1789–1819', *Journal of Modern History* 72/4 (December 2000), pp. 890–943.

Wolff, Otto, *Ouvrard: Speculator of Genius*, trans. Stewart Thompson (London: Barrie and Rockliff, 1962).

Woodhouse, C.M., *Capodistria: the Founder of Greek Independence* (London: Oxford University Press, 1973).

Yamada, Norihito, 'George Canning and the Spanish Question, September 1822 to March 1823', *The Historical Journal* 52/2 (June 2009), pp. 343–62.

Yapp, Malcolm, *The Making of the Modern Middle East, 1798–1923* (London: Longman, 1987).

York, Elizabeth, *Leagues of Nations; Ancient, Mediaeval, and Modern* (London: The Swarthmore Press Ltd, 1919).

Zak, L.A., *Monarkhi protiv narodov* [Monarchy against the People] (Moscow, 1966).

Zakythinos, D.A., *The Making of Modern Greece: From Byzantium to Independence*, trans. K.R. Johnstone (Oxford: Blackwell, 1976).

Zamoyski, Adam, *Holy Madness: Romantics, Patriots, and Revolutionaries, 1776–1871* (London: Weidenfeld and Nicolson, 1999).

——, *Rites of Peace: The Fall of Napoleon and the Congress of Vienna* (New York: HarperCollins, 2007).

Zawadzki, W.H., 'Prince Adam Czartoryski and Napoleonic France, 1801–1805: A Study in Political Attitudes', *The Historical Journal* xviii/2 (1975), pp. 245–77.

——, 'Russia and the Re-Opening of the Polish Question, 1801–1814', *The International History Review* 7/1 (February 1985), pp. 19–44.

——, *A Man of Honour: Adam Czartoryski as a Statesman of Russia and Poland, 1795–1831* (Oxford: Oxford University Press, 1993).

INDEX

A'Court, William, 1st Baron Heytesbury (1779–1860), 135, 233–236, 268–269, 274, 276, 320, 333
Aix-la-Chapelle, Congress of (1818), 180–205: evacuation of France, 179–181, 184; France and the Alliance, 183–190; British vs Russian views of Alliance, 183–189, 190–194; Ancillon's proposed treaty, 194–197; Spanish-American colonies, 197–201; other questions, 201–203; subsequent assessments, 203–205
Alexander I, Tsar of Russia (1777–1825), 29, 31–33, 37–40, 43–44, 46–47, 50, 52–56, 60–63, 69–72, 75–79, 82–83, 86–89, 95–96, 98–107, 109–120, 122, 124–29, 137, 139, 141–42, 145–49, 153–156, 160–61, 163–64, 166–68, 171–88, 190–93, 196–97, 199, 201–04, 207, 214, 216, 219, 222, 227–231, 236–237, 239–242, 244–250, 253–255, 257–259, 264–265, 267–68, 271–272, 264, 278, 280–281, 283–285, 288, 290–296, 298–308, 314–316, 319, 321, 325–328, 331, 333, 335, 337, 344–347, 354, 356–357, 360, 364, 366, 378
Ali Pasha of Janina (1740–1822), 289, 291, 303
Altensteig, Baron Franz Hager von, 96
ambassadorial conference, 145, 164, 169–170, 181, 194, 200, 201–02, 205, 230, 240–241, 300, 305–306, 314, 334–335, 338, 340, 342, 343, 345–346, 348, 351, 358–359, 369
Amiens, Peace of (1802), 27, 28
Ancillon, Johann Peter Friedrich von (1767–1837), 195–96, 212, 214, 217, 299–300, 373, 381, 385
Angoulême, Louis Antoine, Duc d' (1775–1844), 341–342
Arakcheev, Count Alexis (1769–1834), 257–258, 344, 347
Armée du Nord, 161, 163
Assembly of Notables, 19, 55, 213
August, Karl, Grand Duke of Saxe-Weimar (1757–1828), 212, 216
Austerlitz, Battle of (1805), 29–30, 53, 77–78, 162
Austria, 9–11, 13–14, 18, 21–22, 25–26, 28–30, 32–34, 38–49, 52–57, 60, 65, 71–72, 77–78, 84, 86–89, 92, 94–96, 98–129, 131–37, 141–142, 146, 153–157, 160, 173, 177, 180, 200, 209–210, 211–212, 216–219, 222, 231, 233, 235–237, 239–245, 248, 250–55, 260, 262–264, 266–268, 270, 274–277, 279–285, 288, 290, 292, 295–296, 298, 300–303, 305, 308, 310, 312, 315–323, 325, 327, 329, 332, 334, 336–337, 339, 343, 345–348, 351–352, 356–357, 360, 364, 367–368, 375–376
ayans, 287–288

Baden, 10, 28, 30, 71, 128, 132, 201, 211, 213, 215
Bagot, Sir Charles (1781–1843), 297, 302, 304, 306, 346
Bagration, Princess Katrina, 76, 96, 128
balance of power, 9, 17, 35, 40, 50, 57, 63, 65, 85, 87, 108, 116, 125, 128, 131, 150–151, 153, 229, 361, 363, 375
Balbo, Cesare (1789–1853), 282
Baring, Alexander (1774–1848), 180, 182
Baruch, Jacob (b. 1763), 141–143
Bastille, 20, 74
Bathurst, Henry, 3rd Earl (1762–1834), 123, 167, 188
Bavaria, 10, 28, 30, 34, 71, 88, 94–95, 103, 106, 110–111, 114, 119, 124, 132, 141–142, 148, 171, 179, 201, 211, 213, 215, 217, 348
Beethoven, Ludwig van (1770–1827), 95
Belgium, 10, 22, 24, 31, 40–42, 50, 52–55, 64, 65, 86–87, 152–56, 159, 350, 367
Bernadotte, Jean (*see* Charles John of Sweden), 29, 52–55, 63, 103, 139, 140, 155, 203, 322
Bernstorff, Christian, Count von (1769–1835), 182, 216, 248, 255, 261, 272, 275, 298, 302, 321, 323, 334–335, 340
Berri, Charles Ferdinand, Duc de (1778–1820), 227, 258
Bessarabia, 288, 293, 303
biens nationaux, 59
Blacas d'Aulps, Pierre Louis, Comte de (1771–1839), 161, 264–273, 275, 277–278
Boislecomte, Charles Joseph Edmond Sain de (1796–1863), 322–323, 325–327, 331–333
Bolívar, Simón (1783–1830), 224, 310
Bonaparte, Caroline (1782–1839), 133, 135
Bonaparte, Jérôme (1784–1860), 31–32
Bonaparte, Joseph (1768–1844), 30, 32–34, 133

Bonaparte, Napoléon (*see* Napoleon)
Borodino, Battle of (1812), 43
Bremen, 6, 141–43
Brougham, Henry (1778–1868), 238, 367
Bucharest, Treaty of (1812), 288, 292, 294
Buchholz, Dr. Carl August (1785–1843), 142–143
Buda, 106, 107, 110, 351
Burke, Edmund (1729–97), 20–21, 23, 63, 81, 83
Burschenschaften, 211–12, 217

Cadiz, 14, 223, 225, 341
Cambrai, 69, 179
Camden, Charles Pratt, 1st Earl (1713–94), 75, 81
Campochiaro, Duke of, 235, 268–69
Canning, George (1770–1827), 77, 112, 137, 138, 188, 238, 307, 317–319, 321, 327–328, 338, 340–347, 350, 363, 366
Canning, Stratford, 1st Viscount Stratford de Redcliffe (1786–1880), 77, 80, 137–138
Capodistrias, Count John (1776–1831), 77, 100, 118, 125, 137, 138, 164, 166–67, 174, 177, 180–82, 184–85, 190, 199–201, 219, 224, 228, 242, 245, 248–526, 258–261, 264–273, 275, 277, 280, 285, 287, 290–94, 296–301, 303–06, 315, 335, 348, 352, 375, 378
Caraman, Louis Charles Victor, Marquis de (1762–1839), 182, 248, 258–259, 261, 266, 271–273, 321, 337
Carbonari, 233–235, 269, 281, 282
Carlsbad Decrees (1819), 181, 209, 217–19, 222, 262, 348–349
Caroline, Queen Consort (1768–1821), 238, 317
Castle Opočno, 46
Castlereagh, Robert Stewart, 1st Viscount and 2nd Marquess of Londonderry (1769–1822), 1, 18, 21, 45–47, 50, 52–56, 60–61, 64–65, 68, 72, 74–75, 77–78, 80–82, 86–87, 90–94, 100–131, 134–136, 142–149, 154–156, 159–163, 165–168, 170–174, 176–191, 193, 195–205, 207, 219–223, 228–230, 234, 237–246, 248, 253, 259, 261–262, 322, 340–341, 345–347, 350, 354–357, 361–362, 364–369, 373–379
casus belli, 246, 296, 335
casus foederis, 123, 167, 185, 189, 191, 194, 240, 246, 330–331, 333–335, 364
Catherine the Great (1729–96), 5, 8–9, 26, 75, 82, 256, 287
Catherine, Grand Duchess of Russia (1788–1819), 72, 127
Caucasus, 5, 288, 303
Caulaincourt, Armand de (1773–1827)
'Cecil Draft', 370
Champ de Mai, 160–62
Charles III, King of Spain (1716–88), 13–14
Charles X, King of France (1757–1836), 85, 227, 313, 341, 344, 348

Charles Albert of Piedmont (1798–1849), 283, 285, 337
Charles John of Sweden (1763–1844)
Charte, 62, 160–61, 167, 187, 213, 228, 239, 249, 264, 314, 319, 325
Chateaubriand, François-René de (1768–1848), 1, 178, 290, 313, 321–322, 325, 333, 337, 338, 339, 341–345
Châtillon, Congress of (1814), 54–57, 60, 63, 70, 84
Chaumont, Treaty of (1814), 47, 56–57, 72, 94, 127, 159, 164, 184, 355, 369
Chiffon de Carlsbad (1830), 349
Christian Frederick, Prince of Denmark (1786–1848), 140
Civil Code (or Code Napoleon), 27, 32, 98, 282
Clancarty, Richard Trench, 2nd Earl of (1767–1837), 116, 129
Clausewitz, Carl von (1780–1831), 1, 182
Committee of Four (*see* Vienna, Congress of)
Committee of Eight (*see* Vienna, Congress of)
Committee of Public Safety, 23
Comte d'Artois (*see* Charles X)
Concordat (1801), 27, 233
Confederation of the Rhine (*Rheinbund*), 30–32, 48, 131, 141
Congress of Aix-La-Chapelle (*see* Aix-la-Chapelle, Congress of)
Congress of Laibach (*see* Laibach, Congress of)
Congress of Troppau (*see* Troppau, Congress of)
Congress of Verona (*see* Verona, Congress of)
Congress of Vienna (*see* Vienna, Congress of)
'Congress System', origins, 164–178; Quadruple Alliance, 166–169; end of, 344–352; characterization and assessments of, 353–363; explanation for failure of, 363–369; legacy of, 369–379 (*see also* Aix-la-Chapelle, Troppau, Laibach, Verona, Congress of; Holy Alliance)
Constantine Pavlovich, Grand Duke of Russia (1779–1831), 75, 114, 118, 247, 347
Constantinople (Istanbul), 5, 148, 171, 287–93, 299, 303, 321, 337, 345, 348
Continental system, 32, 43, 133, 192
Convention, 23–25, 144, 259
Cornwallis, Charles, 1st Marquess (1738–1805), 82
Courland, Duchess of, 76
Czartoryski, Prince Adam Jerzy (1770–1861), 8, 18, 35, 37–39, 41–43, 52, 57, 76–77, 82, 86, 98–100, 102, 105, 107–109, 111, 113, 115–118, 120, 127, 139, 146–147, 154, 186, 243, 246–247, 249, 350, 354–355, 373–374, 378

Index

Dalberg, Emmerich Joseph, Duc de (1773–1833), 116, 129, 138
Danubian Principalities (Moldavia and Wallachia), 5, 287–306, 345
Danzig (Gdańsk), 96
Denmark, 3, 6, 52, 95, 138–141, 145, 179, 203, 385
Doceañistas, 309–312
Dohm, Christian Wilhelm von (1751–1820), 84, 141
Dresden, 45–46, 73, 111, 126, 129, 291

'Eastern Question', 307, 334, 336, 345, 351–352, 357
Elba, 27, 62, 158
émigrés, 23, 59, 158
Enghien, Louis Antoine Henri de Bourbon-Condé, Duc d' (1772–1804), 28, 321
Erfurt, 33, 61, 129
Esdaile, Charles, 224
Estates General (France), 19–20, 74, 79
Esterhazy, Prince Paul (1786–1866), 207, 237, 244, 262, 279, 321
European Union, 353, 369, 372, 373, 377
Exaltados, 309, 311–313, 339

Federal Diet (German)
Ferdinand IV, King of Naples (1751–1825), 13, 134–136, 231
Ferdinand VII of Spain (1784–1833), 85, 198, 223, 224, 228, 309, 312–314, 316, 318, 325, 337, 342–343, 356
Finland, 4, 6, 32, 138–139, 141
Fontainebleau, Treaty of (1814), 61–62, 158
Fouché, Joseph, Duc d'Otrante (1759–1820), 160–161, 163–164
'Four Points' (1821), 294–295, 301
France, 1, 3, 9, 11–35, 38–58, 60–65, 68–70, 72–74, 80–81, 86–95, 99–100, 103, 105, 107, 110, 112, 114–116, 118–120, 122–125, 127–131, 133–134, 136–141, 143–147, 151, 153–174, 178–186, 188–192, 194–199, 209, 212–213, 221–224, 227–231, 235–236, 239–242, 245–246, 250, 252–254, 256, 258, 264–267, 270–273, 275, 277–278, 284–285, 287–288, 293, 295–296, 298, 304, 306–307, 310, 313–316, 318–321, 323–345, 347–360, 363–364, 366–368, 371–372, 374–376, 378
Francis, Emperor of Austria (1768–1835), 28–29, 33–34, 55, 60–61, 73, 95–96, 101, 105–106, 108–109, 111, 113, 115, 119, 121, 135–36, 146, 160, 173–174, 176–177, 182, 184, 210, 216, 231, 233, 236, 240, 248, 251, 261, 267, 269, 272, 281, 283, 292, 295, 300, 325, 349, 356
Frankfurt Proposals (1813), 49–50, 55–56
Frederick Augustus I, King of Saxony (1750–1827), 31, 99, 103, 115–116, 126, 130

Frederick the Great (1712–86), 9, 11, 12, 15, 74, 98
Frederick William III, King of Prussia (1770–1840), 30, 44, 48, 60–61, 74, 101–103, 107, 109–110, 127, 129–130, 141, 146, 154–155, 173–174, 176, 182, 184, 187, 190, 196, 213–218, 240, 248–249, 281, 321

Gagern, Heinrich von (1799–1880), 211
Gallo, Marzio Mastrilli, Duc di, 269, 275
Gatchina, 75, 345
Geneva, 26, 64, 134, 137–138
Genoa, 13, 26, 28, 40, 50, 65, 86, 131, 134, 136, 155, 283, 285
Gentz, Friedrich von (1764–1832), 21, 40–41, 84–85, 93, 96, 129, 142–143, 147–149, 153, 157, 159–160, 182, 190, 195, 197, 200, 203–204, 212, 214, 216, 218, 248, 255, 263–264, 273–74, 276, 305, 321, 330–331, 338, 344, 356, 363, 374
George III, King of England (1738–1820), 27, 77, 238
George IV, King of England (1762–1830), 55, 71–72, 114, 117, 171, 173, 176–177, 189, 192, 196, 229, 238, 274, 301–302, 317, 384, 387
German Confederation, 69, 71, 87–88, 102–103, 105, 110, 112, 114–115, 119, 131–133, 142–143, 154, 182, 195–196, 210–213, 216–217, 219–220, 298
Germanos, Bishop of Patras (1771–1826), 293
Germany, 3, 10, 12, 15, 25–28, 34, 38, 41, 44, 46, 48, 52, 57, 65, 69, 71, 84–85, 87–89, 91–92, 94, 102–103, 105, 110–112, 121–122, 129–132, 143, 147, 150, 156–157, 202, 210–212, 217, 223, 231, 236–237, 263, 267–268, 284, 325, 352–353, 368–369, 371–372, 374, 377, 383
Ghent, Treaty of (1814), 119, 381
Ghervas, Stella, 219
Girondins, 22–23, 259, 335
Golitsyn, Prince Alexander (1773–1844), 128, 258, 280–281, 291
Golovkin, Count Yuri (1762–1846), 248
Gordon, Robert (1791–1847), 272–73, 277, 279–280, 284, 321, 361
Grande Armée, 29, 44, 140
Great Britain, 3, 15–19, 21–22, 25–28, 30–32, 38–40, 45–47, 50, 52–54, 56–57, 64, 72, 81–82, 87–89, 101, 104–105, 110, 112–113, 115–120, 122–124, 127, 129–131, 137, 139–140, 144, 146, 148, 151–153, 155–157, 229–231, 233, 237–238, 241–244, 248, 252, 256, 258, 262–266, 270–271, 273–274, 279–280, 285, 287–288, 296, 300–302, 306, 308, 314, 316–321, 323, 326, 329–333, 336–338, 340–348, 350–352, 355–356, 359, 364–368, 370–371, 375–376

517

Greece, 5, 286, 289–290, 292–293, 297, 300, 302–306, 321, 345–348, 350, 375
Greek question, background, 287–290; Ypsilantis' revolt, 290–93; uprising in the Peloponnese, 293, 303, 306; murder of the Patriarch, 293; Russian 'Four Points', 294–295, 301; negotiations among European powers, 292–307, 345–348; intervention of Ibrahim Pasha, 346–47; continuing atrocities (1822), 306–307; Canning and Greece, 345–347; conferences at St Petersburg (1824), 345–346; Anglo-Russian rapprochement, 347–348; independence, 348 (*see also Phanariot*; *Philiki Hetairia*; Ypsilantis)
Grigorios V, Patriarch of Constantinople (1746–1821), 293–294, 296
Grotius, Hugo (1583–1645), 69
Grouchy, General Emmanuel de (1768–1847), 162–163
Guadeloupe, 140, 144
Gulick, Edward Vose, 150
Gumprecht, J., 142

Habsburg Empire (*see* Austria)
Haiti, 28, 144
Halet Effendi, Mohammed-Sayd (1761–1822), 288
Hanover, 6, 10, 17, 28, 30, 46, 52, 71, 74, 77, 87, 94, 103, 112, 116, 119, 126, 129–30, 140, 148, 171, 179, 285, 301, 316
Hardenberg, Prince Karl August von (1750–1822), 52, 60, 63, 71–72, 74, 77–79, 83–84, 87, 90, 100, 101–07, 109, 110–116, 118–120, 122, 124–132, 141, 142–143, 149, 154–155, 181–182, 195–196, 209, 211, 213–218, 248, 252–253, 255, 261, 270, 321, 347
Helvetic Republic, 26–27
Henry IV, King of France (1553–1610), 16, 35
Hofburg, 95, 109, 376
Hoffmann, J.G., 116
Holy Alliance (1815), 128, 164, 173–74, 176–78, 185, 193, 204, 239, 243, 279, 281, 285, 292, 299, 306, 308, 322, 352, 354, 358, 367–68
Holy Roman Empire, 10, 12, 28, 30, 71, 78, 85, 103, 131–132, 210, 380
Hone, William (1780–1842), 367
hospodars, 287, 291
House of Commons, 17, 21, 65, 136, 140, 144, 146, 149 220–222, 284, 307, 317, 340, 342–243, 350, 367; Irish House of Commons, 75, 77, 205
Humboldt, Wilhelm von (1767–1835), 83–85, 90–91, 102, 107, 112–115, 120, 128, 138, 141–143, 148–149, 182, 211, 215, 217–218
Hundred Days (*Cent Jours*), 125, 136, 138, 155, 158, 164–65, 170–71, 179–180, 191, 252, 262, 273, 284, 376

Ikenberry, G. John, 152
Ireland, 3, 16–17, 26, 75, 77, 81–82, 176, 220, 385, 389
Irish Rebellion (1798), 81–82, 297, 355
Isabey, Jean-Baptiste (1767–1855), 95
Italy, 3, 12–13, 25–28, 31–32, 34, 38, 40–42, 49–50, 57, 62, 65, 71–72, 85, 87–88, 92–93, 107–08, 110, 120, 122, 133–136, 147, 150, 154–157, 209, 216, 231–232, 235–37, 239, 250, 255, 263, 267, 275–78, 282–285, 292–293, 295–96, 304–05, 307, 309, 321, 325, 331, 343, 352–353, 367, 369, 374

Jacobins, 25, 80, 160, 212, 233, 325
Janissaries, 287–288, 347
Jena, 30, 79, 171, 212–213, 215–216
Jervis, Robert, 360–61, 363
Jewish emancipation, 84, 141–143, 202–203
Jung-Stilling, Johann Heinrich (1740–1817), 128
juntas, 198, 223, 309

Kalisch, Treaty of (1813), 44–45, 98, 126, 173
kapoi, 289
Kaunitz, Prince Wenzel Anton (1711–94), 34, 73
Kiel, Treaty of (1814), 140–141, 201, 203
Kissinger, Henry, 78, 150, 157, 374–376
klephts, 289, 293
Knesebeck, General Karl Friedrich von dem (1768–1848), 109
Korais, Adamantios (1748–1833), 289
Kościuszko, Tadeusz (1746–1817), 9, 99
Kotzebue, August von (1761–1819), 215–216
Kraehe, Enno, 105, 153–54
Kraków, 8, 70–71, 98–99, 100, 107, 110–111, 115, 118, 125, 130
Kreis system, 103, 105, 107, 112, 132
Krüdener, Baroness Julie von (1764–1824), 128, 174, 176, 178, 299
Krusemarck, General Frederick William Ludwig (1767–1822), 248
Kutchuk Kainardji, Treaty of (1774), 287, 294

La Ferronnays, Pierre Louis, Comte de (1777–1842), 207, 248, 250, 259, 261, 266, 271, 278, 295, 299, 321–322, 326, 331–333, 335
La Harpe, Frédéric César de (1754–1838), 40, 75, 82, 100, 137
La Tour du Pin, Frédéric-Séraphin, Marquis de (1759–1837), 228
Labrador, Don Pedro Gómez, Marquis of (1755–1852), 92–93
Laibach, Congress of (1821), opening 270; French policy in disarray, 271; early sessions, 272–273; King Ferdinand of Naples at Laibach, 268–270, 275–77; fictitious Conference journal, 273–274; British protests, 274–275, 278–280;

other Italian states, 275–276; Austrian occupation of Naples, 276–277, 280, 316, 336; revolution in Piedmont, 281–285
Landständische Verfassung, 132, 210, 216, 218
Landwehr, 213–214
Lawrence, Sir Thomas (1769–1830), 182
League of Nations, 195, 353, 366, 369–374
Lebzeltern, Ludwig, Count (1774–1854), 137, 182, 248, 251, 258, 267, 269, 315, 321, 327
Leipzig, Battle of (1813), 48–49, 69, 95, 102, 137, 140, 182, 212
Leopold II, Holy Roman Emperor (1747–92), 73
Lieven, Count Christopher (1774–1839), 117, 182, 244, 262, 302, 304, 305, 321, 333, 346
Lieven, Countess Dorothea (1785–1857), 182, 302, 317, 322, 346
Ligne, Charles-Joseph, Prince de (1735–1814), 95, 113, 140
Liverpool, Robert Banks Jenkinson, 2nd Earl of (1770–1828), 52, 90, 105, 121–123, 125, 127, 130, 154, 166, 207, 242, 302, 317, 350
Lombardy-Venetia, 134, 236–237, 282–283
London, 21, 28, 33, 38–40, 45, 50, 64, 70–74, 80, 94, 105, 117, 120, 122–123, 126, 128, 130, 142, 145, 147, 159, 161, 167, 171–72, 180–81, 183, 198–199, 201–202, 215, 219–220, 222, 238, 242, 244, 251, 261, 263, 265, 279, 289, 297, 304–305, 310, 317, 338, 341–342, 345–348, 350–351
London, Treaty of (1827), 347–48, 382
Louis XIV, King of France (1638–15), 15–16, 22, 263
Louis XVI, King of France (1754–93), 11, 16, 19–22, 52, 58, 73–74, 82, 95, 227, 261, 341
Louis XVIII, King of France (1755–1824), 30, 52–53, 60–64, 71–72, 85, 88, 92, 106, 112, 116, 119, 122, 134–136, 144–145, 159–161, 163–164, 167, 172–173, 179–180, 182–184, 188, 190, 199, 227–228, 230, 254, 256, 259, 266, 314, 320–321, 330, 339–340, 344, 347–348, 377
Louis Philippe, Duc d'Orléans and King of the French (1773–1850), 161, 348–349, 351
l'Ouverture, General Toussaint (1743–1803), 144
Lübeck, 32, 141–143

Mackintosh, Sir James (1765–1832), 279
Mahmud II, Sultan (1785–1839), 288–289, 292–296, 299–308, 345–347, 351, 378
Mainz, 71, 73, 80, 87–88, 103, 106, 110–11, 171, 194, 217, 237
Marie Antoinette, Queen of France (1755–93), 11, 23, 34, 173, 341
Marie Louise, Empress of France (1791–1847), 34, 45, 53, 60, 62–63, 135–36, 161, 322
Merveldt, Maximilian Count von (1764–1815), 105, 120, 122

Metternich, Prince Clemens Wenzel Lothar von (1773–1859), 12, 17, 21, 34, 40, 45–49, 52–55, 57, 60–61, 70–73, 75–78, 80–81, 86, 88, 90, 92–96, 100–107, 109–113, 115–120, 122–123, 125, 127–129, 132–135, 142–143, 149, 153–156, 158, 160–161, 163–165, 173–178, 180–184, 186, 195–196, 200, 203–204, 207, 209, 212, 214–221, 227–228, 230–231, 233–237, 239–243, 248–259, 261–283, 285, 291–292, 296–306, 308, 310, 313–338, 340, 344–351, 354, 356–357, 364, 369, 375–376
Metternich, Princess Eleonore von
millet, 287, 293
Mirabeau, Honoré Gabriel Riqueti (1749–91), 74, 79, 280
Moldavia, 5, 287–88, 291–292, 303
Monroe Doctrine (1823), 342–343
Montmorency, Mathieu, Duc de (1767–1826), 313–314, 318, 320–326, 328–336, 338–339, 343
Mulgrave, Lord Henry Phipps (1755–1831), 123, 125
Münchengrätz Agreement (1833), 351, 382
Münster, George Herbert, Count of (1766–1839), 112, 114, 116, 129, 171
Murat, Joachim (1767–1815), 32–33, 49, 71, 85, 88, 133–136, 145, 231, 233

Naples, 13–14, 26, 30, 32–33, 46, 49, 71, 85, 88, 91, 129, 133–136, 145, 231, 233–245, 250–256, 258–260, 264–279, 281–285, 292, 296, 298, 308–310, 312, 314, 316, 318–320, 322, 327, 329, 337, 342, 344–345, 356, 359, 367, 376–378
Napoleon I, Emperor of the French (1769–1821), 1, 25–35, 38–39, 43–49, 53–64, 69, 71–72, 74, 76–81, 83–86, 88, 98–99, 101, 104, 125, 129, 133–137, 139–141, 144, 146, 148, 150, 157–167, 172–174, 177, 179, 198, 201, 203, 209, 212, 216–217, 220, 224, 246, 261, 265, 267, 269, 280, 285, 288, 321, 323, 333, 341, 344, 349, 351, 355, 359, 361, 375
nationalism, 38, 42, 86, 88, 111, 131, 134, 136, 141, 150, 153, 155, 210, 211, 290, 296, 360, 367–368, 375
'natural frontiers' of France, 16, 33, 38, 49, 54–55, 156
Navarino, Battle of (1827), 348
Neapolitan Revolution, 231–36, 268–69, 276–77, 280
Nesselrode, Count Karl Robert (1780–1862), 64, 77, 90, 101, 122, 142, 165, 182, 199–200, 248–252, 255, 261, 272, 275, 300, 304–305, 320–321, 323, 329, 331–335, 349

519

Ney, Marshal Michel (1769–1815), 162, 170, 377
Nicholas I, Tsar of Russia (1796–1855), 308
Nicolson, Sir Harold, 205
Norway, 6, 86, 131, 138–141, 203
Novalis (1772–1801), 178

occupation of France (1815–1818), 178–180, 184
Orléans, Duc d' (*see* Louis Philippe)
Osiander, Andreas, 151–52, 157
Ottoman Empire, 3, 5, 9, 18, 31–32, 38, 104, 148, 156, 197, 201, 247, 249, 282, 285, 287–291, 295–300, 302–309, 326, 332, 346, 348, 352–353, 360, 368
Owen, Robert (1771–1858), 182, 345

Papacy, 13–14, 20, 27–28, 34, 85, 136, 145, 176, 233, 266–267, 269–270, 275, 282, 337
Paris, 20–23, 25–26, 28, 32, 34, 45, 52, 55–56, 58–62, 70–72, 76, 84–85, 87–89, 91–94, 108, 113–114, 118–119, 122, 133–138, 141, 144–145, 149, 155–156, 159, 162–164, 170–171, 173–174, 179–182, 186, 190, 194, 197–198, 201, 213, 228, 230, 240, 242–243, 245, 249, 254, 258, 265–266, 271–272, 289, 292, 295, 297, 299–300, 306, 314–316, 318–319, 321–322, 327328, 333–336, 338, 340, 342–343, 346, 348–352, 364, 369, 372, 374
Paris, First Peace of (1814), 63–65
Paris, Second Peace of (1815), 164–165, 171–173, 178–179, 181
Parish, David, 182
Parliament, 16–17, 27, 82, 90, 126, 130–131, 135–136, 144–145, 147, 156, 159, 166–168, 188–193, 198, 201, 219–220, 222–223, 239, 241, 244–246, 268, 274, 279, 307, 323, 331–332, 343, 350 356, 360, 364–365
Pasquier, Étienne-Denis, Duc de (1767–1862), 239, 242, 248, 254, 259, 266, 271, 278, 295
Paul, Tsar of Russia (1754–1801), 26–27, 75, 257
Peloponnese, 289–91, 293, 298, 303, 346–347
Pepe, General Guglielmo (1783–1855), 233–235, 280
Peterloo (1819), 220–223
Phanariot, 287, 291–292
Philhellenism, 347
Philiki Hetairia, 290–293
Piedmont, 13, 26–27, 38–41, 50, 65, 85, 87, 120, 133–34, 147, 157, 172, 270, 281–85, 303, 312, 315–316, 318–320, 325, 327, 337, 377–378
Piedmontese Revolution, 281–285
Pilbeam, Pamela, 150–51, 155
Pitt 'the Younger', William (1759–1806), 21, 27, 29, 35, 39–43, 50, 52, 57, 67, 75, 77, 82, 85, 100, 130, 147, 186, 230, 350, 355, 373
Poland, 3, 5–12, 18, 22, 24, 26, 30–31, 37–38, 44–45, 48, 52, 70–72, 85–88, 93, 96, 98–113, 118, 120, 122–124, 126–127, 129, 139, 147, 150, 152, 154–157, 246–247, 253, 346, 350, 354, 368, 378
Polignac, Jules de (1780–1847), 342–343, 348
Polish-Saxon question (*see* Vienna, Congress of)
Poniatowski, Stanisław (*see* Stanislaus Augustus)
Portugal, 14–15, 33, 50, 65, 72, 145–146, 198–199, 201–202, 230, 243, 254, 258, 275, 304, 307, 310, 316–17, 323, 340, 343, 351, 353, 378
Portuguese Revolution, 243
Pozzo di Borgo, Charles Andrea (1764–1842), 315, 321, 326–327, 331–32, 334, 338, 342
Pradt, Dominque-Georges-Frédéric, Abbé de (1759–1837), 41
Prague Talks (1813), 46–47
Prince Regent (*see* George IV)
Procedural question (*see* Vienna, Congress of)
'Profession of Faith' (*see* Troppau, Congress of)
Protocole préliminaire (*see* Troppau, Congress of)
Prussia, 3, 6, 8–12, 15, 18, 21, 25, 28–32, 34, 38–42, 44–48, 52, 56, 60–61, 63–64, 70–75, 77–79, 83–84, 86–90, 92, 94–96, 98–107, 109–116, 118–132, 140–142, 146–147, 149, 152–157, 160–163, 171, 173–174, 176–177, 180–182, 186–187, 190, 194–197, 200, 202–203, 209, 211–218, 240, 246, 248–250, 252, 270, 276–277, 281, 298–299, 302, 310, 320–321, 325, 329, 334, 339, 347, 349–350, 352, 356–357, 364, 368, 378
Pufendorf, Samuel (1632–1694), 69
Puławy, 100

Quadruple Alliance (1815), 164, 166, 173, 181, 183–186, 188–191, 194, 196, 240, 348–349, 351, 355, 359, 366, 370–371
Quadruple Alliance (1834), 351

Radetzky, General Joseph (1766–1858), 351
Razumovsky, Count Alexei Grigorievich, 118–19, 126, 128, 167
Rechtstaat, 75, 186
Reichenbach, Treaty of (1813), 46, 50, 104, 107–108
Reign of Terror, 23
reparations (from France), 172, 178–180
Rhine, 29–30, 32–33, 48–49, 64–65, 70–71, 114–115, 121, 129, 131, 141, 146–147, 163
Rhineland, 11, 24, 28, 31, 40–41, 52, 54, 55, 71, 73–74, 77, 80, 87, 112, 114–116, 118–119, 126, 128–130, 182, 214
Richardson, Louise, 161
Richelieu, Armand-Emmanuel du Plessis, Duc de (1766–1822), 16, 172–173, 179, 182–184, 188–190, 194, 198–200, 228, 234, 239, 242, 248, 252, 254, 259, 271, 278, 306, 313, 315, 352

Index

Riego y Nunez, Rafael del (1784–1823), 225, 227, 312–313, 342, 377
Rieti, Battle of (1821), 280, 283
Riga Memorial (1807), 83
'right of visit', 145, 202, 337
Robespierre, Maximilien (1758–94), 22–25, 177
Robinson, Frederick John, 1st Earl Ripon (1782–1859), 205
Rosa, Francisco Martínez de la (1787–1862), 312–313
Rossini, Giachino (1792–1868), 322
Rothschild, Nathan (1777–1836), 141–142, 182, 203, 276, 322
Rousseau, Jean-Jacques (1712–1778), 19–20, 22, 36, 40, 75
Ruffo, Prince Alvaro, 270, 272–275, 277–278
Russia, 3–6, 8–9, 15, 17–18, 26–32, 34, 37–39, 43–49, 53, 57, 64, 70–72, 78, 86, 88–89, 96, 98–103, 106–118, 120–123, 125, 127–130, 135, 137, 139–141, 147–148, 151–153, 173, 176, 181, 184, 186, 190, 195, 196, 199, 201, 203, 209, 217, 219, 225, 231, 236, 239, 241, 248–250, 255, 258–259, 262, 264, 271–272, 276–277, 284, 287–288, 291–307, 310, 316, 318, 320–321, 325, 327, 329–330, 332, 35, 339, 345–357, 359, 366, 368–369, 371, 374, 377–378

Sagan, Duchess Dorothée von (1793–1862) 76
Sagan, Duchess Wilhelmine von (1781–1839), 76, 96, 109, 119
St Helena, 164, 201, 203, 269, 285
Saint-Pierre, Charles-Irénée Castel, Abbé de (1658–43), 35–36, 40, 146, 195
San Martín, José de (1778–1850), 224
Sand, Karl Ludwig (1795–1820), 215
Sardinia, 13, 39, 65, 85, 133, 280
Saxony, 8, 10, 31–32, 44–45, 48, 52, 71, 86–88, 91, 93, 98–99, 102–103, 105–107, 109–13, 115–116, 118–119, 121–124, 126–130, 132, 142, 152, 154–156, 179
Scheldt, 22, 50, 64
Schroeder, Paul, 148, 150–53, 157, 201, 307
Schwarzenberg, Karl Philipp, Prince of (1771–1820), 120–121, 128, 351
Sejm, 8–9, 246–247, 258
Selim III, Sultan (1761–1807), 288
Serbia, 287–288, 291, 303
Sierakowski, Józef (1765–1831), 105
Sieyès, Emmanuel Joseph, Abbé (1748–1836), 19, 26, 84, 314
Silesia, 11–12, 18, 98, 111, 157, 248
Six Acts (1819), 220–122
Sked, Alan, 153, 172, 210, 357, 363
slave trade, 144–146, 202, 318, 337
Spain, 3, 13–15, 18, 22, 25, 28, 32–35, 43, 46, 48–50, 57, 64–65, 72, 85–86, 90–91, 136, 145–146, 149, 180–181, 184, 197–201, 209, 223–235, 237, 239, 243, 250, 253, 254, 258, 260, 267–268, 275, 278, 293, 304, 307, 309–311, 131–316, 318–320, 322–335, 337–345, 347, 351, 353, 356–357, 359, 376–378
Spanish Constitution of 1812, 223, 233–234, 236–237, 243, 269, 283, 310, 324, 339
Spanish Revolution of 1820, 225–231, 309–316, 341–342
Speransky, Mikhail (1772–1839), 82, 139, 209
Spina, Cardinal (1756–1828), 275, 327
Srbik, Heinrich von, 81
Staël, Madame de (1766–1817), 58, 84, 179
Stanislaus Augustus, King of Poland (1732–1798), 8–9, 99
State Paper of 5 May 1820, 228–231, 237, 244, 262, 279, 284, 318, 341
Statistical Committee (*see* Vienna, Congress of)
Stein, Friedrich Karl vom und zum (1757–1831), 74, 77, 100, 111, 113, 115, 121, 125, 138, 209
Stewart, Charles William, 3rd Marquess of Londonderry (1778–1854), 124, 138, 171, 182, 230, 237, 240–241, 244, 248–249, 257, 260–262, 270, 274–276, 320–321, 327, 364, 366
Stourdza, Alexander (1791–1854), 174, 177–178, 212, 214, 219, 249, 291, 293, 299, 306
Stourdza, Rozanne (1786–1844), 128, 174
Strangford, Percy Smythe, 6th Viscount (1780–1855), 294, 301, 306–307, 320–321, 332, 337, 345
Stroganov, Baron Gregory (1769–1857), 292–295, 301, 305, 321
Selim III, Sultan (1761–1808), 288
Semenovsky Regiment, 256–257, 347
Sully, Duc de (1560–1641), 35–38, 40, 146, 195
Sutzo, Michael (1778–1864), 291–292, 303
Sweden, 3–6, 9, 12, 18, 28–29, 32, 44, 46, 53, 55, 72, 98, 138–141, 145, 201, 203, 322
Switzerland, 3, 12, 26, 32, 39, 52, 57, 65, 69–70, 93–94, 136–138, 152, 172, 176, 268

Taganrog, 347
Talleyrand-Perigord, Prince Charles-Maurice de (1754–1838), 24–26, 28, 32–33, 61–64, 68, 72–74, 76, 79–80, 83, 88, 91–94, 96, 100, 103, 106, 112, 116–120, 122, 124–125, 128–129, 134–135, 142, 144–145, 153–155, 160–161, 164, 172–173, 233, 243, 350–351, 376
Tarnopol District (Poland), 15, 118, 129
Tatishchev, Count Dmitri (1767–1845), 197, 304–306, 321, 327, 332–333
Teplitz, 48, 50, 216–17, 249
Third Coalition, 28–30, 39–42
'Third Germany', 211
Thorn (Toruń), 70–71, 96, 98, 101, 107, 110–111, 118, 125, 129–130

521

Tilsit, Treaty of (1807), 31, 33, 74, 79, 82, 98, 139, 288
Trauttmansdorff, Ferdinand, Prince von (1749–1827), 95
Treaty of 25 March 1815, 159, 168, 246
Treitschke, Heinrich von (1834–1896), 105, 216
Trienio Liberal (Spain), 225–228, 309–313, 341–342
Triple Alliance of 3 January 1815, 119–125, 160
Troppau, Congress of (1820), preliminary negotiations, 239–245; opening session, 250; Metternich and Capodistrias, 248–256, 258–259; invitation to King of Naples, 255–256; Semenovsky mutiny; 256–257, 347; Capodistrias' 'System of Conduct', 252–254; *protocole préliminaire*, 259–262; Troppau Circular, 264–65, 278–280; Metternich's 'Profession of Faith', 267–268; reactions in Naples, 268–270
Troyes, 55–56, 94
Tugendbund, 114, 214
Tuscany, 11, 13, 41, 88, 131, 136, 238, 270, 283

ultra-royalists, 85, 180, 280, 313–314, 321, 339, 341–344, 348
United Irishmen, 81
United Netherlands, 87, 147, 349
Urgel regency, 313, 319, 322, 324, 336, 338

Vansittart, Nicholas (1766–1851), 123
Vasquez, John, 152
Vaud, 12, 137
Venice, 13, 26, 38, 65, 171, 287, 337, 345, 351
Victor Emmanuel, King of Piedmont (1759–1824), 85, 282–283
Verona, Congress of (1822), background, 309–319; negotiations at Vienna, 319–321; death of Castlereagh, 316–318; arrival of sovereigns and statesmen, 321; festivities, 321–323; Montmorency and Villèle, 313–314, 318, 321, 324, 328, 333–334, 338–339; Montmorency's 'Three Questions', 323–326; allied responses to 'Three Questions', 329–330; Chateaubriand, 313, 321–22, 325, 333, 337–39, 341–343, 345; instructions to allied ambassadors, 328–329, 331–332, 335, 339; other issues, 336–337; French expedition to Spain, 338–343; 'Verona Circular', 338
Vienna, Congress of (1814–1815), decision to convene, 65, 69–70; the statesmen, 72–84; aims of powers, 84–89; procedural question, 89–94; Committee of Eight, 94, 145; festivities, 94–96; Polish-Saxon question, 96–131; conspiracy of 23 October, 106–110; war scare, 113–115, 120–123; Rhineland proposal, 115–116, 118, 129; Statistical Committee, 115–116, 126, 130; Committee of Four, 117–118, 122–124, 126; Secret Treaty of 3 January 1815, 119–125; German Confederation, 131–133; Switzerland, 136–138; Scandinavia, 138–141; Italy and Murat, 133–136; status of German Jews, 141–143; slave trade, 144–146; rivers and diplomatic precedence, 146; question of a general guarantee, 146–149; Vienna Final Act, 149
Villèle, Jean-Baptiste, Comte de (1773–1854), 318–322, 324, 327–328, 333–336, 338–339, 342–343, 345
Villepin, Dominique de, 374, 376
Vitrolles, Eugène François, Baron de (1774–1854), 180, 344
Vladimirescu, Tudor (1780–1821), 292
Vorontsov, Count Semyon (1744–1832), 40, 67, 248

Wagram, Battle of (1809), 34, 78, 88
Wallachia, 5, 287, 292
Warsaw, 8, 31–32, 34, 40, 44, 46, 48, 71, 96, 98–101, 103–104, 106, 108–109, 111, 114, 116, 118, 130, 187, 240, 242, 246–247, 249, 254, 258, 293
Waterloo, Battle of (1815), 1–2, 162–163, 176, 179, 348–349
Way, Lewis (1772–1840), 182, 203
Webster, Sir Charles, 125, 138, 348, 357, 370–371, 374
Wellesley, Sir Henry, 225, 227–228, 310–311
Wellington, Arthur Wellesley, 1st Duke of (1769–1852), 46, 49, 52, 116, 145, 149, 162–163, 165, 168–171, 179–181, 186, 193, 194, 197, 200–201, 225, 228, 238, 317–321, 323, 325–328, 330–338, 340–341, 347, 349–350, 364
Wessenberg, Johann Philipp, Freiherr von (1773–1858), 116, 129, 138, 143
Wieliczka salt mines, 118
Wilberforce, William (1759–1833), 72, 144–145
Wittgenstein, Wilhelm Ludwig, Prince (1770–1851), 214
Woodhouse, C. M., 374–375
Württemberg, 10, 28, 30, 71, 94–95, 103, 114, 127, 132, 179, 211, 213, 219

Ypsilantis, Prince Alexander (1792–1828), 291–294, 308

Zamość, 98
Zamoyski, Adam, 150, 153, 155, 363
Zichy, Count, 182, 248, 321
Zurlo, Giuseppe (1759–1828), 234, 268–269

www.ingramcontent.com/pod-product-compliance
Lightning Source LLC
Chambersburg PA
CBHW051802230426
43672CB00012B/2596